Understanding
GENERALIST
PRACTICE

Understanding GENERALIST PRACTICE

Karen K. Kirst-Ashman
University of Wisconsin-Whitewater

Grafton H. Hull, Jr.
University of Wisconsin-Eau Claire

Nelson-Hall Publishers/Chicago

Project Editors: Rachel Schick and Richard Meade
Cartoonist: Don Baumgart
Photo Researcher: Randall Nicholas
Illustrator: Bill Nelson
Cover Painting: *Platform* by Betty Ann Mocek

Library of Congress Cataloging-in-Publication Data

Kirst-Ashman, Karen Kay.
    Understanding generalist practice / Karen K. Kirst-Ashman, Grafton
H. Hull, Jr.
       p.   cm.
    Includes bibliographical references (p.   ) and index.
    ISBN 0-8304-1268-9
    1. Social service. 2. Social case work. I. Hull, Grafton H.
II. Title.
HV40.K465 1993
361.3′2—dc20   92-34831
                                          CIP

Manufactured in the United States of America

10 9 8 7 6 5 4

The paper used in this book meets the
minimum requirements of American
National Standard for Information
Sciences—Permanence of Paper for
Printed Library Materials, ANSI
Z39.48-1984.

To Mabel and Judy

Contents in Brief

Contents

CHAPTER 3
Mezzo Practice Skills: Working with Groups 80

CHAPTER 4
Macro Practice Skills: Working with Organizations and Communities 114

CHAPTER 5
Assessment in Generalist Practice 146

CHAPTER 6
Planning in Generalist Practice 188

CHAPTER 9
Understanding Families 308

CHAPTER 10
Working with Families 342

CHAPTER 11
Making Ethical Decisions 372

CHAPTER 12
Ethnically and Racially Sensitive
Social Work Practice   398

CHAPTER 13
Gender Sensitive Social Work
Practice   422

CHAPTER 14
Advocacy 464

CHAPTER 15
Brokering and Case Management 492

CHAPTER 16
Recording in Generalist Social Work Practice 522

Preface

This book is a guide to generalist social work practice. Oriented toward students, it provides a framework for them to view the world from a generalist perspective, intending to concur with Council on Social Work Education accreditation standards. A major concern in social work today is the tendency for students to veer away from thinking about helping communities and enabling social change. Instead, aspiring social workers are frequently drawn to the perceived psychological drama and intensity of clinical practice. The text, while stressing work with individuals, should help make them aware of other exciting aspects of the profession.

Understanding Generalist Practice pursues two primary goals. First, it aims to teach students the relationship-building, interviewing, and problem-solving skills necessary for them to work with individual clients. The perspective assumes that group (i.e., mezzo) skills are built upon a firm foundation of individual (i.e., micro) skills. Likewise, skills involved in community organization and social planning (i.e., macro) skills rest upon a solid base of both micro and mezzo skills.

The text's second primary goal is to introduce students to other dimensions of generalist practice. It orients them to think not only in terms of individual needs but also of group and community needs. The book's intent is to structure how students think about clients and their problems so that they automatically explore alternatives beyond the individual level. Links are clearly made among these three levels of practice. A systems approach aids students' understanding of how perspectives shift when changing from one practice level to another.

This book is primarily geared for use either in a course stressing micro-level skill develop-ment or in one intended as an introduction to generalist social work practice. It serves to ground students from the very beginning of the practice sequence with a strong generalist perspective.

Content is intended to be highly practical. The backbone of the proposed Generalist Intervention Model is the problem-solving method. This approach provides clear guidelines for how students might proceed through the helping process. Yet, it allows a wide range of flexibility for the application of theoretical approaches and specific skills. Students should gain a foundation upon which they can continue to add and build skills. The Generalist Intervention Model, as a unifying framework, is intended to help students make sense of the breadth and depth of the social work profession.

Understanding Generalist Practice aims to avoid the pitfall of focusing most of its attention on explaining a complicated theoretical model. Rather, the book addresses a core of micro skills which were carefully chosen. These skills are deemed the most useful to generalist practitioners in a wide variety of settings. Such core skills include, for example, those involved in recording and working with families.

Social work ethics and values provide another major dimension in the text. Sensitivity to human diversity and populations at risk is paramount. Chapters are devoted both to ethnic/racial and gender sensitivity. Additionally, content on human diversity is incorporated throughout the text. An entire chapter addresses professional values. Content goes on to examine ethical dilemmas commonly encountered in practice and to suggest solutions. Moreover, another full chapter stresses advocacy in response to oppression.

In order to be usable and practical, content is presented clearly. Numerous reality-based case examples demonstrate how skills are applied in real social work settings. The problem-solving model itself is graphically illustrated to provide the clearest picture possible of its implementation. Research applications in terms of evaluating one's own practice are emphasized. An entire chapter is devoted to developing relevant evaluation skills.

Additionally, content and specific skills are elaborated upon in a number of practice areas (for example, child abuse and neglect, crisis intervention, and chemical dependency). Such content areas are emphasized for a number of reasons. Either they are among those often encountered in practice, they present excessively difficult situations for untrained workers to address, or they are not consistently covered in another area of the required social work curriculum.

Available with the text is a Student Manual filled with classroom exercises and assignments. These are designed to coincide directly with text content and can be used to help students integrate reading material. The Student Manual also contains detailed outlines of each chapter. The intent is to help students organize the material and take notes if they so choose. Also available is an instructor's guide containing suggestions for using the exercises and a comprehensive test bank.

In summary, we hope that *Understanding Generalist Practice* will be a practical and flexible tool for students. We hope to emphasize the unique nature of social work as a helping profession. Finally, we hope students will find its content interesting and even enjoy it.

Companion Texts

Understanding Generalist Practice introduces generalist practice and targets micro-level skills. In like manner, two additional texts focus the generalist perspective on mezzo and macro skills. *Generalist Practice with Organizations and Communities* will be issued following publication of the present volume, and *Generalist Practice with Groups* shortly thereafter. Both stress the Generalist Intervention Model for problem-solving introduced in this book. However, each concentrates on the specific skills necessary for its respective level of practice. Each text will review the model and reinforce the generalist perspective by establishing numerous linkages among the three practice levels.

The three texts can be used in sequence, as one can build upon the other. On the other hand, each of the three texts can be used independently in conjunction with other practice textbooks, even those not reflecting a generalist perspective. Each can be used to integrate a generalist perspective at any point in the practice sequence. Student Manuals complete with classroom exercises and assignments will be available for each text.

Acknowledgments

We wish to express our heartfelt appreciation to the following people. Sincere thanks to illustrator Don Baumgart whose genius and artistic talent capture the heart of this book through his drawings. Many thanks to Lloyd Sinclair for writing chapter 11, "Making Ethical Decisions." We wish to express our sincere thanks to Carol Modl and Vicki Vogel for their exceptional supportive help. We also appreciate support provided by the University of Wisconsin—Eau Claire which included release time and financial assistance for Grafton H. Hull, Jr. We extend our earnest thanks to Judy Hull and Nick Ashman who sustained us with their monumental support, encouragement, and patience. We express our genuine indebtedness and appreciation to Steve Ferrara who encouraged us to pursue this endeavor and provided invaluable assistance and advice throughout the project. Many thanks to Richard Meade, Tamra Campbell-Phelps, and Rachel Schick whose steadfast help and creative consultation greatly facilitated the writing process.

Grafton H. Hull, Jr.
Karen K. Kirst-Ashman

1 Introducing Generalist Practice: The Generalist Intervention Model

A visual riddle: Assembling the tools of the profession. Subsequent chapters explore the generalist practice skills that these tools represent.

A fifteen-year-old can hardly make it through the morning until he can meet with his dealer and get some crack. He thinks briefly that it didn't used to be this bad, that he didn't used to "need" it this much. But he doesn't want to think about that for very long. It's too uncomfortable. He rationalizes that life is short and he wants to make the most of it. Besides, all of his friends use drugs, too. He's no different.

Forlorn homeless people are starving in the streets. Public funding for a community mental health program has been drastically cut back. That program had provided a halfway house where people could stay, receive counseling, and have their medication monitored. Years ago the long-term, inpatient mental institution had been shut down. It was much too expensive. Now with the cutbacks, the community program can barely survive. People with serious mental and emotional problems have been turned away and are roaming the streets with nowhere to go.

A family of four—the fifth generation to live on their family farm—is dispossessed. They had several years of crop failures and were unable to pay back the loans they so desperately needed to survive at the time. They're living in their '84 Chevy station wagon now. They can't find any housing they can possibly afford even though both parents work full-time, minimum wage jobs.

CHAPTER ONE

Introduction: What Is Generalist Practice?

These are situations that confront generalist social work practitioners everyday. Social workers don't pick and choose problems and issues they would like to address. They see a problem, often a very difficult problem, and try to help people solve it.

Social workers are generalists (Johnson,

┌─ HIGHLIGHT 1.1 ─────────────────────

Generalist Practice Involves Systems

There is a tendency for people to balk at theory. They prefer to focus their interest on the exciting aspects of practice, the actual doing of social work. However, theory provides social workers with a way of viewing the world. It gives direction to understanding why problems are occurring. Even more important, it provides clues for how to proceed in order to get the problems solved.

In order to understand how a systems model can provide the framework for intervention, one must understand some of the major concepts involved. These include the terms "system," "dynamic," "interact," "input," "output," "homeostasis," and "equifinality."

A *system* is a set of elements which forms an orderly, interrelated, and functional whole. Several aspects of this definition are important. The idea that a system is a "set of elements" means that a system can be composed of any type of things as long as these things have some relationship to each other. Things may be people or they may be mathematical symbols. Regardless, the set of elements must be orderly. The elements must be arranged in some pattern which is not simply random.

The set of elements must also be interrelated. They must have some mutual relationship or connection with each other. Additionally, the set of elements must be functional. Together they must be able to perform some regular task, activity, or function and fulfill some purpose. Finally, the set of elements must form a whole, a single entity. Examples of systems include a large nation, a public social services department, a Girl Scout troop, and a newly married couple.

The concept of a system helps a social worker focus on a target for intervention. The system may be an individual or it may be a state government.

The fact that the target is conceptualized as a system means that an understanding of the whole system and how its many elements work together is necessary. View, for example, an individual named Bill as a functioning system. Bill says he's depressed. The psychological aspects are only one facet of the entire functioning system. Physical and social aspects are among numerous other system characteristics. A worker who looks at the person as a total system would inquire further about Bill's health and social circumstances. The worker finds that Bill is suffering both from a viral flu infection which has been "hanging on" for the past three weeks and from a chronic blood disease. Both elements affect his psychological state. Additionally, the worker discovers that Bill has recently been divorced and misses his three children desperately. He has only partial custody of them. These aspects, too, relate directly to Bill's depression.

Thus, a systems approach guides social workers to look beyond a seemingly simple presenting problem. Workers view problems as interrelated with all other aspects of the system. Many aspects work together to affect the functioning of the whole person.

A systems perspective also guides workers to view systems as *dynamic*—that is, having constant dynamic movement. Problems and issues are forever changing. This provides workers with a flexible outlook. They must be ready to address new problems and apply new intervention strategies. For instance, a worker's assessment of Bill's situation and of intervention strategies would probably change if he were fired from his current job or re-united with his ex-wife.

Systems constantly *interact* with one another. A system can be an individual, a group, or a large

1989). That is, they need a wide array of skills at their disposal. They are prepared to help people with very individualized personal problems and with very broad problems that affect whole communities.

This book is about generalist practice. It involves what social workers do to help people with problems in virtually any setting. There are many ways to describe what social workers do. They work with individuals, families, groups,

organization. A systems focus provides the worker with a framework that extends far beyond that of the individual as the sole target of intervention. A systems perspective diverts attention from the individual to the interaction between that individual and the environment (Hartman, 1970). There is a constant flow of *input* and *output* among systems. Input is the energy, information, or communication flow received from other systems; output is the same flow emitted from a system to the environment or to other systems.

Reconsider Bill, the depressed man. His relationship with his ex-wife and children is seriously affecting not only him, but also his interactions at work. Co-workers who were once his friends are tired of hearing him complain. They no longer like to associate with him very much. Bill feels that he is in a dead-end, low level white-collar job which requires minimal skill. Even worse, his boss has cut back his hours so he can no longer work overtime. Now he can barely scrape by financially. The courts have mandated support payments for his children which he hasn't been able to make for three months. His ex-wife is threatening not to let him see his kids if he doesn't get some money to her soon.

(Of course, it should be noted that Bill's ex-wife Shirley views the situation from a totally different perspective. She attributes the divorce to the fact that Bill had a long series of affairs throughout their marriage. She had sacrificed her own employment and career in order to remain the primary caretaker of home and children. She just couldn't stand his infidelity any longer and filed for the divorce. Her serious financial situation is magnified by the fact that she has no employment or credit history of her own. She remains

very angry at Bill. She feels it is her right to demand support payments.)

Bill, on the other hand, is expending much energy to hold his life together. This is his output. However, he is receiving little input in return. As a result, he is unable to maintain his *homeostasis*. Homeostasis refers to the tendency of a system to maintain a relatively stable, constant equilibrium or balance.

A systems perspective takes these many aspects of Bill's life into account. It focuses on his input, output, and homeostasis with respect to the many systems with which he's interacting. Sitting in an office with this man for fifty minutes each week and trying to get him to talk his way out of his depression will not suffice in generalist practice. His interactions with his family, impinging mezzo systems (for instance, his co-workers) and macro systems (for example, the large company he works for and the state which mandates his support payments) provide potential targets of intervention and change. Can visits with his children and his support payment schedule be renegotiated? Can reconciliation with Shirley be pursued? Are the policies mandating his support payments and controlling his visitation rights fair? Are there any support groups available whose members have situations similar to his own and from whom he could gain support? Is there any potential for job retraining or job change?

Equifinality refers to the fact that there are many different means to the same end. In other words, there are many ways of viewing a problem and thus many potential means of solving it. Bill's interaction with friends, family, co-workers, governmental offices, and health care systems all affect his psychological state. Therefore, targets of intervention may involve change or interaction with any of these other systems.

organizations, and social systems. Their work is based on a body of knowledge, practice skills, and professional values. They work in settings which focus on children and families, health, justice, education, and economic status.

Johnson (1989) speaks of the "generalist approach" as requiring that the social worker assess the situation with the client and decide which system is the appropriate *unit of attention,* or focus of the work for the change effort (p. 1). She explains that this means that attention could be devoted to "an individual, a family, a small group, an agency or organization, or a community."

The *Encyclopedia of Social Work* (Sheafor & Landon, 1987, p. 666) defines the generalist perspective as one in which "the social worker has an eclectic theoretical base for practice," one which "is grounded in a systems framework suitable for assessing multiple points for potential intervention," one which "perceives that productive intervention occurs at every practice level (individual to community) and that frequently the most effective and beneficial changes occur through multilevel interventions"; and which recognizes that "a central responsibility of social work practice is the guidance of the planned change or problem-solving process." Although this definition is a mouthful, there are major themes involved. First, generalist social workers need to be infinitely flexible. Second, they require a solid knowledge base about many things. Third, they must master a wide range of skills and have these skills at their disposal.

The social work profession has been struggling with the concept of generalist practice for many years. There has been a tendency to educate new practitioners so that they are tracked into emphasizing only one area of skills (for example, work with individuals, groups, or communities) or one area of practice (for instance, children and families, or policy and administration). A generalist practitioner needs competency in a wide variety of areas instead of being limited to a single track.

Generalist social work practice may involve almost anything. A generalist practitioner may be called upon to help a homeless family, a sexually abused child, a pregnant teenager, an elderly person who's sick and unable to care for herself any longer, an alcoholic parent, a community that's trying to address its drug abuse problem, or a public assistance agency that's struggling to amend its policies in order to conform to new federal regulations. Therefore, generalist practitioners must be well prepared to address many kinds of difficult situations.

Proposed here is a problem-solving model. It presents practice from a systems perspective. The intent is to clarify in a practical manner what occurs in generalist social work practice. The model addresses the qualities that make social work unique and special. It demonstrates how a social work problem-solving approach can be applied to virtually any situation, no matter how difficult or complex. Finally, the model integrates an orientation to advocacy and a focus on more than just an individual as the target of change. Mezzo systems such as small groups and families (which we place somewhere between the micro and mezzo levels of generalist practice), and macro systems such as communities and large organizations are also potential targets of intervention.

This book emphasizes practical skills based on a solid foundation of knowledge and professional values. Specifically, this chapter will:

- Define and explain generalist practice;
- Describe the uniqueness of social work;
- Examine the foundation of knowledge, skills, and values upon which generalist social work practice is built;
- Propose a Generalist Intervention Model which employs a problem-solving focus;
- Review other practical generalist skills including making ethical decisions; practicing ethnically, racially, and gender sensitive social work; advocacy; brokering; case management; and recording.

Figure 1.1: Social Work and Other Helping Professions

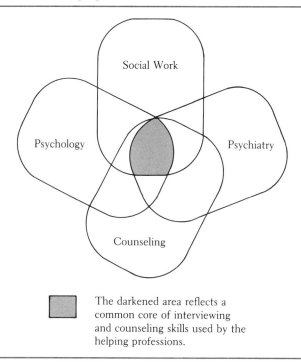

The darkened area reflects a common core of interviewing and counseling skills used by the helping professions.

The Uniqueness of Social Work

The purpose of social work is "to (1) enhance the problem-solving and coping capacities of people, (2) link people with systems that provide them with resources, services, and opportunities, (3) promote the effective and humane operation of these systems, and (4) contribute to the development and improvement of social policy" (Pincus & Minahan, 1973, p. 8). In other words, the purpose of social work is to help people in need by using any ethical means possible. It's impossible to specify a cookbook recipe for social work practice because of the variety of problems encountered and the methods employed. Flexibility and creativity are key qualities for generalist social work practitioners.

Other fields also perform some of the same functions as social work. For instance, mental health clinicians in psychology, psychiatry, and counseling use interviewing skills. Some use a problem-solving approach. Figure 1.1 illustrates how social work overlaps to some extent with other helping professions. All, for example, have a common core of interviewing and counseling skills.

However, social work involves much more than having a clinician sit down in her office with an individual, group, or family and focus on solving mental health problems. (This is not to imply that this is all the other helping professions do. Their own unique thrusts and emphases are beyond the scope of what is included here.) Social work has at least four major dimensions which make it unique.

First, social workers may focus attention on *any problem* or cluster of problems, even those which are very complex and difficult. Social workers don't refuse to work with clients or refer them elsewhere because those clients have unappealing characteristics. There may be a family in which sexual abuse is occurring. That abuse must stop. Likewise, there may be a community where the juvenile crime rate is skyrocketing. Something needs to be done.

Generalist practice doesn't mean that every problem can be solved. But some of them can be—or can at least be alleviated. Generalist practitioners are equipped with a bag of skills to help them identify and examine problems. They then make choices about where their efforts can be best directed.

The second dimension which makes social work unique involves a focus on *targeting the environment* for change. The system that social workers need "to change or influence in order to accomplish (their) goals" is called the "target system" or target of change (Pincus & Minahan, 1973, p. 58). Targets of change are not limited to individuals or families. Sometimes services are unavailable or excessively difficult to obtain, social policies are unfair, or people are oppressed by other people. Social workers look at where change is needed outside the individual and work with the environment to effect that change.

One example involves a midwestern city of about half a million people. Several dozen teenagers in the city have been expelled from several schools. They all have lengthening delinquency records and serious emotional problems. These young people have been attending a private day treatment program which provides special education and counseling at the individual, group, and family levels. The fact is that "day treatment" allows them to live at home in the community yet still receive special treatment. The program has been paid for by public funds. The county department of social services purchases treatment services from the private agency. The public schools have no special resources to handle and help these teens. Suddenly, money becomes scarce and community leaders decide they can no longer afford a day treatment program. The result is that these teenagers have nowhere to go.

This problem involves many children and their families. The social environment is not responding to their desperate needs. A generalist social worker addressing this problem might look at it from several perspectives. First, the city with its various communities might need to be made acutely aware both of the existence of these teens and of the sudden cuts in funding. Newspapers may need to be contacted. Second, the public school system may need to develop its own program to meet these children's and families' needs. Third, the parents of these children may need to band together and lobby for attention and services.

In this case, social workers involved in the agency whose funding had been cut off mobilized immediately. They contacted the parents of their clients and told them about the situation. The parents were outraged. They demanded that the community provide education for their children as it did for all the other children. Several parents became outspoken leaders of the group. Assisted by social workers, they filed a class action suit. The court determined that until the situation had been evaluated, funding for services must continue. Eventually, the public school system (also with the help of social workers) developed its own programs to meet the needs of such teenagers, and the private program was phased out.

The third dimension which makes social work unique is related to targeting the environment. Social workers often need to *advocate* for their clients. Advocacy involves actively intervening in order to help clients get what they need. Most frequently, this intervention focuses on "the relationship between the client and an unresponsive 'system'" (Epstein, 1981, p. 8). Clients have specified needs. Social agencies, organizations, or communities may not be meeting these needs. These unresponsive systems must be pressured to make changes so needs can be met. Specific techniques of advocacy will be addressed in much greater detail in chapter 14.

The fourth dimension which makes social work unique is its emphasis on and adherence to a *core of professional values*. The National Association of Social Worker's (NASW) Code of Ethics is illustrated in Figure 1.2 (see p. 23). This Code focuses on the right of the individual to make free choices and have a good quality of life. Social workers do not track people into specific ways of thinking or acting. Rather, they assist people to make their own decisions about how they will choose to think or act.

The Generalist Intervention Model

The Generalist Intervention Model (GIM) is characterized by four major features. First, the model is based on a foundation of knowledge, skills, and values which reflect the unique nature of social work. Second, GIM is oriented toward solving problems which involve not only individuals, but also groups, organizations, and even major social policies. In other words, the model involves micro, mezzo, and macro systems as targets of change. Third, the model's generalist approach means that virtually any problem may be analyzed and addressed from a wide range of perspectives. Fourth, GIM uses a specific problem-solving method which is infinitely flexible in its application.

The Foundation of Social Work: Knowledge, Skills, and Values

Social work has a growing and progressive knowledge base. More and more is being researched and written about how social workers can more effectively help people solve problems. Additionally, the field has borrowed much knowledge from other fields like psychology and sociology. Social work then applies such knowledge to practice situations.

Knowledge involves understanding the dynamics of people's situations and recognizing the skills that work best in specific situations. We've emphasized that generalist social workers need a broad knowledge base because they are called upon to help people solve such a wide variety of problems.

Fields of Practice

There are a number of ways to classify the kinds of knowledge generalist social workers need. One is by means of fields of practice. These are broad areas which address certain types of populations and needs. Each field of practice is a labyrinth of typical human problems and the services that attempt to address them. The seven fields of practice currently characterizing the profession include: family and children's services; health; mental health; occupational social work; aging; education; and corrections (Compton, 1983). Generalist social workers require information about people who need help in each of these seven areas. Workers must also be knowledgeable about the services available to meet needs and the major issues related to each area. A social worker may be called upon to work with a problem that clearly falls within one field of practice. On the other hand, a problem may involve several of these fields.

For example, the Steno family comes to a social worker's attention when a neighbor reports that Ben, a five-year-old child, is frequently seen with odd-looking bruises on his arms and legs. The neighbor suspects child abuse. Upon investigation, the social worker finds that the parents are indeed abusive. They often grab the child violently by a limb and throw him against the wall. This problem initially falls under the umbrella of family and children's services.

However, the social worker also finds a number of other problems operating within the family. The mother, Natasia Steno, is seriously depressed and frequently suicidal. She needs mental health services. Additionally, the father, Eric Steno, is struggling with a drinking problem which is beginning to affect his performance at work. A program is available at his place of employment where an occupational social worker helps employees deal with such problems. Thus, occupational social work may also be involved.

There is a maternal grandmother, Emma, living in the home with the Steno family. Emma's physical health is failing. Although her daughter Natasia dreads the idea of nursing home placement, the issue must be addressed. Emma, who is also overweight, finds it increasingly difficult to move around by herself. She is demanding more and more physical help and support from Natasia. Natasia, who has back problems herself, is finding it increasingly burdensome to help her mother. Finally, Vernite, the twelve-year-old daughter in the family, is falling behind in school. Truancy is becoming a major problem. The last issue falls under the umbrella of education.

Most of the problems that social workers face are complex. They may involve a variety of practice fields all at one time. In order to understand clients' needs, social workers must know something about a wide range of problems and services.

Curriculum Content Areas

There is another way of classifying the bodies of knowledge social workers need: one can look at the educational content of social work programs. The Council on Social Work Education (CSWE) is the organization that accredits social work programs throughout the country and specifies required content. Major required areas of content currently include practice, human behavior and the social environment, research, and policy.

Practice and Practice Skills

Social work practice is what this book is all about. It's the *doing* of social work. It involves how to form relationships with clients, help them share information with you, identify and evaluate numerous alternatives for action, make specific plans, implement these plans, evaluate progress, terminate the client-worker relationship, and follow up to make certain intervention is no longer necessary.

Practice involves working with individuals, families, groups, organizations (both large and small), and large social and governmental structures. The acquisition of practice skills is what makes social work useful and practical. Skills are the muscle that makes social work practice effective.

The social work knowledge base includes knowledge of skills in addition to knowledge of problems and services. A social worker must know which skills will be most effective in which situation.

Consider a family whose home suddenly burns to the ground. Its members need immediate shelter. The social worker decides it's necessary to use brokering skills; that is, skills involving seeking out and connecting people with the resources they need. The immediate crisis must be resolved by finding a place for the family to stay. In this situation, brokering skills take precedence over other skills. For instance, using less directive counseling techniques to explore the relationship between the spouses is inappropriate at this time. There is no current evidence of need. Such intervention may be necessary in the future, but only after the immediate crisis has been resolved.

Likewise, there is increasing evidence that a behavioral approach, in which tasks and goals are clearly specified, proves more effective than the less structured, vaguer procedures used in the past (Blythe & Briar, 1987). There are multitudes of helping techniques and theories about these techniques from which social workers can choose. Knowledge about the effectiveness of techniques is critical in choosing those which can accomplish the most in a specific situation.

Human Behavior and the Social Environment

Knowledge about human behavior and the social environment (HBSE) is an essential foundation on which to build practice skills. The first step in the problem-solving process is accurate assessment of the person, problem, and situation. The environment is vitally important in the analysis and understanding of human behavior. As social work has a person-in-environment focus (Council on Social Work Education, 1983), the interactions between individuals, systems, and the environment are critical. Such a conceptual perspective provides social workers with a symbolic representation of how to view the world. It provides ideas on how to assess clients' situations and identify their alternatives.

Both systems theory and the ecological perspective provide relevant models for conceptualizing social work practice. This text assumes a systems theory approach. However, it takes and utilizes selected concepts and ideas that are exceptionally useful in describing human interaction with other systems. For instance, the concept of social environment is grounded in ecological theory. Generalist practitioners work with clients in the context of their social environments.

People are constantly and dynamically involved in social transactions. There is ongoing activity, communication, and change. Social work assessment seeks to answer the question, "What is it in any particular situation that causes a problem to continue despite the client's expressed wish to change it?" A person-in-environment perspective allows social workers to assess many aspects of a situation. Assessment may involve not only individual, personal characteristics and experiences (micro events), but also mezzo and macro events (Kirst-Ashman, 1989). These concepts are grounded in systems theory.

Mezzo events involve interactions with other people in the immediate environment. These experiences often concern relationships with peer groups and immediate work groups.

Family events lie somewhere between the micro and mezzo levels of generalist practice. Because of the intimacy and intensity of family relationships and the importance of the family context to individuals, families deserve special status and attention.

Macro events involve people's transactions with large organizations and systems around the individual. An individual's place in the total scheme of things can be analyzed. Such macro events may include poverty, discrimination, social pressures, and the effects of social policies. This means that clients' problems are not viewed as each client's own fault. The forces surrounding the client frequently cause or contribute to problems. Thus, social workers need to focus their assessment on many levels. How the client and the problem fit into the larger scheme of things is critically important.

For instance, take a fifteen-year-old gang member, Kevin, in an urban inner-city. The gang is involved in drug dealing which, of course, is illegal. However, when assessing the situation and what might be done about it, a broader perspective is necessary. Looking at how the environment encourages and even supports the illegal activity is critical to understanding how to solve the problem. Kevin's father is no longer involved with the family. Now it's only Kevin, his mother, and three younger brothers. Kevin's mother works a six-day-per-week, nine-hour-per-day second shift job at George Webb's, a local all-night diner where she slings burgers. Although she loves her children dearly, she can barely make ends meet. She has little time for their supervision, especially Kevin's, as he is the oldest.

It seems that all of the neighborhood "kids" belong to one gang or another. It gives them a sense of identity and importance. It provides social support, where, in many instances, such support is almost completely lacking. Easy ac-

---

HIGHLIGHT 1.2

Differences Between Systems Theory and the Ecological Perspective

The Issues

Terms and concepts from both systems theory and the ecological perspective offer useful frameworks for generalist practice. There is some debate regarding the relationship between systems theory and the ecological perspective. That is, to what extent are the theoretical approaches similar and dissimilar? The ecological approach assumes a person-in-environment focus. Each perspective has, at various times, been described as a theory, a model, or a theoretical underpinning. Some similarities and differences will be briefly discussed below. Subsequently, a number of major concepts involved in the ecological perspective will be explained. Finally, the question of which approach is best will be addressed.

Similarities Between Systems Theory and the Ecological Perspective

Some very basic similarities exist between systems theory and the ecological perspective. Both emphasize systems. Likewise, both focus on the dynamic interaction among levels of systems. Some terms and concepts (for example, the term "input") are similar. Additionally, each provides social workers a framework with which to view the world. Finally, both perspectives emphasize external interactions instead of internal functioning. In other words, from a social work point of view, both emphasize helping people improve their interactions with other systems. This is very different from focusing on fixing or curing the individual.

Differences Between Systems Theory and the Ecological Perspective

In the simplest sense, there are two major differences between systems theory and the ecological perspective. First, the ecological approach refers to living, dynamic interactions. The emphasis is on active participation. People, for example, have dynamic transactions with each other and with their environments. Systems theory, on the other hand, assumes a broader perspective. It can be used to refer to inanimate, mechanical operations such as a mechanized assembly line in a Coca-Cola bottling plant. It can also be used to describe the functioning of a human family.

There is a second difference between the ecological perspective and systems theory. Although some terms are similar, different terms are emphasized. For example, the ecological approach focuses on transactions between individuals and the environment at the interface or point at which the individual and environment meet. Systems theory, on the other hand, addresses boundaries of subsystems and the maintenance of homeostasis or equilibrium within a system. Some theoreticians might posit that the ecological model is an offshoot or interpretation of systems theory, because it is a bit more limited in scope and application.

Ecological Concepts

In order to understand similarities and differences between the two perspectives, you must know the terms and principles involved in each. We've already reviewed some systems theory terminology including: system, dynamic, interaction, input, output, homeostasis, and equifinality. Below are some commonly used ecological concepts:

Social Environment

The social environment involves the conditions, circumstances, and human interactions which encompass human beings. Persons are dependent on effective interactions with this environment in order to survive and thrive. The social environment includes the type of homes people live in, the type of work they do, the amount of money available, and the laws and social rules they live by. The social environment also includes all the individuals, groups, organizations, and systems with which persons come into contact.

Person-in-Environment

A person-in-environment focus sees people as constantly interacting with various systems around them. These systems include the family, friends, work, social services, politics, religion, goods and services, and educational systems. The person is portrayed as being dynamically involved with each. Social work practice, then, is directed at improving the interactions between the person and these various systems. This is referred to as improving person-in-environment fit.

Transactions

People communicate and interact with others in their environments. Each interaction or transaction is active and dynamic (that is, something is communicated or exchanged). However, they may be positive or negative. A positive transaction may be the revelation that the one you dearly love loves you in return. A negative transaction may be being fired from a job that you've had for fifteen years.

Energy

Energy is the natural power of active involvement between people and their environments. Energy can take the form of input or output. Input is a form of energy coming into a person's life and adding to that life. For example, an elderly person in failing health may need substantial physical assistance and emotional support in order to continue performing necessary daily tasks. Output, on the other hand, is a form of energy going out of a person's life or taking something away from it. For example, a person may volunteer time and effort to work on a political campaign.

Interface

The interface is the exact point at which the interaction between an individual and the environment takes place. During an assessment of a person-in-environment situation, the interface must be clearly in focus in order to target the appropriate interactions for change. For example, a couple entering marriage counseling may first state that their problem concerns disagreements about how to raise the children. On further exploration, however, their inability to communicate their real feelings to each other surfaces. The actual problem—the inability to communicate—is the interface at which one individual affects the other. Each person is part of the other's social environment. If the interface is inaccurately targeted, much time and energy will be wasted before getting at the real problem.

Adaptation

Adaptation refers to the capacity to adjust to surrounding environmental conditions. It implies change. A person must change or adapt to new conditions and circumstances in order to continue functioning effectively. As people are constantly exposed to changes and stressful life events, they need to be flexible and capable of adaptation. Social workers frequently help people in this process of adaptation. A person may have to adapt to a new marriage partner, a new job, or a new neighborhood. Adaptation usually requires energy in the form of effort. Social workers often help direct people's energies so that they are most productive.

People are affected by their environments, and vice versa. People can and do change their environments in order to adapt successfully. For instance, a person would find it hard to survive a Montana winter in the natural environment without people-made shelter. Therefore, those who live in Montana change and manipulate their environment by clearing land and constructing heated

HIGHLIGHT 1.2 (continued)

buildings. They change their environment so they are better able to adapt to it. Therefore, adaptation often implies a two-way process involving both the individual and the environment.

Coping

Coping is a form of human adaptation and implies a struggle to overcome problems. Although adaptation may involve responses to new positive or negative conditions, coping refers to the way we deal with the problems we experience. For example, a person might have to cope with the sudden death of a parent or the birth of a new baby.

Interdependence

Interdependence refers to the mutual reliance of each person on each other person. Individuals are interdependent on other individuals and groups of individuals in the social environment. Likewise, these other individuals are interdependent on each other for input, energy, services, and consistency. People cannot exist without each other. The business executive needs the farmer to produce food and customers to purchase goods. Likewise, the farmer must sell food products to the

executive in order to get money for seed, tools, and other essentials. People—especially in a highly industrialized society—are interdependent and need each other in order to survive.

Which Perspective Is Best?

Both systems theory and the ecological perspective are useful for social work. The important thing is that both emphasize interactions with the environment. Depending on the circumstances, one perspective might be more helpful than the other. For example, systems theory might be more helpful when addressing problems within a family. Using concepts like subsystems and boundaries helps social workers understand the ongoing family dynamics. Likewise, analysis of a particular family system using these concepts provides cues for how to proceed to improve family functioning.

On the other hand, an ecological perspective can also be helpful. The concept of transactions with the social environment helps provide focus when a homeless family is not getting the resources it needs. A focus on the interface between family and environment leads a social worker to emphasize getting the family the services and support it requires to survive.

cess to drugs offers a readily available chance to escape from impoverished, depressing, and apparently hopeless conditions. Finally, gang membership gives these young people a means of getting hold of some money. In fact, they can get relatively large amounts of money in a hurry.

The gang members' alternatives appear grim. There are few, if any, positive role models to show them other ways of existence. They don't see their peers or adults close to them becoming corporate lawyers, brain surgeons, or nuclear physicists. In fact, they don't see anyone who's going or has gone to college. Finishing high school is considered quite a feat. Neigh-

borhood unemployment runs at more than 50 percent. A few part-time, minimum wage jobs are available—cleaning washrooms at Burger King or hauling heavy packages off of trucks at Pick 'n' Save. These options are unappealing alternatives to the immediate sources of gratification provided by gang membership and drug dealing. Even if another minimal source of income could be found, the other rewarding aspects of gang membership would be lost. Also, there's the all-consuming problem of having no positive future to look forward to. The future looks pretty bleak, so the excitement of the present remains seductive.

This is not to say that it's right for people like Kevin to join vicious gangs and participate in illegal activities. Nor does this mean that Kevin's plight is hopeless. Going beyond a focus on the individual to assess the many environmental impacts and interactions gives the social worker a better understanding of the whole situation. The answer might not be to send Kevin to the state juvenile correctional facility for a year or two, and then put him back in the same community with the same friends and the same problems. That focuses on the individual in a very limited manner.

A generalist social work practitioner views Kevin as part of a family and a community. Kevin is affected, influenced, supported, and limited by his immediate environment. Continuing along this line of thought, other questions arise. For example, how might Kevin's environment be changed? What other alternatives are available to him?

Many potential alternatives would involve major changes in the larger systems around him. Neighborhood youth centers with staff serving as positive role models could be developed as an alternative to gang membership. Kevin's school system could be evaluated. Does it have enough resources to give Kevin a "good education"? Is there a teacher who could single Kevin out and serve as his mentor and enthusiastic supporter? Can a mentor system be established within the school? Are scholarships and loans available to offer Kevin a viable alternative of college or trade school? Can positive role models demonstrate to Kevin and his peers that alternative ways of life may be open to them? Where might the resources for implementation of any of these ideas come from?

Concerning Kevin's family environment, can additional resources be provided? These might include food and housing assistance, good daycare for his younger brothers, and even educational opportunities for Kevin's mother so that she, too, could see a brighter future. Is there a Big Brother organization to support Kevin and his siblings? Can the neighborhood be made a better place to live? Can crime be curbed and housing conditions improved?

There obviously are no easy answers. Scarcity of resources remains a fundamental problem. However, this illustration is intended to show how a generalist social work practitioner would look at various options and targets of change—not just at Kevin.

In summary, knowledge of human behavior and the social environment is essential in generalist practice. With that foundation, the total picture can be better understood and a wider range of options identified.

Research

Research is the third major area of curriculum content. It accompanies practice and HBSE as a necessary component of the knowledge base for generalist practice.

Knowledge of social work research is important for three basic reasons (Reid, 1987). First, it can help social workers become more effective in their practice. It can help them get better and clearer results. Framing social work interventions so that they can be evaluated through research produces information about which specific techniques work best with which specific problems. When work with a client is clearly evaluated, social workers can determine whether they are really helping a client with his or her problem; additionally, they can monitor their progress during the actual intervention process (Hudson & Thayer, 1987).

There is a second reason why knowledge of research is important for generalist practice; accumulated research helps build a foundation for planning effective interventions. Knowledge about what has worked best in the past is a guideline for approaches and techniques to be used in the present and in the future. Research is the basis for the development of whole programs and policies which affect large numbers of people. Such knowledge can also be used to generate new theories and ideas to further enhance the effectiveness of social work.

The third reason for research's importance is that it "serves the practical function of providing situation-specific data to inform such actions as practice decisions, program operations, or efforts at social change" (Reid, 1987a, p. 474). In other words, at any point in the problem-solving intervention process, it can provide guidelines for what to do. It gives information about what has worked in the past and clues about how to proceed.

The content of social work research tends to fall within four major categories (Reid, 1987a). First, many studies involve the behavior of individual clients and their interactions with others close to them, including families and small groups. Second, much research focuses on how services are provided to clients, what such services involve, and how successful they are in accomplishing their goals. Third, many studies address social workers' attitudes and educational backgrounds, in addition to what's occurring in the entire social work profession itself. The fourth research category involves the study of "organizations, communities, and social policy" (p. 478). This latter category emphasizes the influence of the larger social environment upon the behavior and conditions of clients.

Thus, research is important to social work practice. Research informs and supports intervention approaches. It identifies theories and programs which are likely to be effective. Finally, it helps workers ensure that the client is being helped, rather than hurt, by what workers do.

Each social worker needs to master three dimensions of basic research skills. First, social workers need research skills to effectively evaluate the work they do with clients on both the micro and mezzo levels. Evaluation is the fourth step of the problem-solving process em-

phasized in this book. It involves determining whether what you do as a practitioner is effective. On a micro level, are your clients' needs being met? Are they generally attaining their goals? On a mezzo level, is the group you're running effective? Are individual members and the group as a whole accomplishing their respective goals?

The second dimension of basic research skills necessary for generalist practice involves the evaluation of macro system effectiveness. On a macro level, is your agency generally effective in providing services? Are clients really getting what they need? Practitioners, thus, need research competence to evaluate the effectiveness of service provision at all three levels of practice.

A third dimension of required research skills is the ability to understand, analyze, and critically evaluate social work literature and research. A wide variety of competing intervention approaches and techniques is available. Practitioners require research competence to make effective choices in their own generalist practice. How much faith can you place in specific research findings, considering the research methodology used? How useful is the research for your particular client population? How relevant are the findings for your own generalist practice?

Policy

Social policy is the fourth major area of curriculum content and knowledge base for generalist social work practice. Policy, in its simplest form, might be thought of as *rules*. Our lives and those of our clients are governed by rules. There are rules about how we drive our cars. There are rules about when we must go to school. There are rules about how we talk or write sentences.

Policies, in essence, are rules which tell us which actions among a multitude of actions we may take, and which we may not. Policies guide our work and our decisions. Social welfare policies tell us what resources are available to our clients and what kinds of things we may do for clients.

Policy might be divided into two major categories—social policy and agency policy. Social policy includes the laws and regulations that govern which social programs exist, what categories of clients are served, and who qualifies for a given program. It also sets standards regarding the type of services provided and the qualifications of the service provider.

Social policy involves "decisions of various levels of the government, especially the federal government, as expressed in budgetary expenditures, congressional appropriations, and approved programs" (Morris, 1987, p. 664). In other words, it involves the rules for how money may be spent to help people and how these people will be treated. Policies determine who is eligible for public assistance and who is not. Likewise, policies specify what social workers can do for sexually abused children and what they cannot.

Morris (1987) identifies several current trends in social policy, many of which restrict what can be done for people. For example, social policies have allowed programs which serve both rich and poor people to increase their resources, although at a slower pace than in prior decades. On the other hand, policies have restricted and decreased those services aimed primarily at poor people. Likewise, "new tax policies shifted more and more of the tax burden onto the poor and away from the wealthy" (p. 674).

Generalist practitioners must be well versed in social policy. Social workers must know what is available for a client and how to get it. In order to get what's needed, they must understand the rules or policies for getting it. For example, Adam, a social worker for a county social services department, has a young female client with three small children who has just been evicted from her apartment. Although the rent was relatively low and the

apartment small (one bedroom), she had been unable to pay the rent for the past three months. All her money had gone to clothing and feeding her children.

Adam needs to know what, if any, other resources are available for this client and whether the client is eligible to receive these resources. Policies determine the answers to these questions. Will the client qualify for temporary additional general assistance in order to help her relocate? Is there a local shelter for the homeless whose policies will allow the client and her children admission? If so, what is the shelter's policy regarding how long she can stay? Is low-rent housing available? If so, what does its policy designate as the criteria and procedure for admittance? Such questions may continue on and on.

In addition to social policies, there are agency policies. Agency policies include those standards adopted by individual organizations and programs which provide services (for example, a family service agency, a Department of Human Services, or a nursing home). Such standards may specify how the agency is structured, the qualifications of supervisors and workers, the rules governing what a worker may or may not do, and the proper procedures to follow for completing a family assessment.

The point is that knowledge of policy is vitally important. An organization's policy can dictate how much vacation an employee gets and how raises are earned. An adoption agency's policy can determine who is eligible to adopt a child, and who isn't. A social program's policies determine who gets needed services and resources and who does not.

One more thing should be said concerning social workers and social policy. Sometimes, for whatever reasons, social policies are unfair or oppressive to clients. Sometimes a social worker decides that a policy is ethically or morally intolerable. In those events, the worker may decide to advocate on behalf of clients to try to change the policy. More will be said in later chapters about advocacy and making changes in larger systems and their policies.

Generalist Practice Skills

We've reviewed the knowledge base needed by practitioners as part of their foundation for generalist practice. A second part of the foundation involves the skills needed to implement the problem-solving process. That is the primary thrust of this book. Later chapters will address a variety of generalist skills in much greater depth. A brief summary of the skills is related here.

Historically, social work skills were clustered into three major categories. First, *casework* primarily involved direct interaction with individual clients. This is analogous in many ways to the micro level of practice. Second, *group work* involved organizing and running a wide variety of groups (for example, therapeutic groups or support groups). The mezzo level of practice might be said to comprise this cluster of skills. Third, *community organization* involved working with organizations and communities. This is analogous to the macro level of social work practice.

Under this old model of practice, social workers considered themselves experts in only one approach. They were either caseworkers, group workers, or community organizers. They did not see themselves as having a sound basis in all three areas.

The intent of generalist practice is to provide a solid base of skills for working at the micro, mezzo, and macro levels of practice. Social workers are no longer divided and channeled into one of the three methods. This text will concentrate on the basic skills needed in working with individuals, groups, larger organizations, and communities, with the assumption that generalist social workers must be prepared to approach a problem from a wide variety of perspectives. Many times problems can be

To continue progress in a case, generalist practitioners must be prepared to view problems from many levels.

viewed on many levels. Additionally, as we will see, mezzo skills are based to some extent on micro level skills. Likewise, macro level skills have a basis both in mezzo and micro skills.

Common Generalist Skills

Specific skills characterize each level of practice. However, six core activities are also necessary regardless of the type of intervention (Landon, 1987, p. 668). First, generalist practitioners must *prepare* for the intervention before they begin. They need to get information and make plans, not just rush in haphazardly and "do something." What they do must be based on professional knowledge, skills, and values.

Secondly, generalist social workers must know how to *communicate*. It is essential to know how to form a relationship and talk to clients, whether they are single teen mothers receiving public assistance, state senators, the board of directors of a major social agency, or a crowd of nine hundred persons marching to gain resources for persons living with AIDS. Effective communication involves understanding the issues and problems. It also involves understanding how others view these same issues and problems. Communication allows you to make your intent clear to others. Words must be used in such a way that others can understand. Both verbal and nonverbal communication (for example, posture, eye contact, and gestures) must cohere to help deliver the intended message. Finally, communication involves good listening skills. Not only must you hear what others are saying to you, but you must also listen to what they mean.

Thirdly, generalist practitioners need to *analyze* the problem situation regardless of whether individuals, groups, or communities are involved. This involves "sorting and thinking through the various factors that have an impact on the client system and selecting the appropriate intervention approach" (p. 668).

The fourth skill common to all levels of practice is formulating a *contract* with the client system. Problems must be clearly identified and goals established with clients. Procedures to attain goals—including who is to do what by when—should be clearly specified.

Fifth, the generalist practitioner may need to assume a variety of *roles* when addressing a problem. If the client system needs active solicitation for help, the worker may need to function as an "advocate"; other possible roles include "enabler, educator, manager, broker, [and] mediator" (p. 668). All of these roles will be described more thoroughly in later chapters.

The sixth skill needed, regardless of level of practice, is *stabilizing*. The social worker needs to continually guide and monitor the intervention and its progress. Goals may need to be modified when relevant conditions change. New roles may be assumed in order to continue progress. Additionally, workers must evaluate interventions. Evaluation is necessary whether clients are individuals, groups, or entire communities. Likewise, workers need to recognize when goals are attained and termination achieved.

Micro Skills for Generalist Practice

We mentioned earlier that generalist practice skills are to some extent built upon each other as we move from micro to mezzo to macro levels. Social work obviously involves working with people. In order to work with people, basic interpersonal skills, including good communication skills, must be mastered. These basic skills are the same, whether you're working with one individual, a small or large group of people, or the representatives of a large organization or a community.

Chapter 2 will focus on these micro level skills. Relationship-building skills will be explained. The importance of displaying warmth, empathy, and genuineness will be discussed. Various aspects of communication will be examined, including verbal, nonverbal, and discrepancies between the two. Basic interviewing skills with a problem-solving orientation will be explained. A broad range of possible verbal responses to clients will be reviewed. Finally, a number of issues and hurdles in interviewing will be examined.

Mezzo Skills for Generalist Practice

Building upon the basic interpersonal skills established in chapter 2, chapter 3 will examine mezzo level skills. First, basic group dynamics (that is, what tends to go on in any actively functioning group) will be explored. Before group work skills can be applied, how groups form rules and expectations, select leaders, and distribute power must be understood.

The application of micro level relationship-building and communication skills will then be specifically applied to group settings. We will review the types of groups social workers frequently encounter and explain common social work roles. Finally, we will discuss specific skills social workers often need to help groups func-

tion and work effectively toward achieving their goals. For instance, how can goals be formulated to satisfy the needs of all group members? How can conflict among group members be managed?

Macro Skills for Generalist Practice

In order to solve problems involving organizations or communities, mastery of both micro and mezzo level skills are necessary. Working with macro level problems requires working with other individuals and working with groups of individuals. Chapter 4 will introduce you to the types of situations social workers frequently encounter in working with larger systems and

---

HIGHLIGHT 1.3

The Macro Level Approach: Promoting Social and Economic Justice

It's very easy for social workers, especially when they're just beginning in practice, to focus on changing the individual. Applying interviewing and problem-solving techniques to an individual in a practice situation is exciting. Figuring out how an individual client thinks and functions is fascinating. Additionally, the individual is right in front of you. The other systems with which the client is involved are much more abstract. Their interactions and effects may seem vague and distant. Because of the complexity of outside systems, it often seems more difficult to pinpoint them as targets of change.

However, generalist social work practitioners must also think in terms of needed changes beyond the individual client system. The individual is only one focus for potential change.

Macro system changes are seldom easy. They often involve influencing large numbers of people. Sometimes conflict arises. However, focusing on large system change is a unique aspect of social work which may open up multitudes of new problem-solving alternatives.

Three situations are described below. For

each one, think in terms of how the problem might be solved through macro level changes. For this exercise, do not change or move the individual. Think in terms of what major organizations or community groups can do to effect change. What policies might be changed? What community services might be developed? What strategies might achieve these changes?

Remember, do not change the individual. Focus only on macro system change.

1. You are a public social services worker in a rural county. Your job includes everything from helping the elderly obtain their Social Security payments to investigating alleged child abuse. Within the past six months, six farm families in the county have gone bankrupt. Government farm subsidies which used to be available have been withdrawn. It's been a bad two years for crops. Now the banks are threatening to foreclose on the farm mortgages. If they do, the six families will literally be put out in the cold with no money and no place to go.

What do you do?

organizations. The relationship between micro and mezzo level skills to those involved in macro level interventions will be described. Finally, we will examine the specific skills useful in macro practice and the roles social workers frequently assume.

Macro practice most frequently involves issues concerning a number of people or a specific group of people. For example, illegal drug use might be identified as a major difficulty in an urban neighborhood. Violence over drug sales is escalating. More and more people, including teens, are being shot as dealers and users squabble. The incidence of persons diagnosed with AIDS is abruptly increasing as addicts share needles and contaminate each other. Child neglect and abuse in the community is skyrocketing. Truancy rates are soaring. Parents on a "high" fail to attend to their young children. Parents' anger at themselves, at unsatisfied needs, and at the world in general is taken out on the easiest scapegoats—their children.

Approaches to solving these problems may reach far beyond helping an individual break a drug habit. Drug rehabilitation programs may be needed. Policies regarding the treatment of dealers may need to be addressed. Alternatives to a drug-related lifestyle may need to be pursued and developed for community residents. A youth center may be needed as a place for younger people to socialize, participate in activities, and have fun. Community residents may need job training and help in finding adequate employment.

---

2. You are a social worker for Bumpkin County Social Services. It's a rural county with a few towns of ten thousand people and no large cities. Your job as intake worker is to do family assessments when people call in with problems (anything from domestic violence to coping with serious illnesses). Your next task is to make referrals to the appropriate services.

You have been hearing about a number of sexual assaults in the area. Women are expressing fear for their safety. People who have been assaulted don't know where to turn. The nearest large cities are over eighty miles away. You have always been interested in women's issues and advocacy for women.

Now what do you do?

3. You have a seventy-year-old client named Harriett who lives in an old inner-city neighborhood in a large city. Since her husband died seven years ago, she's been living alone. She has no children, is still in good health, and likes to be independent.

The problem is that her house has been condemned for new highway construction. The plans are to tear it down within six months. There is no public housing available for the elderly within five miles of where she lives. She would like to stay in the area because she has a lot of elderly friends there.

Now what? (Remember, don't move Harriett.)

A Commentary

The scenarios above are very difficult to solve. They are not designed to frustrate you, but rather to encourage you to think about interventions beyond the micro and mezzo levels. Sometimes, macro system service provision is inadequate, ineffective, or simply wrong. The generalist practitioner's unique perspective is one of potential system change at all levels.

This text is designed to help you clarify that perspective and assimilate a wide variety of practice skills. The dimension of macro skills focuses on targeting the environment, not the person in the environment, for change.

The list of needs and possibilities is endless. A social worker involved in the community needs skills for organizing residents to come together and plan solutions. Skills in approaching community leaders and policymakers are important, because they may be persuaded to support and to help finance needed services. Fundraising skills are often necessary when other funding sources are unavailable. Skills are needed for a variety of macro practice roles including: initiating action when no one else is doing it; negotiating solutions; advocating on the behalf of clients who are unable to do so adequately for themselves; speaking on behalf of groups to make their issues and needs clear to those in decision-making positions; organizing people into groups that seek to get their own needs met; mediating among parties so that differences will be resolved; and, finally, providing necessary consultation to people in need of information.

Professional Values and Ethics

Along with knowledge and skills, professional values comprise the third basis for the foundation of generalist social work practice. Values involve what you do and do not consider important. They concern what is and is not considered to have worth. They also involve judgments and decisions about relative worth—that is, about what is more valuable and what is less valuable.

Ethics involve principles which specify what is good and what is bad. They clarify what should and should not be done. Social workers have a specific *Code of Ethics* (see Figure 1.2) which is based on professional values. Ethics and values are clearly related, although they are not synonymous. Loewenberg and Dolgoff (1985, p. 15) explain, "Ethics are deduced from values and must be in consonance with them. The difference between them is that values are concerned with what is *good* and *desirable*, while

ethics deal with what is *right* and *correct*." Values determine what beliefs are appropriate. Ethics address what to *do* with, or how to *apply*, those beliefs.

Social work values focus on "a commitment to human welfare, social justice, and individual dignity" (Reamer, 1987, p. 801). This frames the perspective with which social workers view their work with people. In other words, the well-being of people is more important than making the largest business profit or becoming the most famous actor. Social workers care about other people and spend their time helping people improve the conditions of their lives.

Social work values address both individual needs and concerns, those of communities, and those of society in general. Professional values are interwoven throughout micro, mezzo, and macro levels of practice. The individual well-being of a victim of child abuse is critical, as is the way public services and laws generally treat child abuse victims.

The *Code of Ethics* addresses six aspects of professional responsibility. In other words, ethical guidelines for how to make decisions and practice social work are given in six general areas. These areas include "the social worker's conduct and comportment as a social worker" and "ethical responsibility to clients, . . . colleagues, . . . employers and employing organizations, . . . the social work profession," and, finally, to "society" (National Association of Social Workers, 1987, p. 952).

Superficially, this situation appears simple. The profession provides ethical guidelines for how to help people. Theoretically, all you should have to do is adhere closely to those guidelines and ethical practice should be easy. You are simply supposed to look out for the well-being of your clients, right?

It is a cliché to say that people are complicated, as is life in general. However, it can also be said that the application of ethics to actual decision-making is often tremendously complicated. Many times the monster of ethical con-

Figure 1.2: National Association of Social Workers Code of Ethics (As adopted by the 1979 NASW Delegate Assembly, Effective July 1, 1980)

Summary of Major Principles*

I. **The Social Worker's Conduct and Comportment as a Social Worker**
A. *Propriety*
The social worker should maintain high standards of personal conduct in the capacity or identity as social worker.
B. *Competence and Professional Development*
The social worker should strive to become and remain proficient in professional practice and the performance of professional functions.
C. *Service*
The social worker should regard as primary the service obligation of the social work profession.
D. *Integrity*
The social worker should act in accordance with the highest standards of professional integrity.
E. *Scholarship and Research*
The social worker engaged in study and research should be guided by the conventions of scholarly inquiry.

II. **The Social Worker's Ethical Responsibility to Clients**
F. *Primacy of Clients' Interests*
The social worker's primary responsibility is to clients.
G. *Rights and Prerogatives of Clients*
The social worker should make every effort to foster maximum self-determination on the part of clients.
H. *Confidentiality and Privacy*
The social worker should respect the privacy of clients and hold in confidence all information obtained in the course of professional service.
I. *Fees*
When setting fees, the social worker should ensure that they are fair, reasonable, considerate, and commensurate with the service performed and with due regard for the clients' ability to pay.

III. **The Social Worker's Ethical Responsibility to Colleagues**
J. *Respect, Fairness, and Courtesy*
The social worker should treat colleagues with respect, courtesy, fairness, and good faith.
K. *Dealing with Colleagues' Clients*
The social worker has the responsibility to relate to the clients of colleagues with full professional consideration.

IV. **The Social Worker's Ethical Responsibility to Employers and Employing Organizations**
L. *Commitments to Employing Organizations*
The social worker should adhere to commitments made to the employing organizations.

V. **The Social Worker's Ethical Responsibility to the Social Work Profession**
M. *Maintaining the Integrity of the Profession*
The social worker should uphold and advance the values, ethics, knowledge, and mission of the profession.
N. *Community Service*
The social worker should assist the profession in making social services available to the general public.
O. *Development of Knowledge*
The social worker should take responsibility for identifying, developing, and fully utilizing knowledge for professional practice.

VI. **The Social Worker's Ethical Responsibility to Society**
P. *Promoting the General Welfare.*
The social worker should promote the general welfare of society.

*Constitutes a summary of the Code of Ethics effective July 1, 1980, as adopted by the 1979 NASW Delegate Assembly. The complete text, including preamble and expanded definition of principles, is available upon request.

flict will raise its hoary head. Adherence to one aspect of ethics will strikingly contradict adherence to another.

Reamer (1987, p. 804) cites an example of a typical ethical quandary:

> . . . the NASW Code of Ethics states that the "social worker should not engage in any action that violates or diminishes the civil or legal rights of clients." However, the code also states that the "social worker should adhere to commitments made to the employing organization."

Consider a situation in which a client, David, reveals that he has contracted AIDS. He has just been given the diagnosis. This condition is almost certainly fatal, and the social worker knows that the client has been having unprotected sexual relations with several people over the past months. During their meetings David has specifically named these people. After discussing options, the client refuses to tell his sexual partners about his diagnosis. Additionally, for a variety of reasons, the social worker doubts that the client will now begin to use precautions against spreading the disease. Agency policy mandates that social workers may not violate clients' confidentiality. This means that according to policy the social worker may not tell anyone about the AIDS diagnosis

---

┌ HIGHLIGHT 1.4
Ethical Dilemmas

One of the ethical dilemmas commonly faced by social workers is deciding who is to get help when resources are limited. In many instances there is a given amount of money to spend, and a social worker must choose who will receive help and who will not.

Below is an exercise designed to help you understand how difficult ethical dilemmas can be. Later, chapter 11 will help you work through some of the dilemmas social workers commonly face. It will also provide suggested structures for making difficult decisions.

The Exercise

You have $25,000 to spend. Below are ten situations. Each situation requires the full $25,000. Dividing the money would be useless and would help no one. You must decide where to spend the money.

To whom should the $25,000 be made available?

1. A premature infant (born three months early) who needs to be maintained in an incubator.
2. A fifty-two-year-old man who needs a heart transplant.
3. Your fifty-two-year-old father who needs a heart transplant.
4. A five-year-old child with AIDS.
5. You yourself who have graduated and have been out of work for six months.
6. A divorced single mother with three children, a tenth grade education, and nothing but the clothes on her back.
7. A mentally retarded person who needs to be placed in a group home for the developmentally disabled.
8. A fourteen-year-old runaway, addicted to cocaine and alcohol, who has been prostituting herself to survive, and needs the money to enter a drug treatment program.
9. A convicted child sexual abuser who was himself sexually abused as a child and seeks rehabilitation.
10. A dispossessed urban family—a couple in their late twenties and their three small children.

There are no easy answers.

without David's clearly expressed written permission. The worker worries that, among other things, prior sexual partners unaware of the AIDS diagnosis and their potential exposure may continue to spread the disease. Which ethical concept is most important—respect for David's privacy, commitment to the employing organization and its policy, or ethical responsibility to the general welfare of society and the well-being of other people? There is no easy answer.

Ethical dilemmas are numerous. For instance, the law may dictate a lengthy procedure for removing the perpetrator in a case of alleged sexual abuse. However, what about the immediate critical needs of the victim? Or a public assistance agency may require that applicants maintain residency for a specified time before they become eligible for help. The single parent of a family of five comes in and says her children are starving. She has not lived in the area long enough to satisfy the residency requirement. What should the social worker do? Should the family be allowed to starve?

The potential for ethical dilemmas is endless. Professional values and ethics offer some basic guidelines. However, many times a social worker will have to decide what is *more* ethical or *more* critical. Chapter 11 will address the issue of ethical decisions. Suggestions for evaluating problems, breaking down potential solutions, and prioritizing ethical principles will be discussed.

The Problem-Solving Method

The Generalist Intervention Model uses a problem-solving approach. A problem may be defined as an "intricate, unsettled question" or a "source of perplexity, distress, or vexation" (*Webster's New Collegiate Dictionary*, 1977, p. 917). Social workers help people deal with problems ranging from personal relationships to lack of resources to blatant discrimination. A social worker may need to address the problem of a battered woman who is economically and emotionally dependent on her abusive husband and who also has three children to protect. In another instance, a social worker might have an adolescent client who has committed a number of serious crimes and is heavily involved with an urban gang. At yet another time, a social worker may need to advocate and fight for change in a public assistance policy that discriminates against people who don't speak English very well and are thus unable to follow an intricate, exasperating process of applying for benefits.

Regardless of what kind of problem is addressed, the problem-solving process presented here involves six major steps. Each will be defined briefly now with later chapters providing more extensive elaboration. The problem-solving steps include assessment, planning, intervention, evaluation, termination, and follow-up.

Step 1: Assessment

According to Siporin (1975, p. 224), assessment is the "differential, individualized, and accurate identification and evaluation of problems, people, and situations and of their interrelations, to serve as a sound basis for differential helping intervention." Sheafor et al. (1988, p. 222) define assessment as "the process of interpreting or giving meaning and conceptual order to data; it is an attempt to make sense out of the data that have been collected." They continue that assessment "is an activity directed toward understanding the client's problem or situation and developing a plan of action" (p. 224). In other words, assessment refers to defining issues and gathering relevant information about a problem so that decisions can be made about what to do to solve it.

Identify Your Client

The first step in assessment is to determine who your client is. At first glance, this may sound overly simplistic. It seems logical to say your clients are those people cited on your client list (i.e., your caseload). However, we've already established that people, their lives, and their problems are often very complicated. The designation of who is really your client and who is not may become blurred and vague.

For example, say you are a probation officer. Justin, age fifteen, is a client on your caseload. He was adjudicated delinquent because he had stolen over a dozen cars. Since Justin is clearly listed on your caseload, he is your client, right?

However, you determine that Justin needs support and guidance from his parents. He currently lives at home with them, and both parents are currently abusing illegal drugs. Both also have conviction records for drug dealing. Additionally, Justin has three younger siblings also living in the home. You worry that they are likely to follow in Justin's footsteps and become involved in theft and other illegal activities.

Who is your client? Who do you need to help? Is it just Justin? Or is his entire family your client? Is your client really the community that employs you to monitor lawbreakers and help them fit into the community more appropriately?

To answer these questions, it is helpful to think in terms of a "client system" (Pincus & Minahan, 1973; Lippit, 1958). Pincus and Minahan (1973, p. 56) define a client system as "the individual, family, group, organization, or community that, in addition to being the expected beneficiary of service, is a system that asks for help and engages the services of a social worker as a change agent." They continue that "people become clients only when a working agreement or contract has been established between them and a change agent" (that is, the social worker).

The probation officer may decide that Justin alone is the client system. Or that Justin and his entire family will become the client system. Whoever is identified as "those who have sanctioned (or asked for) his services, are expected to be beneficiaries of the change efforts, and have entered into a working agreement or contract" with the social worker (Pincus & Minahan, 1973, p. 57) become the client system.

It should be noted that clients may be voluntary or involuntary. Justin surely didn't choose to have a personal probation officer. His family may not be thrilled with the idea either. Rather, society forced the probation situation upon Justin and his family. Nonetheless, in this case Justin and his family are intended to receive the benefits of the intervention effort. Additionally, the probation office will make agreements with whomever is identified as part of the client system by establishing a contract with them. This situation fits the definition of client system which was provided earlier.

Assess the Client-In-Situation and Identify Issues

After the client system is established, a generalist practitioner will continue with the assessment. This process of gathering information is tied directly to what the social worker does about the problem. How social workers intervene is based on the information they have and on the judgments they have made about that information. Assessment in generalist practice focuses on understanding the many aspects of a problem. Information is needed about the client and about those aspects of the client's environment which the worker feels are significant.

For example, a social services worker in a rural county receives a call about Hilda from Hilda's neighbor. Hilda, eighty-four, lives in an old farm house in the country where she has lived for most of her life. Hilda's health is deteriorating. She is falling more and more frequently, and her eyesight is failing. The neighbor worries that Hilda may fall, break something, and lie helpless and alone for days.

The worker visits Hilda and does an assessment of her and her situation. The worker needs information to make decisions about what he

Aspects of an elderly client's problems which the generalist practitioner may need to assess include the client's being confined to a house and living in an isolated area.

and Hilda can do. Hilda may need some supportive services or even health care center placement.

The information needed falls into four major categories. These include micro, mezzo, and macro levels of assessment in addition to consideration of elements of human diversity. In each category, problems need to be defined and strengths identified.

Micro Aspects

First, the worker needs to explore the micro aspects of the situation. What are Hilda's most critical problems? What things about Hilda con-

tribute to her problems? On the other hand, what are Hilda's strengths? What does she do well? What aspects of her life does she consider important?

The worker explores both biological and psychological aspects of Hilda's situation. In Hilda's case, the biological aspects primarily involve her current health problems. Yes, Hilda admits she falls occasionally, but she thinks that a cane might help. Her failing sight is especially difficult for her. She talks of how she is not eating very well lately because she can't see well enough to cook.

Also, from the micro aspects perspective,

the worker explores Hilda's psychological situation. How does Hilda feel about herself and her situation? The worker finds that Hilda, too, is finding it increasingly difficult to take care of herself. She loves her home and expressed the strong desire to remain in it. However, she feels she could use some help, especially with food purchase and preparation. The worker finds that Hilda expresses herself well. Although Hilda is somewhat discouraged about her eyesight, she appears to be emotionally stable.

Micro/Mezzo Aspects: Families

The worker asks Hilda about her family. Does Hilda have any relatives in the immediate vicinity? Does she have children who are available to help out? What are her relationships with relatives who might be accessible?

The worker discovers that Hilda has three children in the area. They call and visit frequently, but haphazardly. They occasionally take her shopping or to visit their homes.

Mezzo Aspects

The worker then pursues questions about the other mezzo aspects of Hilda's situation. Does Hilda have friends she can talk to? Do people visit her? How often? Does she have opportunities to get out of the house at all?

The worker establishes that Hilda has a number of friends in the area. However, she rarely sees them because of the transportation difficulties for both her and them. She is, however, affiliated with a church and participates in church activities as frequently as she can.

Macro Aspects

Thirdly, the worker explores the macro aspects of the situation. What services might be available to help Hilda with her identified problems? Is there a Meals-on-Wheels program available? Meals-on-Wheels provides regular delivery of hot meals to elderly people throughout a designated area. Is there a Visiting Friends program through which paraprofessionals regu-

larly visit elderly residents in their homes and help them with shopping, paying bills, making medical appointments, and so on?

The worker determines that no such services are readily available at this time. He decides that the system is not designed to meet Hilda's needs or the needs of other elderly people in similar positions.

Aspects of Diversity

The worker needs to consider a fourth dimension while assessing Hilda and her situation: are there any significant aspects of diversity? Human diversity refers to "the range of differences between peoples in terms of race, ethnicity, age, geography, religion, values, culture, orientations, physical and mental health, and many other distinguishing characteristics" (Barker, 1991, p. 105). The worker finds that Hilda is of German heritage. This is a relevant aspect of ethnic and cultural diversity. Hilda also feels strongly about her membership in a local Lutheran church which many other elderly people of similar heritage also attend. For many reasons, Hilda's church involvement is very important to her.

Another aspect of diversity is Hilda's age. Is Hilda being treated differently or in a discriminatory manner because of ageism? Ageism refers to discrimination based on predisposed notions about older people, regardless of their individual qualities and capabilities. The worker closely evaluates his own attitudes. For instance, is he tempted to make assumptions about Hilda's mental capability because of the stereotype that older people can no longer think as clearly as they could when they were younger?

Likewise, the worker must be aware of any sexist biases he might harbor. Sexism refers to predisposed notions about a person based on that person's gender. For instance, does the worker feel that Hilda is a dependent person who needs to be taken care of simply because she's a woman? Such a bias fails to take into account the client as a unique individual with particular strengths and weaknesses.

Assessment and Planning

After reassessing the client and her situation, the worker and Hilda together establish the following plan. First, regarding micro intervention, Hilda needs a cane. Hilda also needs some supportive care related to micro/mezzo (family) and macro interventions. The worker and Hilda decide to meet with Hilda's children and their families to work out a schedule for visitation and assistance. In this way, her relatives can regularly check to make certain Hilda is all right. Hilda feels strongly about remaining in her home as long as possible. The worker, Hilda, and Hilda's family agree that until/unless her health deteriorates further, they will try to maintain her in her own home.

The macro intervention in Hilda's case involves the lack of supportive services available to her. The worker and his supervisor bring Hilda's situation to the attention of the social services department's administration. On further investigation, a substantial number of other elderly people are found to be in positions similar to Hilda's. Thus, the change process is initiated to pursue funding for new resources to help elderly people.

Hilda's example provides only a brief summary of the social service worker's assessment. However, it does highlight the basic categories of information needed in virtually every assessment. The assessment model is illustrated in Figure 1.3. Once again, four general categories of information should be considered: *micro information* which includes both biological and psychological aspects; *mezzo information* which involves immediate groups with which clients have interaction; *macro information* which concerns the impact of the broader social environment, organization, laws, and policies upon the client(s); and finally, *aspects of diversity* which focus on special qualities or characteristics which may place clients in a designated group.

Concerning the last category, the potential for discrimination must also be considered.

The crucial task of generalist practice is to look beyond the individual and examine other factors that impinge on the client's environment. In any individual case, the emphases upon one or the other assessment categories may vary. However, each category must still be reviewed and considered for its potential contribution to the problem.

For instance, a couple may come to a social worker for help in their marital relationship. Thus, assessment of the mezzo aspects or relationship issues of the situation would be emphasized. However, a generalist practitioner would also consider both the micro aspects—such as the strengths, needs, and issues of each partner—and the macro aspects impinging upon their situation. Macro aspects might involve the fact that both spouses have been laid off their jobs at the local Case International tractor factory. They've held these jobs for over ten years, and the lay-off was probably due to a serious depression in farm prices. In this case the social worker might not be able to do much about the current economy. However, the economic impact on the couple is vital in an assessment of the current conflictual situation.

We've already established that the problems social workers deal with are seldom easy to solve. We've also identified an underlying theme in generalist practice which provides a whole new array of potential alternatives: the generalist practitioner focuses on how clients are integrally involved with their social environments, on both the mezzo and macro levels.

Many specific assessment instruments and techniques are available. They vary by agency, clientele, and problem area. Within the framework of the Generalist Intervention Model, chapter 5 will discuss a variety of more specific assessment methods and issues commonly encountered during the assessment process. Specific case examples will illustrate the application of assessment principles.

Figure 1.3: Assessment in the Generalist Intervention Model

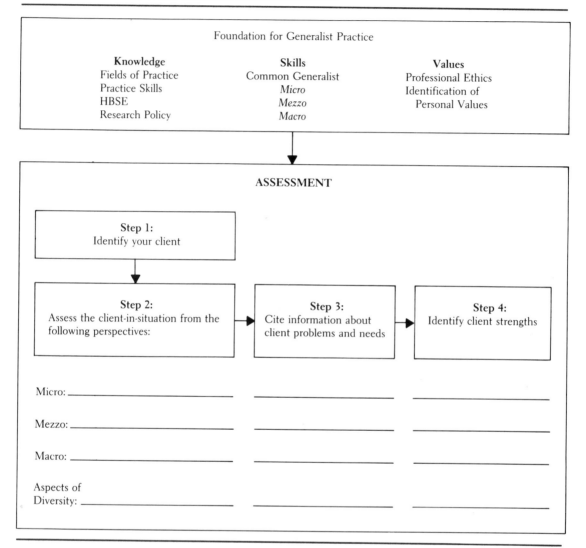

Step 2: Planning

The second step in the Generalist Intervention Model involves planning what to do. Planning follows assessment in the problem-solving process. Assessment sets the stage for the intervention. Planning specifies what should be done. Chapter 6 elaborates on the planning process in greater depth.

Work with the Client

The generalist practitioner follows seven sub-steps in the planning process. Figure 1.4 illustrates these sub-steps. First, it is important to work *with* the client, not *at* the client. The client must be involved in problem definition and must agree as to which problems merit attention. Additionally, the planning pro-

Figure 1.4: Planning in the Generalist Intervention Model

Foundation for Generalist Practice

Knowledge
Skills
Values

Assessment

PLANNING

Step 1: Work with the client.

Step 2: Prioritize problems. ⟶

> Problem
> 1.
> 2.
> 3. etc.

Step 3: Translate problems into needs.

Problem ⟶	Need
1. ⟶	1.
2. ⟶	2.
3. ⟶	3.

Step 4: Evaluate levels of intervention for each need.

Need #1: _____ etc.

a. Identify Alternatives: ⟶	b. Propose Solutions ⟶	c. Evaluate: Pros	Cons	Client strengths
Micro				
Mezzo				
Macro				

Step 5: Establish primary goals

Step 6: Specify objectives

	Who?	Will do What?	By When?	How will you measure success?
1.				
2.				
3.				

Step 7: Formalize a contract.

cess should take advantage of the client's strengths.

Prioritize Problems

The second sub-step in planning is to prioritize the problems. Again, the client must be a partner in this process. Many times what the worker feels is important differs drastically from what the client thinks is most significant. For example, a social worker may be most concerned about Carol's potential for abusing her small children and about her alcohol consumption. Carol, on the other hand, may be most interested in solving her financial problems. She has been cut back on the hours she works, so she now works only part-time. Meanwhile, her rent is rising astronomically, she owes growing debts on her credit cards, and she sees herself as a failure because she can't take adequate care of her family. Part of the worker's job is to examine the various aspects of the problems at hand and focus on problems and issues considered significant by the client and the worker.

Translate Problems into Needs

Sub-step 3 in the planning process involves translating problems into needs. Clients come to you because they are suffering from problems. The way you can help them is to establish what they *need* to solve the problem. This relatively simple step in planning helps to restructure how you look at the situation so that it's easier to figure out solutions.

Evaluate Levels of Intervention (Micro, Mezzo, and Macro)

Sub-step 4 in the planning process involves first focusing on one client need at a time, beginning with those of highest priority. Possible alternative solutions should be discussed with the client.

Alternative solutions may focus on the micro, mezzo, or macro level of change. The proposed alternative, thus, may involve what the individual can do at the micro level. For instance, one alternative solution aims at having Carol change her own behavior. She might enter an alcohol and drug treatment program. Another tack might be to help her find a new, more suitable job.

Or the worker and client might address the problem at a mezzo level. Carol could join a support group for people dealing with similar issues. Still another option may involve proposed change at the macro level. The worker might advocate to get Carol into low-rent housing. Another strategy might be to develop a plan for instituting rent control in the community. This last idea would make life more affordable for people facing financial conditions similar to Carol's.

Each proposed alternative solution should be evaluated regarding its pros and cons. How feasible or doable is it? What are the chances of success? Client strengths should be constantly kept in mind and involved in the solutions whenever possible. One result should be the selection of an alternative plan of action.

Establish Primary Goals

The fifth sub-step in the planning process is to establish primary goals. Goals provide you and your client with direction regarding how to proceed with the intervention. What do you really want to accomplish? How can your client's major needs be accomplished? What are your primary, necessary end results?

Specify Objectives

Goals can probably never be too specific. They should be so clearly stated that it is as easy as possible to determine when they've been attained and when they have not. However, many times goals are very basic and broad. For instance, consider the goals "find adequate housing" or "obtain needed medical attention." These primary goal statements and other statements like them don't give you a clue regarding *how* to achieve them. Where would you go to meet these needs? How would you begin the planning process?

Thus, primary goal statements should be translated into *objectives*. You might think of objectives as sub-goals, or smaller steps specifying how you might achieve a primary goal. For example, a sub-goal might be for you as a practitioner to call six specified medical clinics and hospitals to determine the availability of medical attention for your client—and to complete these calls by next Thursday. Objectives are very specific. They should include *who* should do *what* by *when*, and *how* they should do it. For instance, Ms. Schultz will complete a one-page, typewritten statement of her positive qualities and characteristics by 3:30 P.M. next Thursday.

The "how" portion of accomplishing an objective is perhaps the hardest part. It is very difficult, for example, to determine exactly when an individual has achieved the objective of "attaining a positive attitude." This is much too vague. When does a "negative attitude" suddenly turn into a "positive" one? Is there some twilight zone in the middle where the person is simply neutral? What is "neutral" anyway? Must the attitude be just a little positive or very, very positive, and what is the difference between the two?

On the other hand, an objective which specifies prioritizing and writing down five tasks to accomplish each day is easier to evaluate. If four tasks are recorded or if the tasks remain unprioritized, the objective has not been fully met. Objectives should be stated with as much behavioral specificity as possible. They should reflect very clearly specific behaviors which can be easily measured. In this instance, "how" Ms. Schultz achieves her objective is clearly stated. She does it by writing and prioritizing a specified number of tasks.

Formalize a Contract with the Client

"A contract is a working agreement that usually is negotiated by the client, the worker, and other service personnel who will be involved in the service process" (Seabury, 1987, p. 343). The contract can be used to specify the many ways in which the worker and client are going to work together toward their goals. A contract formalizes the agreement between client and worker. It also clarifies their expectations.

A wide variety of items can be included in a contract. These include specific aspects of the plan—such as who will do what by when, intended goals, fees or financial responsibility, meeting times, types of services provided, and virtually any other condition involved in the intervention. As in other aspects of the problem-solving process, it's critically important for "the client to be actively involved in developing the terms" of the contract (Seabury, 1987, p. 344). The worker must make certain that the client understands all of the specific words used in the contract. Technical jargon (or "psychobabble" as a business major friend once labeled it) must be clearly explained to the client or paraphrased in words the client readily understands.

Contracts are flexible agreements. In this manner, they are strikingly different from "legal" contracts which require that all parties concur with their terms. This latter type of contract cannot easily be altered. Contracts with clients must be formal enough to clarify expectations but informal enough to let the worker respond flexibly to the client's changing needs or conditions.

Step 3: The Intervention

The third step in the Generalist Intervention Model involves the actual *doing* of the plan. Client and worker follow their plan to achieve

Figure 1.5: Intervention in the Generalist Intervention Model

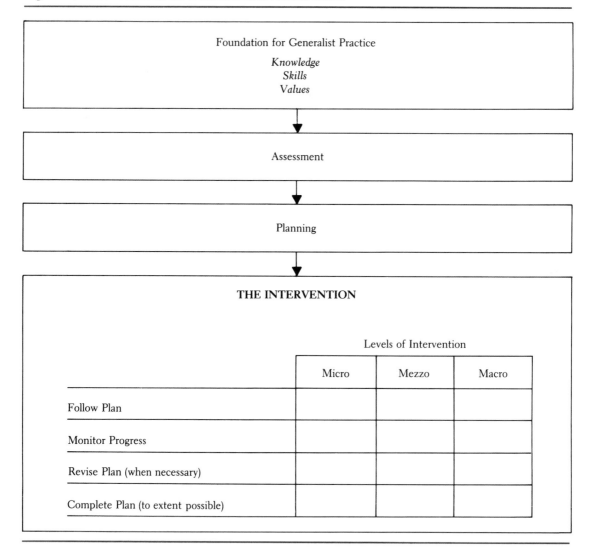

their goals. Progress during the intervention must be constantly monitored and assessed. Sometimes new issues, situations, and conditions require that the plan be changed (see Figure 1.5).

For example, take a case in which the intervention plan involves the goal of determining custody and visitation rights following a divorce. The couple suddenly decides to stay together. Determining custody rights is no longer relevant. However, new goals might need to be developed concerning more effective behavioral management of the children to prevent family feuding and future disruptions of the marital relationship.

Chapter 7 will examine three applications

of intervention. They include risk management in the context of child maltreatment and protective services, assessment and treatment of alcohol and other drug abuse, and crisis intervention.

Step 4: Evaluation

Evaluation of an intervention, Step 4 in the Generalist Intervention Model, is critical for accountability. Social workers need to be account-

Figure 1.6: Evaluation in the Generalist Intervention Model

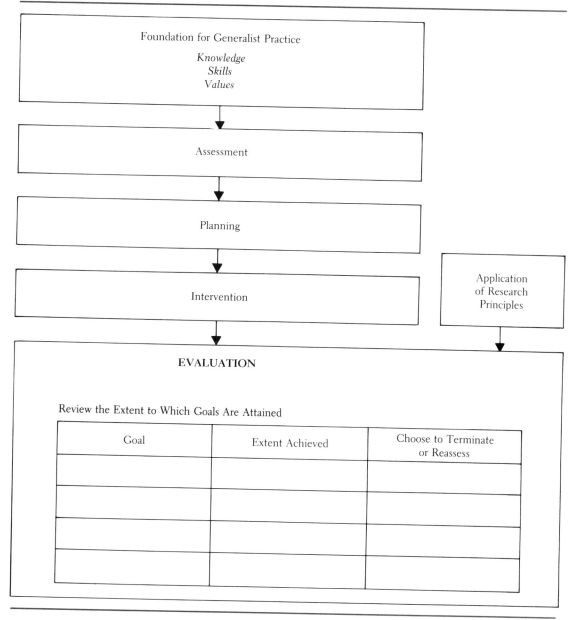

able. That is, they must prove that their interventions have been effective. Each goal is evaluated in terms of the extent to which it has been achieved. The decision then must be made about whether the case should be terminated or reassessed to establish new goals (see Figure 1.6).

Evaluation techniques are becoming increasingly more effective. They involve the application of research principles to generalist practice. Chapter 8 will explore a variety of evaluation designs both for direct service practitioners and for whole programs. Evaluation

Figure 1.7: Problem-Solving Steps in the Generalist Intervention Model

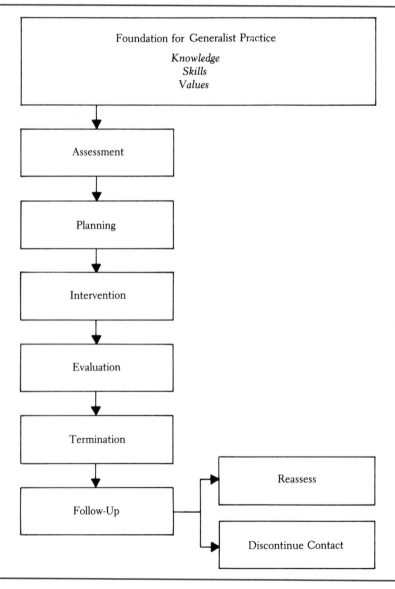

issues commonly faced by practitioners will also be addressed.

Step 5: Termination

Step 5 in the Generalist Practice Model concerns termination. The worker/client relationship must eventually come to an end. It is not a good ending for a worker to get up one day and, out of the clear blue sky, say, "Well, good-bye." Termination in generalist practice involves specific skills and techniques. This is true regardless of the level of intervention (see Figure 1.7).

Appropriate timing of the termination is important. Hellenbrand cites at least three basic types of termination (1987, p. 765). First, some terminations are "natural." That is, goals have been achieved, and it is time for the clients to take what they have learned and go out on their own. Other terminations are "forced," as, for example, when a worker leaves the agency. Another example involves the client leaving an institution for some reason or losing eligibility for services. Finally, there are "unplanned" terminations. The client just does not come back. The family moves. The client is no longer motivated to return. Other aspects of a client's life take precedence over the problem he or she came to the social worker to solve.

The most effective terminations follow a process of disengagement and stabilization. Chapter 8 discusses this process. Social workers need to acknowledge that endings are near before they abruptly occur. They must encourage clients to share feelings about the termination, and in turn share their own. Additionally, practitioners must clearly identify whatever progress has been made. This increases the chance that the client will use what has been learned during this intervention to help solve other problems in the future.

The client may be an individual, a group member, or a large agency. Regardless, each needs help in the transition from dependence on the worker for support or guidance to making decisions and functioning independently.

Step 6: Follow-Up

Follow-up is the sixth and final step in the Generalist Intervention Model. Many times it is the most difficult step to follow. Caseloads may be too heavy and too filled with crises. The worker may be distracted by other issues and demands. Follow-up information might be hard to get.

Follow-up is an important step in the intervention process. It involves checking to find out whether clients have maintained progress and are still functioning well on their own. Does a client need to be reassessed for another intervention? Chapter 8 will address the barriers often encountered in follow-up, present guidelines for how to determine the need for follow-up, and offer suggestions for how to sample a limited number of cases instead of contacting them all.

Other Practical Generalist Skills

After the Generalist Intervention Model's problem-solving process has been explained, remaining chapters in this book will address other practical skills necessary for competence at any level of practice—micro, mezzo, or macro. These include:

Understanding and Working with Families

The family forms the core of people's lives. It is the framework in which they grow and learn. It gives, or fails to give, the support needed in the most intimate relationships. Generalist practitioners inevitably work directly or indirectly with families. Therefore, they merit special attention.

The scenario may be a family in which incest is suspected. It may be a family in the process of deciding what to do for and about a member who has been seriously disabled in a motorcycle accident. Brain damage may be so severe that both physical and mental capabilities are significantly impaired. The scene might also be a community which discriminates against certain racial and ethnic groups; families in these groups receive a lesser quality of service than do other groups. Regardless of the specific situation, a generalist practitioner must understand the underlying dynamics occurring in families, the significance of the family upon an individual's behavior, family values related to race and ethnicity, the basic skills necessary to assess a family, and what intervention techniques to use.

Making Ethical Decisions

We've already discussed professional values and ethics as a major portion of the foundation for generalist social work practice. We've also pointed out how often social workers must make decisions about what is considered ethical behavior and what is not. Even more difficult are the choices which have to be made among ethical principles. Sometimes professional loyalties are divided. Practitioners may have to choose between loyalties to their agency's policies, to their client's needs, and to society's best interests. Generalist practitioners need to examine some of the ethical dilemmas commonly encountered in practice. They also need guidance regarding how to make decisions and proceed under such circumstances.

Ethically and Racially Sensitive Social Work Practice

Sensitivity to human diversity is essential in generalist practice. Membership in an ethnic or racial group poses a special set of environ-mental circumstances. A Chicano adolescent from an inner city neighborhood has a different social environment than an upper middle-class adolescent of Jewish descent living in the well-to-do suburbs of the same city.

The values and orientation of a particular group affect individual choices and pressures. Social workers must understand and appreciate group differences so they will not impose inappropriate expectations upon people culturally different from themselves. Nor should workers, based on their own group membership, make stereotyped judgments about people. Additionally, members of a diverse group may be subjected to prejudice, discrimination, and oppression solely because of their membership in the group. Many times practitioners advocate on behalf of people and groups who differ from those in the mainstream.

Gender Sensitive Social Work Practice

Gender differences reflect another aspect of human diversity. Just as it's important for practitioners to be ethnically and racially sensitive, so is it important for them to be sensitive to differences and discrimination based on gender. Gottlieb (1987, p. 562) states, "Sex inequality is based essentially on the belief that a woman's role is a family role." She continues that expecting women to primarily fulfill the nurturant functions of wife and mother leads to expecting them to have certain characteristics related to these functions. Such traits include many traditional stereotypes such as being warm, dependent, emotional, and supportive. These stand in stark contrast to stereotyped characteristics traditionally attributed to men. For instance, men should traditionally be strong, unemotional, independent decision-makers.

Gender stereotypes have negative effects on both women and men. The problem is that such stereotypes often limit alternatives. It is well documented that women are "in a disadvantageous power position" which "results in serious social, economic, and political consequences for women as a group" (Gottlieb, 1987, p. 562). For instance, much attention has recently been given to the *feminization of poverty*. This concept is based on the fact that, for many gender stereotype-related reasons, women are significantly more likely than men to be poor. This status is an outgrowth of oppression.

Gender stereotypes also negatively affect men. For instance, men are expected to pursue women and expose themselves to the pain of rejection. Men are supposed to be strong and decisive whether they feel like it or not. Additionally, men are not supposed to express emotion because such expression implies weakness. Crying is traditionally considered a terrible thing for men to do. Thus, men, too, are seriously constrained by gender role expectations.

Although generalist practitioners must be aware of stereotypes imposed upon both men and women, they especially need to understand women's status as an oppressed group. Women often experience difficulties overcoming traditional stereotypes and expectations. When working with women such special issues as low self-esteem and nonassertiveness must often be addressed. Many, indeed probably most, of a generalist practitioner's clients will be women. Therefore, workers need to be sensitive to women's special needs and master the skills needed to address these needs.

Advocacy

Advocacy involves defending clients' rights and often pleading their cause. Many times advocacy concerns battling oppression and promoting social and economic justice. Social workers will see that people are treated unfairly or are not receiving the resources and support they need to maintain an adequate quality of life. One of the tasks for generalist practitioners is to help people get what they need and deserve. Frequently, this involves expending significantly more than minimal effort. It means fighting obstacles and manipulating systems. It also means making choices regarding when and when not to advocate on a client's behalf. Techniques of persuasion and confrontation are essential. Advocacy is a critically important dimension of social work.

Brokering and Case Management

Much of what generalist practitioners do involves connecting clients to the resources they need. Most frequently a social worker will not be able to fulfill all of a client's needs by herself. Therefore, she or he must be able to identify the client's needs, know what resources are available, know the eligibility requirements, understand how to contact the resource, articulate the client's needs to resource representatives, and finally, make connections between the client and the resource so that the client can get what she or he needs. Brokering involves this entire process.

Recording

Social workers often are what they write. In other words, the worker may not be there in person when decisions are made about the client. Others will have to rely on what the worker has written as their primary source of information. Therefore, written communication is frequently the major, or even the only, means of helping clients. It follows, then, that it is especially important to have good writing skills, to express oneself clearly and accurately, and to be familiar with the formats used to convey information as effectively and efficiently as possible.

Chapter Summary

This chapter has examined what makes social work special and unique. The knowledge, skills, and values that form the basis for social work practice have been summarized. A model has been presented to establish the framework for the rest of this text.

Generalist social work practice involves working with people on many levels. These include: micro practice which emphasizes individuals; mezzo practice which focuses on interpersonal relationships in groups; generalist practice with families, which lies somewhere between the micro and mezzo levels on the practice continuum; and, finally, macro practice in which organizations and large systems are the primary targets of intervention.

The Generalist Intervention Model guides workers through the problem-solving process. Throughout the intervention process, attention is given to all three levels of practice. Generalist practitioners are infinitely flexible. Their foundation of basic skills allows them to function in a wide range of social work roles and positions.

2

Micro Practice Skills: Working with Individuals

Shall we talk?

How can you get people to open up and tell you about their problems?

Do you have to have an answer to every question?

What if you don't know how to solve someone's problem?

How do you work with a client who doesn't want to be there?

What if the client won't say anything?

How do you handle a hostile or angry client?

What should you do if a client starts to cry?

How much should you tell a client about your personal life?

What if a client wants to be friends with you?

What should you do if you think a client isn't listening to what you're saying?

These and many other questions arise in the interpersonal relationship between a social worker and a client, and are especially important for beginning practitioners. Being able to work with individuals is the first step in learning how to practice generalist social work. You must understand interpersonal dynamics and have interviewing skills before being able to work with groups of people and larger systems.

Introduction

Undertaking an actual social work intervention involves assessment, planning, intervention, evaluation, termination, and follow-up. Chapters 5 through 8 will elaborate on what occurs during each of these phases. The worker needs to direct and control each worker/client interview during all of these stages. Interviewing provides a major means for gathering data during the assessment phase of a problem situation. There are a number of specific interviewing techniques which help workers do this and this chapter will focus largely on those basic skills.

Sometimes interviewing is broken up into beginning, middle, and ending phases. Most of the techniques described here are useful at almost any point of the interviewing process. However, some—such as how to introduce yourself to a client or how to terminate your relationship with a client—are more oriented toward a particular interviewing phase.

This chapter focuses on the techniques necessary for communicating with individuals. Later chapters discuss how these techniques are useful throughout the intervention process. Also, keep in mind that these techniques form the foundation for learning and applying mezzo skills (working with groups) and macro skills (working with agencies, organizations, communities, and social systems). Learning how to communicate well and work with individuals is a necessity for any type of social work practice.

Chapter 2 will address numerous questions like the ones listed at the beginning of the chapter and discuss techniques to answer them. Specifically, this chapter will:

- Explore how to establish rapport and build a relationship with a client;
- Examine issues in verbal and nonverbal communication;
- Suggest effective ways to initiate the interviewing process;

- Describe and illustrate a variety of interviewing techniques;
- Propose techniques to deal with difficult situations such as confidentiality issues, confrontation, hostility, uncomfortable periods of silence, and involuntary clients;
- Relate how micro practice techniques are involved in the generalist problem-solving process.

Beginning the Worker/Client Relationship

Communication with clients is obviously necessary to work with and help them. Interviewing provides a primary means for such communication, and is a core skill in micro practice. Interviews involve "social interactions . . . ; communication processes, or a series of linguistic actions leading toward a result that is cognitive, affective, and behavioral; and interventions of a problem-solving nature" (Epstein, 1985, p. 7). In generalist social work practice, the interview is more than a pleasant conversation with a client. The interview's purpose is to "exchange information in order to illuminate and solve problems, promote growth, and plan strategies or actions aimed at improving people's quality of life" (Hepworth & Larsen, 1987, p. 996).

When learning how to work with clients it is useful first to examine how to establish a good worker/client relationship. Some people are naturally popular. Others aren't. There are some basic behaviors and characteristics which make a person more appealing to others. Similarly, in worker/client situations, certain behavior and personal qualities tend to nurture interpersonal relationships. When manifested by the worker, these traits and deeds tend to put the client at ease and make him or her feel important and cared about. This chapter begins by discussing how verbal and nonverbal behavior can enhance worker/client relationships.

Verbal and Nonverbal Behavior

At the most basic level, human interaction and communication involve both verbal and nonverbal behavior. Verbal behavior is what is being said. Nonverbal behavior is communication in ways other than spoken words. People communicate by facial expressions, hand movements, eye contact, the manner in which they sit, and how close they stand to you. Any aspect of a person's presence that conveys ideas or information without being spoken is nonverbal communication.

An example is a student who is ten minutes late for a statistics exam (she was up until 4:30 that morning "cramming" in a panic and her alarm didn't go off for some reason). She runs into her academic advisor, a talkative individual who starts to chat about next semester's registration. The student doesn't want to offend the advisor by dashing off. However, she needs to get to her exam right away. She fidgets, looks repeatedly at her watch, frequently glances in the direction she needs to go, and starts edging away step by step. Without actually using words, she is trying to nonverbally tell the advisor, "I don't want to be rude and I appreciate the time you're taking to talk to me, but please stop talking and let me sprint to my stats exam." The advisor finally gets the nonverbal "hint" and asks, "Oh, are you in a hurry?" It probably would have been much more efficient, thoughtful, and straightforward to have verbally stated those words to the advisor in the first place. Assertiveness will be addressed in a later chapter.

There are many aspects of nonverbal behavior. Here we will focus on four of them: eye contact, attentive listening, facial expressions, and body positioning.

Eye Contact

It's important to look a client directly in the eye. Direct eye contact means that you hold your head straight and face the client. This establishes a rapport and conveys that you are listening to the client.

You must know people who have difficulty looking you in the eye. This often conveys that they are afraid or insecure. It might also imply disinterest or dishonesty. On the other hand, maintaining continuous eye contact can make a person uncomfortable. Additionally, it can also be tedious as if you were in a who-can-hold-out-and-not-blink-the-longest contest. Eye contact is a complex nonverbal behavior. Moderate eye contact, somewhere between no eye contact and constant eye contact, seems to put people at ease most (Epstein, 1985, p. 29). Thus, direct eye contact with an occasional glance away at your hands, a bookcase, or simply into nowhere is probably most appropriate.

One more point about eye contact must be mentioned. In some cultures, direct eye contact is considered "rude and intrusive" (Whittaker & Tracy, 1989, p. 133). This reinforces the need to become knowledgeable about and sensitive to cultural differences between you and your clients. Chapter 12 addresses how to work with people of different cultural backgrounds from your own.

Attentive Listening

Of course, you're supposed to listen to what a client is saying, right? In reality, it's not so simple. First, the distinction must be made between *hearing* and *listening*. Listening implies more than just audio perception of words that are said. It focuses on comprehending the meaning of what is said.

There are a number of barriers to attentive listening. They involve three aspects of communication. First, the person sends a message with some *intent* of what needs to be conveyed. The word to remember here is the "intent," or what the sender hopes the receiver will hear. Second, the receiver of the message tries to decipher the meaning of what has been said. Thus, the message has some *impact* on the receiver. The important word here is "impact," which refers to what the receiver thinks the sender said. What the receiver actually hears may or may not be what the sender intended the receiver to hear. Third, there may be environmental barriers impeding communication of the message (see Figure 2.1).

The first cluster of communication barriers mentioned involves the sender, in this case, the client. The client might not be using words, phrases, or concepts which are clear to you. The client may say something very vague. The sender's *intent* may not be the same as the *impact* on the receiver.

Or, the client may view things from a different cultural perspective where the same words have different meanings. For instance, a Chicano father says, "The problem is that my daughter disobeys me and goes out with boys." A white middle-class social worker may interpret this statement to mean that the daughter is seeing a number of men. Sexual activity and related issues such as pregnancy and sexually transmitted diseases may enter the worker's thinking. Finally, the possibility that the father is overly domineering may be a concern. However, what the Chicano father really means is that his daughter thinks she is in love with a boy and is sneaking out to see him. In their Chicano culture, such behavior

Figure 2.1: Barriers to Attentive Listening

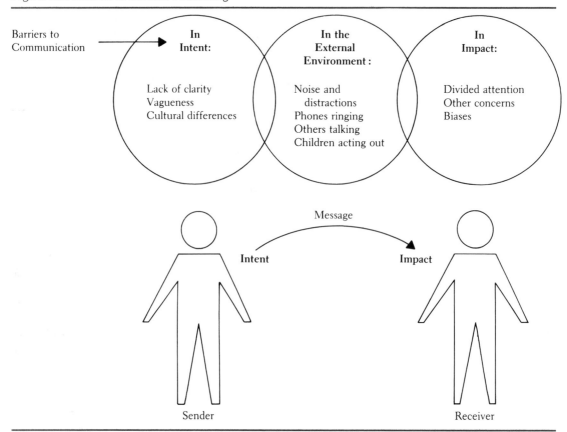

is inappropriate if a couple is not engaged to be married and, in any case, a chaperon is still needed to supervise them.

The second type of communication barrier involves the receiver, in this case, the social worker. The worker's attention may be divided between what the client is saying, and what the worker is going to say next. Likewise, the worker may be focusing on what direction the interview should go in the future. It's easy not to pay full attention to the client and listen to all that is said.

The third cluster of communication barriers to attentive listening involves the external environment and potential noise and distractions. For example, a social worker visits a client's home. The television is blaring and four young children are running through the house with toy rifles playing "GI Joe." Such environmental distractions make it very difficult to organize one's own thoughts, let alone listen to what the client is saying.

In summary, listening is not always easy. It demands concentration, perceptiveness, and the use of a range of interviewing skills. A number of these skills will be described in this chapter.

Facial Expressions

Facial movements and expressions provide an excellent means of communicating. A furrowed brow may convey intense concentration, uncertainty, or concern. A casual smile may indicate pleasure and even warmth. Raising the eyebrows can indicate surprise or sudden interest. In contrast, a blank expression conveys little or no information about what you mean or think.

Facial expressions can be used to reinforce what is said verbally and corroborate the fact that you mean what you say. However, two aspects about using facial expressions should be noted. First, it is very important to be aware

of your facial responses so that you know how you're communicating. Second, make certain that your facial expressions correspond with both your other types of nonverbal behavior and with what you're saying verbally. It's not helpful to give a client a mixed message and *say* one thing while *looking like you mean* another. Such action can convey doubt that you're being truthful. For instance, if you say, "Oh, I'm so glad to see you," with a scowl on your face, you communicate very inconsistent messages.

Body Positioning

Body movement and positioning also provide information to others. The tense/relaxed and formal/informal continuums are especially important.

Body tension involves how rigid or tense our muscles appear as we position ourselves and most frequently coincides with emotional tension. If we look "uptight," we probably feel "uptight" inside. Such tension can be demonstrated by sitting perfectly straight and allowing minimal movement of extremities. Tension is also apparent when a person makes quick, nervous gestures, such as continuously tapping a foot or finger, or jingling loose change in his or her pocket.

The opposite of a tense stance is a relaxed one. Relaxation can be portrayed by slow, loose movements and a decidedly casual, informal presentation of self. The most extreme form of a relaxed stance would probably be to lie down. The term "laid back" is often used to refer to such a relaxed approach.

When working with a client, it's important to be aware of how you nonverbally present yourself. Extreme tension may convey lack of confidence or excessive nervousness. It may put distance between you and your client and make it difficult for him or her to feel comfortable and trust you.

On the other hand, an extremely relaxed stance may convey to a client that you don't care much about what happens. It may also damage your professional credibility.

Ideally, it's best to present yourself somewhere in between the two extremes. To some extent it's a matter of personal style. You need to appear genuine, that is, that you are reflecting aspects of your true individual personality to the client. It is important to be aware of your body positioning and how it affects your interaction with clients.

The second continuum, formal/informal, relates to some extent with the tense/relaxed continuum. Being more rigid and tense reflects formality while being relaxed is associated with informality. Formality implies greater structure and less warmth. To the extent that you are more formal with a client, you are less personal. You allow less of your true personality to show through the professional facade. On the other hand, complete informality or lack of structure impedes getting anything done. A worker/client relationship is not a friendship; it exists for the purpose of solving a problem or attaining a goal. This implies some degree of formality and structure.

As with the tense/relaxed continuum, the extent of formality often relates to personal style. The best approach lies somewhere between being extremely formal and extremely informal. The important thing is to be aware of how you're presenting yourself, how you feel most comfortable, and how the client reacts and relates to you.

A student once asked me a question before undertaking her very first interview (which happened to be a relatively simple, very structured social history). She wondered if, while doing the interview, she should act like a "social worker" or act like herself. I thought to myself, "Hmmmm, what does a social worker act like?" The answer is to use the techniques and problem-solving focus inherent in generalist social work practice (which the rest of this book is all about), yet to do so as yourself. Ask questions in the manner and tone of voice you feel comfortable with. Smile when you feel like smiling. Use the gestures and personal presentation that reflect your true personality.

The use of personal space is another part of body positioning. This is the actual space or distance between you and the client. Hall (1969) identifies four distances or zones that we set in our daily interactions: the intimate zone, the personal zone, the social zone, and the public zone. Each zone respectively demonstrates more formal and less intimate relationships. The intimate zone is just that. It ranges from skin contact to about eighteen inches. It obviously is reserved for very close personal relationships. The personal zone ranges from about eighteen inches to four feet, the social zone from four feet to twelve feet, and the public zone outward from twelve feet. Contact with clients most likely should occur in the closer half of the social zone. This allows for comfortable discussion yet it provides an adequate degree of personal space so that a client does not feel threatened.

Another aspect of body positioning and defining personal space involves where workers sit in their offices in relationship to where clients sit. Typically, an office has a desk and you as a worker may have some flexibility regarding placement of that desk. Sitting behind the desk and talking to a client seated in front of the desk implies greater formality and difference in status and may be appropriate in some settings where the worker feels such formality is needed. For instance, a worker who is a probation officer might find it useful to sit behind a desk in a more formal situation where the goal is to monitor a client's adherence to prescribed probationary conditions. However, in many other situations, having the desk's front side abutting the wall, sitting behind the desk, and being able to turn your chair in order to talk to a client can convey greater informality and warmth.

Warmth, Empathy, and Genuineness

In generalist social work practice a variety of relationship-enhancing characteristics can be defined and learned. Demonstrating these characteristics involves employing the appropriate corresponding verbal and nonverbal behavior. Three specific relationship-enhancing traits are warmth, empathy, and genuineness. These attributes characterize the social work literature as among the most basic and important in developing relationships with clients (Austin et al., 1986; Fischer & Gochros, 1975; Hepworth & Larsen, 1987, 1990).

Warmth

Displaying warmth involves conveying a feeling of interest, concern, well-being and affection to another individual. It is often difficult to find specific, accurate words for feelings. For example, *Webster's New Collegiate Dictionary* (1977, p. 1320) defines warmth as "the quality or state of being warm in feeling" such as "a child needing human warmth and family life." We do have a tendency to define a word by using the same word in the definition. There's often no exact synonym available. Conveying warmth, however, does involve enhancing the positive feelings of one person toward another. Warmth promotes a sense of comfort and well-being in that other person.

Warmth can be communicated to a client both verbally and nonverbally. Such behaviors can be defined, practiced, and learned. The following are examples of verbally communicating warmth:

"Hello. It's good to meet you."
"I'm glad we have the chance to talk about this."
"It's pleasant talking with you."
"It's good to see you again."

"Please sit down. Can I get you a cup of coffee?"

These are just a few of the many statements you can make to show that you respect the client and are glad he or she is there. These statements help to convey a sense of concern for the client and for the client's well-being. Similarly, there are many ways to communicate warmth to a client nonverbally. We've discussed how eye contact, attentive listening, body positioning, and tonal quality can all be used to a worker's advantage.

Empathy

Empathy is the second basic characteristic which has been found to enhance a worker/client relationship. Hepworth and Larsen (1987) refer to it as "the workhorse of interviewing" (p. 998). Empathy involves not only *being in tune* with how a client feels, but also *conveying to that client* that you understand how she or he feels. It does not necessarily mean that you think the client's feelings are positive or negative, nor does it mean that you're having the same feelings yourself. Empathy is purely acknowledgment that you understand the client's situation. For instance, consider the case of Ms. Wilson, who has been referred to a protective services worker for abusing her two-year-old son, Tyrone. A neighbor reported Ms. Wilson after seeing odd, strap-like, black bruises on the child's arms two weeks in a row. During the interview, Ms. Wilson says, "Tyrone never does what he's told. He runs away from me when I call him. He gets into all of my things and breaks them. Sometimes I get so angry, I could kill him. I tie him up to the bed with old ties just so I can get some peace."

The worker empathetically responds, "Two-year-olds can be very difficult and trying. I understand how sometimes you feel like you're at your wits' end." This response conveys that the worker *understands* the situation and

Ms. Wilson's feelings. However, it does not *condone* Ms. Wilson's behavior. Empathy can be used to demonstrate to a client that you're on her side. Once the client feels that you've listened to how she feels and you're not against her, she is much more likely to be willing to work with you toward finding a solution to the problem. Empathy communicates to a client that you are there to help her solve her problem.

In this example, what do you think Ms. Wilson's reaction would have been if the worker had responded to her statement by saying, "How can you hurt your own child like that? What kind of mother are you? Don't you have any feelings?" The latter statement criticizes Ms. Wilson and communicates to her that the worker does not understand her feelings and her situation. It totally lacks empathy. Ms. Wilson could easily view the worker as "the enemy," someone to fight with or avoid.

Establishing initial rapport is only the first among a number of reasons for employing empathy; Hepworth and Larsen cite several other uses (1987, 1990). Empathy enables the worker

---

HIGHLIGHT 2.1

Practicing Empathic Responses

There are a number of leading phrases which you can use to begin an empathic statement. Here are some examples:

"My impression is that . . ."
"It appears to me that . . ."
"Is what you're saying that . . .?"
"Do I understand you correctly that . . .?"
"I'm hearing you say that . . ."
"Do you mean that . . .?"
"Do you feel that . . .?"
"I feel that you . . ."
"I'm getting the message that . . ."
"You seem to be . . ."
"When you say that, I think you . . ."
"You look like you . . ."
"You sound so _____. Can we talk more about it?"
"You look _____. What's been happening?"

The following are several vignettes about client situations. Formulate and practice your own empathic responses for each one. The first vignette provides an example.

Example: You are a social worker in foster care. You're visiting one of the foster homes on your caseload. The purpose is to talk with both foster parents and determine how things are going with their nine-year-old foster child, Katie. The couple has three children of their own, all of whom are in college. In the past the foster couple has expressed interest in adopting Katie. When you arrive at the home, only the mother is present. After polite greetings, the foster mother says, "Katie certainly doesn't like to read very much like the rest of us. I think she gets bored when she's not doing something active. Many times I just don't know what to do with her."

Possible empathic responses include:

"You sound like you're having some problems with Katie that you didn't expect. Can we talk more about it?"
"It seems like you're somewhat frustrated with Katie these days."
"I feel like you're telling me that Katie's more difficult to take care of than perhaps you thought."

Vignette 1: You are a social worker in a health care facility for the elderly. Helen is a resident who has been living there for approximately two years. All rooms have two residents which has consistently been a problem for Helen. Her current roommate is Emma, a quiet woman who rarely interacts with any of the other residents. Helen is very possessive of her things and wants no one else to

to keep up with the client and the client's problems and concerns throughout the worker/client relationship.

Empathizing with positive emotions can also be helpful. For example, if a client appears exceptionally happy one day, an empathic response may get at the reason. Maybe some problem has already been solved. Perhaps, a new client strength can be identified that can be used in the change process. Acknowledging positives may help in the maintenance of the worker/client relationship.

Additionally, empathic responding may elicit feelings and discussion about previously unmentioned issues. Empathy provides the worker with a means of getting at feelings which aren't expressed verbally. For example, a worker can say, "When you frown like that, it looks like you're very worried about something." The client now has an opening to talk about what's on her mind, even though she has not expressed it verbally.

Yet another use of empathy involves "making confrontations more palatable" (Hepworth

touch them. Additionally, Helen does not like to share the bathroom which is also used by the two residents in the next room. Helen, a strong, outspoken woman even at age ninety-seven, approaches you and says, "Emma keeps using my bathroom and moves my things around. I want her out of there right now! You do something right now!"

You empathetically respond . . . (Remember that you *do not* have to solve the problem right now. You only need to let your client know that you understand how she feels.)

Vignette 2: You are a school social worker. Romy, age sixteen, was in the men's bathroom when several other students were caught using drugs. Romy insists the others are guilty and he is innocent, he just happened to be in the restroom at the same time. The teacher who found the boys couldn't distinguish who was guilty and who was not so he put them all on "penalty," which means detention after school and exclusion from any sports for two weeks. Romy is furious. He comes up to you and says, "It's not fair! It's just not fair! I'm innocent and I'm getting punished anyway. I should've used the drugs if I'm going to get the punishment."

You empathetically respond . . .

Vignette 3: You are a social worker at a diagnostic and treatment center for children with multiple disabilities. Your primary function is to work with parents, helping them to cope with the pressures and connecting them with resources they need. A mother of a five-year-old boy with severe cerebral palsy talks with you on a weekly basis. Her son is severely disabled and has very little muscular control. He can't walk by himself or talk, although the other therapists feel he has normal intelligence. The boy's father belongs to a religion that denies the existence of disease and physical impairment. Thus, he denies that his son is disabled. The burden of caretaking rests solely upon the mother. She loves her son dearly and is generally enthusiastic in doing what she can for him. She enters your office one day, says hello, and sits down. She immediately puts her hand to her eyes and breaks down in tears.

You empathetically respond . . .

Vignette 4: You are an intake worker at a social services agency in a rural area. Your job is to take telephone calls, assess problems, and refer clients to the most appropriate services. You receive a call from an adult male. After identifying who you are and asking what you can do for the caller, he responds, "I just lost my job. Nothing's going right. I feel like I want to kill myself."

You empathetically respond . . .

& Larsen, 1990, p. 105). Empathy can be used to disperse hostility. For example, a client enters a worker's office and demands his financial assistance check right now instead of five days later when he's supposed to receive it. He's breathing fast, his face is red, and his vocal tone is loud, gruff, and hostile. The worker chooses not to respond initially to what the client said. The worker does *not* say something like, "You're here five days early and you can't have the check until it's ready." Instead, the worker can make an empathic response by saying, "Mr. Carlton, you sound so angry. It seems like you desperately need the money right now." This latter response is much more likely to help Mr. Carlton calm down and talk about his problem. The worker may or may not be able to get Mr. Carlton his check. However, an empathic response is much more likely to convey to Mr. Carlton that the worker is on his side. He should be much more likely to settle down, talk about what's wrong, and pursue possible alternative courses of action.

Nonverbal communication can also be used to enhance empathy. A worker's gestures can mirror how a client feels. For instance, furrowing the brow can convey a serious focusing of attention and reflect a client's grave concern over some issue. Nonverbal communication can also emphasize or enhance verbal empathic responses. For example, consider a client who appears happy. Smiling while making an empathic verbal response indicates more convincingly to the client that you really understand how she or he feels.

Genuineness

The third quality found to enhance client/worker relationships is genuineness, which involves "sharing of self by relating in a natural, sincere, spontaneous, open and genuine manner" (Hepworth & Larsen, 1987, p. 998). Genuineness simply means that you continue to be yourself, despite the fact that you are working to accomplish goals in your professional role.

Personality refers to the unique configuration of qualities and attributes that make you an individual. Some people have effervescent, outgoing personalities. Others have more subdued, quiet temperaments. Some people relate to others using a sense of humor while others prefer to relate in a more serious manner. The point is that there is no one type of personality that is best for a professional role. Rather, it is important that you be yourself and not pretend to be something or someone that you're not. Genuineness conveys a sense of honesty to clients and makes them feel that you're someone they can trust.

Two sisters, Karen, a social worker, and Susie, an occupational therapist, illustrate this point. Both women have worked with very similar clients, primarily children and teenagers with behavioral problems. Karen is extremely outgoing, fast-moving, excitable, and tries to make jokes at every opportunity. Others have often labeled her "hyperactive" and frequently complain that she talks too fast. Susie, on the other hand, is very calm, evenly paced, and sedate. Her manner has often been labeled "dignified." If Karen would accidentally put her hand on a hot burner, she'd utter a piercing scream, dash around frantically, and spew forth a stream of colorful obscenities. If Susie placed her hand on the same hot burner she would calmly lift her hand, look at it, and quietly reflect, "Oh, I burned my hand." (It might be noted that Susie's husband has commented that if you put Karen and Susie into a giant blender together, mixed them up, and poured them into two equal portions, they'd turn into two "normal" human beings.) The point is that despite extreme differences in personality and style, both sisters worked effectively with similar clients. Each was herself while still performing her professional functions (although Karen did have to monitor carefully her tendency to utter obscenities).

Being conscious of one's emotional response to difficult clients can help one deal with these clients appropriately.

Starting the Interview

The major goal of any interview is "interpersonal communication with the client" (Pippin, 1980, p. 48). Interviews make use of communication with clients to solve problems, encourage positive change, and maximize clients' "quality of life" (Hepworth & Larsen, 1987, p. 996). We've talked about the importance of both verbal and nonverbal behavior in communication. We've also established that warmth, empathy, and genuineness are qualities which help foster professional relationships with clients. Now we will propose some very specific suggestions for *starting* and, subsequently, *conducting* the interview. The emphasis is on planning and action. You as a practitioner are there to help your cli-

ent clearly identify what the problems are and what can be done to solve them. In this section we will discuss typical interview settings, how to dress and prepare for interviews, initial introductions, alleviating clients' anxiety, conveying confidence and competence, and stating the interview's purpose.

The Interview Setting

Interviews may occur in a variety of settings, depending on the field of practice and type of agency. Some interviews take place in hospitals or schools. Many occur in the worker's own office, which gives him or her more control over the environment. We've already discussed positioning the desk and chairs to enhance the client's comfort level. Offering the client a cup of coffee, whether he accepts or not, is another way of displaying warmth.

Social workers need to be sensitive to the overall impression their office environment itself presents. There are no absolute guidelines for dictating office decor. It's appropriate to put pictures you like on the walls and trinkets you enjoy on the shelves. However, you need to be aware of their potential effect on clients. If you paint your office bright orange and put giant posters of your favorite rock stars on the walls, you need to be aware that this may be unnerving to some clients. On the other hand, if your clients are primarily adolescents who like some of the same rock stars you do, such posters may provide a means of making a connection with your clients. The orange walls, however, probably should go.

Some interviews will take place in the client's own home, which provides the advantage of seeing where and how he or she lives. However, home visits may have the disadvantage of distraction such as children, pets, and television which can make it more difficult to control the interview. Home visits often provide an excellent means of making assessments and are discussed more extensively in chapter 5.

How to Dress for the Interview and for the Job

The main thing to remember when deciding how to dress for interviews with clients and for social work positions in general is that your appearance will make an impression and it's to your advantage to make a good one. The rule of thumb is to start out dressing "nicely" and "relatively conservatively." What this means is up to individual interpretation. It's important to note how other workers in your agency dress because each agency has its own personality. Some agencies are very formal while others are very informal.

It's also important to note clients' reactions to how you and the other workers in your agency dress. If you are a woman who works in a corrections institution for delinquent youth, wearing three-inch high heels and short skirts may be very inappropriate. You may be expected to participate in recreational activities with clients, or, in the event that they "lose control," help to physically restrain them. More informal clothing would then be to your great advantage.

Or, if you are a practitioner working in a protective services unit who must go out and interview families in poverty-stricken areas of the city, you may not want to flaunt wealth. In other words, wearing expensive three-piece gray flannel suits may not enhance clients' impression of you or your relationship with them. On the other hand, it might. Some clients may perceive such efforts and formality as a demonstration of your professionalism and respect for them. Jeans and a T-shirt might have the opposite effect. Thus, it's important to carefully watch clients' reactions to you and dress in a way that enhances your professional performance.

Thinking Ahead about an Interview with a Client

Before the interview begins, the worker needs to think ahead about at least three variables. First, is there any specific information which will be needed such as addresses and phone numbers of specific resources? Can you anticipate any questions the client might ask for which you should be prepared?

Second, the interview's time frame should be clearly specified. The time frame means when the interview is scheduled to begin and when it needs to end. The meeting should start punctually. Making the client wait beyond the scheduled starting time may imply that the client's time is not very important and that you have better things to do. A timely start conveys common courtesy and respect for the client. In the event that you are late for whatever reason, an appropriate apology should be made.

The interview should have a timely ending and the next client shouldn't be kept waiting. One means of alerting the client that the interview is coming to a close is to make a statement such as, "Well, we only have another ten minutes left, so perhaps we should talk a bit about our next meeting."

The third variable which needs consideration prior to the interview is the interview's purpose. According to Kadushin (1972, pp. 119–20), "Preparation involves operationalizing and specifying the interview's purpose, translating objectives into the specific items that need to be covered." He continues, "How, in general, can the purpose be achieved, what questions will need to be asked, what content will need to be covered, and what is the most desirable sequence with which such content might be introduced?" In other words, the worker must have some general idea about what he or she wants to accomplish by the end of the interview.

Interviews generally are either "diagnostic, informational, or therapeutic" in purpose (Pippin, 1980, p. 72). Diagnostic interviews assess a client's situations and problems. Informational interviews are used to collect specific data, while therapeutic interviews focus on solving a problem. If the worker has a purpose clearly in mind, it's much easier to direct the interview and accomplish that goal. For example, if the purpose is to get specific information, the worker can think about questions to ask to get that information.

Initial Introductions

Initial introductions resemble those in other formal and informal interactions. Names are exchanged with typical pleasantries such as "It's nice to meet you." It's usually best to use surnames as they imply greater respect. Handshakes are also often appropriate. However, it's important to be aware of the client's levels of comfort and anxiety. If a client cringes as you extend your hand, nonchalantly take it back and continue with a verbal interchange.

Sometimes ethnic or cultural differences require you to behave differently than you normally would. For instance, the Hmong, who have migrated to the United States during the past two decades from Southeast Asia, abhor the type of physical contact involved in shaking hands. Working with clients from a variety of cultural backgrounds will be described more thoroughly in chapter 12.

When beginning the interview, it may also be appropriate to initiate brief, innocuous exchanges about some bland topic like the weather. For example, "I'm glad you made it here despite the heat (or the blizzard)." Such comments must be brief, however, because you can't afford to waste valuable time. A short interchange can be used to soften the formal edge of the interview and make the situation warmer and more human.

Alleviating the Client's Anxiety

"Starting where the client is" is a phrase social workers often use to describe how they begin an interview. The first important aspect of this concept is to think about how the client must feel coming into the initial interview with you. Put yourself into the client's shoes. You too would probably be anxious about approaching an unknown situation and would not feel in control. The client may wonder, "Will this "professional" interrogate me under bright lights as if I were a foreign spy? Will this social worker criticize all the things I'm doing wrong? Will she attack me for something I did or didn't do?"

Many clients will approach the interview with anxiety; others, however, may arrive with resentment or hostility. For instance, if clients

---

HIGHLIGHT 2.2
Using Direct and Indirect Questions

Questions can also be categorized as being either *direct* or *indirect*. Direct questions are those that clearly ask for information and usually end in a question mark. Examples are:

"Did your mother ask you to see me?"

"What do you see as the major problem areas?"

"How did you arrange for your transportation here?"

"When do you intend on completing that plan?"

Indirect questions ask questions without seeming to. They provide an excellent vehicle for gathering information. Examples include:

"Many mothers would find having three children under the age of five difficult."

"You seem like you're under a great deal of stress today."

"Taking care of your brother after school each day must make it hard to find time to play with your friends."

"I wonder how you manage to care for little Johnny and your aging mother at the same time."

In each of these indirect questions, the interviewer is asking the client to respond, but is not stating a direct question. Notice there are no question marks ending the sentences. This technique can be helpful in gathering information from clients without asking a tediously long list of direct questions.

---

are forced to see you for some reason, it's logical for them to have negative feelings. The important thing is for you to pay close attention to their nonverbal and verbal behavior. Empathy is essential to communicate and begin the problem-solving process. Specific suggestions for how to deal with difficult situations such as hostility are discussed later in this chapter.

Other conditions which may be affecting a client's perspective and attitude should also be considered. Is your office hard to find? Did the client have to wait a long time before you could see him? Did he have a bad experience with your agency in the past? Did the client have a flat tire on the way in to see you? It's important to be aware that these and many other variables may be affecting his feelings.

Portraying Confidence and Competence

A common situation many new workers, especially those who are in their early and middle

twenties, encounter is a client questioning their level of competence. A client might think and/or say, "How can somebody your age possibly help me? I'm old enough to be your parent." In some cases the last part of the statement is true.

A similar situation arises when a worker without children of his or her own must work with clients who have problems with their children. Such clients may ask how a childless individual can possibly understand and help them.

There are at least five things a worker can do about these types of situations. First, when a client says something that's true (even if you don't want to make an issue of it), acknowledge that it is the truth. You can do this at least silently to yourself or make a statement to that effect. For example, you might say, "Yes, I am younger than you are," or, "No, I don't have any children." This gets the cards out on the table, so to speak, and prevents you from seeming defensive.

A second approach to addressing client concerns is to respond to the client with a question. You might say, "Is it important to you that I have children?" or, "Does my being younger pose a problem for you?" Again, this tactic gets the issue out on the table without making the worker appear defensive.

The third thing a worker can do is to follow up the true statement with another statement of truth. You might share examples of your competence. For instance, you could say, "I have an undergraduate degree in social work and have been trained to help solve problems just like yours. Why don't you give me a chance to show you what I can do for you?"

The fourth thing a worker can do in a situation where his or her competence is questioned is simply to rely on the relationship-building skills which we've already discussed. Keep warmth, empathy, and genuineness in mind. Be assertive verbally and nonverbally. Speak calmly and look the client in the eye. As the client gains trust in you as a professional, the question of competence will cease to become an issue. The best way to convince a client of your competence is by your own behavior. Austin et al. (1986) summarize this point by stating, "When you actually help a consumer (a client), you are perceived as competent" (p. 233).

The fifth thing you can do to demonstrate competence is to be knowledgeable. Planning the interview conveys to the client a sense of organization and purpose. Knowing your role and where to find information the client needs also reflects your competence.

Beginning Statement of Purpose and Role

Not only must the purpose of the interview be clearly identified in the worker's own mind, it must also be clearly understood by the client. There are four major tasks that should be undertaken at the very beginning of the interviewing process (Schwartz, 1976; Sheafor, 1988; Shulman, 1984). The first, as we've already indicated, is to clearly explain the interview's purpose to the client. An example of this involves a worker in an alcohol and other drug abuse (AODA) assessment unit in a large urban social services agency. The worker meets with her twenty-seven-year-old male client for the first time. After the initial introductions, the worker says, "I'm happy to talk with you today. I understand that you voluntarily came in for some help with controlling your drinking. What we need to do today is to find out more about you and your drinking, so I'd like to ask you a few questions."

In this example, the worker expressed warmth and concern. Without blaming the client, she indicated the need to work together. Finally, she explained in straightforward terms that their goal was to assess his drinking problem.

The second major task in an interview's beginning phase is to explain the worker's role to the client. We've discussed how clients often have significant apprehension about interviews for a wide variety of reasons. Explaining your role does not mean reciting a job description. However, it does mean describing in general terms to the client what you intend to do and talk about.

For example, let's return to our original example of the AODA assessment worker with the twenty-seven-year-old client. After clarifying the interview's purpose, the worker might say, "I will be asking a number of questions that are typically asked when someone wants to work on controlling their drinking. Some of the questions may seem odd to you. They ask about a lot of things from work to friends to family to personal interests to the drinking itself. These questions help me get to know you better and give me a better idea about where we can start in helping to change."

The third important task in the initial interviewing process concerns "encouraging the client's feedback on purpose" (Sheafor et al., 1988, p. 101). This means that the worker should ask the client how he or she feels about the identified purpose. It is necessary to actively involve the client from the beginning of the change process. Back to our AODA example, the worker might say, "I feel like I've done most of the talking so far. How do you feel about what I've said. Do the plans so far sound good to you? Is there something you'd like to change or add?"

The final task in the initial interview involves making a statement about the usefulness of the intervention process. In other words, the worker can convey to the client that there is hope to begin to solve his or her problems. For example, the worker might say, "When you talk about your drinking, I can hear you say how worried about it you are. I think it is a serious problem. However, I give you lots of credit for having the courage to come in and talk to me about it. There are a number of excellent techniques we can use and alternatives we can look at. It's hard, but I think we have a good chance at helping you over the next few weeks and months."

These statements reflect only one combination of words and ideas for accomplishing the four tasks. In other words, there are many ways to define the purpose of the interview or to ask for feedback. The interview may indeed have any number of purposes. The intent may be to help a fifteen-year-old decide whether to have an abortion or to assist an eighty-five-year-old in deciding where it would be best for her to live. The words used to define purpose vary as dramatically as the actual intent of the interview. The important thing is for the client to understand why he or she is there and what you intend to do.

The discussion of the four tasks mentioned above is oriented primarily toward one of the initial interviews with clients. Subsequent interviews with clients may not require such extensive, detailed explanations of purpose and other facets of the interviewing process. Clients already will have learned about your general intent. However, these tasks are good to keep in mind even with clients whom you've seen a number of times. In review, the four tasks include defining the interview's specific purpose,

explaining what you will be doing, asking clients for feedback, and expressing hope that things can improve. All four help provide direction to interviews and enhance your positive interaction with clients.

Conducting the Interview

Regardless of the specific purpose of the interview, its major function is communication with the client. Communication, of course, involves exchange of information. There is a variety of specific skills and techniques which can facilitate the exchange of information. Using these techniques helps to maximize the chances that the worker's *intent* matches her *impact* on the client and vice versa.

There is a vast array of communication techniques for workers to use. These include ways to initiate a communication with a client or respond to something a client says. We will define and explain a number of specific methods of responding to clients which place the focus of attention on the client. Next, we will examine a number of issues and difficulties frequently encountered in interviews.

Verbal Responses to the Client

There are a number of techniques used to enhance worker/client communication. Some are used to solicit information while others encourage the client and enhance the worker/client relationship. The proceeding approaches include simple encouragement, rephrasing, reflective responding, clarification, interpretation, providing information, emphasizing clients' strengths, self-disclosure, summarization, and eliciting information.

Simple Encouragement

Many times a simple one word response or nonverbal head nod while maintaining eye contact is enough to encourage a client to continue. Okun (1976, p. 52) indicates that "verbal clues such as 'mm-mm,' 'I see,' 'uh-huh,' . . . indicate that the helper is listening and following what the client is saying." Such responses may also be used to keep a client on the right track in conjunction with the purpose of the interview.

Rephrasing

Rephrasing involves stating what the client is saying, but using different words. Rephrasing has a variety of purposes. It can communicate to the client that you're really trying to listen to what she is saying. On the other hand, if you had not heard the client's real intent, it can let the client know so she can clarify her meaning. It can also help the client take time out and reflect on what she just said.

One example of rephrasing is a client who says, "I feel really miserable today." The worker may respond, "You really don't feel well at all today." Rephrasing does not involve offering an interpretation of what the client has said. It simply repeats a statement by using other words.

Reflective Responding

Reflective responding concerns translating what you think the client is feeling into words. It is a means of displaying empathy. Such responding conveys that you understand what a client is going through and how he or she feels about it. A typical scenario involves a client who is *talking about* his problems, but doesn't really articulate how he *feels about* his problems. Part of your job as the worker is to bring these feelings out into the open so he knows they're there and can begin to work on them. Both verbal and nonverbal behavior can be used as cues for reflective responding. For example, a client comes to you with her shoulders slumped and her eyes downcast. She slumps into a chair and says, "Yep, he dumped me. He finally told me

to get lost. He's been talking about it for months, but the old coot finally did it."

As a worker, you might respond, "You sound like you feel crushed and angry that your boyfriend left you. You also sound like you're a bit surprised even though he's been threatening for a long time."

Clarification

Clarification involves making certain that what the client says is understood. Clarification is typically used in one of two ways (Benjamin, 1974). First, the worker can help the client articulate more clearly what he or she really means by providing the words for it. This is clarification for the client's benefit. Second, the worker can use a clarifying statement to make what the client is saying clearer to the worker herself. This latter type of clarification is for the worker's benefit. Many times clarification will benefit both worker and client. An example of this involves a client who comes to a worker and says, "I just lost my job. Everything's gone. What will I do? Where will I go?"

The worker may respond, "You mean you just lost your income along with your job and you're wondering about how to pay the rent and other bills this month?" This example depicts the worker's attempt to clarify what the real issues are that must be addressed and to help the client proceed "from the general to the specific" (Shulman, 1981, p. 14). It's difficult to try to solve the problem of losing "everything." However, determining the exact amount needed to pay the rent and other bills, or even finding an alternate residence, are more concrete, doable goals. Helping the client to specify what she really means makes a problem much more workable.

Clarification is used when there is a question about what the client means. Restatement, on the other hand involves understanding the client and simply paraphrasing what he has said. Finally, reflective responding adds the dimension of emotion and feeling to clients' statements.

Interpretation

Interpretation involves seeking meaning beyond that of clarification. To interpret means to help bring to a conclusion, to enlighten, to seek a meaning of greater depth than that which has been stated. Interpretation helps lead clients to look deeper into themselves and their problems. It enhances one's perception of one's own situation.

For example, a client says, "I hate it when my mother tells me what to do. And, yet, if I don't do what she says, she makes me feel guilty. She makes me feel like I don't care about her anymore."

The worker might respond, "It seems like you have very ambivalent feelings toward your mother. You want to be independent, yet you don't want to hurt your mother's feelings. Perhaps, on some level, she realizes that, doesn't want to lose you, and is able to manipulate you."

To interpret means to take a statement a step beyond its basic meaning. In the preceding example, the worker went beyond the client's feelings of anger, guilt, and resentment. Instead, the worker focused in on both the client's and her mother's motivations for their behavior. The worker attempted to provide some insight into both of their feelings.

Providing Information

Sometimes it is appropriate to provide information to clients. They may ask you a frank question. They may not know where to find resources or how a social services system works. Or, they may not understand why they must provide certain information or follow some rule. Sometimes they will be misinformed and accurate information will need to be provided.

For example, a female teenager asks a worker, "My friends tell me you can't get pregnant the first time you do it. Is that true?"

To this the worker might respond, "No, that's not true. You're just as likely to get pregnant the first time as any other time. There are some other things to consider, though, any time you choose to have sex. Let's take some time and talk about it."

Emphasizing Clients' Strengths

Social workers deal with the most difficult human problems. Their clients are often those people who are the most oppressed and have the most obstacles to living healthy, happy lives. Many clients are so overwhelmed by their problems that it's difficult for them to focus on anything but problems. They assume a "tunnel vision," that is, they have difficulty focusing on anything but this long, dark, entrapping tunnel of stressful life issues.

Sometimes it will be quite difficult to identify client strengths because their problems will seem so insurmountable. However, as we will discuss in later chapters which focus on the problem-solving process, emphasizing client strengths is critical throughout intervention (Sheafor, et al., 1988; Shulman, 1984) and helps in several ways. First, it reinforces a client's sense of self-respect and self-value. Second, it provides rays of hope even in "tunnels of darkness." Third, it helps identify ways to solve problems by relying on the specified strengths.

Client strengths may be found in three major areas. The first involves behaviors and accomplishments. The second concerns personal qualities and characteristics. Finally, the third revolves around the client's material and social resources. Highlight 2.3 illustrates how to focus on client strengths.

Self-Disclosure

Many generalist practitioners, especially those new to the field, wonder to what extent they should disclose information about themselves. Johnson (1986) defines self-disclosure as

┌─ HIGHLIGHT 2.3 ──────────────────────────────

Stressing Client Strengths

The following examples are statements workers might use to emphasize a client's strengths in three basic areas.

Client Behaviors

"You've done a nice job of following those suggestions. Look what you've accomplished."

"Sometimes you emphasize all the things that have gone wrong, but look at all the things you've done well. You've kept your family together even when your husband left you and you lost a primary source of income. You've managed a tight budget and kept your children fed, housed, and in-school. You're going back to school part-time. I think that's wonderful."

Personal Qualities

"You're very bright and easy to talk to."

"I think you're very motivated to work on this thing."

"It's nice to work with you. You're so cooperative."

"You have a very pleasant personality. I think you will do very well in the group."

"You brighten up when you're happy. It makes people feel good to see your cheery smile."

"You look very nice today."

Client's Resources

"I know it's been hard, but you've found yourself a part-time job and have worked out a schedule for paying your bills. That's a great start."

"It's really good that you have close friends (or a minister or a relative) to talk to. It helps."

"Your family is very supportive. That's really good."

"There are several resources available to you here at the agency which can get you off to a good start."

──

"revealing how you are reacting to the present situation and giving any information about the past that is relevant to an understanding of your reactions to the present" (p. 18).

Historically, what and how much about yourself should be disclosed during a professional interview is a controversial issue (Okun, 1976). On the one hand, there is substantial research indicating that some amount of self-disclosure enhances relationships (Johnson, 1973, 1986)—people are more apt to like others who reveal things about themselves. Similarly, the more you reveal to someone, the more likely he or she will be to self-disclose to you. On the other hand, we all know people who seem like they never stop talking about themselves. They are so interested in their own issues and activities that they never think of asking how you are. We also all know our

reactions to people who behave this way: "Let me out of here!"

We've already established that warmth, empathy, and genuineness are important characteristics to demonstrate in professional worker/client relationships. To some extent self-disclosure is necessary to give feedback to the client. Feedback involves providing input about how the client is functioning and how others perceive the client. This is an important aspect of working through the problem-solving process.

Hackney and Cormier (1979) cite four major types of self-disclosure. The first three involve communicating something about the worker/client relationship and the ongoing interviewing process. These types of self-disclosures also frequently overlap with some of the other interviewing techniques mentioned earlier. They focus directly on the worker/client role and the purpose of the interview.

First, you can give information about *your professional role*. Second, you can share your feelings and impressions about the *client* and the client's behavior by giving feedback. Third, you can provide feedback about your perceptions concerning *your ongoing interaction and relationship with the client*. These latter two types of self-disclosure are especially useful when you can't think of anything else to say during an interview. You can share your feelings about what's happening with the client inside or outside of the interview. Or, self-disclose what you feel is happening in your relationship with the client at that point in the interview.

The fourth type of self-disclosure, however, differs significantly from the other three. It involves *relating aspects about your own life or problems* in some way to the client's feelings or situation. This approach can convey empathy to the client and indicate that you really understand. It can also provide a "positive role model" under some circumstances by showing the client that others have learned to live through similar problems (Okun, 1976, p. 199).

The amount you choose to self-disclose about your own life is, ultimately, an individual decision. Some people are naturally more outgoing and self-disclosing than others. Regardless, when you as a worker choose to self-disclose, there are some basic guidelines.

The first guideline is to make certain that the self-disclosure is really for the client's benefit and not for your own. Friendships provide arenas for mutual self-disclosure and support but professional worker/client relationships exist to benefit the client only (see Figure 2.2).

A second guideline is to make the self-disclosure relevant to the client; this involves demonstrating both "genuineness" and "timeliness" (Ivey, 1983, p. 183). In other words, self-disclose for some definite purpose. For example, the client may need some reassurance that it's all right to talk about a particular issue. Or at some specific point you can make an empathic self-disclosure about an issue related to that of the client and he or she will feel more comfortable.

The third guideline for making self-disclosures is that they should be short and very simple. You want to share a small slice of your life, feelings, or experience for a specific purpose. Details are unimportant. Most likely you just want to convey to your client that to some extent you really do understand how he or she feels.

Sometimes clients will initiate asking you uncomfortable personal questions such as, "Are you married?" "Are you going with anybody?" "Did you sleep with your spouse before you were married?" or "Did you ever drink when you were under age or try any drugs?"

Under such circumstances, you have two choices. First, you can answer honestly, briefly, and simply. Then you can say something like, "I think we'd better get back on track. The important thing we're here to work on is your problem and what to do about it."

Your second choice is to avoid answering the question by instantly focusing on something else such as the client or the interviewing process. In other words, you can ignore the question and talk about the client and how he is participating in the interviewing process (Hackney & Cormier, 1979). For example, you might say any of the following:

> "You seem really anxious to get off the topic today. What's on your mind?"
> "It seems as though you don't feel like talking about the problem right now. Is something bothering you?"
> "That really doesn't have much to do with what we're talking about here. We don't have that much time. Let's get back to the subject."
> "I feel like you're trying to avoid my questions. What do you think are the reasons for that?"

This second approach of avoiding the answer may or may not work. If it doesn't, you may have to simply and honestly say something like, "I really don't feel comfortable answering that. Let's get back to the matter at hand."

Summarization

Summarization involves restating the main points of an interview or a portion of an inter-view in a brief and concise manner. Periodic summarization helps the client focus on the main points covered during a portion of the interaction and also helps keep the interview on track. It can be used "as a transition to new topics, or to review complex issues" (Whittaker & Tracy, 1989, p. 137). Summarization is difficult in that the worker must carefully select and emphasize only the most important facts, issues, and themes.

Figure 2.2: Personal versus Professional Relationships

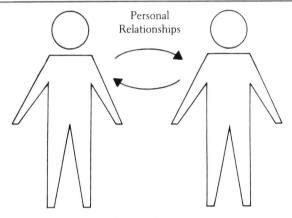

Personal Relationships

Both people need their needs met

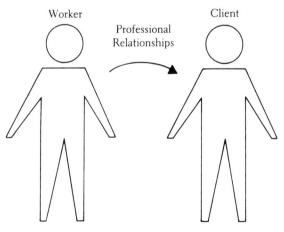

Worker

Client

Professional Relationships

The purpose is to meet the client's, not the worker's needs.

Summarizing what has been accomplished during the interview is very helpful when bringing it to a close because it allows the client to leave on a positive note. Also, summarizing recommendations about who is to do what before the next meeting crystalizes the plans that have been made in both the client's and the worker's minds. Summarization as a major aspect of terminating the intervention process is also covered in chapter 8.

Eliciting Information

As part of the communication process, a worker must encourage a client to reach for and share information. One way of doing this is simply to ask questions. There are two basic types of questions, open-ended and closed-ended. Closed-ended questions include those which seek simple "yes" or "no" answers, such as:

> "Are you coming tomorrow?"
> "Did you have a nice time?"
> "Is Harry here?"
> "Did Francesca take the dog out yet?"
> "Are you getting along better with your wife?"

Closed-ended questions may also involve those where there are a number of clearly defined answers to choose from. They do not encourage or even allow for an explanation of why the answer was chosen or for an elaboration of thoughts or feelings about the answer. For example, consider these questions:

> "Are you male or female?"
> "Do you want chocolate, vanilla, or super-duper tutti-frutti ice cream?"
> "Are you working at Burger King, Mac's, or Heavenly Hash Heaven next summer?"
> "How many brothers do you have?"
> "What is your birthdate?"

In each of the above instances, a simple response is required. The choices for the response are established ahead of time and have a closed number of options. Your job is simply to choose one. Even the last two questions have a limited number of responses. The number of brothers must be from none to probably under twenty. A birthdate is limited to specific days in the twelve months of the year.

It's easy, especially for beginning interviewers, to "machine-gun" or bombard the client with one closed-ended question after the other. Frequently, this occurs when a worker is anxious and trying to keep the interview going. Often, the worker wonders why the client isn't saying much or isn't initiating any discussion on his or her own.

The answer to this dilemma is to use the open-ended question. Instead of requiring simple, established answers from a pre-determined selection, the open-ended question seeks out the client's thoughts, ideas, and explanations for answers. It encourages elaboration and specifics about answers unique to particular clients and situations. Consider the following examples:

> "What are your reasons for wanting to leave home?"
> "How are you feeling about the situation?"
> "What do you plan on doing in the future?"
> "What are the people in your family like?"
> "How are you planning to accomplish this?"

Each of these questions allows for a more detailed answer, unique to every individual and situation. For example, how you would describe your family members at any particular point in time would be different from the way anyone else would.

HIGHLIGHT 2.4
Telling a Client What to Do

Can you make suggestions to clients without interfering with their right to individual choice? Should you give a client advice? Should you urge a client to pursue an alternative when you're absolutely certain it's the best thing for him or her to do?

These are often difficult questions to struggle with. There is some controversy regarding the extent to which a worker can direct a client into taking some particular action. A major problem is that if you tell a client what to do, in a way you are taking responsibility for the result. In other words, if it turns out that the result of the action is bad for whatever reason, the client has you to blame.

Another problem involves the difficulty of putting yourself in another person's shoes. Can you really understand what it's like to be that person and understand his or her values and ideas? Is it ethical for you to tell someone else what route is best for them to take when you don't have to suffer any possible consequences yourself?

It's one thing to help a client identify the alternatives available to him or her. It's another to direct the client as to which one is the best. An underlying theme in the problem-solving process is to help clients explore the pros and cons of the various alternatives available to them. As a worker, you can help them think through what each possible action really would mean to them.

Consider a teenager with an unwanted pregnancy. It's most likely that each of us has a strong opinion about what the teenager *should* do, or, rather, about what *we think we would do* in her situation. However, she has her own life situation with worries about her future, parents, friends, school, guilt, and religious ideas. The choice needs to be hers.

This is not to say that there are never times when it is appropriate to encourage a client to pursue the alternative he or she has chosen to be the best. Sometimes it's difficult and scary for a client to get going and move onward. In those circumstances a worker needs to use professional judgment regarding how forcefully to encourage the client to proceed. A helpful thought is to emphasize to the client that taking no action is indeed a decision to take one alternative. Making no decision has definite consequences. For example, if the pregnant teen decides not to make a decision and ignore her pregnancy, at five or six months gestation, she has already narrowed the alternatives available to her. She has begun to make a decision by not making a decision.

There will be times when clients will pressure you to tell them what to do. For instance, I once worked with a woman who had a variety of crises in her life and in her marriage. She spoke about a married man with whom she once had an affair. She said that she still thought about him often, even though the affair had ended over five years ago. She hadn't seen him since then because he lived in another city. She asked me point-blank if I would call him if I were her. Bewildered, I replied, "I can't answer that because I'm not you." The woman never spoke to me again.

After much thought, it has occurred to me that there would have been a number of more effective replies. For instance, I could've said, "That's a difficult thing for me to answer. Help me think through how you feel about this man, your husband, and your marriage, so that I can better understand your situation." In this way, I could have gotten back on the track of helping her think through her own decision.

There are some instances where encouragement to take some action may need to be more forceful. One example of this approach is crisis intervention, which will be discussed more thoroughly in chapter 7. In a crisis situation, clients may need to be pushed out of their frozen, emotional, and perhaps illogical state. Once again, however, this is a matter of professional judgment.

There's one other thing to consider when thinking about telling a client what to do. Namely, how do *you* feel when someone tells you what you *should* do. Do you run right out and do it readily? Or, do you resent the intrusion and ignore the advice, or even take off in the opposite direction?

The Use of "Why?"

One thing to consider when formulating questions for clients is if and when to use the word "why." This word can be very threatening to clients because it often implies that the person to whom it's directed is at fault. For example, a student enters a classroom three minutes late. The instructor asks in front of the whole class, "Why are you late?" This question places a demand on the student to explain his reasons for doing something wrong by not being on time. The following are other examples:

"Why do you beat your children?"
"Why do you drink so much?"
"Why don't you get a job?"
"Why don't you get straight A's?"
"Why do you always nag me so much?"

The word "why" also can put the burden of seeking out a solution on the individual to whom it's directed. The solution often involves reaching inside of one's mind for facts, organizing one's thoughts and ideas, and presenting them in an understandable form right then and there. The following questions illustrate this:

"Why does it take at least four years to graduate from college?"
"Why does the sun shine?"
"Why don't I have enough money?"
"Why do they have that rule?"
"Why can't I do what I want to?"

In summary, it's best to be cautious in using the word "why."

Overlap of Techniques

Sometimes it is difficult to label a technique specifically as being a "clarification" or a "self-disclosure." Some responses fulfill only one purpose and fit obviously into one category, while others combine two or more techniques if they fulfill two or more functions. The important thing is to master a variety of techniques and thereby become more flexible and effective.

Interviewing, Specific Techniques, and the Problem-Solving Process

You may be asking yourself at this point, "Okay, how do these specific interviewing techniques work in real interviews? How will they fit into the problem-solving process with real clients?" The answers to these questions are given in later chapters which address each phase of the problem-solving process. The phases are assessment, planning, intervention, evaluation, termination, and follow-up. The first and most basic step before beginning the intervention process is mastering how to communicate with a wide range of clients.

Issues and Hurdles in Interviewing

The fascinating thing about working with and helping people is that you never really know what to expect. Every person, problem, and situation is different but there are a number of issues that frequently must be dealt with in order to continue with the problem-solving approach. They often pose dilemmas for workers about how to proceed. Among these issues are confidentiality, silence in the interview, confronting clients, involuntary clients, and suspicion of untruth.

Confidentiality

The National Association of Social Workers Code of Ethics (NASW, 1980) clearly states, "The social worker should respect the privacy of clients and hold in confidence all information obtained in the course of professional service."

This sounds simple enough, but what if a client tells you that he is sexually abusing his five-year-old child, that he can't control himself, and that he does not want anyone to know about it? Or, what if a client tells you that she made twenty-five hundred dollars last week in her cocaine dealings? Or, what if a married client tells you he's really gay, has had numerous unpro-

---

HIGHLIGHT 2.5
Confidentiality and Persons Living with AIDS

AIDS has posed some special problems of confidentiality that differ from those of any other illness.* AIDS is deadly. It's spreading at an explosive rate. It's associated with issues of secrecy such as "homosexuality, bisexuality, promiscuity, or intravenous drug use" (Abramson, 1990, p. 170). Finally, people with AIDS dread *discrimination* because of the disease second only to fear of the disease itself (Presidential Commission on the Human Immunodeficiency Virus Epidemic, 1988).

Abramson (1990) interviewed social workers who spent from 20 to 100 percent of their caseload time working with persons diagnosed with AIDS. She found that *secrecy* was by far the most dominant problematic issue addressed by these workers.

This secrecy primarily concerned three areas. First, secrets were kept from those diagnosed with AIDS. Second, there were secrets kept from people close to those with AIDS who were unknowingly at risk of contracting the disease. Third, secrets about the AIDS diagnosis were kept from society at large.

Evident were numerous dilemmas concerning confidentiality. Some involved not telling people about their own positive diagnosis because of the negative emotional ramifications. Others involved not telling people at risk of contracting AIDS from the client in order to keep the client's confidentiality. Still others concerned hiding the diagnosis from other staff, agencies, and organizations. For example, such information might be kept confidential in order to allow the client continuity of health insurance benefits.

Abramson emphasized what a horrible quandary secrecy imposed for practitioners. Although secrecy might maintain an individual's confidentiality, there are numerous negative effects. She continued that "on a practical level, secrets can impede understanding, foster isolation, prevent access to services, increase stigma, and interfere with a sense of community, keeping society separated into 'us' and 'them.' More important, the energies that should be invested in finding a cure, changing behaviors, and fighting discrimination are drained by the demands of secrecy by patients, families, and health providers" (p. 172).

People are often terrified by AIDS. They want no one to know about it. They fear, often realistically so, that they will be ostracized and discriminated against. Fear may force them to cling doggedly to confidentiality.

However, questions must be raised about the well-being not only of the client, but also of those interfacing with the client and of society at large. People who are positively diagnosed need to know about their condition in order to maximize the treatment and prevention aspects which maximize longevity. People who are at risk of contracting AIDS need to know in order to prevent contraction. Finally, society, with its many facets and organizations, must know in order to combat the disease and help its victims. Confidentiality concerning AIDS becomes a most complex and difficult issue. There are some laws which now restrict the amount of information which can be shared about a person with AIDS. These further restrict and affect confidentiality and the freedom of the worker.

---

*This is certainly not to imply that confidentiality in all areas of social work (for example, child abuse reporting, chemical dependency, and mental health) are not critically important. However, AIDS is such a new and rapidly developing issue that many questions concerning confidentiality have not yet been identified, let alone addressed.

tected sexual encounters with other men over the past fifteen years, worries about having contracted AIDS, but absolutely does not want to tell his wife about his fears?

In chapter 1, we posed a number of ethical quandaries which may confront generalist practitioners. Many involve dilemmas concerning confidentiality issues. Although we will discuss ethics more thoroughly in chapter 11, because of its significance, some comments about confidentiality are important here.

According to Pippin (1980), "In its simplest form, confidentiality means that all that takes place between the professional and the client is the property of the client and cannot be publicized in any way" (p. 40). However, he continues that, "Caseworkers have no privileged information protection. In the public welfare agency, confidentiality does not mean that all that takes place in the casework relationship is the property of the client.... The caseworker is the agent of the agency. Anything that the caseworker is privy to, the agency is privy to as well" (p. 41). In other words, in principle, what goes on between worker and client should be confidential. However, in reality this often is not possible.

Wilson (1978) identifies two types of confidentiality, *absolute confidentiality* and *relative confidentiality*. Absolute confidentiality means all that transpires between client and worker goes no further. There is absolutely no sharing of that information. Because of the lack of legal protection for many social workers concerning privileged communication, the necessity to record certain types of information, share information for supervisory purposes, and provide "continuity of service" in the event the case is transferred, such absolute confidentiality is rare in actual practice (Sheafor et al., 1988, p. 64).

Relative confidentiality is much more common. Sheafor et al. (1988) describe this type of confidentiality as when "the social worker can only promise to be responsible about his or her own communication regarding a situation and

should work to assure that the agency will carefully protect the information prepared for its records" (p. 64). In other words, the worker should do his or her best to ensure the client's confidentiality but can't guarantee it.

Austin et al. (1986) emphasize that this means that the client's information and situation should *not* be shared informally with the worker's colleagues, friends or family. The information should be considered very serious and should not be used as "juicy" tidbits in social conversation.

Johnson (1989) stresses the concept of "informed consent" (p. 399). This involves making the client fully aware of the fact that any disclosed information may have to be shared under certain circumstances. The client should also have some idea about what these circumstances are. How to gain the client's consent is discussed further in chapter 16.

In summary, a generalist practitioner should make every effort to keep information about the client confidential. However, the worker should also be aware that, depending on the particular situation, there are many constraints about what really can and can't be kept secret. Constraints include those imposed by the agency and other legal restrictions regarding what must be shared. The worker should clarify to the client what these constraints are. Thus, the client may have the choice of whether or not to share personal and other information.

Silence in the Interview

What if, try as you might, the client won't say much? Kadushin (1972) makes some important comments about how silence can operate within human interaction such as an interview. First, silence "generates social anxiety, felt as embarrassment, in people who have come together with the intent of talking to each other. But the social worker, in addition, feels a professional anxiety at the thought that continued silence signals a failing interview" (p. 193). In other words, a worker may feel threatened, inadequate, or out of control if long periods of silence occur during the interview. It's almost as if such silent times demonstrate the uselessness or lack of substance of the interview. However in reality, Kadushin continues, "something is happening all the time, even when participants appear totally passive in their silent interaction. It is a period filled with nonspeech, in which both interviewer and interviewee participate" (p. 193). In other words, silence is meaningful, and may occur for a number of reasons.

Client-Initiated Silence

Silence in the interview is either client-initiated or worker-initiated (Hackney & Cormier, 1979). Client-initiated silence means that the client is taking responsibility for having the silent period happen. This silence occurs for different reasons (Kadushin, 1972). First, the client may be addressing an issue and then come to a point where she's not certain where to go and needs time to organize her thoughts. Second, the client may be trying to pressure the worker to give some answer, response, or solution to a problem. A third use of silence is to offer resistance. It may be used as a way to "frustrate the interviewer," "exert control" over him or her and the interview, or defend "against anxiety" (p. 196).

Negative Worker-Initiated Silence

The second type of silence in an interview is worker-initiated. This means that the worker has been talking and feels responsible for the silence. This silence usually occurs in one of six scenarios, two of which are negative and four of which are therapeutic. (Hackney & Cormier, 1979). The first negative scenario involves a worker who demonstrates a quiet, non-involved, non-assertive personality style. For this worker it is not natural to work that hard at directing the interview. Such behavior is inappropriate and a "cop-out" for a professional. Professional skills must transcend individual personality styles.

The second negative type of worker-initiated silence occurs when the worker's mind becomes a blank and he or she cannot think of anything to say. This form of silence occurs more frequently with new workers who are anxious about their own performance.

Focusing on the Client Instead of Yourself

When a social worker comes upon a new situation or a new type of problem, it's easy to become anxious if you're not sure about what to do next. The answer to this dilemma is to tune in to your anxiety and do one of two things. First, you can allow yourself a brief period of silence in order to get your thoughts together. (This type of silence will be discussed further in the next section under therapeutic silence.) Second, you can think about what's happening in the interview and label it. For example, you might say, "It's pretty quiet in here. Where are your thoughts?" or "It seems like you're taking some time to think about the issue. That's all right. We can start again when you're ready."

Therapeutic Worker-Initiated Silence

Hackney and Cormier (1979, pp. 72–73) cite four ways in which worker-initiated silence can be beneficial or therapeutic: "pacing the interview," "silent focusing," "responding to defenses," and "silent caring." Each type assumes that the worker initiates or is in control of the silent period.

Sometimes conversations and information move very rapidly during the interview and there's not enough time for the client to keep up or to absorb all that is transpiring. *Pacing the interview* involves using small periods of silence to allow time to think about and assimilate what's occurring.

A second type of therapeutic silence involves *silent focusing*. This period of silence is a bit longer than those used to pace interviews and is only allowed to occur after some significant revelation has surfaced. Silent focusing enables the client to focus in on and think more intensively about an issue without having to rush right into something else.

The third type of therapeutic silence concerns the worker *responding to defenses* in the client. This occurs when a client has an emotional outburst toward the worker. Usually, the client is angry at something else (for example, the spouse, children, the agency which is denying benefits, the landlord, the in-laws, etc.) However, clients may vent their intense emotions at you the worker just because you are there. It may be tempting to become defensive yourself or immediately try to provide insight into the client's behavior. However, a period of silence with congruent nonverbal behavior (for example, maintenance of direct eye contact with the client and a somber facial expression) may give clients time to think about how and why they're acting the way they are.

Silent caring is the fourth type of therapeutic silence. Sometimes there will be a period of intense emotion during an interview, often involving profound sadness, grief, or regret. Many times a client will cry during these moments. Culturally, we are often taught that crying implies weakness and is essentially bad. This is a misconception, however, because crying allows for an honest expression of emotion and an opportunity to let pain out and experience it. Unless such poignant emotions are identified and allowed expression, people can't work through them and get on with life. A period of silent empathy during an interview may best convey your caring and understanding. Incidentally it also may be appropriate to subtly offer the client a Kleenex.

Finally, it should be noted that there are distinctive cultural differences regarding the treatment of silence in conversations and interviews. It's important to be sensitive to these nuances and respectful of the client's values about silent communication.

Silent focusing on the client can enable both parties to get their thoughts in order.

Confronting Clients

Confrontation in almost any situation is difficult for many people. To confront means to disagree with another person and make a point of stating that disagreement. Confrontation also involves risking a negative or hostile reaction from the person you're confronting.

Nonetheless, confrontation is an important

tool in the problem-solving process of generalist practice. Johnson (1986) defines a confrontation as a "direct expression of one's view of the conflict and one's feelings about it while inviting the other person to do the same. Confrontations involve clarifying and exploring the issues, the nature and strength of the underlying needs of the participants, and their current feelings" (p. 222). A confrontation in social work practice most often "involves directly pointing out to a client a discrepancy or an inconsistency between statements and actions" (Compton & Galaway, 1984, p. 301). Any confrontation first involves clearly identifying the existing discrepancy and then working toward some resolution (Ivey, 1988). In other words, confrontations are necessary to help clients face "factors that contribute to their problems or that block progress toward goal attainment" (Hepworth & Larsen, 1987, p. 1005).

There are four major types of discrepancies that practitioners frequently target for confrontation including those: "(1) between two statements; (2) between what one says and what one does; (3) between verbal and nonverbal behavior; and (4) between two or more people" (Whittaker & Tracy, 1989, p. 136; Ivey, 1988). The following are examples of such discrepancies:

- A client states, "I want to stay here and work on the problem. I really want to go home now."
- After having gone out to "hang one on in a big way" the prior evening, a client says, "I don't drink anymore."
- While chewing her fingernails, tapping her foot, and grimacing, a client says, "I feel so at ease here talking with you."
- A worker is interviewing two parents. The focus is on child behavior management techniques. One parent states, "I really am responsible for all the discipline of the children." The other parent replies, "You're all talk and no action. I'm the one who does all the disciplining around here."

There are a number of reasons for these discrepancies (Whittaker & Tracy, 1989). Sometimes confrontations are necessary when clients are trying to resist intervention for a certain reason. At other times, clients may not be certain whether they want to be helped and are hesitant to cooperate. Still other times, for reasons of their own, clients won't want to follow through on recommendations. Sometimes clients will find it too difficult to make actual changes in their behavior. Clients may also make excuses for behavior which you feel are unacceptable. Finally, clients may be behaving in ways which are contrary to their own best interests.

Hepworth and Larsen (1990) postulate that confrontations involve four components. First, the worker should communicate that she or he cares about the client and is interested in the client's well-being. Second, the worker should clearly express the client's stated goal within the problem-solving process. Third, the worker should illustrate exactly what the discrepancy is. Finally, the worker should indicate the realistic results of the discrepancy.

For example, a worker in a sheltered workshop for developmentally disabled adults might say to a client:

1. "I like you and I care about how you perform here" (*communication of caring*).
2. "You've told me that you'd like to continue working here for a long time" (*client's stated goal*).
3. "However, you say you like working here, but after every half hour of work you take a half hour break" (*identification of the discrepancy*).
4. "You know that everybody here is expected to work two hours straight and then they get a half-hour break. You know that you and everyone else must follow these rules or you can't continue working here" (*realistic results of the discrepancy*).

There are several additional suggestions for maximizing the use of confrontation. First, as a worker, consider whether your relationship with the client is strong enough to withstand the potential stress caused by confrontation (Johnson, 1986). For instance, it would probably be unwise for you to confront a client within 10 minutes after the initial interview with the client has begun.

Second, be aware of the client's emotional state. If he or she is extremely upset, agitated, or anxious, a confrontation probably would have little value (Hepworth & Larsen, 1990). Clients who are preoccupied with other issues probably will have little energy left to respond positively and helpfully to confrontations.

Third, use confrontations infrequently and only when you have to (Compton & Galaway, 1984; Hepworth & Larsen, 1990). Confrontations are often difficult and imply some risk to the relationship. If they are used as an integral part of a confrontational style, the client may feel downtrodden and terminate the worker/client relationship.

Fourth, continue to demonstrate respect for the client throughout the confrontation (Nunnally & Moy, 1989). This involves listening to what the client is saying whether or not you agree with it and also acknowledging the fact that the client ultimately has the right to choose his or her own course of action. Finally, respect concerns keeping in mind that you as the worker are there to help the client, not to get the client to do what you want him or her to do.

Fifth, remain empathic with the client throughout the confrontation (Hepworth & Larsen, 1990; Johnson, 1986) and don't get overly involved in trying to get your own way. Continue to work on understanding how the client feels and how he or she views the problem from his or her own perspective.

Sixth, use "I" statements during the confrontation (Hepworth & Larsen, 1990). Simply rephrasing your thoughts to include the word "I" enhances the quality of personal caring and empathy. This technique emphasizes the fact that you are giving feedback instead of criticizing or blaming. For example, a worker might say, "*I* would like to share with you some inconsistencies I've noticed between what you've been saying and what you've actually been doing." This is far more personal and far less blaming than a statement such as, "*You've* been saying one thing and doing another."

Seventh, have patience and allow the client some time to change (Hepworth & Larsen, 1990; Johnson, 1986). Applying intense pressure for a client to change may be a "turn off" because people are likely to resent being told what to do. Johnson (1986) emphasizes that a worker should not demand change unless she is God. Additionally, expecting instantaneous change is inappropriate. Clients need time to integrate new information, think things through, and make gradual changes in their lives and behavior.

Involuntary Clients

Many social workers find themselves in the position of trying to help involuntary clients who don't want to be there. Epstein (1985) describes involuntary clients as "individuals or families who have come to public attention because they are part of a social problem that is currently of official public concern" (p. 250). Examples include child abusers, people on probation or parole, rapists, men who beat their spouses, adolescent delinquents, alcohol and other drug abusers, and clients in various residential settings (for example, nursing homes, mental health inpatient facilities, prisons, and residential treatment centers).

There is no question that it is difficult to work with people who don't want to work with you. However, there are a number of suggestions which can help the intervention process along even when clients are involuntary.

First, acknowledge to yourself that the client is indeed involuntary. Don't ignore the fact that the client doesn't want to be there. Rather, accept it. Instead of trying to force the client to like being there with you, start where the client is.

Second, try to put yourself in your client's shoes. We've already discussed some of the negative feelings clients may come to interviews with. They may be wary and suspicious. They may have had bad experiences with your agency or others before. They might be trying desperately to maintain their own homeostasis and thus strongly resist any attempt to change. Just looking at the reality of the situation instead of trying to fight it is a good start.

HIGHLIGHT 2.6
Handling Hostility

Sometimes clients will be angry when they arrive for your interview. They may raise their voices and even scream, shake their fists, scowl, snarl, be sarcastic, or behave aggresively in other ways. Displaying hostility is one way a client has of dramatizing a conflict. Conflicts may involve disagreements, disappointments, or general displeasure. What is certain is that something is making the client mad.

Johnson (1986) points out that, although conflicts are generally viewed as being unpleasant incidents to be avoided, there are some positive aspects to conflict. For example, conflicts bring to the surface issues which are of serious concern to clients. Instead of hiding their negative feelings, clients may voice some hostility. A worker then knows what he's up against and can begin to address the issues involved. Additionally, conflict can provide motivating arenas for change. If a client is uncomfortable enough with a situation to voice hostility, that client may be more motivated to work to resolve the problem causing the discomfort. Only then can the client revert to a calmer, more comfortable state.

The following are ten suggestions for dealing with client hostility:

1. *Don't get angry or defensive.* Recognize your own reactions. Remember that this is a professional and not a personal issue.
2. *Focus on the client's hostile* behavior *instead of labeling the client a hostile* person. Label the hostile behavior and other dynamics as they occur.

3. *Allow the client briefly to voice his or her anger.* Be empathic. See the situation from the client's perspective.
4. *Emphasize the client's personal strengths.* Do not attack the client. You want to close, not widen the rift in communication.
5. *Know the facts regarding the client's situation and the parameters of your role.* To help the client deal with reality, you must know what reality is.
6. *Focus on the present and future.* Avoid allowing the client to dwell on the past. Emphasize what can be done positively—not what has already happened negatively and can't be changed.
7. *Look at the various alternatives open to the client and their consequences.* Help the client evaluate the pros and cons of each alternative.
8. *Don't moralize.* (It helps to remember the times someone has moralized to you about what you *should* do and how annoying it was.)
9. *Summarize what has occurred during the interview* and what recommendations have been made. Sometimes this helps the client to keep on track. You want to help the client deal objectively with his or her reality, not go off on tangents of emotional outbursts.
10. *Establish very short-term, initial goals* with a hostile client. These might include calming the client down and establishing short-term goals such as making a basic agreement to discuss a particular issue or to come to another appointment. This is quite different from addressing major problems as part of the intervention process.

The third suggestion for working with involuntary clients involves labeling and helping them express their negative feelings (Whittaker & Tracy, 1989). If the client is resistant, bring that out into the open. For example, you might say, "I get the strong impression that you don't really want to be here. I'd like to know how you're feeling right now."

It's also helpful to identify the reasons you suspect for the client's resistance. For example, if appropriate, you might say, "I know it's been difficult for you to come in and see me. I realize that you're required to do this by the court." Once again, labeling the reality of the situation often both disperses anxiety and introduces opportunities for clients to get their real feelings out on the table.

A fourth suggestion involves knowing the limits of your authority and, in effect, power over the client (Epstein, 1985). Giving the client the idea that you are the master and he or she must do what you say is usually a turnoff. However, you do want to clarify, at least in your own mind, the ultimate consequences of the client's involvement or lack of involvement with you. Depending on the circumstances, you may even want to state these consequences in the interview. For instance, the client's alternative to working with you might be incarceration. As a worker you might say, "I hope you choose to work with me on this problem. As we both know, your alternatives are limited to this or going to jail. That's a pretty coercive situation."

The fifth suggestion for involuntary client situations involves figuring out what you can do for the client that he or she wants. You might first think about why the client is *ambivalent* about seeing you (Epstein, 1985). This requires careful *listening* to what the client says. What is really important to him or her? What can you do for the client which will make the intervention worthwhile? Your usefulness is often best demonstrated to the client in "an immediate and concrete way (e.g., by arranging for a needed service such as transportation, medical or dental care, etc.)" (Sheafor et al., 1988, p. 213).

The sixth suggestion concerns "cultivating hope and conveying encouragement" (Whittaker & Tracy, 1989, p. 143). You might try suggesting some potentially positive outcomes of the intervention which the client may never have thought of. You might indicate that, although it's difficult at the beginning of the process, you've seen many other people work their problems out and make great gains.

The seventh suggestion involves allowing the client time to gain trust in you and in the intervention process. It's illogical to expect instant motivation. Allowing the client to get to know you as a competent professional while you establish a positive worker/client relationship is important.

The final suggestion for working with unwilling clients involves accepting the fact that it is ultimately the client who has the right to choose whether or not to cooperate with you. After you've done your best, the client still may decide not to work with you. This is his or her right and the client must live with the consequences of his or her decision. You can help the client explore the negative and positive consequences of that decision. The bottom line, however, is that it is the client's decision to make.

Suspicion of Untruth

There may be times when a worker has a *gut reaction* that a client is not telling the truth. Gut reactions involve feelings that you get in reaction to situations where you feel in the back of your mind that something is occurring or something is wrong. It's useful to become adept at identifying your gut reactions because they often provide excellent clues about what's happening in any given situation.

Kadushin (1972) points out that, although

we would probably prefer it otherwise, clients are not perfect. They may choose to lie for various reasons. Kadushin says that unfortunately workers don't like to address the issue of clients' lying; it makes workers "feel guilty and unhappy because skepticism seems to violate the professionally dictated need to be 'accepting' and to treat the client with respect" (p. 201). It's uncomfortable to confront a possible lie. For one thing, you may be wrong. The client may really be telling the truth.

Regardless, lying sometimes occurs. There are four suggestions regarding what to do if you think a client may be lying to you. First, evaluate the situation logically. Do you have a feeling that something isn't right? Are there discrepancies in facts? Or does the client's story not have a realistic sense to it?

Consider a three-year-old child with odd-looking, round burn marks on the tops of his hands. The parent explains that the burns are the result of accidentally spilling some hot water on his hands. Your gut reaction, however, is to question how such a hot water burn resulted in small circular burn marks instead of a large reddened area. Logically you might think such burns are more likely to result from a lighted cigarette. Such a gut reaction may give you a clue that child abuse may be occurring. At least it's a possibility to investigate.

The second suggestion for dealing with possible lying is to examine the client's pattern of prior behavior. This, of course, can only be done if you have a history of interaction with the client or if you have access to records about how the client has behaved in the past. Has the client omitted facts or lied before? Have you suspected lying before? Or is this the first time such behavior is suspected?

The third suggestion is that you may choose not to confront the client if this is the first time the possibility of lying has come up. You might give the client the benefit of the doubt.

The fourth suggestion about a client's lying is to evaluate the costs of believing or not be-

lieving your client. Is it more costly to lose the client's trust if you express disbelief? Or is it more costly to ignore what you think is not true and risk possible severe consequences? For example, if you strongly suspect that a pregnant mother is lying about abusing cocaine, can you afford to ignore the lie at the expense of the fetus's health?

Terminating the Interview

Sometimes it is difficult or uncomfortable to bring an interview to a close. You may think the client is finally feeling comfortable with you. During the last five minutes of an interview, the client may raise strikingly significant issues. The client may express the strong need to continue talking.

Terminating the intervention process in general is addressed in chapter 8. However, Shulman (1981) makes four points about how to end interviews and worker/client relationships which are relevant here.

First, before the actual interview termination (for example, five, ten, or even fifteen minutes before) mention exactly how much time is left. You might say something like, "We're starting to get into some things you feel very strongly about. We've got another ten minutes to talk about them today, and then can continue our discussion next week." This "points out the ending" to the client (p. 27). It acts as a guide-post for how much more the client will be able to pursue and it also sets a time limit so that the client is not abruptly surprised when the interview draws to a close.

The second suggestion involves "sharing ending feelings" (p. 27). You can tell the client about how you feel as the interview is coming to a close. Statements may include positive feelings you have toward the client and about what the client has accomplished. Of course, these statements must reflect genuine feelings. For example, you might say, "I've really en-

Figure 2.3: Social Work Roles with Micro Systems

Social workers have many roles. The boxes below illustrate some of the roles commonly assumed in micro practice. Circles are used to represent worker, client, and macro systems. Lines and arrows depict how systems relate to each other. Macro systems are usually organizations or communities. Client systems illustrated in these particular diagrams are individuals.

However, it's important to note how working on the behalf of individuals often involves helping your clients deal with the many other systems with which they interact. The distinctions between micro, mezzo, and macro practice blur. Your goal as a professional social worker is to help your clients solve problems, obtain resources, and address issues by using the most effective means possible. This is what being a generalist practitioner is all about.

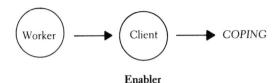

Enabler

The *enabler* role involves providing support, encouragement, and suggestions to a client system so that the client may proceed more easily and successfully in completing tasks or solving problems. The diagram above illustrates how workers can provide such support. An arrow pointing from the worker circle to the client system circle depicts the worker's support. The desired result is that the client system will be better able to cope with problems and to pursue some course of action.

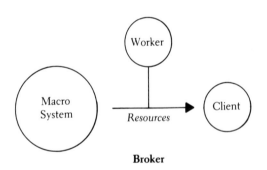

Broker

The *broker* role involves linking clients with needed resources. The line from the worker circle to the arrow in the above diagram portrays the worker's role. It illustrates the worker's active involvement in obtaining resources for the client. The arrow points from the macro system circle, which provides resources, to the client system circle, which receives them.

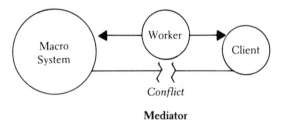

Mediator

Mediators work to help conflicting parties settle disputes and agree on compromises. A mediator maintains a neutral stance between the involved parties, taking no one's side. In the above diagram, the broken line beneath the worker circle depicts the two parties; broken lines of communication and their inability to settle differences.

Here the worker is mediating between a client system and a macro system. However, mediation can occur between virtually any size systems including that between two macro systems or two micro systems. Consider, for instance, divorce mediation where disputes are settled and agreements made between divorcing spouses.

Educator

As an *educator,* a worker conveys information to a client, as the diagram above illustrates.

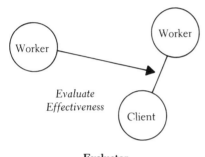

Evaluator

All practitioners need to assume the role of *evaluator* in terms of the effectiveness of their own practice. The arrow in the above diagram portrays the worker evaluating her own intervention with a client.

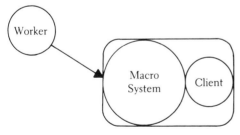

Case Manager/Coordinator

Many clients have multiple problems and are involved with many other systems. One role social workers often assume is that of *case manager* or *coordinator.* This role involves seeking out resources, planning how they might be delivered, organizing service provision, and monitoring progress.

The box enclosing the macro and client systems represents the coordinated interactions between these two systems. The arrow pointing from the worker to the box depicts the worker's active involvement in coordinating all the systems involved. Although the diagram above illustrates the coordination of one macro and one micro client system, such coordination can occur among any number of macro, mezzo, and micro systems.

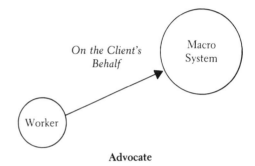

Advocate

Advocates champion the rights of others. They usually advocate with the goal of empowering their clients. The arrow in the diagram above which leads from the worker to the macro system is exceptionally thick. This represents the significant amount of energy it often takes to impact larger, more powerful systems. Advocacy is an extremely significant role in generalist social work practice.

joyed working with you. I think you've made great strides toward achieving your goals."

A third recommendation for terminating interviews concerns "asking for a review of the learning" (Shulman, 1981, p. 28). In other words, ask the client to summarize what he or she thinks has been learned and accomplished. As the intervention progresses, the client should become increasingly articulate about what goals have been established and attained. How to identify and monitor goals is discussed more thoroughly in chapters 6 through 8. Summarization helps a client focus in on the core meaningfulness of the intervention. Additionally, it helps a client clarify exactly what has been learned so it can be used to address new problems and situations again in the future.

The final suggestion for terminating interviews involves "reaching for ending feelings" (p. 28). Not only can you as a worker share your feelings about the interview and intervention process, but you can also draw out your client's reactions. As we've discussed earlier, expressing feelings openly allows clients to deal with them and move on with their lives. For example, a worker might say, "You seem awfully anxious right now. We've been working together for quite a while. Sometimes it's scary to move on alone. How are you feeling?"

Chapter Summary

This chapter introduced some of the basic skills for micro level generalist social work practice. The impacts of verbal and nonverbal behavior were described, as well as the relationship-enhancing qualities of warmth, empathy, and genuineness. The need to have the *impact* on the receiver match the *intent* of the sender in any communication was stressed. Various aspects of starting the interview were described. These included the interview's setting, how to dress for the interview, thinking ahead about the interview, initial introductions, alleviating clients' anxiety, portraying confidence, and stating the interview's purpose and role.

A variety of interviewing techniques were explained including simple encouragement, rephrasing, reflective responding, clarification, interpretation, providing information, emphasizing clients' strengths, summarizaton, eliciting information, and self-disclosure. Questions were raised regarding both the use of the word "why" and telling clients what they should do.

A number of issues and hurdles involved in interviewing were addressed including confidentiality issues, silence in interviews, confrontation, involuntary clients, client hostility, and suspicion of untruth. Finally, suggestions for terminating interviews were proposed.

3

Mezzo Practice Skills: Working with Groups

"Ya-hoo!"

Six young adults sat around the room fidgeting nervously and avoiding each other's eyes. Each wondered what the other was thinking. All would describe themselves as shy, inadequate, and depressed. This was despite the fact that their individual personalities varied drastically. All had tried to kill themselves at least once. This is why they were gathered together in that room. The six were about to begin their involvement in a treatment group. The group's initial purpose was to help the participants explore the reasons for their sadness and begin to build more fortified self-concepts and lives. The social worker entered the room. Group treatment was about to begin.

The chairperson of the group tapped her foot nervously on the floor. She had already interrupted Mr. Fischer twice. There he was rambling on again about irrelevant details. He simply would not stop talking. The chairperson glanced at her watch. She had only twenty-three more minutes to bring the group to a consensus. This was a task group trying to initiate a plan for publicizing a new child abuse prevention program. Finally, at her wit's end, she stated loudly and assertively, "Excuse me, Mr. Fischer. I appreciate your ideas and input. Our time is very limited and we need to hear what the other group members have to say." It seems like the rest of the people in the room breathed a simultaneous sigh of relief. The meeting proceeded.

Jimmy is certainly a tough case. He is a developmentally disabled nine-year-old who has lived with foster parents almost since birth. Jimmy has a number of serious delays in development including intellectual, language, social, and physical (both fine and gross motor). Even though he resides in foster care, he still remains very involved with his biological parents and his seven siblings still living with them. The biological family has a multitude of problems including poverty, truancy, illness, and developmental disability on the part of the mother. The foster parents and the biological parents don't like each other very much and quarrel regularly. Jimmy visits his biological family on a weekly basis.

A number of professionals sit around a large rectangular table discussing Jimmy and his situation. They had all had the opportunity to evaluate his case and now will make their recommendations for his treatment. They all are participating in an interdisciplinary team staffing (that is, a planning meeting involving a number of different professional disciplines). A social worker is the case coordinator. This means it is her job to run the meeting and help bring the team to conclusions regarding the best plan to help Jimmy. The speech, physical, and occupational therapists along with the nurse, physician, psychologist, and psychiatrist would all share their findings. Together they would formulate plans to help Jimmy, his foster family, and his biological family. As case coordinator, the social worker is responsible for pulling together a broad range of information so that it makes sense. Her task is to lead the group in formulating effective intervention plans.

Introduction

The previous examples illustrate the types of groups which social workers might be responsible for leading. Much of social work occurs within, by, or for groups. A social worker, therefore, needs both group knowledge and skills. Increasingly, social workers use groups for a variety of purposes. A group is defined as "a collection of people brought together by mutual interests, who are capable of consistent and uniform action" (Barker, 1987, p. 66). Groups help chemically dependent people and those trying to lose weight. Groups help children cope with the divorce of their parents, teach new foster parents about the effect of separation and placement on foster children, and help family members deal with many problem areas. Social workers also play a role in some self-help type groups such as Parents Anonymous.

In addition, social workers use groups to gather information about clients and to help plan interventions. In many settings social workers participate in staffings where colleagues from other disciplines share their knowledge about a particular client. Case conferences are common in medical settings and other types of agencies.

Finally, most social workers will participate in agency staff meetings where the focus may be on new policies, in-service training, or agency problems. In each case, the social worker will need specific knowledge and skills to participate as an effective group member, leader or facilitator.

This chapter will:

- Examine two major types of groups, treatment and task;
- Describe the various roles generalist practitioners frequently assume in groups;
- Formulate a framework for understanding groups;
- Outline the skills needed to work effectively with groups;
- Discuss basic elements which impact group dynamics such as group culture and norms, group size and composition;
- Explore various decision-making approaches used in groups;
- Review micro skills essential for working with groups.

Types of Groups

There are different ways to categorize the types of groups with which social workers are frequently involved. Perhaps the most common approach is to divide groups into either *task groups* or *treatment groups*. Each of these two basic types can be further divided into more specific categories. We will deal first with task groups.

Task Groups

By their title, task groups exist to achieve a specific set of objectives or tasks. Concerted attention is paid to these goals and attainment of the desired ends assumes great importance. The goals help determine how the group operates and the roles played by members. The following list is not exhaustive, but provides examples of the types of task groups with which the social worker may come in contact. The possible roles the social worker might play are described under each type.

Boards of Directors

A board of directors is an administrative group charged with responsibility for setting the policy governing agency programs. The board is a legal entity established by the bylaws, organizational charter, or articles of incorporation. Normally the board hires and supervises the agency director and determines policy within which the agency must operate. Such policy has direct impact on what agency practitioners can and cannot do for clients.

Members of the board are not usually experts in the operation of the agency, but are elected or selected based upon other contributions they may make. For instance, they are often prominent citizens in a community, and may include benefactors who financially support the agency. Boards often establish subgroups or committees responsible for such things as personnel policies, finance, and building.

Social workers working with a board of directors for the first time often find it a challenging experience. Board members know a great deal less about the organization than many staff members of the agency and must be kept well informed. As laypersons, they may not understand why a program is proposed and may not share the values of members of the agency staff. Since their position is one of authority (remember, they hire and fire the director and he or she can hire or fire you and your supervisors) it takes tact and finesse to work with board members. Since they provide the agency with a strong connection to the community and are often instrumental in fundraising, board members are an irreplaceable asset for the agency.

Task Forces

Task forces are groups established for a special purpose and usually disbanded after completion of their task. They may be created by any of the other task groups mentioned in this section. For example, a board of directors might appoint a task force to explore new funding approaches for the twenty-first century. A United Way task force may be established to consider better ways of distributing funds to new agencies. Members of the task force usually are appointed because of their special expertise or interest in the topic under consideration. They are expected to study the idea or problem, consider alternatives, and prepare a report. After completion of the report, the task force usually goes out of existence.

Committees and Commissions

Committees exist to deal with specific tasks or matters. They may be formed by people in virtually any agency or group. Members of a committee may be selected or elected, depending upon the type of committee. As mentioned before, a board of directors may create a personnel committee to develop personnel policies for the agency and evaluate the agency director's performance. An agency may appoint a committee to plan the annual Christmas party. Committees typically work in a particular area and may be either standing or ad hoc. A standing committee is one which exists on a continuous basis. It may be provided for in an organization's bylaws (for example, an executive committee or finance committee) or it may be established by an agency (for example, a speakers committee).

An ad hoc committee, like a task force, is set up for one purpose and expected to cease operation after completion of its task. A committee to revise an organization's bylaws is a good example of an ad hoc committee. Committee members may be selected because they have a particular interest in the committee's task or because of their expertise.

Commissions are similar to committees in that they are responsible for a particular task. They are usually ongoing in nature. Examples of commissions include the Council on Social Work Education's (CSWE) Commission on Accreditation and the NASW's Commission on Inquiry. A community may have a city planning commission, a nondiscrimination and affirmative action commission, and/or a police and fire commission. These last three groups exist to help city officials with particular tasks. The planning commission may review all requests for new buildings or consider only those falling into a certain category. The nondiscrimination committee may investigate charges of discrimination in application of city laws and regulations. The police and fire commission may help set policy for the police and fire departments. Commission members may be elected, but usually are appointed by an administrator with approval of the governing board. Members of the CSWE's Commission on Accreditation are appointed by the president of CSWE after consultation with the board of directors. Members of such groups are called commissioners.

Legislative Bodies

Legislative bodies include city councils, county boards of supervisors, state legislatures, and the Congress of the United States. Composed of elected representatives, these bodies have legal responsibility for establishing laws and appropriating funds for programs established by law. A social worker's interaction with these bodies can occur in many ways. Social workers currently serve as elected members of each of these bodies. The also may be called upon or choose to testify before legislative bodies considering laws affecting clients. This might include funding for the WIC (Women, Infant, Children) Program, family leave legislation, or social security policy. Sometimes a social worker may serve on the staff of a legislative body, handling details such as scheduling, locating meeting sites, and ensuring that identified tasks are carried out. Because legislative bodies (Congress primarily) establish policies (laws) that affect which social programs are created and funded, it is important for social workers to be familiar with how these bodies operate. They also must be prepared to testify about the need for programs and to work with members of legis-

lative bodies to achieve social work purposes. Such purposes might include licensing of social workers at all levels (BSW, MSW etc.), and funding for social programs such as food stamps, etc. Finally, they must be willing to serve as members of legislative bodies.

Staff Meetings

Staff meetings are composed of agency staff members who assemble periodically for some identified purpose. Some agencies have meetings of all staff members on a regular basis. Others assemble only small groups regularly (such as all supervisors or all members of the foster care staff.) Staff meetings occur for the purposes of explaining new policy, keeping all participants informed about changes in the agency, or introducing new staff. Sometimes the meetings have the social or emotional function of bringing all staff members together to enhance the sense of commonality or "we" feeling. Often the agency director or other supervisory personnel preside over the staff meeting. Depending upon the type of agency (and preferences of the director) the meeting may consist of an administrator announcing new policies and everyone else listening or it may be a discussion session where all members are equally free to contribute ideas and reactions.

Multidisciplinary Teams

Multidisciplinary teams, or M teams as they often are called, consist of professionals from various disciplines. They often meet to discuss specific clients or patients with whom team members are working. In a state institution for the severely developmentally disabled, a team may consist of a social worker, nurse, medical doctor, psychologist, and aide. In a hospital healthworks program the M team may include a registered nurse, social worker, dietician, and psychologist. One member of the team often serves as the leader, but all members are respon-

HIGHLIGHT 3.1
Social Action within a University

The staff members in the university counseling and health office were becoming increasingly concerned about policies and procedures being initiated and supported by the program director. The policies and procedures did not seem directed toward helping students and appeared increasingly erratic. The director often threatened to fire staff who disagreed with him and implied that all his actions had the backing of his immediate supervisor. Although he possessed a nursing degree, the director was also making decisions beyond his level of training and competence. After several failed attempts to talk directly to the director, staff members met and decided that additional steps would be necessary to change the situation and restore harmony within the program. Each staff member wrote to the vice-president for Health and Counseling Services (the program director's supervisor) and identified individual concerns. A copy of the letter was sent to the director so that he was made aware of the staff's continuing concern. The letter also made it clear the staff had decided to follow the appropriate chain of command to create change. In other words, the staff was committed to take the issue up to the director's supervisor and even higher levels, if necessary. Following discussions between the vice-president, the director and members of the staff, the director chose to resign his position and a search was conducted for a replacement.

sible for their specific area of expertise. Typically, the team meets on some regularly scheduled basis.

Case Conferences and Staffings

Case conferences, also called staffings, are similar to multidisciplinary teams. One difference is that, unlike the M team, the members who compose the case conference may not be perceived as, or see themselves as, a team. They may meet on an as-needed basis instead of regularly. Depending upon the type of agency, members participating in the case conference or staffing may not represent different disciplines.

Sometimes a client will be staffed by the social work department. Here all members can contribute to the decision making. For example, one juvenile probation department staffs all cases where the probation officer has made a recommendation for incarceration in a presentence investigation. Other probation officers look at the same evidence gathered by the investigating officer and consider whether the recommendation was appropriate. The purpose of a staffing is to bring the wisdom of others to bear on a particular situation and to arrive at the best solution or recommendation.

Social Action Groups

The purpose of social action groups is to change the physical or social environment (Toseland & Rivas, 1984). The goals sought may benefit either members of the social action group or other nonmembers. Goals might include getting the city to enforce health and building codes, changing the eligibility requirements for a specific social program, or modifying rules or laws that discriminate against a particular class of persons. Highlight 3.1 provides an example of a social action group.

Another example of a social action group might be composed of social workers testifying before a legislative body requesting funds for drug and alcohol treatment programs. Yet another example would be citizens asking the city council to rezone their neighborhood to stop the conversion of existing homes into multifamily housing. The social worker may be a group member or serve as the group's leader. Another possible role is a staff or resource person to the group. In this role the worker might help arrange meetings, provide the names of contact persons within existing agencies and organizations, or assist the group in whatever ways are needed. It is important for the worker to have the skill to help the group reach its goal while ensuring sufficient stability of the group until completion of the task (Toseland & Rivas, 1984). For example, the worker might help the group over rough spots such as early setbacks or failures by encouraging and supporting their efforts. He or she might follow up on all decisions to make certain that the group's wishes are carried out.

Treatment Groups

The term treatment group is very broad and includes groups with similar goals. Five types of treatment groups will be discussed: growth, remedial, educational, socialization and mutual aid (Toseland & Rivas, 1984; Barker, 1991). In each group there is a presumption that the individual member of the group is going to benefit directly from the existence of the group. Usually individual change occurs within group members and that change is often the reason for the group's existence.

Growth Groups

As the name suggests, growth groups are designed to encourage and support the growth of the individual group member. The presumption is that this can be done through helping the member achieve insight or self-understanding. The group experience may consist of various activities designed to help the participants reach their goals. One example would be a group focused on helping couples learn to communicate better. A series of exercises might be

done emphasizing listening skills, value clarification, and sending clear messages. Another example is a group composed of women who have sought refuge in a domestic violence shelter. The group meets twice a week with a focus on helping the members explore what they want from their lives. Activities include a time for each person to talk about their immediate and long-term goals and didactic presentations on the pattern of violent relationships. The group also makes the women aware of alternatives open to them such as court-imposed restraining orders and financial resources in the community and supports them in their efforts to be free of abuse. Growth groups focus on helping individuals achieve their potential and there is no presumption that members necessarily have a "problem."

In growth groups the worker is a facilitator, simply helping the group members attain their goals. As with all groups, the worker's role involves a higher level of activity in early stages and less activity as the group develops.

Remedial Groups

Remedial groups, sometimes referred to as therapy groups, help clients who have an identified goal of changing some aspect of their behavior. The term includes groups where the objective is recovering from problematic life experiences. Such groups include those sponsored by a hospital for clients 20 percent or more overweight, an inpatient group for chemically dependent patients, and a group for people who abuse their children. The focus is on correcting a perceived intrapersonal or interpersonal problem or learning better problem-solving and coping styles.

The worker role is one of higher visibility in this type of group. The worker may begin as a director, expert or leader, depending upon the needs of the group, but it is likely that he or she will become more of a facilitator as the group progresses.

Educational Groups

Educational groups include an enormous number of groups designed to provide members with information about themselves or others. The purpose, as suggested by the name, is to educate or teach the group members about some issue or topic. This may be done through didactic presentations, role plays, activities, and discussions. Examples include a group for prospective adoptive parents, natural childbirth groups, and practical parenting groups. Educational groups are similar to growth groups in that there is no presumption that members have a "problem." Educational groups tend to have less interaction among leaders and members than growth or remedial groups.

As in the remedial group, the worker in an educational group is often very much a group leader. She or he may be doing much of the presentation of new information and serve as the group expert. In one group focused on teaching parents new child nurturing skills, a BSW field student developed the curriculum after reviewing similar programs, put together the charts and exercises to be used by participants, and led the group through each session.

Socialization Groups

Socialization groups assist participants in acquiring skills necessary to become "socialized" into the community. The presumption is that the group members have a deficit of some sort in social skills. For example, a group might be developed for adolescents who have been involved in delinquent behavior. By their actions they have demonstrated an inability to abide by society's norms. Socialization groups frequently make great use of structured experiences or activities as a medium for change and rely less on member-to-member discussion. In some cases the activities become the primary or only intervention that occurs. Adventure-based counseling programs are one example. These adolescent programs include heavy emphasis on physical skill, testing one's courage, building teamwork, and self-reliance. They increase the self-confidence of group members, improve their social skills, and redirect their energies into socially approved activities. In these programs group members are challenged by a series of physical hurdles including climbing over barriers, rappelling down a cliff, and crossing a stream on a rope.

A current events group at a nursing home is another example. In this case, group emphasis is on getting the residents to interact with one another by discussing current events. The group also has a goal of helping to keep the residents' minds active and oriented to the present.

The social worker role in socialization groups is often one of highest visibility. She or he serves as director or expert designing the program and leading members through the process and exercises. As with other types of groups, that role may change as the group enters later stages of development.

The role of the social worker in each of these treatment groups has some similarities and some differences. To summarize, the leader will have the highest visibility in educational, remedial, and socialization groups. In each case the worker may be a director, expert, or leader. In the growth group and some remedial groups the leader may be more of a facilitator, simply helping the group members attain their goals. It is common, however, for the worker to be much more active in the early stages of all groups. Once a group becomes established the worker's role often changes to that of a consultant, expert, and role model. Group needs usually determine the role to be played by the social worker. Thus social workers must be flexible and modify their type and level of involvement as needed. They also need to use a variety of skills depending upon the group's stage of development, the skills of the members, and the type of group.

Mutual Aid Groups

Mutual aid groups are groups of people sharing certain characteristics who get together "to provide one another with advice, emotional support, information, and other help" (Barker, 1991, p. 149). They typically have a professional leader and may be formally or informally organized. Because they exist to accomplish a variety of goals, they may share some characteristics with the groups we have discussed above. For example, one mutual aid group is the La Leche League. This group is devoted to encouraging breast feeding of infants and to helping parents better understand the advantages of this method over the use of baby formula. In some ways, this organization is similar to the educational group in that members are not presumed to have a "problem." Rather, they share the characteristic of being parents (or prospective parents) of infants. As might be expected, much of the activity in group meetings is educational in purpose.

The term "mutual aid group" is sometimes used interchangeably with "self-help group" since both share a goal of having members provide support to one another. Self-help groups, however, are less likely to have professional leadership. To further complicate matters, you will recognize that many different types of groups provide members with "advice, emotional support, information, and other help." Thus, mutual aid might be considered a component of many different types of groups. As a result of this confusion around the term "mutual aid group," it is less delineated than the other types of groups previously discussed. What is most important to remember is that the term is frequently used in social work to refer to groups with a strong mutual support emphasis.

Worker Roles in Groups

It will be clear from the many examples in this chapter that social workers play multiple leadership roles in groups. This section briefly discusses some common social worker roles and describes how they are used in work with groups. The roles are broker, mediator, educator, and facilitator.

Broker

The primary function of a broker is to help the client obtain needed resources. This requires that the worker be familiar with community resources, have general knowledge about eligibility requirements, and be sensitive to client needs. A broker may help the client obtain emergency food or housing, legal aid, or other needed resources. A worker may act as a broker either in one-to-one situations or in a group.

Community resource books can prove helpful to new and experienced workers. These books typically describe most services in a community including eligibility requirements, contact persons, address and telephone numbers. A broker can use such listings to augment those with which he or she is familiar. To be most helpful, the worker should attempt to aid the client through referral to specific staff members. If a client goes to a new agency without having a contact person or much information about how to use the resource, he or she can have a bad experience and become discouraged from using the agency. A more detailed review of the broker role appears in chapter 15.

Mediator

As a mediator the social worker helps group members with conflicts or other dissension (Toseland & Rivas, 1984). To be most successful in this role, the worker must believe that different sides to a disagreement are legitimate and help each side recognize that their views are valid. Avoiding win-lose situations described earlier is an important task of the social worker as mediator. To do this the worker must help the parties identify the points of disagreement and of mutual interest. The worker then must focus on finding a solution that meets the needs of all. Finally, on another level, the worker may help group members negotiate with the environment or other systems. This is especially important when the client finds resource systems intimidating and impersonal. The worker can help bridge this gulf and build on the broker role described above.

Educator

As a teacher, the social worker provides group participants with new information, structures the presentation of that information, and uses modeling to help members learn new skills. The task of a worker as educator is described later and will not receive further elaboration here.

Facilitator

The concept of facilitator shares some of the same characteristics as that of the mediator. The facilitator, as the name suggests, eases or expedites the way for others. This is true when the problem is between individuals and their environment or when it is between members in the same group. In a task group the facilitative role may involve helping the group stick to the

To avoid win-lose results in a group, the worker acts as a mediator to help the parties identify points of both disagreement and mutual interest.

agenda, encouraging all to participate, supporting their contributions, helping members test new skills, and summarizing what has been accomplished (Friesen, 1987).

As noted, the social worker must play a variety of roles depending upon the needs of the group and the problems confronted. It's important to conceive of social work as being made up of a series of roles. This coincides with the idea that generalist social workers have numerous responsibilities. It also helps the worker think more clearly about what a group needs at any given time in its developmental life.

Basic Group Dynamics

Social workers who have dealt with various types of groups frequently comment about how the group seems to develop a life of its own. Each group has its own unique configuration of varied individual personalities, as well as its own set of dynamics that affect what is said or done, the roles that members play, and how the group relates to the leader. There have been repeated efforts to provide a framework for understanding group dynamics and help those working with groups. Most frameworks attempt to explain group development through a single model. Each of these approaches has strengths and weaknesses. This section focuses on five broad areas: group development; group culture, norms and power; group size, composition, and boundaries; decision-making patterns; and group roles.

Group Development

Most groups proceed through an identifiable set of steps or stages. This pattern of development has allowed group observers to describe the stages and to predict what may occur in each stage. In the first stage of development most groups display a strong reliance on the leader. Members expect the leader to provide direction and they tend to be more hesitant or reluctant to participate actively. The leader assists members in this stage by encouraging participation, supporting positive groups norms (informal rules of behavior), and helping members rely more on one another.

In the second stage, the group members begin to assert themselves more. During this time some level of conflict is common. Power and control issues become more frequent as members become more comfortable with each other and take greater responsibility for what happens in the group. There may be disagreement over goals agreed upon in the previous stage and challenges to the leader that can be unsettling to him or her. It is important that the leader encourage open discussion of the conflict so that the group will ultimately be responsible for its decision. It is important to recognize that conflict is expected, acceptable, and perhaps even healthy.

Once past the conflict stage, the group is ready to go ahead with the primary work facing it. Group productivity increases and there is greater attention to achieving its goals. This is stage three, the "working" phase of the group. Members frequently feel positive about the group, may have developed affection or liking for it and its members, and are more willing to share their ideas and reactions. Trust has developed among members as roles become more clear and a group culture has developed. The role of the leader is likely to become different during this phase. There is more need for a leader who can serve as consultant, advisor, or resource to the group instead of a director.

Finally, there is usually a fourth phase, separation, where the group has reached its goals and members begin to separate emotionally from the group. In this phase there are often feelings of loss when the group ends, but there also may be angry feelings. Again, the worker should expect and realize members may need help to accept and discuss their feelings.

The group stage model (Highlight 3.2 to Highlight 3.5) appears to apply well to growth or treatment groups (groups which focus on changing the individual group member) and to many task groups (committees, teams, social action groups). However, the ongoing nature of task groups (agency staff meetings, boards of directors, etc.) may complicate or mix-up some stages. Because some staff groups do not have a separation phase where members prepare to leave, there is less likely to be the same kinds of reactions found in other groups with a defined ending period. Open-ended groups, such as Parents Anonymous, where members enter and leave the group at different times, may change how the group develops. The model above fits

---

HIGHLIGHT 3.2

Stage 1 in a Teen Group: Encouraging Participation

As she looked around the group of teenagers, Mary was reminded once again about the effect a group can have on its members. Mary had been assigned to work with this group because she had previously had some group experiences during her field placement. Having read the files on all of the members, Mary knew something about each of the girls present in the teen center meeting room. Jacque was quiet, which for her was unusual. She was always the most talkative person in any group. Belinda was whispering to Angel and both were smiling knowingly. Cindy was looking down and flipping absent-mindedly through her notebook. Alice stared out the window. When Mary got up to close the door, the room became as quiet as a tomb. Each girl looked up at Mary expecting her to say something.

HIGHLIGHT 3.3

Stage 2 in a Teen Group: Addressing Conflict

Mary had asked the group to agree on the major activities they would pursue during the next six weeks. Although there had been ample time to decide, the group seemed hopelessly deadlocked. Jacque was arguing that the group should hold a party and Cindy testily reminded her that they were in this group because they partied too much. Belinda asked if they could have a session focused on getting along better with parents. When Mary responded favorably to Belinda, Angel said she did not want to even talk about her parents. After ten more minutes, the group was no closer to a decision than when the meeting started.

HIGHLIGHT 3.4

Stage 3 in a Teen Group: Working

When Alice said she felt her parents did not care what happened to her and began to cry softly, Jacque reached over and put an arm around her. "Maybe they just don't know how to show they care," said Cindy. "I mean, we can't know what's in someone else's head." "That's right," said Belinda, "don't assume anything about parents." As the group meeting came to an end, Mary smiled and said quietly, "I'm very proud of how the group reached out to Alice and used the ideas we've been talking about the last few weeks. You've really supported one another."

┌───┐

HIGHLIGHT 3.5

Stage 4 in a Teen Group: Separation

For the last meeting, Mary had asked the girls what they wanted to do that would appropriately conclude their work together. They decided to write each other a brief note stating what good qualities they learned about one another during the past few weeks. This method of saying goodbye was encouraged by Mary, who had also arranged for milk and brownies for the meeting. The group had spent the last week talking about their feelings as the group ended and reviewing the various plans group members had for the summer. Mary told them she would miss their weekly meetings and encouraged them to stay in touch with her and with each other.

└───┘

most closely those groups where members join and leave the group together (closed groups) such as the teen group described previously.

There also may be a difference in group development between formed groups and those that exist naturally. One type of natural group, a family, already has an established pattern of interacting with one another. This also may be true of a gang. Formed groups composed of clients with similar problems or characteristics (for example, chemically addicted or delinquent girls) are perhaps more likely to fit the model described. Thus, when group members achieve their treatment or personal goals the group will enter phase four where separation occurs.

It is important to realize that any developmental model for groups is only an abstraction. Individual groups may not proceed exactly as outlined above. Some groups will seem to skip a stage or move backward instead of forward from time to time. It is important to remember that failure to proceed in the precise manner described earlier is neither an unhealthy sign nor necessarily problematic. The social worker must be flexible and adaptable when working with groups because they vary so drastically in purpose, composition, and dynamics.

Group Culture, Norms, and Power

All groups develop an individualized culture which includes the traditions, customs and values/beliefs shared by group members. This culture affects how members react and interact with one another and the leader, how work is done, and how status and power are distributed (Olmstead, 1959). Sometimes this culture exists prior to the worker's involvement, as happens with families or groups of friends. At other times, it occurs after group formation. A norm of openness and a willingness to admit mistakes can be encouraged by a worker who models these characteristics for group members. Evidence of a positive group culture includes free expression of ideas, open disagreement, and a safe atmosphere in which the contributions of members are respected and considered. The worker can help ensure development of such a culture by describing for members what is desired or expected in the group, modeling appropriate behavior, and supporting group members as they interact within the group.

Value differences among group members may contribute to difficulties within the group. For example, within a group of teens discussing sexual behavior it is likely that some members will view sexual activity as a part of adolescence and others may (because of religious or other values) not want to talk about the topic. The worker should encourage members to discuss the values they brought to the group and to listen carefully to the values of other members. When a climate of trust and safety exists, members are more likely to accept individual differences and allow fellow members to express their individuality. If members do not sense such a climate, they are less likely to be honest in expressing their opinions and will be more guarded in what they say and do. This is less likely to lead to positive outcomes. The leader should help to establish a culture where members are free to talk and are supportive of each other. This permits the business of the group to be accomplished in an open and frank manner.

Power issues always exist within groups. In many groups there is a period in which the group or individual members of the group vie with the leader for power. In most groups individual members have different levels of status and power. Those accorded the highest status by other group members are more likely to be listened to. Subgroups may develop as two or more members find themselves holding similar views and feeling at odds with other group members. Struggles over decisions may occur, exacerbated by these divisions.

Group Size, Composition, and Duration

Sometimes both the size and composition of a group are established ahead of time and the worker lacks control over these elements. For example, consider families and other pre-existing groups. The size of the family is not within the control of the worker, nor is the composition. In other situations, the worker is responsible for making decisions about who will be included as members and how large the group will be. For instance, a worker leading a parent nurturing group may set the limit on members at seven or nine and not allow a larger group.

Group size has a definite impact on what occurs within a group. It affects both the level and type of interaction in addition to members' feelings about the group. Large groups tend to be less popular with members because of lessened opportunity for discussion and interac-

tion. Members of larger groups are more likely to feel inhibited and will often participate less than members in smaller groups. While members rate a group of five as most satisfactory (Slater, 1958) this size is not necessarily ideal for all situations. Many social work groups have as many as ten members and some groups are much larger. Larger groups may be more effective at handling difficult and involved problems because the number of possible contributors is greater. Thus, the task or objectives of the group may be a governing factor affecting group size.

While composition of a group may be beyond the control of the worker, many situations do allow the leader to select the members. Formed groups lend themselves nicely to this kind of selection since the worker often chooses individual members. The worker must decide the degree of heterogeneity and homogeneity appropriate for a given group. A heterogeneous group has members with different problems and personality characteristics. A homogeneous group has members with similar problems and personalities. Practically speaking, few groups are completely homogeneous because as human beings we all differ from one another in many ways. Workers must take these differences into consideration when selecting members for a group.

We also must remember that there may be real advantages in selecting people for a group who are alike in some ways and different in others. For example, it might make sense to select people who share similar problems (e.g., child abusers) but who have differing personalities. It would not be wise, for example, to select seven nonverbal group members. A healthy mix of talkers and listeners is likely to be more useful.

Age also may be a factor in composition. Different levels of development probably preclude starting a group composed of children ranging in age from eight to fifteen. The difference in interests and attention spans would be especially problematic. Ultimately, the purpose of the group should be considered when deciding group size and composition.

Gender also may be an important consideration. Gender similarity may be important in groups of children but gender diversity is desirable among adolescents when the objective is helping group members develop socialization skills. Bertcher and Maple (1974) provide a useful rule of thumb for selecting group members. They suggest selecting members with similar descriptive characteristics such as age, sex, and level of education but with dissimilar behavioral attributes. Behavioral attributes include aggressiveness, verbal ability, and leadership skills, among others. It might be preferable to have some group members who will serve as models for other members. Social workers need to give this matter careful consideration when they are composing a group.

Determining the duration of a group requires that the worker decide how many sessions will be held and how long they will last. It is common to have groups meet for one and one-half to two hours per session. This allows enough time to conduct the business of the meeting without becoming drawn out. Specifying in advance the length and number of sessions helps members focus on the topic and discourages nonfunctional behavior such as wasting time on irrelevant topics. A group planning to meet for six sessions is more likely to stay on task than one meeting for twenty sessions. A general observation is that the closer to the ending point a group gets, the more likely group members will attend to the task. This is a phenomenon familiar to many students who find their interest in, and efforts to write, a class paper increase as the deadline approaches.

Flexibility is helpful in the matter of duration. If a pre-selected length of time proves counterproductive, the worker should feel free to suggest a change. The judgment of the worker and clients about what works best is as important as any set of guidelines.

Decision Making in Groups

How groups, especially task groups, make decisions is important to understanding why some groups are more successful than others. Task groups, which include committees, administrative groups such as boards of directors, delegate assemblies such as the NASW Delegate Assembly, teams, treatment conferences, and social action groups (Toseland & Rivas, 1984) must often make decisions. These task groups share some similarities, yet each is different from the others in some important ways, including how they interact and come to decisions. In this section, several common approaches to group decision making will be discussed: consensus decision making, compromise, decision making by majority, rule by an individual, persuasion by a recognized expert, averaging of opinions of individual group members, and persuasion by a minority of the group (Johnson & Johnson, 1975). (See Highlights 3.6 to 3.12.) In addition, we will review three special techniques to help groups make decisions and solve problems: nominal group technique, brainstorming, and parliamentary procedure.

Decision Making by Consensus

An attractive, albeit time-consuming, approach to making decisions is through consensus. Consensus refers to "the process in which individuals and groups achieve general agreement about the goals of mutual interest and the means to achieve them" (Barker, 1987, p. 32). Consensus decision making is attractive because, when concluded, all members accept and support the decision even if they were not initially so inclined. To make decisions by consensus requires an atmosphere of openness in which all members have an opportunity to be heard and influence the ultimate outcome. This presumes that members can present alternate ideas, that opposing views are solicited, and that creative solutions are encouraged. The emphasis is on finding the best solution instead of getting one's way. The real advantage of consensus decision making is that it increases the commitment of group members to the decision. In situations where this commitment is particularly important, there is no other adequate substitute.

Decision Making by Compromise

Most of us have been involved in decision making by compromise. In these situations the group attempts to reach a solution that most, if not all members, can support. In some cases the compromise pleases no one entirely, but is viewed as the best that can be done under the circumstances. Each side gives up something to

reach an agreement with the other side. Groups that begin with an idea, amend it repeatedly to satisfy divergent points of view, and then approve the final product usually are making decisions by compromise. (See Highlight 3.7.)

Decision Making by Majority

Most deliberative bodies, (for example, legislatures, boards of directors) make decisions by majority rule. In this model, a decision occurs when just over one-half of the decision makers support (or vote) for an idea. Decisions made in this fashion typically are accepted by the winning side and disliked by the losing side. Losers do not necessarily feel as compelled to support

---

HIGHLIGHT 3.6
Decision Making by Consensus

The Blackwell City Council was at an impasse. After almost a year of study, debate, and argument, the new library was no closer to fruition than it had been when the council started discussing the idea. The primary issue which had stymied the group was the proposed location. The library board had proposed that the new building be located on an undeveloped site near Lake Prosper, a recommendation supported by two or three council members. Other members wanted the new library adjacent to the old library, a location which many felt

was too small to meet future needs. After a lengthy debate, Greg Hanson, a social worker on the city council, suggested holding an advisory referendum on the location, allowing the residents of the city the opportunity to voice their opinion. Council members were all in agreement with this proposal, a consensus decision that was unusual for this body. At least temporarily, it got the issue off their agenda and offered hope of a clear mandate from the voters.

HIGHLIGHT 3.7
Decision Making by Compromise

"Finally, a package we can live with." Lenore was exhausted. As president of the social work union she had been deeply involved in the negotiations for the contract for the next year. After an initial (and unacceptable) offer from the finance committee, the union representatives had been going through the usual process of making proposals and rejecting them. Finally, a package was agreed to.

It contained salary increases agreeable to the union and gave management more flexibility to move workers within the agency. It was a compromise for both parties since it did not give either side exactly what they would have liked. It was a classic labor agreement, something for everyone, but less than each side had desired.

HIGHLIGHT 3.8

Decision Making by Majority Rule

The five agency supervisors were in the second hour of what was supposed to be a one hour meeting. The issue which had stymied efforts to conclude the meeting was a proposed reorganization of services and service units. Don was unhappy with the proposal because it would increase the workload of his unit slightly at a time when he felt his workers were already overloaded. Still, the proposal would give the agency an opportunity to offer a very specialized service, which a previous needs assessment had determined was missing in

the county. Finally, the agency deputy director asked for a show of hands for those who supported the proposed change. All supervisors but Don voted in favor of the proposal. The deputy director said, "Don, I know you are not crazy about this idea, but it has the support of the others and we're going to go with the majority this time. I will see, however, what I can do about getting another position assigned to your unit to help with the overload."

HIGHLIGHT 3.9

Rule by an Individual

The Millard School Rec Club was having difficulty choosing an activity to mark the end of the high school year. In past years the group had held pizza parties, donated gifts to the school, and contributed their time to a neighborhood clean-up project. Mike, the captain of the baseball team and a respected student, argued forcefully that the club should donate money to the school to purchase a

pitching machine. Other members of the group were reluctant to express their opinions for fear of appearing to oppose Mike's suggestion. When no one spoke up, Mike then said, "Well, then it's settled. I'll tell the principal and the coach." The group had just allowed one member to rule (make a decision) for the entire club.

---

the outcome of the group decision making as is true with consensus. Because it is a less time-consuming method, large groups often use majority rule. When a matter is of little consequence, majority rule may be a satisfactory method for making a decision. When the matter is complex or requires a high level of commitment from the group to the decision, this method is problematic. Losers may not support the decision and may passively undercut the proposal. In some cases, losers may be resentful and actively work to make the idea fail. Alternate methods of arriving at majority rule involve increasing the percent of votes required for passage (revisions of bylaws or constitutions of organizations frequently require a two-thirds majority) or developing a weighted system of voting.

While these methods help increase the percent of members who support a decision, they do not truly overcome the disadvantages of this style of decision making. (See Highlight 3.8.)

Rule by an Individual

Many groups make decisions by default and allow one individual to make choices that affect the entire group. This may occur because of the forcefulness of the speaker, members fear of offending the decision maker, disinterest in the decision itself, or lack of assertiveness. Essentially one member makes a decision and the rest of the group acquiesces. Sometimes there is discussion among the members about the options; at other times there is none. (See Highlight 3.9.)

Persuasion by a Recognized Expert

Many groups have members with expertise in a certain area. For example, one member of an educational group may have had experience placing a loved one in a nursing home. Other group members typically listen to members who are perceived to be knowledgeable about a given subject. When it comes to making a decision a group may accede to the recommendations of the "expert." (See Highlight 3.10.)

Averaging of Individual Opinions

In some groups, decisions are made by averaging the opinions of individual group members. This is done most easily when the opinions are really able to be averaged. That is, the opinions may be in the form of numerical ratings which can be averaged using standard mathematical techniques. Unlike a compromise, there is really no giving in by individual members, but rather an acceptance that one's opinion will be merged with those of the rest of the group. This technique has the advantage of not requiring anyone to give up their opinion or change it in response to group pressure. (See Highlight 3.11.)

Persuasion by a Minority

Persuasion by a minority often occurs when one or more members of a group feel strongly about a particular decision. It happens more frequently when a subgroup has intense attitudes and the rest of the group has less invested in the

---

HIGHLIGHT 3.10
Persuasion by an Expert

When it came time to discuss how the new social work program would be evaluated, everyone on the administrative staff looked to Gerry for guidance. He was considered the resident expert on program evaluation, and was familiar with a variety of approaches that could be used in different situations. Though Jack had some reservations about a couple of Gerry's ideas, his opinions did not sway the staff group very much. Jack knew in advance that Gerry's recommendations would be accepted by the group based on his reputation and past experience. Sure enough, when the meeting was over, Gerry's ideas were approved and his plan for evaluation accepted.

HIGHLIGHT 3.11
Averaging of Individual Opinions

Mary had asked her foster care unit to evaluate her performance as a supervisor. Mary had only recently been a supervisor after several years of work as a line social worker. Most of the people in the foster care unit had been her friends before her promotion six months ago. Now she wanted to get their feedback on her work as their supervisor.

After much discussion, unit members decided to rate Mary on five different characteristics they considered important in a supervisor. When they were done they decided to present Mary with a composite picture of how the unit felt about her leadership. Rather than give her their individual ratings, the unit members decided to average their individual ratings on each of the five characteristics and give her one set of ratings. This method eliminated extremes at both ends (for example, very high or very low ratings) and gave a more "middle of the road" view of her performance.

┌─ HIGHLIGHT 3.12 ───
  ### Persuasion by a Minority

  It was getting quite late as the Franklin Avenue Neighborhood Association neared the end of its agenda. The last item to discuss was what to do about the vacant house at the end of the block. The property had been abandoned by its owner and was attracting children and local teenagers who sought access through its broken windows and door. Since the house was really on the edge of the neighborhood, many members did not see it as a matter of great concern. There was even a question of whether the property was part of Franklin Avenue since it faced a side street.

  Quietly, but firmly, Mr. Alison and Mrs. Gonzales spoke of the dangers to the neighborhood children, and the way the property detracted from the quality of the neighborhood. Ms. Washington, usually rather quiet, then spoke passionately about how this house was a danger to her small children. She angrily asked how the other members would feel if the house was next door to their homes. She demanded that the group take a position and ask the city to have the house torn down or renovated. The group decided to follow her recommendation, less out of commitment and more because of her ardent and outspoken position on a matter of relatively less concern to them.
└──

matter at stake. A vocal and persuasive individual (or group of individuals) thus may be successful in swaying the opinions of a larger group.

Nominal Group Technique

One of the most interesting techniques used to help groups make decisions is the nominal group. Its intent is to help "assess existing problems, needs, interests, or objectives" (Barker, 1987, p. 107). Developed by Delbecq and Van de Ven (1975), this approach can be used by groups of various size. To begin, members receive a problem statement and list their ideas about the problem. Each member does this without consulting other members and once completed, the leader goes around the group one by one asking each member to provide one of the ideas from his or her list. This continues until all items on each person's list have been exhausted. Members may choose to pass when they no longer have any ideas to contribute. They are also free to contribute additional ideas they thought of while listening to other members. The worker writes each idea on a board or flip chart visible to all members. No evaluation of ideas occurs during this round-robin procedure.

Once all the ideas are collected and listed for the members, the leader begins to go through each idea briefly. This helps ensure clarity and allows each member to explain the merits of an idea. No lengthy discussion of any idea occurs at this point.

In the third stage, members review the ideas on the board and list those they believe are the most important or have highest priority. They may be asked to select a specific number such as five or fifteen. The goal is to reduce the overall list by one-half to three quarters. Once completed, the leader places a check mark by each idea supported by a member. This tabulation may be accomplished by the member listing the best ideas on a card and handing the card in or by going around in round-robin fashion again. When completed, the group has a list of those ideas that showed the most promise.

In the final stage, members rank the new list of ideas. Usually the priority list will be small, with only five ideas permitted. These are listed on an index card, one idea per card. The cards are collected and the leader tallies the results on the flip chart. The highest priority idea receives a point value of five and on down to the lowest priority item which receives a one. A mean rank for each idea is computed by adding the numbers together and dividing by the number of members. Once completed, it is usually clear which idea or ideas have the greatest support and should be undertaken by the group.

The nominal group technique can produce a larger number of alternatives than most other approaches (Scheidel & Crowell, 1979). In the authors' experience, this approach also is usually enjoyable for the participants. It is an effective technique for developing alternatives because it encourages participation of all members. It also allows all points of view to be expressed. It discourages making decisions without adequate discussion. Finally, it increases members' commitment to the outcome.

Brainstorming

Brainstorming is a well-known approach for developing alternate solutions to a problem. Useful in both large and small groups, brainstorming begins with a problem to be solved. Each member presents one idea and then another member has a turn. This continues until the leader lists all ideas on the board or flip chart. No attempt is made to rate or evaluate the ideas. Members should be free to present ideas they thought of after hearing other members' contributions and should raise their hand before participating. The leader should encourage all contributions and clarify any ideas that are not clear.

Unlike the nominal group approach, the evaluation phase does not closely follow the idea-generating phase. Ideas tend to be better if the problem is clearly and specifically defined. Brainstorming can produce large numbers of ideas and works best when the goal is generation of multiple alternatives. It does not work as well with complex situations or those in which there is only a single correct answer. There is no clear evidence that brainstorming is more or less effective than the nominal group approach. Because both methods rely on an atmosphere of openness to new ideas, it is important that the worker encourage this and resist premature attempts to evaluate the ideas presented. In either case, ideas that receive immediate evaluation, especially that which is negative, are less likely to be followed by other ideas. Members may feel threatened because someone ridiculed or challenged their idea and will be less likely to risk offering other ideas to the group.

Parliamentary Procedure

Parliamentary procedure is a highly structured technique used by groups of various sizes to make decisions and conduct business. The model of parliamentary procedure described in *Robert's Rules of Order* (Robert, 1970) was devised over one hundred years ago. It remains the most common set of guidelines in use today. Groups agree in advance to use the rules so that there is no last minute disagreement about how decisions will be made. Most deliberative bodies (legislatures), large task groups, and many smaller task groups use *Robert's Rules* to facilitate their work. While parliamentary procedural rules are clear and designed to help the group, they are not always followed closely. Sometimes the procedures called for in the rules become barriers to accomplishment of group goals. For example, smaller committees may decide to operate by consensus and dispense with voting on items where the group is in agreement. In legislative bodies it is possible for a person to waste the body's time by endlessly speaking on a matter before the group. Often called *filibustering*, this method may stymie a body and prevent it from conducting its normal business. In these situations groups may adopt other less cumbersome methods or decide to temporarily suspend some of the usual rules of parliamentary procedure.

In parliamentary procedure the business of the group occurs in the form of motions, which are proposed actions that the group is asked to support. A member of the social work student organization may make a motion to buy paint to refurbish the child-care center. The motion might be stated as follows: "I move we purchase three gallons of paint for the child-care center." If others support this motion, one member would say, "I second the motion." The motion or proposal would then be open for debate or discussion by the members. Motions generally fall into two major categories, primary motions and secondary motions. Primary motions bring business to the group for consideration. The motion to purchase paint is an example of a primary motion. Primary motions include both main motions (example above) and incidental motions. Incidental motions are used for such purposes as adjourning the group and repealing an action already taken.

Secondary motions are used to act upon the primary motion. They include motions to amend a main motion, to refer a matter to another body, or to defer action on a motion (postpone or table). They also are used to limit debate on a motion, to reconsider a motion, or to bring up for discussion an item that had been previously tabled. Lastly, secondary motions include motions to challenge improper actions and to request information (for instance, point of order or point of information). For example, a member might wish clarification on why the body is dealing with a matter that seems to belong to another group. In this case she or he would raise a hand and address the presiding officer by stating "Point of Information." The chair would then ask the member to state the point of information and would attempt to respond to the question the member has raised. Similarly, if a group strays in their debate and is now discussing a matter that is not related to the motion on the floor, a member might state "Point of order." The member would then remind the group that they have not yet voted on the motion before them and have begun to debate some other matter. The chair would then rule on the member's point of order, ask if there is any additional debate on the motion on the floor, and then call for the vote.

Other motions do exist, but they are used too infrequently to mention in this chapter. *Robert's Rules of Order* should be consulted by those who frequently use parliamentary procedure.

The primary principle established by parliamentary procedure is that each person has a right to be heard without interruption. The person who makes a motion speaks first on a topic. All members must have an opportunity to speak if they so wish. Debate must be related to the motion on the floor and cannot be on superfluous matters not before the group. Once each person who wishes has had a chance to speak, the leader (chair) asks if there is any further debate. If there is none, the group will then vote on the proposal. Sometimes a member of the group will wish to stop debate and bring a matter to a vote. This is achieved by saying "I call the question." This motion is not debatable. It immediately halts discussion on a matter if supported by two-thirds of those present.

When it is time to vote, the chair will say "All those in favor of the motion, say aye." It may be best to state the motion to be voted on or to have the secretary read the motion. At that point all favoring the motion will respond "aye." Then the chair will call for all no (or nay) votes and abstentions. The chair will decide which side prevailed based on this voice vote and announce the results. Sometimes members vote by raising their hands or by using paper ballots, especially when the vote appears to be close. Normally a simple majority must approve a motion. If a tie occurs in the voting, the motion does not pass. Sometimes the chair may vote to break a tie or to create a tie.

As mentioned above, a motion may be amended. This means it may be changed by a member proposing to add or delete something in the original motion. To amend the motion above, a member might say "I move to amend the motion to place a limit of fifty dollars on the amount to be spent for paint." This amendment also needs a second and would be voted on. If approved, the amendment would then become a part of the original main motion. After all amendments are considered, the main motion would be voted on.

There are other rules governing parliamentary procedure. These include specification of a quorum (the minimum number of group members that must be present to conduct business and make decisions) and use of an agenda (an ordered list of the topics to be covered in the meeting). Most groups have a leader or chairperson responsible for helping the group conduct its business. A secretary is charged with the task of keeping the minutes (official record of a group's actions). Other officers, such as a treasurer or vice-chairperson, may be needed depending upon the type and size of group.

In larger groups there may be subgroups or committees to which certain business is sent for review. It is common, for example, to have both standing committees (such as finance committee and personnel committee) and special ad hoc committees set up to handle specific bits or categories of business. Committee members and the chairperson of the committee are appointed by the chair of the larger group. The smaller the committee, the less likely it will use more formalized parliamentary procedures.

A social worker skilled in the use of parliamentary procedure can be of enormous assistance to task groups. Knowing how to make and amend motions and otherwise properly handle the group's business can make the group's task go smoothly. Parliamentary procedure provides a set of rules to guide groups in their deliberations; it was never meant to serve as an obstacle. In the final analysis the wishes of the group must prevail even if a violation of *Robert's Rules* occurs.

Group Roles

Observers of most groups have concluded that there are two types of basic functions that each group must fulfill: task functions and maintenance functions. Task functions help to keep a group on task and working toward agreed upon ends. Maintenance functions, on the other hand, ensure that the needs of group members receive attention. Both task groups and treatment (therapeutic) groups require members who attend to task and maintenance functions. In task groups we are typically less concerned about the needs of the individual member and more focused on the group task. In contrast, within treatment or growth groups, the needs and interests of individual members receive more attention. It is important to remember that no group operates without attending to both functions. The emphasis placed on each function will vary depending upon the group.

In practice, it is often the members of the group who carry out the various functions described above. This occurs through one or more roles that members (and leaders) play in the group.

Task Roles

As mentioned previously, task roles are functional roles designed to help the group reach agreed upon goals. Many different typologies have been used to describe these and other role types (Benne & Sheats, 1948; Shulman, 1979). Benne and Sheats' typology divides task roles into the following: instructor, information seeker, opinion seeker, evaluator, elaborator, energizer, recorder, and procedural technician. The titles describe quite accurately the behaviors performed by group members playing each role and only a brief discussion will be provided here.

The *instructor* often clarifies and reminds the other members about what they have agreed to do. *Information seekers* frequently question the leader and other members on various topics. The *opinion seeker* is likely to want to know what other members think about an idea before expressing his or her own opinion. The *evaluator* likes to make judgments about ideas presented to the group and often comments on the wisdom or appropriateness of any particular idea. *Elaborators* expand on almost any idea proposed to the group. They help ensure that a complete explanation is provided for all ideas. *Energizers* serve as the spark plug for the group. They frequently show excitement and enthusiasm for projects and by force of their interest bring other members along. *Recorders* are a bit like unelected secretaries, keeping a log or record of decisions reached or actions taken. They help keep things on target and become unofficial historians of the group. *Procedural technicians* help ensure the group will act according to any set of rules or procedures previously agreed to.

Persons playing task roles are interested in the group completing its agreed upon task and try to help this process. They tend to be more committed to the task and may be less concerned about the importance of group maintenance.

Maintenance Roles

Group maintenance is an important function needing attention in any group. Group maintenance roles are more concerned with improving, enhancing, or increasing group functioning. Task groups often pay less attention to this facet than treatment groups do, but the function of group maintenance cannot be ignored. Group maintenance roles include harmonizer, compromiser, encourager, follower, tension reliever, and listener. The titles assigned to these different roles are less important than the behaviors that members perform to accomplish the group maintenance function. As suggested by the titles, group members focusing on group building and maintenance encourage other members to participate (*encourager*) and they listen carefully (*listener*). They also follow the directions of others (*follower*), emphasize harmony and compromise (*harmonizer* and *compromiser*), and relieve rough moments in the group, often through humor (*tension reliever*). The goal is to attend to the group's socioemotional climate and help the group maintain its "we" feeling.

Paying attention to the needs of individual members naturally occurs in most remedial or treatment groups. Members are selected for, or join, these groups with the expectation that their social and emotional needs will be given concerted attention. Task groups, on the other hand, often assume that members' personal needs are secondary to the group's purpose. A balance between meeting the two types of needs, task and socioemotional, must occur in all groups. There almost always will be more attention to the task of the group and less to individual needs of the members in a board of directors or a multidisciplinary care conference in a hospital. Likewise, a group for men who abuse their spouses or a group for women surviving breast cancer will have a greater emphasis on individual needs and feelings of the members. Ultimately, all groups need members who attend to both functions. Task groups that ignore the feelings and needs of members are not likely to endure because members will drop out or otherwise avoid participating. Treatment groups without sufficient task focus will not reach their goals of changing individual behavior. Group members will become frustrated because they see no progress. Eventually, a therapeutic group that does not maintain a task focus will lose members, or funding, or both.

Individual Roles

Not all the behavior of group members can be classified into the two categories described previously. Some roles played by members meet only the needs of the individual playing the role. These behaviors include aggressiveness, blocking, seeking recognition for self, dominating the group, seeking help, and confessing past errors.

The *aggressive* member attacks others and, by putting them down, raises himself or herself. This member is likely to challenge the ideas and motives of others and soon become a problem for the group. The *blocker* is usually the one to say "Yes, but . . ." to all the ideas or solutions proposed in the group. No matter what the proposal, he or she will always have a reason why it will not succeed. The *recognition seeker* will engage in a variety of behaviors, all of which are designed to focus the group's attention on him or her. Like the person who dominates (*dominator*) the group by talking incessantly or the person who seeks help from the group for his or her own problems, the person seeking recognition has personal needs that are not being met. Their behavior indicates a need to which the group cannot respond. The person who confesses (*confessor*) past mistakes often embarrasses the group by inappropriately disclosing personal behavior. The confessor is similar to a student the author once knew. At the first class session, when members took turns introducing themselves she remarked that she had an abortion once. This disclosure made some members of the class uncomfortable and showed the student's insensitivity to the usual boundaries experienced within such groups. These roles are important because they indicate the needs of the individual member, but they often don't help the group toward its goal. A member who behaves in this fashion often risks rebuke from the group and slows the group in its achievement of objectives.

Nonfunctional Roles

Besides some of the individual roles that can become nonfunctional if they aren't stopped, there are other roles that almost always are nonfunctional. These include the scapegoat, deviant member, defensive member, quiet member, and internal leader (Shulman, 1979). The *scapegoat* is a person who draws upon himself or herself the wrath of the other members.

This person serves as someone to blame when things are not going well. *Defensive members*, on the other hand, do not accept blame for anything and deny responsibility for their actions. *Deviant members* engage in behavior they know the group will oppose or find annoying, such as continuing to speak out of turn, interrupting others, or refusing to participate in group activities. *Quiet members* simply do not participate and make it impossible for anyone to get to know them. Finally, the *internal leader* may vie for leadership of the group and attempt to wrestle control from the designated leader. Internal leaders are often members with significant natural leadership ability or influence over other members.

Groups need guidance and help from the leader to recognize and confront nonfunctional roles. They also need assistance to learn how to help members playing individual roles. At various times in the developmental history of a group (that is, as a specific group develops and changes over time), different roles may be needed. The leader must be familiar with task and group building or maintenance roles and skilled enough to model them for group members. Leaders also must be keenly aware of what the group needs at any time. They then must either address that need themselves or draw upon other group members who will play the proper role. Continued nonfunctional role playing by a group member usually suggests that the group itself is not functioning well. Such behavior should not be ignored or allowed to continue unabated. Figure 3.1 summarizes the wide variety of potentially positive and negative group roles as well as those considered nonfunctional.

Micro Skills in Groups

Chapter 2 discussed a wide variety of skills important for micro or one-on-one practice. These include skills needed to build relationships with clients (such as warmth, empathy, and genuineness), and attending skills (including eye contact, active listening, facial expressions, and body position). In addition, chapter 2 describes a number of interviewing skills including encouragement, reflective responding, rephrasing, clarification, interpretation, providing information, summarizing, and self-disclosure. As might be expected, these skills are as applicable in groups as they are in one-on-one interviews. In therapeutic or growth-oriented groups the worker is likely to use these skills and to encourage group members to do the same. Part of the

worker's function, indeed, may be to teach these skills to members of the group. For example, members of a parenting skills group will benefit from learning how to listen actively to their children. Members of chemical dependency treatment groups will need to engage in self-disclosure; it is not uncommon for the leader to model this behavior.

Task groups typically have less emphasis on such matters as self-disclosure because this is not usually related to the purpose of the group. Likewise, interpretation of behavior and reflective responding is used less often in a staffing for a nursing home patient. Listening skills, the ability to summarize, clarify, and provide information are, however, just as important in task groups as they are in one-on-one interviews and in treatment-oriented groups. It is important to view the development of skills as a continuing process. Some skills essential for one-on-one situations must be used in small groups and when working with larger system levels such as an agency or large governmental organization. At the same time, a worker with a group must use additional skills that include playing task and group maintenance roles, using parliamentary procedure, nominal group, and brainstorming techniques.

Figure 3.1: A Variety of Group Roles

Potentially Positive Roles
Instructor
Information Seeker
Opinion Seeker
Evaluator
Elaborator
Energizer
Recorder
Procedural Technician
Harmonizer
Compromiser
Encourager
Follower
Tension Reliever
Listener

Potentially Negative Roles
Aggressor
Blocker
Recognition Seeker
Dominator
Help Seeker
Confessor

Nonfunctional Roles
Scapegoat
Deviant Member
Defensive Member
Quiet Member
Internal Leader

Task and Treatment-Group Skills

Whether the social worker is leading a task group or facilitating a treatment group, there are several essential skills, including conflict resolution, modeling, coaching, guiding, team building, confrontation, planning, consulting, coordinating, and using structure.

Conflict Resolution

Conflict is a fact of life. It occurs routinely within relationships and can have positive or negative consequences depending upon how it

┌───

HIGHLIGHT 3.13 ─────────────

The Family Treatment Program: Recognizing Conflict

The new specialized family treatment program was barely six months old when problems began to appear. It was designed to provide intensive in-home treatment by a team of family workers with low caseloads. The program had initially been greeted as a very positive approach to working with multi-problem families. Within a few months the team was beginning to prove the merits of the idea. At the same time, workers who were not part of the specialized unit began to complain. Soon the source of the complaints became clear. With several workers attached to the special program, those remaining were being asked increasingly to handle larger caseloads. Many saw the benefits of the new program but felt their extra work was unfair. Those with larger caseloads felt they were assuming too much of the caseload burden and resented it.

When designed, the new program had no alternative plans to handle an increased caseload. Nor was any thought given to how removing workers from the regular family unit would affect the workload of those who remained. Clearly, the agency administration had a problem.

└───

is handled. Conflict may arise from power or status differences, personality disagreements, or from opposing values or belief systems.

Conflict tends to be viewed as negative because too often it is not resolved or managed successfully. Friesen (1987) has suggested applying a four-step problem-solving framework to conflict management. The four steps include recognition of actual or potential conflict, assessment of the conflictual situation, choosing a strategy, and intervening.

Recognizing Conflict

Recognizing conflict is easy when people don't talk to one another, or are openly hostile, unnecessarily polite, or outright rude. Ideas suggested by one side may be routinely rejected by the other. The conflict may be between individuals or groups. It may be created by jealousy and other personal reactions or it may be caused by confusion or misunderstanding. The example in Highlight 3.13 suggests how even the best plans can create conflict.

Assessing Conflict

Assessing conflict usually involves talking directly to the parties involved. Often the source becomes clear during this process. In the preceding situation, the source was identified readily. Sometimes other problems mask the source or the problem is the result of miscommunication. In the latter case, the problem can be more easily resolved. Highlight 3.14 gives a simple example.

It does not take much to create a problem. It follows that unclear messages between sender and listener cause their share of conflictual situations.

Choosing a Strategy and Intervening

Identifying the source of a conflict is an important step in resolving it. Once identified, appropriate strategies can be considered or devised. For example, if the problem is simply between people a variety of approaches can be used. These include bargaining or negotiating (discussed in chapter 4), and other methods designed to separate those in conflict. When a structural problem (one related to agency design or organization) is causing the conflict, the solution must also be structural. For example, a disagreement over assignments may be resolved by modifying the assignment system or redistributing an unfair workload. Sometimes an interpersonal problem can be resolved through structural means. Highlight 3.15 illustrates this.

While positive outcomes are not always possible and some conflicts cannot be managed, progress can usually be made. In some cases the strategies listed below under resolving win-lose situations will prove effective.

Win-Lose and Win-Win Situations

One of the ways we can avoid becoming involved in conflict is to recognize when a win-lose conflict situation is developing. The nature of competition often produces a win-lose mentality. Much of our society is structured around

---

HIGHLIGHT 3.14

That's Not What I Said: Assessing Conflict

John was in his second month as director of the Eastern Washington Service Center (EWSC). The agency had been racked with scandal before John became director. Under a recent director, the agency had lost its entire building fund because of poor stock investments. John's task was to return the agency to a healthy financial footing and restore its reputation. In his first report to the board of directors, John explained recent changes in EWSC and tried to highlight some of the accomplishments. To help improve staff morale and pro-

ductivity, he announced he had recently bought some chairs. Almost immediately one board member at the other end of the room exclaimed angrily, "What?" John was momentarily perplexed. Surely purchasing a couple of office chairs was not a matter of major concern to a member of the board of directors. Then the board member asked, "Did you say you bought shares or chairs?" John quickly assured the board that he had indeed purchased desk chairs, not shares of stock, the cause of the earlier scandal.

HIGHLIGHT 3.15

Square Peg in a Round Hole: Choosing a Strategy

Both workers and clients complained about the treatment they received from Ann. With responsibility for the reception area, Ann was supposed to greet all clients and visitors, notify workers of the their arrival, answer phone calls and direct them to other staff, and keep track of clients when the worker came to the front desk to meet them. Workers considered her rude to clients and felt she was impatient and irritable most of the time. She was likened to Charles Dickens' character Scrooge.

The agency administrative staff had discussed the situation before, and the supervisor had talked to Ann, all to no avail. Ann would try to improve, but things always seemed to end up the same. The administrative staff was working on a reorganization plan that would require assigning new responsibilities to one supervisor and reassigning an additional experienced clerical staff member. After a

brief discussion the group decided to reassign Ann to new duties and move her from the reception desk to the clerical pool. A new receptionist would be hired, and Ann would be working with day-care providers and foster parents. She would handle financial details and report to a new supervisor. Within days of the administrative reorganization, Ann was hard at work on her new tasks. She stopped complaining, treated everyone with respect, and underwent a remarkable transformation. This change continued and Ann was never again reported for abusive or rude behavior. The agency reorganization had not been designed to end the problem in the reception area, but had the effect of doing so. Once away from the stress of being receptionist, Ann developed into a highly valued member of the agency team.

HIGHLIGHT 3.16
Win-Lose Resolution Strategies

Zander (1983) has suggested some strategies that are often successful for resolving or avoiding win-lose situations in groups. They include:

1. Asking each person to listen actively to the other. Active listening requires that you demonstrate your understanding of what the other person has said by paraphrasing it.
2. Role playing for the parties to show how their communication looks to an outsider.
3. Asking both sides to list their areas of similarity and agreement.
4. Attempting to identify goals that transcend

the differences between the parties and working for solutions that fulfill these goals.
5. Finding objective criteria or values that can be used to evaluate other solutions.
6. Seeking agreement from each side to make concessions that will meet the needs of the other.

Source: Adapted from A. Zander, *Making Groups Effective.* Copyright 1983. Reprinted with permission from Jossey-Bass Inc., Publishers. San Francisco.

---

the idea of winning or beating the competition. In group meetings there are always clues to win-lose situations. When you feel yourself lining up on one side or the other, you are probably becoming involved in a win-lose incident. Sometimes our language gives us away. If we say or believe that our way is the only way or the best way, we are implicitly giving a message that the other person's point of view is wrong. Eventually win-lose situations become lose-lose situations because neither side benefits. The side that loses feels bad and may be resentful. They often lose their sense of being part of the group and may even sabotage things if sufficiently upset. Losers stop listening to the other side and soon see additional areas where they disagree. Resolving win-lose situations requires that we first be aware of them. Once alerted, there are a number of skills and techniques that can be employed to defuse the situation. Highlight 3.16 lists some possible approaches.

Once agreements appear to be reached, it is important to test to make sure this has happened. Asking each side to describe explicitly their understanding of the agreed upon solution is wise. Miscommunication that originally caused a problem can just as easily disrupt the

solution. The ability to resolve conflict successfully, or at least to manage it, is an important skill for any social worker.

Modeling and Coaching

Albert Bandura's (1977) work on modeling suggests the enormous importance that watching others has on our behavior. Social workers may find modeling helpful in a number of situations including teaching new skills, showing clients alternative methods for resolving problems, and helping clients develop a repertoire of responses to problematic situations. An example of this is presented in Highlight 3.17. Bandura has identified conditions that enhance the likelihood that a model's behavior will be copied. These include (1) the attention level or awareness of the model by the observer; (2) the observer's retention of the modeled behavior; (3) the observer's ability to perform modeled behavior; and (4) the observer's motivation to perform the behavior. Awareness of the factors that influence effective modeling allows the social worker to increase the likelihood that the modeled behavior will be performed by the observer.

HIGHLIGHT 3.17
Teaching Disciplinary Techniques

The second meeting of the practical parenting group began with a review by the social worker, Marjorie, of what had been learned in the first session. Marjorie then discussed the program for the day. The major goal was to learn two new, non-punitive techniques for disciplining children. The first technique was a time-out procedure. Marjorie told the group they would see a brief videotape of a mother using the time-out technique with her child. Group members were asked to watch the mother carefully and take notes on what she did. Marjorie emphasized the importance of this technique for managing certain kinds of situations that commonly arise between parent and child. She quickly summarized the research on this approach as well as her own experience with its use.

(Using this approach described, Marjorie was demonstrating two of the guidelines for modeling: asking the observer to pay special attention to the model and describing why the modeled behavior was important.)

After the videotape had been played twice, Marjorie asked one of the parents to volunteer to model the time-out technique with Marjorie playing the child's role. Then each parent took a turn playing the roles of parent and child. Marjorie praised good examples of the time-out technique and suggested improvements for group members who were having more difficulty.

In this last section, Marjorie used the remaining guidelines. She asked the group members to role play the desired behavior and used praise or corrective feedback depending upon how well the person performed the desired behavior.

In groups, this can be achieved by several methods, including:

1. Asking the observer to pay special attention to the model's behavior;
2. Describing for the observer why the modeled behavior is important;
3. Having observers role play the modeled behavior to ensure that they understood and can perform it;
4. Using praise both for the observer and for others who perform the appropriate behavior;
5. Giving observers immediate corrective feedback when they attempt a new behavior.

Corrective feedback, or simply feedback, is one element of a skill called *coaching*. In coaching, the worker may choose to intervene immediately after a client has engaged in a behavior. If the behavior to be changed includes verbal communication, the worker may wish to ignore the content and focus on the process (Hepworth & Larsen, 1986). It is always appropriate to describe the group member's behavior instead of evaluating it. Evaluative comments typically exacerbate problems instead of assisting communication skills. People often resent direct criticism.

One approach to coaching would be to ask a group member to speak directly to another member, rather than to the group as a whole or to the worker. This is especially helpful if the group involves family members or others with whom the speaker frequently interacts. For example, in the couples group John tells the social worker that he would like his wife to be more affectionate. The social worker asks John to turn directly to his wife and tell her specifically what he would like her to do. In this way, John must address his wife, who is ultimately the only person who can solve his problem. This approach forces John to be more specific since "being more affectionate" has many meanings.

Coaching also involves encouraging members to try new behavior. A common barrier to behaving differently is fear that one will look stupid or perform poorly. The worker can help overcome this by encouraging and supporting the member. This is especially effective if the behavior to be copied has already been modeled. Assertiveness training typically uses a combination of modeling and coaching to help group members develop and use new skills. When used by the worker in tandem, these skills can increase the likelihood that the members will adopt and continue the new behavior or communication patterns.

Team Building

The importance of working as a team member should be clear by now. The use of multidisciplinary teams, staffings, and similar work groups is sufficiently common in social work that every worker can expect to become a member of one such team or another. Whether the team works effectively is often a result of the team-building efforts that have occurred. Johnson (1989) and others have identified some of the problems that frequently interfere with the ability of a team to develop. Our emphasis here is on strategies to build a team while overcoming common barriers.

Team building can best occur when there is strong organizational support for the team. This support can be shown through several means. First, it is important that the place of the team within the organization is clear. This requires providing sufficient time for the team to meet independently of their case-handling responsibilities so that team meetings won't be an additional burden competing with their regular job responsibilities. If the only time the team meets is around individual cases, there will likely be limited ability to develop the "we" feeling so important to effective functioning. Adequate

Effective team building often depends on the expertise and motivating skills of the team leader.

time for team building also allows the team to agree on goals and roles and responsibilities ahead of time. This includes not only decision-making processes but also who will assume leadership responsibilities.

Leadership for the team can be handled in a variety of ways. The leader can be selected by the team members or appointed by an outside supervisor. It's important that the leader be well qualified. That is, she or he should have experience working on teams and making decisions as part of a team. Although members bring varying levels of expertise to the team, all should be seen more or less as equal participants. If there are clear status differentials among members, functioning may be impaired.

Some team building will occur as members become more familiar with their colleagues. This includes familiarity with communication patterns, terminology, disciplinary jargon, and interpersonal styles. Quite simply, it involves getting used to each other and how the team interacts. A well-functioning team will be composed of members who understand and respect one another's expertise, carry out agreed upon tasks, and are cooperative. Individual members must be comfortable working in an interdisciplinary environment and not lose sight of their professional orientation. A social worker on an interdisciplinary team is still a social worker; no other professional is likely to bring an identical perspective to the team's deliberations. Social work is the only profession with a primary focus on the person within the environment and a concomitant obligation to work for change in that environment.

The work of teams is achieved in the same problem-solving steps described earlier in this text. The team must define the problem, select appropriate goals, use their collective knowledge to consider alternatives, develop an intervention plan, and carry it out. Evaluation of the plan and process must follow the implementation phase. Team members should agree in advance how this process will occur. If this is done

and the other tasks mentioned above are performed, it is likely that an effective team will result.

Confrontation

Confrontation within a group tends to be more discomforting than confronting individuals on a one-on-one basis. Yet to be effective as a team player, group leader, or member, the worker must be able to use confrontation. Chapter 2 described some of the situations where confrontation is appropriate. In this section we will discuss briefly the importance of confrontation in groups.

Chapter 2 described confronting discrepancies, primarily in relation to working with individuals. Discrepancies that occur within groups also require some level and type of confrontation. If the worker in a treatment group determines that a member has engaged in behavior warranting confrontation, the worker has a responsibility to follow through and confront that individual. There are, however, at least two ways to do this that can make the confrontation palatable and effective. When workers choose to confront a client directly, for example, because of a discrepancy between his or her verbal and other behavior, this provides a good opportunity to model appropriate confrontation for other members. The worker engages in a non-blaming type of confrontation by pointing out the discrepancy and how it affects the worker, for example, by using an I-statement.

A second manner of confrontation involves having the worker in a group ask the entire group to take responsibility for problem solving. Thus, a worker might say, "Is anyone else bothered by Mike's assertion that he is going straight, after saying that he was arrested again last night?" This approach places responsibility for confronting Mike on the group instead of the worker, underscoring an important principle in treatment groups.

Confrontation in task groups is also essential. Members must be able to confront other members who do not carry out agreed upon tasks or who engage in other behavior that threatens the group. In one case known to the authors, a team member represented himself to the public as having more authority and responsibility in the group than was true. In other words, he said he did most of the work and, therefore, wanted most of the credit. The group, charged with planning a conference, took responsibility for telling the errant member that no single member was appointed as a conference coordinator and that the group reserved the role for itself. In their view, they all put in a lot of effort and deserved to share the credit accordingly.

While there will usually be a brief moment of discomfort when confrontation is used, the costs of not being confrontational are too high to avoid this responsibility. As always, confrontation should be used judiciously and tactfully. One should have both empathy and respect for the sensibilities of the person being confronted.

Consultation

As described throughout this chapter, the worker may serve as a consultant to the group while acting in a leadership role. Consider a worker who provided consultation to a Parents Anonymous group (Hull, 1978). The group's goal was to provide a supportive experience for parents who abuse their children and to help these parents avoid such behavior in the future. The worker's role included providing consultation on available community services, strategies for successfully negotiating agency bureaucracies, and non-punitive ideas for child management. The worker informed group members about local resources, shared his knowledge of agency eligibility requirements, and helped clients assess the appropriateness of the service for meeting their needs. The consultant role is basically that of an advisor who provides information, suggestions, ideas, and feedback. A consultant lacks administrative power over the consultee, but has special knowledge or expertise that is of value to the recipient. The consultee is free to accept, modify, or reject the advice.

Consultation may be either case consultation or program consultation, or it may include elements of both (Shulman, 1987). In *case consultation* the focus is on a specific client or situation and the consultation may be provided to either social workers or non-social workers. An example would be consultation provided to a nursing home staff on a particular client.

Program consultation may occur when the consultant works with supervisory or administrative staff about ways to improve service. In this case the focus may be on agency policies and practices instead of a specific client.

In one instance, a social worker was asked to serve as a consultant by the director of a family planning agency. The director believed that the intercession of a consultant could help ameliorate problems occurring among volunteers serving the agency. The problems seemed to focus on disagreements between and among members of the volunteer group and the director. Volunteers appeared resistive to suggestions and direction provided by the agency director. The consultant met separately with the director and then jointly with the director and the volunteers. Several salient issues that were of concern to the volunteers were identified during this meeting. The primary issue involved a perception that the director was favoring one member of the volunteer group over the others. The consultant suggested that the director address this issue directly with the group. The director publicly announced his engagement to the "favored" volunteer and took pains from that point on to ensure that his interactions with the group did not show favoritism. The end result was improved service delivery to agency clients, increased openness on the part of the director, and a greater sense on the part of the volunteers that they were making a valued contribution to the agency.

Rapoport (1977) captured the essence of consultation by observing that although no single model of social work consultation has emerged, consultation does involve a purpose, a problem, and a process. Ultimately, the success of the consultation depends upon the relationship between consultant and consultee. The expertise and capability of the consultant is only as effective as the relationship between the two allows. Once again, skills important for one-on-one interventions are important when working with groups.

Coordination

Johnson (1989) describes the coordinating function of social work as encompassing both collaboration and teamwork. To be successful, coordination requires that all parties have a common goal. The goal may relate to a particular client or include provision of services to a target population. There is an expectation that all parties believe that improvements will occur if coordination of services is accomplished.

Case management often involves coordination of services provided by a variety of professionals. The focus is on assuring that all services provided to a client are accomplished in a way that achieves common goals and meets client needs. Often it is the social worker who has the case management responsibility and ensures that agreed upon services are provided. (Case management will be discussed further in chapter 15.) Coordination is especially important when the service providers have different professional orientations or when both formal and informal resources must be used to help the client. To be most effective, the social worker providing coordination must value and believe in the competence of services provided by others. The worker must also ensure that all important information is communicated to all par-

ties. It is important that sufficient time be made available for building relationships among the participants, in addition to participants having support for their efforts (Johnson, 1989).

Using Structure

Structure describes the use of "planned, systematic, time limited interventions ..." (Toseland & Rivas, 1984, p. 196). One of the facets of structure is the use of time. Group meetings should begin and end at an agreed upon time. Material brought up at the last minute is best held for the next meeting.

Agendas help structure time, ensuring that topics or activities to be covered are known to all. This places responsibility on all members to stay on task. Sometimes the amount of time to be spent on each topic is specified, further structuring the use of time. In treatment groups structure may include spending different amounts of time on the problems of each client. In many groups, all members take turns sharing their progress since the previous meeting, with major focus on one member. This process will be followed in successive meetings so all members have opportunities to focus on their problems.

The worker is largely responsible for enforcing time constraints and models this for the members. Frequently, the entire intervention is highly structured. Many educational groups are well-structured and include blocks of time allocated for specific topics, group activities designed to teach important concepts, and even role playing. The degree of structure needed may vary from one type of group to another. The worker will need to be flexible in planning and working with groups.

Chapter Summary

This chapter began with a discussion of two broad categories of groups, task and treatment. Several examples of each type were given. Important skills for both types of groups were discussed along with worker roles in groups. These included: broker, mediator, educator, and facilitator.

The chapter also included an introduction to basic group dynamics including group development, culture, norms, and power. Group size and composition were discussed along with the decision-making process in groups. Group roles also were described.

The chapter then looked at micro skills that are important in groups. These included skills needed to build relationships with clients (warmth, empathy, genuineness), attending skills (eye contact, active listening, facial expressions, and body position), and interviewing skills.

The intent of this chapter was to suggest that there is a continuum of knowledge and skills needed for generalist practice. Many skills used in one-on-one interventions are just as applicable to various types of groups. However, there are additional skills needed for work with groups. The chapter concluded with a discussion of these additional skills, which included conflict resolution, modeling and coaching, team building, confrontation, consultation, coordination, and using structure. Combined with the one-on-one skills, these mezzo level skills help provide the worker with a formidable array of tools for social work practice. In the next chapter we shall see how this combination of skills serves as a base for interventions with larger systems.

4

Macro Practice Skills: Working with Organizations and Communities

Moving mountains

Georgiana Harrison was dog-tired. Her primary job was to license foster homes, make foster home placements, and oversee her agency's receiving homes for children. The receiving homes provided temporary shelter for up to three weeks while other, more permanent arrangements could be made (for example, foster care or return to the child's own home). But this had been an especially bad year for Janna, as her friends called her, as well as for the county human-services agency for which she worked.

First, Janna had become aware that fewer people were applying to be foster parents. She didn't know the reasons for this, but the lack of homes was becoming serious.

Second, she recognized that her agency badly needed a group home for adolescent boys. The number of referrals for group-home care was increasing, and none of her traditional foster homes were designed to handle half a dozen delinquent boys.

Janna found that her colleagues were also confronting many problems. Too many sexually active young people had no access to family planning services. Many clients could not afford to see a physician.

Finally, her own agency seemed reluctant to provide clients with adequate resources unless administrators were legally pressured to do so. Past efforts to get the agency director to be more flexible were not particularly successful.

As a line social worker (i.e., not a supervisor or administrator), Janna didn't think of herself as a community organizer or organizational change agent. However, in the next three years, Janna would be involved in all of the following macro-level change activities:

1. Development of a family planning clinic for low-income clients (She later served as vice chair of their board of directors.);
2. Creation of community education programs designed to increase the number of licensed foster homes (She prepared radio and newspaper ads and appeared on local talk-radio shows.);
3. Writing of a grant to establish a group home for delinquent boys (She wrote the grant, defended it before a review panel, and supervised operation of the group home.);
4. Pressuring of her agency's director to recognize client rights and provide better service;
5. Creation of a new program to provide part-time jobs as tutors for delinquent adolescents.

CHAPTER FOUR

Introduction

Macro practice in generalist social work involves working on behalf of whole groups or populations of clients. It transcends working with individual clients or small treatment groups. Macro-practice involves questioning and sometimes confronting major social issues and global organizational policies. Sometimes the services your clients need are not being provided; at other times the policies under which you're expected to work are unfair or inhumane. At these times, you will need to consider whether to try to change the organization, policy, or system on behalf of your clients. You may need to assess the situation from a very broad perspective, and you may have to evaluate how "the system" (whichever one may be involved) is impacting your clients.

Many, perhaps most, social workers, especially as they begin their practice, focus on working with individual clients or groups of clients. Thinking about changing "the system" is vague or overwhelming. The specific "system" that needs changing may be hard to define. (For example, "the system" may be the organization you work for, a county social services agency, your state government, or a federal bureaucracy.) How to go about making changes in "the system" may be unclear. The work necessary to implement changes may not be included in your written job description. You might be awed by the amount of effort such change demands.

Core value themes in social work include the fundamental rights of people to have their basic needs met, to make their own choices (assuming such choices harm neither others nor themselves), and to maintain their human dignity. There will be times when you will find these value themes violated. You will see inequities and unfairness that you will be ethically unable to tolerate. These will most likely be the times when you will call upon your macro practice skills to implement changes outside the individual client or client group. Something in the environment, in some part of "the system," will need to be the target of your change effort.

This chapter focuses on the skills needed to work *with* and *within* the various systems enveloping us. Most macro change efforts will be pursued within an agency context. Therefore, we will view macro practice primarily from an organizational perspective. Specifically, this chapter will:

- Introduce an organizational context of practice;
- Define and discuss major perspectives of macro practice, including social reform, social action, case advocacy, and cause advocacy;
- Examine the concept of community and its relevance to social work;
- Describe the application of micro and mezzo practice skills to macro practice;
- Examine and illustrate the skills necessary for effective macro practice, including building and maintaining organizations, evaluating results, fund-raising, budgeting, negotiating, mediating, assessing needs, planning, using political skills, and working with coalitions;
- Emphasize those skills necessary to exercise influence, including petitioning, using the media, educating, persuading, confronting, collaborating, and letter writing;
- Examine those roles most useful in macro practice, including initiator, negotiator, advocate, spokesperson, organizer, mediator, and consultant.

Defining Macro Practice

Meenaghan (1987), in the *Encyclopedia of Social Work*, states that macro practice concerns itself primarily with four basic applications: "planning, administration, evaluation, and community organizing" (p. 83). On the other hand, one of the concerns of macro practice involves "looking for ways to promote professional relationships between macro social workers and clinical social workers" and "looking for ways to increase the relationships among the components of macro practice" (p. 88). Social work involves so many facets that there are many ways of defining what it's all about. The Generalist Intervention Model proposed in this book seeks to integrate the macro perspective in an ongoing manner throughout everything generalist practitioners do. Separating and categorizing different types of workers and types of social work practice is avoided. The intent is to orient the new generalist practitioner to view the world through multiple perspectives, including, micro, mezzo, and macro.

Thus, we will explain macro practice in a different way. In the *Social Work Dictionary*, Barker (1987) defines macro practice as "social work practice geared toward bringing about improvements and changes in general society" (p. 92). We will add four dimensions to this definition. First, macro practice usually targets one of three tasks. The first involves changing or improving policies and procedures which regulate distribution of resources to clients. In other words, clients aren't getting what they need as effectively or efficiently as they should. Perhaps some clients aren't getting the resources they need at all.

The second task concerns developing new resources when what clients need is unavailable. Sometimes, new policies and procedures must be developed and implemented. At other times, whole new groups, agencies, or organizations must be established.

The third task most common in macro practice is helping clients get their due rights. Changes need to be made in "the system" so that clients' rights can be exercised. Change is needed whether for the benefit of one client or ten thousand clients.

The second dimension of macro practice involves targeting "the system" to determine where and how changes need to be made. Numerous systems make up our "general society." They include political systems like town, county, state, and federal governments. They also include legal systems involving the police, legislature, and courts. Additionally, they involve social service delivery systems like county social service agencies, residential mental health facilities, and federal Veterans' Administration services.

The third dimension of macro practice concerns the frequent need for advocacy on behalf of clients. Advocacy involves intervening in order to help clients get what they need. Sometimes it means going much further and working much harder than the specifications of your job description. This is one of the elements of social work that makes it special and distinct from other fields.

The fourth dimension of macro practice embraced by this book is an organizational perspective. In other words, most macro practice is performed by those in agencies or organizations. Agencies have policies or constraints which often act to limit workers' behavior. This is very different than a worker who can act as an independent agent, attack a problem, and do whatever she or he wants to. Following is a detailed exploration of this issue.

The Organizational Context of Social Work Practice

Most social workers spend all, or part, of their professional careers within formal organizations. Similarly, all persons live and practice within a community (rural, urban, suburban). The benefits of formal organizations include such tangible resources as office space, salary, clerical support, paper, telephone, and the like. They also provide such less tangible benefits as sanction for one's professional efforts.

Consider, for example, that the social worker in a child welfare agency must complete

┌─ HIGHLIGHT 4.1 ─────────────────────────────────────
When the Agency You Work for Is Part of the Problem

Glen had worked only a short time for the Manitou County Department of Human Services. As foster care coordinator, he was responsible for recruiting, screening, training, and licensing of foster homes. It was a job of which he was very proud. Glen put in many extra hours meeting prospective foster parents in the evening, so neither foster parent would have to take off from work to meet with Glen. During one of their regular supervisory conferences, Glen's supervisor, Peggy, said he was accumulating too much compensatory time and should stop the evening visits.

Glen liked Peggy and generally felt that she was supportive of his work. Peggy said that if people cared enough about becoming foster parents, most would come in during regular business hours. The new policy troubled Glen. In his view, foster parents were providing an important and irreplaceable service to the community and agency. Foster parents were always badly needed, and most of the couples interested in becoming foster parents had at least one parent working during the day. Most were in what some might call the lower-middle class, hardworking people with limited financial resources. Glen saw them in the evening because he was reluctant to ask parents to take time off from work and possibly lose income. Glen felt an obligation to the foster parents and a duty to follow the rules of his agency, and now these responsibilities seemed in conflict.
└──

investigations following allegations of child abuse. She was hired for that job, supported by the agency in her performance, and is generally respected by the agency and community for her efforts to protect vulnerable children. In pursuing the mandate for child protection, the worker has an office, telephone, mileage allowance, secretarial support, salary, and fringe benefits. These are provided because the agency and community believe in the potential good to be accomplished by the worker. Clearly, such formal organizations as social and other human service agencies provide much of value to the social worker.

With the benefits of belonging to, or working for an organization, however, come drawbacks. These include policies, rules and regulations that circumscribe behavior, and procedures that sometimes become a source of difficulty. It is the rare worker who has not found working within an organization sometimes troublesome or downright antithetical to professional obligations to the client. Highlight 4.1 illustrates how an agency can sometimes become part of the problem.

Professional-Organizational Conflicts

Conflicts such as the one Glen experienced are common for workers in most human service agencies. Frequently, the problem is even more serious than the one in our example. The social worker who feels a sense of professional identity with the social work profession and subscribes to the NASW Code of Ethics may find serious conflicts arising between her professional role as change agent and her responsibilities to the employing agency. These naturally occurring conflicts reflect the reality of professional practice within formal organizations. All social workers have an obligation to follow the policies of their agency, and most of the time this is not a problem. The conflict described above was real, and the dilemma faced by the social worker was challenging. Formal organizations require rules and regulations (policies) to function effectively. Similarly, the profession of social work has established guides to professional behavior to ensure a minimum level of service to all clients. When these two obligations collide, the worker (and often the client) are frequently in the middle.

Limitations and Risk Assessment

When such a situation arises, the worker must decide how to handle the situation. The problem-solving process explained earlier in this text is applicable here. The worker must assess several items. It would be important to know, for example, whether Glen's view is correct, that foster parents should not have to take off from work to participate in the interviews. Glen's position, however, rests largely on his values and nothing stronger. It might be important to know whether scheduling meetings during the day discourages foster parents from participating. It might also be helpful to learn why the supervisor felt the amount of compensatory time was excessive. Was there some agency rule which set the maximum amount that could be accrued or was the supervisor just worried about how much evening work Glen was putting in? Glen needed to know where the problem lay in order to find a solution. Also, Glen was a new worker, albeit a valuable one. He felt it would be difficult to challenge his supervisor because of his newness.

Glen's reluctance illustrates the importance of assessing the risk inherent in trying to change any part of an organization. Glen was also aware of other rules that were equally problematic, but seemed more intractable. Glen knew that there are limitations in how many, what type of, and how fast problems within an agency can be solved. A new worker is in a vulnerable position if he tries to change some part of an agency. Before making efforts to change an organization, the worker must realistically assess the probability of success, the importance of securing this change, and the risks to himself for pursuing such a change. This last risk cannot be accurately assessed without considering the strategies Glen might undertake to challenge the rule. Some strategies carry increased risk to the worker. Angering a supervisor is risky. Getting fired is unappealing. The worker is more vulnerable at certain times. Many agen-

cies, for example, place a new worker on probation for six months. During that time, the worker may be fired for almost any reason without recourse to the usual protections afforded more experienced workers (union contract, personnel policies, etc.).

Changing any organization or community is often complicated. Historically, the types of change might be viewed within four spheres: social reform, social action, case advocacy, and cause advocacy. In each of these, the goal is change, but the nature and extent of the change vary dramatically. In the next pages, we will briefly explore each of these ideas.

Social Reform

Garvin and Cox (1987) have briefly discussed the history of social reform movements in the United States. The basic concern of the social reformer is the development and improvement of social conditions. Early efforts at social reform included creation of kindergartens, recreational programs for children and adults, and educational programs for adults. The early social reformer fought large scale problems related to immigration and the impact of urbanization. Social workers helped develop vocational education, hot lunch programs, neighborhood playgrounds, and community housing codes. These changes came about through the reformers' involvement in the political process.

Like their forebears, social workers today actively pursue a legislative agenda designed to improve client services and meet large-scale problems with large-scale programs. The social reformer's focus is on modifying the conditions of society that seriously threaten the well-being of citizens or prevent them from developing their potential. The social worker-reformer today works to maintain and strengthen such programs as Headstart, WIC, and family planning. He or she fights homelessness, drug abuse, and opposes changes in programs like Aid to Families with Dependent Children (AFDC) that will hurt or penalize these programs' recipients. In summary, social reform is more concerned with problems on a larger scale and focuses efforts in such legislative arenas as Congress, state legislatures, county boards of supervisors, and city councils.

Social Action

Social action is a term given to three different but related types of activity. They include (1) advocacy around specific populations and issues such as the homeless and food and hunger, (2) working in local and national elections to elect sympathetic representatives and to support new programs designed to combat large-scale problems, and (3) networking with other groups pursuing a similar agenda (Burghardt, 1987, p. 292). The latter may include organizations of women or gays and lesbians who combine efforts to combat such problems as sexist or homophobia-induced rules. Clearly, overlap exists between the roles of social reformer and social activist, although the latter model emphasizes greater involvement in the change effort by the intended beneficiaries. Social reform frequently focuses on doing good *for* the client, while social action more often values doing good *with* the client.

Cause Advocacy

Barker (1991, p. 7) defines advocacy as the "act of directly representing or defending others." Cause advocacy is a term used to describe advocacy efforts by social workers on behalf of an issue of overriding importance to a *group* of clients. It assumes that the expected beneficiaries are likely to share certain common characteristics. Examples of causes for which advocacy might be appropriate include education for handicapped children and/or expanded medi-

cal insurance coverage for the elderly. Sometimes the terms cause advocacy and class advocacy are used interchangeably. The latter term also suggests that one is advocating for all members of a particular class or grouping of persons (for example, poor people, physically disabled people, or people of a particular ethnic group).

Case Advocacy

Case advocacy, as the name implies, refers to activity on behalf of a single case: an individual, family, or small group. Case advocacy typically involves different strategies from those used to advocate for a cause. For example, the focus may be on the way a particular rule is preventing a client from receiving services to which he or she is otherwise entitled. The expectation is that this client will benefit from waiving the rule or interpreting it differently, but there is no general sense that a large group of clients will benefit in a similar fashion. Because of its significance to generalist social work practice, chapter 14 is devoted to discussing advocacy in much greater depth.

The ideas discussed above share at least one characteristic—the desire to produce a change that will benefit an identified client or group of clients. For the purposes of this chapter, this commonality will be highlighted and the differences among the various concepts minimized. The key point is the obligation of the social worker to work for change that will benefit clients, not just because of the client, but also because of the worker's identification with the profession of social work.

Theoretical Base for Organizational and Community Change

Kettner, Daley, and Nichols (1985) have identified two broad theoretical perspectives that underlie practice with large systems—organizational theory and community theory. Organizations include any structures with staff, policies, and procedures, whose purpose in operating is to attain certain goals. For example, schools, public social welfare departments, and an agency operating four group homes for developmentally disabled adults are all organizations.

Organizational theory is concerned with how organizations function, what improves or impairs the ability of an organization to accomplish its mission, and what motivates people to work toward organizational goals. Some approaches to organizational theory have focused on management or leadership style, while others have dealt with such structural issues as organizational hierarchy, planning, staffing patterns, budgeting, policies, and procedures.

Community theory has two primary components—the nature of communities and social work practice within communities. Warren argues that a community is a "combination of social units and systems that perform the major social functions" important to the locality (Warren, 1984, p. 28). The first major social function includes the *production, distribution,* and *consumption of goods and services.* According to his formulation, all community institutions (churches and business, professional

This group rallying in support of a shelter for the homeless exhibits the community's mutual support function.

and governmental organizations) provide a variety of goods and services.

The second function of a community is *socialization*, or the process in which knowledge, values, beliefs, and behaviors are taught to members of the community. Socialization is particularly important to children, since this is the way they learn the community's expectations for them. Families are one of the primary socialization units in the community.

The third function, *social control*, is designed to ensure that community members live within the norms of the community. Social control is exerted through laws, police powers, and the court system.

Social participation, the fourth function, is achieved through religious organizations such as churches, social clubs such as the League of Women Voters, membership organizations such as NASW, and friendship groups. In addition, many businesses and governmental agencies encourage social participation through organized events such as sporting activities.

The final community function is *mutual sup-*

HIGHLIGHT 4.2

Community Organization: The Traditional Focus on the Community in Macro Practice

Historically, community organization has been the term used to refer to macro practice in social work. The methods and directions of social work practice have changed and evolved, just as the economic and social realities of the times have drastically changed. However, the concept of *community* continues to be very significant for social workers. You might ask how the word *community* can be clearly defined. Is it a neighborhood? Or is the community a group with common issues, problems, and concerns? For example, there is the social work community or the community of physically disabled persons. Does the word community connote a certain ethnic, cultural, or racial group? How large or small should a community be? Can the U.S. be considered a world community?

Barker (1987, p. 28) defines the community as "a group of individuals having common interests or living in the same locality." We have already described Warren's (1984) formulation of the city. His is perhaps the best articulated and most well-respected perspective on the community.

Because of the wide range of possible meanings associated with the term *community*, we will focus here on some of the major concepts inherent in the Barker and Warren definitions. First, both Barker and Warren's definitions concern a group of people related in terms of locality. Second, these people also have some interests or functions in common. Third, because of their common locality, functions, and/or interests, people in the community interact together on some level, or at least have the potential to interact.

A fourth concept involved in community is important from a social work perspective. A community can be organized so that its citizens can participate together and solve their mutual problems or improve their overall quality of life. Social workers can use their macro practice skills to mobilize citizens within communities to accomplish the goals they have set for themselves. Social workers have been involved in efforts to encourage the growth of new businesses and to counteract the human toll that occurs when a major employer goes out of business.

Historically, the three methods of community organization engaged in by social workers have included social action, social planning, and locality development (Rothman & Tropman, 1987). *Social action* has already been discussed. Using macro practice skills to advocate on behalf of communities of people is one logical application of social action. Frequently, social action can be used to remedy imbalances of power. For instance, sometimes a city will draw its voting boundaries to guarantee that minorities will not be the majority in

port, which involves caring for the sick, helping the poor or homeless, and providing for a variety of health and human services. Mutual support activities are carried out by individuals and families, social and religious organizations, and the government. It is easy to see how problems could occur in carrying out any of these functions. One can also see the ways in which social workers might become involved in solving these problems.

Warren has also helped us conceptualize communities from multiple perspectives. For example, one may think of a community as having spe- cific geographical boundaries, like a city, or as denoting a group with shared interests and beliefs, such as the social work community. Cox suggests that the community may be seen as a target for change, as the problem, or as the context within which change occurs. The advantages of these perspectives become more apparent when assessing the problem, deciding among several possible interventions, and evaluating the outcome.

Because of the similarities between organizations and communities, the problem solving model discussed in chapter 1 is clearly applica-

any single district. Some minority groups have forced communities (sometimes through legal action) to rewrite the boundaries for city voting districts so that they have an opportunity to elect a representative who would uphold their interests.

Social planning involves "a technical process of problem solving with regard to substantive social problems, such as delinquency, housing, and mental health" (Rothman & Tropman, 1987, p. 6). The emphasis is to call in experts or consultants to work with designated community leaders to solve specific problems. People in the general community would have little, if any, participation or input into the problem-solving process. For example, a city might call in an urban renewal expert to recommend what should be done with a blighted area of the community.

Locality development emphasizes "community change . . . pursued optimally through broad participation of a wide spectrum of people at the local community level" (Rothman & Tropman, 1987, p. 4). The idea is to involve as many people as possible within the community in a democratic manner to define their own goals and help themselves. Locality development is consistent with social work values since individual dignity and participation and the right of free choice are emphasized.

There is considerable debate regarding the paths social work macro practice should take. National and world politics have changed drastically since the three traditional methods of community organization were enthusiastically espoused. Resources continue to shrink, and hard decisions must be made regarding their focus. Many argue that macro practice in the real world is substantially different than it was a few decades ago.

The position of this text is that macro practice, which involves interventions with large systems and organizations on behalf of people, is still a major component of generalist social work. Systems and their policies need change and improvement. Oppressed populations need advocacy. The focus of change must not be limited to changing the behavior of individual clients or client groups. Rather, there is a cluster of macro practice skills which social workers can use to effect change. As we've already indicated, today, most macro practice takes place within an organizational context.

The basic concept of community is no less important now than it was twenty or thirty years ago. It remains just as important to focus on the benefits of large groups of people, their overall well-being, their dignity, and their right of choice. Community provides a wider, more global perspective within which social workers can view the world and set their goals.

HIGHLIGHT 4.3
Social Workers Can Help Improve Delivery of Services

The meeting room of the Algoma City Council was full, an unusual event since hardly anyone ever attended the council's bimonthly meetings. Residents of the small community simply allowed the council the freedom to conduct business and rarely asked to address the body.

Tonight, the situation was different. Residents in the Knollwood subdivision were out in force to protest a business park proposed for property next to their residential neighborhood. Each resident spoke and shared misgivings about the potential effect this development might have on their property values. They also expressed anger at not being formally notified about the proposal. Council members stated their sensitivity to the plight of the residents and agreed to gather additional information before making a decision. They also promised that residents would have an opportunity to review any proposed building in the business park.

When a speaker said that many members had attended this meeting because their neighbor had seen the topic on the Council agenda, another potential problem surfaced. If residents did not know about a proposed development, they could not voice their concerns. The present system relied mainly on word of mouth to inform people about issues pending before the Council. Suspicion existed in such circumstances and prevented an impartial review of the proposal.

Finally, the social worker proposed a solution. A brief amendment to the zoning law would provide for residents within three hundred feet of a proposed development to be notified about the changes under consideration. Most residents believed this would provide ample warning, allow citizens to voice concerns, and allay fears that some secret development would adversely affect their lives. The result would be better communication between city government and the citizen and prevention of the angry and disenfranchised feelings that emerged tonight. Over time, both sides would benefit from the change.

ble. However, Kettner et al. (1985) emphasize that a problem need not exist for intervention to occur. A worker might, for instance, choose to intervene after identifying a potential problem, to prevent future difficulties, or simply to improve an already existing program or condition. The advantage of this is that it allows the social worker to be *proactive* instead of *reacting* to problems or issues. Thus, a social worker may recognize that a change in a particular program or policy might produce additional benefits or that greater efficiency could be achieved by modifying some aspect of the services provided.

Micro Skills for Organizational and Community Change

Earlier chapters have explained some key skills necessary for intervention at all system levels.

The intent of this chapter is to briefly summarize the ways in which these skills apply when working for organizational and community change. Chapter 2 identified warmth, empathy, and genuineness as important attributes for working with individuals. Much of the work of organizational or community change occurs in face-to-face interactions. This might be worker to client, worker to administrator or supervisor, or worker to elected or appointed official. The capacity for genuineness and empathy are equally important in these situations. The worker mentioned in Highlight 4.3, who was attempting to modify local procedures, must be perceived as genuine and sensitive to the problems of decision makers. Most people respond better to warmth than to criticism. This applies to administrators or others in positions of power. There may be situations where the worker does not wish to be considered sensitive to the target's position or where clear adversarial strategies are most appropriate. These situations, however, are much less common.

Usually, positively reinforcing others and the ability to form relationships with people from vastly different backgrounds and orientations are essential for work in the community. Finally, the capacity to observe and understand verbal and nonverbal behavior, to interpret and summarize the words of others, and the ability

to portray oneself as confident and competent are important skills for organizational or community change.

Mezzo Skills for Organizational and Community Change

Much of the work of social workers occurs on a one-on-one basis or through working in small

---

HIGHLIGHT 4.4
Saving a Community: A Task Group at Work

Clearwater had once won an award for its beauty. The growth of the university and the concomitant destruction of Victorian-era homes had left many in the town in a state of despair. Not only were the remaining homes being converted into student housing, but the lovely elm trees lining the streets had died, leaving a denuded landscape.

At the request of local officials, the community development specialist called a meeting at which citizen concerns would be explored. Using techniques such as nominal group (a combination of brainstorming and prioritizing issues by the group), the worker helped the group identify three major problem areas. Three groups were formed, each in response to a particular problem. One group focused on trying to save the remaining historic homes, a second worked on community beautification, and a third looked at downtown business development. The worker met separately with each group to help them get started. Periodically, all three groups met together to discuss accomplishments and future tasks. The historic preservation task group studied the problem and considered the work of other cities with similar problems.

Eventually, this group wrote an ordinance protecting historic buildings from destruction or unsympathetic remodeling. They lobbied the city planning commission and the city council, organized mailings to council members, and spoke at various public meetings. Despite vigorous opposition from the most powerful property owner in town, the council adopted the ordinance and es-

tablished a permanent landmark commission to enforce it.

Achieving this was not easy. Overcoming opposition and resolving areas of conflict were formidable tasks. Conflict resolution, described in chapter 3, is equally important at both the organizational and community levels. The ability to diffuse potentially problematic situations, to find a satisfactory middle ground, is critical. Win-win outcomes, where all parties benefit, are desirable and should be the worker's goal whenever possible.

Similarly, the ability to use the disparate strengths of many individuals and to build an effective task group requires skill in team building. In this case, the worker assessed the strengths and weaknesses of each group member and helped the group accomplish its goal by building on the former and overcoming the latter. Thus, members who were more comfortable speaking in public presented the group's ideas to the city planning commission, the city council, and the chamber of commerce. Others wrote letters, telephoned people, and addressed envelopes.

After the historic preservation group became an effective body, the worker's role changed to that of a consultant, offering ideas and providing feedback to the group leaders. Skill in offering consultation is important, because the worker will usually not continue indefinitely as leader. Yet he will want to provide for a certain degree of continuity or stabilization of the change effort.

task groups. These groups have several advantages. Groups are often better equipped to handle complex activities or to undertake projects beyond the ability of a single person. In addition, participants in the group are usually more committed to the outcome when they are involved in the decision-making process. Chapter 3 discussed groups in greater detail, and no attempt will be made here to recap that material. Instead, an example of a successful project involving a task group within a community is provided in Highlight 4.4.

As our example in Highlight 4.4 suggests, mezzo skills useful for organizational and community change include the following:

- Conflict resolution
- Developing win-win outcomes
- Team building
- Public speaking
- Consultation

The final mezzo skill needed is coordination. In Highlight 4.4, several steps had to be achieved simultaneously, while others followed a sequence. The worker sought examples of other landmark ordinances that could be used as a model. He arranged meeting times and places for the group. He also helped plan a lobbying campaign and assisted the group in each of its chores. Since some members of this task group were also members of other community groups, it was essential to avoid overlap in meeting times. It was also important to ensure that each member knew exactly who they were to talk to regarding the ordinance. Skill in coordinating the efforts of group members is essential to any organizational or community change effort.

Macro Skills for Organizational and Community Change

This chapter will address eleven major skills important in macro practice: building and main-

taining organizations, evaluating results, fundraising, budgeting, negotiating, mediating, influencing decision makers, needs assessment, planning, political skills, and working with coalitions.

Building and Maintaining Organizations

Little occurs without concerted effort by many people. The ability to build a workable organization and to maintain that entity is a task all who attempt to change organizations or communities face. Rubin and Rubin (1986) have identified a set of technical skills that comprise the ability to build and maintain an organization. Included are fund raising, managing a budget, gathering information through surveys, and using specific tactics to accomplish one's goals. Negotiating the best outcome for one's organization is necessary, and the worker must know *when* and *when not* to give in. The worker must recognize that she speaks for her group and is not completely free to express alternate positions. When the worker disagrees with the group, there are two ethical choices: resign the leadership or accept the will of the other members. This does not ignore the importance of arguing forcefully for what one thinks is best. Rather, it is acknowledging that when one speaks for the group, what is said must reflect the group's decision.

Evaluating Outcomes

Evaluating the outcome or results of one's practice has become increasingly important. Clients have a right to expect their social worker to be competent for the task at hand. It is also incumbent upon the social worker to want to improve her practice. It is essential to learn what does and does not work and in what situations. The social worker should always operate under the dictum that governs medical doctors: "First, do no harm." Without a plan for evaluating interventions, we run the risk of inadvertently hurting the people and causes we are trying to help.

Chapter 8 will take a more concentrated look at types of evaluations available to the social worker. For purposes of this section, however, we will identify two major approaches: *practice evaluation* and *program evaluation*. Practice evaluation focuses on evaluating the effectiveness or results of what individual social workers do. It may take the form of single subject designs, task achievement scaling (Reid & Epstein, 1972), client satisfaction surveys, or goal attainment scaling (Hagedorn et al., 1976), also called goal accomplishment (McMahon, 1990).

Program evaluation addresses the effectiveness and results of entire programs. Program evaluation techniques might include needs assessments, evaluability assessments, process analysis, outcome analysis, and cost-benefit analysis (Grinnell & Williams, 1990). These approaches will be discussed further in chapter 8.

Fund-raising

For most people, asking for money is a difficult task. In the social work context, asking for money is called fund-raising. Social programs usually cannot exist without financial support. Money is needed to pay staff, buy equipment, and rent space. It is also required for such consumables as paper, pens, etc. Many social programs depend upon a combination of public funding and private donations to cover operating costs. In addition, political campaigns require money. Social workers may be called upon to raise funds and should be familiar with the basics of fund raising.

The fund-raiser should keep multiple sources of funds in mind. Flanagan (1980) divides these into individual donors, corporate do-

nors, foundations, membership dues, and benefits. In addition, church organizations and service clubs often provide funding if the area to be supported falls within their sphere of interest. Foundations and corporations are most likely to have the resources to make major contributions to a cause or program. On the other hand, they are also the most difficult and time consuming to solicit. Individual donations are more easily acquired, but generally, the amounts received are likely to be limited. While individuals typically give once for a cause, corporations are often more willing to provide continuing funds. Foundations are also more likely to give matching funds if the program promises to raise an equal amount from other sources. This is often an effective way to start up a program but does not guarantee any long-term support. Service clubs and church groups often provide small donations for specific projects. They may offer to purchase a piece of equipment or provide time and money to build a wheelchair ramp.

Membership dues are generally free of the restrictions that other kinds of donations carry. Because they depend upon membership, size of the member pool becomes important. Membership dues are ongoing, but often the dollar amount raised is less when compared to other sources. Equally limiting are benefits. Most of us are familiar with benefits of one type: the bake sale or car wash. While benefits can take this form, the most successful benefits in terms of money raised are those involving some activity in which the public can participate. A musical program, comedy show, raffle, dance, or some similar activity that will attract the public holds more promise than such things as bake sales. Held annually, benefits can be very successful and become a continuing source of funding.

All fund-raising takes time, hard work, and dedication by the social worker. There is only one real secret to fund-raising—you must ask for money. Asking others to donate is scary; it is a taboo subject with many people. Flanagan

(1980) suggests starting by selling a product, such as a sweatshirt or cookbook. The product is produced at minimal cost and sold at a good profit. Later, it may be possible to request money specifically for support of your cause. Some organizations sell memberships to the public, knowing that the purchaser will not likely attend any of the organization's meetings. Joining the organization allows one to give indirectly to support the group's goals.

In many situations, it will be necessary for the fund-raiser to make the program's request through a formal presentation. The audience may be the entire membership, such as with a service organization or a select group such as a foundation's board of directors. In other scenarios, all fund-raising may be achieved through mail solicitations. This is not uncommon when raising money for political campaigns. In these situations, the fund-raisers begin by listing those likely to support the cause. Next they decide the best person to make the request. Direct person-to-person solicitation uses a similar process. If the contact is through a letter, it is important to make it clear why the potential donor should give to this cause. Making the request as relevant to the individual donor as possible is desirable. Some letters suggest an amount to be donated while others leave this up to the donor. In fund-raising drives dedicated to purchasing equipment, it may be helpful to list the cost of the items. Some who receive the solicitation may choose to donate money for a specific item or to donate the equipment itself.

In more extensive solicitations, especially to foundations or corporations, a packet of materials about the program may be developed. Formal presentations may include visual aids or videotaped information and printed materials. Whatever the source of funding, it is critical for the donor to receive a thank you. This should include at least a note of appreciation, preferably handwritten, and perhaps a verbal thank you as well.

Finally, it is important to remember that people usually do not give to a cause without being asked. The person doing the asking must believe in the cause and be willing to explain to potential donors why they should support the project. Once begun, the process of asking for money becomes easier, and even the novice fund-raiser becomes more self-confident. Remember, if you want something, you have to ask for it.

Budgeting

Budgeting involves money, which is critically important to all agencies and organizations where social workers function. Budgeting is an important concept to understand. Most beginning generalist practitioners will not be responsible for actually making up a budget. However, the budget and the budgeting process will *always* affect them.

A budget is "a statement of probable revenues," that is all types of income "and expenditures during a specified time period" (Barker, 1987, p. 18). We all have budgets, that is, specific allotments of money we can spend for rent or food or fun. The important thing about budgets is that they involve some predetermined and limited amount of money. If more money is spent on one thing, such as rent, there is less money to be spent on other things, such as food and fun.

The same principle applies to social agencies and organizations. Each has a budget regarding how much money it can spend and on what. When more money is spent on one item (for example, provision of financial assistance to clients), then less money is available to spend on other items (for instance, social workers' salaries). The amount of money allotted to you (as salary and benefits) and to your clients (as services or resources) is critically important.

In effect, different parts and functions of

an organization compete for the same money or portions of that money. When you work for an agency, there will be times when you strongly feel that clients have needs that either aren't being met at all or at least not satisfactorily. When advocating for these clients, you will need to understand budgets and this competition for funds.

For instance, a social worker at a private day-treatment center for behaviorally disordered children and teenagers was concerned about the "snacks" given to the children each morning when they arrived at the center. Day treatment provided troubled children with therapy and special education during the day. Yet, the children returned to their own homes each night. Many of the children came from severely impoverished homes with little, if any, food in the house. When they arrived at the center in the morning, they were hungry. The "snack" they received then was often the only nourishment they'd get until the lunch the center provided at noon.

The day treatment program was owned by a private individual who sold the agency's services to surrounding counties that didn't provide these services themselves. (This is referred to as "purchase of service," in that public agencies buy some kind of service from someone else who provides it.) All staff at the day treatment center, including social workers, received exceptionally high salaries. However, this was at the expense of the other services. For instance, the offices and classrooms were poorly furnished, and the building was badly in need of repair.

Additionally, there was the problem of the "snacks." The owner of the agency apparently had gotten a "deal," whereby he had purchased a whole truckload of crumb cakes at very little expense. After three weeks of crumb cakes every morning, the center's clients were becoming tired of them. Despite their hunger, the children began to refer to the cakes by a quite vile term. The teachers and social workers, also quite sick of the cakes, found it difficult to reprimand the children for their vocabulary, as the staff was beginning to feel the terms were almost appropriate.

The social worker we initially talked about was concerned over the lack of adequate nutrition provided, since these cakes were all most of the children were getting. She was also concerned about the sugar-initiated "high" the children experienced immediately after eating the cakes and the subsequent drop in energy level a while later. These children already had problems with being overly active, controlling their behavior, and attending to classroom tasks. Should the worker approach the higher-level administration about this problem? Was the issue important enough to do so? She didn't want to seem like she was the type of person who complained about everything.

She finally did approach the center's director (who was one level below the owner). His response was that having the crumb cakes at such a reduced rate helped to keep the agency within its budget. Was she willing to take a cut in salary to improve the quality of morning snacks?

How would you have responded to the director's question had you been this social worker? Would you have said, "Oh, sure, I'll gladly take a cut in pay"? Would you have sheepishly backed away? Or would you have countered the director's question with a statement suggesting that money could be redistributed from some other part of the budget?

The point is that budgeting is very important. The greater the depth of your understanding of your agency's budget and of the budgeting process, the more potential you will have to impact budgeting decisions.

The task of preparing and managing a budget for any enterprise is similar. Usually, one establishes the budget for a given period (such as a year). Four types of budgeting may be encountered: line item, program or functional, incremental, and zero-based (Sheafer, Horejsi, & Horejsi, 1988).

Line-Item Budgets

Line-item budgets categorize each source of income and area of expenditures. Thus, one might have a category called personnel (further divided into salary, fringe benefits, etc.), another called equipment, and as many other categories as needed. An agency may operate multiple programs, such as protective services, foster care, and juvenile court services, but the costs of each program are not separated and identified. In effect, costs of these programs (and any new ones) may be invisible, because everything is lumped together into one big budget.

Setting initial budgets or continuing budgets may represent something of a guess. In the former situation, there is no existing budget to use as a model. With continuing budgets there is an existing budget, but the estimates for future years must be prepared before the current year has been completed. Many social agencies use this method of budgeting.

Program Budgets

A program budget, also known as a functional budget, uses the same structure as line-item budgets. It also identifies cost centers, such as the adoption program, delinquency project, or group home. This allows the cost of each program to be identified and is useful in making decisions about spending priorities. Such a system is not perfect, because it relies on estimates of certain items. For example, the secretary spends a portion of her time typing for the adoption program and another portion doing bookkeeping for the group home. To assign her salary into the proper categories depends upon the accuracy of the estimates of the time she contributes to each program. This is not always a simple chore. When accomplished, program budgets are helpful for accountability, in that they indicate where money is actually being spent. They also allow some measure of cost-effectiveness.

In short, they can help establish that money is being put to the best use.

Line-item budgets and program budgets are common ways of describing existing budgets. In other words, they describe how the current budget is organized. Once a budget exists, there are two common systems for dealing with requests for budgets for subsequent years—incremental and zero-based budgets.

Incremental Budgets

Incremental budgets rest upon assumptions about anticipated income and expenditures. Typically, one would plan for the next year's budget by starting with the existing budget and then acting according to assumptions. If one assumes, for example, that income and expenditures will rise at the same rate as inflation (e.g., 3 percent), then the existing budget will be increased by 3 percent for next year. If the rate increases differently across categories, e.g., personnel or equipment, these differences should be reflected in the increment used. If salaries are going up at the rate of 5 percent and equipment at 2 percent, one would raise the amount budgeted for both categories accordingly.

Similarly, a decrease in revenues would result in reductions of anticipated income and expenditures of a given amount. This is a very common method of budgeting.

Zero-Based Budgets

Unlike incremental budgets, this approach assumes that one starts fresh each year (zero budget) and justifies a budget based on activities to be accomplished or goals to be reached. Such a system does not guarantee the continuity of a budget (or program) and places them at risk each time a new budget must be submitted for consideration. Because the instability of funding does not allow an agency to plan for more than one year, zero-based budgeting is generally considered inappropriate in social service areas. For example, an agency engaged in adoption studies must be reasonably certain that the studies they began one year can be finished in the next year. The inability to plan for continued operation inherent in this model would seriously hamper most social programs where clients and workers expect to have an ongoing relationship.

Negotiating

Negotiating is a process in which at least two individuals participate in a face-to-face interaction in order to reach an agreement acceptable to both parties (Kettner, Daley, & Nichols, 1985). Negotiations occur over any issue where people disagree or conflict with each other. Sometimes disagreements are marginal. For example, you might think your client needs a clothing allowance of fifty dollars and your supervisor thinks twenty-five dollars is sufficient. At other times, disagreements reflect opposite opinions. For instance, you think your client needs services; another worker thinks she does not.

Negotiating and bargaining can be problematic. When one side gains and the other side loses, bad feelings often result. Such outcomes contribute to a long list of problems and interfere with future working relationships. Fisher and Ury (1981) suggest using principled negotiation wherever possible.

There are four steps to principled negotiating. First, it is important to *separate the problem from the people involved.* In practice, this means we cannot personalize the differences that exist. To do otherwise is to create an adversarial situation in which a problem-solving approach would be more effective. It is possible to dislike *the ideas* or *demands* of others without disliking the *person.*

The second step is to direct attention to the *mutual interests* of both parties and not to the positions they are taking. Both sides have goals they value highly and others that they feel are less important. Negotiating based on this approach allows for creative problem solving and increases the likelihood that both sides will be pleased with the outcome.

The third step requires *devising new options or choices* that benefit both sides. The value of this approach is that it steers away from the tendency to think there is only one answer. It also creates alternatives that help meet the needs of both sides in the negotiation.

Finally, both sides must agree to using *objective criteria* for deciding an issue. In practice, this means that two people might take turns or allow an impartial party to make a certain decision. They may also agree to rely on standards, prior court decisions, or published information for reaching this decision. Thus, the value of a piece of property could be established by having it professionally appraised. Similarly, a disagreement over lot lines can be resolved by using the services of a surveyor. NASW standards could be used for deciding what salary to set for a position requiring a BSW or MSW degree. In each case, there is an identifiable measure available to assist in judging the merits of various positions.

Principled negotiation allows both sides to win and makes it more likely that each will be satisfied with the outcome. Achieving this goal is not always easy, but will result in more positive feelings in the long run.

Mediating

Mediating is a process used to resolve disputes between opposing parties and is becoming a more common approach to solving differences of agreement in many areas. Mediating is common in divorce situations where the husband and wife disagree over such things as custody arrangements, child support, and maintenance.

Mediation settles disputes between neighbors, vendors and customers, and landlords and tenants. The limited research on mediation suggests that it produces positive outcomes from the perspective of the individual parties (Pearson & Varderkooi, 1983). It is not yet known why some parties accept mediation and others do not. Compton and Galaway (1979) discuss the value of helping each person in conflict to recognize the legitimate interests of the other party. As in bargaining and negotiating, the goal of mediation is to work toward common interests of each member, focusing on the specific areas of disagreement. The goal is to produce an outcome satisfactory to both sides (Toseland & Rivas, 1984). Social workers may be involved in mediating between clients and such institutions as schools, social agencies, and government agencies. Johnson (1989) has described the interaction between the two parties involved as the target for change. In such instances, the difficulties may be compounded by characteristics of large systems that include complexity, pursuit of self-interest, and communication problems (Shulman, 1984). The worker's task is to motivate and help each side reach out to the other.

Influencing Decision Makers

Influencing others is a common role for social workers. Sometimes this influence is direct—as in the role of probation officer. At other times it is indirect—such as when one models behavior for a client. In many areas of social work practice and in one's life, there is a need to influence other people, particularly those with decision-making power. This includes supervisors, administrators, elected and appointed officials, and others in similar positions. The tactics one adopts often depend upon several factors: the target, the ability of the social worker, the likelihood of success, and the risk to both client and worker.

If the target is an individual, the tactics may differ from those used when dealing with an organization. We also must consider our own ability to bring about change, including such aspects as our ability to influence others, our power, and resources. In addition, some approaches may be more or less likely to bring success in certain situations. For example, a letter-writing campaign may not be effective against entrenched individuals who do not care what others say or think.

Finally, all large system interventions carry some risk to both the client and worker. In many situations, the risks are minimal, entailing no more than perhaps a few ruffled feathers for a short time. Yet other cases may involve the risk of losing a job or position. In all cases, we must recognize that the decision to select a strategy is a serious one with a variety of components.

In the next section, we will discuss seven strategies for influencing decision makers, although each is not equally effective in all situations.

Petitioning

Petitioning the decision maker is the first strategy. This involves placing one's ideas or positions in writing and seeking others to add support to the position. Petitions have a section where supporters may sign their names as a show of support for the ideas presented. Petition signatures are somewhat easy to obtain and therefore not as effective as other methods. For example, it is not uncommon for a person to sign a petition when asked by a friend, even though he may hold views opposite to those expressed in the petition. In a recent situation, a group opposed to an elected official gathered enough signatures to force a recall election. When the election occurred, the recalled candidate's opponent received fewer votes than there were signatures on the recall petition. In some situations, however, petitions can be very effective. The example in Highlight 4.5 illustrates this.

HIGHLIGHT 4.5
Petitioning Works

The Clearwater City Council was preparing to vote on whether to build a bypass highway around the city. Several members of the council had already stated their support for the bypass. They argued that it would reduce congestion on the city's main street and make it easier to cross a dangerous street. Prior to the vote, Mrs. White, who owned a small antique business on Main Street, presented the council with a petition signed by most of the businesses located on Main Street. The petition opposed building the bypass highway because it might negatively affect some businesses along the street. During balloting, not a single member of the council voted to build the bypass. Even council members who supported the bypass were influenced by a petition signed by so many business leaders.

Using the Media

Any type of media, including television, radio, and newspapers, can be employed with good results. Using the media is an effective way to bring attention to one's cause and to influence decision makers. For instance, the media could be used to help get transportation services to therapy sessions for physically disabled children when their parents can't afford transportation costs. A newspaper article or a segment on television illustrating the plight of these children can gain public support. The public might subsequently pressure the city or county government to provide the money for transportation services, whether they like it or not.

The media can also be used to inform the public and promote one's own agency. For example, one large urban children's hospital sponsors a five-mile run each year. The purpose is not only to raise funds but also to publicize its services and increase public use and support.

The decision to use media often occurs when no other method has proven effective or when no other method will have the same degree of effectiveness. There are several general guides to using the media (Church, 1981). First, reach out to the media. Contact them early before problems arise and provide ideas for stories regarding your agency (This author used both radio and newspapers to publicize a need for foster parents and television to promote the formation of a Parents Anonymous chapter.)

Second, build contacts within the media. Just as we develop resources of other agencies to which a referral can be made, media contacts should also be nurtured.

Third, if you are speaking for an organization or agency, be certain you are authorized to do so.

Fourth, provide ease of access for media representatives to contact you. Give them both home and office phone numbers and addresses and suggest the name of someone else they may contact if you are unavailable.

Fifth, learn the timetables necessary for all media. Newspapers have deadlines as do radio and television. Reporters appreciate timely notice of newsworthy events.

Sixth, don't play favorites. Give all forms of media the same opportunity to present your story, unless you are granting an exclusive interview. In these cases, no one else will have access to the story until it appears in the media.

Seventh, if the media makes a mistake, consider your reactions with care. If a correction is necessary, be tactful and explain the reasons for your request. Usually, minor errors should be left alone. Like everyone else, media representatives react to praise and support. If you thank them for the exposure and express satisfaction with the result, they are more likely to cooperate in the future.

Finally, if you gave your story, posed for pictures, and waited in vain for the article to appear, you are not alone. Many articles do not get printed or used because more important news supersedes the story. Reporters do not like this to happen since it affects them as well, but they recognize this is an occupational hazard. Again, thank the reporter for the effort and indicate your willingness to work with them again.

In certain situations, you will have to prepare a media release. A media release is a public announcement that may acknowledge the opening of an agency, the creation of a new program, or a problem which needs attention from the community. A sample press release is shown in Figure 4.1.

Educating

Often, decision makers are not as familiar with every aspect of a situation as others may be. Thus, it may only take educating a decision maker about a situation to produce the desired outcome. This is often true with such public officials as legislators, who must represent many different points of view. For example, a legislator may not feel it's important to allocate resources to combating child abuse and neglect if she doesn't feel there's a problem. You as a social worker may need to inform or educate that legislator about how serious the problem is before she's convinced it's worthwhile to spend the necessary money.

In some situations, simply presenting the information in written form and in person will convince the decision maker of the validity of your position. In other situations, it will require repeated efforts. It is important to remember that no one likes to appear ignorant nor to be treated as if they were. Avoid talking down to the decision maker, but present the information as matter-of-factly as possible. Sometimes, sending a written position statement as background

is helpful before proceeding to the point of an in-person interview. It allows the target to become familiar with your ideas and to have some basis for beginning a dialogue with you. Often, the educating function is an adjunct to the next skill, persuading.

Persuading

Persuading people or organizations to change may be easy or difficult, depending upon several variables. Persuasion is easiest when there is *issue consensus,* or when the target or decision makers share your values and agreement on solutions is likely. Persuasion is more difficult when the target shares similar values but does not perceive the problem in the same light (*issue difference*). Persuasion is most difficult when the target neither shares similar values nor accepts your identification of the problem (*issue dissensus*) (Patti & Resnick, 1972). These variables must be carefully considered when attempting to persuade. A more detailed discussion of persuasion appears in chapter 14.

We are not suggesting workers persuade clients to adopt a position similar to their own. Client self-determination is still a cardinal value. Instead, we are suggesting that this knowledge can be put into practice on behalf of client systems, especially when the target for change is an agency or larger system. Persuasion is a positive alternative to the next skill to be discussed, confrontation.

Confrontation

Few of us like confrontation. When asked why they decided to become social workers, many students reply, "Because I wanted to help people." Helping people and confronting people sometimes seem like opposing ideas. In actuality, much of social work practice involves confrontation. The clinician confronts a client about his lying or confronts a patient who says

Figure 4.1: Using the Media: An Example of a News Release

Rural Mental Health Clinic
12 East North Street
East North Overshoe, Vermont
(802) 658–0371

For Immediate Release:

Drug and Alcohol Program a First in State

EAST NORTH OVERSHOE, VT—December 28, 1992. The Rural Mental Health Clinic has added a drug and alcohol program to their new service center in East North Overshoe. According to the director, Jim Stevens, the new program is the first in the state to offer both inpatient and outpatient service to chemically addicted individuals. The clinic has added three staff members and will be hosting an open house on Friday, January 14th from 1:00 P.M.–3:00 P.M. The office for the new program is located at 232 Spring Street.

For further information, contact Jim Stevens at 658–0371 or 658–9981.

###

Note: The release should be typed double-spaced with margins of at least $1\frac{1}{2}$ inches on each side.

┌─ **HIGHLIGHT 4.6** ─────────────────────────────

Embarrassing a Landlord

Tenants in the Smith Apartments were angry. No matter how much they complained to the city and their landlord, their living conditions remained the same. The building in which they lived was in violation of many city ordinances, and the landlord refused to make any changes. The city did not follow through on its enforcement responsibilities and the situation remained deadlocked. Finally, the tenants decided to try a different approach. Late one afternoon, they gathered in front of the land-

lord's home in an exclusive suburban neighborhood and picketed, their signs expressing anger with his neglect. The group called the news media, and television crews appeared at the site to record the event for the evening news. Both city officials, who had been lax in their enforcement of the building codes, and the landlord himself, experienced enough embarrassment to undertake the changes demanded by the tenants.

└───

one thing and does another. Confrontation is common in work with the chemically dependent, correctional clients, and others who have in some way violated community standards. Confrontation requires certain assumptions concerning action and target systems (Patti & Resnick, 1972). An *action system* is "the people and resources in the community with whom the social worker deals in order to achieve desired changes. For example, the action system for a client being evicted might include the other residents of the apartment building, local city housing officials, and the newspaper reporters contacted by a worker in an effort to change a landlord's policies" (Barker, 1987, p. 2). A *target system*, on the other hand, is "the individual, group, or community to be changed or influenced to achieve the social work goals" (Barker, 1987, p. 163). Confrontations may be appropriate under the following circumstances:

1. *Action system goals* and *target system goals* are in sharp contrast to one another.
2. The action system poses a credible threat to the target system. (This usually means that there is an availability of coercive power the action system can use against the target system.)

3. The target system's position is somewhat immutable (unchangeable) because of its investment in the status quo or fear of the outcome of the proposed change. It may also lack information about economic costs of the change, or be concerned about loss of support from groups that favor the existing system.

Confrontation can take many forms, but the two most difficult are *legal action* and *public embarrassment*. In taking legal action, the social worker is proceeding with the belief that the target has violated a law, code, or other regulation and that other methods have not borne fruit. Legal action may involve reporting a landlord for violating city building or health codes by failing to provide hot water or allowing vermin to exist within a building. It may include pressing charges against the target for violation of a criminal law, such as battery or violation of a court order. Another possibility is filing a civil suit against a person for violating one's rights. Examples include getting fired from a job because of one's race or gender. Pursuing the latter forms of legal action are potentially expensive, time consuming, and lengthy. The outcome is uncertain, and there is always some risk for the worker and client. Other strategies should be used whenever possible, since they provoke less emotion and are more likely to lead to win-win results.

Another form of confrontation is *public embarrassment*. This occurs when the target system's shortcomings or errors become public knowledge through efforts by the worker. An example of this is shown in Highlight 4.6.

Such tactics are dramatic and extreme and do not always succeed. Yet, in certain circumstances, they may be effective in forcing change in larger systems. Confrontation may not be an easy route to follow. The needs of clients and the worker's obligation to the client should take precedence over any initial discomfort about tactics.

Collaborating

If the target system is rational and will listen to new or challenging ideas and is acting with good faith, collaboration is the preferable route. Collaboration is the procedure in which two or more persons work together to serve a given client. The client may be a community, individual, group, or family. Collaborative strategies include all of the following (Patti & Resnick, 1972).

1. Supply facts about the actual problem. This assumes that the target knows nothing about the existence of a particular problem.
2. Offer options for resolving the problem. This helps the target consider other solutions that the action system believes are or will be effective.
3. Ask permission to try a solution on a trial basis. Often this is helpful because it does not commit the target to an open-ended agreement with unknown consequences.
4. Request permission to set up a committee to consider the problem and possible alternatives. This approach increases the target's involvement in the problem and

expands the number of people aware of the situation. It is less threatening, since the only request is for a study committee.
5. Request increased opportunities for target and action (or client) systems to get together and share interests. This may be a bit more threatening to the target, but it gets the two parties talking about their respective concerns.
6. Appealing to the values, ethics, or scruples of the target system. This assumes that the values or ethics of the target are consonant with those of the action system.
7. Convince the target system through rational debate and discussion. This is most effective when the target and action system share certain values or when the data presented leads to a conclusion the target system can accept.
8. Identify adverse outcomes arising from continuation of the present situation. The negative outcomes must be realistic or have a realistic probability of occurring.

Collaborative strategies should be attempted before using adversarial approaches to problem solving. Adversarial approaches run the risk of alienating both the target and those not directly involved in the situation, such as co-workers. Collaborative strategies are good faith efforts to change the target system based on positive assumptions about the target. Only when they fail should other approaches be used.

There may be times when collaborative and adversarial strategies work together or when a given tactic may be used differently than described above. For example, the petition case described above was not an adversarial tactic as defined by Patti and Resnick, but a collaborative effort to let the target system (city council) know of a potential problem that could be caused by

┌─ **HIGHLIGHT 4.7** ───
Letter-Writing Strategies

To be effective, letters should:

1. Be carefully planned, revised, polished, and proofread.
2. Include letterhead (with address), date, salutation (Dear _____), body, complimentary close (Sincerely), and both typed and written signature.
3. Be businesslike and pleasant.
4. Be brief (preferably one page) and discuss only one topic.
5. Open with a positive comment.
6. Be factual and simply written.
7. Request a response.

Letters that are less likely to be effective include those that appear identical, those copied out of newspaper advertisements, or clearly mass-produced letters (e.g., duplicated copies instead of original). Letters attacking the reader are less likely to work and may backfire. Some people advocate handwritten letters, but the advantages of a clear, typed message outweigh those of handwritten communication.

If letters are to be mass produced, as might be desired when a group is trying to sway the reader, vary the letters so that they don't appear identical. Written letters are helpful in certain situations and help create a record of communication with the decision maker. They should be used as an adjunct to, not instead of, other more personal forms of contact. Person-to-person communication is still superior to written messages as a means of influencing people.

their decision to relocate the highway. Ultimately, the actual mechanisms used to cause change depend on many factors. These include the competence of the worker, the desires of the intended beneficiary, assumptions about the target system, and the risks of one strategy versus another.

Letter Writing

Letter writing is not always recognized as a strategy for influencing decision makers, yet it can be effective in certain situations. Elected officials frequently receive letters on topics, and often keep a tally of how many letters arrive on a particular subject. Virtually any issue—from the need for alcohol and other drug abuse prevention programs to nuclear war—may be addressed. Sheafor, Horejsi, and Horejsi (1988) provide suggestions for writing better letters. These are shown in Highlight 4.7.

Needs Assessment

Needs assessments are used for a variety of purposes, but their primary role is to estimate the extent of demand for a particular service or program. Barker (1987) describes needs assessments as: "systematic appraisals, made by social workers and other professionals in evaluating their clients, of problems, existing resources, potential solutions, and obstacles to problem solving. In social agencies, needs assessments are made on behalf of the clients who receive clinical services; in communities, on behalf of all the residents. The purpose of needs assessments is to document needs and establish priorities for service. The data come from existing records, such as census and local government statistics, as well as from interviews and research on the relevant population" (p. 106).

There are a variety of ways to conduct a needs assessment. The five primary methods include the *key informant* approach, the *com-*

munity forum approach, the *rates-under-treatment* approach, the *social indicators* approach and the *field* study. Each method is briefly described below using the models explicated by Warheit, Bell and Schwab (1977).

1. The *key informant* approach assumes that certain individuals are especially knowledgeable about the needs of a given community. This might include such local officials as a county judge, mayor, or social service provider. Thus, these individuals would be approached to provide their knowledge about needs in a particular area.
2. The *community forum* approach assumes that the public also has knowledge of a community's needs. In this approach a series of widely advertised meetings are held, designed to bring in a cross section of the population.
3. The *rates-under-treatment* approach is a time-honored way of determining the need for a particular service. It assumes that counting the people who seek and receive a given service (e.g., supportive home care) is an accurate estimate of the actual need in a community.
4. *The social indicators* approach uses information in existing public records, such as the census, to estimate the actual need for a service.
5. A *field study* needs assessment relies on gathering actual data in the community through interviews and observation.

All but the last of these methods are relatively easy to use and inexpensive. When undertaking a needs assessment, it is important to think through the exact information that one wishes to gather. One must define goals and decide how the goals will be measured and what data should be collected. Sometimes those collecting the data will need special training or orientation. A needs assessments is an effective method for determining

unmet need in a community and, sometimes, for determining the existence of an overlap of services. Each social worker should be able to conduct a needs assessment using one or more of the above approaches.

Planning

Planning hardly seems like a topic that deserves much attention in a social work text. After all, everyone plans something and most people have had experience in various activities for which planning was required, whether it be a party, a picnic, or a trip. Planning with large systems, however, requires a higher level of skill than the aforementioned activities. Several techniques exist to assist the planner identify all steps, establish a time frame, and assign specific tasks to responsible parties. One of the more useful approaches is the Program Evaluation and Review Technique, or PERT (Federal Electric Corporation, 1963). PERT assists the planning process for both business and social services. (The author used the technique to plan a group home program and to prepare for accreditation of two social work programs.) In PERT, there are a series of steps that must be undertaken. They are: (1) identifying major tasks to be accomplished, (2) placing them in sequential order, (3) determining the probable time needed for completion of each step, and (4) identifying those responsible for completing each specific task.

Once these steps are completed, it is possible to map out the total project graphically showing what will occur, when it will occur, and who is responsible. The sample PERT chart in Figure 4.2 uses planning for a party as the project.

The chart shows the tasks to be accomplished and the date by which each step is to be completed. If a committee planned this party, each task might be delegated to a particular subcommittee, and the chart would reflect this as-

Figure 4.2: A Sample PERT Chart

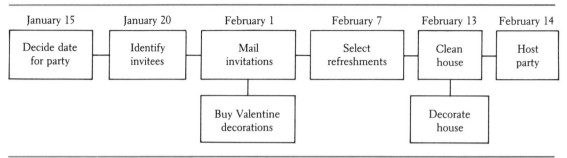

signment. Assignments may be shown by coloring in the chart, a different color for each responsible party, or by placing initials in the lower corner of a square. Sometimes two or more tasks occur simultaneously, and this would be reflected by a vertical line connecting the two boxes, one box placed under the other as shown above. If the tasks are complex, a detailed work plan can be drawn up to show the activity, describe the steps within, identify those responsible, and specify the date for completion. The PERT system allows larger projects to be planned and allows for constant monitoring of tasks. It shows what will be accomplished and helps hold people responsible for their assignments. It is simple, easy to use, and can be applied to any number of tasks or projects.

Working with Coalitions

Many tasks associated with changing large systems require the concerted efforts of more than one group. A coalition is "an alliance of various factions or ideological groups in a society brought together to achieve a goal" (Barker, 1987, p. 26). The types of groups that form a coalition may be similar or very diverse. For instance, well-to-do business owners as a group and single parents receiving public assistance might form a coalition to help their community combat drug abuse.

Rubin and Rubin (1986) note that coalitions may be effective when problems cannot be solved by a single organization. It is very common to have several groups with like interests work together to achieve ends that each group desires. For example, the efforts to create licensing laws for social workers often involve coalitions between social work organizations, such as NASW, and other groups, such as marriage and family therapist associations, and nursing home social workers. This frequently occurs because few laws pass through the efforts of only one group (League of Women Voters, 1976). Coalitions are often essential when the task is large and will require a complex effort by several participants. Perhaps the primary advantage of working with coalitions is the increased strength that occurs when several groups combine forces.

Coalitions may be designed to be ongoing or developed to respond to a specific problem. Sometimes, a coalition created to respond to particular problem may continue indefinitely as the groups or individuals involved recognize advantages of the new structure. Of course, any coalition may cease to exist after achieving the initial goal. Permanent alliances are difficult to maintain but are potentially very effective in uniting diverse interests in a common cause.

Deciding which groups to include in a coalition is not very difficult. One must be aware of the network of community groups already in existence. It is important to know the primary goals of each group and to assess the compatibility of those goals with those of your organization. It is also important to know which groups are influential and to attempt to align with them if possible. Begin by listing organizations already working in a specific area. An organization focused on youth might determine that it shares interests with many other groups. Examples include groups focused on the developmentally disabled, service clubs giving to youth causes, scouting organizations, teacher organizations, YMCA's or YWCA's, etc. Arranging a meeting with the leadership of these groups to explore the possibility of working together may be desirable. It is helpful when the leadership of several organizations can work together well. Individual personalities or styles can be either a barrier or an asset to this collaboration.

After the coalition is created, the real work begins. While there is enormous strength in coalitions, they also suffer from serious shortcomings. It is sometimes easy to break apart a coalition by playing up the differences among or between organizations that form it. Opponents use this tactic to try to sidetrack or otherwise weaken the group.

Similarly, it is important to keep every coalition member informed of what is happening. This is especially true where there is a history of organizations not working together or where there is an unequal balance among the various subgroups.

If one group is clearly the strongest and has the most to gain from the effort to organize and use the coalition, it is essential that the leaders of the stronger group keep the others apprised of what is happening. If the weaker partners fear being left out of significant decisions, there is greater likelihood that they will drop out.

The importance of shared leadership is obvious. Making certain that all groups in the coalition are represented on some sort of coordinating board or steering committee helps them to feel they have a stake in the outcome.

The governing committee members must often take any plans developed by the governing body back to their respective groups for approval. This process is cumbersome, but it ensures that no group will be dragged into a project against the wishes of its members. For ongoing coalitions, the decision by one group not to participate in a specific project is unlikely to threaten the coalition. On the other hand, an ad hoc coalition formed to pursue a specific purpose is vulnerable to dissolution if one or more of the component groups withdraw.

Coalitions are most effective when the task is clear and the responsibilities are specified. Coalition members may continue to work on other projects while engaged in a coalition. Individual goals, however, must be sacrificed for the good of the coalition. This means that each organization in the coalition must agree that the primary goal is of sufficient importance that achieving it supersedes the petty jealousies and difficulties that traditionally exist. A decision must also be made about the contributions to be provided by each group. In addition, it is important to assess which group is more likely to be effective with which tasks. Just as in any other endeavor, it makes sense to assign tasks to those most competent to carry them out. An effective coalition can multiply exponentially the capacity to achieve desired ends. It is easier to create a coalition from existing groups than to build an individual membership organization with the same goal. In the end, the former is more likely to accomplish its goals, to shorten the time needed to achieve desired ends, and to build a reputation for effectiveness.

Worker Roles in Organizational and Community Change

It is possible, and sometimes helpful, to think of the work of the social worker as a series of roles. This section will briefly describe several key roles assumed when working for change in organizations and communities.

Initiator

Kettner, Daley, and Nichols (1985) define the initiator as the person or persons who call attention to an issue. The issue may be a problem existing in the community, a need, or simply a situation that can be improved. It is important to recognize that a problem need not exist before attention can be called to it. Often, preventing future problems or enhancing existing services are satisfactory reasons for creating a change. Thus, a social worker may recognize that a policy is creating problems for particular clients and bring this to the attention of his supervisor. A client may identify ways that service could be improved. In each case, the person is playing the role of initiator. Usually, this role must be followed up by other kinds of work because just pointing out that a problem exists is no guarantee that it will be fixed.

Negotiator

In some situations, the worker may find herself in the role of negotiator, representing an organization or group trying to wrestle something from another group. As mentioned earlier, negotiators who can construct a win-win situation are more likely to be successful than those who adopt a win-lose approach. Successful negotiators also remain calm when others are more emotionally involved. The negotiator cannot personalize the attacks or comments of the other person or group with whom he or she is negotiating. The task is to find a middle

The role of the listener is important in working for change in organizations and communities. To create win-win solutions to problems, one must carefully absorb and process the information and views of others.

ground both sides can live with. Negotiators need the skills of an advocate to push for achievement of organizational goals and those of a mediator to find a satisfactory compromise.

Advocate

An advocate decides what one's client is entitled to and what problem is keeping the client from receiving what she needs. The worker must also assess the adversary to figure out its strengths and weaknesses. While some adversaries may quickly meet the requests (demands) of an advocate, it is more likely that additional work will be required. This may include assessing the client's situation to determine if advocating for the client is likely to cause further problems. The client may be in a vulnerable situation, and the worker would not want to worsen things. Sometimes, it is possible to document a problem so that the adversary understands the reasons for the client's concerns. In other situations, documentation alone will not suffice. As discussed earlier, an opponent who does not share your values or perception of the problem is unlikely to accede to your wishes. In addition, very few people or organizations give up power willingly. Thus, the advocate must expect to use skills other than simply marshalling evidence. The worker may have to negotiate or bargain with the adversary or use pressure tactics to achieve desired ends (Connaway & Gentry, 1988). Advocacy is discussed in much greater depth in chapter 14.

Spokesperson

The role of the spokesperson is sometimes a troublesome one. Too often, the spokesperson begins to personalize the information provided until it reflects the spokesperson's ideas more than those of the organization. A spokesperson should seek to present the organization's views and positions without coloring them with his. This is not always easy. In addition, a special problem exists when one disagrees with the position taken by one's organization or group. The dilemma can be resolved in two ways. First, you can cease to speak for the group and give up the role as spokesperson. Second, you can reflect accurately the organization's position and submerge your own hesitation or disagreement. Doing anything else, such as presenting the organization's opinion in a way that satisfies your own beliefs, is violating the principle of representing the group.

Organizer

The organizer may be organizing individuals or groups. As mentioned earlier, organizing existing groups is easier and usually more effective than creating groups from scratch. Organizers' tasks include developing the potential of others to serve as leaders, stimulating others to act, identifying likely targets for change, serving as a staff member or facilitator, and linking the organization with others sharing their interests (Rubin & Rubin, 1986). The tasks vary depending on the nature of the problem and the strengths and limitations of the components to be organized. Where indigenous leadership already exists, the worker may serve as a consultant or advisor; where it is not present, the worker may become a mentor or teacher. In either case, organizing others is a formidable role.

Mediator

Mediators can achieve several desired ends. A mediator may help two sides work out a compromise, much like the negotiator, except that the latter is clearly on one side of the disagreement. The mediator's role is one of neutrality. He must understand the positions of both parties and attempt to find a suitable compromise.

This requires listening to each side, drawing out feelings and beliefs about the disagreement (Hepworth & Larsen, 1990). The worker as mediator can clarify positions, recognize miscommunication about differences, and help both parties present their ideas clearly. The mediator helps take the emotion out of the situation, allowing better problem solving. As discussed earlier in this chapter, mediation skill is becoming increasingly important in such situations as divorce and child-custody disagreements.

Consultant

A consultant provides advice, suggestions, or ideas to another person, group, or organization. Consultants advise cities on zoning laws, suggest better ways of structuring human service programs, and help groups become more effective. There are two requirements for consultants. First, they must know more than the individual consultee. This may be specific knowledge on a particular topic, such as zoning laws, or knowlege of better ways of problem solving. Second, the consultant must be able to see her advice ignored without becoming offended. A consultant does not have supervisory or administrative power over the consultee. If the consultee chooses to ignore the consultant's advice, no matter how good, the consultant must accept that the client has this right. The principle of self-determination is clearly operable in such situations. With accepting consultation comes the concomitant right to take or ignore the advice provided.

Chapter Summary

This chapter has reviewed the organizational context of social work practice and various conceptualizations of practice with large systems. It has introduced ideas, such as social reform, social action, case and cause advocacy, that are basic to social work practice with larger systems. The theoretical base for organizational change was described, as were micro skills including empathy, positive reinforcement, relationship building, observing, and evaluating, all of which are helpful to social workers working within organizations and communities. Mezzo skills, such as working with task groups, conflict resolution, team building consultation, and coordinating, were also discussed.

Macro skills for organizational and community change were also described. They include building and maintaining organizations, evaluating, fund-raising, budgeting, negotiating, mediating, influencing decision makers, assessing needs, planning, and working with coalitions. Finally, several role conceptions for social workers working with large systems were discussed.

5 Assessment in Generalist Practice

. . . And how are we feeling today?

Elisha White, a protective services worker called in to assess a reported case of child abuse, looked around the room. An emaciated child, age three or four squatted in the corner. Her long, dark hair was snarled and greasy. Whimpering, she hid her eyes with her hands. Her skin was mottled with dirt and what appeared to be purplish bruises. The floor and walls were barren and smeared with dirt. Tattered drapes fluttered at the open windows. The autumn air was nippy with early morning frost. The archaic radiator in the corner emitted no heat.

An anonymous neighbor had called in and reported that the girl's mother was a "coke freak" who frequently left the little girl home alone. In her brief, initial assessment of the situation, Elisha noted the girl's apparent neglect (the apparent lack of appropriate physical care, food, and heat) in addition to potential abuse (the bruises from some unidentified cause).

A number of thoughts went through Elisha's mind. They included the procedures for reporting this situation and removing the little girl from the premises. How was the little girl feeling inside? What damage had already been done to her? Elisha approached the tiny body slowly and spoke in a calm, soothing tone, trying to assure the child that everything would be "okay."

Other thoughts swept through Elisha's consciousness. Where was the mother? In what condition was she? How could she be contacted? What would the mother's chances be in a drug rehabilitation program, if that were indeed one of the woman's problems? Were there relatives available who could help?

If there was no one else, how fast could Elisha place the little girl in temporary foster care? What kind of care was available? Sometimes, good foster placements were hard to find. What effects would placement have on the little girl?

Child abuse and neglect were massive problems in the large city where Elisha worked. Elisha's and her colleagues' caseloads were large. Treatment services were too limited.

Elisha decided that something needed to be done. She herself knew of dozens of cases similar to this one. The needs of these children had to be publicized. The community needed to do more about this increasingly serious problem. Elisha decided to talk to her supervisor as soon as she returned to the agency. Her supervisor just might be receptive to setting up an agency task group to work on the problem. Maybe, if these children's needs could be more obviously identified, people in the community would respond positively to supporting more services. Perhaps then, the community and city leaders would listen and devote more resources to this problem. Even members of her church might respond to her pleas. She decided she would bring the topic up at the next church meeting.

CHAPTER FIVE

Elisha was committed. First, she must attend to this small child's immediate needs. But, the problem was much larger than this. The entire community should be forced to confront the problem and the issues. Next, she would set out to assess the problem on a macro basis. How extensive was child abuse and neglect? What services were already in place to combat the problem and provide intervention for the children and their families? How effective were these services? Were there other resources in the community that could be called upon for help?

Introduction

Assessment is the first step in the problem-solving process. It involves "acquiring an understanding of a problem, what causes it, and what can be changed to minimize or resolve it" (Barker, 1987, p. 11). The generalist social worker evaluates problem situations within an environmental perspective. A problem not only involves individuals and families, but also the larger communities and systems in which these people live. From the onset of the problem-solving process, generalist practitioners focus on problems from the macro and mezzo perspectives, in addition to the micro.

People are dramatically affected by the people, groups, and organizations around them. A young child may be devastated by a sharp scolding from a parent. The presence or lack of friends and social supports within an office work environment may affect whether people love or hate their jobs. Which president is elected may affect the amount of taxes an individual is required to pay, the types of freedom a person can enjoy, and the absolute quality of life itself.

This chapter will discuss the assessment step of the problem-solving process from a generalist perspective. Potential micro, mezzo, and macro dimensions of assessment should be considered throughout the assessment process.

However, since this text emphasizes micro skills in generalist practice, they will be the primary focus of this chapter.

Specifically, this chapter will:

- Identify the major goals inherent in any assessment preceding intervention;
- Discuss a variety of micro assessment issues, including defining problems, types of problems, the importance of identifying various client strengths, and locating sources of assessment information;
- Explain several commonly used micro assessment mechanisms, including DSM-III, the Rathus Assertiveness Schedule, and an alcoholism test;
- Propose means for deciding to work with families and review a variety of areas critical to the assessment of families;
- Describe the use of home visits as an assessment mechanism;
- Discuss assessment from a mezzo practice perspective focusing on groups;
- Appraise the value of home visits, provide some suggestions to maximize their effectiveness, and describe suggestions for your own safety;
- Discuss aspects of assessing both task and treatment groups, including appraising potential sponsorship and targeting potential membership;
- Describe how to do a community needs assessment from a variety of approaches;
- Formulate and demonstrate the steps necessary in analyzing a community or neighborhood.

How to Approach Assessment

Accurate assessment of the person, problem, and situation is well documented as a critically important step in the social work process (Baer, 1979; Loewenberg, 1977; Richmond, 1917). Information about the problem or situation needs to be gathered, analyzed, and interpreted. Such situations may involve parents who have difficulty controlling the behavior of their children or families not receiving the public assistance they desperately need. Regardless of the type of situation, careful thought is necessary in order

---

HIGHLIGHT 5.1
The Difference Between Diagnosis and Assessment

Social work education in the early 1900s, when its courses were first offered at colleges and universities, was very different from what it is today. From the 1920s to the 1960s, most social work programs used a medical model, first developed by Sigmund Freud, to understand human behavior and human problems.

The medical model views clients as "patients." The social worker's first task is seen as making a *diagnosis* as to the causes of a patient's problems and then providing treatment. The patient's problems are viewed as being inside the patient. The diagnostic process is analogous to how physicians work. Namely, medical doctors will examine patients to identify problems. Problems are viewed as illnesses or diseases based inside the patient.

In the 1960s, social work began questioning the usefulness of the medical model. Environmental factors were shown to be *at least* as important in causing a client's problems as internal factors. During this time, social work shifted its attention from individual pathology (that is, the idea that there is something wrong with the client) to problems in the client's environment. Social workers began to identify inequities and unfairnesses to which clients were subjected. The need to advocate for clients oppressed by systems and to try to change or reform these systems became paramount. Social workers began to *assess* problems by viewing clients in their situations instead of *diagnosing* what was wrong with the clients themselves.

Assessment differs from diagnosis in at least four major ways. First, the environmental surroundings of the client, which include the mezzo and macro aspects of the client's situation, are considered at least as important as the micro aspects when trying to understand any problem situation.

Second, since it's recognized that problems exist outside of the client, the outside systems can become targets of change. In other words, organizational policies or public laws may be the source of the problem. Thus, social workers often focus their efforts on changing these laws rather than trying to "cure" clients.

The third major difference between diagnosis and assessment involves the client's involvement in the problem-solving process. Using the medical model, a client is diagnosed as having a problem. Then a social worker provides some kind of therapy to help cure the client. The client responds to therapy and thus expends some effort. However, the client is the target of change, rather than a partner in the change process. Assessment in generalist practice emphasizes that practitioners work *with,* not *on,* clients. The social worker and client work together in the change process. Both work to assess the problems not only in an individual client's life but also those systemic problems outside of the client. Thus, both can work together to make changes and solve the problem.

The fourth primary difference between diagnosis and assessment concerns the approach to client's strengths. Diagnosis focuses on pathology. What are the *problems?* What's *wrong* with the individual client? Assessment, on the other hand, targets not only the client's problems, but also the client's strengths. Emphasizing strengths allows the social worker both to tap "clients' potentials for growth" and to "help in enhancing their self esteem" (Hepworth & Larsen, 1986, pp. 195–96).

In summary, social work's focus on assessment rather than diagnosis is one of the dimensions which makes social work unique. Assuming an approach which stresses analysis of mezzo and macro systems in addition to micro provides a very different view of the world and of how that world might be improved.

to make effective decisions about how to proceed.

Assessment in generalist practice should always involve four considerations. These include: micro, mezzo, and macro dimensions of a client situation, in addition to aspects of human diversity. This chapter will focus primarily on the first three. Human diversity will be covered more thoroughly in chapter 12. Each dimension requires a focus on two broad categories of information. The first involves clients' problems and needs. The second entails clients' strengths. Figure 5.1, orginally proposed in chapter 1 (The Generalist Intervention Model), illustrates this approach.

Before describing specific assessment techniques, five major points need to be made. First, *involvement of the client is absolutely essential*

Figure 5.1: Assessment in the Generalist Intervention Model

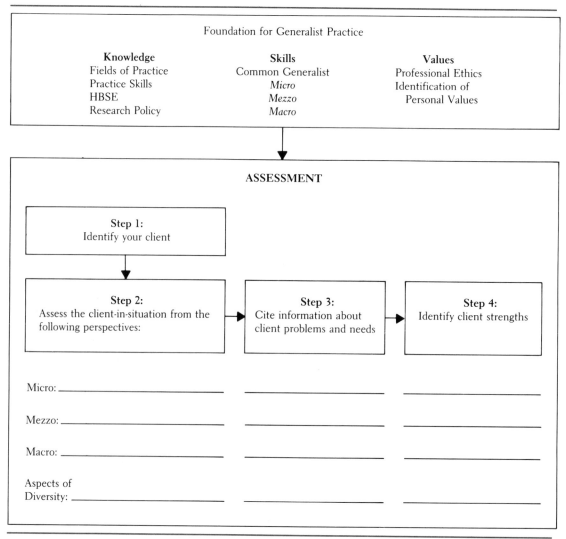

Foundation for Generalist Practice

Knowledge	Skills	Values
Fields of Practice	Common Generalist	Professional Ethics
Practice Skills	*Micro*	Identification of
HBSE	*Mezzo*	Personal Values
Research Policy	*Macro*	

ASSESSMENT

Step 1:
Identify your client

Step 2:
Assess the client-in-situation from the following perspectives:

Step 3:
Cite information about client problems and needs

Step 4:
Identify client strengths

Micro: _____

Mezzo: _____

Macro: _____

Aspects of
Diversity: _____

(Northen, 1987; Siporin, 1975). It's tempting to formulate in your own mind what you think the client's problems really are, however, these formulations may differ radically from what the client sees as the problems. For example, you might determine that the client has an alcohol addiction problem. The client, however, may feel that the real problem is abject poverty. Drinking to him provides an escape from his stark, cold reality. Thus, part of the art of social work intervention is to view any problem from a variety of perspectives and to develop a mutually agreed upon plan.

A second major point is that social work *assessment always involves making judgments* (Johnson, 1989; Siporin, 1975). It would probably be easier if there were a recipe book for problem solutions—you could look up some designated problem and follow a clearly specified, step-by-step process to reach a solution. However, we know that people, their lives, and their situations are complicated entities. Each configuration of strengths, weaknesses, and issues is different. You need to make decisions regarding what appears to you to be relevant and what does not. This involves isolating certain aspects of a problem for assessment and intervention. It also involves prioritizing what you feel is important to pursue. On the one hand, this isn't always easy. But on the other hand, it's one of the things which makes social work so interesting.

The third significant point to be made about assessment involves *strengths*. We've already established that highlighting strengths is one of the striking ways assessment differs from diagnosis. You have clients because they have problems. Therefore, it's easy to concentrate on these problems. It can't be emphasized enough how attending to strengths is as important, perhaps, even more important, than attending to problems. Strengths provide you with an already available means of finding solutions.

A fourth important point about assessment is that *a single, clear definition of the problem may not exist*. Later, we will explore the complexity and variety of problems social workers

address. It is up to you as a skilled social worker to do the best you can to identify, define, and prioritize problems. Frequently it is not an easy task. Problems can be vague and multi-faceted. Even problems aren't perfect.

A fifth major point is that *assessment needs to be an "ongoing process"* (Hepworth & Larsen, 1990, p. 194). We identify assessment as the initial step in problem-solving, which it is. However, because problems, strengths, and issues can be vague, and aspects of any situation can change over time, social workers must be vigilant. They must be ever-watchful, regularly fine-tuning, modifying, even making major changes in their plans and interventions. They must continue to make judgments about what might be the most effective plan and intervention approach as time goes on. In other words, you, as a generalist practitioner, may need to focus on and assess different aspects of a client's situation as your work with that client progresses. Social workers must be infinitely flexible.

Figure 5.2 illustrates assessment as an ongoing process. Arrows below each of the other problem-solving steps lead back to the assessment phase.

A single, pregnant teenager provides one example of the importance of assessment as an ongoing process. When the young woman initially discovers her unplanned pregnancy, you, as a generalist practitioner working with her, may need to help her evaluate her various alternatives (abortion, adoption, or keeping the baby). If her decision is to have and keep the baby, your focus of attention changes. You would then likely decide to assess her current environment. From a micro perspective, this would include health and nutritional status. You might also assess her family relationships and support systems. If you deem support lacking from a mezzo perspective, you might refer her to a support group of other single, pregnant teenagers. Finally, from a macro perspective, you might assess the programs and services available to her and other young women in similar circumstances. You may determine that they can function as strengths for her. You then would try to involve her with the appropriate services and resources. On the other hand, if you found resources lacking, you might turn your attention to assessing and improving these resources.

Goals of Assessment

During any assessment, a generalist practitioner should aim to accomplish four major goals (Siporin, 1975). First, the worker needs to articulate a clear "statement of the problem"

Figure 5.2: Assessment in Problem-Solving Is an Ongoing Process

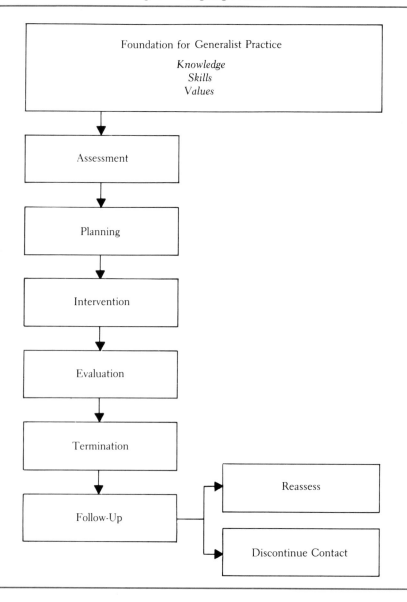

(p. 229). This allows the worker to know what to focus attention upon. For example, is the problem in a particular client situation drug dependency, drug dealing, child abuse, marital interaction, truancy, or lack of sufficient resources? How the worker frames the problem will provide direction for intervention.

Second, the worker needs to formulate a clear description of the client system. This is true whether that client system is an individual, a family, a support group, a social services agency, or a community. On whose behalf is the worker intervening? Does the delinquent child, the parents, or the entire family make up the client system? Is the worker trying to get resources for a single family or an entire community?

Third, the generalist practitioner needs to illustrate how the client system functions with other interacting systems. Is the client system, in this case a family, isolated from friends, family, and other support networks? Has the client system, in another case a community, been deprived of adequate state, county, and social service support and resources?

The fourth goal of assessment is to put all of this information together. We assess client situations in order to formulate intervention plans. In turn, plans provide guidelines to solve client problems. This process involves making a number of judgments. The practitioner must prioritize different aspects of the situation. Likewise, the practitioner must decide whether intervention is best approached from a micro, mezzo, or macro perspective, or requires some combination of these three.

Assessment from a Micro Practice Perspective

This section will focus on assessment of individual client systems. First, how to define the problem will be described. A classification of common problem areas will then be identified and a number of areas targeting potential client

strengths will be recognized. Finally, a variety of assessment instruments for assessing individual characteristics will be discussed.

Defining Problems and Issues

To begin assessment, the client system must be clearly identified. Problem definition immediately follows. Johnson (1989) suggests that it takes three steps to define a problem. First, the worker must recognize the client's unmet needs. What does the client lack that's causing a problem? Second, the worker must identify the "blocks to need fulfillment" (p. 279). What is it about the client and the client's situation that prevents the client's needs from being fulfilled? Third, the worker must formulate "the problem in terms of removing the blocks to need fulfillment" (p. 279). How can the problem be described so that the worker acquires some direction for how to proceed with the planning and intervention? Looking at the problem in terms of what needs are lacking provides suggestions for how to proceed. One example is a homeless client needing shelter. The problem is homelessness or lack of needed shelter. The worker knows that one intervention goal will be to meet that client's unmet need, namely to find some kind of shelter.

Types of Problems

It's important for generalist practitioners to be aware of the types of problems clients typically have. You as a worker need to know what to look for. What areas should you assess? Here, we will look at nine categories of problems commonly confronting clients (Northen, 1987; Northen, 1982; Reid, 1978; Reid & Epstein, 1972).

It should be noted that micro, mezzo, and macro aspects of practice are frequently intimately intertwined. Therefore, it is not possible to identify any particular category of problems with only one of these practice perspectives. For example, take a person addicted to cocaine. From the micro perspective, a worker would focus on the personal habits and impacts on the individual. The mezzo perspective, on the other hand, would accentuate the addicted client's interactions with the people close to him. Additionally, it would address the impacts his addiction was having on these people. Family, friends, work groups, and neighbors might all be affected by the client's behavior. Finally, a macro perspective would direct attention to the major social problems in society which foster cocaine addiction, the ease with which cocaine can be purchased, and the treatment services available to the client.

Interpersonal Conflict

The first category of problems involves "interpersonal conflict" (Reid & Epstein, 1972, p. 42). These involve individuals having difficulty relating to each other. A delinquent teenager may be unable to form friendships with peers. An elderly woman in a nursing home may refuse to cooperate with health-care staff desperately attempting to meet her increasingly serious health-care needs. A developmentally disabled adult may get into frequent fights with his peers at a sheltered workshop because of his poorly developed social and communication skills. Finally, a married couple may be in almost constant verbal conflict.

Interpersonal conflicts may involve both communication and behavior. Problems may exist regarding how information is conveyed and received between two people. Likewise, problems may center on how people treat or act toward each other.

Dissatisfaction in Social Relations

Even when no overt conflict exists, people may identify "dissatisfaction in social relations"

as a primary problem (Reid & Epstein, 1972, p. 43). One may feel unable to get as close to others as she'd like. Another may feel that lack of assertiveness prevents his needs from being met the way he'd like. Still another might feel unable to divorce himself from the guilt that he feels his mother imposes upon him.

Problems with Formal Organizations

"Problems with formal organizations" are frequently cited by clients (Reid & Epstein, 1972, p. 44). Clients may not feel they are getting the resources they need. A Social Security check may be received late or be for an amount less than anticipated. Adequate health care services for pregnant teens may be unavailable. A client may feel that she is being treated rudely or abruptly when signing in to see her caseworker. Or the client may feel that she has been made to wait an inordinately long period of time to see a worker.

Difficulties in Role Performance

Sometimes, clients will have "difficulties in role performance" (Reid & Epstein, 1972, p. 45). A *role* is a culturally expected behavior pattern that characterizes people having a particular position and status in society. For example, people who assume the role of social worker are expected to behave in certain ways.

Most problems in role performance involve "family roles, usually roles of spouse or parent, although roles of student, employee, and patient also receive considerable emphasis" (Reid & Epstein, 1972, p. 45). A difficulty in role performance can best be distinguished from interpersonal conflict by the fact that it is more one-sided. An example is a father who is physically abusing his five year old daughter because "she just won't behave." He is having difficulty fulfilling his role as parent. One intervention tactic would be to train him in more appropriate and effective child management techniques. He, not the daughter, would be the target of intervention.

Problems of Social Transition

Sometimes clients will have problems making "social transitions" (Reid & Epstein, 1972, p. 46). In other words, they will experience difficulty dealing with some major change in their lives. Such changes may include divorce, having a baby, moving to a new locale, adjusting to a new job requiring higher skill levels, or coping with a loved one's death. Any of these may involve serious emotional upset and disruptions in clients' coping abilities.

Psychological and Behavioral Problems

Clients may experience "psychological or behavioral problems" (Northen, 1987, p. 173; Reid, 1978). These involve a broad gamut of emotional upheavals and inappropriate, self-defeating, criminal, or uncontrollable behavior. A client may be seriously clinically depressed. Another may be struggling with anorexia nervosa, "a psychological and endocrine disorder primarily of young women usually in their teens that is characterized especially by a pathological fear of weight gain leading to faulty eating patterns, malnutrition, and usually excessive weight loss" (*Webster's Ninth New Collegiate Dictionary*, 1991, p. 88). Or a client may have uncontrollable agoraphobia, "an abnormal fear of crossing or of being in open or public places" (*Webster's Ninth New Collegiate Dictionary*, 1991, p. 65). People with severe cases of the latter may feel trapped in their own homes, as they are terrified of leaving.

Many of these conditions affect both psychological state and behavior. Depressed people often isolate themselves emotionally and physically from others. Anorexics allow food, or the lack of it, to become the focus of their whole lives and behave accordingly. Agoraphobics experience both psychological terror and severely restricted behavior.

Inadequate Resources

The problem of "inadequate resources" may reflect a number of deprivations of basic needs (Reid & Epstein, 1972, p. 48). Many times, this problem is related to poverty. If you don't have enough money, you may not be able to buy enough food, visit a physician when you're sick, or pay this month's rent.

Inadequate resources may also refer to a lack of resources or services available to the client. On the one hand, the service may not exist. For example, a Native American community may have no health services available to them within a realistic distance. On the other hand, the existing resources may not cover the need. Consider a family of six that needs a minimum of $450 each month to provide adequate nutrition. They receive only $200 in public assistance and food stamps. Thus, their need is not being met, and they are subject to inadequate resources.

Problems in Decision Making

Sometimes clients will find themselves in emotional dilemmas in which they experience serious difficulties in making important decisions (Northen, 1987; Reid, 1978). They may come upon life crises that create emotional turmoil and for which they see no positive solution. When under such duress, it is easy to lose objectivity. Emotional crises can blind people to their rational choices. Such emotion-laden decisions include an infinite number of scenarios: whether to have the baby if the pregnancy was unwanted; whether to follow through on the divorce if he's unfaithful but you still love him; whether to place a person recently paralyzed in a car accident in his own home, a group home, or some other residential setting.

In any of these instances, a generalist practitioner can help a client immobilized by emotion to identify the various alternatives available. Because of her training, likewise, the worker can assist the client in evaluating the pros and cons of each realistic alternative and come to a decision.

Cultural Conflicts

"Cultural conflicts" provide a final category of problems typically encountered by clients (Northen, 1987, p. 173). Sometimes they involve discrimination and oppression by majority groups. For instance, urban African American students may be denied access to similar educational benefits available to white suburban students. At other times, these conflicts concern difficulties in relating to and becoming acclimated into the larger society. For instance, consider the Hmong people who emigrated here from Southeast Asia after the Vietnam War. They had to learn a new language and customs while still striving to maintain their own values and cultural integrity.

Prioritizing Problems

When working with real clients, the actual number of potential problems may seem overwhelming. However, there are approaches for prioritizing which problem to work on first, second, etc. Such prioritizing is part of the planning phase in the problem-solving process and thus will be discussed in the next chapter.

Some Final Notes

These categories of problems are intended to provide ideas about what aspects of client's lives require assessment. They are not necessarily distinct from each other. An example is a two-parent family where the father is sexually abusing his two adolescent daughters. This situation involves at least the following: difficulties in role performance, dissatisfaction in social relationships, and psychological/behavior problems.

Identifying Clients' Strengths

Jones and Biesecker (1980, pp. 48–49) emphasize the importance of identifying strengths in the assessment process. Such strengths include "what the person can and likes to do" and "people who are available to help" in addition to any other potential resources you can poinpoint (p. 21). Strengths can be divided into the following nine categories:

1. *"Family and friends"* (Jones & Biesecker, 1977, p. 48). Does the client have family and/or friends available to provide support and resources? How motivated might these family members and friends be to help the client? Is their help potentially significant to helping the client deal with the situation at hand?

For instance, take Blake, a nine-year-old developmentally disabled child living with his single, alcohol-addicted mother, Stephanie. Stephanie has been accused of neglecting Blake on four occasions. She has previously been told that unless she undergoes inpatient treatment for her addiction, Blake will be removed from her home. The court warns her that the removal may be permanent. Stephanie states that she loves Blake dearly and does not want to lose him. She just can't stop her addiction on her own. She is finally willing to seek help.

The problem involves who will care for Blake while Stephanie is in treatment. Good foster homes, especially those equipped to care for children with special needs, are hard to find. Stephanie's worker explores potential support systems with Stephanie. It's discovered that Stephanie's mother lives in the same city and has expressed willingness to care for Blake, even on a permanent basis. Additionally, Stephanie's sister Sabrina lives within several blocks of Stephanie's home. Both sister and mother are terribly concerned about Stephanie's addiction and have urged her to seek treatment many times. Although Sabrina has three children of her own in addition to a full-time job, she is willing to assist their mother in Blake's care. Both Sabrina and her mother can now serve as significant resources. In addition to taking care of Blake, they can be used as sources of significant emotional support as Stephanie seeks help.

2. *Education and employment background.* This is especially significant in cases where unemployment or financial need is a major problem. Does the client have educational prerequisites, skills, or work experience which would qualify him or her for work with adequate or better compensation? Can former skills used in one setting now be transferred to and applied in a different setting?

Jennifer, age fifty-four, provides an example. Her husband Brian died suddenly in a car crash. Not only was she emotionally distraught, but she found herself in serious financial turmoil. Brian had handled the finances (at least she had thought he had) throughout their twenty-one year marriage. Upon his death, she abruptly discovered that they were deep in debt, having lived way beyond their means for years. She suddenly needed to find a job, and fast.

Jennifer had not worked full-time since she married Brian. However, she did have a college degree in biology. For the past three years, she'd been working for a small, local hardware store. Her job was to do the ordering and keep the accounts. She had discovered that she was exceptionally good at such activities. In fact, she had revamped the store's entire accounting system. She found she had a knack for working with computers. Such assessment of Jennifer's life experience thus established strengths including organization skills, dependability, and computer skills. These, in addition to her college degree and her mature, well-developed social skills, made her an attractive job candidate for a number of potential positions.

She initially found a job as an administrative assistant for a firm assisting companies in computer system installation. Although this was an entry-level job with relatively low pay, she soon worked her way up. Eventually, she became a consultant to companies all over the country.

The point here is that many times, people have valuable skills and qualities which can be applied to jobs even when they've never formally held those specific jobs. You, as the worker, need to investigate specific qualities they've developed. Many times, people will be surprised that they do have valuable assets. You can help them clarify their strengths and the value of such strengths. Resulting enhanced self-esteem can help make clients stronger and better able to pursue their goals.

3. *Problem-solving and decision-making skills.* The extent to which clients have experience solving difficult problems in the past can also be useful. What means have they used to remedy similar situations before? Can this approach be used again? Assessing their handling of previous problems can provide significant clues regarding how they can proceed once again.

4. *Personal qualities and characteristics.* Many strengths fall within the personal realm. For instance, is your client articulate and pleasant? Is he intelligent? Does he appear to be a good listener? Does he keep appointments dependably and punctually?

Labeling and emphasizing positive qualities can educate the client about him or herself and build self-confidence. Additionally, this can provide clues about ways to proceed in the problem-solving process. For instance, will he be able to approach the landlord in a rational manner and request necessary repairs? Will she check back at the unemployment office regularly in search of work? Will his or her pleasant, caring manner toward others enhance his ability to make friends (despite his lack of self-esteem)? Is she well-respected in her neighborhood and able to assume leadership responsibility?

Physical strengths can also be pertinent.

For example, is she strong enough to accomplish a job requiring some degree of physical strength? Is the client attractive in appearance?

Health is also an important asset not to take for granted. Even for those with some physical disability, it's important to define and emphasize what people *can* do, instead of dwelling on what they can't.

5. Physical and financial resources. Because clients most frequently stress their problems to social workers, it's easy to overlook strengths. Does the client currently reside in adequate to good housing? This can provide a sense of security and continuity. What kinds of property does the client own? Does he own a car or other vehicle? Are there any savings upon which to rely? Does she have a source from which she could borrow money, should the need arise?

6. Attitudes and perspectives. Does the client appear motivated to work on solving the problem? Has he indicated willingness to cooperate with the agency? Does he seem willing to talk and work with you? Motivation and positive attitudes toward change are critically valuable assets.

Some clients maintain strong values, which sustain them during difficult times or motivate them to make changes. For instance, an extremely religious client may rely on her beliefs, minister, and fellow parishioners to help her cope with the death of her father. This can provide her with strength. Likewise, parents who maintain a strong belief in the value of education can provide substantial support for a teenage son contemplating dropping out of school to join a neighborhood gang.

7. Miscellaneous other strengths. We know that each individual is unique. Thus, there are innumerable possibilities regarding strengths which may neither occur to you nor be readily apparent. It's important to listen carefully to what clients indicate are important to them. Sometimes, strengths appear or develop during the course of the assessment and even during the intervention process.

For example, take Abe, age fifteen. He was in a special education and treatment program because of violently uncontrollable physical attacks on peers and some minor delinquent acts. He had been seriously physically abused by a stepfather as a child. Thus, he was trying to cope with the awesome rage he felt within.

Abe moved in with his natural biological father upon entrance into the special program at age thirteen. Major therapeutic goals involved getting in touch with his feelings and in control of his temper. He became involved with Junior Achievement. There he made friends, gained confidence, and developed innovative projects. One of his other strengths was that he was exceptionally bright. By age seventeen, Abe returned to regular public school and later successfully graduated.

Other strengths may involve athletic ability, musical talent, acting ability, or special interests. Interests may range from collecting old beer cans to counted cross-stitch to deer hunting. Any of these may provide potential sources of satisfaction, motivation, and enhanced self-esteem.

Which Problem Should You Work On?

Many of your clients will have multiple problems on multiple levels. In view of the numerous categories of problems, how will you choose which to work on?

The first thing to do is to ascertain that the problems to be considered fulfill three criteria (Northen, 1987). First, the client must recognize that the problem exists. Second, the problem should be clearly defined in understandable terms. Third, you and the client should realistically be able to do something to remedy the problem.

Reid and Epstein (1972) make several suggestions concerning how to decide which problem will be worked on (that is, which problem

---

HIGHLIGHT 5.2

Examples of Questions You Can Ask During Assessment

The following are examples of the types of questions you can ask as you assess the client and his or her situation (Hepworth & Larsen, 1990). Of course, each situation is unique. These questions are simply examples. They are merely intended to provide you with some direction regarding how an assessment interview may progress.

"What do you feel are your major problems at this time?"

"How would you rate these problems in terms of their severity?"

"How are other people involved in the problems?"

"Have you been involved with other agencies or received services before? If so, what were they?"

"How do you think this particular problem affects you?"

"In what situations is the problem most likely to take place?"

"How often does the problem occur?"

"How long does the problem usually last?"

"How do you usually react when the problem occurs?"

"How have you tried to solve the problem in the past?"

"Has anything you've tried been at all helpful? If so, what?"

"What do you think you need to solve the problem?"

"What are your strengths (for example, you work hard, you have a good, supportive family, or you're easy to get along with)?"

"Do you think any of these strengths can help to solve the problem?"

"What kind of help or resources do you feel you need (for example, financial, health care, legal, etc.)?"

"What are you willing to do to solve the problem?"

"What things about your situation are preventing you from solving the problem?"

---

will be the "target problem"). After exploring with the client the range of problems of most concern, each problem is defined in "explicit behavioral terms" (p. 58). In other words, the precise nature of the problem should be clear in your mind. Additionally, the problem statement should include descriptions of behaviors which will later allow you to measure your progress and determine when you succeed in solving the problem. Chapter 6, which discusses planning and goal-setting in generalist social work practice, will elaborate further on the importance of behavioral specificity.

Finally, problems should be ordered in terms of their priority *to the client*. This alerts you to which problem you should address first. For example, a client may be concerned with the following problems in order of priority: paying the rent, her husband's drinking, her child's truancy, and an overweight condition which is resulting in a number of health problems. Pay-

ing the rent, is probably the problem you should address first.

This is not as easy as it sounds. Frequently, you will rank the client's problems differently than the client will. In these cases, it's up to you to explore the problems with the client. You will need to establish a list of priorities satisfactory to you both. Once again, this process involves both good communication skills and making judgments.

Gathering Information: Sources of Assessment Data

There are at least seven basic "sources of information" about your clients (Hepworth & Larsen, 1990, p. 196). First, many agencies require clients to fill out forms to provide information. Virtually any type of information may be requested. Information ranges from age and address to family history to descriptions of current crises.

Second, of course, you, as the worker, can obtain much information from clients' responses to questions during your interview. The third means of gleaning information can also occur during the interview. Observe the client's nonverbal behavior. Is the client fidgeting? Does he avoid eye contact when approaching certain topics? Do his nonverbal and verbal behavior coincide?

Fourth, if you have the opportunity, you can observe the client's interactions with other people. Observing interaction with other family members can provide you with useful insights about the client.

Fifth, information is sometimes available from outside sources. Such "collateral information" includes that "from relatives, friends, physicians, teachers, employers, and other professionals" (p. 196). Perhaps, there is a referral source which can give you information. Or there may be prior reports available from other agencies.

Sixth, sometimes the client has gone through psychological and other testing. If so, what information does this provide about the client's emotional state and behavior? Later on in this chapter, we will discuss specific instruments, including the Rathus Assertiveness Scale and an alcoholism test.

Finally, your seventh source of information about the client is based on your own interactions with him or her. Does the client react with hostility to your questions? Does she appear extremely needy or dependent? Is she speaking irrationally? Here, your own "gut reactions" may be useful. If you have certain types of reactions to or impressions of the client, it's very likely that other people will have similar responses.

Assessment Instruments

Multitudes of assessment instruments are available to evaluate various aspects of clients'

lives. Mental health, suicide potential, assertiveness, self-esteem, a child's need of protection from abuse, interaction between spouses, and availability of resources are among the many variables frequently assessed by generalist practitioners. Of course, the worker's field of practice will dictate which variables are most important to evaluate. For instance, a protective services worker must make assessments regarding the extent to which children are in danger of abuse. Likewise, a worker in public assistance must primarily assess the extent to which a client has access to financial resources.

Three assessment instruments have been selected for discussion here. They reflect the varied types of approaches to assessment available today and include some likely to be used in social work practice. The specific assessment approaches addressed here include: the Diagnostic and Statistical Manual (DSM-III); the Rathus Assertiveness Schedule; and an alcoholism test.

DSM-III

According to Barker (1987), DSM-III "represents the American Psychiatric Association's official classification of mental disorders. Each disorder is labeled and given a numerical code and systematic criteria for distinguishing it from other mental disorders" (p. 45). Mental disorders (another term for mental illness) involve "impaired psychosocial or cognitive functioning due to disturbances in any one or more of the following processes: biological, chemical, physiological, genetic, psychological, social, or environmental" (Barker, 1987, p. 97). The American Psychiatric Association originally published the manual in 1980. A 1986 revision is entitled DSM-III-R.

Earlier editions were published in 1952 and 1958. However, the current edition "represents the first time an official diagnostic manual has been widely adopted by mental health professionals in the United States" and it, therefore, "has had a major impact on the field of mental health" (Williams, 1987, p. 389).

As a generalist social work practioner you will not practice "therapy" in a private office with comfortable couches. Rather, you will intervene with clients *and* the multiple systems with which they're involved. You will probably not be called upon to make a formal assessment using DSM-III-R. In other words, you won't have to figure out the specific numerical code that best reflects a client's mental status. However, you will be expected to work both with clients who have been diagnosed and with the system of other professionals working with those clients.

Mental health professionals use DSM-III-R to assess individuals by concentrating on five major dimensions or axes (American Psychiatric Association, 1980, 1986). The reason for formulating assessments according to axes is that "each axis serves as a reminder to clinicians to pay attention to a particular aspect of functioning so that none of these important areas is overlooked" (Williams, 1987, pp. 389–90).

The first axis involves "clinical syndromes" and "conditions not attributable to a mental disorder that are a focus of attention or treatment" (Williams, 1987, p. 389). These include conditions for which people seek professional help, but are not considered mental disorders. Examples are "Borderline Intellectual Functioning" (V62.89), "Academic Problem" (V62.20), "Marital Problem" (V61.10), or "Parent-Child Problem" (V61.20), in addition to many others (American Psychiatric Association, 1986).

DSM-III-R's second axis involves *personality disorders* (for example, schizophrenic or paranoid disorders) and *certain developomental disorders* (for instance, some language disorders or autism). The third axis concentrates on any *physical conditions* which may affect the individual's emotional health. Examples include a knife wound, AIDS, or diabetes.

The fourth dimension "provides a coded number to indicate the *overall severity* of stresses that are judged to contribute to the current disorder" (Barker, 1987, p. 45). This involves an arbitrary professional judgment about the individual's situation and functioning. Scores range from one, which indicates no evident stressor, to seven, which conveys that there are "catastrophic" psychological and social stressors involved (an example is an individual who recently experienced "multiple family deaths") (Williams, 1981, p. 104).

Finally, the fifth axis describes the client's *"highest level of functioning* (socially, vocationally, and in use of leisure time) during the past year" (Barker, 1987, p. 45). Possible ratings range from a score of one, which portrays "superior" functioning (for example, take a "single parent living in [a] deteriorating neighborhood [who] takes excellent care of [her] children and home [and] has warm relations with friends") to a score of seven, which relates "grossly impaired" functioning (for instance, consider an "elderly man [who] needs supervision to maintain personal hygiene and is usually incoherent") (Williams, 1981, p. 105).

Together, these assessment dimensions can depict a relatively clear picture of an individual's behavior, life functioning, and emotional status. DSM-III-R emphasizes characteristics of the various mental disorders without specifying causes; this allows professionals to maintain their own theories regarding why such mental illnesses occur (Williams, 1987).

There are at least four reasons why DSM-III-R is relevant to social workers (Williams, 1987). First, it provides a means for a variety of professionals (for example, nurses, psychiatrists, psychologists, and social workers) to communicate with each other about specific mental, emotional, and behavioral problems. Giving a client's problem a diagnosis makes it easier for each professional to know what others are talking about when they discuss that problem.

A second benefit of DSM-III-R is its helpfulness in evaluating and treating clients with mental disorders. The manual focuses more on descriptions of the symptoms and behaviors of a particular disorder rather than on what causes that disorder. Therefore, it helps to define the specific problem requiring intervention.

A third benefit is DSM-III-R's utility in teaching about mental disorders. Classifying a disorder by describing its symptoms enhances our understanding of that disorder.

Finally, DSM-III-R provides better opportunities to do research on mental disorders. For instance, it enables researchers to place people receiving treatment into specific categories. They can then investigate whether specific treatments or interventions are effective with specific disorders.

Generalist practitioners, however, should be wary of at least three factors when using the DSM-III-R. First, it only describes particular conditions. It does not provide intervention strategies and is only an assessment mechanism upon which specific interventions can be built.

Second, there can be some tendency to focus on the individual pathology or "mental illness" instead of on a client's interaction with the environment. The manual does use the term "client" instead of "patient." Earlier in the chapter, we discussed the difference between "diagnosis," a medical term focusing on individual pathology, and "assessment," which in generalist social work practice also stresses the environment's impact upon the client. Additionally, the manual uses the terms "clinician" and "mental health professional" instead of "physician" and "psychiatrist" (Williams, 1987, pp. 390–91). Still, the manual targets sole individuals. There may be some tendency to "cure" the individual, rather than intervene in the systems intimately intertwined with the client. People using the manual as a formal assessment tool are primarily psychiatrists, psychologists, and "psychiatric social workers." The psychiatric tradition is rooted in the medical model. Thus, generalist practitioners must be cautious to maintain their orientation toward the environment and its profound impact on clients. As

we know, this is one of the dimensions which makes social work unique and special.

A third reason for wariness when using DSM-III-R concerns imperfections in its categories. Professional discretion is involved in assigning diagnoses to individual clients. Individuals and their behaviors are complex and difficult to place in neat, compact categories. Questions also can be raised regarding the potential hazards of labeling people. How might such labels affect and bias expectations? Labels tend to interfere with the notion that each individual is unique, having a unique combination of strengths and weaknesses.

Assessing Assertiveness

Assertiveness involves being able to state your thoughts, wants, and feelings straightforwardly and effectively. It concerns the ability to establish an appropriate stance between being too aggressive and too timid. Aggressiveness in this context implies taking only your needs into account. Essentially, you ignore the needs and rights of others. Timidity, on the other hand, concerns placing the needs and wishes of others far before your own. Assertiveness, then, means that you reach a balance. The implication is that you take both your needs and the needs of others into account. You then try to make some objective judgment about what behavior, response, or plan of action is fair to you both.

The Rathus Assertiveness Schedule (RAS) is an instrument composed of thirty items that measure an individual's assertiveness. It can be a useful tool to gauge clients' ability to determine how well they can speak on their own behalf assertively without aggression. The scale is illustrated in Figure 5.3.

Assessing Alcohol and Other Drug Abuse

Drug abuse involves improper use of some chemical substance in a manner that's harmful physically, mentally, or emotionally. Alcohol

Figure 5.3: The Rathus Assertiveness Schedule (RAS)

Directions: Indicate how characteristic or descriptive each of the following statements is of you by using the code given below.

+3 Very characteristic of me, extremely descriptive
+2 Rather characteristic of me, quite descriptive
+1 Somewhat characteristic of me, slightly descriptive
−1 Somewhat uncharacteristic of me, slightly nondescriptive
−2 Rather uncharacteristic of me, quite nondescriptive
−3 Very uncharacteristic of me, extremely nondescriptive

_____ 1. Most people seem to be more aggressive and assertive than I am.
_____ 2. I have hesitated to make or accept dates because of "shyness."
_____ 3. When the food served at a restaurant is not done to my satisfaction, I complain about it to the waiter or waitress.
_____ 4. I am careful to avoid hurting other people's feelings, even when I feel that I have been injured.
_____ 5. If a salesman has gone to considerable trouble to show me merchandise which is not quite suitable, I have a difficult time in saying "no."
_____ 6. When I am asked to do something, I insist upon knowing why.
_____ 7. There are times when I look for a good and vigorous argument.
_____ 8. I strive to get ahead as well as most people in my position.
_____ 9. To be honest, people often take advantage of me.
_____ 10. I enjoy starting conversations with new acquaintances and strangers.
_____ 11. I often don't know what to say to attractive persons of the opposite sex.
_____ 12. I will hesitate to make phone calls to business establishments and institutions.
_____ 13. I would rather apply for a job or for admission to a college by writing letters than by going through with personal interviews.
_____ 14. I find it embarrassing to return merchandise.
_____ 15. If a close and respected relative were annoying me, I would smother my feelings rather than express my annoyance.
_____ 16. I have avoided asking questions for fear of sounding stupid.
_____ 17. During an argument I am sometimes afraid that I will get so upset that I will shake all over.
_____ 18. If a famed and respected lecturer makes a statement which I think is incorrect, I will have the audience hear my point of view as well.
_____ 19. I avoid arguing over prices with clerks and salesmen.
_____ 20. When I have done something important or worthwhile, I manage to let others know about it.
_____ 21. I am open and frank about my feelings.
_____ 22. If someone has been spreading false and bad stories about me, I see him (her) as soon as possible to "have a talk" about it.
_____ 23. I often have a hard time saying "no."
_____ 24. I tend to bottle up my emotions rather than make a scene.
_____ 25. I complain about poor service in a restaurant or elsewhere.
_____ 26. When I am given a complaint, I sometimes just don't know what to say.
_____ 27. If a couple near me in a theater or at a lecture were conversing rather loudly, I would ask them to be quiet or to take their conversation elsewhere.
_____ 28. Anyone attempting to push ahead of me in a line is in for a good battle.
_____ 29. I am quick to express my opinion.
_____ 30. There are times when I just can't say anything.

(continued next page)

Figure 5.3 *(continued)*

To score:

1. Take the RAS.
2. Change the sign from positive (+) to negative (−) or negative (−) to positive (+) for your answers to the following questions: 2, 4, 5, 9, 11, 12, 13, 14, 15, 16, 17, 19, 23, 24, 26, 30.
3. Add up your total.
   a. A score of −90 to −20 means you're generally unassertive and probably too much so. The lower your score, the less assertive you are.
   b. A score of −20 to +60 indicates that you're within the realm of being appropriately assertive much of the time.
   c. A score of +60 to +90 mean you're very assertive or possibly aggressive. This is a warning category.

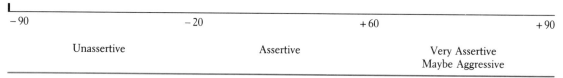

−90	−20	+60	+90
Unassertive	Assertive	Very Assertive Maybe Aggressive	

Source: D. B. Hull and J. H. Hull. "Rathus Assertiveness Schedule: Normative and Factor-Analytic Data." *Behavior Therapy*, Volume 9 (1978) page 673. Copyright 1978 by the Association for Advancement of Behavior Therapy. Reprinted by permission of the publisher and the author.

abuse, of course, is a form of drug abuse. It can be detrimental to the user and to others. Frequently, it, as the "nation's . . . greatest drug problem, leads the abuser to cause accidents, become physically assaultive and less productive, or to deteriorate physically" (Barker, 1987, p. 6).

Because of the prevalence of alcohol and other drug abuse, it is important for a generalist practitioner to assess the extent to which it is a problem for a client. There are numerous assessment instruments available. One is illustrated in Figure 5.4.

Family Assessment

The family is "a primary group whose members are related by blood, adoption, or marriage and who usually have shared common residences, have mutual rights and obligations, and assume responsibility for the primary socialization of children" (Barker, 1987, p. 53). Family membership is intimate. Family members share tasks and responsibilities which contribute to the maintenance of the family's identity and functioning. On one hand, families are made up of unique individuals. On the other, each individual family member is a subsystem of the larger family system. Therefore, anything impacting an individual member also has repercussions upon the entire family and all its members.

Because of their unique qualities involving identity and intimacy, families are considered special types of groups. In one respect, families, as groups, are part of mezzo practice. In another, the importance of the family to individual clients often places family intervention within the realm of micro practice. For our purposes, we will consider work with families to lie somewhere on a continuum between micro and mezzo practice.

Choosing to Work with Families

Working with the family system is one of many intervention alternatives in the problem-solving process. A worker may choose during assessment (Step 1 of the Generalist Practice

Model) to plan (Step 2) and intervene (Step 3) to address the family as the primary target of attention. Other options, of course, involve the assessment of other micro and mezzo aspects of potential intervention in addition to macro dimensions. This may lead you to the question

of when should a generalist practitioner choose to work with a family and when with either the individual alone or with some other external system?

There is no easy answer to this question. However, there are some variables to take into

Figure 5.4: An Alcoholism Test

Please honestly answer the following questions about your use of alcohol and other drugs:

1. Have you ever tried or decided to stop drinking or using drugs for a week or so only to find that this lasted a couple of days?
   Yes ____ No ____
2. Do you think people pay too much attention to how much you drink or use drugs?
   Yes ____ No ____
3. Have you ever switched brands of alcohol ot types of drugs in an effort to control your use?
   Yes ____ No ____
4. Do you need a drink or a drug to get started in the morning?
   Yes ____ No ____
5. Do you admire people who can control drugs and alcohol?
   Yes ____ No ____
6. Have you had problems with drugs and alcohol during the past year?
   Yes ____ No ____
7. Has your drinking or use of drugs ever caused you problems at home with your family?
   Yes ____ No ____
8. Do you take a few drinks before you go to parties, or try to get extra drinks at a party?
   Yes ____ No ____
9. Do you tell yourself you can stop drinking any time you want to, even though you keep getting drunk when you drink?
   Yes ____ No ____
10 Have you missed days at work or school because of your drinking or use of drugs?
   Yes ____ No ____
11. Do you have "blackouts"; that is, are there times when you were drinking or using drugs which you cannot remember, or things that happened to you while you were drinking that you can't account for?
   Yes ____ No ____
12. Have you ever had the feeling that your life would be better if you stopped using and drinking?
   Yes ____ No ____
13. Do you hide alcohol?
   Yes ____ No ____
14. Do you drink alone?
   Yes ____ No ____
15. Do you feel guilt and remorse after you drink and use, or after a night of heavy drinking?
   Yes ____ No ____
16. Have you ever been to a hospital or institution because of your drinking or use of drugs?
   Yes ____ No ____

If you answer yes four or more times, you are probably in trouble with alcohol and drugs. (This test is a combination of questions contained on the National Alcoholism Test and in the twelve questions A.A. asks in its short pamphlet "Is A.A. for You?")

Source: This material is adapted from *Treating Alcoholism* (1987) by Norman K. Denzin (Newbury Park, CA: Sage), pp. 128–129. Copyright 1987. Reprinted by permission of Sage Publications, Inc., Newbury Park, CA.

Many people living in a tiny apartment is a special challenge to the generalist practitioner assessing whether to work with them on an individual or a family basis.

account when making an assessment and planning an intervention. First, you need to ask yourself to what extent the problem affects other family members. Second, do you have the time and resources to work with other family members? Third, in terms of prioritizing problems, are those aspects of the problem involving other family members among the most critical to be addressed? Finally, to what extent do you think family intervention is likely to be successful?

Family Assessment Skills

We've established that the family is a special type of system. It has momentous significance concerning individual members' physical and emotional well-being. Working with families is a major dimension of generalist social work practice. Therefore, chapter 9 is devoted to assessing families (additionally, chapter 10 concentrates on skills for working with families). Only a brief summary of assessment concepts

will be provided here. They include the following:

Family Communication

Family communication involves how well each family member conveys feelings and ideas to each other. To what extent does each sender's *intent* match the *impact* on the receiver? The effectiveness of a family's internal communication is important, not only for assessment purposes but also for planning and undertaking the intervention. Improving communication is frequently a core goal when working with families.

Family Structure

Family structure involves the organization of relationships and patterns of interaction within the family. Assessment of five dimensions of family structure is especially relevant. First, the family's *functioning as a system* with intact, appropriate boundaries and subsystems is important. The second dimension involves *family norms.* These are the rules that specify proper behavior within the family group. Third, there are *family roles.* These concern both the status differential and behavioral expectations the family has for each of its members. The fourth dimension involves the appropriate *balance of power* within the family and among its members. Finally, *intergenerational aspects* and the impact of family history upon current family functioning is vital.

Life-Cycle Adjustments

Assessment of how the family adapts to various predictable phases of its life cycle is important. Births, deaths, marriages, and grown children's departures are included among the many events that call upon the family's coping abilities.

Impacts of the Social Environment

How good is the family's *fit* with its social environment? Does it have adequate social supports, or is it isolated? Is the family receiving satisfactory resources to survive and thrive? How well integrated is the family with its surrounding community? These and related questions are critical for assessing family functioning and planning interventions.

Key Areas of Family Conflict

Chapter 9 will also examine four key areas of family conflict: marital difficulties; parent/child relationship difficulties; personal problems of individual family members; and external environmental stresses.

Home Visits

Home visits involve calling upon clients in their own homes in order to provide some type of professional service. This content is included here because of the significance home visits can have in assessing a family's environment (or an individual's, for that matter). Striking information can be gained during a home visit that is simply not available in the more sterile, agency interview situation.

It should be noted, however, that there are other reasons for making home visits than to do assessments. Barker (1987) cites a number of them. First, the clients may be physically disabled. It may be extremely difficult or impossible for them to leave their own homes. Second, some workers make home visits "because they believe the helping process can be more effective and efficient if conducted in an environment familiar to the client." Finally, some home visits are made "because the worker seeks to mobilize a neighborhood or county toward a social cause" (p. 71). In the latter case, workers need to get involved in the community in order to gain community members' trust and commitment.

Workers' Reactions

One aspect of home visits that can be difficult for workers is the shocking nature of what people must endure as a result of their impoverished environments or their state of physical or mental health. Many social workers come from middle-class backgrounds where there is a certain level of learned expectations regarding cleanliness and household organization. Of course, clients vary drastically regarding their values, just as any group of people vary. However, generalist social workers address and deal with the very worst of people's problems. Thus, there are times when workers must be prepared to look beyond extreme circumstances, remain objective, and try to see things from the client's point of view.

For instance, during her internship, one student confided in her faculty liaison about a serious problem she was having with one of her clients. Her placement involved providing supportive services to a caseload of elderly clients so that they might remain living in their own homes. The student would regularly visit clients and help them get groceries, pay their bills, see friends, visit physicians when needed, and complete other daily living tasks. The student described this particular client as living in an old house trailer cluttered with cast-off clothing, broken furniture, and garbage. The sink was piled high with dishes filled with rotting remnants of food. Although the student found the environmental situation difficult to visit, this was not the major problem. She stated that she was horrified at how cockroaches seemed to be crawling everywhere throughout the trailer. She continued that the very last straw was seeing a cockroach crawl out of her client's ear, up the side of her client's face, and across her forehead.

The faculty liaison acknowledged that this was an extremely difficult situation. Together with the student's field supervisor, the student and liaison planned an evaluation of the client and her living conditions. Frequently, such evaluations were done at the field placement agency. Together with the client, living conditions were assessed and decisions made. Some alternatives for this particular situation included providing the client with additional homemaker services, involving a visiting nurse to assess health conditions, considering removing the client from the trailer, and arranging for alternative living conditions. One of the things discovered was that the elderly woman's intellectual functioning appeared to be deteriorating. This was magnified by her almost total isolation, except for the visits by people providing her with supportive services.

A major issue which the faculty liaison helped the student address involved the student's own perceptions and reactions to the cockroach situation. The student worked to shift her focus of attention from fear of the cockroaches to concern for the well-being of the cli-

ent. This had to be done despite its difficulty. The client was the person who was suffering and in desperate need of help. The situation was alleviated, of course, once the cockroaches were exterminated.

Another example of a difficult home visit situation involves a thirty-four-year-old single, extremely obese mother of four male children, ages seventeen, twelve, nine and four. The twelve-year-old son was currently in a day treatment center for behaviorally disordered ("emotionally disturbed" or delinquent) children and adolescents. There, he received therapy and special education while residing in his own home. The seventeen-year-old son had spent several years in a residential treatment center for emotionally disturbed children. He currently resided in the state correctional facility for youth because, among other things, he had sexually abused his two-and-one-half year old niece.

The purpose of the home visit was to assess the home situation and to talk to the mother about the twelve-year-old's attendance at the treatment program. The worker functioned as the child's counselor at the program. Truancy was becoming an increasingly serious problem. After making an appointment with the mother, the worker came to the home for the interview. The mother answered the door and invited the worker inside. As in some of the other examples cited, filth was a problem.

It is important to be behaviorally or descriptively specific regarding what is considered dirty and what is not. We all have slightly or drastically different expectations concerning what level of dirt is tolerable. The worker in this situation was not renowned for her own housekeeping abilities. However, she based her observation that the house was filthy on a number of observable facts. The colors of the furniture and walls were barely discernible due to the covering of dirt. About one half-dozen odorous bags of garbage resided on the blackened kitchen floor. Unwashed dishes streaked with food remnants overflowed the kitchen sink and were scattered throughout the house. Finally, there were three or four piles of animal feces scattered about the living room floor.

The worker proceeded to discuss the truancy situation with the mother. Despite trying to use the helpful hints she had learned, the worker was unable to establish with the client a workable plan of action. The worker then ended the interview and was escorted by the mother out of the door onto the outside porch. At this point, a small puppy standing on the porch lifted its leg and urinated directly onto the porch floor. As the worker was ending the meeting by making plans for another visit, she watched the puppy in amazement. The mother, who was also watching the puppy's behavior, looked up at the worker and said, "Well, at least he didn't do it inside the house." The worker then said good-bye and left.

This situation did indeed shock the worker, who found it hard to accept that a person could effect such little control over her and her family's environment. This was an extremely difficult case. The many problems involved included abject poverty, depression, physical child abuse, sexual abuse, and alcoholism. Although it is beyond the scope of this book to do a lengthy case analysis, let it be said that this mother felt she had little control over her environment. This was manifested by the dirty house and the urinating puppy. She felt she had little control over her children. Finally, she felt she had little control over herself. The whole point of this is that it is critically important for generalist practitioners to focus on the client and the client's problems rather on their own uncomfortable reactions. This woman and her family desperately needed help.

Although dirt seems to be the emphasis in the prior examples, it must be stressed that many other things can be learned from a visit to the client's home environment. Two examples also involve adolescent males who attended the day treatment center for "emotionally disturbed" youth mentioned earlier.

The first case involves a thirteen-year-old. His primary problems involved his insensitivity to the feelings of others and his long history of delinquent behavior. The latter included shoplifting, battery, and theft. He was extremely bright and seemed to enjoy manipulating his peers so that they would get into trouble. For example, he would goad one peer whom he knew to be extremely impressionable into shooting a spit wad at another peer whom he knew would get angry, jump up, and try to punch the spitter. Meanwhile, he'd sit back, watch, and enjoy the activity.

A home visit revealed some interesting information. He lived alone with his single mother and seventeen-year-old brother, the latter of whom was not very involved with the other two. His mother was very straightforward, terse, and sarcastic. She refused to answer most of the questions the worker asked. The interview was very short, due to the fact that after fifteen minutes, the mother abruptly asked the worker to leave her home. The worker's impression was that she was a very cold, uncaring person who kept any emotions carefully in check. The interesting and striking observation of the home environment was that not only was each piece of furniture carefully covered with transparent plastic but so were the lampshades and the drapes. Additionally, there were plastic runners on the carpet over the major walkways. The rooms were spotless and covered in plastic. The worker noted that it was the coldest "home" she had ever been in.

Several therapeutic implications of the home situation for the thirteen-year-old's treatment were established. It appeared that he had never had the chance to learn how to care about anyone but himself. Apparently, he had rarely if ever been the recipient of love, caring, and warmth. How could he learn such feelings and behaviors if he had never experienced them? It was almost as if he had a lack of conscience. He made certain that he was taken care of but cared little or nothing about anyone else.

Another example of a home visit illustrated what can be learned about the family environment. This sixteen-year-old male client also attended the aforementioned day treatment center for emotionally disturbed adolescents. He had been enrolled in the program for two primary reasons. First, he was significantly behind academically. Second, he had broken into several of his neighbors' garages to steal tools.

In the program, he had much difficulty relating to peers but was very cooperative with staff. He never misbehaved and would volunteer for extra tasks.

A home visit revealed some interesting things about this client. He lived with his single mother and his eleven-year-old sister, the latter of whom had Down's syndrome. The family lived in the second story of an ancient house in one of the poorest areas of the inner city. The furniture was old and mismatched but neatly arranged. There was a pervasive aura of warmth throughout. For instance, crocheted doilies were carefully arranged under knickknacks and lamps. When the worker arrived, there was a pleasant aroma of something being fried in the kitchen. The walls were carefully spotted with paint designs made to look like wallpaper. Most of the other rooms had doors onto the living room so their walls could also be seen. Each room had similar painted designs. Each was painstakingly painted in a different color.

The mother, a short, frail-appearing woman, greeted the worker at the door with a wide smile. She proudly introduced her daughter, who was observably developmentally disabled. The sixteen-year-old client was also in the room. When talking and answering questions, each, especially the mother and son, looked at each other, smiled at each other, and talked to each other about which answers would be most correct. At two points during the interview, the mother asked her son to get something for her. Each time he did so immediately and apparently very willingly. The mother appeared to be very concerned about both of her children and very willing to help.

The worker found out a lot about her sixteen-year-old client. Apparently, until about one year earlier, he had lived with his father somewhere in the rural Deep South. One day, for no determinable reason, his father purchased a Greyhound bus ticket for him and put him on the bus to live with his mother in a northern urban city. It continued to be unclear how long he had initially lived with his mother before going to live with his father.

When he got to the city, he felt, frankly, like "a fish out of water." Although he happened to be African American and lived in a primarily African American neighborhood, he was totally unsophisticated regarding urban living. As a result, he hated school, had no friends, and resorted to stealing tools so that he would have something to do. He loved to tinker with wood and machines, and seemed to have some talent in that area.

This home visit revealed much about this client. Apparently, he received much warmth and support from his mother. It also appeared he was in no way a discipline problem to her. He was very unlike most of his peers in the treatment center. Although they came from a variety of racial and ethnic backgrounds, they virtually all were oriented toward urban living, came from dysfunctional families, and had serious, long-term mental health problems. Intervention implications for this client involved examining his interpersonal skills and interactions with his peers. Among other things, he needed to build his self-confidence. Other implications concerned improving his academic performance and looking at possible vocations involving skilled trades.

Scheduling Home Visits

Home visits should be at a time as convenient as possible for family members. Oftentimes, this is not during typical nine-to-five office hours. Evenings or even weekends might be the only times family members are usually home. Here, it's helpful if you have a job where such flexible scheduling is possible. Otherwise, you must work overtime or accept the fact that some home visits are impossible to make within your job specifications.

Home visits can be scheduled by phone. During the initial conversation, you should identify who you are and clearly state the purpose of the visit. For instance, you would like to talk about son Hampton's progress in school.

Some clients will not have phones. This makes it more difficult to arrange for a visit. In this case, one possibility is to write the family and schedule a time which you anticipate to be most convenient for them. Simply notify them that since you can't contact them by phone, you would like to meet with them at a specific time and date in their home. You might then ask them to notify you if that time is bad for them. You also might ask them to suggest another time which they feel is better for them.

Sometimes this won't work. I once attempted to visit a family four times without success. Each time, I notified them by mail as suggested above. Each time, I stopped by their house and rang the doorbell to no avail. They were either not at home or were pretending this. The bottom line is that they simply did not want to see me, for whatever reason. On this occasion, I had to accept the fact that I would be unable to make that particular visit.

Taking Care of Your Own Safety

It is important to consider your safety when visiting various areas and neighborhoods. Some areas are simply "rougher" than others. You must weigh the extent to which you need or are required to make a home visit against the potential danger in which it will place you. For instance, a home visit in a gang-ridden, urban neighborhood at night is probably a bad idea.

You should also be aware of areas with high crime rates and take as many precautions as possible. Be aware of where you are and who is around you. If racial tensions are high and you are of a minority race in a neighborhood, it's especially important to be aware of this.

This warning is not meant to scare you. Neighborhoods, as we know, vary drastically regarding these safety issues. It is important to be aware of facts and make rational decisions. Highlight 5.3 identifies a number of safety tips.

Assessment in Mezzo Practice: Assessing Groups

In the assessment process, a generalist practitioner identifies a need and then may determine that this need can best be met through formulating and working with a group of individuals. Needs involve virtually any issue. A category of clients may have some kind of treatment need because of problems they have (for example, alcohol addiction, incest, or lack of assertiveness). There may be a need to structure a group within an agency to work on policies needing revision. Or there may be a need to formulate a group for lobbying a state legislature to change an excessively restrictive public assistance policy.

In chapter 3, we recognized the two major types of groups, task and treatment. Task groups, of course, are designed to do just that. They are formed to accomplish some specified task or goal. Treatment groups, on the other hand, focus on goals targeting growth, remedying problems, providing education, or enhancing socialization (Toseland & Rivas, 1984).

Assessment in groups is an ongoing process carried out prior to the group's formation, throughout intervention, and after completion of the group (Rose, 1981; Toseland & Rivas, 1984). As we know, assessment and evaluation are two sides of the same coin. During the initial assessment phase, problems, strengths, and needs must be clearly established so that progress may later be evaluated. Regardless of the type of group, two dimensions must be the first focus of attention. These are *potential sponsorship* and *potential membership*.

HIGHLIGHT 5.3
Be Alert, Streetwise, and Safe

You can do a great deal to reduce your risk of becoming a victim of crime. The most effective weapons against crime are *common sense, alertness,* and *involvement.* Armed with these, you can protect yourself by reducing the opportunity for muggers, purse snatchers, and other street criminals to strike.

Elementary Street Sense

- Wherever you are, be alert to what's going on around you. Don't get distracted or daydream. Look to see who is ahead of, beside, and behind you.
- Communicate visually that you are a calm, confident individual. Stand tall with your head erect, and walk purposefully. Make quick eye contact with the people around you, so that you give the impression of awareness.
- Always trust your instincts. If you feel uncomfortable in a place or situation, leave as soon as possible.
- Don't drop your guard because you feel that you are in a familiar area. Crime knows no boundaries.

Walking Smart

- Plan the safest route to your destination and USE IT. On the sidewalk, use the part farthest away from shrubs, doorways, and alleys, where people can hide.
- Walk with a companion whenever possible. There is safety in numbers.
- Learn the neighborhood. A few minutes to notice what stores are open, the type of street lighting, and the locations of telephones may be important if you need help later.
- If you are carrying a purse, hold it close to

your body or wear it under your coat. Keep a firm grip on the purse, and don't let it hang loosely by its straps. Wallets should be carried in an inside coat or front trouser pocket.
- Don't overburden yourself with books, backpacks, or packages. Avoid wearing shoes or clothing that restricts your movements. Notice how many women executives wearing five-hundred-dollar suits walk the city streets in designer sneakers. Three-inch high heels would make them easy prey for attack.
- Have your key in your hand when entering your residence or car. This allows quick access and also provides a weapon if you're attacked. Remember to look into the back seat before getting into your car to make sure nobody is hiding there.
- Avoid carrying large amounts of money. Don't wear expensive jewelry or clothing when going on home visits. Thieves give in easily to temptation.
- Consider buying and carrying a shriek alarm.
- Leave all headphones at home. You need to use all your senses. Headphones eliminate sounds which would alert you to danger.
- Don't give money to people who ask for it on the street. Your "loose change" is not really going to help their situation. Instead, volunteer some time to a local program designed to help the homeless.

Elevator Sense

- Familiarize yourself with the emergency buttons of the elevators you ride frequently. Always stand near the controls.
- Look inside the elevator before you get on board to make sure nobody is hiding inside.
- Get off the elevator if someone suspicious en-

ters. If you are uneasy about someone who is waiting with you for the elevator, pretend that you have forgotten something and don't get on the elevator with the person. Listen to your gut reactions and intuition about what and who is around you.

- If you're attacked while in the elevator, hit the alarm button and as many floor buttons as possible.

Defensive Driving

- Always lock your car doors, even when driving. Don't put your purse or other valuables on the seat next to you. Thieves have broken windows, even while a car is waiting at a stoplight, to reach inside and steal. Keep your windows rolled up whenever possible.
- Keep your car in good running condition and always have enough gas to get where you're going and back again. If you do have car trouble, raise the hood and sit in the locked car. If someone offers to help, always stay in the car. Ask them to call the police to help you.
- Park in well-lighted areas which will still be well-lit when you return to your car. If you expect to return to your car after dark, park near or under a light.

Tips for Buses

- Use well-lighted and busy bus stops. Stand with other people whenever possible.
- Sit near the front, close to the driver. Do not fall asleep.
- If someone is harassing you, tell him firmly and loudly, "Leave me alone!" Persistent persons should be reported to the driver.
- Be alert to who gets off the bus with you. If you feel uneasy, walk directly to a place where there are other people.

If You Are Threatened

- Remain calm—try not to panic or show any signs of confusion.
- Don't resist if the attacker is armed or is only after your valuables. You don't want to escalate a property crime into a violent confrontation.
- If resistance is an option, don't get scared. Get mad! Shout, "No!", "Stop!", "Fire!", or "Call the police!" loudly and forcefully. Try to incapacitate or distract your assailant long enough to escape. A jab to the throat or eyes, even a swift kick to the knees or groin may give you a few minutes to get away or attract attention for help.
- After the attack, call the police *immediately*. Identify yourself and your location. During the attack, make a conscious effort to get a good look at the assailant: his facial features, type of clothing/shoes, height and weight, race and sex, or anything distinctive about him (for instance, a large nose or obvious scars). If a vehicle is involved, try to get the license number.
- *Remember* that any crime is a traumatic experience, even if you're not hurt. Turn to others for help and support. Tell your field supervisor and faculty liaison. Allow others to help you get in touch with such supportive services as a victim assistance program.

Source: This material has been adapted from the pamphlet *How to Be "Streetwise"—and Safe,* published by the Marquette University Public Safety Department. Used with permission of the Marquette University Public Safety Department, 1212 W. Wisconsin Ave., Milwaukee, WI, 53233.

Potential Sponsorship

Almost all practitioners function under job descriptions, summaries of the duties and responsibilities inherent in the particular worker's job. Working with task and treatment groups may or may not synchronize well with the worker's primary job responsibilities. The extent to which the job description incorporates working with groups directly impacts the ease with which a worker can run groups.

Consider the worker responsible for multitudinous duties, none of which directly correlate with formulating groups. Work with groups may be difficult or impossible for that worker to do. She may have no time flexibility in view of her other duties. Likewise, the agency may see working with groups as an activity of relatively low priority for that worker. On the other hand, a job description which includes the responsibility of teaching parenting skills to individuals and *groups*, thereby, includes group work as a natural part of the worker's expected activities.

The agency's sponsorship or support of group work is very important (Shulman, 1984). Before beginning work with groups, a worker must assess the extent to which this support exists. Toseland and Rivas (1984) explain, "Treatment groups rely on agency administrators and staff for sanctions, financial support, member referrals, and physical facilities for the group. Similarly, task groups are intrinsically linked to the functioning of their sponsoring agencies and must continually refer back to the agency's policies for clarification of their task, charge, and mandate" (pp. 119–20).

Treatment groups may be incorporated into the goals of agencies geared to working with some category of clients' problems. Running such groups may then be part of the worker's normal routine. On the other hand, the agency administration may be oriented toward working with *individuals* on their specific problems. Strong resistance on the part of the administration makes the formulation of groups very difficult and, sometimes, impossible. When you consider forming a treatment group, it's very important to assess your agency's support of such an endeavor. If support is seriously lacking, you should ask yourself if the time and effort it will take are worth it.

Assessment regarding agency support of task groups is also important. If you determine that a task group is needed to accomplish some purpose or fulfill some need, you must first assess how open the agency is to evaluating issues and implementing changes in policy and practice. A number of questions may be appropriate: Do agency decison makers typically react positively to innovative suggestions? Or does the agency usually adhere tightly to how things have been done in the past? Which decision makers might be most likely to provide support for a task group? What kinds of information would be helpful to them? Are the chances of successfully formulating a task group worth the effort it will take to persuade the administration to support it? In summary, the practitioner must assess the potential agency support, how that support might best be mustered, and, in the end, whether it's worth the effort.

Who Should Be Members of the Group?

Assessing agency support should be done very early in the assessment process. Another early step concerns figuring out who the group members should be. This involves clearly defining the proposed group's purpose and addressing a number of questions: What characteristics should group members have? How will their needs be met by the group's purpose? How motivated will they be?

Toseland and Rivas (1984) suggest that the practitioner collect information about potential group members. What are potential members' problems, needs, and strengths? Information can be gathered through interviewing, consultation with colleagues about the problem or issue, and reading any available information and documentation about the issue.

Selection Criteria for Treatment Group Membership

Unfortunately, there appears to be no clear-cut recipe for perfect group membership. Shulman (1984) reflects upon this by telling an entertaining story. He relates how he once led a group of five couples having marital problems. A group of students observed the counseling sessions on video in a nearby room. Following the first session (which, by the way, had gone very well), students flooded him with a number of specific questions about how the group was formed.

First, the students asked how the group had been composed, as members of couples ranged in age from their twenties to their seventies. The students apparently wondered what kind of prescribed plan had led the group leader to compose the group so creatively and successfully. Shulman replied, "much to the disappointment of the group" of students, that these were the only five couples available (p. 186).

One of the students then asked how the magic number of five couples was established, once again in view of the excellent and dynamic interaction observed during the first session. Shulman replied that the room available to them only had space enough for five couples.

Finally, the students asked how the group leader had arrived at such a specific plan, namely, that the group would be run for exactly twenty-three sessions and then terminate. One might imagine a complex algebraic formula filled with x's and n's and hieroglyphic-like symbols. The group leader responded that for administrative reasons they couldn't get started any earlier than they did and there were only twenty-three weeks until the end of the semester. So much for concise scientific assessment and planning.

On a more serious note, the point is that most groups are formed and run while dealing with limited resources, infinite variation of individual characteristics, and agency or job constrictions. A precise formula involving exacting measurements is unrealistic and virtually impossible. However, there are a number of "common sense" principles which can help to determine group composition. These include motivation, group purpose, common communication skills, and a generalized assessment of the potential rewards and punishments of the group.

Motivation

Yalom (1985) stresses that the most critical variable in including a particular member in a group is motivation. If the individual is not committed to the group and not willing to work on behalf of herself and the group, little can be accomplished in the group.

However, oftentimes generalist practitioners will be in the situation of running treatment groups where members are wary or simply involuntary. For example, take groups run in residential treatment centers or group homes for children with behavioral and emotional problems. Or consider a deferred prosecution group where first-time offenders are given the choice of paying a large fine, going to jail for a while, or participating in a group (such a group would focus on increasing self-awareness, understanding one's motivation for committing the crime, and designing ways to avoid committing the crime in the future).

It's important for a worker to make an accurate assessment of a client's motivation for participating in a group. Often this involves more than the decision of whether a member will or will not become a member of a group. It will also involve the extent to which the worker needs to work on enhancing the motivational level of an individual or that of the entire group.

Group Purpose

It makes sense that people are assessed and selected for membership in a particular treatment group for some clearly specified reason. The reason might be to work on marital issues as mentioned above. Likewise, any number of other reasons might be pertinent (a social skills improvement group, a child management group, or a support group for children with parents placed in a nursing home). The important thing is that group members are there to work together on some common problem or issue (Rose, 1981).

Common Communication Skills

Group treatment is based on communication. Whatever is accomplished in a group is done through this medium. Therefore, group members must be able to communicate effectively with each other (Rose, 1981). This implies that group members should have a similar ability to use language and express themselves. The important thing is for you to determine that group members will be able to communicate ideas and feelings to each other adequately.

Group Rewards versus Punishments

Yalom (1985, p. 248) proposes "a simple punishment-reward system" as a perspective on assessing an individual's potential for group membership. If the rewards of the group exceed the punishments or unappealing aspects of the group, then that individual member will probably be motivated to continue in the group. Such rewards might include the potential for seeing improvement in the handling of the problem, decreased emotional pain, enjoyment of other group members, or increase in self-confidence. Punishments, on the other hand, might include the time and effort it takes to participate, dislike of or lack of communication with other group members, or resentment about feeling forced to participate.

Toseland and Rivas (1984) suggest some approaches for dealing with resistance on the part of group members. "Discussions that center on the reasons for the mandatory nature of the group are . . . sometimes helpful in overcoming resistance. The worker can ask members to discuss their perceptions of why they are required to attend, their feelings about mandated participation, and how they might best use the group experience that they are required to attend" (p. 121).

Gathering Information about Potential Treatment Group Members

For treatment groups, Rose (1981) suggests at least two primary assessment mechanisms. First, interviews with potential group members prior to beginning the group are helpful. Assessment regarding the clients' problems, communication skills, social interaction skills, prior experience with groups, attitudes toward such a group, and motivation to participate can all be assessed.

A second mechanism involves the use of "self-rating tests" (p. 32). There are many such highly developed and widely used instruments available. The appropriate instrument would be chosen, of course, in view of the problem to be addressed. For example, earlier in this chapter in a section on assessment in micro practice, several such instruments were mentioned, including the Rathus Assertiveness Schedule. Yalom (1985) mentions traditional psychological testing as another possible means of providing useful information about potential group members.

Selection Criteria for Task Group Membership

Selection criteria for task groups are similar to that for treatment groups. Toseland and Rivas (1984) suggest a number of variables to consider, including the individual's interest, areas of expertise, homogeneity versus heterogeneity of group members, prestige in the community, relationship with the sponsoring agency, and potential members' demographic characteristics.

Sociograms

A common technique for assessing children's interaction is referred to as *sociometry* (Rose, 1981). This involves asking children questions about their relationships and feelings toward other people. After information is gathered, the relationships can be illustrated on a diagram called a *sociogram*. Sociograms can be extremely useful for assessing children's interactional patterns. This is especially true for those who have low self-esteem and difficulty relating to their peers. A sociogram can be a "sensitive instrument for demonstrating change of behavior in children" after treatment (Rose, 1981, p. 33).

Children in a group might be asked such questions as which three peers do they like the best, which three do they like the least, who do they most admire, who would they like to sit next to, and who are they most afraid of. Each child can be represented by a circle. Arrows can then be drawn to the people they indicate in answer to each question.

A sociogram of a special education class is depicted below. A sociogram can be created to illustrate the results of each question asked. Our example plots out two questions. Sociogram A reflects students' feelings about who they thought was the strongest leader in the group. Sociogram B illustrates which peer they most liked in the group.

Sociogram A clearly illustrates that Toby was thought to be the strongest leader in the group. He is bright, energetic, and very "street smart." However, Sociogram B clearly illustrates that he is not the most popular or best-liked in the group. Both Tom and Gertie shine there. They are more mature than the other group members. They are assertive and fairly self-confident yet don't impose their will on the others. They are among the brightest in the group. Toby, on the other hand, is more feared than respected in the group. The others admire his apparent sophistication yet don't trust him. He doesn't let anyone get close to him either emotionally or even spatially.

Vince's opinions differ radically from the other group members. Vince stays by himself most of the time. He loves to wander off whenever he can sneak away. He sees Dean as being both a strong and likable leader. Dean is a very active, verbal person who is always in the center of activity. He has some trouble controlling his behavior and tends to provoke the other students. Perhaps Vince admires Dean's involvement.

These two sociograms are examples of how a group's interaction can be assessed and visually pictured. Although they only begin to portray some of the complexities of the group's interaction, they do provide some interesting clues upon which later interventions can be planned.

Sociogram A

Sociogram B

Individual Interests

It's essential for a group leader to assess the extent to which a potential member is genuinely interested in the group and the group's task. This is directly related to motivation—a motivated individual is more likely to cooperate and work in the group. In assessing potential motivation, a worker might ask himself or herself a number of questions. For instance, what interest has the individual expressed in this or similar tasks before? How important will the potential member view the tasks? What direct or indirect benefits might the individual get out of the group (for example, increased status, enjoyable or profitable interpersonal contacts, or greater visibility)?

Expertise

As discussed in chapter 3, task groups often need a range of competencies or expertise to best accomplish their goals. For instance, a task group aimed at establishing a rape crisis center could benefit by inclusion of a physician concerning the medical implications, a police officer regarding legal aspects, and representatives from local women's groups regarding advocacy.

Homogeneity versus Heterogeneity

There are no clear guidelines regarding the extent to which a group should be homogeneous (composed of people with similar characteristics) or heterogeneous (consisting of people with dissimilar characteristics). On the one hand, group members need to be homogeneous enough to communicate and work with each other. Members must also be dissimilar enough to provide the necessary range of both skills and ideas. The group leader needs to attend to these issues, weigh the pros and cons of various alternatives, and make final decisions regarding what is potentially best for the group and its purpose.

Prestige in the Community

Many times, depending on the group's purpose, it's important to gain outside public support in order to accomplish a task. This can involve inviting important or well-respected community members to join the group.

An example involves a task group aimed at developing a stronger sex-education program in a school district. Appropriate members might not only include such experts in sexuality education as teachers in that area, but also local religious leaders, lawyers, physicians, and business people. Sometimes this task is very controversial. Recruiting religious leaders might lend increased public trust to the group.

Likewise, involving respected professionals leads to enhanced credibility. Finally, tapping local businesses for membership can sometimes gain financial assistance.

Relationship with the Sponsoring Agency

Some task groups are formed within an agency. For example, a task group for updating staff policies might best be composed of an agency's own staff members. However, other task groups might be more effective if they involve a cross section of various agency and community members.

For instance, consider a task group whose purpose is to reestablish funding of a special treatment program for adolescents with behavioral and emotional problems. The urban county which had previously supported the development and maintenance of the program slashed the program from its budget during a financial crisis. The most effective task group in this case might include agency personnel who had been providing the service, parents of children whose treatment had been cut off, and any other professional, religious, and business community leaders who support the program.

Demographic Characteristics

At least two demographic variables are often important when assembling a task group: gender balance within the group and "sociocultural factors" (Toseland & Rivas, 1984, p. 129).

The worker, of course, needs to use his common sense regarding the extent to which such demographic characteristics are important. Sometimes, potential members with diverse characteristics will not be available. Other times, such members will not want to join the group.

However, it's generally important for the worker to attend to both gender and ethnic/racial/cultural balance within a group. Task groups aimed at providing services to women should have adequate representation of women in their membership. Likewise, task groups working on an issue involving some ethnic, racial, or cultural group should have adequate representation from the relevant group or groups in their membership. What "adequate" means is at the discretion of the worker's professional judgment.

Gender and sociocultural balance is especially important because of traditional oppressive power imbalances. In other words, it is no longer acceptable (and it never was just) for white males to make decisions about women or racial minorities. Members of oppressed groups must be involved in and in control of decisions that affect them.

Recruiting Task Group Members

The next step involves the recruitment process for potential members (Toseland & Rivas, 1984). Task group members can be targeted using the variables described above. The worker can personally invite the individual to become a member of the group via a meeting, phone call, or letter. Additionally, the worker can publicize the need for members with certain areas of expertise or interests through fliers, notices in newsletters and newspapers, and even announcements in the radio and television media.

Ongoing Group Assessment

We've established that assessment in groups is an ongoing process. A practitioner is responsible for monitoring the ongoing group climate. This climate includes the breadth of variables discussed in chapter 3. One especially relevant area for assessment involves "communication and interaction patterns" (Toseland & Rivas, 1984, p. 174). This involves many of the concepts discussed in chapter 3. The practitioner's responsibility as group leader is to monitor the openness of communication and the appropriateness of interactions. This involves encouraging participation of all group members yet not allowing domination. It also concerns establishing and maintaining group structure so that progress can continuously be made toward accomplishing group goals.

Ongoing Assessment in Treatment Groups

A number of ongoing assessment mechanisms have been developed for treatment groups (Rose, 1981; Toseland & Rivas, 1984). First, the individual self-rating questionnaires previously mentioned can be administered periodically to monitor progress in specific areas.

Second, clients may keep diaries of daily events concerning the problems addressed in treatment. This approach helps clients focus on their problems and their progress toward solving them.

A third assessment mechanism involves charting their improvement. This is discussed more thoroughly in chapter 8. Simple charting might involve noting on a chart whenever a specified behavior occurs. For example, a client involved in an assertiveness training group might note on a chart each time she musters up enough confidence to contact another person by phone outside of the group.

Role-playing within the group provides a fourth assessment mechanism. The group leader can ask group members to practice what they've learned in the group. The worker may then observe their progress, share his or her perceptions with the clients, and provide suggestions for improvement. After role playing, the worker can also solicit feedback from other group members. This can be useful both to the role players and to the individuals assessing them and articulating their feedback.

Finally, the worker can bring in outside observers to assess treatment groups. Observers can be used either in the group or to report clients' observed progress outside the group. An outsider observing the group, for instance, can note how frequently each group member speaks and for how long.

Another example concerns assessment feedback outside of a socialization group for children. The worker might contact the children's teachers to determine the extent to which they apply what they learn in the group to outside situations.

Assessment in Macro Practice

Micro practice, mezzo practice, and macro practice are all intimately intertwined. Any practice, of course, involves working with other people, which necessitates the mastery of micro skills. Macro practice does not involve a focus on individuals or even on groups of individuals. Rather, as we've established in chapter 4, macro practice focuses on making positive changes which affect large numbers of people. To implement these changes, generalist practitioners must work together with other individuals and groups. Thus, macro practice is both based upon and highly interactive with the other two practice modes. Hence, we have the generalist social work practitioner.

In the recent past and current eras of shrinking resources, the profession has become increasingly focused on the social environment and the context in which social workers practice. Meenaghan (1987) states that macro practice "denotes a range of interrelated competencies in designing and evaluating services and in administering them in a community and interorganizational context" (p. 83).

In other words, generalist practioners need to attend to the environment in which they work. The remainder of this chapter will focus on one example of macro system assessment, namely the assessment of a community's needs.

Assessment of Community Needs

Social workers often need to confront the environment in which they work. Absolutely necessary services may be unavailable. Public bureaucracies may be detachedly unresponsive to clients' needs. Archaic policies may significantly interfere with clients' lives.

Thus, the generalist practitioner may need to work to make changes within the community in which clients live. It's difficult at first for many students to focus on community change instead of trying to change the client or something about how the client lives. Nonetheless, combating inequities in the system can be a productive way to initiate changes for large groups of people.

When trying to assess clients' needs within a community, the first thing to do is to define what a community is. As we've discussed in chapter 4, there are a number of ways of conceptualizing communities, including those focusing on geographical boundaries and those emphasizing groups of people with common interests and needs. For our purposes, the important thing is for generalist practitioners to clearly define the communities with which they work, regardless of the definition they choose to use.

Community needs assessment entails evaluation of "problems, existing resources, potential solutions, and obstacles to problem solving . . . on behalf of all the residents. The purpose of needs assessments is to document needs and establish priorities for service" (Barker, 1991, p. 153). Essentially, then, a community needs assessment does just what the name implies—

it involves assessment of a community's needs. Northwood (1964) makes an interesting distinction between the concept of "need" and of "problem." He states, "A need usually refers to a lack of something, which lack contributes to the discomfort of members of the group. A problem usually refers to the presence of something, which presence contributes to the discomfort of members of the group" (p. 202). In other words, needs involve what's missing, while problems concern negative happenings already in existence.

There is no one best approach to community needs assessment. Each situation and approach is unique. However, there are at least four general variables to take into account when considering a needs assessment—"information," "resources available," "state of program development," and "community attitudes" (Siegel, Attkisson & Carson, 1987, p. 72).

Information

Before attempting a needs assessment, it's important to know what kind of information you're after. If you're working for a local agency, what information would be most relevant in terms of what that agency will be able to do? What are the best ways of obtaining the most useful information? How difficult will the information be to obtain? Will the information be accurate enough to make effective decisions?

Resources Available

A second variable to consider involves resources. On the one hand, you'll need enough support and financial backing to conduct the assessment. On the other hand, how desperate is the community to have its needs met? In other words, are the needs extremely grave and meriting immediate attention? Will the potential rewards of the assessment merit the time and expense it will take to conduct it?

State of Program Development

Consideration of the current state of the community's resource system is also important. Are there other already existing resources in the community which could potentially meet the community's needs at lesser costs? Would a needs assessment provide information useful for changing or improving the current state of the resource provision system?

Community Attitudes

Finally, community attitudes are important to consider prior to conducting a needs assessment. Will relevant community members be willing to provide information and participate in the assessment process? Does the community have the potential to respond positively to the implications of such an assessment? Will you find support in the community to carry out the assessment and implement recommendations? Or will you encounter such massive resistance that the process will seem like fighting on a battlefield?

An Example of a Community Assessment

In order to work with people in a community and understand their needs, it's important to be familiar with the culture, values, priorities, issues, and problems characterizing the community. Warren and Warren (1984) propose one process for analyzing a community or neighborhood, which includes the assessment of needs. Their step-by-step assessment guide can be used "to capture the distinctive interwoven helping patterns—the networks crisscrossing the neighborhood fabric" which makes each neighborhood or community unique (p. 27). First, the four-step process of performing a needs assessment will be explained. Next, a format for gathering information will be provided in Highlight 5.5.

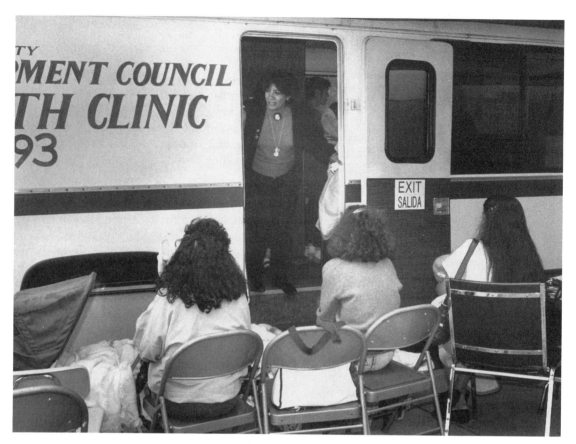

A social worker may need to assess the capability of a mobile medical van in meeting the health-care needs of a community's low-income citizens.

Step 1: Exploring the Nature of the Neighborhood

The first step in the investigatory process involves finding out how people in the neighborhood function. Before you *do* anything, you need enough background information to know *what* you're doing. How do people in the neighborhood or community solve their problems? What resources are available to work with? Answers to these questions begin to provide you with information about the community's strengths and weaknesses. They can also help you determine the community's needs.

Local centers of government are good places to get information during this phase of your community assessment. A city hall, local courthouse, branch of social services, the chamber of commerce, and even a library all have useful information. There might be pamphlets available about the community. Or notices about community events and services might be posted to inform the public (and you) about what generally goes on within the community.

Getting maps can be tremendously helpful. This can increase your confidence and agility in getting around the community. Maps also can give you information about how the community you're assessing fits in with surrounding communities or neighborhoods.

Telephone books also provide useful information. Not only can you find out where government offices are but you can also find and explore the types of businesses in the community, the health-care services available, and such other resources as churches and activity centers.

Newspapers harbor a lot of information. Advertisements reflect what businesses are available and what appears to be significant in the local culture. News items reflect what the community feels is important. For instance, consider the fact that local cow prices are regularly posted on the front page of the small rural paper, the *Benjamin Key*. This implies that many community residents are rural farmers interested in this type of news.

Even if your job is more oriented toward micro or mezzo levels of social work practice, getting to know your clients' community is significant. Getting information and thinking about a community can prepare you much more effectively for working with its people. You begin to know what to expect.

Step 2: Getting to Know the Area and Its Residents

Getting a general impression of the community is probably the most useful thing to do at this point. Drive around the area and pay attention to what it's like. What are the buildings like? Are they well-kept or in disrepair? Do some buildings look abandoned? Where do people seem to congregate? What businesses characterize the community? What are your general impressions of the community as a whole? Does it appear to be thriving or desolate, safe or unsafe, well-managed or disorganized?

As you continue to explore, establish the community's boundaries in your own mind.

What areas in the community will be your chief concern? Are there geographical boundaries which characterize the community? For instance, is there a main street on which community members focus their attention? Or, do rivers, valleys, or industrial sections cut the community in half or in sections?

Step 3: Identify the Community's Strengths

We've already established that in generalist social work practice, assessing strengths is just as important as evaluating problems or needs. Healthy businesses, homes kept in good repair, social clubs and organizations (for instance, Boy Scouts, bowling teams, or the Polish Nationalist Society), churches, and even friendly interaction with community residents all contribute to the community's strengths.

Step 4: Talk to People in the Community

Identifying major community figures is critical. Talking with these people can give you substantial insight into the fabric and values of the community.

Warren and Warren (1984) emphasize that the elementary school principal is "a MUST" (p. 32). The person in this position is in regular contact with the core of community residents. The principal must work integrally with community families and understand their issues. You can obtain information about the economic situation, what types of recreation people generally enjoy, religious affiliations, racial tensions, and other concerns from this person.

Other individuals to contact include a range of community leaders. You should not force yourself to contact every leader. Rather, identify those whom you feel might have information most relevant for your needs. These might include local ministers and priests, such public officials as aldermen, the town board chairper-

---
HIGHLIGHT 5.5

A Format for Analyzing a Community or Neighborhood

Below is a prescribed format for analyzing a community. It addresses community characteristics and community life. Additionally, it assesses the public welfare and social service system available in the community. Suggestions for assessing a community have already been provided. Now we will provide a format for the specific types of questions to ask and how to organize that information.

The questions asked in the various sections are not exhaustive nor all of equal importance. They are suggested as beginnings in a search for change. Some of them may not be useful or may not fit your particular local government. However, most can be adapted. Some may uncover issues that require more careful study than this format allows.

One other thing to remember is that a community is not an isolated entity. Rather, it is part of a much larger social, legal, and political system. What's decided at the national, state, and even county levels can have awesome impacts upon a community's functioning. The following format directs attention only to the community itself. It will at least, however, give you a jumping-off point for beginning to understand your community:

A. Community Characteristics
   1. *Ethnic/Racial Configuration*
      What are the major population characteristics (for example, what percentage is white, African American, Vietnamese, American Indian, or Hispanic)?
      What are the principal ethnic and religious groups?
      What is the age composition?
      How do the population characteristics compare to state and national demographics?
   2. *Economic Factors*
      What are the principal economic characteristics of the community?
      How are most of the people employed?
      What are the major industries?
      What other sources of wealth are there?

Have there been recent changes in the economic life of the community (for example, having industries moving in or out of the area, or having major expansions or cutbacks)?
   3. *Unemployment*
      What is the unemployment rate?
      How does this rate compare with state and national rates?
      What variables tend to characterize the unemployed population (that is, is it largely African American, Hispanic, female, or within the eighteen to twenty-two-year-old age range)?
      Have there been recent changes in this unemployment rate?
      If so, to what can these changes be attributed?
      Are there sections of the community where the rate is appreciably higher than the average?
   4. *Income levels*
      What is the median or per capita income?
      Is the average skewed because of large numbers of wealthy people?
      Are there large numbers of poor people in the community?
      How does the community's median income compare to state and national averages?
   5. *Housing Patterns*
      What are the housing patterns within the community?
      What percentage of residential property is high, moderate, or low-cost?
      What is the condition of the community's housing (for instance, mostly new, well-kept and maintained, or deteriorating)?
      What pattern characterizes the range of rents in the community?
      How available is moderate and low-cost housing?
      Is the community dependent on a large metropolitan area for employment?

Is the community dependent on a large metropolitan area for the housing of those who work in this community?

B. Community Life

1. *Communication and Interaction*

How many newspapers are there?

If there is more than one, are they independently owned?

How many radio and television stations are there?

Are radio and/or television stations owned by newspapers?

Is community news carried on a regular basis in a metropolitan newspaper?

What are the principal out-of-town media influences?

How does one learn about local governmental activities, hearings, meetings, or cultural activities?

2. *Social Services*

What private social service agencies exist in the community?

Are there specific organized groups aimed at improving social services within the community?

Is there joint fund-raising in the community, such as that provided by United Way?

What types of fund-raising exist in the community and why?

3. *Civic and Service Organizations*

What are principal community-wide civic and service organizations?

Are there fraternal groups?

Are there labor organizations?

Are there business organizations?

Are there cultural groups?

Do such groups work together on community-wide problems?

Are there coalitions among these groups on common interests?

Are such coalitions ad hoc groups or groups of longer standing?

Which groups are more likely to be aligned and on what kinds of issues?

Are there neighborhood groups?

If so, around what are they organized—cultural, school, political, or other interests?

C. Available Social Services

1. *Administration*

What governmental agencies are involved in operating the public welfare/social services in the community?

What employees are engaged in public welfare/social service activities?

How are these employees selected?

What qualifications are required?

What are these employees' salaries?

2. *Interagency Cooperation*

What cooperative programs, if any, exist between public welfare agencies and the juvenile court, probation officers, school, day-care centers, nursing homes, public health services, and other agencies?

What cooperation, if any, exists between public and private social service agencies?

If so, what form of cooperation exists?

Is there regular exchange of information?

Is there any joint planning going on?

3. *Non-Institutional Care*

What agency or agencies administer services for children who are abandoned or who have been abandoned?

Are foster homes used?

What is the rate of pay to foster homes?

How are such foster homes chosen?

How are such homes supervised?

What money is available for Aid to Families with Dependent Children?

What General Assistance is available?

What is the average amount available for each child?

What is the caseload per worker for income maintenance and social service workers?

Are there efforts being made to help parents find jobs?

┌─ **HIGHLIGHT 5.5** (*continued*) ──────────────────────────

If so, what kind of efforts?

Are there adequate day care centers?

Is there an adoption service?

4. *Other Public Assistance Programs*

What programs are there for blind and deaf persons?

What programs are there for permanently disabled persons?

What programs are there for partially disabled elderly persons who don't qualify for Social Security?

What other assistance programs exist (for example, temporary assistance, special and corrective needs, exceptional needs such as bus fares and help during emergencies, employment services, legal services, or others)?

What money is available for such assistance?

From what sources is it available?

How do individuals apply for such assistance?

How is information about such special assistance made available to the people?

D. Summary

In one to two paragraphs, summarize your major perceptions about this community.

───────────

Source: Most of this format for analyzing a community or neighborhood was adapted from *Know Your Community* (1972), published by the League of Women Voters of the United States. Used with permission of the League of Women Voters of the United States, Washington, DC.

son or the mayor, presidents of clubs and organizations (for instance, the Kiwanis Club or the Parent/Teacher Association), the heads of the homeowners' associations or Neighborhood Watch groups, prominent business people, and other social workers in the area.

Sometimes, there are extremely vocal community members whom others feel complain all the time. Talking to these people can be useful in targeting some of the community's hot spots. Oftentimes, these people are relatively easy to talk to because they want to have their gripes heard.

It's important to obtain information about a broad cross section of the community. This includes the wide range of age groups represented in the community. As we know, people's concerns vary according to their life's developmental stage. Additionally, it's critical to find out about all the primary ethnic and racial groups within the community. You need to know about values and customs. You also need to know about conflicts between groups in order to examine how the community really functions.

*Interviewing Persons
in the Community*

Warren and Warren (1984) make at least seven specific suggestions for things to say during your interviews with key community people. First, take time for "chit chat" (p. 34). The generalist practitioner utilizes micro practice skills even when pursuing a macro practice objective. In other words, it's important to gain a rapport with any new person you're interviewing. Warm, friendly, informal small talk about the weather, the place you're meeting, or the neighborhood itself is usually appropriate.

A second interviewing suggestion is to provide your interviewee with a clear definition of your purpose. Why are you there? Why should he take the time to talk to you? Your purpose might be to familiarize yourself with clients' community life because you've started a new job and will be working with them. Likewise, it might be that you're interested in initiating some new services within the community and would like to find out how to begin.

The third interviewing suggestion involves clearly explaining to your interviewee what community of people or neighborhood you're interested in. Is it a public school district (especially, if you're talking to a school principal)? Or, is it a geographical neighborhood delineated by specific streets marking off a specified number of city blocks? Or is it an entire town? Regardless, it's important for you and your interviewee to be talking about the same thing to avoid misunderstandings and inaccuracies.

A fourth suggestion for interviewing involves getting "leads" from your interviewee (Warren & Warren, 1984, p. 34). Who might better be aware of other people most involved in and knowledgeable about the community than those who are already integrally involved with that community? Get names, telephone numbers, and addresses, if available. Make decisions about who might be most helpful to you and follow through on contacting them.

The fifth suggestion involves the art of interviewing. Your micro practice skills will come in handy here. You want your interviewee to feel comfortable with you, open up to you, and share what he knows about the community. Sharing some information about yourself can be helpful. For instance, you might share how you lived in a similar neighborhood once or you might contrast this neighborhood with the one in which you now live. Your intent is to find out information about a community, not to fill in blanks on an established questionnaire. Therefore, you want to give your interviewee opportunities to talk and raise new topics. Providing some relevant information about yourself can enhance the interviewee's comfort with the interview. It can also convey to the interviewees that such initiation of their own thoughts, ideas, and other topics is appropriate.

A sixth suggestion for interviewing concerns getting specific information you need. You might "propose a hypothetical situation" (Warren & Warren, 1984, p. 35). For example, you might ask, "What if I contacted the person you suggested? Do you think she would be willing to take time and give me some information?" In another case you might say, "I'm thinking about plans for the future. What if I initiated the program we were talking about? How cooperative do you think the community would be?"

The seventh suggestion involves closure of the interview. It's easy to become very goal-oriented and press methodically for the information you need. However, it's also important to encourage your interviewee to share his or her feelings about the information already given or about the interview itself. You might simply ask if there's anything the person would like to add. In other words, make sure the interviewee has the opportunity to express himself and to conclude the interview.

Chapter Summary

This chapter discussed various micro, mezzo, and macro aspects of assessment in the problem-solving process. The difference between assessment and diagnosis was clarified and a model for assessment in generalist practice reviewed. Micro aspects of assessment include defining problems, discussing the many types of problems, identifying clients' strengths, and finding sources for gathering assessment information. Three specific micro assessment approaches were identified.

Choosing to work with families and necessary family assessment skills were discussed. The importance of home visits, their effectiveness, and suggestions for enhancing your own safety were examined.

Assessment issues in mezzo practice focused on both task and treatment groups. Ways of soliciting potential sponsorship and targeting potential membership were proposed.

Finally, assessment in macro practice was discussed, using a community needs assessment as an example. A process of analyzing a community or neighborhood was detailed.

6 *Planning in Generalist Practice*

Piecing it together and pinning it down

How would you plan to work with this case?

Robby, age six, has cerebral palsy. Cerebral palsy is a "disability resulting from damage to the brain before or during birth," which results in "muscular incoordination and speech disturbances" (*Webster's Ninth New Collegiate Dictionary*, 1991, p. 222). Robby can't walk and has difficulty controlling his hands. He lives with both parents and three sisters. His family is poor, despite the fact that his father works two minimum-wage jobs. His mother is unable to work outside of the home because of the extensive care her children, especially Robby, need.

Here is one way to plan what to do:

1. *Work closely with Robby and his parents.* They must believe in and be committed to the plan for it to succeed.
2. *Prioritize the problems.* Together with Robby's parents, you determine that Robby's physical disability is the top priority. Other prioritized problems and needs include respectively: inadequate finances; father's low skill level; mother's inability to work outside the home; the need for day care; and poor housing.
3. *Translate the problems into needs.* Work with the top priority problem first, Robby's disability. Robby needs a thorough evaluation to determine the extent of his disability. Depending on the findings, he may need such services as physical therapy, speech therapy, occupational therapy, or special education.
4. *Evaluate the level of intervention (micro, mezzo, or macro).* Will you initially plan to pursue a micro, mezzo, or macro approach to intervention? At this point, you select a micro intervention. You know that evaluation and therapeutic services are available. You also know that Robby's family will qualify for financial aid to receive these services because of its low income level. Thus, you determine you don't need to address problems in agency policies or the social service system's delivery of services (some potential macro approaches). Robby and his needs become the focus of attention right now. Such mezzo aspects of intervention as family counseling or support groups might be options in the future, but you determine they are inappropriate at this point in the intervention process.
5. *Establish primary goals.* You and the family decide that your primary goal will be to have Robby's capabilities thoroughly evaluated so that you will know what services he will need.
6. *Specify objectives.* You will schedule an evaluation through your agency and let the family know when it will be by one week from today.

CHAPTER SIX

7. *Formalize a contract.* You and Robby's parents establish a verbal contract. You will initiate and set up the evaluation process within the next week. Within that time period you will contact the family about the details. They are committed to bringing Robby in as soon as the evaluation can be scheduled.

Introduction

The example of Robby and his family portrays one way that you, as a generalist practitioner, might formulate a plan for intervention. This chapter will concentrate on seven basic steps that form the core of planning in the generalist intervention model. Planning involves establishing goals, specifying how such goals will be achieved, and selecting the most appropriate courses of action.

In the problem-solving process, planning immediately follows assessment and precedes the actual intervention. Your plan is based on your assessment of the client's situation, problems, needs, and strengths. Subsequently, your plan serves to guide how you proceed to help your client.

Specifically, this chapter will:

- Examine the seven-step planning process;
- Demonstrate how each of these steps can be applied in generalist practice;
- Employ a generalist perspective which integrates a micro, mezzo, and macro approach to social work practice;
- Discuss how goals and objectives are established and demonstrate the importance of specificity;
- Describe how to formulate contracts using various formats;
- Discuss special aspects of planning involved in mezzo practice;
- Examine program development and relate it to planning in macro practice.

Steps in the Planning Process

The seven steps in the planning process are working with your client(s), prioritizing problems, translating problems into needs, evaluating the level of intervention (micro, mezzo, or macro), establishing primary goals, specifying objectives, and formulating a contract. These steps are illustrated in Figure 6.1.

Step 1: Work with Your Client(s)

The importance of involving the client in every part of the intervention process cannot be emphasized enough. Jones and Biesecker[1] (1980) stress, "Clients should participate in the assessment and development of Goal Plans as much as possible. Plan *with* the person, not *at* or *for* him or her" (p. 7). This suggestion is pretty straightforward. However, it is easier to say than do. Especially with busy caseloads and numerous distractions, it's easy to pressure clients to accept the plans *you* would like them to make without soliciting adequate input from them. It takes time to talk with clients and clarify their needs and wishes. Be courteous to your clients, and make them feel that you are interested in what they have to say. If clients don't feel that they are included and, indeed, *own* the plan themselves, they will probably not be motivated to cooperate.

---

1. Martha Jones and John Biesecker have developed an excellent training workbook entitled *Goal Planning in Children and Youth Services* (1980) published by Training Resources in Permanent Planning Project (TRIPP), Millersville State College, Millersville, PA. Their work was supported by U.S. Department of HEW, Office of Human Development Services, Administration for Children, Youth and Families, Children's Bureau, Grant No. 90-C-0144. Much of the material in the goal planning section of this text is based upon their work. It is felt that the material can be applied not only to the broad range of services provided to children and youth, but to other fields of social work practice as well. It is especially relevant as a case management technique.

Figure 6.1: Planning in the Generalist Intervention Model

Foundation for Generalist Practice

Knowledge
Skills
Values

Assessment

PLANNING

Step 1: Work with the client.

Step 2: Prioritize problems. ⟶

Problem
1.
2.
3. etc.

Step 3: Translate problems into needs.

Problem ⟶ Need
1. ⟶ 1.
2. ⟶ 2.
3. ⟶ 3.

Step 4: Evaluate levels of intervention for each need.

Need #1: _____ etc.

a. Identify Alternatives: ⟶	b. Propose Solutions ⟶	c. Evaluate: Pros	Cons	Client strengths
Micro				
Mezzo				
Macro				

Step 5: Establish primary goals

Step 6: Specify objectives

	Who?	Will do What?	By When?	How will you measure success?
1.				
2.				
3.				

Step 7: Formalize a contract.

Step 2: Prioritize Problems: Which Problem Should You Work On First?

Many clients will have multiple problems on multiple levels. In the last chapter we defined nine categories of problems: interpersonal conflict, dissatisfaction in social relations, problems with formal organizations, difficulties in role performance, problems in social transition, psychological and behavioral problems, inadequate resources, problems in decision making, and cultural conflicts. In view of the numerous categories of problems, how can you choose which to work on?

The first thing to do is to focus on only those problems which fulfill three criteria (Northen, 1987). First, the client must recognize that the problem exists. You may or may not agree with your client about where the problem stands in a prioritized list of all the problems involved. However, the client should at least agree that the problem is significant enough to merit the attention of both of you.

Clients who deny problems or fail to see their importance won't want to waste time on them. For instance, a client who denies his alcohol addiction will probably refuse to discuss the subject in an interview with you. However, you may be able to identify related problems, such as child abuse (while drinking) or lack of money (due to job loss because of the drinking), which are significant to the client.

A second criteria for addressing a problem is that the problem should be clearly defined in understandable terms. You and your client both need to know exactly what you're talking about in order to find a satisfactory solution. The importance of clarity and specificity in goal setting is an ongoing theme throughout this chapter.

A third criteria is that it be realistically possible that you and your client will be able to do something about the problem. Fixating on hopeless problems is just a waste of time for you and your client. For example, dwelling on the problem of a spouse who left home three years ago and hasn't been heard from since is probably useless. It might better merit your time to discuss problematic aspects of your client's situation as it stands right now. For instance, she might currently be very concerned about child care, finances, and housing.

Reid and Epstein (1972, pp. 58–59) make several suggestions regarding how to decide which problem to work on (the "target problem"):

1. *Identify with the client the range of problems which are most significant to the client.* This may be a long or short list. The important thing is to explore with clients all of their concerns. You will probably perceive some of the problems as being much less significant than others. Include them anyway. You'll address them later.

2. *Restate each problem using "explicit behavioral terms"* (p. 58). In other words, the precise nature of the problem should be clear in your mind. Additionally, the problem statement should include descriptions of behaviors, which will later allow you to measure your progress and determine when you have succeeded in solving the problem. We will discuss the importance of behavioral specificity in more depth later in the chapter.

3. *Prioritize the problems in order of their importance to the client.* This alerts you to which problem you should address first, second, etc. For example, a client may be concerned with the following problems in order of priority: paying the rent, her husband's drinking, her child's truancy, and her overweight condition, which is resulting in a number of health problems. Paying the rent, then, is probably the problem you should address first.

Once again, this is not as easy as it sounds. Frequently, how you rank the client's problems will be quite different than how your client ranks them. In such cases, it's up to you to further explore the problems with the client. You will need to establish a list of priorities satisfactory to you both. Once again, this process involves both good communication skills and making judgments. Reid (1987b) relates a typical scenario when practitioner and client are not in complete agreement regarding problem priority:

"The focus is on what the client wants and not on what the practitioner thinks the client may need. The practitioner may point out, however, potential difficulties the client has not acknowledged or the consequences that may result if these difficulties are allowed to go unaddressed. In other words, the target problem is not necessarily defined by what clients say they want initially, but rather by what they want after a process of deliberation to which the practitioner contributes his or her own knowledge and point of view. As a result, clients may alter their conception of their problem or . . . may realize they do have difficulties they may wish to work on" (p. 758).

4. *Establish an initial agreement with the client regarding which problem you will attend to first.* This needs to be a problem in which the client is interested. It should be a problem that you determine can be solved, even if it's not the very first one on your list. For instance, take a client who states the problem most critical to her is finding a job. She indicates her second most critical problem is that her landlord has turned off her heat in the middle of an icy winter. After exploring the matter you determine that finding her a job is a more complicated task than it initially might seem. Your client is unskilled, has no high school diploma, and is responsible for several small children. Such issues as job training, trans-

portation, and day care will require more effort to resolve.

However, you see the heat (or lack thereof) problem as being more amenable to intervention than the unemployment problem. For one thing, it is illegal for landlords to turn the heat off in apartment rentals in your state during midwinter. Therefore, calls to the landlord and, perhaps, the appropriate authorities have a good potential for resolving this problem. You can help your client explore potential solutions for both problems. Hopefully, you can come to an agreement to work on a problem which you feel can be solved in a relatively short period of time.

Sometimes, you determine with the client that more than one problem can be addressed at the same time. For instance, consider the client mentioned above. Her third problem might be that she doesn't have enough money to feed her children. You think she qualifies for assistance which she currently is not receiving. You can proceed to investigate the possibility of getting her these resources at approximately the same time you're working on the heat problem.

Step 3: Translate Problems into Needs

Problems, of course, involve any source of perplexity or distress. Many times they are initiated by lack of resources. Clients will come to you because they have problems they need to solve. It's your job to help them accomplish that.

Needs, on the other hand, are "physical, psychological, economic, and social requirements for survival, well-being, and fulfillment" (Barker, 1987, p. 105). To figure out what to do, you must translate your clients' problems into their needs.

Take, for instance, the lack of adequate resources—not having enough money. Dwelling

Figure 6.2: Examples of Related Needs Translated from Identified Problems

Identified Problems	Related Needs
Alcohol addiction ───────────────→	Ongoing sobriety
Child abuse ──────────────────→	Stop abuse, emotional control, child-management techniques
Unemployment ─────────────────→	Employment
Homelessness ──────────────────→	Place to live
Depression ───────────────────→	Treatment for relief of depression
Grief at death of loved one ──────────→	Grief management
Misbehavior of children ─────────────→	Improved parental control of children, child-management techniques
Poor performance in school ──────────→	Improved school performance, motivation, family stability
Compulsive stealing ──────────────→	Treatment for compulsivity, access to adequate resources
Alzheimer's Disease and loss of control ─────→	Placement in supportive setting

on the problem does not help you figure out what to do about it. However, if you translate the problem into what the client *needs to solve it*, you can formulate ideas about what to do. The problem of lack of money means that the client *needs* better access to resources. The next logical step, then, is to ask yourself the question, "Where might such resources be acquired?" Possible sources include public assistance, food stamps, paid employment, and charitable organizations, among many other resources. These ideas orient your thinking to possible goals for the client and strategies for achieving these goals. For example, you might then discuss with your client the possibility of applying for assistance or seeking job training. Figure 6.2 illustrates a variety of identified problems and their translation into related needs.

Problems, needs, and goals are all interrelated. Your goal will be to satisfy the need causing the problem. Simply translating problems into needs orients you toward establishing goals. It turns your thoughts from focusing on what's wrong to concentrating on how what's wrong can be remedied. Your major goal is usually to satisfy your client's needs.

Step 4: Evaluate Levels of Intervention: Select a Strategy

Together with your client, you need to identify and assess various strategies with which to achieve the major goals related to the specified problems. A "strategy is an overall approach to change in the situation" (Johnson, 1989, p. 302). In other words, your strategy is the route you and your clients will take to meet your client's needs. You can develop a strategy by doing the following:

1. Focus on the need you've selected with your client to work on first.
2. Review the need and consider identifying micro, mezzo, and macro alternative strategies to arrive at a solution.
3. Emphasize your client's strengths when establishing strategies.
4. Evaluate the pros and cons of each strategy you've considered with your client.
5. Select and pursue the strategy that appears to be most efficient and effective.

First, you and your client need to identify and review potential strategies which may involve micro, mezzo, or macro aspects of practice. You want to decide what your "unit of attention" will be; the unit of attention is "the system being focused upon" as a target of change (Johnson, 1989, p. 301). It's important not just to focus on the micro aspects of the client's problem situation, namely what you and your client can do yourselves on your client's behalf. Perhaps your client's family needs to become involved. This, of course, involves a mezzo approach to intervention. Or, perhaps your client could benefit from a treatment or self-help group. Take, for instance, a gambling-addicted client who could benefit from involvement in Gamblers Anonymous. This is a national self-help organization (similar in some ways to Alcoholics Anonymous) for people having problems because of gambling.

Instead of micro or mezzo approaches, strategies involving macro skills might provide the

most appropriate route for solving a particular problem. For instance, take a Hispanic client, Jorge Quiero, whose young children have not been allowed to enter a neighborhood school, despite the fact that the family has lived in that school's district for over a year. You feel that this entails blatant discrimination on the basis of culture and race. You might pursue advocating with the school system on behalf of your client. Or you might determine that educating school-board members about the problem and collaborating with them to change policies is the most effective course of action. You might even decide that legal confrontation is necessary to affect change in the school system's policies.

In some cases, more than one strategy may be needed to attain a particular goal. In the case of the Quiero family, you and Mr. Quiero might conclude that he and his spouse could benefit from English lessons. They speak English just

Selecting a strategy to help a homeless family may require macro skills involving the community.

barely well enough "to get along." They indicated they had difficulty expressing themselves adequately. Lessons could provide them with an enhanced ability to negotiate the difficult school system themselves. Note that this tactic would add a micro strategy (namely, the clients learning English) to the macro strategy already discussed (that is, changing the school system's policy), although both are directed at the same goal. The goal, of course, is for the Quiero children to attain education.

There will probably be many potential strategies possible to achieve any particular goal. You must depend on your professional judgment, expertise, and creativity to formulate the best possible strategy.

Sometimes, "brainstorming" with clients helps generate ideas. Brainstorming is "the creative process of mutually focusing efforts on generating a broad range of possible options from which clients can choose" (Hepworth & Larsen, 1990, p. 380). However, it should be noted that practitioners probably provide most of the resource information and technical help; clients wouldn't need your help in the first place if they had all the answers (Hepworth & Larsen, 1990).

Strengths

Emphasizing and incorporating your client's strengths when establishing strategies is useful in several ways. First, strengths provide blocks upon which to build intervention plans. Instead of focusing on problems, needs, and deficits, strengths provide you with something positive you can use to empower clients. Second, emphasizing client strengths allows you to give your client positive feedback. You can talk about their strengths with them and build up their confidence. Emphasizing strengths can be used to convey your respect to clients. Third, incorporating clients' strengths into strategies provides you with something concrete to work with and think about. To non-

professionals, the intervention process (along with the professional jargon and fancy words involved) can appear vague and confusing. Highlight 6.1 elaborates upon nine areas you can explore with your clients to identify their strengths.

The following example illustrates how strengths can be incorporated into planned strategies. Harvey is a homeless Vietnam veteran with posttraumatic stress disorder. This disorder involves "a psychological reaction to experiencing an event that is outside the range of usual human experience" (in Harvey's case, the horrors and massacres of brutal combat); symptoms include "having difficulty concentrating, feeling emotionally blunted or numb, being hyperalert and jumpy, and having painful memories, nightmares, and sleep disturbances (Barker, 1987, pp. 122–23). Harvey manifests virtually all of these symptoms. Harvey hasn't been able to hold down a job or even remain in the same residence for more than a month since the war ended. He has serious problems.

How can you, as a social worker, figure out how to help Harvey? First, translate his problems into needs. He needs therapy to deal with his stress disorder, emotional support from family and/or friends, a place to live, and a job. Because his disorder affects virtually every aspect of his life, it is easy to be overwhelmed by his situation. However, elaborating upon his strengths provides inklings about what to do.

Harvey's strengths include: his status as a veteran (allowing him free access to help through Veterans' Administration [VA] hospitals and facilities), physical good health, a high school diploma, and an extremely supportive and concerned family. To figure out strategies to meet his needs (your ultimate goal), take his strengths into consideration.

First, Harvey can be referred to the VA hospital for evaluation and therapy. The VA also has a program that provides temporary housing for veterans suffering from similar disorders. His family can be involved in his treatment to provide support in his continuation of it. His good physical health and high-school diploma indicate that he is qualified for a number of blue-collar, physically oriented jobs. A related strength, we find out, is that when he was able to get and hold a job for a few weeks, it was usually in construction. He indicates that this is the kind of work he most enjoys when he is in better control of his disorder. Thus, perhaps a long-term goal is to involve him in this kind of work when he's ready.

Pros and Cons

In the process of planning strategies, you need to evaluate the pros and cons of each. You and your client won't be able to do everything at once. You will probably need to determine what the most efficient and potentially effective strategies would be. For example, take the case of the Quiero family. Major problems included enrolling their children in school and poor English-speaking skills. Consider the pros and cons of two of the possible strategies identified:

HIGHLIGHT 6.1
Potential Areas of Clients' Strengths

Jones and Biesecker (1980, pp. 48–49) cite the following nine categories you might explore with clients to identify and elaborate upon their strengths. After each appears a series of questions. These are the types of questions you might consider asking your own clients.

1. *Special interests and activities.* Do you have special interests on which you would like to spend time? What skills and talents do you feel you have? Do you belong to any organizations or groups? If not, have you in the past? What types of activities do you participate in which make you feel good?

2. *Family and friends.* What family members are you particularly close to? Who can you call on for support? Who do you feel comfortable enough to confide in? Do you have any close friends? Are you friends with any of your neighbors?

3. *Religion and values.* Is religion important and meaningful to you? If so, with what creed or denomination are you involved? Do you have a minister or priest you feel comfortable in going to for support or guidance? What values in life are especially important to you? Honesty? Being close to others? Supporting your children? Being dependable?

4. *Occupation and education.* What educational level have you achieved (as opposed to what level you have *not* achieved)? What work experience have you built up? What marketable skills do you have?

5. *Reaction to professional services.* What, if any, social services have you been involved with that you found helpful? How have you benefited from these services? Were there any particular professionals whom you especially liked or found exceptionally helpful?

6. *Emotional and mental health.* What things make you the happiest? During what times do you feel the strongest and most capable? What types of events or happenings help improve your mood? How do you usually go about making decisions or solving your problems?

7. *Physical condition.* What kinds of physical activities do you like most? What kinds of physical activity makes you feel good? Which aspects of your health are especially good?

8. *Support system.* Where does most of your income come from? Do you have other assets you can rely on in needy times? Who can you depend on to help you when you need it?

9. *Other.* What strengths do you have other than the ones we've already covered?

Macro Strategy 1

Advocate with the school system on behalf of your clients.

Pros

- The school system cannot legally deny children access on the basis of language, so the legal system is on the family's side. The system, therefore, might respond to additional pressure from the worker.
- The worker knows the school's vice principal and two school board members. The school board, of course, has the greatest authority over what goes on in the school system. The worker feels there is good potential here to exercise influence in order to change the school's prior decision and overall policy.

Cons

- The school's principal and a number of other school board members are renowned for their conservative approach to changing policy. Thus, they might bristle and balk at additional pressure.
- Advocacy takes a lot of time. The worker's caseload is large, and there are numerous crises to attend to.
- The advocacy process is vague. The worker would need to sit down and develop a well-specified plan for who to contact and how.
- The children might not be accepted into school for an inordinate period of time. Thus, their education could be drastically impeded.

Micro Strategy 2

Enroll parents in English classes so they may better advocate for themselves.

Pros

- This would enhance the Quieros' empowerment, ability to communicate, and prowess to fight for their own rights.

- The difficulties they experienced in dealing with a primarily English-speaking community would be decreased.

Cons

- No English classes are readily available at low cost in their area.
- Such classes are time consuming and require high motivation to continue with them over a substantial period of time.
- Although such education may be of some use to the Quieros in the long run, its usefulness in the current problem is questionable.
- There is some debate, especially in certain areas of the country with large Hispanic populations, whether English must be the primary language. Is this country not a melting pot of peoples and cultures? Is it fair or right to force English upon people already adept in Spanish?

The pros and cons noted in the above two examples of strategies are arbitrary. That is, there are many other approaches for you to consider. However, these examples are intended to convey the idea of what it's like to identify, struggle with, and finally decide on an actual course of action in real practice situations.

Step 5: Establish Primary Goals

Hepworth and Larsen (1990) cite five basic purposes for establishing goals. First, specifying goals guarantees that worker and clients are in concurrence regarding what they want to pursue. Second, goals "provide direction and continuity in the helping process and prevent needless wandering" (p. 337). Third, goals aid in the identification, formulation, and evaluation of relevant strategies to proceed with the intervention. Fourth, they help practitioners observe and appraise the progress being made in the intervention. Finally, goals "serve as outcome criteria in evaluating the effectiveness of specific interventions and of the helping process" (p. 337).

In summary, goals are established to clarify the purpose of an intervention. A clearly stated goal allows you to determine whether or not your intervention has been successful. Goals are necessary whether your intervention strategy involves micro, mezzo, or macro practice. In micro practice, goals guide your work with individual clients. Mezzo practice intervention may require goals involving each individual member and the entire group as a whole. Finally, in macro practice, a generalist practitioner might use goal-setting to help a community or organization target what it wants to accomplish and how it will go about doing this.

Social workers set goals to help a client system identify and specify what it wants to achieve within the worker/client relationship. Worker and client must be moving in the same direction. They must clearly understand what they are trying to accomplish.

The importance of specifying goals should be emphasized regardless of whether you're participating in micro, mezzo, or macro interventions. You and your client system (be it individual, family, group, agency, or community) need to establish clearly and straightforwardly what you want to accomplish.

Examples of goals include:

- Get landlord to fix leaking plumbing.
- Improve parents' child behavior-management skills.
- Participate in support group for spouses of alcoholics for six months.
- Change agency policy to include home visits for work with families.
- Develop program for rural homeless children.

Thus, your goal is a broad statement of what you and your clients want to achieve.

Step 6: Specify Objectives

Primary goals are usually so broadly stated that it's virtually impossible to identify how they will be achieved. For instance, take the goal "get landlord to fix leaking plumbing." The goal statement gives no indication of how that goal can be accomplished. Will the client picket the landlord's office to demand attention? Will you call the Health Department to complain and demand that the landlord comply with housing codes to maintain plumbing in good working condition? Will the landlord suddenly see the error of his ways and get the pipes fixed?

Both you and your client know what needs to get done. The client needs plumbing that works adequately. The next step, then, is to break that primary goal down into smaller objectives. An objective is "something toward which effort is directed, an aim or end of action" (*Webster's New Collegiate Dictionary,* 1977).

You might think of objectives as subgoals—smaller, more easily met goals which lead up to being able to accomplish a primary goal. Additionally, objectives are behaviorally specific regarding what is to be done and how success will be measured. In the following discussion, objectives and subgoals will be considered identical.

For example, take the goal "get client a job paying at least three hundred dollars a week." In order to attain this goal, you might have to set objectives or subgoals with your client to help prepare him to achieve this major goal. If he hasn't completed high school, one subgoal might be to gain his high school equivalency certificate. A second subgoal might be to subsequently complete six months of job-skill training at a technical school.

Subgoals may have their own subgoals. Thus, the objectives might be specified for any particular subgoal. For instance, refer again to the client needing employment. In order to complete his education and training, he might need some form of financial assistance. He also might need a part-time job to "hold him over" while he is going to school and getting training. Each of these would also be subgoals.

This might seem confusing. The important thing to remember is that goals and subgoals should be used to keep you and your client on track. They can help to clarify tasks and responsibilities. They also can help to prevent you both from wasting time and energy. All your efforts should be expended with the intent of meeting your client's basic identified needs.

Writing Clear Objectives

Establishing objectives involves specifying the steps that are necessary in order to achieve those objectives. In order to achieve this, involved individuals will need to get things done. The basic formula for delegating responsibility is to specify *who* will do *what* by *when*. "Who" is the individual specified for accomplishing a task. "What" involves the tasks the individual has to complete in order to achieve the goal. Finally, "by when" sets a time limit so that the task is not lost in some endless eternity.

The following are examples of objectives:

Ms. M (*who*) will call her mother about helping care for the children (*what*) by 3:00 P.M. next Monday (*when*).
I (*who*) will contact my supervisor and establish a location for the group to meet (*what*) by Wednesday, November 23 (*when*).
Mr. S (*who*) will survey the agency's clientele to determine their primary needs and be ready to make a report (*what*) by the February staff meeting (*when*).

You might be asking yourself, Why is it so important to be so precise and "picky"? The answer is that if you aren't explicit regarding who has the responsibility for accomplishing the task, it's likely that the task won't get done.

As a student you are probably very busy.

You are not likely to have much time to do anything but the required coursework. It would be nice to do a lot of in-depth reading on topics that interest you. However, you probably assign this a relatively low priority. You do what you *have* to do first. It's the same with generalist practitioners in the field. You, as a social worker, will probably have an abundance of clients and will constantly strive to prioritize what needs to get done first. If it's not your specifically identified responsibility to complete a task by a certain deadline, it's easy to put it off . . . and off . . . and off. Such tasks rarely, if ever, get done.

For example, let's say you're at a staff meeting where you're discussing the progress of a developmentally disabled client of yours. Other professionals at the meeting include your supervisor, a psychologist, a vocational counselor, a physician, a speech therapist, an occupational therapist, and a physical therapist. The goal of the meeting is for each professional to report what progress has been made with this particular client to formulate plans and goals for the future. One of the goals established by the group is to "make a referral to another agency for intensive vocational testing." Such testing would determine your client's specific skills, abilities, and job interests. However, it's not clearly specified who's supposed to make the referral.

Two months later, the same group meets again to reevaluate this client's progress. Your supervisor, who is leading the staff meeting, asks for a report on the vocational testing results. You gaze at the psychologist with a blank expression on your face. The psychologist looks at you. The occupational therapist looks at the vocational counselor. The vocational counselor looks at the psychologist. And so it goes. Each staff member assumed that some other staff member would make the referral. All were terribly busy with their own job responsibilities and had no time to do anything they didn't absolutely have to do. As a result, no one "naturally" assumed responsibility for completing the task.

Thus, the task didn't get done. The client had lost two months of precious (and expensive) time.

It's interesting to note the phrase "get done." It's as if the task will magically do itself without any human intervention. In other words, this phrase is one to carefully scrutinize and probably avoid.

Objectives Should Be Measurable

How will you know whether the goal has been achieved or whether you should continue striving to achieve it? For example, take an impoverished, single parent client with three small children. Her *problem* is poverty. She *needs* money. Her *goal* is to get enough financial assistance to supply her family with food, shelter, and clothing. You and your client establish three specific *objectives* for helping her solve her problem. They include obtaining Aid to Families with Dependent Children (AFDC),[2] becoming involved in a housing program,[3] and receiving food stamps.[4] Have your objectives

been met when she begins receiving AFDC payments and food stamps, but remains on a long waiting list for housing assistance? Or, have your objectives been met when she receives $237 a month in AFDC payments, $90 a month in food stamps, and $100 in rent subsidy, even if this total amount is inadequate for her to survive?

Instead, you could specify a more measurable objective. For example, you could establish the maximum amount she could possibly receive from each of these sources. If the $427 is the maximum she is allowed to receive under current guidelines and you have specified that as your objective, then you have succeeded in reaching it. You then may need to establish a subsequent objective to gain additional resources so that she can feed and house her children adequately.

Specifying goals and objectives, in addition to measuring their success, will be addressed more thoroughly later in the chapter. For example, setting objectives in micro practice involves determination of the specific performance required (What is the basic objective you're trying to achieve?), the conditions under which this objective can be accomplished, and the standards by which its success can be measured. We will also address goals and objectives within the contexts of micro, mezzo, and macro practice. Emphasis will be placed on the importance of establishing clear, specific, and measurable statements regardless of your practice arena.

Sometimes Goals and Objectives Are Synonymous

Sometimes, your client's goal will not be very complex. It will not require a number of subgoals or objectives in order to accomplish it. For instance, an elderly client might need help in filing out a form to apply for Meals on Wheels. This service delivers hot meals to elderly clients on a daily basis. Elderly people often have diffi-

---

2. AFDC is "a public assistance program, originating in the Social Security Act of 1935, funded by the federal and state governments to provide financial aid for needly children who are deprived of parental support because of death, incapacity, or absence. AFDC is administered on the state and local levels, usually through county departments of public welfare (or human or social services)" (Barker, 1987, p. 6).

3. Housing programs are "publicly funded and monitored programs designed to provide suitable homes, especially for those unable to find or pay for them themselves. In the United States most of these programs are administered by the Department of Housing and Urban Development (HUD). These programs include Low-Rent Public Housing, the Rent-Subsidy Program, [and] Lower-Income Housing Assistance" among others (Barker, 1987, p. 72).

4. "The Food Stamp program, which was created to supplement the food-buying power of low-income people, is the nation's response to its hunger problem. Monthly benefits in the form of coupons used to purchase food are entirely federally financed. . . . Eligibility for the program is restricted to households that meet income, resource, and work requirements prescribed by law" (Wells, 1987, p. 628).

culty shopping for and preparing food. Therefore, it's easy for them to suffer from malnutrition. Meals on Wheels is one of a number of supportive services which can help people remain in their own homes or apartments as long as possible.

At any rate, your goal in this case is relatively simple. Namely, it is to explain the application form to your client and help her complete it accurately so that it can be effectively submitted for receipt of the service. This goal will be reached when the form is submitted. Therefore, it's important to state your goal as explicitly as if it were an objective. In this and other simple cases, your goal and objective will essentially be the same statement.

This issue is often confusing because many people use goals and objectives synonymously. For our purposes, an objective should *always* be clear, specific, and measurable. A goal often is too complex to be measurable. Goals should be stated as specifically as possible. Very simple goals should be stated as if they were objectives. From here on, we will refer to objectives instead of goals in order to emphasize the importance of specificity.

Setting Goals and Objectives in Micro Practice

Many of the principles which apply to micro practice (for example, the importance of being very specific) apply to macro practice as well. In this section of the chapter, we will examine objectives within the context of work with individual clients. However, our emphasis on how objectives should be stated will apply to mezzo and macro practice as well.

Throughout this discussion, we will be referring to objectives. However, remember that the principle of being clear and specific applies to both objectives and goals. Remember also that a very simple goal should be stated as if it were an objective.

Establishing Behavioral Goals and Objectives

Establish specific objectives with your clients. What does this mean? For one thing, the objective should indicate exactly how it can be met. It should be easy to tell when you have achieved your objective and when you have not. Consider the following examples:

- *Objective: The client will become happier.* How happy does the client have to be in order to have achieved this objective? Should he get very happy, or is just a little happy enough? Are we talking about one smile a day? Or, can the client be happy without smiling? What does "happy" mean anyway?

  There is obviously a broad range of subjective interpretations possible concerning this objective. It is not a good objective. The point about being specific is that you should have to expend as little thought and effort as possible to determine whether the objective has been met or not.

- *Objective: The client's daughter (Sophia) will behave better.* Does this mean that Sophia, age six, will stop pinching her infant brother (which she does frequently throughout the day) and stop spitting at her mother when being reprimanded? Is the objective met if Sophia pinches her brother only ten times during the day instead of her usual two dozen? What if she stops pinching but continues to spit? Has the objective been met? Is she behaving better *enough*?

  Once again, it's difficult to tell. Like the first example mentioned, this objective is subject to a wide range of interpretation. You would be put in the uncomfortable position of struggling to interpret whether you arbitrarily thought the objective had been met or not.

- *Objective: The client (Mindy) will improve*

her communication skills. This time, the client is an eighteen-year-old developmentally disabled woman. Although Mindy is capable of reading at a fourth-grade level, she is shy and rarely speaks to anyone. Will this objective be met if she speaks more frequently to her parents, with whom she lives? How much more frequently? Is two times a day enough? What if she only says one word each time? Or, should she speak to her parents two times each day for at least five minutes each time? Then would the objective be met? Should Mindy also be more adept at speaking to strangers she meets before the objective is met? What about the *listening* part of her communication skills? Must her capacity to listen and understand be improved before this objective is met? Or, does this objective involve her ability to carry on a full and meaningful conversation?

Once again, it's difficult to establish what is really meant by this objective. You would have to make a subjective decision regarding whether you were successful at meeting the objective or whether you needed to continue striving to achieve it.

What are your thoughts right now? Do you think we're being much too particular and absurd? The intent of these poor examples is not to frustrate or annoy you. In practice you will be responsible for both formulating and achieving goals and objectives. What will you (or your job, for that matter) be worth if you don't accomplish what you're supposed to? You will be accountable to your client, your supervisor, and your agency for achieving your intervention goals and objectives. Therefore, it is much to your advantage to be able to cite clear, concrete, readily understandable objectives. For any of the three objectives mentioned above, questions could easily be raised about whether you

were achieving them or not. A clearly defined, specific objective conveys exactly what has been achieved.

It's thus helpful to specify *behavioral* objectives in the planning process. Behavior, for our purposes, refers to observable actions that are possible to measure in order to monitor progress. Our clients, supervisors, and colleagues should have a graphic, coherent picture in their minds of exactly what we mean.

Objectives then should meet three criteria: objectivity, clarity, and completeness (Hawkins & Dobes, 1975; Kazdin, 1989). Unbiased *objectivity* involves "observable characteristics or environmental events" (Kazdin, 1989, p. 54). In other words, objectives should refer to something that can be seen and measured. For example, take one of our earlier "bad objective" examples regarding improving communication skills for Mindy, the developmentally disabled young adult. In that case, what exactly should be improved? Should she be expected to speak in complete sentences and use correct grammar? Should she be expected to initiate conversations and ask questions in order to achieve "improved" communication skills? Think back to chapter 2, which identified the many attending and interviewing skills used to enhance communication. Which of these should Mindy be expected to master in order to achieve the goal? The objectives leading up to the goal should specify exactly *what* behavior and *how much* of that behavior Mindy would need to learn in order to achieve the goal. In other words, improved communication would have to be behaviorally defined.

The second criterion for a good objective is *clarity*. Clarity means that a goal or objective should be so "unambiguous that it can be read, repeated, and paraphrased by others" (Kazdin, 1989, p. 55). It shouldn't matter who is evaluating whether the objective is achieved or not. All observers should see the same thing and be in agreement. Take Mindy. There should be strong concurrence among anyone knowing what the objective is and observing Mindy's communication behavior regarding whether the objective has been met or not.

Finally, the last criterion, *completeness*, means that enough information should be given about how the objective can be attained. Once more, consider Mindy. The objective should specify the circumstances under which her communication should be improved. Should it involve interactions only with her parents and loved ones? Or should it involve communication and interaction with others? Would it suffice to improve her communication with clerks at stores she visits? Or would she also need to initiate communication with complete strangers in order to achieve the objective?

Behavioral Objectives Can Be Measured

We've established that one of the major purposes of formulating objectives is to provide a means for measuring whether they've been attained or not. The point of having an objective is to reach it and know that you've done so. Three required components in a clear, well-written objective are "performance," "conditions," and "standard or level of performance" (Thompson, 1977, p. 49). Much work has been done in the area of educational achievement

---

HIGHLIGHT 6.2

Using the Concepts of Performance, Conditions, and Standards to Establish Goals and Objectives with Clients

For each of the following scenarios, a client will be described briefly. Subsequently, an arbitrary objective using the performance/conditions/standards formula will be presented. This illustrates an extension of the *who should do what by when* formula for delegating responsibility and specifying objectives. For each scenario, the client is *who*. Likewise, the performance, conditions, and standards specify the *what* and by *when*.

Earl, age eighty-three, resides in a large nursing home. He has arthritis, is gradually losing the use of his hands, and is slowly failing. The *objective* for this client is:

PERFORMANCE: Earl will enhance and maintain eye-hand coordination
CONDITIONS: by participating in a crafts activity hour offered four times each week
STANDARDS: and attend three out of four times each week (75 percent of the time).

Pearl, age twenty-four, has been reported for physically abusing her two small children when they don't obey her demands. The *objective* for this client is:

PERFORMANCE: Pearl will learn parent-effectiveness skills
CONDITIONS: by attending Parent Effectiveness Training Classes every Thursday evening at the local YMCA
STANDARDS: and attend all six training sessions (100 percent of the time).

Johnny, age fifteen, is labeled by his parents as uncontrollable. He has been arrested for selling drugs twice, is frequently involved in gang-related fights, and often gets home after his curfew. The *objective* for this client is:

PERFORMANCE: Johnny will arrive home by his curfew
CONDITIONS: at 9:00 P.M. on weeknights and 11:00 P.M. on weekends
STANDARDS: thirteen out of fourteen nights every two weeks (93 percent of the time).

and behavioral child management, the latter usually applied within family or school settings (DeRisi & Butz, 1975; Jones & Biesecker, 1980; Thompson, 1977). Therefore, our discussion here will relate examples involving children's learning and behavior.

The first component of a well-written objective, *performance*, involves what the client, worker, or other subject involved is to perform in order to attain the objective. The performance component in the context of changing a child's behavior illustrates exactly what it is that you expect the child to do. What specific activity or behavior is involved in achieving the ob-

jective? Examples include, "unties and ties shoelace," "counts to twenty," "recites letters of the alphabet," or "washes dishes" (Thompson, 1977, p. 49).

The second component of a clear objective involves the *conditions* or circumstances under which the behaviors involved in achieving the objective are performed. What materials does the child need in order to finish the activity and subsequently achieve the objective? Must the child perform the activity alone or can someone help her? Is there a limited time frame within which she must complete the task? Examples of conditions include "given shoes with shoe-

---

Ivy, age twenty-one, has three small children. She works a full-time first-shift job at a bakery. Ivy's own mother, who has been caring for Ivy's children, has recently become very ill and can no longer babysit. Ivy does not want to lose her job. The *objective* for this client is:

PERFORMANCE: Ivy will arrange for day care for her three small children
CONDITIONS: by calling five local day care agencies to determine cost and her children's eligibility
STANDARDS: and report her findings to her social worker by next Thursday.

Storm, a twenty-six-year-old developmentally disabled adult, lives in a group home with other adults of similar ability levels. She moved in after the death of her mother with whom she had lived her entire life. The *objective* for this client is:

PERFORMANCE: Storm will complete specified daily living tasks
CONDITIONS: and check off completed tasks on the clipboard holding her

daily log of activities (for example, making her bed, getting to work at the sheltered workshop on time, vacuuming the living room)
STANDARDS: and complete 80 percent of all her required tasks each day.

Commentary

It's very clear when these goals have been attained and when they have not. If Storm, for example, only completes 78 percent of her required tasks, she has not met her objective. Likewise, if Johnny misses his curfew two times in two weeks, he hasn't accomplished his objective.

Clearly specifying how you will evaluate your objective will save you many headaches in the long run. Specifying and agreeing upon goal expectations in advance will help you avoid potential arguments, having to make judgments about excuses, and even being the target of manipulation.

HIGHLIGHT 6.3

Clarifying Vague Goals and Objectives

Below is a case of a client with multiple problems. Following the scenario, there are a series of vague statements which could be incorporated as possible objectives for the client portrayed. The words and phrases used in the vague goal statements are taken from Jones and Biesecker (1980, p. 28). Unfortunately, these phrases are sometimes embodied in the goals proposed in real case records and reports.

For each vague goal statement:

1. Explain why the goal is vague. For example, which specific words are vague? How might their meanings be misinterpreted or interpreted in many different ways by different people?
2. Reformulate these objectives by using behaviorally specific terminology and incorporating the performance/conditions/standards format illustrated in Highlight 6.2.

Sarah, age twenty-four, is a paraplegic. She broke her back in a car accident when she was sixteen. Afterward, she became clinically depressed, withdrawing from family and friends and has isolated herself in her apartment for the past three years. She dresses slovenly, is generally lethargic,

and remains unmotivated to get training for employment or improve her social life. The low-rent apartment building in which she lives is being torn down. Sarah is panic-stricken, hostile to social workers and family members trying to help her, and doesn't know what she will do.

Respond to the following potential goals for Sarah and answer the two questions posed above for each. The first statement is followed by an example of how you might respond to the remaining goal statements.

Vague Statement of Objective (Example): *Improve family relationships.* Reason for Vagueness: "Improve" is a vague term. How can you measure relationship improvement? How can you tell when the goal is achieved? Which family relationships are being targeted? Those with parents? Siblings? Grandparents? What aspects of the relationships should change? What does "relationship" mean?

Improved Restatement of an Objective (Performance, Conditions, Standards): Sarah will speak with her mother by calling her mother on the telephone for at least five minutes three days each week.

Now, do the same thing for the following vague goal statements:

---

laces," "within two minutes," "without prompting," or "for his parents in their kitchen after supper."

The *standard of performance* involves how well, how soon, or how often the performance, activity, or behavior should be done. Does the activity have to be done perfectly? Must it be done every single day? Is the objective still achieved if the child misses one day a week or mixes up two letters of the alphabet?

Highlight 6.2 applies this three-component basis for setting good objectives to situations

typically found in social work. The importance of specificity continues to be a major theme.

Assigning Tasks as Part of the Objective-Setting Process

In micro practice as well as in mezzo and macro practice, the *who* will do *what* by *when* formula should be applied consistently, regardless of who is responsible for the task. The examples provided in Highlight 6.2 illustrate objectives where clients had tasks to complete for themselves. They then assumed the *who* responsibility.

Vague Objective Statement	Reasons for Vagueness	Improved Restatement: Performance/Conditions/Standards
1. Promote emotional well-being:		
2. Increase self-awareness:		
3. Find adequate housing:		
4. Facilitate adequate functioning:		
5. Accept physical disability:		
6. Dress appropriately:		
7. Increase motivation:		
8. Show interest:		
9. Respond appropriately:		
10. Improve self-concept:		
11. Develop a relationship:		
12. Decrease hostile attitude:		

We've already established that you, as the worker, will also frequently have the responsibility for completing specified tasks. In these instances you will become the *who* in this formula.

Step 7: Formalize a Contract

Thus far, we've established six steps in the planning phase of the problem-solving process: work with your client, prioritize problems, translate problems into needs, evaluate levels of intervention (micro, mezzo, and macro), establish

primary goals, and specify objectives. The seventh and final step of the planning phase is to establish an intervention contract.

A contract is an agreement between a client and worker about what will occur in the intervention process. It can include goals, objectives, time frames, and responsibilities of people involved.

Let's break this definition down into its four major components:

1. A contract specifies what will occur during the intervention process;

2. A contract is established by a worker and client making an agreement together;
3. A contract generally contains four types of information including goals, methods, timetables, and mutual obligations;
4. A contract's format can be written, oral, or implied.

The Purpose of a Contract

A contract represents the culmination of the planning step in the problem-solving process. It clarifies and summarizes exactly who is responsible for completing which tasks. Austin, Kopp, and Smith (1986) describe the usefulness of contracts:

> . . . contracts are one way to ensure the consumer's rights, to free the consumer, and to increase consumer control in developing and implementing the plan. Such contracts are not legal documents; rather, they are a way to involve interested persons and to identify each person's roles in the achievement of the desired goals. Contracts help to document who does what and when. Thus, contracts explain to the consumer what will be done by the worker and the agency, as well as clearly what is expected of the consumer and significant others (p. 305).

Contracts identify expectations. They help the client and worker avoid potential misunderstandings. The plan should be very clear to all involved.

Contracts can be used in any arena of practice. In micro practice, they can summarize specific responsibilities of client, worker, agency, and any involved others. In mezzo practice, contracts can specify individual and group goals and tasks. In macro practice, contracts can formalize any number of agreed-upon plans. A contract can, for instance, specify individual responsibilities of task group members advocating for a policy change concerning clients living with AIDS. This group's intent is to lobby for a change in state law which will prohibit insurance companies from canceling the policies of persons diagnosed with AIDS.

A client looks over a written contract documenting the care services to be provided by the county for her child.

Another example of a contract in macro practice is the *purchase of service agreement*. This is a "fiscal agreement between two or more social agencies or between an agency and a government body, usually involving a contract between an agency with funds and another that can provide needed services. Purchaser agencies are thus able to extend services to their clientele, and provider agencies can increase their budgets, extend their services, and, in many cases, increase their profits" (Barker, 1987, p. 132). A more specific example of a purchase of service contract is a rural county social services agency with children in foster care needing speech therapy services. The county was too small and had too few child clients needing such therapy to hire its own speech therapist. The county officials decided to purchase the needed speech-therapy services from a private agency, Catholic Social Services (CSS). CSS was a statewide agency hiring a number of speech therapists to travel around the state and supply part-time speech-therapy services to a number of counties in similar circumstances (that is, needing speech therapy services for only a few clients).

Make Contracts *with* Clients

A contract summarizes what you as a worker and your client system *agree* to do during the intervention process. The emphasis is on the word "agree." We continue to stress involving clients during every phase of the intervention process. The extensive involvement of clients in the development of intervention contracts is simply an extension of this theme.

The contract is not a legal contract as such. It has little to do with the contracts disputed in courts of law. It articulates a commitment valid only within the practitioner/client relationship. On the other hand, an intervention contract "contains more flexibility than a legal document, for it can be changed by agreement between the worker and the client. This flexibility is essential if indicated changes in plans of action are to take place when new information is identified that points to a need for a change in the plan of action and the contract" (Johnson, 1989, p. 315). Thus, the ongoing involvement of the client system is critical.

Johnson (1989) cites two additional advantages of client involvement in establishing contracts. First, a contract can cultivate and enrich clients' motivation for work on problems and tasks because it "gives structure, specificity, and a sense of participation to the client" (p. 314). Second, "the reaching of agreed-upon goals and objectives through the client's own actions (at least in part) enhances self-esteem and the sense of being able to affect a situation. ... The choices involved in developing a plan give clients a sense of some control over their problem and situation" (p. 314).

It is important that clients understand everything incorporated into a contract (Johnson, 1989). All the contract's terms should be clear to them. They should be able to understand all of the words used.

The Format of a Contract

Contracts can be established in three different ways. First, they can be written and signed. Examples of this type will be given later. Second, they can involve a verbal agreement between client, worker, and any others involved. Third, they may be implicit or assumed.

The Written Contract

The written contract is the most formal format. It clearly and visually reflects what client, workers, and anyone involved have agreed upon. It should state specific objectives and follow the *who* will do *what* by *when* format discussed earlier.

A primary advantage of a written contract is that it becomes a clear, virtually indisputable record. There can be no distortions of what earlier agreements involved. It can be brought before worker and client at any time to refresh memories about what they agreed upon.

Another advantage is that participants sign the contract. A signature illustrates commitment. It makes it difficult to later question who agreed to do what by when.

Written contracts have two disadvantages. First, they take time to draw up. (Sheafor et al., 1988). A practitioner may be rushed, extremely busy, late, or overwhelmed. Second, some legal questions can be raised (Epstein, 1980). How binding would any particular contract be if brought before a court? Would a worker be liable if he fails to complete responsibilities recorded in a contract?

Sheafor et al. (1988) reflect on how to respond to some other extenuating circumstances:

> It may be necessary to prepare the contract in the client's first language (e.g., Spanish) if he or she has a poor understanding of English. In cases where the client cannot read, the worker should consider recording the agreement on a cassette tape, in addition to preparing a written statement (p. 313).

Finally, a copy of the written contract should always be placed in the client's file. It should be easily accessible at any time during the intervention process.

The Verbal Contract

Verbal contracts specify essentially the same thing as written contracts, although verbally—the intent is to clearly identify all objectives and responsibilities in the planning process. Verbal contracts should be just as clear as written contracts.

There are two advantages to a verbal contract. First, it can be made swiftly and in a relatively easy fashion. Second, it can be a "help" when working with a "resistant or distrustful client" who refuses to sign a written document (Johnson, 1989, p. 315). You can solicit agreement from such a client without trying to force a signature.

The client's record should still indicate that the verbal contract was made along with a brief summary of what was involved; this summary should include "who participated in the decision making, what decisions were made, [and] what alternatives were considered and why they were rejected (Kagle, 1991, p. 39).

The major disadvantage of a verbal contract is that it's easy to forget the details of an agreement unless they are written down. It might be helpful for workers to jot down informal notes to themselves so that they can remember exactly what transpired.

Implicit Contracts

Implicit contracts are agreements that are implied or assumed, but not actually articulated. Be wary about using them. It's easy to make two assumptions which can be false. First, you can mistakenly assume that your client has agreed when she really has not. Second, you can assume that your client understands all the conditions and responsibilities of your perceived implicit contract when she does not.

Kravetz and Rose (1973) explain the potential use of implicit agreements in groups:

> In addition to the explicit terms which are agreed upon by all the participants, the interpersonal interaction of the group is also governed by implicit norms, rules, or agreements. The group leader must identify and assess the effect of these norms on group process. If the interaction patterns do not interfere with the achievement of goals, these patterns need not be made explicit. However, the group leader may engage group members in discussion of their interaction in order to modify those implicit agreements which interfere with goal attainment (p. 17).

Groups and the interpersonal processes involved can be very complex. There may be numerous assumed agreements concerning how individuals will perform and behave inside and outside of the group. There may be too many, and they may be too subtle to label openly. Such assumed agreements essentially compose an implicit contract. For instance, an implicit contract within a treatment group for alcoholic adults might be a prohibition of encouraging other group members to drink. Another term of the implicit contract for this particular group might be to behave in a socially appropriate manner. For instance, fingers should be kept out of noses, ears, and other orifices, and members shouldn't swear at each other.

What to Include in Intervention Contracts

At the least, intervention contracts should include identifying information about the client, specified objectives and signatures of client and worker. Each type of information merits further discussion. Figure 6.3 depicts an example of an intervention contract.

Identifying Information

An intervention contract must always contain information which identifies the client. This almost always includes the client's name. Sometimes, a case number is involved. Other times, there is a brief description of the problem included, as is illustrated in Figure 6.3. This can help quickly orient a worker, who deals with many cases and many problems, to a particular case.

Contracts involving groups may include all members' names. The type of group may also be used as identifying information.

In contracts with other agencies, sometimes their names are specified as well. At other times, the contract will be identified by a project name.

Specified Objectives

The core of any intervention contract involves specification of objectives. Our previous discussion concerning the writing of objectives applies directly to writing them into contracts. They should be clear and easily understood by anyone reading them. They should indicate who will do what by when, and they should be measurable.

Signatures

All written contracts should be signed. This demonstrates that the participants are both well informed about the plan, its objectives, and each participant's responsibilities. Additionally, a signature indicates commitment to the plan.

Contracts used in mezzo and macro practice may need room for a number of different signatures. All participants in the intervention plan should have a place to sign.

Dates

Finally, all intervention contracts should include the date the agreement was made. This can usually be found directly underneath the participants' signatures. A date will indicate the contract's currency. An old date might indicate that the contract's contents need to be reviewed.

Formats Vary

In reality, contract formats vary radically. For example, Kagle (1991, p. 138) illustrates a contract called a "service agreement" with the following four components: "(1) Purpose(s) or goal(s) of service; (2) plan of service; (3) (client name) agrees to undertake the following responsibilities; (4) on behalf of the agency, (worker name) agrees to undertake the following responsibilities."

Additionally, instructions for filling it out are included. Dates are also recorded a bit differently than those illustrated in figure 6.3. They indicate the time that the contract covers—the date it was signed and the date it should be completed. The contract then ends with signature lines for both client and worker.

You should be prepared to find such different contract formats. Formats may depend on the agency's mission, client needs, and contract purpose. Regardless of the format your agency uses, the principles applying to writing good behavioral objectives should still apply. It should be clear who is responsible for what tasks. Task completion dates should be specified. Finally, objectives should be measurable, so no question exists about whether or not they have been accomplished.

Contracts Often Change Over Time

Contracts continue to change over time. Objectives are reached; new objectives are established. Clients' situations change and, inter-

Figure 6.3: An Example of a Written Contract Format

<u>Contract for Intervention Plan</u>

Client Name: _____

1. Description of the Problem: _____

_____

_____

2. Primary Goals: _____

_____

_____

3. We, the undersigned, agree to the objectives in the following plan:

    A. _____

    B. _____

    C. _____

    D. _____

    E. _____

_____   _____
(Signature of Client)   (Signature of Worker)

_____   _____
(Date)   (Date)

vention plans must be adjusted to meet these changes. You should indicate such changes and the dates they were made either on the old contract or on a revised one.

Figure 6.4 illustrates a series of three monthly contracts used for residents in a halfway house for people recovering from alcohol and other drug abuse. Because the clients reside there, they receive daily supervision in addition to professional counseling. The goal is to help integrate them back into the community. Thus, the contracts focus on gaining employment and saving money.

Several differences are reflected in the three contracts. Some content changes as the months progress. Note six elements about the "First Month Contract." First, the contract starts with a basic commitment to follow the house rules. Second, it structures a statement committing the client to actively seek employment in a specified geographical area. Third, the contract requires that the client strive to put the specific amount of at least one hundred dollars in savings. Fourth, it structures the fact that a new contract will be established within one month. Fifth, it specifies that weekly counseling sessions are required. Sixth, blank spaces two through nine are left for the specification of individualized objectives.

Now view the "Second Month Contract" depicted in figure 6.4. This contract is much less structured. The idea is that clients are gradually encouraged to make more decisions and accept greater responsibility for themselves. This contract omits the item about commitment to house rules. It allows the client to specify how much he will put into savings. Note that putting money into savings is still required. The contract assumes the client has already gotten a job. Likewise, weekly counseling sessions are still required. Additionally, blank spaces two through five are provided for establishing individualized objectives.

Finally, consider the "Third Month Contract." Once again, the client is required to

place a set amount into savings. He is again permitted to determine that amount himself. Next, a new goal is added, namely to work actively on the transition from a supervised living environment to living independently within the community. The contract then requires that the client continue evaluating individual goals and working with his counselor to develop new goals. This contract requires that the client attend group meetings instead of individual "weekly counseling sessions." Places for individualized objectives remain.

This series of contracts provides a good example of how objectives and the contracts which reflect them can change. The contracts go from making specific requirements to enhancing the client's independent decision-making capacity. It is obvious that some of the objectives are highly structured—it is the nature of this treatment program that clients must abide by some rules in order to continue in the program. The agency has found this to be the most effective means of treatment. Client participation in the treatment contract is encouraged as much as possible within this setting.

Preliminary Contracts

According to Kravetz and Rose (1973), a "preliminary contract" is one which allows the client to "explore and develop with the worker possible terms of the contract." They continue that it involves the client's "agreement to explore the terms of the contract, with or without member commitment to change" (p. 21). In other words, sometimes a contract with primary goals and specific objectives cannot be formulated during the first or even the first few sessions with the client. The client may be resistant, resentful, or confused. In these instances, the best you can do is establish an agreement with the client that s/he will at least continue trying to establish preliminary goals. Sometimes, a preliminary contract simply is the client's commitment to come and talk to you one more time. Nonetheless, preliminary contracts

Figure 6.4: An Example of Progressively Changing Contracts

CEPHAS HALFWAY HOUSE
Lutheran Social Services

First Month Contract

In addition to following the House Rules, I, _____,
agree to the following terms in order to keep my residency at Cephas Halfway House.

I will look for employment in the Waukesha area every day until I find a job.

When I become employed, I will open a savings account and try to save at least one
hundred dollars ($100).

Once this is done, I will approach my counselor to negotiate a second month contract,
which will include goals that my agent and counselor want.

1. Weekly counseling sessions _____

2. _____   6. _____

3. _____   7. _____

4. _____   8. _____

5. _____   9. _____

_____   _____
(Staff)   (Date)

_____
(Resident)

Source: This material has been adapted from contracts used by Cephas Halfway House, Waukesha, WI. Used with permission of Lutheran Social Services, 3200 W. Highland Boulevard, P.O. Box 08320, Milwaukee, WI 53208.

Figure 6.4 (*continued*)

CEPHAS HALFWAY HOUSE
Lutheran Social Services

Second Month Contract

I, _____, will agree to increase my savings account

to _____ by the end of my second month. If there is any restitu-

tion, I will sit down with my agent and work out some arrangement and make out a

schedule of payment in addition to the above.

My goals for the second month are as follows:

1. Weekly counseling sessions _____

2. _____

3. _____

4. _____

5. _____

_____   _____
(Staff)   (Date)

_____
(Resident)

Figure 6.4 (*continued*)

CEPHAS HALFWAY HOUSE
Lutheran Social Services

Third Month Contract

I, _____ , agree to increase my savings account
to _____. In addition to this, I will work closely with my
counselor in preparing for the transition from Cephas Halfway House to community
living. Goal achievements will be looked at closely. I will continue to work on
my goals previously set, in addition to what my counselor and I agree on in this
third month. I will continue to attend my group meeting.

1. _____

2. _____

3. _____

4. _____

5. _____

_____   _____
(Staff)   (Date)

_____
(Resident)

are valid and often useful, providing an alternative method of engaging a client in the intervention process.

Planning in Mezzo Practice

Parts of the planning process for working with groups have been discussed in earlier chapters (specifically, chapter 3 and chapter 5). Namely, formulating group membership depends on a number of variables, including motivation of potential group members, group purpose, members' ability to communicate with each other, group size, group structure, and group duration. To avoid redundancy, we won't discuss those variables again here.

The six-step planning process described here can be similarly applied to planning when working with groups. Of course, variations do exist because of the increased complexity when more than one client is involved.

The Complexity of Setting Objectives in Mezzo Practice

As we know, a *client system* can be an individual, group, or large organization. Your "client" is the individual or group you're helping. Working with families and other groups becomes more complicated than working with single individuals, because you need to take all group members' needs into consideration. Nonetheless, the bottom line is to *work with* the client or clients. With task groups, treatment groups, and families, you need to make certain that each and every member is involved in the planning and goal-setting process.

Toseland and Rivas (1984, pp. 153–57) make at least six points about formulating goals and objectives in groups:

1. First, it usually takes substantially *more time* for members in groups to discuss and clarify their goals and objectives. Much depends on the diversity of membership and the individuals' level of motivation. Even group members whose views diverge most strongly from the majority of other members must be satisfactorily integrated into the goal-setting process. Likewise, the least motivated group members must also be included for the group to succeed at its goals and objectives.

2. *Both the clients and the worker* can propose, devise, and refine group goals and objectives. To be effective, the goal-setting process must meet the worker's needs as well as those of the group.

3. Practitioners often propose goals and objectives reflecting their *unique perspective*. "As members of social service agencies, workers are aware of the aims and the limitations of agencies, services, and their functions in communities. Workers' formulations of goals reflect what they believe can be accomplished, given the support, resources, and limitations within which the group operates" (pp. 154–55).

In treatment groups, practitioners "often have an opportunity to meet each member during the planning phase. Potential members are selected, in part, because of their compatibility with the purposes and goals developed for the group. Workers make preliminary assessments of members' needs and capacities, as well as the tasks that face each group member. Goals are formulated on the basis of this assessment process" (p. 155).

Likewise, in task groups, a practitioner can make assessments of the strengths, weaknesses, and areas of expertise demonstrated by individual group members. S/he can then help members to develop goals and objectives that maximize their individual strengths. For instance, take a group whose task is to evaluate an agency's personnel policies and make recommendations for change to the upper-level administration. One member might be exceptionally oriented to minute detail and accuracy. That member might be the one to pursue the objective of evaluating the current agency policy manual for inconsistencies. This would help prepare for the primary goal of overhauling the entire policy manual.

You would not want such a task assigned to a group member who has little tolerance for detail. Accuracy, sometimes tedious accuracy, is necessary to complete this task adequately. The latter member, however, although poor in attending to detail, might be especially adept at developing new ideas and alternatives. This member's objective might be to survey personnel to develop a list of existing problems and suggested changes for the manual. Both members' individual strengths would then be put to their most effective use.

4. Individual group members establish goals and objectives on the basis of "their own perspective on the particular concerns, problems, and issues that affect them and their fellow group members" (p. 155).

When a group meets for the first time, members tend to formulate their goals based on five major variables. First, individual members' proposed goals and objectives are based on their evaluation of their own wants, lacks, and needs. What is it that each wants from the group? What does each want the group to accomplish?

The second variable involves how effective each has been in accomplishing such goals in the past. How likely is future success based on past experiences? How likely is failure?

The third variable involves other pressures and demands influencing group members. How much time and energy can each group member afford to devote to the group and its goals in view of other social and professional responsibilities?

The fourth variable concerns what each member feels he or she is capable of accomplishing. What skills, abilities, or competencies does each bring to the group? What does the member feel capable of doing and what not?

Finally, the fifth variable involves the member's prior involvement with the agency promoting the group and that member's faith in the agency's ability to accomplish goals effectively. Have past experiences been positive or negative? Does this member join the group with an optimistic or pessimistic attitude? Or is this member's attitude more neutral?

5. Groups vary significantly in the degree to which they are capable of developing shared group goals and objectives. Sometimes, individual goals vary to such an extreme that finding common ground is very difficult. Other times, group members have obviously similar needs which can lead to the establishment of common goals.

Consider, for example, a treatment group of agoraphobics. Agoraphobics have extreme and irrational fears of open or crowded places. They often strive to avoid any location where they feel uncomfortable. Extreme cases may feel safe and at ease only in their own home. People subjected to such a desperate condition usually find their daily activities and lives seriously curtailed. Such individuals would probably be highly motivated to establish goals oriented to coping with and ridding themselves of this oppressive state.

In groups where members have unrelated needs and distinctly different perspectives, it will probably be much more difficult to work together and establish common goals. An example is a task group trying to establish a neighborhood recreational center. It is composed of members from a wide cross section of the community. If one member joined the group primarily to create a job for himself, another to find potential dates, and still another to provide a centralized hub of activity for neighborhood adolescents, the group might find it extremely difficult to agree upon its goals.

6. Group goals and objectives can be classified into three major categories (Toseland & Rivas, 1984, p. 156). First, there are goals that involve nourishing the group and keeping it going. These are "group-centered goals." For example, such a goal might be to enhance group members' ability to express their ideas and work out compromises. The second category of goals is made up of the "common group goals" referred to earlier. These involve a goal arrived at and shared by all group members. For instance, all members of a task group might aim to decrease community taxes. A third type of goal is the "individual goal." This is where the individual member works to attain some specific goal for him or herself.

An example of the individual goal involves an eating disorders self-help (treatment) group. Eating disorders encompass a variety of psychological and physical problems involving eating behavior. One disorder, anorexia nervosa, is a condition where people, usually young women, experience a severe fear of gaining weight. This often results in extreme weight loss and sometimes starvation. A group member with this condition might formulate individual goals and objectives concerning her personal eating patterns. Additionally, she might establish a goal for a specific amount of weight gain. A young woman who is five-foot-eleven and 83 pounds might establish a weight goal for herself of 125 pounds.

Contracts in Mezzo Practice

Kravetz and Rose (1973) talk about writing contracts in groups:

In groups, one can identify individual and group goals. Individual goals concern the achievements expected for each member of the group. These may be attitudes and skills to be learned or tasks to be achieved. Group goals are concerned with the expected achievement for the group as a whole or expected patterns of interaction within the group (p. 5).

In groups, then, each member might sign two contracts. One would include group goals and objectives and the other individual goals and objectives. Sometimes, all group members have an identical section on the contract summarizing group goals and objectives. Additionally, each group member's contract is different, because it also summarizes his or her individual goals and objectives.

Planning in Macro Practice

Planning in macro practice follows the same basic steps as planning in micro and mezzo practice. As chapter 4 describes, there are many avenues with which to practice on the macro level. Consider social reform, social action, cause advocacy, and case advocacy. Likewise, there are many ways to change or initiate policies, programs, and organizations. It's easy for a beginning social worker to focus more heavily on the micro and mezzo aspects of practice. Working with people and helping them solve their individual problems is fascinating. Each person and problem is unique.

In order to demonstrate the significance and relevance of macro planning, we'll provide one specific example here, namely that of *program development*. Program development involves establishing some new way of providing a different or new service to clients. Sometimes, new programs are developed within existing agencies. At other times, they require starting up a whole new agency. Programs can entail virtually any type of service provision. Services can range from providing mental-health counseling for veterans to residential treatment for delinquent adolescents to nursing-home facilities for the elderly.

It is likely that you will be part of some program's development. It's also quite possible that you will be in a position to initiate some program yourself.

An Approach to Program Planning

Hasenfeld (1987) proposes a number of specific procedures to follow in the program development process. They include:

1. Articulate the problem, and translate it into what clients need;
2. Marshal support for program development;
3. Allocate "responsibilities to a board or advisory council" (p. 456);
4. Describe the purpose (or overall goal) of the proposed program;
5. Formulate clear subgoals or objectives;
6. Implement a "feasibility study" (p. 458);
7. Solicit the financial resources you need to initiate the program;
8. Describe how the program will provide services;
9. Get the program going;
10. Establish how services will be effectively provided on an ongoing basis.

These procedures comply with our basic planning steps in the problem-solving process. The following discussion describes each of these procedures and integrates them within the planning model (see Figure 6.1).

Work with the Client

Working with the client system means that you need to work closely with those people who will be receiving the service. In macro practice, it entails working with other professionals, orga-

nizations, and agencies that can help you complete your intervention. They can provide you with information about individual clients' needs and assist you in the actual intervention process. Working with the client system means that you remain open to feedback and remain responsive to the needs of others in the process.

Prioritize Problems

It is assumed here that problems have already been identified during the assessment phase of the problem-solving process. You are proceeding to develop a program. You are doing so because you've identified some specific problems. It may be that there are no shelters for the homeless people in your area or that poor people are not getting access to the health care they need. Your intent is to identify the order in which you'll address your specified problems. Your proposed program will take shape according to what problems you determine are most important to solve.

For instance, consider the problem of poor people not getting adequate access to health care. How you define and prioritize problems will significantly impact how your program will eventually work and what services it will provide. You might decide that the most significant problem is that there is no health delivery service in the targeted area. People aren't getting health care because there isn't any. In this case, you may begin initiating an entire health program with facilities to be set up in the area where the care is needed.

On the other hand, you might decide that the primary problem is not that health care is unavailable. Rather, the problem is that poor people have neither money nor health insurance to pay for the health care provided in the community. In this situation, you might try to establish a program to provide poor people with *funding* for health care. Or you could determine that funding is already potentially available. What is needed is a *program to educate* needy people regarding what's available and assist them in applying for the funding.

Translate Problems into Needs

We've discussed how translating the problem into a need helps give you direction on fulfilling that need. It orients you away from dwelling on what's wrong to focusing on what can be done to solve the problem(s).

This is equivalent to Hasenfeld's (1987) first procedure for establishing a new program or service. Namely, *articulate the problem and translate it into what clients need.* You've already established and prioritized problems. Now you need to translate them into needs that can be documented and clearly understood.

Hasenfeld continues with five steps for clarifying and substantiating an unmet need (pp. 454–55):

1. Get data and information to clarify exactly what the need is. Substantiating data can also be used to prove that the need is significant enough to merit intervention. You can obtain "facts" from statistical reports kept by public agencies. Census data is often helpful. Public and private agencies often keep information on the requests for service which cannot be met. Research studies also sometimes document needs. Be creative. Think about what kinds of facts would be helpful to prove the need. Who else might be interested in the problem and need? Where might other interested parties make documentation available?

   For instance, take the *problem* of many community teenagers being heavily involved in drugs. You determine that they *need* the establishment of a drug treatment program within the community. Where could you find facts and statistics to establish this need? One source might be police statistics. How many drug-related arrests have been made? Can the lack of treatment programs and referral sources be documented from their records? Another source might be local schools. What records are available regarding drug problems and seizures? Are research reports available addressing similar adolescent populations, which can support the need for drug rehabilitation programs in general?

2. A second step is to recognize and specify what other agencies or programs in the community are already addressing the identified need. If the need is already being met somewhere else, why go through the effort needed to start a new program? Continue with our adolescent drug problem example. If a local hospital is already offering a program to address the treatment and rehabilitation need, further program development may not be necessary. Rather, your intervention approach might then be to educate teens and parents about the problem and program, in addition to facilitating their access to the already-existing program. On the other hand, establishing that no relevant programs exist only strengthens your position that a program is needed.

3. Talk to other professionals involved with clients. Find out how they perceive the problem and need. They might enhance your understanding of what's involved and give you ideas on how to proceed.

4. This step emphasizes involving clients. Talk to community residents and find out how they perceive the problem and need. For example, parent-teacher associations, church groups, and community businesspeople and professionals might provide further insight and support for your plans.

5. Consider doing a more formal needs assessment. This technique was addressed in chapter 4. Such studies can document

very specific needs in a convincing manner.

Evaluate the Levels of Intervention

In essence, we've already chosen the macro approach as the target strategy in this discussion. The intent of Hasenfeld's program-development formulation is to illustrate one type of planning in macro practice.

Establish Primary Goals and Specify Objectives

The primary goal in program development, of course, is to define and develop a new program. Hasenfeld's Steps 2 through 10 describe objectives to pursue in order to achieve this primary goal. Step 1 concerns determining that the need exists in the first place.

Step 2 concerns *marshaling support for program development*. It is difficult, if not impossible, to initiate and establish a new program or service completely by yourself. You need support from a variety of other sources. One especially useful means of soliciting a steady source of support is to establish an "action group." Such a group "then gathers resources and influence, actively representing the new program's objectives, and fights for its support in the community" (Hasenfeld, 1987, p. 455). Additionally, such a group can help you identify and articulate the primary goals for the proposed program, specify the client systems to receive services, target potential financial resources for the program, and share information about the program and its goals with other groups, agencies, and organizations within the community" (such as city council, county government, mental health board, United Fund)" (Hasenfeld, 1987, p. 456).

Action-group members should be chosen very carefully. Chapter 3 examined task groups and their membership. You will want motivated individuals who are seriously interested in the proposed program. Additionally, you might so-

licit support by including influential community professionals, religious leaders, and businesspeople. They can provide you with credibility. Their views are generally listened to.

Finally, you might select action-group members for their specific areas of expertise. For example, a certified alcohol and other drug abuse counselor could provide valuable input regarding how a drug rehabilitation program needs to be structured. Likewise, a lawyer whose practice targets juveniles or a police officer could contribute relevant information regarding the legal aspects of working with juvenile drug abusers.

From members of this action group, you might establish a more formalized "board of directors, . . . advisory council, or . . . an internal task force within an existing agency" (Hasenfeld, 1987, p. 457). A board of directors is "a group of people empowered to establish an organization's objectives and policies and to oversee the activities of the personnel responsible for day-to-day implementation of those policies. Social agency boards of directors are often made up of volunteers who are influential in the community and reflect the views prevalent in the community" (Barker, 1987, p. 17). In other words, such a formalized group can lend support, credibility, and community influence.

Hasenfeld's Step 3 entails *allocating responsibilities to a board or advisory council*. The *who* should do *what* by *when* formula clearly applies here. Board tasks can include "general direction and control of the agency—policy development, short- and long-term planning . . . , hiring competent administrative staff . . . , facilitating access to necessary resources . . . public relations, [and] evaluation [for] accountability" (Gelman, 1987, p. 207).

Step 4 concerns *describing the purpose (or overall goal) of the proposed program*. A program's mission involves three facets. First, the unmet needs must be clearly defined and documented. Second, the clientele receiving the services must be clearly identified. Third, the services to be provided by the program must be plainly delineated. In other words, the purpose of the program should be well articulated so that everyone involved understands the program's structure and intentions.

Step 5 involves *formulating clear subgoals or objectives*. As we've established, goals or objectives must be very clear. This applies to micro, mezzo, and macro practice. Earlier, we discussed behavioral specificity within the context of micro practice. Goals in macro practice should be just as clear and measurable as in any other type of intervention. Specifying the performance expected, the conditions under which that performance is to occur, and the standards by which success is measured in macro practice corresponds to doing the same thing in micro practice.

For example, return to the illustration of developing a program for adolescent drug abusers. A program objective might be to provide an inpatient, six-week treatment program (performance) for all identified drug-abusing teens within a specified geographic area (conditions) with at least 90 percent of clients remaining drug-free for six months after leaving the program (standards). Inpatient programs are those which require clients in treatment to live right in the facility both day and night.

Such an objective would also require a variety of objectives or subgoals of its own in order to be completed. What steps would need to be followed to develop this program? *Who* would need to do *what* by *when*? Macro practice, of course, involves more individuals and groups in addition to agencies, policies, and organizations, than micro practice. Therefore, you might anticipate having more levels of objectives than, for example, when working with a single individual. These subgoals might involve any number of individuals and groups before primary goals can be accomplished.

Step 6 of program development entails *implementing a feasibility study*. This is "a systematic assessment of the resources needed to accomplish a specified objective and concurrent evaluation of an organization's existing and anticipated capabilities for providing those resources" (Barker, 1987, p. 55). In other words, you need to explore how realistic it is that you can actually develop the program. How much will staffing and facilities cost? What kind of backing can you expect from the community housing the program and from other community agencies?

Additionally, what other types of resources might be available? Hasenfeld suggests five potential sources: grants, assistance from local government, private donations by individuals and agencies, services and goods donated by other agencies, and the use of volunteers.

One especially beneficial resource for many agencies is United Way. This agency is a national union of local organizations that coordinates fund-raising and distribution of those funds to designated social service agencies at the local level.

The main point is that you need to determine that you have enough resources to continue with your program development plan. On the other hand, if you can't possibly afford to implement the program, you might as well halt the process right here.

Soliciting the financial resources you need to initiate the program is Step 7. Earlier, your feasibility study identified possible funding sources. Step 7 involves actually *getting* the necessary funding to start the program. You need to transform the *potential* funding sources into *actual* funding sources. You need to work with these resources and convince the people controlling them that your proposed program does indeed merit their attention, support, and money. Additionally, you may want to instigate some fund-raising crusades, a macro technique mentioned in chapter 4.

Step 8 concerns *describing how the program will provide services*. How will the program actually work? For instance, what types of treatment techniques will the drug rehabilitation counselors be expected to use? What kind of training do they require in order to do their jobs well? Will there be an outpatient program in addition to inpatient? In outpatient treatment programs clients receive health care by visiting the clinic or facility, not by staying overnight or receiving more extended ongoing care. How will the inpatient units be run? What types of treatment programs will clients have (for instance, group counseling, individual counseling, or job-seeking assistance)?

It's important, then, to specify the details that describe how the program will be run. What specific kinds of services will the program deliver to clients? Exactly how will the program reach its specified objectives?

Actually *getting the program going* is Step 9. Staff with the necessary credentials need to be hired and scheduled. These staff need to fully understand how the program is structured and run. All procedures should be stated as clearly as possible.

Sometimes, a trial run is helpful. Trying out the program with a few clients instead of having the program start out at full capacity can identify flaws. Such flaws can be addressed and remedied more easily when programs first begin. Precedents (that is, established ways of doing things that guide how those things are done in the future) have not yet been set. It's very important for the new program to be responsive to needed changes and improvements.

Step 10 in program development concerns *establishing how services will be provided on an ongoing basis. How* services are delivered to clients is just as important as *what* services are delivered. Clients should be able to depend on any service being provided in a timely, predictable fashion. Scheduling appointments and meetings should be done according to clearly defined procedures. Staff should have straight-forward, accurate job descriptions. They should all know exactly what tasks they are responsible for. Finally, billing should be organized and predictable.

Formalize a Contract

Contracts can be useful in program development on a variety of levels. They might be used to solidify the agreements made in action groups or by a board of directors.

The purchase-of-service contracts described earlier might be established with other agencies to provide services your program cannot. For instance, your agency might contract with another agency to provide vocational-rehabilitation counseling. Your program might even employ contracts with food suppliers and professional laundry facilities in order to take care of inpatient clients' daily needs.

Chapter Summary

This chapter examined the seven-step planning process in the generalist intervention model. These steps are work with the client, prioritize problems, translate problems into needs, evaluate the level of intervention (micro, mezzo, or macro), establish primary goals, specify objectives, and formalize a contract.

Establishing primary goals and objectives was discussed. Writing clear, measurable objectives was stressed. Written, verbal, and implicit contracts were described. The types of content to be included in contracts with client systems was identified.

Special aspects of planning in mezzo practice were recognized. Planning in program development as it relates to macro practice was explained.

7 Intervention Applications

Doing it

TWO CHILDREN FOUND LOCKED IN TINY ROOM FILLED
    WITH ANIMAL FECES

DRUNKEN MAN RUNS DOWN TWO TEENS, KILLS BOTH

ECONOMY SLUMPS, SUICIDE CRISIS LINES BUZZING

Any of these headlines might be found in your local evening newspaper. They are included here because they refer to issues that often involve social work intervention. These issues are child maltreatment, alcohol and other drug abuse, and crisis intervention.

CHAPTER SEVEN

Introduction

Barker (1987) describes the meaning of intervention as

> ... interceding in or coming between groups of people, events, planning activities, or an individual's internal conflicts. In social work, the term is analogous to the physician's term "treatment." Many social workers prefer using "intervention" because it includes "treatment" and also encompasses the other activities social workers use to solve or prevent problems or achieve goals for social betterment. Thus, it refers to psychotherapy, advocacy, mediation, social planning, community organization, finding and developing resources, and many other activities (p. 82).

Thus, intervention is the actual *doing* of social work. It's obvious that this can involve a broad range of activities in micro, mezzo, and macro practice. Individual chapters in this text have been devoted to a number of these activities (for example, advocacy, case management, and connecting clients with needed resources, or brokering). Often, you, as a generalist practitioner, will not be responsible for the *counseling* aspects of intervention. Rather, you might be responsible for assessment and referral to other resources or for coordinating the activities of a number of social workers and other professionals working on a specific case.

This chapter will address three different approaches to intervention. Each coincides with the Generalist Intervention Model and its problem-solving focus. However, each approach also embraces its own unique qualities and specific techniques. These intervention approaches are risk management in protective services, crisis intervention, and intervention with alcohol and other drug abusers. All involve problems with which you are likely to come into contact, even if your individual job does not provide services related directly to them.

Specifically, this chapter will:

- Describe risk management in protective services;
- Examine a program that uses the concepts of risk management and family preservation to combat child maltreatment;
- Summarize common goals of risk management;
- Describe how crises develop;
- Explain the major concepts in crisis intervention;
- Examine a model of crisis intervention, identify specific techniques involved, and apply the model to a case situation;
- Recognize the significance of crisis intervention at the mezzo and macro levels in addition to the micro level;
- Review terms commonly used in interventions involving alcohol and other drug abuse (AODA);
- Describe typical characteristics of the alcoholic people and their families;
- Discuss the generalist practitioner's role in intervention with abusers and their families;
- Identify a number of techniques effective in AODA interventions.
- Recognize a number of potential referral sources for AODA clients;
- Relate mezzo and macro aspects of the intervention process with AODA clients.

Risk Management in Protective Services: A Decision-Making Approach

The Child at Risk Field System (CARF) developed by Holder and Corey (1991) provides an excellent example of how social workers might

Figure 7.1: Intervention in the Generalist Intervention Model

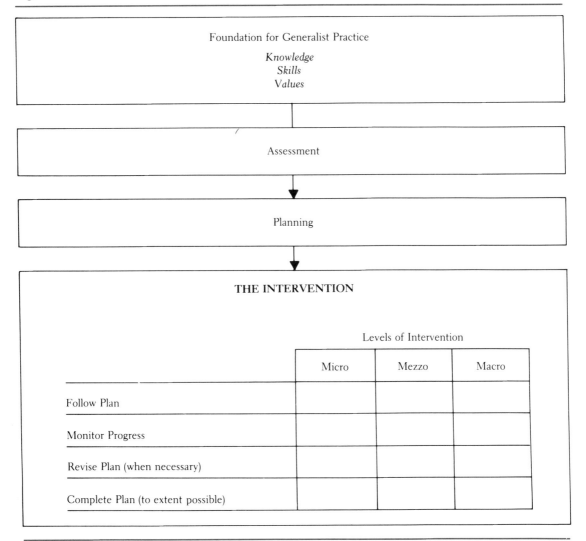

carry out the intervention process.[1] It uses an approach to addressing child abuse and neglect which emphasizes the concept of *risk manage-*

1. The description of the Child at Risk Field System here is reprinted with the permission of Wayne Holder, MSW, ACPS, and Michael Corey, MSW, ACPS, Action for Child Protection, Headquarters, 4724 Park Road, Suite C, Charlotte, NC 28209.

ment. Risk management involves addressing or managing the likelihood or *risk* that a child will be maltreated (Holder & Corey, 1991).

What do you, as a protective-services worker, do when you receive a report that child abuse or neglect has occurred? Child protective services (CPS) involve assessment and interventions by social workers and others in situations

HIGHLIGHT 7.1

A Profile of Child Maltreatment

There are a number of ways in which children can be abused or neglected. The umbrella term which may be used to include all of them is child "maltreatment" (Kadushin & Martin, 1988, p. 226). Maltreatment includes physical abuse, inadequate care and nourishment, deprivation of adequate medical care, insufficient encouragement to attend school consistently, exploitation by being forced to work too hard or too long, exposure to unwholesome or demoralizing circumstances," sexual abuse, and emotional abuse and neglect (Kadushin & Martin, 1988, p. 226). Definitions used by legal and social service agencies vary from locality to locality and state to state. Usually, however, all can be clustered under two headings: child abuse (both physical and sexual) and child neglect.

Child maltreatment is a critical issue for social workers to understand. You need to know the clues that signify maltreatment. Even if you don't work directly in Protective Services, you need a basic understanding of child maltreatment in order to assess the possibility of occurrence in any families you work with. You then can make appropriate referrals to resources that can help.

Definitions and Indicators

Physical abuse can be defined very generally, although it becomes much more difficult to do so upon examination of real-life situations. Kadushin and Martin (1988) define physical abuse as "beating a child to the point at which the child sustains some physical damage" (p. 288). However, they conclude that in reality, there is often a very fine line between physical abuse and parental discipline.

Definitions of physical abuse vary from one place to another. Some definitions focus on whether the alleged abuser's purpose is to harm the child. Other definitions ignore the intent and instead emphasize the potential or actual harm done to the child.

Both physical and behavioral indicators provide clues that a child is being physically abused.

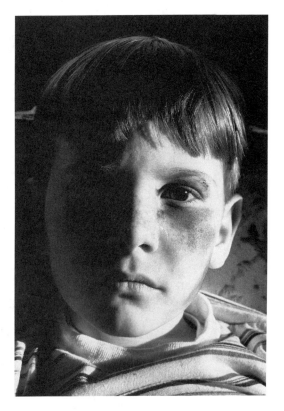

A black eye may be evidence that a child has been physically maltreated and that social work intervention is required.

Physical indicators can be broken down into six basic categories:

1. *Bruises.* Bruises on any infant should be suspect. Infants are not yet mobile, therefore, it's not likely that they can bruise themselves. Bruises in unusual places or forming unusual patterns may be indicators of physical abuse. Bruises that take on a recognizable shape, such as a hand mark or a belt mark, should be noted. Finally, bruises that display a variety of colors may portray abuse. This may be an indication that a series of bruises have been

received over time. Bruises usually progress from an initial bright red to blue to blackish-purple within the first day; they become shaded with a dark green color after four to six days and finally turn pale green or yellow after five to ten days have passed (Davis, 1982).

2. *Lacerations.* Cuts, scrapes, or scratches, especially if they occur frequently or their origin is poorly explained may indicate physical abuse. Lacerations on the face and genitalia should be noted. Bite marks may also indicate abuse.

3. *Fractures.* Bone fractures and other skeletal injuries may indicate abuse. Strangely twisted fractures and multiple fractures are especially telltale signs. Infants' fractures may be the result of abuse. Additional indicators are joint dislocations and injuries where the periosteum, the thin membrane covering the bone, is detached.

4. *Burns.* Burns, especially ones that take odd forms or are in patterns, may indicate abuse. Children have been burned by cigarettes and ropes (from being tied up and confined). Burns that occur on normally inaccessible portions of the body, such as the stomach, genitals, or soles of the feet, are clues to abuse. Patterned burns may indicate that the child has been burned with some hot utensil. Sacklike burns result when a hand or foot has been submerged in a hot liquid (Davis, 1982). A doughnut shaped burn will occur on the buttocks if a child has been immersed in very hot water. The central unburned area results from where the child's skin touched the bottom of the receptacle holding the water (Schmitt, 1980).

5. *Head injuries.* Head injuries which can indicate abuse include skull fractures, loss of hair due to vigorous pulling, and subdural hematomas (that is, blood which has collected beneath the outer covering of the brain after strenuous shaking or hitting has occurred). Black eyes should be suspect. Retinas may detach or hemorrhage if a child is shaken vigorously.

6. *Internal injuries.* Children have received injuries to their spleen, kidneys, and intestines due to hitting and kicking. The vena cava, the large vein by which blood is brought from the lower extremities to the heart, may be ruptured. Peritonitis, where the lining of the abdominal cavity becomes inflamed, can be another indicator of abuse.

In summary, some of the major questions to ask yourself if you think a child may have been physically abused are:

Does this child get hurt too often for someone his or her age?
Does the child have multiple injuries?
Do the injuries occur in patterns, assume recognizable shapes, or look like some of the injuries described here?
Are the injuries such that they don't seem possible for a child at that stage of development?
Do the explanations given for the injuries make sense?

If something doesn't seem right or logical to you, it may mean something is wrong. It might be called a "gut reaction." If a little voice way in the back of your mind is saying, "Oh-oh, that certainly is odd," perhaps you should pay attention. It might be a clue to abuse.

In addition to physical indicators, behavioral indicators provide another major dimension of clues to physical abuse. A physically abused child tends to adopt behavioral extremes. Virtually all children display these extreme behaviors at one time or another. However, the frequency and severity of these behaviors in abused children are clearly notable. Four categories of behavioral indicators have been established (U.S. Department of Health and Welfare, 1979, pp. 25–27). The categories are (p. 25):

1. "Overly compliant, passive, undemanding behaviors aimed at maintaining a low profile, avoiding any possible confrontation with a parent which could lead to abuse." Abused children can be exceptionally calm and docile.

HIGHLIGHT 7.1 (*continued*)

They have learned this behavior in order to avoid any possible conflict with the abusive parent. If they are invisible, the parent may not be provoked. Many times, abusive children will even avoid playing for fear of drawing too much attention to themselves. Martin and Beezley (1976) call this approach "hypervigilance."

2. "Extremely aggressive, demanding, and rageful behaviors, sometimes hyperactive, caused by the child's repeated frustrations at getting basic needs met." Other physically abused children assume an opposite approach to the overly passive manner identified earlier. These children are so desperately in need of attention that they will try almost anything to get it. Even if they can only provoke negative attention from their parents, their aggressive behavior is reinforced.

3. "Role reversal behavior or extremely dependent behavior in response to parental emotional and even physical needs." Some physically abused children form behavioral patterns in reaction to their parents' own needs. For instance, parents who are seriously immature and in need of nurturing themselves may elicit overly mature, responsible, almost adultlike behavior from their children. These parents will expect their children to assume the parental role. The children will then act like little adults. On the other hand, some abusive parents will desperately need to keep their children dependent and to feel themselves in control. Children of these parents will behave in ways appropriate for children much younger than their actual age. They will cling to their parents and often display babyish behavior.

4. "Lags in development." Because abused children are forced to direct their attention and energy toward coping with their abusive situation, they will frequently show developmental delays. These may appear in the form of language delays, poorly developed social skills for their age level, or lags in motor development.

Helfer et al. (1976) state that abusive parents have failed to learn several basic skills in order to become good parents. In addition to not knowing how to meet their own emotional needs, they haven't learned to separate their feelings and emotions from their behavior. Therefore, if they get mad, they don't talk about it; they hit.

Another unlearned skill involves the appropriate delineation of responsibility. Their perception of who is responsible for whose behavior is blurred. On one hand, there is a tendency to blame others for their mistakes. For example, "It's the child's fault he got hit and broke his arm, because he was naughty." On the other hand, abusers tend to accept the blame for others' behavior. For instance, "It's my fault that Honey hit the child because I didn't have his supper hot enough when he got home."

Still another unlearned task involves decision making. Abusers tend to have little confidence in their own ability. Therefore, they tend to have little faith in their own judgment. They have difficulty articulating and evaluating their alternatives with the respective pros and cons of each choice.

One other skill abusers often fail to master is how to delay their own gratification. The here and now becomes all-important. If a child misbehaves, a kick will take care of it immediately. If their stress level is too high, they need immediate relief. They focus on the moment and have trouble looking at what the consequences of their behavior will be in the future.

Child neglect is "the failure of the child's parent or caretaker, who has the material resources to do so, to provide minimally adequate care in the areas of health, nutrition, shelter, education, supervision, affection, or attention" (Wolock & Horowitz, 1984, p. 15). Two of the most frequent aspects of neglect involve "deprivation of necessities" and "inadequate supervision" (Kadushin & Martin, 1988, p. 230).

Neglectful deprivation entails not providing children with the basic necessities they need to survive and thrive, both physically and emotionally. They may not be getting the food or clothing they need. Likewise, the conditions of their home environment may be inadequate. For instance, the house might not be heated, or children might be forced to sleep on the bare floor for lack of beds.

Inadequate medical and dental care is another dimension of neglect. Parents may not take children to a physician when they're sick or for regular check-ups, or to a dentist when they have toothaches. Neglected children's teeth may be in exceptionally poor condition.

Inadequate supervision can involve almost any aspect of children's lives. For example, small children may simply be left unattended and locked alone in a room for hours or even days at a time. Another aspect of inadequate supervision is neglecting children's hygiene. Children may not be bathed, and their clothes may not be washed.

Finally, children may be neglected in terms of their education. Parents may not provide adequate support for children to attend and succeed in school. Perhaps a parent "forgets" to wake the children up in the morning. Or a parent may provide no encouragement or support for their children to do well in school.

Sexual abuse involves "contacts and interactions between a child and an adult in which the child is being used for the sexual stimulation of the perpetrator or another person (Kadushin & Martin, 1988, p. 292–93). *Incest*, a form of sexual abuse, is "any sexual contact or interaction between family members who are not marital partners" (Mayer, 1983, p. 4). Three categories of symptoms indicate that sexual abuse may be occurring—physical problems, behavioral indicators, and inappropriate sexual behavior.

A variety of physical problems are indications of sexual abuse. For instance, a small child may become infected with a sexually transmitted disease. There may be pain, bleeding, or bruises in genital or anal areas. Pregnancy is still another indicator, especially if it occurs when a child is of an unusually young age to have sexual intercourse.

Behavioral symptoms provide the second category of symptoms. Many of these resemble those commonly demonstrated by physically abused children. For instance, sexually abused children may be either extremely withdrawn from others or exceptionally aggressive in their interactions. Likewise, their relationships with parents may be excessively dependent or overly involved.

The third category of indicators involves inappropriate, sexually related behavior. Sexually abused children may "display bizarre, sophisticated, or unusual sexual knowledge or behavior" (U.S. Department of Health, Education, and Welfare, 1979, p. 73). For example, one eight-year-old child's teacher expressed concern when she had to stop the child several times from mimicking sexual intercourse with another child (the term this teacher referred to was "humping") on the playground. Another teacher was alerted when one of her fifth-grade female students handed in eighteen poems. The assignment had only required one. Each of the poems was saturated with sexual images and terminology.

At the other extreme, sexually abused children may demonstrate fear, avoidance, or disgust concerning almost anything sexual. For instance, a student may refuse to undress for physical-education class or take showers afterwards with the other students. A sexually abused child may cringe when touched. Or a child will leave the room whenever any sexual topic is raised or sexual issue discussed.

Incidence of Child Maltreatment

The actual number of child maltreatment cases is difficult to determine. Specific definitions for who can and can't be included in specific catego-

HIGHLIGHT 7.1 (continued)

ries vary. How cases are reported and data gathered also vary dramatically. One thing, however, is certain. Any figures that are reported reflect a minimal number of actual cases. All indications are that vast numbers of cases remain unreported.

Some of the best statistics available indicate that nearly two million cases of child maltreatment were reported in 1985 (Kadushin & Martin, 1988, p. 244). Of these, 55.7 percent were for neglect, 33 percent for physical abuse, and 11.7 percent for sexual abuse.

A Profile of the Victim

Kadushin and Martin (1988) summarize the typical profile of the maltreated victim. They state, "The average age of the maltreated child is slightly over seven years of age. Younger, more vulnerable children are disproportionately underrepresented. Boys are more frequently abused than girls, but this is true only for children up to age ten or eleven. Girls are more frequently reported abused from ages eleven to seventeen" (p. 245). Kadushin and Martin continue that the increase in abuse to girls is due to the fact that sexual abuse begins to be reported at about that age level. Girls are much more likely to be reported as victims of sexual abuse than boys.

Characteristics of Abusers

Perpetrators of child abuse tend to have problems in seven major areas, the first four of which are personal and the last three environmental (U.S. Department of Health, Education, and Welfare, 1979). Although no one person may have all seven problems, most abusers will be characterized by at least some of them.

First, they themselves most likely have serious needs for support and nurturance which remain unfulfilled from their own childhood. A basic quality characterizing abusers is low self-esteem. Since they have never had their own needs met, they are unable to meet the needs of their children. They often invite rejection and hostility because they have little confidence in their own abilities. They don't know how to reach out for support. They often feel they are undeserving but still have desperate needs for human support. Many perpetrators have been abused as children themselves.

A second problem characterizing abusers involves social isolation. Their own self-confidence is low. They feel like no one will like them anyway, so they isolate themselves. They reject attention, even though they really need others for emotional support. They fear rejection, so they don't even try to reach out to others. As a result, when normal everyday stresses build up, they have no one to talk to and help them cope.

---

where children are deemed at risk of maltreatment. Usually, an investigation is performed to assess risk and services are provided as necessary. The latter may include providing the family with needed resources or initiating alternative placements for children at risk.

Many times, social work involves other phases of the problem-solving process than a clearly defined "intervention" step. Thus, your primary "doing" task might be assessment and referral to other caregivers. Or it might be case management which focuses on the *coordination*

of all the services and professionals providing those services which a client receives, rather than providing those services yourself (see chapter 15).

CARF structures seven steps that coincide with those in our problem-solving process (Holder & Corey, 1991). *Assessment* is a major thrust of CARF. Therefore, the assessment step is broken down into four substeps. These include "intake," "initial assessment," "safety evaluation and response," and "family assessment" (pp. 33–34). CARF's fifth through eighth steps respectively are *"treatment planning," "service provision,"*

Inability to take care of a child adequately because of their own emotional needs is a third problem characterizing abusive parents. We've already mentioned how abused children display a role reversal with their abusive parents or become extremely dependent on their parents. This is the other side of that coin. Some parents look for parental support from their children. Others feel the need to control their children and keep them dependent. Sometimes the child becomes "an extension of self" (p. 29). Parents see themselves as being bad, and so their children are also bad and deserving of punishment. Children with physical or mental disabilities are at special risk because of the additional resentment they may elicit.

A related problem is the fourth characterizing abusive people. They don't know how to raise their children in a nurturing family environment. Their own family environment of origin may have been hostile and abusive. They may never have observed nurturing behavior on the part of their own parents and caretakers. Their expectations for what constitutes appropriate behavior at the various developmental levels may be lacking. For instance, their demands upon the child for behavioral submission and even perfection may be very inappropriate.

Several environmental problems also tend to characterize child abusers. The fifth of their common problems involves the lack of support systems. Since these people tend to isolate themselves due to their poor self-esteem, they have no one to turn to in times of stress.

The sixth problem involves the marital relationship. Low self-esteem may also impact the marital subsystem. Abusers may not know how to get their needs met. They may allow their disappointments and anger to build up within them because they don't know how to express these feelings more appropriately to others. They may feel isolated and alone even within the marriage. Children may become easy targets for parents to communicate with each other. Children may provide a conduit for the expression of violence and anger actually directed at a spouse.

The seventh problem often facing abusers is that of extreme external stress and life crises. We've noted that some child abuse is related to lower socioeconomic status and single parenthood. Poverty causes stress, as can the lack of a partner to provide emotional support. The abuser may feel isolated and incompetent. Additional life crises like losing a job, illness, a marital dispute, or even a child's behavior problem may push people over the brink of where they can control themselves and cope. They may take out their stress on the easiest, most available targets, namely, their children.

"case evaluation," and "case closure" (p. 12).

In order to understand this system, we will briefly introduce some facts about child maltreatment, explain CARF's philosophy, and explain each of the seven steps in the CARF process.

The Philosophy of the Child at Risk Field System (CARF)

Philosophy involves the concepts and principles about how the world should, or actually does, function. Philosophy provides values and guidelines for what is considered important. Thus, it follows that a philosophy of intervention helps to guide the intervention process. It emphasizes the aspects of a problem situation and the helping process that should be the focus of attention. Child abuse provides an example. A philosophy based on the medical model would orient your focus on the *pathology* of the child abuser. The medical model emphasizes how illnesses (or problems) should be cured (or solved). The focus is on "fixing" the individual.

In the case of child abuse, then, intervention or treatment would be directed at the abuser.

A philosophy based on family systems, on the other hand, would emphasize the importance of the entire family's interaction with each other and the environment. Such a philosophy would guide intervention to involve all family members. It would not limit the intervention to the abuser alone.

A family preservation philosophy also involves concepts and principles about what's important for intervention in cases of child maltreatment. These concepts and principles provide guidelines for how practitioners should proceed with intervention.

The *family preservation* approach refers to "providing services to vulnerable families in order to prevent out-of-home placement of children" (Maluccio, 1990, p. 18). A significant principle concerns the importance of children remaining with their own families if at all possible. Another family intervention concept is that interventions are considered positive. People are considered capable of changing if they have help. Additionally, family preservation emphasizes the importance of positive intervention when crises occur, so that children need not be placed out of their own homes.

CARF views the family within a family preservation philosophical perspective and elaborates upon its philosophy by stressing eight points (Holder & Corey, 1991). First, the problem is seen as a social issue. Child maltreatment occurs within the family not because one or two parents intentionally decide to be mean to their children but rather because of external stresses and pressures upon parents. The focus is on the environment and parents' interactions with that environment. Child maltreatment is more the fault of a difficult and nonsupportive environment than the intentional deeds of particular parents.

A second principle holds that condemning and punishing parents who maltreat their children does no good. Assuming that parents will change their behavior if they are chastised is unrealistic. Rather, the cause of the problem lies in pressures coming to bear upon parents from the outside environment. Thus, these pressures should be the focus of treatment.

A third philosophical perspective is that intervention should not interfere with the family's dynamics and ongoing activity any more than is absolutely necessary. The family should be helped to improve its functioning on a day-to-day basis together. Neither abused children nor an abusive parent should be plucked out of the home. Rather, the home environment should be healed and strengthened so that all family members may flourish within it.

The fourth principle in the CARF philosophy indicates that workers should concentrate only on working constructively with the families. "Helpfulness" is the key word (p. 2). Punishing parents doesn't work. Instead, practitioners should *help* parents become stronger and more effective.

The fifth principle is that workers can help maltreating families by coordinating their intervention efforts with those of other professionals who can also be used to help the family. One way of doing this is through case management (the coordination of the work of all the professionals participating in the intervention). Chapter 15 addresses this activity in more depth. You, then, as the worker, don't have to do everything for the family yourself. Instead, you can be most useful by overseeing and integrating the work of others.

CARF's philosophy is a positive one. The sixth principle dictates that the majority of maltreating child caretakers can improve their conduct with support and assistance. This is very different from approaching a difficult, abusive situation which you feel is hopeless. Instead, you review alternatives for helping the family until you find some that work.

A seventh principle offers the guidance that it is best to keep maltreated children within their own families if at all possible. This relates to the idea that risk can be minimized and the children's safety maximized if internal and external pressures can be controlled and parents are taught coping strengths.

The final guiding principle is that clients should always be integrally involved in the intervention. We, as workers, do not go into their homes and mandate to them what they should do. That approach doesn't work. This coincides with our consistent emphasis in generalist practice on client involvement.

CARF espouses two purposes (Holder & Corey, 1991). One is to maximize children's safety within their home environments. The other is to work to change and control those forces which act to increase risk within the child's environment. Risk is defined as "the likelihood that a child will be maltreated" (Holder & Corey, 1991, p. 2). On the other hand, a child has greater safety when stresses impinging on the family are minimized and family members have been strengthened to better ward off such stresses in the future.

Risk Assessment

We've established that risk involves the likelihood that a child will be maltreated. It, then, is the protective services worker's responsibility to assess how much at risk a child is for potential maltreatment. There are five "forces" which can either contribute to or diminish risk in a home: "maltreatment force," "child force," "parent force," "family force," and "intervention force" (Holder & Corey, 1991, p. 23).

Maltreatment Force

Maltreatment force involves the type and severity of maltreatment that are occurring in the home. Are children being neglected, burned, beaten, or sexually molested? It also focuses on the conditions under which maltreatment usually occurs. Is the abusive parent drunk, depressed, or explosive? Does the maltreatment occur randomly or only in times of crisis?

Child Force

Child force involves the maltreated child's personal characteristics. Is she extremely withdrawn, brashly aggressive, or exceptionally slow to respond? This force also involves the extent to which you, as the worker, perceive the child as being susceptible to maltreatment. For instance, very young children and physically disabled children are exceptionally vulnerable.

Parent Force

Parent force entails the characteristics of the parents in the family. How do they feel about themselves? Do they feel guilty after maltreatment occurs? How do they cope with external stresses?

A second aspect of parent force is the parents' child management skills. To what extent do the parents rely on physical punishment to control their children? How do they interact with the children? How responsive are they to the children's wants and demands?

The third facet of parent force concerns the parents' own upbringing and past experiences. How were they treated by their own parents? Do they have a prison record or record of legal convictions? Do they have health difficulties? The final component of parent force is the interactional patterns of the parents with others. How do they communicate with other people? Do they have friends or neighbors with whom they associate? To what extent are they isolated from others?

Family Force

Family force concerns three elements. First, what variables characterize the family in terms of demographics? Are there one or both parents involved? How many children are there? Is the family a blended stepfamily? What levels of education, job training, and work experience do the parents have? What is their income level? Is unemployment a problem? What are their housing conditions?

The second facet of family force involves how the family can "function, interact, and communicate" (Holder & Corey, 1991, p. 30). If parents are married, how do they get along? How do they talk to each other? How would you describe their life-style? Are they prone to crises?

The third facet of family force is the overall support and nurturance the family receives from the surrounding social environment. What relationships does the family have with extended family members? Do they have access to adequate transportation? Are they socially isolated?

Intervention Force

The fifth force that workers assess in risk management involves the intervention force. This concerns your anticipation of how the family will react to intervention. Will family members be angry, afraid, or wary? Intervention force also entails the outside pressures upon the family that might hinder the intervention process with the family. How large and manageable is your caseload? How frequently can you see the family? Are you readily available to them?

Evaluating the Five Forces of Risk[2]

Each of these five forces are further broken down into two to four "elements." Each element reflects a measurable variable involved in the respective force. For each element, workers are

asked to rate the family on a scale ranging from zero to four on the severity of the element being evaluated. For example, take the "descriptive element" of family force which refers to family demographics (Holder & Corey, 1990, p. 44). The worker is asked to respond to the question, "What are the demographics of the family?" The worker then must rate this element of family force from zero to four. Zero refers to "calm," two to "stressful," and four to "chaotic."

There are a total of fourteen elements for the five forces. Individual scores for each of the elements are reported. An average of these scores is then inserted into a formula. This formula also takes into account four qualifying variables which focus on the intensity of all the negative influences evaluated earlier. A final risk score is calculated which ranges from zero (no maltreatment risk) to four (a very strong maltreatment risk).

The Risk Continuum

The idea behind this assessment system is that maltreating families lie somewhere along a risk continuum. The more pressures the family is under and the less external support it has, the greater the risk of maltreatment for the children. As intervention progresses, the family is strengthened. As the family gains support and strength, the maltreatment risk to children decreases. Hopefully, the worker can eventually make the determination that the family has achieved its intervention goals and is strong enough to cope with external social stresses. Thus, when the maltreatment risk is significantly decreased, the case will be closed.

The Intervention Process

We've established that the intervention process in CARF involves eight steps. These correspond to the six steps in the problem-solving process (see figure 7.2).

---

2. More elaborate explanation of the assessment process is beyond the scope of this book. Manuals describing CARF may be purchased from Action for Child Protection, Headquarters, 4724 Park Road, Suite C, Charlotte, NC 28209 (telephone 704-529-1080; FAX 704-529-1132).

The *assessment* phase of the problem-solving process involves the CARF steps of intake (Step 1) and initial assessment (Step 2). Safety evaluation and response (Step 3) and family assessment (Step 4) are intermediate steps which include *both assessment and planning* facets. Treatment planning (Step 5) coincides with the *planning* phase of problem solving. Service provision (Step 6) relates to *intervention*. Case evaluation (Step 7) coincides with *evaluation* in problem solving. Finally, case closure (Step 8) relates to *termination*.

Step 1: Intake

Intake involves the initial referral with the family. The CPS worker gathers the necessary,

relevant information. This includes family demographics and information concerning the five forces affecting the family. It also involves information about the maltreatment report. Who reported the alleged maltreatment, and what specifically was said?

Step 2: Initial Assessment

During this phase, each element relating to the five impinging forces are carefully scrutinized, and a rating is determined for each. On the basis of this data, a final conclusion is reached regarding the amount of risk present and how to proceed. This includes whether the referral is valid and whether the case should be opened for intervention services.

Figure 7.2: The Problem-Solving Process and Steps in CARF

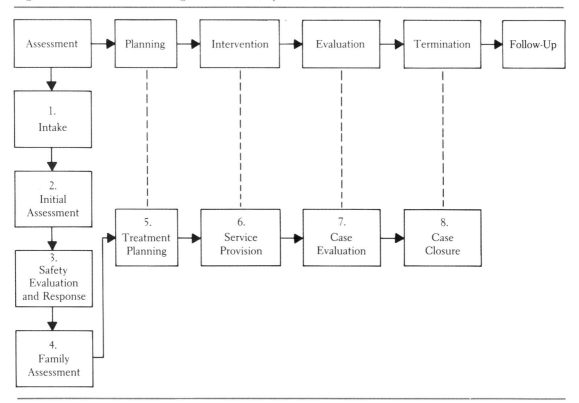

Step 3: Safety Evaluation and Response

This phase involves an extensive investigation of the home and family environment. Holder and Corey (1990) describe the concept of "safety:"

Safety refers to the present security and well-being of a child who has been assessed to be at risk of maltreatment. Security and well-being are evaluated by how controllable the child/family situation is, whether the child's safety is an immediate concern, and based on the kind of mal-

---

HIGHLIGHT 7.2

Common Goals in Risk-Management Treatment Planning

Holder and Corey (Appendix N, 1991, pp. 1–30) cite at least eight dimensions upon which goals are frequently based for families in risk management. They include:

1. *Self-Sufficiency.* Parents and families frequently must enhance their ability to function independently. This dimension has to do with families being better able to fend for themselves and satisfy their own needs. Specific objectives often involve increasing self-esteem and confidence.

2. *Communications Skills.* Goals focusing on improved communication skills among family members are common. Members may be encouraged to identify and express their feelings openly and honestly. Listening skills can be enhanced. Family members' ability to understand the others' points of view can be improved.

3. *Parenting Knowledge.* Parents may not know how to handle and control children. They may have been brought up in emotionally deprived environments themselves, and they may resort to force for controlling children's behavior because they've never been taught any other behavior management techniques. They can be taught not only to control, but to play with and enjoy their children.

    Additionally, parents may need knowledge about normal development. They need to know what to expect in terms of normal behavior at each age level. Appropriate expectations may reduce the frustrations parents feel when children don't behave the way parents think they *should.*

4. *Stress Management.* Parents can be taught to better manage their stress levels. They can be taught to release their feelings more appropriately, instead of allowing emotional pressure to build up and explode. Learning such specific stress management techniques as relaxation approaches can also help them cope with stress.

5. *Impulse Control.* Many parents in families at risk have poor impulse control. They are under tremendous stress. They often need to learn how to direct their energies in more fruitful ways than violently lashing out at their children.

6. *Problem-Solving Skills.* Parents in high-risk families may be so frustrated and stressed that they feel they have little control over their lives and behavior. They can be taught how to analyze problems, translate these problems into needs, establish potential alternatives to meeting these needs, evaluate the pros and cons of alternatives, and, finally, select and pursue their most promising options.

7. *Interactive Nurturing.* Many times, family members need to be taught how to both express their positive feelings and accept affection. They can be taught how to empathize with each other, verbalize their feelings, and reinforce their support and caring for each other.

8. *Resource Enhancement.* A primary means of increasing the strength of families at risk is to increase their resources. Adequate employment, income, housing, food, and clothing all contribute to a family's well-being.

treatment which may be indicated, how severe the maltreatment or its results might be (p. 46).

Other important concepts evaluated during this phase include "influences that negatively affect safety" and "family strengths" (Holder & Corey, 1990, p. 46). Influences that negatively affect safety include any which increase the child's risk of maltreatment. Family strengths include those aspects of the family which can be helpful in treatment. For example, there may be a nonmaltreating parent in the home. Or perhaps the family has adequate resources to meet its basic needs. The final phase of Step 3 is establishing a safety plan, with primary goals being formulated concerning how to maximize the safety factors within the home.

Step 4: Family Assessment

This step involves an extensive review of the forces operating within the family. These involve the family demographics, interpersonal functioning, and the overall level of available support. Family strengths are assessed. Specific risk factors are described. The source of the risk and impediments to intervention are identified. Primary goals for the intervention process are outlined.

Step 5: Treatment Planning

As with any other type of planning in generalist practice, objectives are specified and responsibilities assigned. It's clearly established who will do what by when. Means of evaluating objectives are determined.

Step 6: Service Provision

The intervention approaches specified in the plan are carried out during the service-provision step. This includes tasks for the CPS worker, the client family, and other profession-

als involved with the case. It is quite possible that you, as a CPS worker, may function primarily as a case manager during this part of the intervention.

Step 7: Case Evaluation

During this step, goals and objectives are reviewed. Progress is documented. Intervention plans are amended to meet the current risk situation. Hopefully, the service provision during the intervention process has significantly decreased risk, increased safety, and generally strengthened the family unit.

Step 8: Case Closure

The case is closed when it has been determined that risk is no longer present or has been significantly decreased so that the children are adequately safe. Goals and objectives that have been attained are specified and documented. A final risk assessment of the five forces is concluded and recorded.

Crisis Intervention in Micro Practice

Crisis intervention is "the therapeutic practice used in helping clients in crisis to promote effective coping that can lead to positive growth and change by acknowledging the problem, recognizing its impact, and learning new or more effective behaviors for coping with similar predictable experiences" (Barker, 1987, p. 36). In other words, crisis intervention helps people learn to cope with or adjust to extreme external pressures.

Social workers use the term "crisis" in two ways (Barker, 1987, p. 36). First, it can be "an internal experience of emotional change and distress" (for example, the sudden death of a loved one, job loss, or unwanted pregnancy). Second, a crisis can be "a social event in which a disastrous event disrupts some essential functions of existing social institutions" (for example, a major earthquake, flood, drought, or bombing attack).

Virtually any upsetting event can evoke a crisis. Dixon (1987, pp. 15–16) lists a number of causes for crisis, including family and other interpersonal difficulties, financial problems, physical illnesses, accidents, problems related to age (such as those common in adolescence or old age), alcoholism, and involvement in the legal system.

The Crisis Process

Golan (1987) relates how crises typically progress. First, an individual is exposed to a heavy amount of stress over some period of time. Second, this stress acts to make the person exceptionally "vulnerable" to intimidation and assaults from outside (p. 364). The usual emotional protection from worrisome and painful incidents is weaker than usual. The third aspect is some "precipitating factor," which acts as "a turning point to push the individual into a state of active crisis, marked by disequilibrium, disorganization, and immobility" (p. 364). As the crisis continues, the individual perceives the precipitating factor and other stressors to which he is being exposed as increasingly serious threats. Finally, the person experiences surging anxiety and such accompanying troublesome emotions as depression or grief.

It is at this point that the individual will probably be most receptive to help. Normal defense mechanisms have been weakened. When people become more anxious and emotional, they typically become less objective and logical. Crises breed desperation. Desperation fosters panic and immobility. People in crisis can easily become frozen in their tracks. It then becomes your job to get them moving again.

Crises can happen to individuals, families, groups, communities, and organizations, however, regardless of level, the essential process of crisis buildup remains the same.

Major Concepts in Crisis Intervention

There are many frameworks for crisis intervention. However, virtually all of them have the following themes in common:

1. *The primary goal of crisis intervention is to help the client return at least to the pre-crisis level of functioning* (Dixon, 1984; Golan, 1987).

We have described the crisis process. A person is under a large amount of stress for some period of time. Subsequently, another upsetting event or series of events occurs. The person becomes emotionally shaken, usually loses an objective sense of self-direction, and becomes unable to proceed. Crisis intervention involves helping people in crisis return to the level of functioning they were at prior to the precipitating event. This means that crisis intervention goals are very specific and deal only with issues directly related to the crisis situation.

An example is a situation in which you, as the practitioner, receive a call from a client threatening suicide. Your primary goal would be to help that person return to how she was functioning prior to having suicidal thoughts and feelings. Crisis intervention would not seek to achieve more complicated, long-term goals. For example, you would not try to help the person to become more popular or improve her personality. These goals might be worked on in a longer-term counseling format.

This doesn't mean that you should tell your clients to get worse again if they enhance their level of functioning above its pre-crisis level. If clients make greater improvements, that's wonderful. Your maximum goals with clients would be some improvement above their pre-crisis level of functioning. Goals in crisis intervention should be realistic and focus primarily on the individual's ability to cope with the *crisis*.

2. *Crisis intervention is relatively **short term*** (Wicks & Parsons, 1984).

Because the intent is to return the client to the pre-crisis level of functioning, crisis intervention progresses very quickly. The full crisis process tends to last from four to six weeks (Caplan, 1964). Your length of involvement with the client will be relatively short compared to interventions in most non-crisis situations. If, for example, you're working in a hospital emergency room, your contact would likely be for less than one day (Wicks & Parsons, 1984). In other settings, such as a mental-health center, your length of intervention might last from four to six weeks (Aguilera & Messick, 1974). Regardless, crisis-intervention contacts are significantly shorter than most other client relationships in practice.

3. ***"Specific, observable difficulties** become the target"* of the intervention (Wicks & Parsons, 1984)

Crisis intervention focuses purely on the crisis and those aspects of the client's life directly related to the crisis. Therefore, crisis intervention does little delving into clients' pasts. Only information about the past directly relevant to the crisis is gathered. You can't afford to waste time on anything but resolving the immediate crisis.

4. *When doing crisis intervention, it should be considered the **treatment of choice** and not simply a second-best strategy* (Aguilar & Messick, 1974).

Crisis intervention is a well-defined, viable approach which is indeed the *best* approach to crisis situations. Crises are by nature severe. Their resolution merits the top priority in intervention. Other related stresses and problems can be dealt with later using other intervention methods.

5. *The practitioner in crisis intervention "**must be willing to take an active . . . role** in the intervention," which is often **more "directive"** than that assumed in other approaches to generalist practice* (Aguilar & Messick, 1974).

Throughout this text, we emphasize the importance of client involvement. Integral client participation throughout the problem-solving process is essential. Clients should also be as involved as possible in the crisis-intervention process. However, the key phrase here is *as possible*. You might have to expend more pressure to get the client moving from his or her emotionally frozen position. With crises, you usually don't have the luxury of relaxed discussion time. Consider a bewildered, homeless client living with her family in her car when the wind-chill factor is hitting twenty-five degrees below zero. You probably won't have time to discuss all possible options available in a leisurely fashion. Rather, you may need to pressure her to take some direction you specify in order to keep her family from freezing.

Steps in Crisis Intervention

Aguilar and Messick (1974) propose a clearly defined four-step crisis intervention process which coincides with the problem-solving process in generalist practice.

Step 1: Assessment

The first step in crisis intervention is assessment. The art in crisis intervention is to focus on the specific precipitating event that brought the client to you. Only clearly related aspects of the client's situation should be addressed.

Aguilar and Messick (1974) suggest pursuing at least five specific areas of questioning.

First, you must determine why the person called you or came in to see you *today*. What precipitating event has occurred? The crisis usually occurs less than two weeks before a client seeks professional help. Often, the precipitating event has occurred within the prior twenty-four hours. For instance, one client was just told he is HIV positive, or another client just discovered that her husband is having an affair.

A typical first question to the client is something like, "What brings you in to see me today?" or "What has happened to make you so upset?" The intent is to identify and specify as soon as possible what the crisis is.

A second line of questioning should involve how your client views the crisis situation and precipitating event. How does she feel about the event? What impacts does she think it will have on her life now and in the future? You might ask yourself how objective your client appears to be about her situation.

The third relevant line of questioning involves whether your client has access to support from others. Is there anyone she can talk to? Whom does she feel comfortable asking for help? The general rule of thumb is "the more people helping the person the better" (Aguilar & Messick, 1974, p. 58). Crises are stressful. You have to act fast. The more support you can muster in helping your client return to the pre-crisis level of functioning, the better.

The fourth area of information to pursue concerns your client's history in solving similar problems. Has something like this crisis ever happened to him or her before? If so, how did it get resolved? How does your client usually cope with stressful events in general? Can any of these coping skills be applied to the current situation?

A final and very critical area of information to solicit involves the extent to which your client is either "suicidal or homicidal" (Aguilar &

Messick, 1974, p. 59). If you determine that your client is seriously considering violently harming herself or others, you may need to take more drastic steps. For example, immediate hospitalization or referral to a treatment program might be necessary.

Step 2: Planning

During this step, you must evaluate the extent to which the crisis has interfered with your client's ability to function. Which daily activities will she be able to resume? Will she be able to return to her job, homemaking, parenting, education, or other activities? Additionally, how are others close to your client reacting to the crisis? Is your client receiving any support from them?

The second primary aspect of planning is to review potential alternatives, evaluate the pros and cons, and determine the course of action to pursue. It is important during this phase to review strategies which have worked in the past and decide whether they might not be useful again.

Step 3: The Intervention

Any of a variety of helping techniques can be used in crisis intervention. For example, workers addressing crisis situations vary in terms of the training they've had and in their practice settings. Regardless of background and setting, good interviewing and relationship-building skills are especially important. The crisis demands that you and your client move forward in a hurry.

Aguilera and Messick (1974, pp. 20–21) make the following four suggestions for what to address during the intervention phase of the process:

1. *"Helping the individual to gain an intellectual understanding of his [or her] crisis."* People in crisis are in turmoil. When

HIGHLIGHT 7.3

An Example of Crisis Intervention in Micro Practice

Mildred's husband, Marvin Murphy, was killed abruptly in a car accident two weeks earlier. Mildred, age thirty-five, and Marvin, age thirty-nine, had been married for seventeen years. They had two children Monty, age seventeen, and Michael, age fourteen.

Mildred was distraught with grief. She didn't know what to do next. She had lived with Marvin for almost half her life and just assumed he would always be there for her. They had had their ups and downs, but generally she felt it had been a steady, fairly happy marriage (that was, of course, except for his one extramarital "fling" fifteen years earlier). But even the "fling" had become ancient history to Mildred.

Marvin had been the family's primary breadwinner. He was an accountant who earned $40,743.67 a year. Mildred had almost always worked outside of the home. However, it had consisted of doing nearly minimum-wage jobs on a part-time basis. They owned their midsized home in a suburb of Milwaukee. Rather, they owned about twelve thousand dollars in equity and made one-thousand dollar monthly payments.

Mildred had spent the past two weeks coping with the immediate crises commonly caused by sudden tragic deaths. She had had funeral arrangements to make, in addition to a multitude of insurance and legal issues to settle. This was the first time she really had time for the momentous impact of the event to hit her. What would she do now? She was lonely. She was acutely grief-stricken. She was worried about her two children, both of whom were also seriously affected by their father's abrupt death. She couldn't afford to maintain the style of life the family had become accustomed to. She panicked. She also had the wherewithal to seek help. She called the crisis-intervention unit of the local community mental-health center.* The intake unit set up an appointment for her with Homer Simpson, a social worker and crisis counselor.

Step 1: Assessment

Mildred met with Mr. Simpson early the next day. After cordial introductions, Mr. Simpson asked what brought her in to see him today. She explained her situation to him.

They began the assessment process. Mr. Simpson's intent was to crystalize the *problems affecting Mildred* and *how she felt* about them. After some discussion, they established the following list of prioritized problems: an immediate financial crisis, her extreme level of grief, worry about her children, worry about her future (specifically, her living arrangements), and her loneliness.

Mr. Simpson continued by gently asking Mildred about her friends and family. He was investigating her *current access to support* from others. Had people generally been supportive to her during this time of great need? Were there any friends or family members in particular to whom she could turn for help? Were she and her sons able to provide each other with support?

Mr. Simpson empathized with Mildred concerning the depth of her grief. He emphasized it was indeed difficult to have an intimate partner of so many years plucked from her so hastily. Searching for her innermost feelings, he indicated how this might be the most difficult loss she had ever had to deal with. Mildred responded that it was. Only the death of her own mother five years ago before reminded her of how she felt today. Mr. Simpson then asked in a soft and warm manner how she had managed through the difficult times of coping with grief for her mother. He was seeking to *identify coping mechanisms Mildred had used in the past.* Mildred responded that her sister and one special old friend had both been exceptionally helpful to her at that time. She continued that she had not had much time to talk with either of them during the past two weeks.

Finally, Mr. Simpson asked gently, yet straightforwardly, if Mildred was having any de-

─ **HIGHLIGHT 7.3** (*continued*) ────────────────────────

structive thoughts about herself or others. He explained how easy it was for some people to turn their grief and anger at what had happened toward themselves, or others close to them. Mildred indicated that she had not had such thoughts. Mr. Simpson, at this time, of course, was *evaluating the extent to which Mildred might be suicidal or homicidal.*

Step 2: Planning

Mr. Simpson determined that although this crisis situation had temporarily immobilized Mildred, she probably had the potential to carry on with her life if she was given adequate direction. Prior to her husband's death, Mildred had held her regular, although low-paying, receptionist position for the past four years. She reported having no major difficulties with her children other than what she termed "typical parent-adolescent spats." She was regularly involved with her own extended family members, many of whom lived in nearby areas. Thus, Mildred had a number of strengths upon which to base her plans.

Mr. Simpson and Mildred discussed alternative solutions to some of her problems at this time. Her primary problem was that of financial crisis. He referred her to a financial planner, right within his agency. The planner could help her determine the minimum amount of money she needed in order to live, review her total assets (for example, current income, house equity, savings, insurance payments, and cash), and identify what alternatives she could pursue about her housing situation. Later on, Mildred might pursue with him the possibility of job training and financial resources to assist in solving her financial problems.

Mildred's second major problem involved her grief. Mr. Simpson referred her to a self-help group for survivors of the death of a loved one (held at another social-services agency). He cited the specific time and place the group met. If they chose,

her sons could also attend. Mildred indicated that she would pursue this idea.

Mildred's other problems involved worry about her future in general and her living arrangements in particular. Both of these were directly related to her financial decisions. Mr. Simpson urged her to put off consideration of the two former problems until she had time to establish clearly the state of her financial affairs. Then she could review the options available to her.

They articulated specific objectives regarding who Mildred was to call by specified dates. Finally, they set up another appointment to meet one week from that day.

Step 3: The Intervention

Altogether, Mildred met with Mr. Simpson four times over four weeks. Mildred indicated that her meetings with the financial planner were going well. After including her husband's life insurance benefits, her assets were greater than she had anticipated. The planner was helping her develop short-term and long-term goals regarding living arrangements and employment.

Mildred and Mr. Simpson talked about other realistic alternatives available to her. He helped her to start working through the emotional turmoil that was immobilizing her. She remained very sad. However, she began to understand that she would persevere through this very difficult time in her life. Mr. Simpson's intent was to help her *gain a more realistic, objective perspective on her life* so that she could go on.

Additionally, during their meetings, Mr. Simpson encouraged Mildred to stop desperately trying to contain her feelings. Rather, she should *let her emotions out* so that she could begin to deal with them and recover. Sometimes, she cried sorrowfully. Mr. Simpson encouraged this as a natural expression of her grief.

Together, they continued to *explore coping mechanisms*. Mr. Simpson encouraged Mildred to frequently contact her sister and her close friend, both of whom were so comforting to her after her mother's death. Additionally, she and her sons did attend the self-help group Mr. Simpson had suggested and she said that it was beneficial to her. She indicated that she was motivated to continue for the next few weeks and possibly even months.

In her discussions with Mr. Simpson, Mildred recognized the fact that she had much respect for the minister of her church. Although she had never discussed such personal matters with him before, she went to talk to him about her grief. Afterward, she told Mr. Simpson that her pain was still raging. However, her minister had helped her gain some peace.

In terms of *reopening her social world*, Mildred was not ready to entertain other people or enjoy herself regardless of the circumstance. However, she was able to return to work. She continued to attend her sons' sporting events, as both boys were actively involved in school sports. She spoke with her sister and good friend regularly.

Step 4: Anticipatory Planning

During Mildred's final session with Mr. Simpson, they *summarized together the progress she had made* in so short of a time. She was coping with her financial "crisis" by obtaining help from an expert. She and her sons discovered that self-help groups can be beneficial. Additionally, Mildred worked on maintaining open communication with her sons so that they might support each other in their grief. Finally, she maintained strong and regular contact with those persons identified as being especially helpful to her in times of crisis—her sister, good friend, and minister.

Mr. Simpson emphasized how well Mildred had "pulled herself together." He commended her for having the strength to do so. He also *suggested how the coping methods she had discovered and was using might help her again in future times of need.*

Mr. Simpson wished Mildred the best. This case of crisis intervention was terminated.

A Few Words about Helping People Cope with Grief and Loss

There are a number of suggestions for how you, as a professional, can help someone coping with death, a terminal disease, or virtually any type of extreme loss. They are summarized below.

1. Encourage clients to talk about their loss, both with you and supportive others. Talking about grief eases loneliness and allows them to vent their feelings. Talking with close friends gives people a sense of security and brings them closer to others they love. Talking with people who have had similar losses helps put a client's problem in perspective. They will see that they are not the only ones with problems. Other people with similar crises may be able to give them positive suggestions about coping. Finally, clients may enhance their own self-esteem and sense of well-being when helping others.

2. Understand that many negative feelings may surface when a person is struggling to cope with a crisis. They might include anger, depression, or grief. Encourage expression of even these negative feelings so that clients might begin coping with them and moving forward.

3. Convey verbally and nonverbally that you are willing to talk about any concerns of the client. What you want to convey to clients is that you are emotionally ready to help them cope with their grief and to provide them with support. Remember, however, that clients may always choose not to share their feelings with you. You can encourage, but you can't force them.

4. Don't discourage crying. Rather, people should be encouraged to cry as they feel the need. Crying releases tension that is part of grieving.

┌─ **HIGHLIGHT 7.3** (*continued*) ──────────────

5. Answer questions as honestly as you can. Sometimes, this is especially difficult. For instance, if you're dealing with a crisis where a client or someone close is dying or very ill, questions may be unpleasant. Answers may be awkward and even painful. Nonetheless, it's important to be as honest and straightforward as you possibly can. If you don't know an answer, seek out someone (for example, a physician) who will accurately provide the requested information. Evasion or ambiguity in response to a dying person's questions only increases his or her concerns. If there is a chance for recovery, this should be mentioned. Even a small margin of hope can be a comfort. The chances for recovery, however, should not be exaggerated.

6. If the crisis involves a dying person, help that person become the *star* of his or her own death. In other words, provide the person with requested information and help the person participate in decisions concerning death. Many people, when dying, reach a point where they want to "tie up their loose ends."

They want to consciously set their affairs in order, clarify their will, and discuss their wishes regarding their funeral. It's easy for other people, because of their own fears of death, to avoid such topics. Instead, many people feel more comfortable avoiding the painful topics and trying to remain unrealistically cheery. You, as a helping professional, can help your clients continue to appreciate their personal significance even when death is near. You can also urge your clients' loved ones to remain involved with your clients until the very end.

───────────

*A community mental health center is "a local organization, partly funded and regulated by the federal government, that provides a range of psychiatric and social services to people residing in the area. These include inpatient, outpatient, partial hospitalization, emergency, and transitional services, programs for the elderly and for children, screening and follow-up care, and programs that deal with alcohol and substance abuse" (Barker, 1987, p. 29).

──────────────────────────────

you're in emotional turmoil, it is difficult to think clearly and objectively. A primary function of crisis intervention is to help clients look objectively at their crisis situation. Are they blowing it out of proportion? You can help clients evaluate their strengths and weaknesses more objectively and begin moving toward crisis resolution.

2. *"Helping the individual bring into the open his* [or her] *present feelings to which* [s/]*he may not have access."* Stress frequently results in anxious discomfort and strong negative feelings. People trying to cope with stress will often desperately try to control these feelings, to hold them inside. They may fear the pain associated

with anxiety, worry, grief, disappointment, and sadness. All such restrictive retention of feeling does is immobilize people. Before they can deal with their feelings and make logical choices regarding how to proceed, clients need to acknowledge that these feelings exist. Part of your role in crisis intervention is to help clients explore their emotional state. What blockages are preventing them from returning to their pre-crisis level of functioning? What feelings are making them "stuck?"

3. *"Exploration of coping mechanisms."* What methods of coping have your clients used successfully in the past? Can these be applied to the current crisis?

Additionally, what new methods of coping might you suggest your clients try? Perhaps, in their emotional turmoil, they are having difficulty seeing what alternatives exist.

After the problem and precipitating factor for the crisis are clearly defined for the client, you, as the crisis-intervention practitioner, can suggest potential alternatives to solve the problem. Part of the intervention process is to enable the client to make changes. Because crisis intervention is more directive than many other forms of intervention, "specific directions may be given as to what should be tried as tentative solutions" (Aguilar & Messick, 1974, p. 59). If you are in the position of meeting with the client again, you can later evaluate progress made and the effectiveness of the attempted alternatives. If the alternatives didn't work, you can help your client to identify and assess the potential of new ones.

4. *"Reopening the social world."* The fourth suggestion for what to pursue during intervention involves helping the client establish or reestablish a social support system. If the crisis involved a loss such as a death or divorce, you can help the client identify people who can help them through the crisis. Likewise, you can help clients call upon those people closest to them in such crises such as job loss or major health problems.

People in crisis need as much social support and nurturance as possible. Identify and use the support that is already there. If such support is scanty or nonexistent, help the client open up new avenues of relationships. It should be stressed that during the crisis intervention process, you may choose to pursue any or all of these four options. There may be crisis cases where none readily

apply. It's up to your professional judgment regarding the best way to proceed.

Step 4: Anticipatory Planning

Anticipatory planning helps clients prepare for future crises. The final phase in crisis intervention focuses on articulating and summarizing what clients have learned during the crisis-intervention process. What means have they developed to cope with stress? What have they learned from working through this crisis situation that they may be able to apply to stressful times in the future? One task of the worker is to help clients clearly identify and articulate coping behaviors so that these skills are more readily available when needed next.

In essence, the anticipatory planning phase of crisis intervention includes the evaluation and termination steps of the problem-solving process. Because of the fast-moving nature of crisis intervention, these phases are accomplished quickly. Often they are melded together. For instance, the summarizing involved in anticipatory planning incorporates evaluation, as only effective coping mechanisms are included. Termination promptly follows.

Follow-up, of course, is the last phase of the problem-solving process. Because of the nature of crisis intervention, follow-up is not always possible. Practitioners often don't have time. Follow-up may not be part of their job responsibilities. Sometimes, agencies have alternative mechanisms for follow-up. Since referral is an integral part of the crisis-intervention process, often the responsibility of follow-up rests on those providing the service for which the client has been referred.

Crisis Intervention in Mezzo Practice

The example involving Mildred Murphy in Highlight 7.3 is portrayed as an example of crisis intervention in micro practice. However, in many ways, this example converges with mezzo practice. Mildred's two sons were also indirectly and integrally involved in the helping process, even though they didn't actually meet with the crisis-intervention practitioner.

Golan (1987) summarizes the relevance of crisis intervention to mezzo practice with families:

> In general, whether a family is considered to be in a state of collective crisis because of the role disruption of one of its members or whether one member's state of crisis acts as the hazardous event that disrupts the rest of the family system, interventive efforts should include evaluation of the family's strengths and weaknesses, of their capacities and motivation for change, and of the resources at their disposal, no matter who the designated client may be (p. 368).

A crisis affecting one or more members of a family impacts the entire family. Likewise, intervention efforts directed at some member or part of a family will influence the entire family group.

Golan (1987) continues that crisis intervention is also relevant within the context of small groups. She explains:

> Crisis-oriented groups are frequently used as support systems to avoid hospitalization or institutionalization, to deal with potentially hazardous crises, such as impending surgery and dislocation, to resolve parent-child or marital conflicts, and to mitigate acute eruptions among members of chronically disordered families or groups (p. 368).

Crisis Intervention at the Macro Level

In our introduction to crisis intervention, we cited how the approach is frequently used in response to crises involving major population groups suffering from natural disasters. Floods, earthquakes, droughts, and famines all require crisis intervention efforts on a massive scale. A macro perspective on crisis intervention could potentially involve counties, states, nations, and even continents, depending on the scope of the natural disaster. These other systems could contribute food, clothing, shelter, medical supplies, or funds to purchase what people in the crisis area need. This is crisis intervention at the macro level.

Crisis intervention could also be applied in economic and political situations. For example, human-service workers or agencies are often involved with groups coping with plant closings and other economic emergencies. At another macro level, the former Soviet Union was in need of economic assistance when it disbanded its political structure and was coping with massive economic repercussions.

Crisis intervention in most of these situations requires a multi-disciplinary approach. Many professionals and citizens are called upon to pool their efforts and address major crises. Social work practitioners may become one segment of the total intervention effort.

Alcohol and Other Drug Use and Abuse

Generalist practitioners need a background in alcohol and other drug abuse (AODA) for two basic reasons. First, many social workers are employed in alcohol and other drug abuse treatment agencies. Roffman (1987) explains,

> In addition to focusing on general counseling issues, the social worker's role emphasizes intervention with the client's family and with the occupational, health, criminal justice, employment, and social systems in order to facilitate both short- and long-term opportunities for change and improvement in functioning. Graduate-level social workers also function as program or agency administrators, as analysts with local or state government bureaus responsible for drug abuse services, and as aides to legislative committees (p. 484).

HIGHLIGHT 7.4
Definitions of AODA Terms

It's useful to be familiar with a number of terms commonly used in AODA intervention. The jargon tends to revolve around three types of substances. First, there is *alcohol*. In everyday usage, the term refers to any type of liquor containing alcohol, such as whiskey or beer. Technically, alcohol is "a colorless volatile flammable liquid C_2H_6O that is the intoxicating agent in fermented and distilled liquors and is used also as a solvent" (*Webster's Collegiate Dictionary*, 1977, p. 27). It receives special significance because it is the most prevalent and serious of all drug problems.

Second, there is the term *drugs*. Drugs, in the context referred to here, include a wide range of chemical substances, including alcohol, ingested to obtain some psychological effect. The third term commonly used is *substance*, preferably, *psychoactive substance*, because such substances are used to effect a psychological change in perception or mood.

These three substances have four terms typically employed concerning their usage. Because there is some overlap, they're often confusing. The first term, "abuse," implies either *physical* or *psychological* harm to the user. The emphasis is on some kind of real harm caused by consuming the substance. The second term "addiction," involves *physiological dependence* on the substance. An addicted person's body physically needs the drug in order to avoid negative symptoms if the body is deprived of the drug. The third term, "dependence," involves a condition where a person requires the substance, either *physiologically and/or psychologically*. Physiological dependence involves addiction. Psychological dependence means that people feel they absolutely must have the drug to survive regardless of whether their bodies are physically addicted to it. Finally, the term "habituation" involves *psychological*, but not physiological, dependence.

People, then, can *abuse*, *become addicted to*, *become dependent upon*, or *become habituated* to one or more types of psychoactive substances. For example, *alcohol abuse* means that the individual is imposing some physical or psychological harm to him or herself. The person may or may not be addicted, dependent, or habituated. Likewise, *drug dependent* people feel they require a psychoactive substance for psychological or physical (or both) reasons. Often, people have a substance of choice. That is, they prefer the type of mood alteration produced by one drug over that by another. For instance, one person may prefer beer over cocaine. Another person may feel just the opposite.

Two other terms are important to understand. *Tolerance* to a psychoactive substance entails how more and more of a drug is needed to reach the same level of mood alteration as drug use proceeds over time. *Withdrawal symptoms* are those physical and psychological effects experienced by an addicted person who stops using the psychoactive substance. Despite discontinued use, the addict's body still physically craves the drug. Withdrawal symptoms include severe abdominal pain, convulsions, anxiety attacks, depression, and uncontrollable trembling.

Finally, it's important for social workers to be aware of the resources available to psychoactive substance abusers of any type. A large-scale self-help organization is Alcoholics Anonymous (AA). Anyone who feels that he has encountered difficulties due to alcohol may join. Two alcoholics started the organization in 1935. It now has thousands of chapters throughout the country. More will be said about AA's approach and principles later in the chapter.

Related to AA is Al-Anon. Anyone can choose to join this self-help group if they feel they need help because of problems related to alcohol caused by someone other than themselves. Most members are family members of alcoholics. As with other self-help groups, Al-Anon allows members to provide each other with support, encouragement, and suggestions for dealing with problems related to alcohol.

The second reason for needing some background in AODA involves your role as a referral agent (*See* chapter 15). Even if you don't work in a specialized AODA setting, you will still probably have clients or family members of clients with alcohol and drug problems. Thus, you need to be able to identify such problems when they occur and know how to make appropriate referrals to treatment programs.

Raskin and Daley (1991) explain how alcohol and other drug abuse is often masked by and interrelated to many other problems.

> The addicted person may seek help in a medical setting, a crisis clinic, a mental-health agency, a family service agency, or from a private practitioner or a public assistance agency. In the medical setting, the presenting problem may be pancreatitis, liver disease, traumatic injury, or broken bones. In the mental-health setting, the person may present depression, suicidal feelings, self-destructive behavior, anxiety, psychotic symptoms, or problems associated with an organic brain syndrome. Each of these problems may be the result of alcoholism or drug addiction (p. 25).

Thus, regardless of your practice setting, you will probably need to address AODA problems. It's far beyond the scope of this text to train you to be an AODA counselor. However, we will discuss some of the basic terms, individual and family dynamics, and treatment trends involved.

There are many similarities between alcohol abuse and other drug abuse in terms of the psychological and interpersonal dynamics. It is also beyond the scope of this book to elaborate upon the effects of the numerous varieties of drugs available today. Therefore, we will primarily focus on alcohol abuse and alcoholism.

The Alcoholic Person

Denzin (1987) incorporates three components into his definition of an *alcoholic*. First,

alcoholics are consciously aware that they are alcoholics, even if they don't admit it to others. Second, they no longer can govern their drinking; once they start, they can't stop until they're intoxicated. Third, they can't stop drinking for any significant period of time.

He continues to describe four progressive phases of alcoholism: *prealcoholic, prodomal, crucial,* and *chronic* (p. 10). The *prealcoholic,* phase involves drinking in order to reduce anxiety or stress. During this phase, the person will look for social experiences that involve drinking. The person enjoys drinking and may drink more than those she's associating with.

The second phase, *prodomal,* signals increasing loss of control. Blackouts occur, in which memory losses mark blocks of time. During this phase, once the individual starts drinking, she finds she can't stop.

The *crucial* phase reflects even greater loss of control over drinking. The individual drinks more and more frequently. She is increasingly less able to restrain herself.

Finally, the *chronic* phase "occurs when the drinker begins morning drinking and feels the need to drink every four or five hours. He or she has become physiologically dependent upon alcohol. If a drink is not taken, nausea and shaking of the hands may concur. Alcohol removes these withdrawal effects" (p. 10).

With each of these phases comes increasing loss of control. Drinking begins as a means of escaping stress and becomes the alcoholic's only way of coping with reality. Denzin emphasizes that "alcoholism is but a symptom of the alcoholic's other problems of living" (p. 10). He continues, then, that there must be a two-pronged approach to treatment. First, the alcoholic must quit drinking. Second, the problems from which the alcoholic tried to escape in the first place by turning to drinking must be addressed.

Kingery-McCabe and Frances (1991) stress that each individual responds differently to addiction in terms of severity of physical and psychological effects and the length of time it takes to become addicted. They continue that four major facets of life are typically affected including: "physical and medical, psychological or emotional, social or family, and spiritual" (p. 58).

Kingery-McCabe and Frances (1991) elaborate on these effects. Physical repercussions of alcoholism may involve a number of organ systems, including the digestive, cardiovascular, nervous, endocrine, reproductive, respiratory, and immune systems.

Psychological consequences are massive. Kingery-McCabe and Frances (1991) explain:

> Addiction affects virtually every area of psychological functioning, including cognitive, emotional, and behavioral areas. The alcoholic or drug addict typically utilizes defense mechanisms (e.g., denial) that allow the addiction to continue. Self-esteem is adversely affected, and developmental tasks may be impeded or delayed as a result of impairments associated with the addiction. And in many cases, addiction can exacerbate or mask psychiatric disorders (p. 67).

Alcoholics and other drug abusers typically adopt a series of defense mechanisms to protect themselves from having to deal with the problems caused by alcoholism. They include "denial," "rationalization," and "intellectualization" (Kingery-McCabe & Frances, 1991, p. 67). Each serves to avoid taking responsibility for one's own behavior.

The most prevalent technique is *denial*. This simply entails insisting to oneself that there really isn't a problem or that the problems really aren't that bad. *Rationalization* involves making excuses for the problems caused by the addiction. For example, an alcoholic might say to himself, "I really didn't flunk that exam because I had a hangover; the professor made the questions much harder than she said she would." Finally, *intellectualization* entails becoming very philosophical about drinking or some related issue. Talking can keep the addict's mind off the real problem. For example, "to avoid feeling guilty about drug use, an addict

The preferred drug becomes the addict's "best friend"—something the addict can always depend on being there.

may engage in philosophical debates about what's wrong with society's drug laws" (p. 67).

Numerous social and relationship problems result from alcoholism. They include marital and family difficulties, disruptions in friendships, trouble in work and school performance, accidents when operating vehicles, and being arrested for crimes committed while under the influence.

Alcohol or another drug of choice (that is, the preferred drug) becomes the addict's "best friend." It is something the addict can always depend on. The effects are pleasantly predictable, and the addict can escape from life's stresses whenever she wants. People can be disappointing or place pressure on you, but a drug always acts the same.

Addiction also impacts a person's spiritual life. This involves the core of how people feel about themselves, God, and the world. Addicts are out of control, but they are desperately trying to avoid the responsibility of dealing with that fact. Addicts frequently report having feelings of "guilt and shame" (Kingery-McCabe & Frances, 1991, p. 75). They know that they are doing something wrong but can't allow themselves to face up to it.

Guilt entails feeling bad about something you've done that wasn't right. For example, an addict gets into a fight while drunk which he regrets seriously the following day. He really feels guilty having to pay the $250 fine he received when arrested for fighting. Guilt also might involve something you should have done but failed to do. For instance, while drunk you "forgot" to attend your little sister's birthday party.

Shame, on the other hand, involves feeling that you're a bad person. It's not feeling badly about *something*, but, instead, feeling badly about *yourself*. Additional spiritual effects can include losing religious faith, becoming inactive in your church, becoming unable to display caring and concern for the ones you love, decreasing your expectations regarding how you and others around you should behave, and generally feeling that life has less and less value.

Alcoholism and Family Relationships

Families of alcoholics traverse through seven phases that synchronize with the four phases of alcoholism; they include "denial, adjustment, disorganization, attempts to reorganize, attempts to escape the problem, reorgani-

---

HIGHLIGHT 7.5

Dynamics in the Families of Substance Abusers

Sharon Wegscheider (1981) maintains that alcohol abuse is a family disease, involving and affecting each family member. Although she focuses on the families of alcoholics, much of what she says is also frequently applied to the families of other types of substance abusers. She identifies a number of rules or norms with which alcoholics' families struggle to comply. In reality, these norms serve to sustain the drinking problem.

First, the dependent person's alcohol use becomes "the most important thing in the family's life" (Wegscheider, 1981, p. 81). The abuser's top priority is getting enough alcohol, and the family's top priorities are the abuser, the abuser's behavior, and keeping the abuser away from alcohol. The goals of the abuser and the rest of his family are at completely opposite poles.

A second norm in an alcohol abuser's family is that alcohol is not the cause of the problem. Denial is paramount. A third family norm maintains that the dependent person is really not responsible for his or her behavior and that the alcohol causes the behavior. There is always someone or something else to blame. Another rule dictates that no one should rock the boat, no matter what. Family members strive to protect the family's status quo, even when the family is miserable. Other norms concern forbidding discussion of the family problem either within or outside of the family and consistent avoidance of stating one's true feelings.

Wegscheider (1981) also identifies several roles typically played by family members. These roles act to support family norms which, in turn, support the alcoholic's dependency problem. These norms prevent the dependent person from taking responsibility for his or her behavior.

Six roles typically characterize members of alcoholics' families. All fit well with the family's norms, which support continuation of the dependency problem. In addition to the person dependent on alcohol, there is the chief enabler, the family hero, the scapegoat, the lost child, and the mascot.

The *chief enabler's* main purpose is to assume the primary responsibility for family functioning. The abuser typically continues to lose control and relinquish responsibility. The chief enabler, on the

zation of part of the family, and recovery and reorganization of the whole family" (Denzin, 1987, p. 12). Like the addicts themselves, family members first try to deny that there is a problem or minimize how bad it really is.

The second phase, adjustment, involves family members trying to get rid of the problem. A spouse may nag the alcoholic to stop drinking or even threaten to leave for good. Family members might try hiding the alcohol. They might try to minimize the problem by making jokes about it. Such tactics are hardly ever successful.

Meanwhile, the problem continues to worsen. During the third phase, disorganization, family members find it difficult to pretend that the problem doesn't exist. Instead, they adopt roles to try and maintain their denial.

These roles are explained more thoroughly in Highlight 7.5.

The fourth stage through which the alcoholic family progresses, namely, reorganization of part of the family, involves attempts to restructure the family. During this phase, the chief enabler takes over. The addict assumes little or no responsibility anymore. The alcoholism problem may not seem as severe as before, because family members' expectations for the alcoholic's behavior are extremely low.

The fifth stage entails attempts to escape from the problem. Many times, the spouse will leave. Sometimes, the family fixates at this stage for some time. The alcoholic has had most responsibilities usurped. Again, because of low expectations, the problem may appear less severe.

---

other hand, takes more and more responsibility and begins making more and more of the family's decisions. A chief enabler is often the parent or spouse of the abuser.

Conditions in families of substance abusers often continue to deteriorate as the abuser loses control. A positive influence is needed to offset the negative. The *family hero* fulfills this role. The family hero is often the person who does well at almost everything. The hero works very hard at making the family look like it is functioning better than it is. In this way, the family hero provides the family with self-worth.

Another typical role is the *scapegoat*. Although the alcohol abuse is the real problem, a family rule mandates that this fact must be denied. Therefore, the blame must be placed elsewhere. Frequently, another family member is blamed for the problem. The scapegoat often behaves in negative ways (for example, gets caught stealing, runs away, becomes extremely withdrawn) which draws much attention. The scapegoat's role is to distract attention from the dependent person and on to something else.

This role helps the family avoid addressing the real problem of alcoholism.

Often there is also a *lost child* in the family. This is the person who seems rather uninvolved with the rest of the family yet never causes any trouble. The lost child's purpose is to provide relief to the family from some of the pain it is suffering. At least there is someone in the family who neither requires much attention nor causes any stress. The lost child is simply just there.

Finally, alcoholics' families often have someone playing the role of *mascot*. The mascot is the person who probably has a good sense of humor and appears not to take anything too seriously. Despite the fact that the mascot might be suffering inside, he or she provides a little fun for the family.

In summary, alcoholism and other drug abuse are problems affecting entire families. Each family member suffers from the abuser's dependency, yet each assumes a role in order to maintain the family's status quo and to help the family survive. Family members are driven to maintain these roles, no matter what. They eventually associate these roles with survival.

Thus, family members may escape from the problem by avoiding it.

The sixth stage in the alcoholic family involves family members reorganizing the family without the alcoholic member's involvement. If the alcoholic seeks treatment and begins recovering, the family will begin the seventh and final stage, recovery and reorganization of the whole family, including the recovering alcoholic.

Your Role in Intervention with Alcoholics and Other Drug Abusers

We've already indicated that your career path may or may not lead you to become a specialized AODA counselor. However, your chief usefulness concerning these issues may be to maintain an awareness of the problems involved, include related information in the assessments you do regardless of your practice area, and make necessary referrals for treatment interventions elsewhere.

The following section will address the professional attitudes necessary for effective work with alcoholics and other drug abusers. It will also discuss assessment of dependence, some specific micro intervention techniques used by AODA counselors, the significance of mezzo interventions, and possible macro approaches to intervention.

Effective Professional Attitudes

Denzin (1987) articulates nine basic guidelines for working with alcoholics. They help to shape the appropriate professional attitude for working with alcoholics and their families. They are:

1. *An alcoholic is able to recuperate and improve.* Many alcoholics don't recover. On the other hand, many do. It's important to maintain an optimistic attitude. It's very difficult working with alcoholics be-

cause of denial, relapses, and the resulting frustrations. Yet, to see a person return to a useful, productive, caring life can be infinitely rewarding.

2. *View alcoholism for what it is, namely, a disease which is out of the alcoholic's control.* It's easy to demean alcoholics and blame them for their own problems. To help them get better, don't rebuke and doom them. Rather, help them to regain control. Remember that they are not rotten people. They are desperate people struggling to get better.

An important concept related to that of disease is *recovery*. A recovering alcoholic "is a once-active alcoholic who has stopped drinking" (Denzin, 1987, p. 11). The assumption is that if you have the disease, you can only recover by stopping all drinking. Recovering alcoholics remain in recovery the rest of their lives.

3. *Be aware of telling symptoms which indicate an alcoholic problem.* Be sensitive to the signs of alcoholism (we will discuss assessment issues later). Does the person seem to be out of control when drinking? Does the person drink in secret? Does the person get in trouble during or after drinking? Is the person involved in arguments about drinking with those close to him or her?

4. *Remember that alcoholics have lost control.* You may think it odd that an alcoholic will get "plastered" at obviously noticeable and inappropriate times. For instance, take the dean who staggered up to the stage to address 180 parents of incoming college freshmen. His speech was slurred beyond recognition. Or take the woman who passed out cold at a party honoring her promotion. Once alcoholics start drinking, they can't stop. Drinking often starts as a means of relieving stress.

5. *Confrontation is the most effective approach for dealing with alcoholics.* We've

talked about how other family members can easily start assuming responsibility for an alcoholic's behavior. That's the worst thing they can do. The core of treating alcoholics involves making them responsible for their own behavior. If they are protected from all the negative consequences, they may never allow themselves to face their problem.

You, as a social worker, need to confront alcoholics and help to raise their awareness about their dependency problem and its effects. You also need to encourage those people close to the alcoholic to provide the alcoholic with feedback, in effect, to confront him or her. Such confrontation isn't easy. Whining and scolding should not be used. Scolding is worse than useless in that it probably will push the abuser away from you. The best approach is to remain calm and factual. The alcoholic needs to know how he insulted his boss the night before or how embarrassed you were when she spilled spaghetti all over your new suit. Alcoholism is extremely difficult to combat. An alcoholic will only muster up enough courage to try if she comprehends how bad the problem really is.

6. *The alcoholic must assume responsibility for his or her own behavior in order to get better.* This is related to the previous point. Alcoholics must be confronted with the effects of their behavior in order to be forced to take responsibility for it. Until they become responsible for behavior, they won't be able to change it.

7. *The entire family is part of the alcoholic problem.* We have established how an alcoholic's family passes through stages. Maladaptive roles and rules are established. Children can suffer and take their pain with them into adulthood. Thus, other family members need to address the abuse problem as early as possible so

that they don't develop related problems of their own. The entire family needs attention in intervention.

8. *Know what resources are available.* Multiple problems are involved in alcoholism, as it touches so many aspects of people's lives. Become aware of counseling facilities, inpatient programs, and such self-help groups as AA and Al-Anon. Highlight 7.6 reviews a number of resources available to assist in recovery.

9. *Avoid placing any labels on the alcoholic.* It's likely that alcoholics have already been blasted with accusations and slurs about their drinking. Part of the denial process involves becoming increasingly resistant to being called an alcoholic, drunk, or addict. If you plaster a label on them, they're likely to turn you off. AA emphasizes the importance of their coming to the conclusion that they are alcoholics. Only then can they begin the recovery process.

Assessment of Dependence

Chapter 5 described the Diagnostic and Statistical Manual of Mental Disorders (DSM-III-R), the primary manual used for psychiatric mental health assessments. It cites nine criteria for assessing whether an individual is AODA dependent. The rule of thumb is that at least three criteria must be evident for at least thirty days prior to the assessment. The nine criteria are (American Psychiatric Association, 1986):

1. Regular attempts to stop or persistently expressed longings to decrease or stop using the substance.

2. Frequent use when at work or social functions, where the person is expected to carry out social responsibilities, or substance use when such use is dangerous (for instance, while driving a car, op-

erating potentially hazardous machinery at work, or missing work because of substance use).

3. Increased tolerance to the substance,

thereby requiring increasingly greater amounts to attain the same effects achieved in the past.

4. Evidence of withdrawal symptoms com-

HIGHLIGHT 7.6
Your Role as a Referral Agent

When you assess that alcohol or other drug abuse is a problem for a client, you need to know what resources are available to help them. We've indicated that chapter 15 addresses brokering or referral skills in depth. Most resource agencies have similar goals in treating substance abusers. Their intent is "to educate the . . . [client] and significant others, to raise self-awareness, and to assist in the change process" (Marion & Coleman, 1991, p. 115). Marion and Coleman (1991, pp. 115–25) cite at least nine resources commonly available in communities which you can use for referrals:

1. *Detoxification.* Detoxification is "the process of removing drugs or other harmful substances from the body for a sufficient length of time to permit the restoration of adequate physiological and psychological functioning." The client is forced to refrain from the addictive substance while being given "rest, proper diet, nursing care, suitable medication, psychological support, and social services" (Barker, 1991, p. 61). Education about the drug and its use is also provided. Detoxification usually takes place in a hospital setting, where clients are retained from three to seven days. Strong encouragement is also provided to enter a rehabilitation program at the end of the stay.

2. *Outpatient Services.* Outpatient services involve "treatment at a health-care facility without being admitted for overnight stays or assigned a bed for continuous care (Barker, 1991, p. 164). People who are drug dependent can remain in their own homes and still have services made available to them. There are four types of clients usually suitable for outpatient treatment (Marion & Coleman, 1991): drug dependent people not yet ready to com-

mit themselves to a more extensive level of treatment; people making a transition from inpatient treatment back into the community; people who seek treatment early enough in the progression of dependency that they can respond to this level of treatment; and family members of drug dependent people.

3. *Intensive Outpatient Rehabilitation.* Dependent clients may still remain in their own homes, but receive ten to thirty hours of rehabilitative services each week. Thus, treatment is more concentrated than ordinary outpatient services.

4. *Inpatient Treatment.* Clients remain in inpatient treatment all day and night. It provides a comprehensive, structured environment which maximizes control of the treatment process. In essence, it is "a safe, behaviorally oriented environment in which the patient begins to look at what addiction has done to his or her life," with the entire staff actively participating in the treatment process (Marion & Coleman, 1991, p. 117).

5. *Specialty Programs and Tracts.* Specialty programs target the needs of specifically designated populations. For instance, they may involve "programs for adolescents, the elderly, pregnant women, . . . relapsers," or specifically designated ethnic or racial groups (Marion & Coleman, 1991, p. 117).

6. *Halfway Houses.* Halfway houses are "transitional residences for individuals who require some professional supervision, support, or protection but not full-time institutionalization" (Barker, 1991, p. 99). Recovering abusers reside with other recovering abusers in a supportive setting, where they begin to adjust to life outside such a structured setting in the real-life community. Emphasis is on gradually

monly associated with the substance when use is stopped.

5. Regular and excessive absorption both in

having the substance be readily available and in using the substance.

6. Choosing to use the substance instead of

increasing each resident's ability to handle responsibility at his or her own pace.

7. *Personal Care Homes.* People with extensive physiological damage caused by drug abuse may be admitted to personal care homes. Such facilities focus more on meeting basic, daily physical needs than on the provision of treatment for recovery.

8. *Mutual Self-Help Groups.* Self-help groups are "voluntary associations of nonprofessional people who share common needs or problems and meet together for extended periods of time for the purpose of mutual support and exchange of information about activities and resources that have been found useful in problem solving. These groups usually meet without the direction of a professional" (Barker, 1991, p. 210). Specific programs include AA, Narcotics Anonymous (NA), and Cocaine Anonymous (CA). These groups provide exceptionally relevant treatment approaches in view of their established success. Support from peers in the process of recovery is especially critical.

In view of its prevalence, we will focus on AA here. This nationwide group provides support, information, and guidance necessary for many recovering alcoholics to maintain their recovery process. The organization's success rests upon several principles. First, other people who "really understand" are available to give the recovering dependent person friendship and warmth. Each new member is given a "sponsor," who can be called for support at any time during the day or night. Whenever the dependent person feels depressed or tempted, there is always the sponsor to turn to.

Additionally, AA provides the recovering alcoholic with a new social group with whom to talk and enjoy activities. Old friends with well-established drinking patterns usually become difficult to associate with. The recovering alcoholic can no longer participate in drinking activity. Often, social pressure is applied to drink again. AA provides a respite from such pressure and the opportunity to meet new people, if such an opportunity is needed.

AA also helps the recovering person to understand that alcoholism is a disease. This means that the alcoholic cannot cure himself or herself. She need no longer feel guilty about being an alcoholic. All that needs to be done is to stop drinking.

AA also encourages self-introspection. Members are encouraged to look inside themselves and face whatever they see. They are urged to acknowledge that they have flaws and will never be perfect. This perspective often helps people to stop fleeing from the pain of reality and hiding in alcohol and drugs. It helps them to redefine the expectations for themselves and to gain control. Within the context of this honesty, people often can also acknowledge their strengths. They learn that they do have some control over their own behavior and that they can accomplish things for themselves and others.

Organizations are also available to provide support for other family members and to give them information and suggestions. For example, Al-Anon is an organization for the families of alcoholics, and Alateen is designed specifically for teenagers within these families.

9. *Pharmacological Adjuncts.* Some addicts need the help of prescribed medications (for example, Antabuse, used to combat alcoholism) to help them begin the recovery process. This medication, of course, must be carefully monitored by medical staff.

attending some consequential social or work-related event.

7. Frequent use of some mood or mind-altering substance to eliminate withdrawal symptoms after substance abuse.

8. Frequent use of the substance in larger quantities and for more prolonged periods than initially intended.

9. Continued use of the substance even after suffering from significant emotional, social, legal, or physical problems, even when the person clearly understands the negative effects of the substance.

It should be noted that the definition of dependence in this recent revision (DSM-III-R) differs from earlier manuals. In the past, being diagnosed as dependent required manifesting physical symptoms (for example, physical withdrawal symptoms) in addition to psychological dependence. This revision no longer requires physical symptoms to be present before a diagnosis of drug dependent can be made.

Also note that there are numerous AODA assessment instruments available. An example of one of them is provided in chapter 5.

Raskin and Daley (1991) suggest that information on the pattern of use is vitally important in a thorough assessment. Such information can be obtained either directly from the client or from others involved with the client. The following questions illustrate the types of information which can be gathered:

"What drugs have been used?"

"How old were you when you first started using?"

"What was the last day that you used the drug?"

"When do you usually use the drug? At what time of the week or day? How often during the day? Do you use every week or every day?"

"How do you consume the drug?" (Obviously, you drink alcohol. However,

other drugs can be injected, inhaled, smoked, or swallowed.)

"Are you certain that the needles you used were clean? Do you ever use needles after they've been used by other people?" (If applicable)

"Have you noticed any change in your drug tolerance level (you need to take more or less of the drug than before to achieve the same effect)?"

"Do you suffer from any withdrawal symptoms (for example, physical symptoms like "the shakes" or nausea, or psychological symptoms like radical mood swings) when you don't use the drug for a long period of time?"

"Do you ever experience more serious consequences of your drug use? For example, have you ever overdosed? Do you ever experience blackouts?"

Micro Practice Techniques for Counseling AODA Dependent Clients

Denzin (1987) describes an *interpretive therapy* approach to intervention. Such therapy focuses on four major points. First, alcoholics are excessively "self-centered" (p. 25). They have given their "best friend," alcohol, top priority for a long time. Treatment, then, should focus on examining the alcoholic's sense of self. They need to realign their priorities and give more and better attention to the people they love.

When alcoholics drink, they feel much more important than they do when sober. They also avoid the stresses they dread in everyday life. The second focus of treatment involves the negative emotions the alcoholic is trying to flee. How does the alcoholic feel about him or herself? How can you help the alcoholic more objectively evaluate personal strengths and weaknesses? How can alcoholics learn to accept and appreciate themselves for what and who they are?

Third, alcoholism distorts one's perception of time. Alcoholic time goes much faster or slower than normal time. Additionally, the alcoholic avoids living in real present time by reverting to the past or dreaming about the future. In reality, alcoholics avoid the bad things haunting them in the past and the presumed things threatening them in the future through the drug.

A fourth focus of treatment is the distressed interpersonal relationships alcoholics suffer. They've probably disappointed, frustrated, humiliated, deserted, and disgusted many of the people closest to them. Thus, significant relationship repair work is probably in order.

Jacobs (1981) explains a variety of techniques for addressing problems encountered in micro intervention with alcohol abusers. Discussed here are denial, relapses, client mistrust, and arriving at an interview drunk.

The Problem of Denial

The major symptom of drug dependence is denial (Massella, 1991). Jacobs (1981) suggests an intervention strategy to handle this difficult problem:

> During the early phases of treatment, it can be difficult to differentiate between clients who genuinely do not believe they have a problem and those who privately fear they can no longer control their drinking. One surefire way of losing clients before the distinction can be made is to demand total abstinence. Even if clients are willing to return, they are likely to be hostile and resistant, because the counselor has unwittingly compelled them to entrench their denial more deeply. Early confrontation with deniers is most ill-advised (p. 10).

Jacobs continues that goals of the first sessions should be very basic. For example, the client might simply agree to return for the next session. We have already established the need to help the dependent person accept responsibility for his own behavior and its effects. When working with persons who deny they are alcoholics, any confrontation should be as "unthreatening" as possible (p. 10). The social worker might ask, "If you were to stop drinking, do you think your life would be any different? If so, in what ways?" or "Do you ever get the feeling that you're having trouble controlling your drinking?"

More direct use of confrontation should be used only after a stronger relationship between worker and client has been established. It is crucial to time the confrontation well. A problem at work related to alcohol or a crisis in the marriage might provide good possibilities for confronting the client about the effects of his drinking. The social worker might then say, "It looks as if you're having a serious problem. Let's look at how it's related to drinking."

Many times, working with a genuine denier is tedious. Jacobs warns that the client will sometimes choose to discontinue treatment if the worker places greater demands on self-assessment. However, "the counselor can take solace in knowing that he or she has done all that can be reasonably expected" (p. 12). The bottom line is that it is the client's choice and responsibility.

In conclusion, Jacobs notes that insight-oriented therapy, especially that which addresses reasons for drinking, is generally unsuccessful with denial. On the other hand, becoming involved in a group therapy situation may encourage deniers to assess themselves and their problem, as they compare themselves to others.

What If Your Client Has a Relapse?

Jacobs (1981) provides a series of suggestions for dealing with an alcoholic client who has a relapse. First, a worker should treat the experience calmly, compassionately, and briefly. The alcoholic very likely feels guilty and ashamed even of talking about it. The worst thing to do is to scold your client. When a supervisor or instructor scolds you, how do you usually feel about it? Angry? Downtrodden? Resentful? Rebellious? Clients generally feel the same way.

A second suggestion for addressing a relapse is to treat the ordeal in as beneficial a light as possible. Emphasize what the client has learned from it. Identify the negative consequences he has suffered and relate how awareness of these consequences might help him abstain in the future.

This leads us to the third suggestion. Stress to your client that situations such as the one that led to the relapse should be shunned. Your client can learn that the conditions leading to the relapse (for example, returning to the old tavern with "the boys" after work as he used to do before recovery) only leads to his downfall and loss of control.

A fourth suggestion for addressing relapses entails helping your clients manage the stress which in the past has led to drinking. First, your clients need to become aware of the physical and psychological reactions indicating high stress levels. Next, they need to learn how to control that stress. For example, teaching them such stress-management techniques as specific approaches to relaxation can be helpful.

A fifth suggestion concerns helping your clients avoid relapses in the first place. Using role plays of various alcohol-seductive situations before the situations occur can help clients learn to react to unexpected situations. If they have the chance to think through a tempting situation beforehand, they may be more likely to respond to it in a thoughtful, responsible way.

How Do You Get Your Client to Trust You?

Many alcoholics are used to failure. Perhaps they have tried to quit before with only temporary and limited success. Maybe they've been in treatment with AODA counselors who were unable to help them. At any rate, prior bad experiences together with the alcoholic's tendency toward secrecy and denial paves the ground for mistrust. Because of the severity of their own problems, some clients won't trust you no matter what you do.

Jacobs (1981) makes several suggestions for approaching client mistrust. First, be straightforward and honest about your own abilities. Don't pretend you can wave a magic wand and cure your clients. On the other hand, don't be self-conscious and apologetic. Rather, emphasize that it takes a lot of hard work on the parts of both worker and client to help a person recover. If you have had successes in the past, say so. On the other hand, you can say frankly that you are unable to make any promises. State what treatment will involve. Don't be secretive. One of your objectives will be to give direct feedback to your clients about their behavior. Your intent is to help your client face, rather than hide from, reality.

What If Your Client Arrives Drunk?

Jacobs (1981) emphasizes that counseling can not proceed effectively if a client comes to an interview drunk. He cites four variables to consider when handling any incident: Is the client relatively docile and submissive; is the client "verbally aggressive" (p. 75); is the client physically defiant and threatening; and what should you do about your future work with the client?

Docile clients should generally be calmly told to go home. It is *always* useless to try to work with a client who is drunk. You may decide to confront the drunken behavior at some later time when the client is sober. However, do not chastise the client while he is drunk. This may only make a manageable client volatile.

A client may appear both drunk and verbally assaultive when coming for an interview. In these cases, your main goal should be to minimize the disruption and send the client safely home (that is, in a taxi or with a friend; your client, of course, should not drive his or her own car). If possible, you might take the client aside to a place where he will pose the least disturbance. It's not a good idea to isolate yourselves from others, just in case the client becomes violent. You should never place yourself in physical jeopardy. Allow the client to vent feelings. You might empathize via reflection if appropriate. For example, you might say, "I understand how angry you are right now." Don't disagree with the client. That tact is useless. Rather, let the client settle down until he can be sent home. Once again, you can decide to address this behavior and its ramifications in a subsequent meeting when the client is sober.

You should not take any unnecessary physical risks if a client appears drunk and physically assaultive or aggressive. Stay in an area where others are. You might state your reactions honestly. For instance, you might say, "This is scary for me. I will need to call for help if you won't settle down." Don't try to do any counseling. Simply try to minimize the risk that something violent will happen. Someone other than you should call the police. Likewise, someone other than you (as the focus of animosity) should request that the client depart.

The fourth variable to consider is whether to continue treatment with the client. This is regardless of the type of behavior the client manifested. Jacobs (1981) reflects:

> Should a counselor continue to work with clients who have arrived in an intoxicated state? With the exception of those who presented a direct physical threat, in most instances, the answer is yes. If the anger directed toward the counselor was without any reference to physical threat, whether or how the counselor proceeds depends greatly upon how upsetting the experience was (pp. 76–77).

In a situation in which the practitioner no longer feels safe with the client, that practitioner should discontinue working with the client. When terminating the relationship, the worker should tell the client the truth. For example, the practitioner might say that he no longer feels able to work with the client because he no longer feels safe; additionally, he feels that he and the client would no longer be able to make much progress together.

Intervention at the Mezzo Level

You will most likely fulfill one of two roles in mezzo level practice when working with abusers of alcohol and other drugs. You will make assessments and subsequent referrals to self-help groups such as AA, and you will work with the abuser and his or her family.

Several concepts are critical to direct intervention in families (Wegscheider, 1981). First, family members must first realize the extent of the problem. They need to identify the drug abuse as their major problem. Second, they need to learn about and evaluate their family dynamics. They need to evaluate their own behavior and break out of the roles maintaining the dependent person's abuse. The chief enabler, especially, must stop making excuses and assuming the dependent's responsibility. If the dependent is sick from a hangover and can't make it to school or work the next day, it must be the dependent's responsibility, not a parent's or spouse's, to call in sick.

Third, family members should learn to confront abusers and give them honest information about their behavior. For instance, family members should be encouraged to tell an alcoholic exactly how she behaved during a blackout. If the abuser hit another family member while drunk, this needs to be brought out. The confrontation should occur not in an emotional manner, but in a factual one.

Fourth, the family needs to learn about the progression of the disease. We have already discussed some characteristics of drug abuse. At first, only occasional relief drinking occurs. Drinking becomes more constant. The abuser then begins to drink in secret and feel guilty about drinking. Memory blackouts begin to occur and gradually increase in frequency. The abuser feels worse and worse about his drinking behavior but seems to have less and less control over it. Finally, the drinking begins to seriously affect work, family, and social relationships. A job may be lost or all school classes flunked. Perhaps family members leave or throw the abuser out. The abuser's thinking becomes more and more impaired.

Finally, the abuser "hits rock bottom." Nothing seems left but despair and failure, and the abuser admits complete defeat. It is at this point that the abuser may make one of two choices. Either he will continue on the downward spiral to a probable death related to alcohol, or he may desperately struggle to help himself. Typically, during this period, the abuser will make some progress only to slip back again. Vicious circles of drinking and stopping are often apparent. Finally, the abuser may express an honest desire for help.

Intervention at the Macro Level

Intervention approaches at the macro level are those that go beyond the extent to which alcohol or other drug abusers and their families receive or don't receive treatment. Macro approaches concentrate on how abusers in general are treated and on what solutions to drug-abuse problems society proposes.

Macro issues focus on at least three major areas. The first deals with the adequacy and effectiveness of treatment programs. Are adequate services available to all abusers and their families? Are our clients being served with the resources they need? An answer of no to either of these questions leads to the possibility of macro intervention. Do new programs need to be developed or old programs improved?

A second macro issue involves the accessibility of alcohol and other drugs to abusers. In

the case of illegal drugs other than alcohol, is our legal system adequately regulating their distribution? Obviously, there are problems, or there wouldn't be abusers. What should be done to address these problems? Should abusers, middleperson drug distributors, or major drug kingpins be the target for legal action and control? What policies and programs should be developed to curb drug problems?

In the case of alcohol, a macro issue involves the degree to which social policies should be permissive concerning its use. Should eighteen-year-olds be able to purchase alcoholic beverages? How about if they are only allowed to buy beer? Should nineteen-year-olds be able to purchase beer, or twenty-year-olds, for that matter? Another serious issue related to alcohol involves driving under its influence. What is a permissible blood alcohol level?

A third macro issue concerns prevention of drug abuse. Should more and better drug-education programs be developed? Should prevention focus on "early identification and treatment of alcohol-dependent individuals" or rather, on "education . . . aimed at the entire citizenry" (Anderson, 1987, p. 141)? What might the best methods be to stop drug problems before abuse occurs?

Chapter Summary

This chapter examines three approaches to intervention which address problems frequently encountered by generalist practitioners, regardless of their specific field of practice. The approaches are risk management in protective services, crisis intervention, and working with alcohol and other drug abusers. All three approaches coincide well with the steps in the Generalist Intervention Model's problem-solving approach.

The concept of risk management was explained and the risk continuum described. A specific risk-management program entitled the

Child at Risk Field System was examined. Common goals in risk management treatment planning were identified.

The crisis development process was reviewed. A model of crisis intervention and the specific techniques it employs was explained. An example of how the model could be applied was illustrated with a case example. The relationship between crisis intervention and both mezzo practice and macro practice was reviewed.

The generalist practitioner's role in intervention with alcohol and other drug abusers was discussed. Common terms used in AODA practice were defined. Characteristics of abusers and their families were discussed. Specific techniques for working with abusers were examined. Potential referral resources were identified. Issues involved in the AODA field were related to intervention at the mezzo and macro levels of practice.

8 Evaluation, Termination, and Follow-Up in Generalist Practice

Scoping it out

As a social worker you may be confronted with any of the following tasks:

- Evaluating whether your efforts to help a juvenile delinquent stay out of the criminal justice system are working. (In other words, has he remained out of jail and in the community?)
- Proving to the county board of supervisors the effectiveness of a new parent nurturing program designed to reduce child abuse among low-income parents.
- Determining whether your assertiveness-training program is increasing group members' assertiveness. (To what extent have group members increased their assertiveness without aggressively violating the rights of other?)
- Measuring the effectiveness of a foster parent recruitment program you have implemented. (How many more foster parents have you been able to recruit since the program began compared to the period before the program was instituted?)
- Helping a previously aggressive client in a group home for behaviorally disordered adolescents prepare to return to his home, school, old friends, and community.
- Assisting a family (coping with a recent suicide attempt by its fourteen-year-old member) in the ending phase of a six-week family therapy program.
- Easing the transition of a frightened yet strengthened mother leaving the safety of a battered-women's shelter.
- Following up on your chronically mentally ill adult client who has moved from a residential institution to a community-based program.

CHAPTER EIGHT

Introduction

To be effective as a social worker, you must know whether the interventions you employ are working. This may seem simple enough in the abstract, but developing effective strategies to evaluate our practice is not always easy. Even when we have a clear plan for evaluating the

Figure 8.1: Evaluation in the Generalist Intervention Model

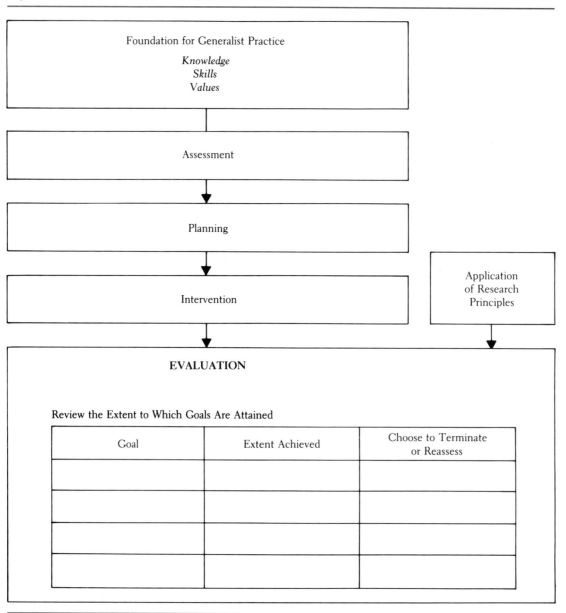

outcomes of our practice or our programs, many things can challenge our conclusions about our effectiveness.

The evaluation process typically is ongoing in that we must always be alert to whether the goals we hoped to reach are being achieved. Evaluation may also be thought of as an end-point activity, often leading to the mutual client-worker decision to terminate the professional relationship. The last part of this chapter focuses on the knowledge and skills needed for effectively concluding professional social worker–client relationships. In summary, this chapter will help you to:

- Identify and use appropriate methods of evaluating your practice;
- Identify commonly used methods for program evaluation;
- Differentiate between various concepts important to evaluation of practice including validity, reliability, generalizability, the baseline, formative and summative evaluation;
- Recognize common problems associated with attempts to evaluate social work practice;
- Prepare the client for the termination phase;
- Help the client recognize and manage termination-related feelings such as anger, anxiety, disappointment, etc.;
- Recognize and manage your *own* termination-related feelings;
- Recognize typical behavior and feelings common to the ending of worker-client relationships;
- Plan for and carry out appropriate termination activities with individuals, families, groups, organizations, and communities;
- Plan for and carry out maintenance of change efforts;
- Carry out the follow-up process in social work practice;

- Recognize and manage barriers to following up on client's functioning once the intervention process is over.

Evaluating Social Work Practice

Evaluation of social work practice has only recently been emphasized. It has been spurred by several factors, including demands for accountability, interest in improving social work practice, and the accreditation requirements of the Council on Social Work Education. We will discuss these factors more thoroughly, as well as describe the purposes of evaluation, in the next few pages.

Purposes of Evaluation

As sources of funding for social programs have become increasingly scarce during the last twenty years, the demand for evaluation of those programs has increased. Governmental and private funding sources wanted proof that their money was being put to good use. They demanded greater assurance that the money they allocated for programs was accomplishing the intended purposes. While many agencies had been providing some kinds of evaluation, their emphasis was largely on output or measuring what the agency did. For example, the worth of an agency might be justified by noting that the agency staff provided ten thousand hours of one-on-one work with first offenders. Therefore, the implication is that the agency is productive. Still another agency might report that its caseload this year increased by 25 percent with no corresponding increase in staff. Thus, the agency implies its current staff is working all the harder. These types of measures supplied us with some information about what agencies do. However, they did nothing to satisfy the basic questions. Did the agency accomplish its purpose, and was it actually successful in helping its clients?

Besides the economic importance of evaluation, political pressures played a role in demanding accountability from social programs. Elected state and federal officials called for increased emphasis on evaluation to justify the continued expenditure of funds. This was especially true for those skeptical of, or opposed to, social programs.

Simultaneously, a growing consumer movement was affecting human-service programs across the country. It maintained that users of products or services had a right to know about their effectiveness. Consumers wanted some assurance that they were getting what they were paying for, whether the product was cornflakes, mouthwash, or counseling.

The result of this confluence of political pressure, economic necessity, and consumer interest is a heightened awareness of the importance of accountability (Hudson & Grinnell, 1989). Accountability involves "the state of being answerable to the community, to consumers of a product or service, or to supervisory groups such as boards of directors"; it also involves the "profession's obligation to reveal clearly what its functions and methods are and to provide assurances to clients that its practitioners meet specific standards of competence" (Barker, 1987, pp. 1–2). How can you, as a generalist practitioner, prove you're accomplishing what you say you are? In the following sections, we will look more closely at what evaluation means and the kinds of things that it achieves. We will also examine its relationship to accountability.

It may seem logical for workers to want to know the outcome of their efforts, or to know that the program in which they work is effective. Still, strangely enough, evaluation has not been an ongoing concern for many workers. There are several reasons for this. First, the very act of evaluating a practitioner's own work leaves the practitioner vulnerable. Workers might ask themselves: What if I'm not success-

The evaluation process enables the social worker to decide if intervention strategies are working.

ful with every client? What if some clients actually get worse? What if my caseload is so large that I don't have time to follow up on my clients' progress? What if my agency charges a lot of money for services I'm not sure really work?

These are all legitimate concerns that have served as obstacles to workers evaluating their own practice. After all, evaluations make judgments about what the worker has accomplished in the change process. These judgments might not always be favorable to the worker, especially if clients were worse off after receiving help.

A second reason for the lack of a routine system of evaluation is that workers are often too busy for any kind of formal evaluation. High caseloads and busy schedules often make it difficult to find time to evaluate results in more than a cursory, haphazard fashion.

A third reason for the lack of effort focused on evaluation is that many agencies have not emphasized its importance. Simply counting cases seen or hours of service given was considered a satisfactory measure of an agency's effort. In addition, agencies did not have the money or time for extensive evaluation studies. Recording information and evaluating it is time-consuming and, therefore, expensive. You're paid for your time, so your time is worth money.

Another likely explanation was that most social workers lacked training in the use of evaluation approaches. Until the Council on Social Work Education enacted standards requiring that social work education programs teach students specifically to evaluate their practice, most schools and universities neglected this content. While students routinely took research classes as part of their work, these courses were generally not focused on evaluation of one's own practice. Rather, the primary goal was to produce a graduate who could read the professional journals and be an intelligent consumer of social-work research. This is no longer the primary research goal of most social-work education programs. Now, most students learn a variety of methods for evaluating their practice and for evaluating agency programs.

Toseland and Rivas (1984, p. 304) identify several reasons for conducting evaluation.[1] These include:

1. Satisfying the curiosity of the worker in the context of one's professional obligation to learn about the effects of specific interventions. For example, was the new family log approach considered beneficial by the family members using it?
2. Providing feedback to workers to help improve their skills. For instance, did the client feel the worker listened to and understood her problem?
3. Proving the usefulness of a program or method to an agency. For instance, a program might be eliminated if its effectiveness cannot be demonstrated.
4. Assessing progress of a client (individually or collectively). Here, we might be concerned about whether a delinquent youngster has improved enough to move from his group home to his own home.
5. Providing means for the clients to express their own views. This might be important to know whether participants in a nurturing skills program felt the program taught them skills they could use effectively at home.
6. Developing knowledge that will guide the practice of others. Newly developed approaches to helping clients are often described in journal articles and presented at conferences. This allows others to become familiar with these approaches and replicate successful interventions.

Typically, evaluations have one of two major thrusts. First, they can *monitor the ongoing operation (effort) of an agency*. Second, evaluations can *assess the outcomes (effects) of a program or intervention*. According to Kettner, Daley, and Nichols (1985, p. 231), the monitoring and evaluation functions are complementary. On one hand, monitoring looks at the process of giving service; on the other, evaluation looks at the effectiveness of the service provided. The ultimate goal is to provide information that increases the effectiveness (and efficiency) of interventions. Effectiveness involves succeeding at what you set out to accomplish. Efficiency concerns doing it at a reasonable cost. In other words, evaluations can focus on effort or activity, outcomes, adequacy of performance, or efficiency.

Evaluations can also focus on the process of giving help (Kettner, Daley, and Nichols, 1985, p. 260). Let's use an example to illustrate how this might work. Assume you are a worker attempting to help a woman become more assertive.

---

1. Reprinted with the permission of Macmillan Publishing Company from *An Introduction to Group Practice* by R. W. Toseland and R. F. Rivas. Copyright 1984 by Macmillan Publishing Company.

HIGHLIGHT 8.1

Evaluating Community Programs

Rubin and Rubin (1986) look at evaluation at the community level. They suggest several additional purposes for evaluation which include:

1. Supplying data to help enhance existing agency programs;
2. Allowing managers to follow the progress of developing programs and undertakings;
3. Helping agencies select activities that are most effectual;

4. Demonstrating to organizational supporters that their support of programs is justified;
5. Meeting conditions imposed by agencies that provide grants. Funding bodies often require the agency receiving a grant to develop some means of evaluating the grant-funded activity. In this way, the funding agency knows whether the money was used appropriately and accomplished its intended purpose.

Cloris describes herself as always being "shy." She is terrified of meeting other people and has virtually no friends. Additionally, she finds it difficult to assert herself at work. As a result, she feels that her colleagues, all health-care aides at a small nursing home, often take advantage of her.

Of course, you care whether Cloris becomes more assertive. This is the outcome the client desired and the goal toward which you both worked for the past six months. Also, you probably want to know which of your interventions proved most helpful and which did not. You want to determine which techniques to continue using in the future and which to omit. Thus, you may be focusing on your *efforts or activities* in the behalf of your client.

Your agency, on the other hand, may be interested in other areas. For instance, the agency might want to evaluate the *adequacy of your performance*. It is possible that the approach you were using with the client might not be as effective as others that are available. Similarly, the board of directors might be wondering whether this service is provided at the *lowest possible cost*. Their interest is in *efficiency* (the relationship between the resources used to effect change and the outcome of the change effort). If another agency provides similar results at lower cost, the board may decide that it

cannot afford you or your program. You, therefore, may be out of a job.

As you can see, there are many facets to this idea called evaluation. In the next section, we will look at the evaluation process itself, focusing on goals and some key concepts in doing evaluations.

The Evaluation Process

Evaluation of practice follows the same problem-solving approach used in the social work practice itself (Duehn, 1985). For example, first we must define the problem to be evaluated. Once this is accomplished, the worker must consider the types of research approaches that might be appropriate (assessment). The best approach is then chosen (planning), and the research is carried out (intervention). Finally, the worker must examine and evaluate the results of the research effort.

As is evident, this problem-solving approach mirrors almost exactly the way in which a worker deals with a problem involving an individual, family, group, organization, or community. Just as with our chapters on micro, mezzo, and macro practice, there are some key terms and ideas that are essential to understand and conduct research on social work practice. These concepts include formative evaluation, summative evaluations, baselines, validity, reliability, data-gathering methods, independent variables, dependent variables, and generalizability.

Key Concepts—Formative Evaluation

We have indicated earlier that evaluations may be conducted for monitoring purposes. Such evaluations assess the adequacy or amount of effort directed at solving a client system's problem. In this type of evaluation, the gathering of data occurs during the actual intervention. We call this a *formative evaluation.*

Formative evaluations focus on the process of providing help instead of the end product of help-giving. For example, Toseland and Rivas (1984) suggest that one can have group members complete a questionnaire following each individual group session. The questionnaire might ask the group members their opinions on what occurred in the group, perhaps focusing on what they learned. The results of the clients' evaluations would be used to help plan subsequent meetings. Formative evaluations help us assess whether the anticipated progress is achieved. For example, in educationally focused groups, the members may be given a pretest at the beginning of a session and a post-test after the session. This would help determine achievement of goals for that specific session. In other words, exactly how much did group members learn during that particular session? Similarly, the worker and client who periodically recall progress made by the client over the past six meetings are engaging in a type of formative evaluation. The PERT chart we reviewed in chapter 4 also is a kind of formative evaluation. As we recall, a PERT chart provides a visual representation or diagram that "looks at program objectives and indicates all the activities that need to be performed, the time required for each, the sequence in which they should take place, and the resources required" (Barker, 1987, p. 119). At any point in the process, one can look at the chart and know what is to be done, by whom, and by what date. This allows us to know whether the process is proceeding as planned. It also enables us to make changes as necessary to reach our goals.

Most students are familiar with one form of formative evaluation, namely, course or instructor evaluations. These evaluations provide the instructor and the instructor's department with information to assess how well that instructor is conveying information to students. Although course evaluations occur at the end of a student's experience with an instructor, they are actually formative evaluations. This is because the evaluations are intended to affect how the instructor teaches the course in the future.

Key Concept—Summative Evaluations

Frequently, we want to know whether the outcome we anticipated at the beginning of our problem-solving process has been achieved. This requires that we conduct an evaluation after completion of the problem-solving process. We call such evaluations *summative,* because they occur at the end of the process. In one sense, end-of-semester examinations in a college course are summative evaluations. They help determine whether you have learned the material outlined in course objectives.

You may be a bit unclear about the distinction between summative and formative evaluations. The important thing to remember is that formative evaluations occur while a problem-solving process is continuing. Summative evaluations, on the other hand, occur at the conclusion of the problem-solving process, looking backward. Their goal is to summarize what has already occurred. Formative evaluations, on the other hand, are oriented toward the future. Their goal is to affect or form what is yet to come.

Key Concepts—Baseline

Another key concept you need to understand is that of baseline. *Baseline* is a term taken from behavioral research, and is very important in assessing the progress of some helping relationships. Take, for example, the case of Virginia Schwartz. Virginia went to a social worker for help because she and her daughter, Mary, fight furiously over Mary's boyfriend, Lonnie. Virginia says the fights occur "a lot, every day." Mary describes the frequency of fights by saying they occur "constantly." If the worker is to judge whether her efforts and those of the family are working, it will be important to learn whether the fights are decreasing or not. Without definitive information on the frequency of the fighting, it will be nearly impossible to know whether things are improving.

What the worker wants is a *baseline*, or a measure, of the frequency, intensity, or duration of a behavior. Before we can tell whether the behavior is changing, we must know how often it occurs. Thus, the worker might ask Virginia and Mary to record individually the number of fights they have in a week. This information would provide some basis for knowing whether the frequency of the fights is diminishing, increasing, or remaining the same.

In some situations, it might be important to have several baselines. Perhaps the fights going on between Mary and Virginia are affecting Mary's schoolwork. Mary's grades in certain subjects must be an additional measure to help determine whether the worker and clients are making progress.

Ideally, a baseline should be based on several observations. These should be made over a period of time prior to intervention. As you can see, baselines can be very important in the helping process and are essential for conducting certain kinds of evaluations. We will discuss these types of evaluations later.

Key Concepts—Validity

When we evaluate a practice situation, it is important that we use appropriate measurements. Assume, for example, that you are a social worker in a deferred prosecution program. This involves working with a group of first-time adult offenders (for example, shoplifters or drunk drivers) referred to your program by the court system. If they successfully complete your program, they will have their records wiped clean. The assumption behind the existence of your program is that early intervention with first offenders will reduce the tendency toward recidivism (further contact with the criminal-justice system).

A new coworker suggests that perhaps one measure of the success of your program is whether the participants feel positively about the experience. He suggests that you ask each member to rate the group experience on a scale of one to ten, with ten being an extremely positive attitude toward the program.

What is the problem with such an approach? The primary problem is that the purpose of the group is to reduce recidivism among this group of first offenders. The measure suggested—that is, a client questionnaire focusing on feelings—has nothing to do with the real purpose of your program, namely reducing actual recidivism. Such a measure is simply not a *valid* means of assessing the outcome of this group.

Validity is another significant concern in evaluation. It is entirely possible, for example, for the group members to have enjoyed the group experience and still continue a life of crime. According to Toseland and Rivas (1984, p. 323) "validity refers to the extent to which a data collection instrument measures what it purports to be measuring." A client questionnaire asking group members to report any contacts with the criminal-justice system would have greater validity than one that asked them to rate the group experience. An even more valid method of knowing whether the goals of the group were met would be to follow up on each group member at periodic points in time (six months, one year, etc.) to see if there were any further arrests. It would be easier to conclude that the intervention worked if only a small percentage of group members had subsequent arrests.

The matter of validity is a bit complicated, since there are really several types of validity. We can speak, for instance, of *face validity*. *Face validity* "refers to a common-sense judgment about whether the measure actually reflects" what it is supposed to measure (Rubin & Rubin, 1986, p. 155). Most of us would react strongly to a social work test containing questions unrelated to our course. If a statistics test asked us to reproduce Einstein's theorem, we would be angry. The test was supposed to measure our mastery of statistics, not the math involved in Einstein's theorem. In this case, the test questions do not have face validity. We would expect the final examination in a history of social welfare course to ask about the Elizabethan Poor Laws, social-security amendments, Hull House, and the War on Poverty. As one might expect, achieving face validity is comparatively easy.

Another type of validity is *concurrent validity*. Let's say a new instrument designed to test for depression is given to a group of patients already hospitalized for depression. If their scores on the new instrument are low (representing a depressed state), then we can say the new instrument has concurrent validity. That is to say, the instrument has a clear relationship to the thing we hope to measure, namely, depression.

Predictive validity is another important form of validity. We can say that a measure has predictive validity when it can be used to predict future events. In theory at least, your performance in field placements should be predictive of how you will do in actual social work positions. Likewise, scores on the Scholastic Aptitude Test (SAT) and the American College Test (ACT) are used to predict how high school graduates will perform in a college or university academic environment. To the extent that an instrument accurately predicts later performance, behavior, or outcomes, it is said to have predictive validity.

Not all the types of validity have been included in this chapter. Your research course will likely provide much greater depth on this matter and further hone your skills as an evaluator of social work practice.

Key Concepts—Reliability

Most of us would probably object to the following situation: A three-credit course on interviewing is required for graduation. The total course grade is based on a onetime observation by one faculty member. That faculty member would be drawn at random from a pool of faculty, including those in psychology, sociology, and social work. The rater would thus be assigned to you by chance. Our objection would probably be based on the realization that each of the potential raters might have different criteria they would use to judge us. The person who rates us on our interview might think we did a good job. Another rater, however, might come to a different conclusion. Even if the whole pool of faculty came from the social work program, there would probably be some differences in their judgments. While all might be competent to judge interviewing skills, there still might be little consistency in their grading. The very same interview might be given an A− by one and a C+ by another. Clearly, we want observer and instruments capable of making consistent judgments. This brings us to another concept of importance—*reliability*.

"*Reliability* refers to the extent to which an instrument measures the same phenomenon the same way each time it is used" (Toseland & Rivas, 1984, p. 323). The key words here are *each time*. In the example above, we might be more comfortable if each observer was using the same rating form with clearly defined criteria. If there is a high level of consistency among the raters, we have what is known as inter-rater reliability, a desirable characteristic.

Let's take a slightly different look at reliability. Assume we have an instrument that purports to measure assertiveness. A reliable instrument will produce similar results each time it is used. If a person scores low on the instrument one week and high the next, we would question whether the measure is reliable. Reliable instruments produce consistent results over time. In theory at least, the only thing which should result in changing one's score on the assertive test is assertiveness training or some similar intervention.

There is also a clear relationship between reliability and validity. If an instrument (or rater) does not produce consistent results on subsequent trials, we can't depend on its accuracy. It is possible, however, for a measure to be reliable but not valid. Let's take an obvious example. Your score on a written test of French vocabulary might be reliable in that it will always produce the same result, namely, a low score. If, however, the purpose of the test is to judge your ability to *speak* French, not read it, the written test is a much less valid measure of spoken vocabulary, since it does not really test this area at all.

Just as you would want to be evaluated in a manner that is both valid and reliable, so too should you want to evaluate your practice in a manner that is both valid and reliable. Sometimes, this is relatively easy to accomplish. If you wanted to know whether a depressed client was becoming less depressed, you might administer to that client one of the available depression scales. You could develop your own instrument, but it would likely prove costly, time consuming, and of less validity and reliability than existing methods. Using instruments where validity and reliability have been demonstrated is certainly an easier course to follow.

Whenever possible, we attempt to use mul-tiple measures or indicators to help ensure that we are getting valid and reliable information. For example, a student doing her field placement in a hospital outpatient setting used both weight loss and cholesterol levels as measures of whether clients were achieving the goals of a health-improvement program.

It is also preferable, if possible, to get independent verification of subjective items. While a client may accurately report a change in his or her behavior, it is sometimes better to have a report from other observers to substantiate the client's claims. A client may report improvement that is not observable to significant others. This, at least, raises a question about the accuracy of the information provided by the client.

Key Concepts—Data-Gathering Methods

The choice of which or how many data-gathering methods to use is determined largely by the goals of the intervention. Social workers use many methods depending upon need. Commonly used methods include surveys, interviews with significant others (parents, teachers, etc.), collected data (such as school attendance records and grades), and observations of the researcher and others involved in the change effort (Gibbs, 1991).

Surveys or interviews may be structured (using a specific set of questions in a structured format) or unstructured (using open-ended questions in an informal discussion). Observations may be direct (person-to-person) or recorded in some way (for example, videotaping). *Self-reports* are used when what must be measured is subjective. Feelings and beliefs of a client are examples of situations where self-reports are appropriate. Since the worker cannot "see" what the client believes, he must resort to asking the client to report on this area. Many instruments have been developed based on this premise. Methods frequently used to gather subjective data include depression scales, assert-

HIGHLIGHT 8.2
Finding Valid and Reliable Instruments

Locating a valid and reliable instrument to assist with your practice and evaluation efforts is sometimes quite easy. There are instruments to measure all of the following:

- assertiveness
- depression
- anger
- fear
- alcoholism
- anxiety
- self-esteem

- peer relationships
- parenting skills and knowledge
- marital happiness
- social skills
- argumentativeness
- sexual interaction

This is only a small sample of the types of measures available. Existing measures such as these usually have information on validity and reliability as well as normative data so that comparisons with "normal" populations can be done.

There are a variety of sources for these instruments. A few of them are listed below.

Pietrzak, J., Ramler, M., Renner, T., Ford, L., and Gilbert, N. (1990). *Practical Program Evaluation*. Newbury Park, CA: Sage Publications.

McCormick, I. A. (1984). "A Simple Version of the Rathus Assertiveness Schedule." *Behavior Assessment*. pp. 7, 95–99.

Magura, S. and Moses, B. S. (1986). *Outcome Measures for Child Welfare Services: Theory and Applications*. Washington, D.C.: Child Welfare League of America.

Corcoran, K. and Fischer, J. (1987). *Measures for Clinical Practice*. New York: The Free Press.

Hudson, W. (1982). *The Clinical Assessment Package: A Field Manual*. Homewood, IL: Dorsey Press.

---

iveness schedules, and other devices. Highlight 8.2 refers to a number of such instruments.

Products, such as achievement of a specific task or change in behavior, are often used in the data-gathering process. A withdrawn child who talks to no one on the playground is exhibiting a specific behavior, that of silence. The worker can certainly assess change in that behavior by noting whether the child begins to talk to other children. Likewise, a client who is trying to lose weight can easily measure progress by stepping on the scale.

Sometimes, *observational measures* are used when it's relatively easy and appropriate to observe specific behavior in a situational context. Consider, for example, evaluations of a student's interviewing technique. One of the most anxiety-producing parts of becoming a social worker is learning how to interview clients. Unlike other courses in college, this requires students to demonstrate that they can conduct an interview meeting the prescribed standards. They can do this using audiotape, videotape, or actual live interviews. Faculty then observe and rate the interview. Such a procedure provides a more valid indicator of interviewing skill than a pencil-and-paper test. The instructor is able to look for certain kinds of skills and judge whether the student has exhibited those skills in the interview. Ideally, the skills must be carefully defined and clearly known to both student and teacher. In addition, the observer must be competent to judge the presence or absence of the skill. In other words, rating must be valid.

Key Concepts—Independent and Dependent Variables

Two other concepts important in practice evaluation are *independent variable* and *dependent variable*. The independent variable involves "the factors that are thought to influence or cause a certain behavior or phenomenon" (Barker, 1987, p. 78). In our context, it is the helping process itself. Our efforts to assist client system represents the independent variable.

The "factor that is being influenced is the dependent variable" (Barker, 1987, p. 78). For our purposes, this is the end product of that helping process. The assumption is that the outcome is dependent upon the helping efforts. Hence, it's called the dependent variable. In practice, we know that the independent variable (our helping) is not totally responsible for the outcome. Too many other intervening variables exist to make such a claim. For example, a client attempting to lose weight may join a weight-loss program that meets weekly. While the weekly sessions are helpful in many ways, other factors affect the client's life. The reactions of other persons (spouse, children, friends) may have an enormous influence on the client. If significant others praise the client's willpower and acknowledge how much better he looks, the results of the group sessions will be enhanced. If, on the other hand, no one shows any recognition of the client's efforts or, worse yet, belittles the effort, the outcome may be negatively affected. It is important to remember that many variables affect people's behavior. The worker's effort to help is simply one of these factors. We will discuss the importance of these alternate explanations for change later in this chapter.

Key Concepts—Generalizability

Assume for a minute that we have been extremely successful in our efforts to help clients or that the program we are part of has had unusual success. Our feelings of success have been supported by the evaluation techniques we've used. It is logical then to begin to think that these methods may prove useful to other similar groups. We are now beginning to *generalize* the results of our research to other groups or populations.

Generalizability is a desirable characteristic of any successful program. However, the very limited size of our sample (a handful of individuals or groups) is too small to make generalizing appropriate. A substantial number of cases is necessary to establish that positive change has not come about simply by chance or other intervening factors.

In addition, for the results of a project to be generalized, we must have confidence that the members of the group are representative of (similar to) others who might benefit from this program. Without this assurance, any attempts to generalize from this group of clients to other clients are pure speculation. We shall refer to this matter again when we look at issues and problems in evaluation.

Key Concepts—A Summary

The concepts we have discussed so far include formative and summative evaluation, baselines, validity (face validity, concurrent validity, predictive validity), and data-gathering methods. We also discussed reliability, independent and dependent variables, and generalizability. Each concept is important to the researcher, whether one is looking at one's own practice or attempting to evaluate an entire program. In the next section, we will be looking at several techniques the worker can use to evaluate his or her practice.

Evaluation Designs for Direct Practice

Most of you will be involved in direct practice with client systems. Those client systems may be individuals, families, groups, organizations, or communities. The nature and level of your practice will be dependent upon your knowledge and skill, level of education, requirements of your agency, and the clientele served by your agency. Therefore, it is important that you be familiar with a variety of techniques to evaluate direct practice. Among the most common are single-subject designs, goal attainment scaling, task achievement scaling, and client satisfaction questionnaires.

Figure 8.2: Single-Subject (AB) Design

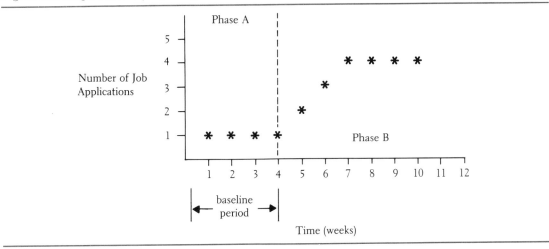

Single-Subject Designs

Bloom and Fischer (1982, p. 7) indicate that *single-subject designs* have had many names, including "single N or N = 1 research, single-subject research, single-subject design, single case-study design, and time-series research or design." To complicate matters a bit more, the "single subject" may really be a family, a group, or some other size system. The structure of single-subject research is fairly simple. In its most basic form we have a client with a problem, the problem is attacked through the intervention of the worker, and we have an outcome of that intervention. The outcome of the intervention is then compared to the state of affairs prior to intervention. Sometimes this is called the AB design, with A representing the preintervention state and B representing the intervention. Figure 8.2 shows an example of this design using a very simple illustration.

The client here is in a halfway house for chemically dependent adults. The primary goal is helping the client find a job. The first objective is to encourage the client to engage in job seeking efforts. The client applied for only one job per week prior to intervention. This information forms the baseline shown in Phase A. Phase B includes the period of time after the worker begins coaching the client in job-seeking skills. The broken vertical line represents the start of intervention. The stars show the number of job applications increased following intervention and then stabilized at four per week.

It is clear that the client has made progress. He now makes significantly more job applications per week. This indicates that the intervention—namely, coaching the client in job seeking skills—has been effective to some extent.

The steps in implementing the single-subject evaluation are straightforward. First, an easily measured goal is identified. (For example, one goal might be to get a nursing home resident out of her room from after breakfast until the noon meal.) Then a baseline is done showing the frequency of the behavior prior to intervention. This is Phase A. Finally, a record of the frequency of the behavior is kept during and following intervention. A graphical representation of the change can be prepared quite readily. Sometimes a baseline can be constructed using information from a case record. However, frequently this is not possible. For example, consistent or easily measurable types of information might not have been recorded.

In the event that there is no opportunity to establish a baseline, the worker can still maintain a record of the behavior following intervention. This is called a B type design (see Figure 8.3). Only the behavior occurring during and at the end of the intervention phase can be measured. The example shown below reflects an intervention with an adolescent who repeatedly violated his parents' curfew restrictions.

It should be noted that we consider results that occur in Phase B to be caused by the intervention. We know from our previous discussion that this is a relatively simplistic notion. Many other variables may be at work helping to cause the changes seen following intervention.

There are other types of designs that fall

Figure 8.3: B Design without a Baseline

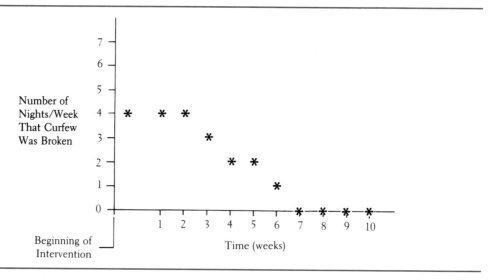

Figure 8.4: ABC Design

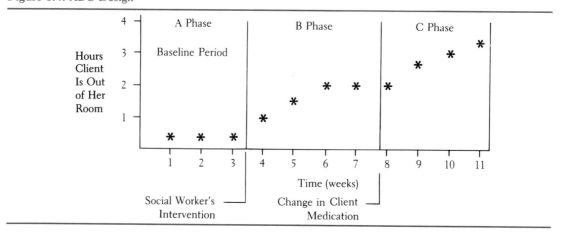

Figure 8.5: ABAB Design

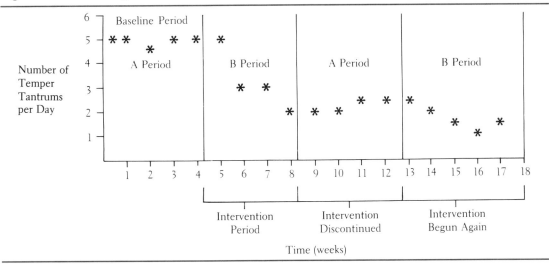

into the single-subject design category. For example, we might have a situation where an ABC design is possible. A baseline is constructed (as might occur when we keep track of how long the client stayed out of her room in the nursing home between the hours of 8:00 A.M. and noon). This is the A Phase. When the social worker begins to provide an intervention, we have the B Phase. Four weeks into the intervention, an additional treatment (C Phase) was prescribed (perhaps the client began to take medication). We now have an ABC design, where C represents the medication phase. Figure 8.4 is an example of this design.

Still another example concerns an ABAB design. This is where a baseline (A) is developed, then the intervention (B) runs its course. Intervention (B) is then discontinued for a period of time (six weeks, for example). Based on the measurement level when the last intervention stopped (A), the intervention (B) is begun again. An example of this design appears in Figure 8.5.

While useful for testing the effectiveness of an intervention, the withdrawal of intervention can be ethically difficult to carry out. It can be used more easily when a worker must discontinue working with the client while the latter is on vacation. Deliberately discontinuing an intervention for the sole purpose of testing the effectiveness of that intervention raises ethical issues that cannot be addressed in this chapter.

Clearly, single-subject designs work well when there is an obvious behavior that can somehow be measured. A student used this method to chart arguments between two residents sharing a room in a nursing home. Both the residents and the nursing staff found the situation intolerable. The nursing staff maintained a record of when and how many arguments occurred.

Efforts to increase or decrease the frequency of a given behavior are particularly appropriate for single-subject design. As was noted, this design can be used with client self-reports or where there is some sort of pre-post data-gathering device employed. That is, some specific instrument is used to measure a behavior prior to intervention and again after intervention. The Rathus Assertiveness Scale (McCormick, 1984) is an example. Scores on this instrument can be used to measure levels of assertiveness prior to and following intervention.

Goal-Attainment Scaling

Sometimes a goal does not lend itself to the kind of charting and evaluation needed for single-subject designs. Perhaps it is a situation where the client has multiple goals, many of which are related to one another. Perhaps the goals are not as easily measured by counting behaviors as was the case in the nursing-home situation mentioned above.

One of the more helpful evaluation methods for these situations is called *goal-attainment scaling.* Here, various steps toward achieving a

goal can be measured. Figure 8.6 provides an example of this. The client is a mother of two children, all of whom are living in a shelter for battered women. The client has three goals she wants to work on: (1) getting a temporary restraining order (TRO) from the court, which prevents her husband from contacting her; (2) finding a job, so she will be less dependent upon her husband for financial support; and (3) reestablishing her social support network (composed of family and friends). The client may not achieve the ultimate goal of leaving her husband, finding a good job, and developing many new friends. However, she may continue to make progress toward increasing her self-esteem and becoming more independent.

McMahon (1990) employs another type of

Figure 8.6: Goal Attainment Scaling

Levels of Predicted Outcomes	Objective 1	Objective 2	Objective 3
Least favorable outcome	Client returns home to abuser, gives up goals	Client returns home to abuser, gives up goals	Client returns home to abuser, gives up goals
Less than expected outcome	Client contacts Court about TRO	Client applies for one job	Client calls one old friend
Expected level of success	Client obtains TRO from court	Client applies for a few jobs	Client spends time with friend
More-than-expected level of success	Client's spouse does not contest TRO	Client offered a job, but turns it down	Client spends time with a few friends
Most favorable outcome	Spouse leaves home so client can live there	Client accepts good job	Client develops new friends

Source: Hagedorn et. al. (1976).

Note: One might substitute the objective listing at the top with a brief description of the problem being addressed.

Figure 8.7: Modified Goal Attainment Scaling

-3	-2	-1	0	+1	+2	+3
Goal given up	Much worse than at start	Little worse than at start	Starting point	Little better than at start	Much better than at start	Goal attained

Source: McMahon (1990), p. 247.

goal attainment scale using a point system. A slightly modified version of her goal attainment scale is shown in Figure 8.7. As you can see, the system is essentially similar to the one in Figure 8.6. The difference is that the possibilities are arranged from the worst outcome (goal given up) to the best outcome (goal attained). This system can be easily modified and used with a wide variety of goals or client problems.

Task-Achievement Scaling

Many intervention activities carried out by social workers are very discrete, or task-oriented. For example, brokering, advocacy, and service coordination–type tasks cannot easily be measured using single-subject designs or goal-attainment scaling. A good example is a hospital social worker doing discharge planning. Her primary goals for a given client may consist of arranging home health care for a client being discharged or checking on financial arrangements needed for admission to a nursing home.

Task-achievement scaling allows us to measure the extent to which the worker and client have completed agreed-upon tasks, such as arranging transportation or filing an insurance claim. This model is especially useful for situations in which there is limited contact between worker and client, as often happens in hospital discharge–planning units. It begins with the expectation that both client and worker agree on the tasks to be performed and who is to perform them. The focus is on results, not on effort. Typically, a five point scale is used. Reid and Epstein (1977, p. 289) use the following description of the points on the scale, ranging from 4 (completely achieved) to 0 (no opportunity to work on task).

A rating of 4 (completely achieved) applies to tasks that are fully accomplished, e.g., a job has been found, a homemaker secured, financial assistance obtained. It may also be used for tasks that are fully accomplished "for all practical purposes." In the case of a couple whose goal was to reduce quarreling, a rating of 4 could be given if they reached a point where hostile interchanges occurred infrequently and no longer presented a problem, and they saw no need for further work on the task.

A rating of 3 (substantially achieved) indicates that the task is largely accomplished, though further action may need to be taken before full accomplishment is realized. Thus, if the task is to improve work performance, significant improvement would merit a rating of 3 even though further improvement would be possible and desirable.

When a rating of 2 (partially achieved) is chosen, this indicates that demonstrable progress has been made on the task but considerable work remains to be done. For example, if the task is to obtain a job, a rating of 2 could be given if the client has actively been looking for work and found a job he could take (and might), but was reluctant to. Or this rating would be appropriate for a couple who had made some headway on a shared task of finding things of mutual interest to do together even though they and the caseworker were dissatisfied with their progress.

A rating of 1 (minimally achieved [or not achieved]) is used for tasks on which no progress has been made or on which progress has been insignificant or uncertain. If a client's task were to enroll in a suitable vocational training program, a rating of 1 would be given if the client were unable to locate a program, even though much effort had gone into searching for one.

A No rating indicates no opportunity to work on the task. An example would be a client who cannot carry out a task in the classroom because school is closed due to a teachers' strike.[2]

---

2. Adapted from *Task-Centered Casework*, W. J. Reid and L. Epstein, 1972, Columbia University Press, New York. Used by permission of the publisher.

Figure 8.8: Task Achievement Scaling

Task	Degree of Achievement	Rating
1. Homemaker services arranged	Client on short waiting list for services. Services will begin in about one week.	3
2. Meals on wheels services secured	Meals will begin the day client is discharged.	4
3. Hospital bed acquired	Hospital bed rented, will be delivered day client is discharged.	4
4. Snow shoveling assistance secured	Have list of possible people who might provide service.	2
5. Contact son and daughter-in-law	No progress—family is out of town for two weeks.	1

Source: Reid and Epstein (1977).

Figure 8.8 shows one example of a task-achievement scale. Here, we are dealing with an elderly client who is confined to her home following a serious injury. She is physically able to care for herself but will need many services in order to remain at home and avoid moving to a nursing home. Five tasks were identified as important in keeping the woman in her own home. Two of the tasks, arranging for meals on wheels and locating a hospital bed have been completely achieved. The client will receive homemaker services in about a week, although the original goal was to have these provided immediately. Snow-shoveling services have not yet been acquired, but the client has a list of people who might provide this service. Finally, the son and daughter-in-law are out of town, making it difficult to contact them.

As can be seen from the example in Figure 8.8, one case may have many tasks that must be accomplished. In some situations, all tasks may be achieved. In other cases, it is possible to complete only a portion of the tasks fully. The task achievement scale allows for a rough assessment of the percent of tasks accomplished.

Here is how progress illustrated in Figure 8.8 might be calculated. There are a total of five goals, each with a maximum point rating of 4 (completely achieved). Multiplying the number of tasks (5 tasks) times the maximum points possible (4 points), we have a total of twenty (20).

Now if we add the number of points under the rating (3 + 4 + 4 + 2 + 1), we find we have a total of fourteen points. If we divide that total (14 points) by the maximum points possible (20) we end up with a 70 percent achievement rating for all goals (14/20 = .70). This is, of course, a very rough form of calculation. However, it does help us get some sense of how we're doing in achieving important tasks associated with a particular case. It is a particularly useful method for task-oriented interventions (that is, where specific tasks are identified to achieve specific goals).

Client Satisfaction Questionnaires

In certain situations, it is important to know the client's reactions to our interventions. Businesses routinely use *client satisfaction questionnaires* to learn the reactions of the customer to various aspects of a product. For example, purchasers of automobiles are commonly surveyed about their level of satisfaction with recent purchases. They may be asked to identify any problems with the vehicle or to provide feedback about the person who sold them the car, or the service department's performance. Similar activities are undertaken by restaurants and other service-oriented businesses.

Client satisfaction questionnaires may be

used with a single case, a group of clients all served by the same worker, or all clients served by an agency. In this way, they can be used for both evaluation of direct practice and evaluation of entire programs. One goal might be to help the agency identify service problems or areas where the service is insufficient. Sometimes such questionnaires help identify unmet needs.

Client satisfaction questionnaires are designed to be used following an intervention. However, they may also prove useful for monitoring progress while service is being given. Toseland and Rivas (1984) suggest that there may be value in using client questionnaires during ongoing group meetings to gather information about the process. The method has been used routinely by some educational groups to help assess the effectiveness of each individual session. One advantage of this approach is that

it can be used during intervention, immediately following termination of services, or at some later point in time.

Figure 8.9 shows one page from a client satisfaction questionnaire provided to clients seen by the admission staff of a nursing home.

Other questions on this questionnaire asked whether the social worker explained admission material clearly enough, and whether the social service department helped to make the admission process as smooth as possible. There was also additional space for extended comments at the bottom of the questionnaire. This particular questionnaire was attempting to gather information both about the social service department itself as well as about the performance of a particular social worker. This shows the potential versatility of client satisfaction questionnaires.

One disadvantage of such questionnaires is

Figure 8.9: A Client Satisfaction Questionnaire

Please circle the number that corresponds to your chosen response.

1. How would you rate the overall quality of your admission process at the Center of Care?

4	3	2	1
Excellent	Good	Fair	Poor

Comments: _____

2. Did you get the kind of service you wanted?

1	2	3	4
No, definitely not	No, not really	Yes, generally	Yes, definitely

Comments: _____

3. To what extent has our social worker met your needs?

4	3	2	1
Almost all of my needs have been met	Most of my needs have been met	Only a few of my needs have been met	None of my needs have been met

Comments: _____

4. If a friend needed a similar nursing home, would you recommend this social service department to him or her?

1	2	3	4
No, definitely not	No, I don't think so	Yes, I think so	Yes, definitely

Comments: _____

their potential for misuse. Asking a cocaine-addicted client and drug dealer whether she benefited from an intervention aimed at keeping her out of the criminal justice system amounts to using the wrong tool for the job. Just as you would not use a screwdriver for driving a nail, you must choose carefully the tools you use in your evaluation efforts. Client satisfaction questionnaires should not be used in lieu of other methods which produce more valid conclusions about the intervention's effectiveness.

Other practice evaluation systems do exist. One is peer review. Peer review involves "a formal evaluation by a relevant peer group of an individual's general competence or specific actions" (Barker, 1987, p. 118). Unlike some of the methods described above, peer review focuses almost exclusively on the process rather than the outcome of intervention. For example, an agency might adopt a system of evaluating monthly whether a worker's case files contain agreed-upon items such as a face sheet, initial contact and assessment information, and written intervention plan. Each month a different worker's files would be reviewed to determine whether the worker was meeting the professional standards adopted by the agency. (For a more detailed description of this method, see Sheafor, Horejsi, & Horejsi, 1989.)

Evaluation Designs for Programs

Up to this point, we have been talking primarily about evaluating direct practice. The data-gathering mechanisms we have described were mostly useful for social workers wanting to evaluate what they do as individual professionals. Some of the approaches discussed also have potential value for evaluating the entire program with which the worker is associated. Program evaluation can help us determine whether one program is more effective or efficient than another. Program evaluation includes periodic as well as ongoing evaluation of the process and the outcomes. In the following section, we will look very briefly at five program evaluation tools: needs assessments, evaluability assessments, process analysis, program outcome analysis, and program monitoring (Evaluation Research Society, 1982, p. 692-93).

Needs Assessments

We discussed *needs assessments* in chapter 4. Needs assessments are considered forms of front-end analysis. In other words, they are employed to help an agency determine whether, and to what extent, a program is needed. They also can be used after a program has been in operation for a period of time to determine if unmet needs still exist. They may be useful for identifying gaps in service and helping an agency decide whether a need for a service still exists.

Evaluability Assessments

Evaluability assessments are designed simply to answer the question, "Can this program be evaluated?" While one might think any program can be evaluated, this is not always true. For example, if either the intervention or the goals are not defined with sufficient clarity, it will be most difficult to arrive at an assessment. Sometimes outcomes cannot be readily measured because the program objectives or products are vague or undefined.

Other factors that might interfere with the ability to evaluate a program are lack of accurate identifying information about clients (which might preclude using client satisfaction questionnaires), high cost of conducting a particular type of evaluation, and poor program record keeping.

You can begin to see the importance of doing an evaluability assessment prior to launching into any evaluation of the program. Once an agency learns that it cannot adequately evaluate itself, it has two options. First, it can make changes which will allow future assessments. Second, it can continue on without change. The latter choice carries high risk, because ultimately some sort of evaluation will be demanded of almost every agency. For a more detailed review of evaluabiliy assessments, see Rutman and Mowbray (1983).

Process Analysis

We briefly mentioned process evaluations earlier in this chapter. You will remember that they are designed to evaluate the way interventions in the agency are carried out. Client satisfaction questionnaires can be used for this goal as well as peer reviews. Both of these have been described above and will not be covered again. At its most basic level, process analysis might be concerned with numbers of clients served or the kinds of services provided. It might also be focused on productivity ratios, such as the actual per-child cost of a program screening infants for malnutrition. Process analysis can also help an agency improve service by looking at the ways in which service is provided. If clients are being transferred from one unit in an agency to another unit, are such transitions conducted smoothly? What could be done to make them better? Process analysis depends largely on gathering information from both the producers and consumers of the process, namely social workers and clients.

There are a variety of instruments available to assist in process assessment. Clearly, the instrument to be used will be affected by the information desired. Pietrzak et al. (1990) contains a fine review of process evaluation and examples of available instruments.

Program Outcome Analysis

Program-outcome analysis helps tell us whether a program is working. It may also help us find out whether a program is cost-effective; that is, if the results merit the expense. There are multiple means of assessing program outcomes. If the program objectives have a consumer-satisfaction component, then we might want to use the client satisfaction scales we discussed earlier.

Perhaps a program hopes to increase the client's knowledge, skills, or attitudes. Consider, for example, a group training program developed to help prospective adoptive parents of hard-to-place children (e.g., handicapped, older). The goal was to help these applicants learn about the difficulties experienced by many of these hard-to-place children. The program began because many prospective adoptive parents did not have accurate information about the problems experienced by these children. In this example, the parents were given a pre-test to determine their knowledge prior to intervention and a post-test at the conclusion of the group training. This information, along with a consumer satisfaction questionnaire, was used to assess the outcome of this program.

There are other questions for which we might like answers. Perhaps we want to know whether the new family resource unit is accomplishing its purpose. Do clients in the nurturing program actually learn any new skills that they use at home? Are the short-term changes noted at termination continued over a six month period? How often do group members served by our Alcohol and Other Drug Abuse (AODA) team reach the goals they set at the onset of intervention? Are there problems or problem areas for which our interventions are not successful?

As you think about these questions, you might realize that an agency whose workers routinely evaluated their practice would be in a better position to respond. Let's say, for example, that *goal attainment scaling* is completed on many or most of the agency clients. This would allow the agency to gather a rather sizable chunk of information useful for program outcome analysis. Similarly, *single-subject designs* routinely used with clients could produce a volume of information as part of an outcome assessment. It should be clear by now that assessing some program outcomes is made easier if there is an ongoing attempt to assess the work of individual components (workers or units) in the agency. Pietrzak et al. (1990) provides excellent examples of outcome evaluation with a specific focus on child abuse programs.

Program Monitoring

Program monitoring is an ongoing activity designed to provide information to the agency on all aspects of its operation. Data may be collected on presenting problems, client demographics, services provided, and outcomes achieved. Agencies develop information management systems so that they can routinely assess how various aspects of their programs are progressing. An agency might decide, for example, that they no longer have sufficient numbers of children placed for adoption to justify continued offering of adoption services. Another agency providing specialized services in the area of sexuality might notice that the type of client has changed over the years. Instead of working with mostly intact couples needing accurate information they are now helping clients with very serious sexual dysfunctions.

From these examples you can see how important it is to maintain accurate and complete records. An ongoing effort at program monitoring is essential to improve services within the agency or organization and to manage agency resources wisely.

Issues and Problems in Evaluation

Any evaluation program, whether employed by the worker or the agency, has the potential to be misused or interpreted incorrectly. Part of this potential is due to the nature of the research tools available to us. Still other parts are inherent in any evaluation effort. For example, normally we are not able to randomly assign clients to treatment and control groups so that we will meet the high, concise standards of the experimental model. Clients often need immediate help. Additionally, there are ethical concerns inherent in refusing clients an intervention because we wish to compare them with a group that is receiving service. The fact that we often must use quasi-experimental methods (that is, experiments in natural social settings where some aspects of experimental design can be applied, albeit less rigorously than in a laboratory situation) rather than experimental methods is an inherent limitation with which we must live. In the next section, we will consider some of these issues.

Problems in Generalizability

As was mentioned earlier in this chapter, there is always a temptation to take evaluation results demonstrating a successful program and apply those results to other groups. We have also suggested that a program that is effective with a given group of clients may not work well with others. We often have no way of knowing whether the clients we work with are representative of other clients. When we decide to evaluate our success with only a subset (sample) of the clients we have served, the potential for threats to generalizability are obvious.

One of the reasons that we attempt to obtain random samples when we survey people is that the mathematical characteristics of random samples allow us to infer from the sample to a larger population. A random sample is one in which all elements in a population have an equal probability of being included in the sample. An agency might wish to obtain a random sample of its clients. Staff can assign each client a different number and then use a table of random numbers to select those to be included in a sample. The idea is for the small subset of people being asked for information to resemble other people in the entire population as closely as possible.

Sometimes, there are problems with this process. Let's say you wanted to know the views of all students majoring in social work. You decide to select a random sample of the majors and to use a questionnaire to gather their views. Although a random sample should result in a subset or group similar to all social work majors, you could end up with no males in the sample simply because males compose only about 12 percent of all undergraduate social work majors. If you think that there may be a difference between males and females in the way they will answer the questionnaire, you might want to ensure that males will be proportionately represented in your sample. To do this, you must assign numbers to both male and female majors, and then, using a table of random numbers (located in most statistics texts), randomly select a proportionate number of males. If there are one hundred social work majors and 88 percent are female, then 88 percent of your sample should also be female. This method of selection is called *stratified random sampling*, and it helps ensure that the sample selected is representative of the larger population. There are a variety of other sampling methods that one may employ in the interests of ensuring that the sample is representative. A more detailed listing of these is included in Grinnell and Williams (1990). Achieving a representative sample is essential if we hope to generalize the results of our evaluation.

Wrong Choices of Evaluation Tools

We have already noted that an evaluation instrument can be used inappropriately. Using a client satisfaction questionnaire to assess whether a program achieved its goal of reducing delinquent behavior is equivalent to hammering a screw into wood. The wrong tool is being used in both cases. It is the wrong tool because the goal was to reduce delinquent behavior, not entertain adolescents. In this case, the most appropriate measure of success should include some means of assessing whether the level of delinquent behavior went up, down, or stayed the same. Asking the client if he liked the group home experience (client satisfaction questionnaire) is of little value. It is conceivable that he liked the group home very much because he learned some new techniques for burglarizing homes. Perhaps, he's even become a more accomplished criminal as a result of this experience. As you might imagine, the use of inappropriate measurement systems is a common problem when agencies first begin to attempt evaluation of outcomes.

Failure to Involve Clients in Evaluation Process

Ideally, clients should be involved in the evaluation process to the extent possible. It is ethically wrong to do research on clients and not inform them that it's being done. Clients should be promised confidentiality. Only aggregate data omitting individual identification should be released. Clients rights should be carefully protected. Moreover, client knowledge of the evaluation process may increase the effectiveness of the intervention.

Staff Distrust of Evaluation

We indicated earlier that many agencies do not routinely engage in evaluation of practice or programs. When a research effort is suggested, it is not uncommon for this to be met with fear or distrust by those who will be evaluated. The motives of the agency in asking for the evaluation may be questioned. Staff may feel they're being criticized or condemned. Unless the agency can gain the trust of those being evaluated, it is likely that the process will be fraught with problems.

Evaluation Process Interferes with Service-Giving

Program evaluation should be accomplished in such a fashion that it does not interfere with the giving of service to clients (Austin et al., 1982, p. 179). An effective management information system can make this process go more smoothly because much of the data needed can be computerized and retrieved with relative ease. If, on the other hand, clients must complete lengthy questionnaires after each session or maintain very detailed logs between sessions, it is possible this will affect the intervention. Clients may find the process overly time-consuming or intrusive. They may cease coming or provide insufficient data to allow the purposes of the evaluation to be carried out. Either way, the evaluation process has begun to interfere with the service giving process.

Alternative Explanations for Program Outcomes

When a client or program achieves the desired objectives, it is tempting to attribute the results to the intervention employed. This is a natural tendency to confuse two events, one following the other, with cause and effect. This thinking implies that since one event precedes the other, it naturally caused the other. This is often not the case. Unfortunately, there are multiple explanations for the occurrence of any event. The outcomes of our interventions are no exception. Highlight 8.3 includes a partial list of those factors, many of which are also called threats to the interval validity of the study design. That is, they represent influences which

can cloud or obscure the real reason that change occurred.

There are many other possible explanations for change which could confound the results of one's evaluation. Gibbs (1991) has developed an extensive list and a very clear explanation of alternative or confounding causes. The important thing to remember is that multiple explanations may exist for changes that we observe following an intervention. These possible explanations should act as a caution to the worker evaluating the results of any intervention.

Unanticipated Consequences

Not infrequently, we discover that a program has had consequences or outcomes we did not envision. These may be categorized as either side effects or regressive effects (Sieber, 1981). Further, side effects may be classified as harmful to clients and others, neutral in their impact, or beneficial. A person learning to be more assertive, for example, may adopt his new approach with his employer. The employer, unused to his employee's newfound assertiveness, reacts by firing the employee. This might be viewed as a negative side effect of the client's assertiveness training. Another example involves a couple learning to communicate their needs more clearly to each other through a marriage-enrichment program. They may discover that they really have incompatible goals in life. This leads them to a decision to divorce. This marriage-enrichment program may then be seen as having an unintended impact on this couple's marriage.

Regressive effects, as the name implies, means that a situation gets worse as a result of the intervention. An example or two should illustrate how this can happen. Mr. Jones was referred to me by another social worker who was moving away. An assessment of Mr. Jones's situation had been made by the previous

HIGHLIGHT 8.3
Alternate Explanations for Outcomes

History. Not infrequently, changes happening in the environment can affect the outcome of an intervention. For example, a 25 percent increase in the number of jobs in an area because of several companies expanding their work force might explain why a job placement program was so successful. In the absence of these new jobs, the rate might have been quite different. It's also possible that the same number of unemployed people would have gotten jobs without the job placement program.

Maturation. Sometimes the results of an intervention can be attributed to changes being experienced by the subject. For example most delinquent children reduce their delinquency as they age. A program which works with children from age thirteen to seventeen might be claiming success with its clients when the results may be more attributable to maturation.

Mortality. This occurs when some of the people in the sample begin to drop out. This means that a select group is now being measured and one cannot extrapolate from this group to the original population. Client self-selection is operating here in that clients themselves may have made the decision about whether to continue in a program. Ideally, a program ought to include as failures those who dropped out along the way rather than just those who stayed to the end without reaching their goals.

Creaming. This problem arises from the tendency of some programs to take only the very best candidates for a program. One danger is that evaluating only the best may reflect significantly greater effectiveness than if all similar candidates in the population were included. Another danger is that perhaps these "best" candidates would have changed anyway. For example, many first-offender programs take those they consider good candidates for the program. Thus, they tend to bias the outcome.

The selection of clients by the worker often creates a form of bias which can be quite powerful. Sometimes workers are not aware they're selecting clients with specific characteristics.

Regression toward the mean. This occurs when those in the program were chosen because they varied greatly from the average. Take, for example, choosing all children with very low scores on a self-esteem scale and exposing them to the treatment. This will almost always result in their having higher scores the next time they are evaluated using the same scale. This is the result of a mathematical or statistical tendency for high scores to move toward the mean (or average) on subsequent testing. Scores far from a mean may be the result of statistical error and a second testing would produce a score more in line with the expected mean.

Reactance. Reactance occurs when people are merely reacting to something new. As soon as people get used to the situation, their reactions change, or they revert to former ways of behaving. Think about how you and your family interact when a stranger is present versus when you are alone together. Often, one behaves differently because of the presence of an observer. Typically, the presence of a new treatment (or worker) may produce something of a honeymoon effect where people begin to act naturally only after they are comfortable with the new situation. Evaluation results may be skewed (distorted) because people are acting unnaturally and will return to their old behavior after they get used to the presence of the worker or the treatment.

In program evaluation, one might be able to control some of these variables by comparing the results of the program with other situations where the program is not being used. This is an attempt to create a control group of sorts and to use the experimental method of research. For example, the results of a first offender diversion program in a city of fifty thousand might be compared with the recidivism rate of first offenders in a city of comparable size that lacks such a program.

social worker and by the consulting psychiatrist. The primary symptom, as described in the record, was anxiety. During the first interview, the author noticed that the client was having trouble sleeping, had lost his appetite, and suffered from disinterest in his work. His relationship with his wife was also deteriorating. He was particularly anxious because his inability to concentrate at work was threatening his job. Mr. Jones had been receiving counseling about his anxiety and was taking tranquilizers prescribed by the psychiatrist. No one, it seemed, had recognized that Mr. Jones was suffering from depression. The medication prescribed for him was helping to depress him further. To make things even worse, he had been treated for the wrong problem. This is an example of a treatment making the problem worse rather than better.

Another example is drawn from the research on program effectiveness. The "scared straight" programs, in which juvenile delinquents are exposed to hardened criminals at maximum security prisons, have been extremely popular in the United States. The goal of these programs is to scare the delinquent youth into a law-abiding life. Adolescents are brought to a prison. Here, experienced criminals verbally threaten them and graphically suggest what their fate will be should they continue their delinquent behavior. Surely such a program would be effective, since it would bring delinquents face-to-face with the future consequences of their actions. Unfortunately, research on the scared straight program indicates that "controls" (that is, delinquents who did not go through this program) committed fewer delinquencies than those who participated in the program (Finckenauer, 1982). In addition, the offenses the controls committed were less serious than offenses committed by delinquents who had been "treated" in this program (Finckenauer, 1982, p. 139–47).

The important thing to keep in mind is that some of our efforts to help may have the opposite effect. Unintended consequences sometimes occur despite our best intentions. Finally, interventions that are effective for one client may not work as well with others. Gibbs (1991) has provided an excellent set of guidelines for practitioners tempted to use untested interventions or approaches which have limited research support.

It is important to attempt identifying the factors that cause harmful side affects and modify the program accordingly. It is also important to offer clients help in overcoming negative experiences arising from prior agency contact.

The completion of the evaluation phase leads to one of two conclusions. Either the client system has achieved the goals previously identified or goals have not been reached. If the goals have not been attained, the worker needs to explore with the client whether continued intervention will be helpful. If both parties decide that continued work is needed this may lead to a new process of problem solving. If goals have been reached or there are other reasons for concluding the intervention, we then enter the termination phase of the helping process.

Termination and Follow-Up

Saying good-bye is often difficult. All relationships between social workers and clients must eventually come to an end. The ending may be scheduled or unexpected, successful or unsuccessful. Despite the circumstances of the ending, the worker must be prepared to manage this phase of the problem-solving process. To do this effectively, social workers need knowledge and skill in two areas: termination and follow-up.

The tasks of termination are similar whether we are working with an individual, a family or group, a community, or an organization. This portion of the chapter focuses on the knowledge and skills needed for concluding effectively the professional social worker-client relationship.

Terminating Professional Relationships

As stated above, all professional relationships must end at some point. When a client no longer needs service, it is expected that the relationship will end. However, not all terminations occur as one might hope. Sometimes, terminations occur unexpectedly and for reasons that the worker could not have predicted. It is

Figure 8.10: Problem-Solving Steps in the Generalist Intervention Model

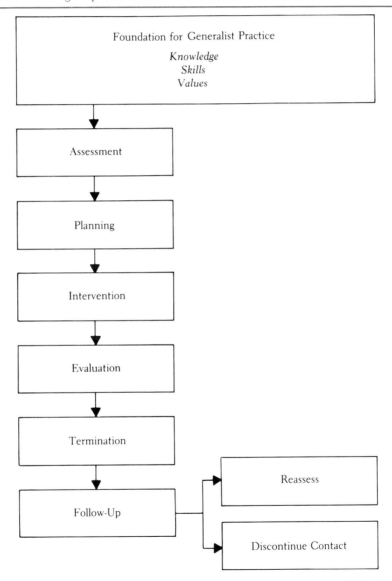

important for a social worker to be aware of these possibilities and prepared to act professionally in any case.

In this section we will look at several issues: the tasks of termination; timing and preparing for termination; reasons for termination; typical reactions to the termination phase; and making appropriate referrals.

Tasks of Termination

Hepworth and Larsen (1990) describe the following termination tasks: determining when to terminate; resolving emotional reactions (client or worker) to termination; evaluating accomplishment of goals; and planning to maintain accomplishments. Brill (1990) suggests a similar list which includes "deal[ing] with unfinished business, deal[ing] with feelings about termination and providing direction for the future" (p. 100). When reviewing the tasks for ending a group, Toseland and Rivas (1984, p. 333) provide a comparable but slightly expanded list. They include the following:

1. *Maintaining and generalizing change efforts.* Here we are concerned with ensuring that progress made during the intervention phase is continued after intervention has been completed. Improvements in one area of the person's life must now generalize to other areas. The person who is more assertive in the group situation should now extend this assertiveness to other areas of her life such as jobs, marriage, etc.

2. *Reducing group attraction and promoting the independent functioning of individual members.* The goal is to encourage the member to function outside of the group without having the group's constant support. The group will thus become less important as a support for the client.

3. *Helping members with their feelings about*

ending. Emotional reactions to the ending of relationships are often acute. People have a multitude of feelings in reaction to the ending of professional relationships. Helping clients express and cope with these feelings is part of a social worker's job.

4. *Planning for the future.* The client needs to focus on a future that does not include the constant support of the social worker or the group. You as a social worker can help the individual group member make specific plans to incorporate what's been learned in the group to other real-life situations completely independent of the group.

5. *Making referrals.* Referrals may be needed when clients face additional problems or when other interventions are needed. You can refer clients to the services they need.

6. *Evaluating the work of the group.* Evaluating progress is a part of all interventions. This is regardless of the size and type of client system.[3]

Finally, Pincus and Minahan (1973) identify three components of termination: disengagement, stabilization of change, and evaluation. Disengagement includes dealing with feelings about ending and summarizing accomplishments. Stabilization of change includes those activities that will assure the change will continue after the worker and client have ceased their professional relationship.

Ultimately, the goal at termination is to empower the client system. This means that clients will learn to use their own resources (instead of those of the social worker) to manage future difficulties they may encounter. This is the real

---

3. Reprinted with the permission of Macmillan Publishing Company from *An Introduction to Group Practice* by R. W. Toseland and R. F. Rivas. Copyright 1984 by Macmillan Publishing Company.

Figure 8.11: Summary of Termination Tasks

Tasks in All Planned Terminations	Individual Clients	Families	Groups	Larger Systems
Deciding when to terminate	XXX	XXX	XXX	XXX
Dealing with unfinished business	XXX	XXX	XXX	XXX
Resolving emotional reactions	XXX	XXX	XXX	XXX
Reducing group attractiveness	NA	NA	XXX	NA
Evaluating achievements	XXX	XXX	XXX	XXX
Maintaining and stabilizing change	XXX	XXX	XXX	XXX
Providing direction for the future	XXX	XXX	XXX	XXX
Making needed referrals	XXX	XXX	XXX	XXX

importance of stabilizing the change effort. Later in this chapter we will discuss each component of termination. Evaluation has already been discussed. Figure 8.11 below summarizes the primary tasks in termination across various system sizes.

As you can see, there is considerable agreement about the activities that must be undertaken as a relationship ends. One of the first steps, however, is to decide when to terminate. We will look at this topic next.

Planned Terminations

As has been suggested, one can easily predict that a worker-client relationship will eventually conclude. Thus, it is expected that the worker will consider the timing of the termination as an important part of the helping relationship. Determining when to terminate is one of the most important tasks the worker must accomplish.

Frequently, an ending point is identified at the start of the professional relationship. For example, in task-centered practice situations it is expected that the sessions will continue for some set time period and then will conclude. Let's look at a family that contracts to see a social worker for six weekly sessions. The family (and the worker) expect that the professional relationship will end after the sixth week. Similarly, consider the situation of a hospital social worker who is doing discharge planning for an elderly patient who will be transferred to a nursing home. She knows that the relationship will terminate following the patient's transfer. The timing of the termination in each of these examples can reasonably be predicted in advance and, by definition, are planned terminations.

Unplanned Terminations

Unfortunately, not all terminations can be planned for and many are unexpected. Terminations may also occur for reasons not under the control of either client or worker. Some terminations occur because no progress has been made or because problems are getting worse, not better. Brill (1990) has suggested that lack of progress may be due to a misunderstanding between client and worker, incorrect or misinterpreted data, or incorrect definition of the problem. Perhaps the wrong problem was selected for intervention or the goals selected were not attainable. Or the alternative selected was inappropriate. Maybe the wrong intervention was made. In other situations the expectations placed on the client by the worker-client contract are too demanding, too complicated, or too simple.

┌ HIGHLIGHT 8.4 ─────────────────────────────

Unplanned Terminations in Groups

Toseland and Rivas (1984) note that "unplanned termination of members (of a group) may be the result of their lack of interest or motivation, particular life circumstances, or other factors beyond the control of the worker that have little or nothing to do with a worker's leadership skills" (p. 329). Yalom (1975) cited a similar list of reasons why members quit coming to a group. They include:

1. Scheduling conflicts;
2. Feeling out of place in the group;

3. Inability to form intimate relationships with others;
4. Fear of emotional contagion (real discomfort with the strong feelings sometimes expressed by others);
5. Inability to share worker with group members;
6. Inadequate orientation to therapy;
7. Subgrouping problems including scape-goating;
8. Problems arising from concurrent individual and group therapy.

└───

Kettner, Daley, and Nichols (1985) indicate that unexpected negative consequences of a change effort may also require premature termination. Other reasons for termination include relationship difficulties between client and worker, or the fact that either the client or worker is moving from the geographical area.

Still other situations may bring about termination before either party would prefer. For instance, a school social worker may not continue seeing a client during the summer. Another example is a field practicum student who ends her placement while the client continues with the agency. Sometimes the worker must terminate with a client who is being referred to another worker or specialist. Additionally, a client may simply quit coming without notifying the worker. McMahon (1990) says that termination may occur when the area being probed is too sensitive and the client cannot tolerate opening the matter up. Some clients end because the feelings associated with ending are too painful to discuss (we will discuss some typical feelings about endings in a later section). Others simply drop out because this appears to them to be a way of controlling the ending. In other words, by taking the first step of quitting, they avoid the pain and discomfort of dealing with the end of a relationship. It's a bit like a person who

quits his job because he anticipates getting fired anyway. Finally, some clients drop out because they are dissatisfied or lack the resources to continue (Blythe & Tripodi, 1989).

Other Points about Termination

Clearly, professional relationships can end for many reasons. Some of those reasons are under the control of the worker and others are not. Some can be anticipated and others cannot. What is most important is that the worker recognizes that unplanned terminations are fairly common. Whenever possible, the worker should plan for terminations and involve the client in that process.

If a client drops out prematurely (in the worker's opinion), it is appropriate for the worker to attempt to discover reasons for this. Perhaps this effort will result in the client returning, perhaps not. Still, it is part of one's professional responsibility to follow up on a client who has terminated early. Ultimately, the client's right to self-determination must guide the worker. That is, the bottom line is that clients have the right to quit if they want to.

Finally, one cannot assume that clients who quit will experience negative outcomes. Research by Toseland (1987) and Presley (1987) seems to indicate that clients who drop out early do so because they are sufficiently comfortable with the changes that have occurred. Given the goal of helping the client become self-sufficient and less dependent upon the worker, it may even be a positive sign when a client decides she no longer needs the worker's help.

Reactions and Feelings in Terminations

Feelings and reactions about termination involve a somewhat controversial topic. Most authors spend a great deal of time declaring that clients experience a significant sense of loss when the relationship with the worker comes to an end. Other researchers have come to opposite conclusions. We shall try to include both perspectives here. Each is based on significant clinical and empirical research.

Extent and Range of Emotional Reactions

Several factors determine the extent to which clients experience given feelings about the termination process. For example, open-ended relationships in which the client and worker have had an extensive, ongoing professional association are more likely to result in stronger emotional reactions (Hepworth & Larsen, 1990). Educationally focused groups experience significantly weaker emotional reactions than is true for treatment groups (Toseland & Rivas, 1984). Task groups (such as committees) frequently experience endings as positive. Members may even feel relieved that their job is done.

Client reactions to terminations are affected by a variety of things. These include the nature of the problem, the duration and intensity of contact, whether the ending was natural or forced, client strengths and support systems, whether goals were achieved or not, and

whether the termination ends service or results from the client being transferred to another worker (Hellenbrand, 1987). Generally, a client system's sense of loss is directly related to the extent to which the relationship focused on personal problems (such as depression, anxiety) as opposed to environmental issues (such as housing).

Amount of Contact

In some situations, the amount of contact between client and worker is so limited that even the concept of termination seems inappropriate. The hospital social worker who simply arranges for a client to get a hospital bed in her home while she recovers from a broken hip may terminate after only one or two short contacts with the client. There often has been such a limited degree of relationship building that perhaps the only reaction of the client would be gratitude.

Size and Type of System

Similarly, the size and type of system with which one is working will have some bearing on the reactions to termination. For example, remember the worker who helped the community of Clearwater described in chapter 4. He had helped the community identify a number of major problems and come to consensus on those of greatest priority. He also left the community with several functioning task groups, each aimed at coping with an identified problem. Thus, he ended his work and moved on to other projects needing his help. The degree of dependency and level of self-disclosure in this relationship were quite low. The relationship had spanned a relatively short period of time. The issues dealt with were related to conditions in the community, not the personal lives of the "clients." Reactions of those with whom he had worked were positive and the amount of emotional content was very limited.

Figure 8.12: Factors Affecting Reactions to Termination

Factors Likely to Produce More Intense Reactions	Factors Likely to Produce Less Intense Reactions
Open-ended relationships	Time-limited relationships
Frequent worker-client contact	Infrequent worker-client contact
Personal problem—focused	Environmental problem—focused
Absence of other client support systems	Presence of other client support systems
Individual or family client system	Organizational or community client system
High level of emotional content	Low level of emotional content
Treatment groups	Task groups

Contrast the termination described in the section above to that found in the termination of a one-to-one relationship between a worker and a client recovering from a depression. In the latter situation, the client and worker have been together for over nine months. The client has talked with the worker about a variety of personal issues. Subsequently, he has gradually developed increased self-confidence and feelings of well-being. Because the nature of the relationship has become so intense from the client's perspective, ending it is likely to be emotionally charged. Figure 8.12 summarizes the factors affecting reactions to termination.

Mixed Feelings

Mixed feelings often characterize the conclusion of professional relationships. The ending of any relationship in which strong emotional sharing has occurred is typically bittersweet. A sense of loss is common. Some clients also experience anger and feelings of rejection in these situations. Others feel pride, satisfaction, optimism, and a sense of achievement or mastery because of what they have accomplished. Some clients report that old problems, long since overcome, reappear. New problems sometimes develop. At other times, clients object to the relationship ending, claiming they're not ready yet. Still others will deny the end is approaching or deny they have any

feelings about the upcoming event, distancing themselves from the inevitable. Some clients report feeling a "sense of abandonment and loss and feelings of rejection and betrayal or hurt or anger. Clients may be anxious about managing alone and sustaining gains . . ." (Hellenbrand, 1987, p. 767).

Epstein (1980) has argued that clients do not routinely experience negative feelings at termination. She is an advocate of task-centered approaches, which are designed to reduce client reliance on the social worker. According to Epstein, "It is a rare client indeed who truly becomes unhappy or adrift when termination occurs. Practitioners tend to overestimate the value they have as persons for the client's well-being. The rewards of termination for a client are great: fewer expenses, more time, more independence. A practitioner may provoke unhappiness in a client about termination if the practitioner has overvalued the relationship and if excess valuation has been communicated to the client by word or deed" (p. 257). McMahon (1990) has effectively summarized the debate over termination feelings by noting that there is a great potential for strong termination feelings to exist.

Worker Reactions to Termination

Interestingly, it is not only the client who has the potential to experience strong feelings at termination. Social workers themselves sometimes experience reactions to the end of a professional relationship. The extent and intensity of those feelings is likely controlled by the same set of factors described above. In other words, the worker is subject to the same potential feelings as a client, depending upon a variety of factors. The social worker may herself feel a sense of disappointment, loss, or guilt. In these situations, a bit of self-disclosure, in which the worker shares her own feelings with the client, may have positive results. Such sharing may free the client to address his/her reactions to the termination. On the other hand, a worker who is having trouble dealing with her own reactions ought to discuss this with a trusted supervisor or colleague.

Helping Clients at Termination

One positive characteristic of termination is that it can always be anticipated. The exact timing of termination may vary but, like death and taxes, it will not go away. Usually the worker can help clients at the termination point, and this section will look at a number of techniques for doing so.

Planning for Termination

Perhaps the most important way in which the worker can help a client at termination is to ensure that the topic of termination is addressed early in the relationship, preferably at the beginning. Planning for the termination and discussing it with the client will help reduce emotional attachment of the client to the worker and any resulting dependency. It also helps to temper the sense of loss we've already described. In time-limited interventions, termination is expected to occur at some specified point. A group that is planned to meet for seven sessions knows at the start when termination will occur. A resident of a halfway house may be told initially that he must move back into the community at the end of nine months.

The worker can help this process along by reminding the client about the approaching date of termination. Ideally, this should occur several sessions before the last meeting. The worker should leave time in later sessions to talk about termination. This is especially true if termination is occurring earlier than expected. This might happen when the worker moves out of the geographical area or the agency discontinues a particular program.

┌ HIGHLIGHT 8.5
Termination Feelings of Family and Group Members

Reactions to termination may vary in groups and families as well as among individual clients. For example, continuing members of a group may react to the departure of another member with guilt or anger. They may also raise questions about the value of the group, thereby challenging the leader.

Loss of several group members may ultimately result in the group ending because of an insufficient number of members. This is the ultimate threat to a group. Family members still have each other to rely on after a family therapy session concludes. However, a group composed of unrelated adults from a large community is unlikely to offer members this degree of continuity. The latter may have lost a significant social support system. A family, on the other hand, continues to perform this supportive function. Members of contrived groups will have different reactions than members of family groups. It is important, however, to recognize that individual family members may each have their own reactions to the loss of an important worker-client relationship (Hellenbrand, 1987).

Addressing Feelings About Termination

As discussed earlier, terminations often produce feelings for both the client and the worker. One task for the worker is to help the client express any feelings associated with termination. The worker might say: "You've seemed a bit sadder the last two times we've met. I wonder what you're feeling." Another way to raise the issue is through what's known as the "generalized other." The worker might state: "Some of the other boys who have left here have said they felt good about leaving. Others said they thought it had been a waste of time. How about you?" Here, the worker lets the client know that other persons in the same situation have felt a certain way. He also invites the client to share his own reactions which may or may not be similar.

Sometimes, sharing the worker's own feelings about the approaching termination can be helpful. For example, consider a practitioner who's been working with a fifteen-year-old adolescent. The boy has been living in a residential treatment center for delinquent and behaviorally disordered adolescents for almost a year. He was admitted to this center after a history of criminal behavior in his home community. Nearing the boy's release and the coinciding termination of the worker-client relationship, the worker might say, "You're going to be finishing the program at the center in another couple of weeks. I want you to know that I feel very good about how hard you've worked here. I also want you to know that I'm going to miss you." In this way, the worker reminds the client of the upcoming termination and shares his own feelings about it. Frequently, this type of modeling by the worker is especially important for clients who have been socialized not to share feelings. It is through this kind of patient, sensitive work that the worker helps the client to address feelings about the ending process.

Summarizing Progress

One of the important tasks of the termination phase is to recognize client accomplishments or achievements. Let's take the example of the boy mentioned in the previous paragraph. The worker might broach the topic of client growth by asking the client to summarize his progress over the time they've worked together. He might ask, "Can you remember back when you first came here? You wouldn't even talk to me. Now you've progressed from Step 1 all the way to Step 10, the highest level in the cottage. What's made the difference between the old Pat and the new?" This helps the client begin to identify the areas of growth that have occurred. It focuses attention on positive experiences and helps to increase the client's sense of accomplishment.

The techniques of planning for termination, uncovering termination-related feelings, and summarizing progress are three primary tasks of the termination phase. Equally important, however, is ensuring that changes that have occurred during an intervention be sustained after the relationship ends. The stabilization of change process will be discussed next.

Stabilization of Change

There is sufficient evidence that changes which occur in the context of therapeutic relationships do not necessarily carry over into the other areas of a client's existence. Changes which have occurred in individual behavior, for example, may not generalize to other situations in a client's life. The young woman who stops using drugs while in a treatment program is going to find it much harder to maintain this when she returns to her old friends. Ultimately, the goal is that change in one area carries over into all others.

Toseland and Rivas (1984) suggest seven things that workers can do to help clients maintain and generalize changes. These include:

1. *Helping clients select relevant and appropriate situations to work on.* This can be

accomplished by helping the client select important problems or concerns to work on. For example, it would make sense to focus on a client's job-seeking skills when the primary problem is unemployment. While other issues (for instance, marital relationships, parenting skills, etc.) might be important, they are not as relevant to the basic problem of being out of work.

2. *Helping clients build confidence in their own abilities.* One of the ways the worker can assist her is through helping the client review their work together. This focuses on achievement of goals and sets the stage to talk about the future. Clients leaving a professional relationship often need reassurance. Discussing the client's progress can help to boost self-confidence.

3. *Using multiple situations and settings when helping members learn new behaviors.* Clients learning new skills and behaviors should be given multiple opportunities to use these. For example, people learning to be more assertive should be given the assignment to practice this with family, friends, coworkers, and strangers. The more situations in which the client can successfully employ her newfound skill, the greater the likelihood the skill will be used following termination.

4. *Using naturally occurring consequences rather than creating artificial ones.* Ultimately, clients will be confronted with the "real world" without the support of the social worker. To ensure that they are prepared for this eventuality, it is important that clients be given every opportunity to practice their new behaviors in natural settings. For example, a client who is trying to improve her communication skills should eventually practice these skills in the "real world." Away from the supportive environment of the

worker or group, the client experiences the very real barriers encountered when people try to change their own behaviors. A client who can be assertive only in the assertiveness-training group has benefitted little from the group experience.

5. *Extending treatment through use of follow-up sessions.* Follow-up contacts between client and worker often serve as "boosters" to help clients maintain their changes over time. Whether the focus is on weight loss, learning new parenting skills, or becoming more assertive, follow-up sessions remind the clients that others remain concerned about their progress. Seeing the worker or other group members may rekindle the client's dedication to her goal or reinforce her efforts to maintain her growth.

6. *Preventing setbacks in other environments such as school, the workplace, or the home.* Sometimes the clients' progress is undermined by other aspects of their environment. An example could be the student who is too easily influenced by his peers and gets into delinquent behavior when around them. To help the client keep his distance from these "friends," the worker might enlist the help of parents or school officials. If multiple figures in the boy's life are working in concert to encourage and maintain positive behavior, it is more likely that the changes will last.

7. *Helping members confront future problems by teaching them a problem-solving process.* Finally, most clients must learn to live without the constant support and encouragement of the worker. One way of reducing dependency is to teach clients the same problem-solving approach the worker uses. Once clients learn to confront problems in a problem-solving framework, many seemingly insurmountable problems disappear. At the very

least, the client learns a system that can be used effectively in most areas of his/her life. In essence, you as the worker are trying to put yourself out of business by teaching clients what you know. The goal is often to teach them practical problem-solving skills. They'll no longer need you and will be able to accomplish goals by themselves.[4]

Stabilizing Change in Small Groups

Most of the approaches described above will work as well with small groups as with individuals. However, there are techniques that are especially effective with groups of various sizes. For example, many community-based programs take clients through a series of ever increasing steps to independence. These steps finally culminate in the client's return to the community with a minimum of formal supervision. A shelter for battered women, for example, operates a halfway house in addition to the shelter itself. Many clients, after staying in the shelter for a period of time, are ready to move into a more independent living arrangement. At this point, the client may elect to move to the half-way house and remain there until she is able to make it on her own. The halfway house serves as a transition between the shelter and full return to the community. It also gradually reduces the role of the shelter staff so that clients do not become overly dependent on them for help.

There are still other effective strategies when working with client groups. One such technique involves varying the use of group activities. For example, in the early stages of a group it is common to have group members engage in activities that are group building in na-

ture (for example, enhancing warmth and trust). Thus, clients may be asked to do ice-breaking activities such as having members interview each other and introduce the interviewee to the group. The ice breaker is designed to increase the "we" feeling of the group.

Conversely, group activities can be used to decrease this "we" feeling. For example, the leader may choose group activities that foster independence and reduce group cohesion. Take the members of an adolescent girls' group that has spent several weeks learning and practicing how to express their feelings to one another. In the last couple of sessions, the worker has asked the members to begin describing the ways their new communication skills are affecting relationships with parents and peers. By asking the members to focus their attention away from the group, she is helping to reconnect them with the larger environment in which they live.

Sometimes groups plan ceremonies to help intensify the sense of ending and to acknowledge the progress of the client in a program. Group homes for chemically dependent clients frequently have "graduation" ceremonies as clients prepare to leave the shelter of the group home environment.

Stabilizing Change in Large Systems

The guidelines described above work well with individuals, families, and groups. However, additional approaches are needed when stabilizing change in communities and organizations. Kettner, Daley, and Nichols (1985) suggest the importance of stabilization of change for work with large systems and provide some important suggestions.

Routinize Procedures and Processes

One of the goals when attempting to change large systems is to ensure that whatever is accomplished continues indefinitely. One way this goal is accomplished is for procedures

---

4. Reprinted with the permission of Macmillan Publishing Company from *An Introduction to Group Practice* by R. W. Toseland and R. F. Rivas. Copyright 1984 by Macmillan Publishing Company.

and processes to become routine. For example, let's recall the case of the city of Algoma noted in chapter 4. Algoma had no system for ensuring that neighbors would be notified when major zoning and land-use proposals affecting them came before the city council. The absence of a procedure for notifying residents about proposed changes in their neighborhood was a continual problem. The adoption of an ordinance (really, a policy) requiring notification by mail guaranteed residents the opportunity to be heard. This ordinance stabilized the desired change.

Clarification of Policies and Procedures

One way to help stabilize change in larger systems is to ensure that newly created policies and procedures are very clear. Sometimes individuals have "understandings" about what was decided or agreed upon. Later, no one can seem to recall exactly what was decided, or there is a major disagreement regarding what

A social worker can act as a stabilizer of change in large organizations. Here a practitioner at a retirement community listens to one of the resident board members.

really transpired. To avoid this, you can follow the old bureaucratic adage and "put it in writing." Policies and procedures that are written down are less likely to be affected by faulty memories.

One approach is to use "memorandums of understanding." These are nothing more than memos or letters which restate in written form what has been agreed to verbally. Let's say the officer of an organization has verbally told you the organization will contribute five hundred dollars toward a new recreation program in your community. You could confirm this by writing the person a letter reiterating what he has told you and thanking him for the organization's generosity. For example, you might simply state, "Thank you so much for your five hundred dollar pledge toward our new recreation program. Your generosity is very much appreciated." This "memorandum of understanding" is just a technique formalizing informal policies, agreements, or procedures. It helps prevent problems later on when people's memories become a bit ragged.

On the same note, if a new policy is agreed to, the sooner it is entered into the organization's policy manual, the better. Most social agencies have manuals containing their policies and operating procedures. These are very important documents because they control what workers can and cannot do. The same is true for most large organizations. Policies that are articulated in policy manuals are more likely to be followed than those that are unwritten.

Reducing the Influence of the Change Agent

There is another way to help maintain change and to increase the client system's opportunities to operate independently, namely reduce the worker's and agency's influence. This is often accomplished by reducing the frequency and intensity of contact between the worker and client systems. The worker in Clear-water gradually reduced the frequency of his attendance at many of the ad hoc committee meetings. Eventually, local members of the community took leadership of the committees and the worker's role became one of consultation. Finally, even this role was dropped as the indigenous leaders developed confidence and skill in leading their committees. The worker had deliberately reduced his level of involvement to facilitate the development of natural community leaders. In this way, positive changes would be maintained on an ongoing basis.

Addressing Ongoing Needs of Clients

The worker in the termination phase of the helping process must attend to the ongoing needs of the client system. We have already touched on the importance of discussing with the client resources for future needs. It also might be helpful to let the client know that the worker and agency remain available should future or ongoing help be required. Reid (1978) suggests that the worker not offer to extend service without clearly knowing that a specific goal can be reached. This prevents the client from becoming overly dependent upon the worker or agency. Still, it is important to keep the door open for the client. If the termination is occurring prematurely, this is especially important. The worker might say, "Denise, I know that you believe we have accomplished what you initially wanted to. I, too, feel we have come a long way. I think we were beginning to get into some other areas that don't seem so critical to you right now. I respect your right to bring this phase of our work together to a close. Still, I want you to know that I am available if you decide you would like additional help." The goal here is to ensure a continued good relationship between the agency and client. Thus, the client can return should she need to.

If necessary, referrals to other service organizations or persons may be made. Referrals should always be made to specific persons, if possible. Toseland and Rivas (1984) suggest calling the contact person in the presence of the client; they also stress making certain the client knows how to get to the agency and has some means of transportation available. Finally, the client should be encouraged to get back to the worker if the service or agency does not provide what the client needs. More will be said about the referral process in chapter 15.

Client Follow-Up

Social work research on the follow-up of clients who are no longer receiving intervention does not paint a very positive picture. Too many clients do not maintain the changes that occurred during the intervention phase (Hepworth & Larsen, 1990). There are several reasons for this. It may be because it was easier to go back to previous ways of doing things than to continue the new behavior. It also can occur because the environment is not supportive of the new changes. Peers, friends, and family may all exert influences that undercut the new behaviors. Sometimes failure occurs because the new behavior was not established long enough to become the norm. It is unfortunate that clients who spend significant periods of time working on a problem are later unable to continue the gains they made. In the next section, we look at one means for dealing with this problem, namely follow-up.

Follow-up is the "acquisition of information about the client's level of functioning in relation to intervention objectives after an intervention is no longer administered or all intervention has been terminated" (Blythe & Tripodi, 1989, p. 136). In other words, follow-up with a client involves learning how the client is doing after your formal relationship with the client has ended. Social workers frequently do not make efforts to follow up on their work with

clients after the point of termination. This occurs because workers are too busy and often overloaded with other cases needing immediate attention.

There are a number of reasons for doing follow-up. One involves first finding out whether the client is functioning without intervention. Then it concerns offering whatever assistance is needed if the client is having difficulty. Austin, Kopp, and Smith (1986, p. 103) identify four possible activities for the social worker when the client needs assistance. These are listed in Highlight 8.6.

Follow-up can also help determine whether an intervention worked. Blythe and Tripodi (1989, p. 137) provide a list of possible intervention outcomes that may be discovered during follow-up.

1. The client may be functioning at the same level in follow-up as at termination. That is, there would be no clinically or statistically significant changes from termination to follow-up.
2. The client may have shown more improvement since termination. This may be attributable to an improvement trend that commenced before termination, a delayed intervention effort, or to other nonintervention factors that might have been responsible for improvement.
3. There may be a gradual deterioration that is a result of premature withdrawal of the intervention or of other unknown factors.
4. Rather than a gradual deterioration, there may be a complete relapse. An example is a recovered addict who is drug-free for a long period but relapses on one occasion and then resumes his or her former drug habit.

For some clients, the follow-up contact acts like a booster shot increasing the effectiveness of the previous intervention. The contact by the worker reminds the client that others are interested in his/her success. It may help the client overcome a temporary hurdle or suggest the need for an additional intervention. In some types of interventions (for example, task-centered), the follow-up is a planned part of the intervention. Both the worker and client are aware that the follow-up will occur.

Wells (1981) recommends that follow-up sessions be discussed during the intervention. The inclusion of discussions about follow-up during the intervention itself may help explain

---

HIGHLIGHT 8.6
Possible Tasks for Worker at Follow-Up

1. *Actively represent the consumer.* This may be necessary when a client is getting "the run-around" from an agency or organization. The worker may have to intervene personally (by phone or in person) to ensure the client receives reasonably timely assistance.
2. *Discuss problems.* Find out why the client is having trouble. Was the referral made to the wrong agency? Did the client present him/herself in a manner that contributed to being denied assistance? Are there critical needs that are still not being met?
3. *Straighten out difficulties.* Once the problems encountered by the client have been discussed, it may be possible to identify means to overcome them. Perhaps the client was not eligible for a service or benefit and another resource can be found. Maybe the client made a mistake on the intake application that resulted in being declared ineligible.

   Often these matters can be straightened out with minimal assistance from the worker. At other times, it will be necessary for the worker to intervene directly with the targeted agency. There may even be situations where the worker must involve his/her supervisor. An example would be when Agency A refuses to qualify the client even though the worker's supervisor specifically suggested the client contact Agency A in the first place. Perhaps the worker's supervisor was incorrect about Agency A's being able to help. Often, the worker's supervisor will have to contact his/her counterpart at Agency A to get that agency to reconsider its decision regarding the client.

   Another example involves a client's complaining to her worker that tenants in neighborhood rental units were parking cars on the front lawn of their duplex. She felt this was unsightly and contributed to the decline of the neighborhood. Seeing this mess during a home visit, the worker suggested to the client that she call the police and report the situation. The police told the client they were reluctant to enforce the ordinance. They hesitated to get involved in an area they considered to be the responsibility of the building inspector. The worker discussed the situation with his supervisor. The supervisor then telephoned the city manager with whom he had a good relationship. Within hours, the police department began enforcing the city ordinance. This is a good example of how involving relevant others and using good contacts can straighten out a perplexing difficulty.
4. *Prepare the consumer.* Perhaps a client will need to return to an agency or organization with which she has already had unpleasant experiences. What should the client expect on this visit? How will s/he respond to agency personnel? Will he or she be uncomfortable? It may be necessary to role play with the client future contacts with the agency. In this way, various scenarios can be anticipated.

From *Delivering Human Services: A Self-Instructional Approach* 2nd ed., by Michael J. Austin, Judith Kopp, and Philip L. Smith. Copyright 1986 by Longman Publishing Group.

the relatively high success rate for task-centered approaches. Follow-up becomes a normal part of the intervention and extends the amount of contact between client and worker.

Overcoming Barriers to Follow-Up

As we have noted above, a major barrier to doing follow-up is the heavy workload carried by many workers. Though this problem is real, there are ways to get around it. When a caseload is too high to follow up on every client, the worker can still sample randomly from the closed caseload. For example, it is possible to select every fifth case closed last December rather than every single one. Alternatively, workers may choose to follow up on only the clients they consider to have the highest risk of experiencing continuing problems. Follow-up can be by telephone or letter, although the first is preferable because it is more personal and less bureaucratic.

In addition to heavy workloads, another barrier to follow-up is the lack of agency policies or traditions which support this activity. Many agencies do not encourage workers to do follow-up. This reluctance may be due to concerns about worker caseload, philosophical objections to making clients too dependent on the worker, or for other reasons. Another barrier to follow-up may be the reluctance of the worker to "intrude" on the client following termination. This problem can be overcome by the method mentioned earlier, namely discussing follow-up during the intervention. This will prime the client to expect a follow-up contact since it is considered part of the intervention.

Regardless of the follow-up method selected, follow-up should be viewed as part of your professional obligation to the client. Even if your agency does not require or encourage workers to follow up on clients after termina-tion, it is your professional responsibility to do so.

Chapter Summary

This chapter has discussed the importance of evaluating both social work practice and social programs. The purposes of evaluation as well as the evaluation process have been described. Key concepts such as formative and summative evaluations, baseline, validity and reliability, data-gathering methods, dependent and independent variables, and generalizability have been defined and discussed. Four evaluation designs for direct practice have been presented, including single-subject, goal attainment and task achievement scaling, and client satisfaction questionnaires.

Five evaluation designs for program evaluation were also briefly described. Several issues and problems in evaluation were identified, including problems in generalizability, wrong choice of evaluation tool, failure to involve client in the evaluation process, staff distrust in evaluation, evaluation processes which interfere with giving service to clients, alternate explanations for program outcomes, and unanticipated consequences of intervention sometimes discovered in the evaluation process.

This chapter has also discussed termination of professional relationships, including both the tasks and timing of termination. We have also described some of the common and possible reactions of clients and workers to termination, in addition to ways of helping clients deal with termination. We have reviewed ways that the change efforts can be stabilized after the intervention is ended. Finally, follow-up of clients following termination was discussed. This discussion included reasons for doing follow-up, barriers to follow-up, and ways these obstacles can be overcome. Also included were steps the worker can take to make the follow-up an effective adjunct to the intervention process.

9 Understanding Families

Getting under their skin

BEHOLD THE BRADY FAMILY Á LA 1970

Mom and Dad are happily married. They are loving parents to six sweet but spirited, smiling (at least most of the time) "little shavers." The youngsters range in age from six to seventeen. Dad's a successful architect. Mom's a "successful housewife." Family life goes along with its little bumps, crises, pleasures, and joys. The "kids" can be impish at times. However, they *never* skip out of school, lie, cheat, take drugs (heavens, no), shoot enemy gang members (because they don't belong to gangs; in fact, there aren't any gangs), get pregnant, or impregnate somebody else.

Yet the Brady family does have its problems. For one thing, those "darn kids" just won't stay off the phone. Jan, the preteen daughter, has sneezing fits in an allergic reaction to the beloved family dog's flea powder. Marcia, the teenage daughter and quite a gorgeous young woman, is madly enamored with sixteen-year-old Harvey Klinger. Harvey, however, is much more enthralled with his bug-collecting hobby than with poor, lovelorn Marcia. Additionally, the whole family is very worried about whether Marcia will indeed be declared head cheerleader or not. Cindy, the youngest, is desperately preoccupied with the enigma of who stole Kitty Carryall, her doll. Peter and Bobby, both somewhere in the middle of the sibling order, seem continuously jealous of Greg, the oldest. Greg, who plays guitar, is torn between going on to college and becoming a teen idol.

Compare this scene with the same family twenty years later. Lovece and Edelstein (1990) contrast the old 1970s television sitcom "The Brady Bunch" with a resurrection of the series aired in 1990. Everyone in the family, of course, is twenty years older. Likewise, the new scene reflects some of the ways in which family life has changed in twenty years. Mom "has finally gotten out of the house and now makes a living selling them" (p. 12). Dad has become a yuppielike entrepreneur. He "has opened his own firm, is mulling a run for city council, and has bought himself a spiffy new camcorder" (p.13). Jan no longer is tormented by her allergic reaction to the beloved pet: The dog has long since "gone to that great kennel in the sky" (p.13). Instead, Jan, now an architect like her dad, is struggling with the fact that she simply cannot get pregnant despite the onerous ticking of her biological clock. Marcia no longer worries about Harvey and his bugs or about becoming head cheerleader. She married somebody who doesn't like to work very much. Unfortunately, Marcia had put more energy into cheerleading than developing a lucrative career for herself. Even shopping at the local Pic 'n' Save Warehouse Foods has become difficult with no money coming in. Baby Cindy, who used to be "cute as a button," now works as a radio disc jockey. She worries about whether she should go to bed with her older, very married boss. Peter is no longer that jealous of teen idol Greg. Now Peter's "a playboy in the age of AIDS" (p.12). Bobby's no longer that jealous of Greg either; rather, he wonders if he'll ever walk again after breaking his back in an auto-racing accident. Greg's major concern, on the other hand, is whether to switch from being an obstetrician to a pediatrician. Finally, someone in the family has the infamous drinking problem. To bait your curiosity, that person will remain a mystery.

The whole point of this is that the nature of the family and of "typical" family problems has changed drastically in the past few decades. There have been awesome technological advances, massive upheavals in world economics, and major shifts in family structure. The problems families now face are very different than those confronted by the two-parent with children, intact, male-dominated, nuclear family in which our culture has traditionally been rooted.

Of course, the Brady example only illustrates some of the changes in family life. For example, there are the changes in gender role expectations with respect to earning a living. Then, there are the moral dilemmas now being faced concerning sexuality and intimacy. Also, there are the effects of advancing technology. Will Bobby ever walk again? Can Jan ever get pregnant?

There are numerous changes in the basic nature of families which the Bradys don't illustrate as well. Mom and Dad are still intact as a couple. Divorce, remarriage, and stepchildren have not created "blended families" for them. Likewise, the Bradys remain very white and very middle-class. They don't reflect the increasing proportion of the population previously labeled as "minorities," in other words, people of nonwhite heritage. Nor do the Bradys clearly demonstrate the increasing proportion of women and children who compose the poor and homeless.

Working with families, regardless of their specific individual circumstances, is a major facet of generalist social work practice. Practitioners need to understand the basic dynamics of today's family relationships and the problems these families face. The family needs to be viewed from several perspectives. These include the family system as an entity in itself, the individual people making up the family system, and the impacts of the social, political, and economic environment upon how the family functions. That's what this chapter is all about.

Introduction

Families continue to remain the foundation of most people's lives. They can provide the security, support, and intimacy people need. Social workers often encounter individual clients who initially appear to have individual problems. However, another way of looking at problems is from a family perspective. That is, you might view a problem not as belonging to the individual, but rather to the individual's entire family.

For example, take a twenty-four-year-old man who abuses alcohol. His alcoholism not only affects him, but his wife whom he slaps around when he returns home from a drunken bout. It also impacts his three children. His primary interactions with them involve hitting, screaming, and ignoring. Finally, it impacts the man's parents and other family members when he typically bursts into fits of alcoholic rage at family gatherings.

An eighty-seven-year-old woman whose health is rapidly failing provides another example. Of course, her health is *her* problem. However, it's also the problem of her middle-aged son and daughter, both of whom live within seventy-five miles of her home. Should one of them take her in and care for her? If so, which one? Both of their spouses hate the idea. The spouses see the older woman's presence as a terrible disruption of their own family's life. So should her children put the elderly woman in a health care facility? Should they force her to go even if she hates that idea? If she does enter a facility, which one? And how often do they need to visit? How can either of the elderly woman's children cope with their burden of guilt over not taking her in themselves?

Still another example involves an active thirteen year-old boy who slips on the mud as he runs down to the river to swim. Although he's run down that same riverbank hundreds of times before, this time he slips and breaks his neck. What impact does his individual problem, namely that of being a quadriplegic, have on his parents, his siblings, his grandparents, and even other members of his extended family?

Thus, generalist social work practitioners will often be called upon to work with an entire family to solve a problem. This does not mean that generalist practitioners are family therapists. In describing what family therapists do, Masson and O'Byrne (1984) state, "Basically we try to intervene in and modify those aspects of a family system which are interfering with the management of the life tasks of the family and its members. We focus on the transactional patterns within families and seek to change them so that people will relate to each other differently" (p. 21).

Family therapists are specialized. Their focus of attention is the family unit. Their goals involve changing family members' patterns of communication and interaction. Family therapists help clients make changes in how they think, both about themselves and about other family members. Therapy typically takes place in the therapist's office and can be somewhat long-term.

Generalist social workers, on the other hand, must address a broader variety of problems. As we've discussed, many of these problems involve outside systems. For example, a client may have lost her job. Part of a social worker's role then might be to help this client find other employment. Linking a client with employment agencies and other potential sources of jobs is one means of doing this. Or the worker might help the client get temporary financial help until she can once again support herself. Still another possibility is helping the client become involved in job training.

A second example of the broad range of problems addressed by generalist practitioners is homelessness. A generalist practitioner can help a homeless client find temporary shelter and resources. Subsequently, that worker might help that client find employment or become linked with other services and financial aid. Likewise, the client may need help in getting needed health care.

Still another example of a problem addressed by generalist practitioners involves helping the thirteen-year-old quadriplegic mentioned earlier. He will likely need help in a variety of ways. He may have difficulty coping with the reality of his disability. Likewise, the impacts of the accident on other family members may need attention. Generalist practitioners may help the quadriplegic and his family deal with these issues or refer them to someone else to do so. The options available to family members (such as pursuing resources) will probably need to be addressed. For instance, a generalist practitioner can work to help the thirteen-year-old get needed physical assistance (such as physical and occupational therapy, and transportation services). A worker can find out what resources are available and help link him and his family with these resources. If services are not available, a generalist practitioner may advocate on her client's behalf so that the community and agencies within the community begin to respond to the client's needs.

Thus, generalist practitioners must adopt a broader view in helping individuals and families solve problems. They need a wide range of skills. They need to be able to tackle a variety of problems and try to solve them in whatever ethical manners they can figure out.

The family remains a significant force in people's lives. Family relationships are intimate and complex. In some ways working with families in social work practice is different than working with individuals, other groups, or larger systems. Working with families is often considered to lie somewhere on a continuum between micro and mezzo practice. Therefore, social workers need a solid base of skills directly related to problem-solving with families.

Specifically, this chapter will:

- Examine information useful in the assessment phase of the Generalist Intervention Model as it applies to families;
- Review a spectrum of communication skills including verbal and nonverbal communication, in addition to specific avenues of communication within families;
- Explore family structure with emphasis on the family as a system;
- Identify family life cycle adjustments;
- Describe common family conflicts and problems;
- Relate policy issues in macro practice to families' basic needs;
- Discuss variations in family structure including single-parent families and step-families.

Family Assessment Skills

Just as with any other generalist intervention, the first in the problem-solving process with families is assessment. As we know, assessment in generalist practice involves getting information about the client and the client's problems in order to decide how best to intervene. Here we will investigate some aspects of assessment which relate specifically to families. The entire family itself will be viewed as the client system.

A family is "a primary group whose members are related by blood, adoption, committment, or marriage and who usually have shared common

residences, have mutual rights and obligations, and assume responsibility for the primary socialization of children" (Barker, 1987, p. 53). Once the family has been identified as your client system, there are a variety of dimensions in which the family's problems and interactions can be assessed. These include communication, family structure, life-cycle adjustments, and impacts of the impinging social environment (Hepworth & Larsen, 1990; Holman, 1983; Janzen & Harris, 1986; Thorman, 1982).

Assessing Family Communication

How family members communicate with each other relates directly to how effectively the family flourishes as a system. Therefore, assessment of communication is essential in preparation for intervention. Several aspects of family communication will be discussed here. They include verbal and nonverbal communication in addition to the various avenues of communication.

Verbal and Nonverbal Communication

As we discussed in chapter 2 regarding skills for working with individuals, communication involves transmitting information from one person to another. Both verbal and nonverbal communication are important in conveying meaning. It is very important that the *impact* on the receiver (that is, what the receiver understands the sender to be saying) closely resembles the *intent* of the sender (that is, what the sender means to say). As we know, inaccuracies or problems at any point in this process can stop the information from getting across to the receiver. At any point, distortion may interfere with the communication process.

Verbal communication patterns inside the family include who talks a lot and who talks only rarely. They involve who talks to whom and who defers to whom. They also reflect the subtle and not so subtle aspects involved in family members' relationships. These qualities might involve hostility, pride, rejection, or overinvolvement.

Nonverbal communication patterns are also important in families. Frequently, a receiver will attribute more value to the nonverbal aspects of the message than the verbal. Nonver-

---

HIGHLIGHT 9.1

An Example of Conflict Between Verbal and Nonverbal Communication

For instance, take Patti and Larry, a married couple. They both work outside the home in professional careers. Because of their involvement in their respective jobs and the long hours they work, they see little of each other during the week. When Friday night rolls around, they typically relax together and enjoy talking about their work and future plans.

Patti made it a point to get home early one Friday and made Larry a relatively elegant beef stroganoff dinner—as elegant as it could get when it was started late Friday afternoon. The two, by the way, usually shared the cooking tasks.

Patti timed the dinner to be ready at 6:30 P.M., about the time Larry usually got home. Patti turned on the television and waited . . . and waited . . . and waited. Seven o'clock came and went. Seven-thirty rolled on by. Eight o'clock passed into oblivion. Time moved on to 9:00 and finally 10:00 P.M.

First, Patti took the dinner off of the stove and let it cool. An hour later she put it in the refrigerator so it wouldn't spoil. Initially, Patti had been worried. What if Larry had been in a car wreck? But, no, the police would have called to let her know. Where was Larry? Why wasn't he calling her to tell her he wouldn't be home?

By 10:00 P.M., Patti had transcended far beyond her initial worry and even her anger. Her fury at Larry's inconsiderateness had escalated to immense proportions. As the evening had progressed she had gone beyond turning the roll of toilet paper in the bathroom upside down, a behavior which really annoyed him. She usually only resorted to such nonverbal behavior to get her point across when it really mattered and verbal communication simply did not work. She not only vigorously squeezed the toothpaste in the middle of the tube (another behavior which really aggravated Larry), but

squeezed it all down to the bottom of the tube. He consistently and carefully liked to squeeze his toothpaste toward the top. By 10:00 P.M., she had taken both the toilet paper roll and the toothpaste tube and thrown them in the garbage.

Patti then heard someone at the door. She, in addition, had also locked the door, another nonverbal means of displaying to Larry her serious disapproval. Someone out there was fidgeting with a key. There was scratching at the lock. Then, suddenly, the door burst open. There was Larry beaming a wide grin. He said with a somewhat alcoholic slur, "Well, hi ya, how're you doin'?"

Patti responded with a face of stone, her eyes black with rage, "I'm fine." She promptly left the room and went to bed.

Larry knew he was in the proverbial "dog house." Even after some unknown number of beers, he knew he should've called to tell Patti about Harvey's going-away party after work. He knew Patti wasn't "fine." He really knew how not "fine" she was when he discovered the missing toilet paper later that night and the phantom toothpaste the next morning.

Patti and Larry eventually talked the situation out. She told him how she thought he knew how she always looked forward to their Friday nights together. She told him how she had wanted to please him with dinner and how worried she had later become when he didn't appear. She told him how she had felt he just didn't care about her feelings. All he would have had to do was call her and tell her he would be late.

Larry apologized and said he would never do it again. He hasn't either. Patti's nonverbal emphasis concerning the issue drove the point home. Later, verbal elaboration helped Larry understand the issue more clearly. However, to this day, Larry emphasizes how Patti *hates it when he has fun.*

bal communication can involve facial expressions, eye contact, and posture. It can also involve seemingly trifling behaviors. See Highlight 9.1 for an example.

The story illustrated in Highlight 9.1 may seem a bit silly. However, it illustrates several points about family interaction and communication. It is a true story.

First, what one family member might say in words to another one may not be what that sender really means. Patti was not "fine," although she verbally stated she was. However, because of her anger and her feelings that Larry didn't care about how she felt, she was not ready to express herself accurately with words.

Second, nonverbal behavior can provide important clues regarding what a sender really wants to convey. Patti did silly, although aggravating, things to convey to Larry that she was angry.

Third, critical nonverbal communication may involve any number of seemingly petty behaviors. Each of us has our "things" which, trivial as they may be, annoy us to no end. An annoyance may be how someone else puts the glasses into the dishwasher the wrong way or forgets to turn out the hall light at night. It might be how someone close to us forgets to put a plastic garbage bag in the waste container before dumping old chicken bones into it. Or, it might be parking the car the "wrong" way in the driveway. Family members can use any of these things to communicate with each other.

A fourth point is that nonverbal behaviors often transcend trivial behaviors. They reflect feelings which the individual is unable or does not want to put into words. Emotions are strong among family members. Petty nonverbal behavior can wield formidable blows to those close to us.

There is a fifth point with respect to the story. Patti and Larry were able to unravel the problem themselves, despite the fact that Larry still feels Patti hates it when he has fun. However, many times a generalist practitioner will

be called upon to disentangle confused verbal and nonverbal communications. It will be up to the worker to help communicators within the family have their *intents* more closely match their *impacts*.

The basic skills for micro practice clearly relate to working with families. In addition to understanding verbal and nonverbal communication, these include: being warm, empathic, and genuine; using interviewing techniques; and overcoming hurdles which often occur during the interviewing and problem-solving processes. Family interaction and communication are more complicated because more individuals are involved.

Avenues of Communication

Perez (1979) cites "five avenues of communication," any or all of which family members may use in a given day; they include "consonance, condemnation, submission, intellectualization, and indifference" (p. 47). Evaluating how a family communicates using these avenues provides clear clues regarding where change is needed.

Consonance

Consonance refers to the extent to which the communication receiver accurately hears and understands the sender of the communication. In other words, to what extent does the sender's *intent* closely resemble the receiver's *impact*? Healthy families are likely to have high levels of consonance in their communications. In other words, family members understand each other well. Unhealthy families, on the other hand, often have low levels of consonance. Members of these families don't communicate clearly with each other.

Condemnation

Condemnation involves family members severely criticizing, blaming, negatively judging, or nagging other family members. More than occurring only once or twice, condemnation involves a regular pattern of family interaction. This pattern may involve any number of the family members. In other words, one person may typically condemn another. Or that one person may typically condemn all the others. Likewise, all other family members may condemn one in particular. Or two or three members may condemn any one or more. Any configuration is possible.

People who form patterns of condemnation frequently do it to enhance their own self-esteem (Perez, 1979). Blaming or criticizing another person makes your own qualities and behaviors appear better or superior. For instance, take the seventy-seven-year-old woman who constantly condemned her husband of fifty-five years. He was eighty-four. She regularly harped on how he was an alcoholic who couldn't keep a job. The strange thing, however, was that he hadn't touched a drop of liquor in over forty years. Additionally, he had worked regularly as a carpenter for most of those years. However, when the woman dwelled on how bad her husband was, albeit for behavior that had occurred over forty years ago, she made herself feel better. If he was so bad, then she looked so good by comparison.

Submission

Submission involves feeling so downtrodden, guilt-ridden, or incapable that you succumb completely to another's will. You don't feel valuable or worthwhile enough to be assertive about your own rights and needs. Instead, you knuckle under the other person's will, submit, and obey. Perez (1979) sums up situations involving submission by saying, "The submissive person, like the condemner, is difficult to live with. His [or her] feelings of ineptness and inadequacy put family members under constant pressure to support, to guide, to direct, to lead him. And again, when the dependency pressure becomes too demanding the family members may well respond via condemnation" (p. 49).

Intellectualization

Intellectualization refers to the process of staging all communication within a strictly logical, rational realm. The existence of any emotion is denied or suppressed. A person who intellectualizes likes to evaluate a problem rationally and establish a solution as soon as possible. This person does not want illogical emotions to interfere with the process of dealing with and controlling reality. The problem usually faced by the intellectualizer, however, is that everyone has emotions, even the intellectualizer. Emotions which are constantly suppressed may build up and explode uncontrollably at inopportune times. Explosions may even result in violence.

Another problem with intellectualization occurs when the intellectualizer is unable to meet the needs of other family members. A person who intellectualizes can seem very cold and unloving. Traditional gender-role stereotypes which direct men to be strong, unemotional decision-makers encourages intellectualization. This often becomes a problem in relationships for women who traditionally have been raised to express emotions. A typical scenario involves a woman who seeks expression of love and emotion from an intimate partner who instead intellectualizes.

Take, for instance, one couple where the man stated point-blank that he has no emotions; he said he was always happy. The woman responded with the question, "Well, then, what are you when you're yelling at me?"

The man replied hesitantly, "Then . . . I'm mad." At this the woman smiled silently to herself. She had made some progress. She had just doubled her mate's emotional repertoire.

Indifference

Indifference involves remaining apparently unconcerned, not caring one way or the other, and appearing detachedly aloof. Two common ways indifference is manifested in families is through "silence" and "ignoring behaviors" (Perez, 1979, p. 51). One or more family mem-

When assessing a family, it is important to consider all of the relationships among individuals.

bers may not talk or respond to one or more other family members.

Indifference can be a very powerful and manipulative means of communicating. A mother who ignores her teenage daughter may convey a number of messages to her. Perhaps, it makes the daughter feel her mother doesn't care enough about her to expend the energy. Or maybe the mother is angry at her for some reason.

In addition to being disturbing, being ignored can be very painful. For instance, take the newlywed wife who was very emotionally insecure. During the first few weeks of marriage, she would ask her husband a dozen times a day if he really loved her. At first, he would answer, "Yes, dear, I do." However, he soon tired of her constant need for reassurance. He began simply to "turn her off" and ignore her. She was devastated. She needed to learn that the impact of her consistent questioning was not eliciting the response she desired. Instead of making herself feel more secure, she was driving her husband away from her. This served only to escalate her insecurity.

Assessing Family Structure

Family structure refers to the organization of relationships and patterns of interaction occurring within the family. Here we will examine five dimensions of family structure. They include the family as a system, family norms, family roles, the balance of power within the system, and intergenerational aspects. Communication might be included as an aspect of family structure. However, because of its significance, not only in assessment but throughout the intervention, we have already discussed it as a separate issue.

The Family as a System

Families are systems. The concepts involved in systems theory, which we discussed in chapter 1, also apply to family systems. Family structure, then, can be assessed by thinking of the family in systems theory terms. As Holman (1983) articulates, "In general systems terms, the family can be perceived as a dynamic system, consisting of a complex of elements or components (family members) directly or indirectly related in a network in such a way that each component (family member) is related to some other in a more or less stable way within any particular period of time" (p. 23).

Thinking of the family as a system is helpful when working with the family to help solve its problems. For instance, as in any system, all parts (family members) have relationships to all other parts (other family members). When assessing a family, it's important then to assess all of the relationships among individuals, even those which appear subdued and less significant.

Additionally, systems theory prescribes that an event affecting one family member will actually have an effect on *all* family members. For example, take Kay, age sixteen. She met a boy at a Friday night high school dance, went out with him for pizza afterward, and later got in a serious car accident. Ironically, the accident happened at about midnight on Friday the thirteenth. Another car pulled out in front of the car in which Kay was a passenger. The driver in the other car tried to cut across the lane of his oncoming traffic to get to the other side of the boulevard. His car hit Kay's car head on. She was sitting in the middle front seat next to her new beau and was not wearing a seatbelt. Upon impact, her face was thrown down onto the radio in the dashboard. The result was a smashed right cheekbone, broken jaw, crushed nose, lost teeth, and several deep facial cuts.

Kay went through about four years and a dozen operations of plastic surgery. Although the experience was very painful, she later reflected that she had learned much from it. For instance, she quickly learned the old cliché that "beauty isn't everything." Her accident helped her to put things of real value such as her religious beliefs and personal relationships into perspective. The insurance money and a two-month trip to Europe wasn't so bad either. She eventually became a social worker.

Her immediate family members, however, were traumatized by the car accident. Kay's twelve-year-old sister promptly fainted dead away upon her initial visit to Kay in the hospital with her ruined face. Her parents were distraught. Not only did the regular trips to the hospital regulate how they could structure their lives over the next few years, but their worry over whether she would ever be able to live a normal life again because of her ugliness was devastating. Kay, now thirty-nine, reflects that her mother (whose name is Gloria) still maintains that Kay's accident was the worst thing that ever happened to her (meaning Gloria). Gloria stresses how it ruined her own life. Kay, of course, thinks this is absurd because it was Kay's, not Gloria's, accident.

Boundaries and Subsystems

Two other systems theory concepts are exceptionally helpful when applied to family systems. They are *boundaries* and *subsystems*. Boundaries are "invisible barriers which surround individuals and subsystems, regulating the amount of contact with others" (Nichols, 1984, p. 474). In a family system, boundaries determine who are members of that particular family system and who are not. Parents and children are within the boundaries of the family system. Close friends of the family are not.

A subsystem is a secondary or subordinate system—a system within a system. The most obvious examples of this are the parental and sibling subsystems. Other more subtle subsystems may also exist depending on the boundaries established within the family system. A mother might form a subsystem with a daughter she feels exceptionally close to. Two siblings among four might form another subsystem be-

┌ **HIGHLIGHT 9.2** ─────────────────────────────────

Family Norms Vary Drastically from One Family to Another

Every family differs in its individual set of norms or rules. For example, Family A has a relatively conservative set of norms governing communication and interpersonal behavior. Although the norms allow frequent pleasant talk among family members, it is generally on a superficial level. The steamingly hot summer weather or the status of the new variety of worms invading the cherry tree is fair game for conversation. However, nothing more personal is ever mentioned. Taboo subjects include anything to do with feelings, interpersonal relationships, or opinions about career or jobs, let alone politics or moral issues. On one occasion, for example, a daughter-in-law asked the family matriarch what her son and other daughter-in-law would name their soon-to-be-born first baby. With a shocked expression on her face, the matriarch replied, "Oh, my heavens, I haven't asked. I don't want to interfere."

Family B, on the other hand, has a vastly dif-

ferent set of norms governing communication and behavior. Virtually everything is discussed and debated, not only among the nuclear family members but among several generations. Personal methods of birth control, stances on abortion, opinions on capital punishment, and politics number among the emotionally heated issues discussed. Family members frequently talk about their personal relationships, including who is the favorite grandchild and who tends to fight all the time with rich old Aunt Harriet. The family is so open that price tags are left on Christmas gifts so each member knows what the other has spent.

The rules of behavior that govern Family B are very different from those of Family A. Yet in each family, all the members consider their family's behavior to be normal and are comfortable with these rules. Members of each family may find it inconceivable that families could be any other way.

───

cause of their exceptionally close and unique relationship.

Boundaries delineate subsystems within a family system. For instance, boundaries separate the spouse subsystem within a family from the sibling subsystem. Each subsystem has its own specified membership. Either a family member is within the boundaries of the subsystem or he is not.

Boundaries between appropriate subsystems in families need to be maintained. For example, parents need to nurture and maintain their own subsystem as a marital couple. In an incestuous family, the marital subsystem boundaries may become blurred. The husband/father may form an intimate subsystem with one or more of his daughters. A family treatment perspective in this case might involve clarifying and strengthening the boundaries of the marital subsystem. Boundaries also need to be

clearly delineated between the parental system and the children's subsystem.

Family Norms

Family norms involve the rules which specify what is considered proper behavior within the family group. Janzen and Harris (1980) define family rules as "relationship agreements which influence family behavior" (p. 24). Many times the most powerful rules are those that are not clearly and verbally stated. Rather, these are implicit rules or repeated family transactions which all family members understand but never discuss. It's important for families to establish norms that allow both the entire family and each individual member to function effectively and productively.

In families with problems, however, the family rules usually do not allow the family or the individual members to function effectively and productively. Ineffective norms need to be identified and changed. Positive, beneficial norms need to be developed and fostered.

The following is an example of a family in which there was an implicit, invalid, and ineffective norm functioning. The norm was that no one in the family would smoke cigarettes. A husband, wife, four children, and two sets of grandparents composed this family. Although never discussed, the understanding was that no one had ever or would ever smoke. One day the husband found several cigarette butts in the ashtray of the car typically used by his wife. Because no one in the family smoked, he deduced that these butts must belong to someone else. He assumed that his wife was having an affair with another man, which devastated him. However, he said nothing about it and suffered in silence. His relationship with his wife began to deteriorate. He became sullen, and spats and conflicts became more frequent. Finally, in a heated conflict, he spit out his thoughts and feelings about the cigarette butts and her alleged affair. His wife expressed shocked disbelief. The reality was that it was she who smoked the cigarettes, but only when no one else was around. Her major time to be alone was when she was driving to and from work. She took advantage of this time to smoke, but occasionally forgot to empty the ashtray. She told him the entire story, and he was tremendously relieved. Their relationship improved and prospered.

This example illustrates how an inappropriate norm almost ruined a family relationship. Of course, there were other dynamics going on between the spouses involved. Relationships are complicated entities. However, such a simple thing as the wife being a "closet smoker" had the potential to tip the balance and destroy the marriage. In this instance, a simple correction in communication solved the problem. The interesting thing is that eventually the entire family learned of this incident. The wife still smokes but still insists on doing it privately. The family now functions effectively with an amended family rule that accepts her secret smoking.

Social workers need to identify and understand family norms so that inappropriate, ineffective norms can be changed. At any point, a social worker can point out such an ineffective norm to family members, help them clarify alternative solutions and changes, and assist them in determining which solution is best to pursue.

Family Roles

A role is "a socially expected behavior pattern usually determined by an individual's status" (*Webster's Ninth New Collegiate Dictionary*, 1991, p. 1021). In families these roles usually involve behaviors that work for the benefit of the family. For instance, the parental role prescribes behaviors helpful in supporting, directing, and raising children. Likewise, parents might assume worker roles to earn financial sustenance for the family by being employed outside of the home. Children, on the other hand, might assume the roles of "student" in school and "helper" in household tasks (Holman, 1983, p. 29).

In addition to these more formal socially acceptable roles, family members may hold a variety of more informal roles, often related to individual personalities and interactional patterns among family members. For instance, such roles may include troublemaker, the oppressed one, the illustrious star, the one to blame for everything (scapegoat), Mr./Ms. Perfection, the old battle ax, or the family's black sheep.

There is a broad range of roles that can be assumed in families. One family comes to mind that has a "white sheep" within its flock. The nuclear family consists of two parents and three children, two females and one male, the latter of whom is also the youngest. At this point, all family members are adults. It's not that the family is "bad," really. However, all members except for the youngest male like to drink, party, and do their share of swearing. None are involved in any organized religion. The youngest male, on the other hand, is a fundamentalist pastor. Hence, he has become the "white sheep" of the family.

Because each person and each family is unique, there is no ideal formula for what roles are best. Each family must be evaluated on how its unique configuration of roles functions to the family's advantage or disadvantage on the whole.

Holman (1983) stresses that "the worker must examine how roles are performed and whether or not they meet the needs of the family" (p. 30); he proposes a series of questions to explore:

What specific roles does each family member occupy?

Do the various roles played work well together for the family's benefit?

Are any of the roles ambiguous, redundant, or left empty?

Is there flexibility among family roles so that the family is better able to adjust to crisis situations?

Do the family's roles conform with basic social norms? (For example, society does not condone a criminal role.)

Do the family's roles function to enhance the family's feelings of self worth and well-being or detract from these feelings?

Chapter 7 explained the roles and norms commonly portrayed in families with alcoholics. These included the chemically dependent person, the chief enabler, the mascot, the family hero, and the lost child. Families of alcoholics are dysfunctional in that massive amounts of energy are wasted in trying to survive with a drug abusing person in the family's midst.

Balance of Power within the Family System

Power is "the capacity of one [family] member to induce change in the behavior of another family member" (Hepworth & Larsen, 1990, p. 273). Power is a vague concept which is difficult to specify clearly. Power is usually related to holding a higher rank, having more prestige, being more respected, and having greater access to and control over resources than others in the system, in this case, the family system.

Power is relative. That is, one individual has more or less power than other individuals. Power is irrelevant to one individual shipwrecked alone on a desert island.

Power is complex and difficult to quantify. Families have "multiple power structures" (Hepworth & Larsen, 1990, p. 273). That is, different family members have more or less power over different matters. For instance, one parent who manages the checkbook and pays all the bills may have more influence over finances than the other parent. On the other hand, the other parent may have more control over family activities, such as what the family does from weekend to weekend. Influence varies depending on the issue.

Children, too, have power to various degrees. They can exert control over the behavior of parents and siblings. Take a five-year-old boy who throws himself on the floor screaming whenever his single-parent mother takes him along to a supermarket. The child has power to the extent that he can force his mother either to leave the place or at least cut her shopping short.

For another example, Christine and Morgan, a married couple. Christine is very outgoing, assertive, and independent, while Morgan, on the other hand, is generally quiet, introspective, and not very socially oriented. Christine will make virtually all of their social plans with little or no input from Morgan. Although Morgan goes along with most of Christine's ideas, he has definite veto power. If he does not want to participate in a social activity, he simply says so. The activity is then either not planned at all or postponed. Hence, there is a balance of power in their relationship, at least concerning this particular issue.

Christine and Morgan also illustrate how power relationships are often hidden or concealed. External appearances don't always accurately represent the reality of the balance of power. Although Christine outwardly appears to lead social activities in the relationship, she does so only with Morgan's consent.

In assessing a family, the important question is whether the balance of power as perceived by each individual is adequate and fair. Situations where family members resent the balance of power may be ripe for problem-solving intervention. Take, for instance, an adolescent who feels hopelessly repressed and unable to express openly any opinions of his or her own. Or, consider one spouse who feels totally impotent and oppressed by the other spouse. Finally, consider a parent, either married or single, who feels she or he has no control over the children's behavior. Each of these families needs help.

Assessing Intergenerational Aspects of Family Systems

Another important aspect of family structure is historical. What is the family's history? Under what conditions were the parents or the single parent in a family brought up? How did the parents' and the grandparents' early environments affect each generation's behavior and way of life? Has there been a history of alcoholism in the family? Or, has corporal punishment to the point of child abuse been considered a family norm?

Assessing Life-Cycle Adjustments

In addition to family communication and structure, assessing life cycle adjustments can give clear insights into a family's problems. As families mature and progress through time, they must successfully complete tasks appropriate to that stage of their development. Problems surface when these tasks can't be completed.

Several decades ago, the family life cycle and the types of experiences family members had during specified phases of the cycle were much more predictable than today. This is no longer the case. There is no "typical" cycle. Carter and McGoldrick (1989) recognize some of the difficulties in describing a *normal* family life cycle:

> An ever increasing percent of the population are living together without marrying (3% of couples at any one point in time), and a rapidly increasing number are having children without marrying. At present 6% or more of the population is homosexual. Present estimates are that 12% of young women will never marry, three times the percent for their parents' generation; 25% will never have children; 50% will end their marriages in divorce and 20% will have two divorces (p. 12).

Women's roles have drastically changed in terms of family roles. Most women work outside the home. Many women have total responsibility for both outside income and inside care of the home. Due partly to awesome technological advances, people are living significantly longer than they did in the past. In stark contrast to past decades, having children need no longer be the central focus of one's marriage or of one's life. All these variables make life within families much different than ever before.

The traditional family life cycle was conceptualized as having six major phases (Carter & McGoldrick, 1980). Each phase focused on some emotional transition in terms of intimate relationships with other people and on changes of personal status.

Traditionally, the first stage involved an unattached young adult separating from his or her family of origin. During this phase, the young adult established a personal identity and developed new interpersonal relationships. Stage 2 concerned marrying and realigning life's joys and responsibilities within a couple's framework. Stage 3 entailed having children and meeting these children's needs. Stage 4 concerned dealing with adolescent children, whose needs and strivings for independence called for very different types of interaction than that appropriate for very young children. Stage 4 also often marked refocusing the couple's relationship and addressing the needs of their own aging parents. Stage 5 involved sending children forth into their own new relationships, addressing mid-life career issues, and coping with the growing disabilities of their own parents. Finally, stage 6 entailed adjustments to aging themselves and addressing the inevitability of one's own death.

Carter and McGoldrick (1989) propose an alternative to the traditional family life cycle. This new approach employs the flexibility necessary for application to a wide variety of family variations. They recognize that the traditional phases of the cycle should not be forgotten. These phases do focus on some of life's major potential transitions. However, included in the family life cycle are a number of other major transitions which are becoming increasingly more common and relevant. These transitions include divorce and remarriage, poverty, and cultural diversity.

Carter and McGoldrick (1989) emphasize how "peaks of emotional tension" involved in divorce and remarriage can lead to additional transitions within the cycle (p. 21). A number of these additional transitions can induce serious stress and merit attention. These "peaks" most likely involve the following times (Carter & McGoldrick, 1989):

1. Making the determination that separation or divorce is inevitable;
2. Telling family, friends, and others about the separation or divorce;

3. Addressing issues such as financial distribution and child custody;
4. Going through the actual process of leaving each other;
5. Participating in the legal divorce process;
6. Addressing significant issues such as "money or children," especially when the interaction involved is uncomfortable or aversive (p. 21);
7. Participating in subsequent events which involve their mutual children, such as graduations, marriages, sicknesses, births, or funerals;
8. Accepting critical points in the life of the ex-spouse, such as remarriage, illness, or death.

In addition to divorce and remarriage, poverty also impacts the life cycle of many families. For instance, a family unable to pay the rent may become suddenly homeless. Such an incident can mark an obvious transition in a family's life. Yet another variable affecting life's transitions involves cultural values and variations. For example, the extent to which an unmarried teen's pregnancy is accepted or condemned by family members might vary according to ethnic or cultural expectations.

Any of these additional pressure points can add a number of "stages" to a particular family's life cycle. Why is it important to be prudently aware of such individualized transitions? Generalist practitioners are often called upon to help families when they are under their greatest stress. Being alert to the broad range of life's transitions and sensitive to families' needs as they progress through these phases can provide workers with significant clues for effective interventions.

Impacts of the Impinging Social Environment

The social environment involves the conditions, circumstances, and human interactions that encompass human beings. A family-in-environment focus provides an important perspective for understanding how families interact with the many other systems surrounding them in the social environment. These systems may include other individuals, families, friends, work groups, social service organizations, political units, religious organizations, and educational systems. All affect how family systems and individual subsystems within the family can effectively go about their daily operations and daily lives. The other point to remember is that what happens to any individual family member ultimately affects the entire family system (Thorman, 1982). Thus, macro systems impact entire families by affecting individual members.

The following is an example of how macro systems influence family systems. The family consists of two parents and three children aged nine, thirteen, and sixteen. Both parents work in a small sausage processing plant in a rural community of about twelve thousand people. Due to deteriorating external economic conditions, the plant is forced to close. Both parents are laid off. Although the parents desperately seek alternative employment, none is available. Unemployment in the community skyrockets. Competition for jobs is intense.

The family's involvement with the many other systems in the environment continues. The family's lack of resources stresses their ability to pay the bills. They get pressure from their landlord and the utility companies. Under such heavy stress, the parents begin to fight. Their children subsequently react to the stress, their parents' fighting, and their newly imposed poverty by starting to rebel. Their work in school suffers and truancy becomes an increasing problem. The school then contacts the parents about these escalating problems, which, in turn, add to the parents' stress. The parents' coping abilities are gradually eaten away.

This is just one of the multitude of examples which portray how family systems are integrally involved with the other systems in their environment. Families aren't isolated units. Each member of a family system must constantly respond to surrounding environmental conditions.

Assessing a Family's Access to Resources

The above example reflects the serious impacts macro systems can have on families. Often, this involves the family's access to adequate resources. Limited resources can have a wide range of serious effects on a family's ability to function. Therefore, generalist practitioners must be acutely aware of any family's resource status.

There are numerous ways of examining how readily a particular family can obtain necessary, available resources. Vosler (1990) has developed the Family Access to Basic Resources (FABR) format illustrated in Figure 9.1, which provides an excellent means of accomplishing this. She explains:

> The . . . FABR assessment tool can enable professionals, families, and individual family members to determine the extent of stress and stress pileup caused by inadequate or unstable basic family resources. . . . The FABR outlines assessment areas for exploration with the family so that both the social worker and the family can begin to understand potential sources of chronic stress from the larger social environment (p. 435).

When using FABR, it's best for the social worker to complete Parts 1 ("monthly expenses for a family of this size and composition") and 2 ("potential monthly family resources) of the instrument before meeting with the family. See Figure 9.1. This can provide the worker with some insights concerning a family's economic status before beginning work with the family.

Part 1 allows for a general estimation of what an average family (of the client family's size and composition) needs every month to

Figure 9.1: Family Access to Basic Resources (FABR)

```
┌─────────────────────────────────────────────────────────────────────────┐
│ PART 1--Monthly Expenses for a Family of This Size and Composition        │
│                                                                           │
│ Work Expenses                    Health Care                              │
│   Transportation:      $_____      Medical:                    $_____     │
│   Child Care:          $_____      Dental:                      $_____     │
│   Taxes:               $_____      Mental Health:               $_____     │
│ Purchases for Basic Needs          Special (e.g., Substance Abuse) $_____  │
│   Decent Housing:      $_____      Education:                   $_____     │
│   Utilities:           $_____      Family and Developmental               │
│   Food:                $_____        (Counseling) Services:     $_____     │
│   Clothing:            $_____      Procurement of Resources/               │
│   Personal Care:       $_____        Services (e.g., transportation       │
│   Recreation:          $_____        Transportation):          $_____     │
│                                                                           │
│                                    Monthly Total                $_____     │
│                                                                           │
│                                                                           │
│ PART 2--Potential Monthly Family Resources                                │
│                                                                           │
│ Money Income                                                              │
│   Wages (If parents' occupa-                               YES  NO        │
│     tions are known, what are    Clothing: Access to Used                 │
│     average monthly wages for       Clothing Store?:       ___  ___       │
│     these types of jobs?):  $_____ Personal Care and Recreation           │
│   Child Support (if applicable) $_____ Access to Free Recreational        │
│   Income Transfers (for those       Facilities:            ___  ___       │
│     unemployed or not expected   Health Care                              │
│     to work)                $_____   Medicare?:            ___  ___       │
│   Unemployment Insurance:   $_____   Medicaid?:            ___  ___       │
│   Workmen's Compensation:   $_____   Health Clinic?:       ___  ___       │
│   Social Security:          $_____   Dental Clinic?:       ___  ___       │
│   Supplemental Security              Mental Health Services?: ___  ___     │
│     Income (SSI):           $_____   Special Services (e.g.,              │
│   Aid to Families with Depen-          Drug Abuse Treatment)?: ___ ___     │
│     dent Children (AFDC):   $_____ Education                              │
│   Other (e.g., general relief,      Public Education?:     ___  ___       │
│     emergency assistance):  $_____   Special Education?:    ___  ___       │
│ Credits, Goods, and Services         Tutoring?:            ___  ___       │
│     (free or sliding scale)          General Equivalency Diploma          │
│   Housing                              (GED)?:             ___  ___       │
│     Section 8:              $_____    Job Training?:        ___  ___       │
│     Other Housing Assistance     Family and Developmental                 │
│       (e.g., public housing,        (Counseling) Services                 │
│       shelter, hotel/motel): $_____  Family Services?:     ___  ___       │
│     Utilities Assistance:    $_____  Support Groups?:      ___  ___       │
│   Food                               Family Life Education?: ___  ___      │
│     Food Stamps:            $_____ Procurement                            │
│     Women's, Infants', and Child-   Transportation?:       ___  ___       │
│       ren's Supplementary Food                                            │
│       Program (WIC):        $_____                                        │
│     Food Bank, Food Pantry, and                                          │
│       Other Food Assistance: $_____                                       │
│                                                                           │
│ Monthly Total:              $_____                                        │
└─────────────────────────────────────────────────────────────────────────┘
```

Figure 9.1 (*continued*)

PART 3--Current Resources

A. Access to Resources Last Month

Money Income		Credits, Goods, and Services	
Wages (use net pay; then sub- tract other work expenses from Part 1 above, includ- ing child care, trans- portation, etc.):	$____	Housing: Food: Clothing: Personal Care and Recreation: Health Care:	$____ $____ $____ $____ $____
Child Support:	$____	Education:	$____
Income Transfers:	$____	Family and Developmental Services: Procurement:	$____ $____
		Monthly Total:	$____

B. Resource Stability

How stable was each resource over the past year (very stable, somewhat stable, somewhat unstable, very unstable)? Discuss for each type of resource.

Wages: Overall access to wages through employment? Types of jobs available? Part-time or full-time? Wage levels? Benefits? How would/do you deal with child care or supervision of youth? Quality of child care? Do you have choices? How would/do you deal with an ill child? How would/do you get to and from work? What education and training are needed for good jobs? What education and training opportunities are available? Have you been laid off or terminated or experienced a plant closing? Number of times unemployed? Length of time unemployed?

Child Support: How is this received? How was the amount decided? Are checks regular? Are payments up to date? Other problems?

Income Transfers: What experiences have you had in receiving benefits? What kinds of attitudes have you encountered? How adequate are benefits relative to your family's expenses? Has a check been cut? Has a check been delayed? Have you been dropped from benefits for reasons you didn't understand?

Housing: Rent or own? Choice. Maintenance a problem? Are utilities adequate? Have you been put on a waiting list or been dropped from Section 8 or other housing assistance? Have you had to move or been evicted because the landlord coverted to higher rents, condominiums, etc.? Have you experienced homelessness?

Food: Quality? Variety? Have your Food Stamps or WIC been cut or delayed? If so, do you understand why? Has other food assistance been cut or changed?

Clothing: Variety for different roles?

Figure 9.1 (*continued*)

Personal Care and Recreation: What kinds of recreation? Individual? Family?

Health Care: High quality? Choice? Available in a crisis? Have you been dropped from health care coverage with an employer or from Medicaid? If so, why? Have you or another family member been put on a waiting list, for example, for medical or dental care, for counseling for a mental health problem, or for treatment for alcohol or drug abuse? If so, how long did the person have to wait for services?

Education: High quality? Available for all ages? For special needs? Choice? Have you participated in education or training paid for with loans? If so, how are you managing loan repayments?

Family and Developmental Services: High quality? Choice? Available in a crisis? Have you or another family member been put on a waiting list, for example, for family counseling? If so, how long did the person have to wait for services?

Procurement: Bus? Car? What's within walking distance? How reliable is transportation (e.g., bus and/or car)? How close are bus lines to home, work, child care, shopping, etc.?

Other Comments and Reflections:

function effectively. Such information can be obtained from a variety of sources. Public agencies may have these figures available as a result of their regular data-collection procedures. Sometimes, census data is helpful. If information is not readily available, "agencies or a local advocacy group could be called upon to develop estimates based on adequate resources needed for a *long-term decent standard of living* for various household sizes and family configurations" (Vosler, 1990, p. 438).

It should be emphasized that the *poverty line* established by the U.S. government probably is significantly lower than what a family actually needs to thrive. The poverty line is "a measure of the amount of money a government or a society believes is necessary for a person to live at a *minimum* level of subsistence . . ." (Barker, 1991, p. 177).

Part 2 of FABR focuses on what resources macro systems in the client family's social environment can potentially provide. What resources are actually available to this family to help them reach the input level they need? What types of local, state, and national assistance can the family potentially use?

Part 3 ("Current Resources") of FABR can be completed by the family itself during one of the worker's early meetings with the family. This portion identifies what resources the family actually has. Part 3 is divided into the family's "access to resources last month" and its "resource stability." The section on resource stability helps establish whether the resources obtained last month were abnormally high or low, or whether the last month's input reflects that which is typical for the family.

A family's actual access to resources, then, can be calculated by taking the family's total "access to resources last month" (Part 3A) and subtracting that from the total "monthly expenses for a [typical] family of this size and composition" (Part 1). The remaining amount refers to what the family needs to function, but is not getting. Subsequently, Parts 2 and 3B help the

worker identify specific problems in the family's access to resources.

Part 2 supplies clues for what resources the family is not getting, but potentially could be. What services has the family not been aware of or taken advantage of in the past? How could the worker act as broker to link family members with the services they need?

Part 3B alerts the worker to problems in ongoing acquisition of resources. For instance, one question asks, "Have your Food Stamps[1] or WIC[2] been cut or delayed?" (p. 437). Such questions can help the worker begin identifying problems in service delivery and exploring potential intervention approaches for positive change. What obstacles exist in impinging macro-systems which prevent the family from getting needed resources? What macro systems are potential targets of change?

On one level, FABR indicates what the family needs in order to function adequately. It provides cues for how the worker should proceed. The worker can target where resources are lacking or not being used, and establish plans to enhance the family's access to them.

On another level FABR indicates what resources impinging macro systems are failing to provide. By emphasizing the importance of the family's access to resources, it highlights the significance of the family's interactions with multiple macro systems. FABR thus establishes links among micro, mezzo, and macro levels of practice. FABR can provide documentation regarding where resources are lacking and changes are

---

1. "The Food Stamp program, which was created to supplement the food-buying power of low-income people, is the nation's response to its hunger problem. Monthly benefits in the form of coupons used to purchase food are entirely federally financed. . . . Eligibility for the program is restricted to households that meet income, resource, and work requirements prescribed by law" (Wells, 1987, p. 628).

2. WIC is the Special Supplementary Feeding Program for Women, Infants and Children administered under the Department of Agriculture. The intent is to provide low-income women and their children at risk of insufficient nutrition with food subsidies.

needed in macro systems. When families have poor or no access to basic resources, interventions may need to involve "social planning, advocacy, and lobbying within larger social systems, including work at neighborhood, local, state, and national levels" (Vosler, 1990, p. 438).

Family Conflicts, Problems, and Their Resolution

Conflict can be defined as "a struggle over . . . resources, power and status, beliefs, and other preferences and desires" (Bisno, 1988, p. 13). Hostility, strife, disharmony, arguments, or disunity all can be involved. Conflicts are destined to occur in any group. As a matter of fact, many times conflicts are positive and desirable. Groups, including family groups, are made up of unique individuals, each with individual opinions and ideas. Conflict can represent the open sharing of these individual ideas. It can serve as a mechanism for improving communication, enhancing the closeness of relationships, and working out dissatisfactions.

Thorman (1982) points out that although each family is unique, conflicts and problems within families tend to be clustered in four major categories (Thorman, 1982). First, there are marital problems between the husband and wife. Second, there are difficulties existing between parents and children. Third are the personal problems of individual family members. Finally, there are stresses imposed on the family by the external environment.

Family problems do not necessarily fall neatly into one of these categories or the other. Frequently, families experience more than one category of problems. Nor are these problem categories mutually exclusive. Many times one problem will be closely related to another. Take, for instance, the wife and mother of a family who is a legal librarian and the primary breadwinner for her family. The law firm at which she has worked for the past eleven years suddenly decides to hire a lawyer to replace her. Despite massive efforts, she had not been able to find another job with similar responsibilities and salary. This can be considered a family problem caused by stresses in the environment. However, this is also a personal problem for the wife and mother. Her sense of self worth is seriously diminished as a result of her job loss and inability to find another position. As a result, she becomes cranky, short-tempered, and difficult to live with. The environmental stress she is experiencing causes her to have difficulties relating to both children and spouse. The entire family system becomes disturbed.

We will now examine each of the four problem categories. They include marital difficulties, parent-child relationships, personal problems of individuals, and external environmental stresses. Some intervention directions will be proposed.

Marital Difficulties

The Family Service Association of America conducted a national survey of troubled couples to determine the major causes of conflict in marital relationships (Beck, 1973). Communication difficulties surfaced as the primary complaint. Other major sources of conflict included disagreements over children, sexual problems, conflicts over recreational time and money, and unfaithfulness. This study provides some clues concerning the content areas practitioners need to address when assessing the marital couple's relationship within the family.

One frequent purpose in interventions involving couples and larger families is to enhance the congruence between intents and impacts as individuals communicate. A practitioner can help each spouse communicate more effectively by giving suggestions about how to rephrase statements using words which reflect more clearly what the speakers really mean. Another suggestion is to encourage feedback, that is, to

HIGHLIGHT 9.3
An Example of Communication Problems within a Marriage

Bill and Linda, both in their midthirties, have a communication problem. They have been married one year. The marriage occurred after a lengthy dating period that was filled with strife. A primary source of stress was Linda's desire for the permanent commitment of marriage and Bill's unwillingness to make such a commitment. In view of Linda's threats to leave him, Bill finally decided to get married.

Prior to the marriage, a major source of difficulty concerned the time that Bill and Linda spent together. They each owned their own condominiums, so they did not live together. Bill was very involved in a physical-fitness program. He went to work out at a health club four nights each week, including Fridays. Bill also had numerous close friends at the club with whom he enjoyed spending his time. Linda was infuriated that Bill restricted the time he spent with her to only some of the days when he didn't work out at the club. Her major concern, however, remained Bill's inability to make a commitment. Linda felt that things would change once they got married.

After marriage, things did not change very much. Although Linda and Bill now lived together, he still worked out at the club with his friends four nights a week. This continued to infuriate Linda.

In a discussion, each spouse expressed their feelings. Linda said, "I hate all the time Bill spends at the club. I resent having him designate the time he thinks he can spend with me. I feel like he's putting my time into little boxes."

Bill responded, "My physical health is very important to me. I love to work out at the club. What should I do—stay home every night watching television and become a couch potato?"

One way of assessing this couple's communication is evaluating the *intent* (what the speaker wants to have communicated to the receiver) and the actual *impact* of the communication, that is, what the listener actually hears (Gottman et al., 1976). Many times the intent and impact of communication are very different. A therapeutic goal is to improve the accuracy of communication, that is, the extent to which the intent of the speaker and the impact upon the listener resemble each other.

There were other difficulties within Bill and Linda's relationship, which are too lengthy to describe. Here we will limit our discussion to some of the issues involved in the simple communication addressed above. In a recent discussion, the following scenario develops. Linda verbally states that she hates seeing Bill go to the health club so often. The impact on Bill is that he feels Linda is trying to control him and tell him what to do. He loves Linda, but is also very wary of losing his independence and what he views as his identity. When Linda places demands on him, he becomes even more protective of his time.

Linda's intent in her communication is very different than her impact; she feels he thinks the club and his friends are more important than she is. This is related to her basic lack of self-esteem and self-confidence.

Bill's response to Linda's statement also has serious discrepancies between its intent and impact. Bill is verbally stating that he loves to work out. The impact on Linda, that is, what she is hearing Bill say, is that he likes the club and his friends more than he likes her. Bill's actual intent is to tell Linda his physical health and appearance are very important to him. He also wants to communicate to her that his sense of independence is important to him. He loves her and wants to be committed to her, yet his long-term fear of commitment is related to his actual fear that he will lose his identity in someone else's. He's afraid of losing his right to make choices and decisions. He fears being told what to do.

pursue "what happens when the listener tells the speaker about the impact a message had" (Gottman et al., 1976, p. 2). For instance, refer back to Highlight 9.3. Instead of responding to Linda's demands defensively, Bill might be encouraged to tell her, "I love you very much, Linda. I need to keep in shape and I need some time to myself. How can we work this out?"

Eventually, Bill and Linda used a problem-solving approach to iron out their difficulties. The accuracy of their communication gradually improved through counseling. Each learned how better to communicate personal needs. Instead of their old standoff, they began to identify and evaluate alternatives. Their final solution involved several facets. First, Bill would continue to go to the club to work out three nights each week. However, Fridays would be spent with Linda. It turned out that she was exceptionally annoyed at not being able to go out with Bill on Friday nights. Linda, who also was an avid believer in physical fitness, would occasionally go with Bill to the health club to work out. This gave her the sense of freedom to join him when she chose to. The important thing was that she no longer felt restricted. In reality, she rarely went with him to the club. Linda also chose to take some postgraduate courses in her field on those evenings when Bill visited the club. She enjoyed such activities and they enhanced her sense of professional competence. The personal issues of Bill's need to feel free and Linda's lack of self-esteem demanded continued efforts on both spouses' parts. Enhanced communication skills helped them communicate their ongoing needs.

Parent-Child Relationship Difficulties

The second major type of family problems involves difficulties in the relationships between parents and children. Sometimes this entails the parents having trouble controlling children. Frequently, especially as children reach adolescence, this involves communication problems.

There are many perspectives on how best to manage children's behavior and improve parent-child communication. Two major approaches include applications of learning theory and Parent Effectiveness Training (PET) developed by Thomas Gordon (1970).

Practitioners can help parents improve their control of children by assessing the individual family situations and teaching parents some basic behavior modification techniques. Behavior modification involves the application of learning theory principles to real-life situations. For instance, it's easy for parents to get into a punishment rut with a misbehaving child. Take Freddie, age four, who spills the contents of drawers and cabinets in the kitchen area whenever he is unobserved. His parents have seen enough flour, honey, silverware, and plastic bags in heaps on the floor to last them several lifetimes. In their frustration, they typically respond by swatting Freddie on the rump. He then cries a little bit until the next time he has the opportunity to be in the kitchen alone and start all over again.

In family counseling Freddie's parents were taught several new behavior-management techniques (that is, behavior modification techniques applied to specific child-management situations). First, they were taught the value of positive reinforcement. These are positive experiences or consequences which follow a behavior and increase the likelihood that it will reoccur. Instead of relying solely on punishment (that is, rump swatting), the parents were taught to react more positively to Freddie during those times when he was behaving well (that is, playing appropriately and not emptying drawers). By closely examining Freddie's behaviors and the circumstances surrounding him, his parents gradually learned to view Freddie in a different way. They learned that he felt he was not getting enough attention in general. In order to get the attention he needed, he resorted to the destructive drawer-emptying behavior. Providing Freddie with structured positive playing times when they gave Freddie their sole attention was much more effective. This, in addition to making positive comments about his good behavior, helped to diminish Freddie's need for getting attention in inappropriate ways. Freddie's parents also learned that their punishment was having the opposite effect of what they had intended. That is, instead of stopping his bad behavior, they were unwittingly encouraging it. Punishing Freddie was actually a form of positive reinforcement because it gave him the attention he wanted. Thus, he continued his drawer-emptying behavior.

As an alternative to punishment, Freddie's parents were taught the time-out technique. Time-out involves a procedure where reinforcement is withdrawn resulting in a decrease in the occurrence of the behavior. Instead of swatting Freddie when he emptied drawers, his parents were directed to place him in a corner with his eyes to the wall for five minutes. A few minutes should be the maximum duration of a time-out, as it loses its effectiveness after a very short length of time. (Kazdin, 1989; White, Nielsen, & Johnson, 1972). It was also important to administer the time-out to Freddie immediately after his inappropriate behavior occurred. This was necessary for him to relate the time-out directly to his misbehavior. Time-outs provided Freddie's parents with a method to deprive Freddie of attention without hurting him. Since attention was what Freddie really wanted, this became a very effective behavioral control technique. It should be emphasized, however, that Freddie needed continued attention and positive reinforcement for appropriate behavior. He would not have misbehaved in the first place had he not been trying to let his parents know about an important need, namely, his desire for attention.

Parent Effectiveness Training is a second method frequently used when parent-child relationship problems occur. Two principles involved in this approach include active listening and the sending of "I-messages" (Gordon, 1975). Active listening resembles the intent-impact communication approach described earlier when discussing couples' communication. It involves two basic steps. First, the receiver of the message tries earnestly to understand the sender's feelings and messages. Another way of saying this is the receiver tries to understand the actual intent of the sender. In the second step, the receiver puts this "understanding into [his/her] own words . . . and feeds it back for the sender's verification" (Gordon, 1975, p. 53).

For instance, thirteen-year-old Tyrone says to his mother, "Dances are boring. I'm not going to that boring old dance on Friday."

His mother works hard at active listening and tries to see the situation from Tyrone's perspective. She replies, "You mean you'd really like to go but you don't think you can dance very well."

Tyrone responds, "Yep." His mother had accurately heard his real concerns.

A second technique involved in Parent Effectiveness Training is the use of "I-messages." Such messages do not blame or threaten but rather tell the receiver how his or her behavior is affecting the sender. They leave responsibility for changing the behavior squarely on the receiver. I-messages should be used to convey both positive and negative feelings, and allow the receiver to get to know the sender.

For instance, a mother is trying to teach her sixteen-year-old daughter how to drive. The daughter gets on the freeway for the first time and pushes the gas peddle to the floor. The speedometer zooms up to eighty-five miles per hour. The mother could choose to say, "You're driving way too fast! Do you want to kill us both?" This is a very blaming, threatening statement. Instead, she chooses to say, "I'm really scared driving so fast." In other words, the mother takes responsibility for her own feelings without placing blame on the receiver of her statement.

Personal Problems of Individual Family Members

Sometimes a family will come to a practitioner for help and identify one family member as being the problem. A basic principle of family therapy is that the entire family owns the problem (Thorman, 1982, p. 87). In other words, sometimes one family member becomes the scapegoat for malfunctioning within the entire family system. The practitioner is then responsible for helping the family define the problem as a family group rather than an individual problem. Treatment goals will then most likely involve the restructuring of various family relationships.

For instance, a family of five came in for treatment. The family consisted of a forty-eight-year-old husband and father, a forty-five-year-old wife and mother, and three children: Bob, age nineteen, Ralph, age sixteen, and Rosie, age twelve. The family came from a rural Wisconsin town of eight thousand people. The father was a successful businessman who was involved in town politics. The mother was a homemaker who did not work outside of the home. Bob was a freshman at the University of Wisconsin at Madison. The identified problem was Ralph. For the past year, Ralph had been stealing neighbors' cars whenever he had the chance and running down people's mailboxes. To say the least, this became annoying to the local townspeople. The family came to counseling as their last resort to try controlling the problem.

After several sessions of family members pointing blaming fingers at Ralph, Rosie quietly commented to her parents, "Well, you never say anything about *his* problem," and proceeded to point at Bob. Suddenly, as if a floodgate had been opened, the entire family situation came pouring out. Rosie had been referring to her parents' difficulties in accepting Bob's recent announcement that he was gay. Bob was going through a difficult period as he was "coming out," in terms of making lifestyle decisions and relating to old friends and family members. Father was terrified that the local townspeople, who had extremely negative and irrational fears of homosexual people, would find out. This attitude is referred to as homophobia. Father feared that he would lose precious social status and that it would damage his political career. Mother turned out to be a serious alcoholic, a secret that the entire family had worked hard to keep. Mother and Father had not had a sexual relationship for ten years; they slept in separate bedrooms. Father was a harsh, stern man who felt it necessary to maintain what he considered absolute control over family members, including Mother. He was very critical of them all and never risked sharing his own feelings. Finally, Rosie was having serious problems both with her grades and attendance in school. She was also sexually active with a variety of young men. Both she and her parents lived in constant fear of her potential pregnancy.

As it turned out, Ralph was one of the better adjusted individuals in the family. He attended school regularly, got straight B's, and was active in high school sports (before being suspended for his delinquent behavior). This family provides a good illustration of a family-owned problem. The entire family system was showing disturbances. Ralph was the scapegoat, the identified problem. All Ralph was doing was calling attention to the family's many more global problems.

External Environmental Stresses: The Impact of Social and Economic Forces

The fourth category of problems frequently found in families are those caused by factors outside of the family in the external environment. These problems can include inadequate income, unemployment, poor housing conditions, poor access to means of transportation and places for recreation, and inadequate job opportunities (Beck, 1973, p. 91). Included in the multitude of other potential problems are poor health conditions, inadequate schools, and dangerous neighborhoods.

To begin addressing these problems, practitioners need sharp brokering skills. That is, they need to know what services are available and how to make a connection with families in need of these services.

Many times appropriate services will be unavailable or nonexistent. Practitioners will need to advocate for clients. That is, they will need to plead actively the cause of their clients often far beyond what is minimally required (Thorman, 1982). Sometimes services will need to be developed. Other times, unresponsive agency administrations will need to be confronted. Legal assistance may be necessary. There are no easy solutions to solving nationwide problems for families such as poverty or poor health care. This is a constant, ongoing process. Political involvement will be necessary. Many external environmental stresses are very difficult to change and diminish. However, such environmental stresses pose serious problems for families that practitioners will not be able to ignore.

Variations in Family Structures

We began this chapter with the contrasting then-and-now stories of the Brady family. The story illustrated some of the awesome impacts changing values, issues, economic support, and technology have had on family life over the past couple of decades. Generalist practitioners cannot assume that the families on their caseloads will consist primarily of intact, two parent families with two to four relatively well-adjusted, blood related siblings. Practitioners today will address a wide variety of family structures and issues. Thus, it's important to be aware of the broad range of dynamics that can operate within these various structures. Here we will

consider two of these variations, namely single-parent families and stepfamilies.

Single-Parent Families

The traditional family configuration (two parents, one a mother who remains in the home

Generalist practitioners cannot assume that the families on their caseloads will consist primarily of intact, two parent families with two or four relatively well-adjusted, blood related siblings.

to provide full-time care) is becoming less and less common. Wattenberg (1987) summarizes some of the statistics:

- Almost one-fifth of American families are supported by single parents.
- The vast majority (approximately 97 percent) of single parents are women.
- Clear demographic differences exist between African Americans and whites. For example, about one-fifth of all white families are headed by single parents. The figure is over one half for all African American families.
- Never-married women compose the fastest-growing category of single parents. Whereas most white single parents are divorced, most African American single parents having their first child have never been married.
- Women and children make up the majority of poor people in this country. Additionally, their proportion of the poverty pie is the fastest growing of all population groups.

This has at least two clear-cut implications for generalist social workers. First, social workers must be flexible regarding what is considered a "typical" or "normal" family. Second, poverty and lack of resources are characterizing a growing number of American women and children.

As in two-parent families, such issues as effective communication among family members and satisfactory child management are vitally important. Likewise, a focus on the family's relationships with other systems in the environment is important. However, two aspects should be highlighted for single-parent families. First, there are often greater pressures brought to bear on a single parent to assume virtually all of the parental responsibilities by herself. Chapter 13, which addresses gender-sensitive social-work practice, will discuss some of the special issues women face.

The second aspect to emphasize in single-parent families is their even greater likelihood of impoverishment. At one level, linking families with needed resources is critically important. Chapter 15 on brokering addresses this in greater depth. On another level advocacy on the behalf of children and their families is often called for. This is described in chapter 14. Highlight 9.4 below discusses the importance of a generalist macro perspective in helping families gain the resources they need.

Single Teenage Parents

A group of single parents deserving special attention is that of single teens. The proportion of births to teenagers is rising compared to births of women past their teens (Chilman, 1988). The increase in teen parenthood is attributed to a variety of factors including "having nonmarital intercourse, not using effective contraceptives or (less usual) experiencing contraceptive failure, becoming pregnant, not obtaining an abortion, carrying a pregnancy to term, failing to marry before the child's birth, and not placing the child up for adoption" (Chilman, 1988, p. 20). Teen parenthood can place momentous responsibility on people who are children or almost children themselves. Chilman (1988) cautions, however, not to blame teen parenthood as "the main cause of early school leaving, youth unemployment, poverty, and welfare dependency" (p. 38). Rather, she continues to say that the real causes of these problems lie in our social structure fraught with "institutional racism" and its serious unemployment problem "especially among minority youth" (p. 38).

Weatherley and Cartoof (1988) propose a series of suggestions for working with single adolescent parents; they focus on "a continuum of services thought to be appropriate at various stages of adolescent pregnancy and parenthood" (p. 39). These include the following:

1. *Preventing pregnancy.* Primary prevention refers to preventing the problem altogether, assuming that the pregnancy is a problem. To do this, adolescents need both information and ready access to contraception so that they can make responsible decisions. Sex education does not seem to have much effect on adolescent sexual behavior, that is, whether teens are sexually active or not (Spanier, 1976). However, there is some support that sex education is related to decreased pregnancy rates and even postponement of sexual activity (Zabin, Hirsch, Smith, & Hardy, 1984; Zelnik & Kim, 1982).

   Access to methods of birth control also seems to be important. Components which appear to increase adolescents' use of clinics includes "free services, an absence of parental notification, convenient hours for students, walk-in service, a diversity of locations, and warm and caring staff" (Weatherley & Cartoof, 1988, p. 39).

   Promotion of chastity has been proposed as a means of pregnancy prevention. However, research has not found that this approach works (Weatherley & Cartoof, 1988). "Just say no" is easy to say but hard to do. Several pictures come to mind. One possible scenario involves just saying no to a hot fudge sundae if you absolutely adore hot fudge, but are desperately trying to stay on your liquid-protein diet. Another is just saying no to a friend offering you a cigarette when you're out at a bar where everyone in the world seems to be smoking and you just quit this morning. One final scene involves one of those hot, passionate, decision-making moments when you're madly in love and you're simply certain it will last forever (again). Just saying no is not always so easy.

2. *Help during pregnancy.* Providing support during pregnancy can be very important.

It's easy to become depressed and isolated during that time. Physical changes may have impacts. This is especially in view of the great emphasis placed on physical appearance, attractiveness, and popularity during adolescence. One junior-high teacher once said that talking about the responsibility of pregnancy and teen parenthood had absolutely no effect on her students. However, the young women sat up with serious faces and widened eyes when told that once you have a baby, you often have stretch marks on your abdomen for the rest of your life. To these young women, stretch marks were serious consequences.

Pregnant adolescents may need help relating to friends and family members. This involves maintaining good communication with and emotional support from others around them. Many times a social worker may need to do active outreach to the pregnant teen. Home visits may be especially useful. Counseling can be provided either individually or on a group basis.

Pregnant teens most often need counseling about good nutrition and the impacts of lifestyle upon the fetus. For instance, they need to be well-informed about the results of alcohol and drug use during pregnancy. Teens also may need help in determining what to do about the pregnancy and other future plans involving living conditions, day care, education, and employment.

3. *Helping adolescent fathers.* It's important not to forget that babies born to adolescent mothers also have fathers. Despite myths to the contrary, most teen fathers are significantly affected by their child's birth and are involved to various degrees in the child's early life (Robinson, 1969; Weatherley & Cartoof, 1988). However, this involvement usually drops off by the

HIGHLIGHT 9.4

Families, Macro Practice, and the Integration of Policy and Practice

Because of the major focus on resources and their availability to families, the importance of macro practice is easily stressed. Needed resources are only available if agencies and organizations provide them. These agencies provide them only if their policies and procedures allow them to do so. Sometimes agency and social policies restrict resources. Other times policies simply deny that such potential resources exist. Hence, as a generalist social work practitioner, you may have to advocate and work for changes in organizational and social policies so that resources are made available to the people who need them.

There are a number of policy areas that critically affect the well-being of families (Kamerman, 1984; Kamerman, 1987; Kamerman & Kahn, 1981).The policies existing in these areas merit careful attention and scrutiny. Each policy issue has dramatic and direct effects upon your clients, including both families and individuals. They include the following six:

1. *Employment.* How family members can work to gain income is dictated by policy. World and national policies determine where jobs will be located and what kind they will be. For example, if the cost of running a farm continues to escalate and small U.S. farmers can't compete with others in the world, small U.S. farmers may go bankrupt. However, the government can subsidize these farmers. For example, the government can (and does) formulate policies to help farmers pay their farming costs. Other policies can add charges to incoming farm produce so that U.S. farmers can compete with foreign prices. Such policies significantly decrease the farmers' potential for bankruptcy.

Another example involves providing money for job training. Programs can be developed to pay for training certain segments of the population for jobs that need to be filled. Training takes money. If poor people in an urban ghetto or a rural enclave

can't afford training, they won't get it. Thus, they won't get the jobs. However, if training is provided and paid for in another way, these same people will get jobs.

What if the unemployment rate in your clients' community is more than 50 percent, as is the case for many young people in urban ghettos? Even then, those who are employed receive minimum wages and no benefits (such as health insurance, sick leave, or vacation). What can you do to help your clients gain adequate employment under such circumstances if no programs and policies exist to help you?

This book is neither an economics nor a policy text. You probably guessed that. However, the book does intend to depict clearly how policy at various system levels directly impacts clients and what they are able to do. It also, of course, affects what *you* can *do* for clients.

2. *Direct provision of income or substitutes for income.* How income is provided or not provided to designated groups of people is a policy matter. A good example is AFDC (Aid to Families with Dependent Children). How much money is provided to a family without resources varies drastically from one state to another. This directly affects the family's quality of life. Thus, the greater level of AFDC payments provided in Wisconsin allows the same family greater potential for a better quality of life there than lower AFDC payments in Louisiana.

Substitutes for income otherwise referred to as "in-kind income transfers" can also provide resources to families. Food stamps, which can be exchanged only for groceries, are a good example. As with AFDC, criteria for who is eligible to get food stamps and how many they can get varies drastically from state to state.

What do you do when your clients aren't eligible for enough cash and in-kind income transfers to survive? What do you do if policies neglect clients who are slowly starving to death?

3. *Health care.* Policies determine who is, or is not eligible and who is not for publicly financed health care such as Medicaid or Medicare. Even those who are eligible find that such programs either don't pay enough or don't cover certain health needs at all. Additionally, many health care facilities won't accept such payments because they don't pay full costs, are administratively burdensome, or "take forever" to actually receive.

Even for those with private insurance (many millions of people have none), policies also determine what is paid for and how much. For instance, a deductible of one thousand dollars (which means you must pay that amount first before the insurance company will begin paying anything) might as well be a billion dollars for clients who don't have ready access to money at all.

Designated maximum amounts for specific health services create other problems. For instance, take an insurance policy which allows five hundred dollars for alcohol and drug rehabilitation services. If the entire program costs five thousand dollars and more, what good will the measly five hundred dollars do?

4. *Homeless people.* More and more families, especially those including only women and children, are homeless. Rents are escalating. Affordable housing is becoming increasingly difficult to find throughout the nation. What do you as a social worker do if there are no programs with policies to provide your clients temporary shelter, food, and longer-term housing? What do you do if families are living literally on the streets?

5. *Day care.* Most women work. More specifically, most women with children work. Adequate day care for their children is difficult, if not impossible, to find. It's also expensive and the quality is highly variable. Should the federal, state, and/or local governments establish policies to provide resources for day care so that parents can work? Are you and others willing to pay taxes to finance these services?

What if your client is a single parent who receives AFDC payments barely allowing her to subsist below the poverty level? What if she wants to go out, get a job, and support herself, but can't because she can't afford the available day care? What policy changes might help her?

6. *Child support maintenance.* Policies dictate how much support divorced fathers provide their children. (Of course, mothers may also be required to provide support to children living with their fathers; however, this occurs infrequently.) Policies also mandate how the receipt of that support is monitored. In other words, if the family doesn't receive the financial support it's supposed to, then what happens? Do existing policies indicate that a portion of the father's salary can be garnisheed, that is, legally removed from his pay and sent to his family before he receives his paycheck? Will policies mandate that this happens automatically or must the mother seek legal counsel to advocate for her? What happens if the father moves to another state? Will that state's policies allow the garnishment of wages?

What if your client, a single parent and mother of two, works for a minimum wage, can't afford adequate housing on that income, and desperately needs support payments to subsist? Even minimum wages are determined by policies. How will policies help or prevent you from helping her get her due resources?

The problems evident in all six policy issues are difficult to solve. The questions raised are very hard to answer. However, these are questions and issues which generalist practitioners must face everyday. It is social work's ethical perspective of seeking the best route for the common good that provides direction. Many times, advocacy on the behalf of clients is paramount. Searching and working for policy change may be critical.

time the child reaches two years of age (Earls & Siegel, 1980).

An adolescent father may need help in expressing his feelings, defining his role, and contributing where he can in taking over responsibilities for his child. Many adolescent fathers have both psychological and psychosomatic repercussions as a result of the pregnancy (Elster & Panzarine, 1983). Because of their tendency to do less well educationally and economically (Card & Wise, 1978), they may need help and encouragement in pursuing educational and vocational goals.

4. *Helping mothers after the pregnancy.* It's important to keep the continuum of service in mind. This mother's needs do not suddenly stop after the baby is born. The case is not automatically closed. Weatherley and Cartoof (1988) cite three major areas where adolescent mothers may need ongoing help.

First, they may need help in learning about positive parenting and child management skills. Several aspects have been found to enhance this training. For one thing, training should be "flexible, informal, and individualized" (Weatherley & Cartoof, 1988, p. 49). For another thing, training is more helpful when provided after the baby's born rather than during the pregnancy (McGee, 1982). Finally, all involved family members and care givers including the child's father should participate in the training (Furstenburg & Crawford, 1978).

The second area where adolescent mothers often need help involves avoiding more pregnancies. Pregnancy is no guarantee that they have an adequate knowledge of decreasing chances of conception or of birth-control methodology. Both information and ready access to contraception is necessary.

The third area where young mothers most often need assistance is in their future life planning. Issues include continuing their education, gaining employment, finding day care for their child, and determining where and how they will live.

Remarriage and Stepfamilies

A stepfamily is "a primary kinship group whose members are joined as a result of second or subsequent marriages" (Barker, 1987, p. 158). Visher and Visher (1988) stress that stepfamilies differ from intact nuclear families in that they are more likely to experience certain problems. Because of the increased prevalence of such blended or reconstituted families, it's important for generalist practitioners to be aware of their special issues and needs. For one thing, loyalty conflicts may arise (Sager et al., 1983). Which parent of the divorced or separated couple should children be loyal to? How does a newly married stepparent fit into the family's scheme of things? Should a remarried spouse devote more attention to her new spouse or to children from her prior marriage?

Defense of territoriality is often another major issue in blended families. How is power and authority reestablished and changed when new parts of family systems are melded together? Many questions arise in newly blended families. Will the stepchildren resent the new stepmother assuming the same parental authority as their biological father and, for that matter, their biological mother? How will the new spouse get along with the stepchildren's other biological parent? Because of old interactional patterns, how difficult will it be for a new stepparent to adjust to all the firmly established interactional patterns of the old family system? How will stepchildren adjust to new stepparental rule?

Visher and Visher (1988) propose that "the

basic struggle for a stepfamily is the search for its identity as a family unit" (p. 224); they go on to identify at lease seven aspects characterizing stepfamilies. Each merits the worker's attention when working with such families.

The first area needing attention is that of *change* on the one hand, and *loss* on the other (p. 225). Members of stepfamilies are subject to massive changes. Place of residence may change. Schools may change. Daily family procedures may be altered. When and what the family eats may be modified by the new stepparent's wishes. Children may have to modify their bedroom sleeping arrangements to incorporate new stepbrothers and sisters. Where the family traditionally spends Thanksgiving, Christmas Eve, Hanukkah, or Easter may change. Members of stepfamilies are forced to make a broad variety of adjustments. These range from major alterations in basic living conditions to minor adjustments in everyday habits.

Additionally, stepfamilies suffer losses. Sometimes it's the loss of regular contact with the absent parent. Other times it's the loss of friends or possessions. Perhaps the children never see their grandparents on one side of the family anymore.

The point is that it's especially important for practitioners to attend to the vast array of changes, including losses, that confront stepfamily members. These changes may provide clear clues regarding what direction interventions need to take.

A second aspect of stepfamily life important to workers to address is the idea of *unrealistic belief systems* (Visher & Visher, 1988, p. 227). It's easy to model our idea of the perfect family on the intact nuclear family. There may be pressure for parents in newly blended stepfamilies to try to make these new families conform to old rules which may no longer be appropriate. For example, there is the idea that stepbrothers and stepsisters should become emotionally close and get along almost immediately like an instant family. This is unrealistic.

Relationships take time to develop. Positive feelings take time to be nurtured and grow. The practitioner may need to help the family set more realistic expectations for its interaction. It might be that some individual family members will never come to like each other.

A third important issue to address with stepfamilies is that of *insiders versus outsiders*. Outsiders may include "a stepparent without children who joins a parent with children, a fourteen-year-old girl who comes to live with her father and stepmother after they have been married for five years, or a mother and her two children who move into her new husband's former home" (Visher & Visher, 1988, p. 228). Practitioners need to watch out for family members placed in outsider roles. Feeling like an outsider in what's supposed to be your own home inevitably causes problems. The social worker may need to help the family define ways in which it can make all members become insiders so that they all can feel "at home."

The fourth important aspect operating within stepfamilies is that of *power* (Visher & Visher, 1988, p. 229). Power is a complicated concept. It's difficult to define concisely. It involves who can control or influence whom within the stepfamily. It concerns the hierarchy of command. In other words, who will be paid attention to before someone else? It also involves the amount of respect various stepfamily members have for each other. Usually, the ranking system places the biological parent living with the children first, the biological parent not living with the children second, the stepparent living with the children third, and the stepparent not living with the children last. More complex custody arrangements such as joint custody may complicate the power hierarchy even more.

Problems arise when people feel powerless in stepfamilies. It's a problem when stepparents feel stepchildren don't listen to them. It causes difficulty when a child feels divided between her two stepfamilies and unable to control her own life. Likewise, it's a problem when a non-custodial parent refuses to follow the terms of the custodial agreement and collects or returns children unpredictably.

At any rate, when power is an issue, the worker needs to help the family clarify to the best extent possible *who has what power* and *what that power involves*. It's important that all family members feel they're valuable family participants and not simply helpless pawns.

Loyalty conflicts involve the fifth problem commonly found in stepfamilies (Visher & Visher, 1988, p. 231). Children may feel pulled between two divorced parents. A parent may

---

┌ HIGHLIGHT 9.5 ─────────────────────────

An Example of Life within a Stepfamily

One stepmother, Cathy, after one and a half years of marriage, made some wise comments about stepfamily life. Cathy married for the first time in her midthirties to someone a few years older than herself. He was divorced and had two teenage daughters.

Both of these daughters lived with Cathy and her new husband. Cathy spoke of how she naively entered the marriage and stepfamily life, never anticipating the struggles which were about to occur.

Cathy described her stepdaughters as beautiful but spoiled. She, by the way, was a social worker by profession. Discrepancies in values between stepmother and stepdaughters were huge. Problematic issues in stepfamily life were ominous. Cathy's stepdaughters would associate only with "upper-class" people (meaning people who had a lot of money) and people of their same race. Neither daughter liked poor people very much. Additionally, one daughter kept things fastidiously clean and the other maintained a disorganized mess. Cathy's own approach to housework was somewhere in between. The daughter who emphasized cleanliness was also anorexic. This made family meals and eating in general a continual struggle. For instance, Cathy confided that sometimes she would bake muffins for her anorexic stepdaughter which the latter loved. On the outside these looked like ordinary muffins high in fiber content and low in calories. On the inside, however, they were packed with a special, highly caloric substance made for people who needed additional nutrition. Hence, the muffin appeared to be eighty calories by looking at the outside, but in reality it exceeded eight hundred. Her anorexic stepdaughter would

eagerly eat two or three muffins at a sitting. In this way Cathy could trick the anorexic into getting her needed nutrition. Cathy said the anorexic probably would've fainted dead away had she had any inkling regarding how many calories there really were in what she considered a "diet" muffin.

Cathy also commented on how difficult it was to feel automatic love toward her stepdaughters. She hadn't had the loving, nurturing childhood years (at least, these years should be such theoretically) to develop a strong relationship with them. The common daily struggles and annoyances of teenagers versus parents in addition to the major differences in values made it very difficult for positive feelings to bloom.

A positive aspect about the family was that Cathy and her husband maintained a good relationship between them. Her husband worked hard at not taking sides against her on the behalf of his daughters.

Due to the conflicts and the anorexia, the entire family entered family counseling. Remember that Cathy also happened to be a social worker. She expressed profuse relief at being able to step out of her social work role and say how she really felt as "the stepmother." She felt the sessions were very helpful to the family as communication began to improve. Although the family did not become blissfully happy, at least it could function and accomplish its daily activities. Cathy continued to work at her marriage. Cathy also recognized that the daily living problems with her stepdaughter will gradually decrease as the girls matured and moved into their own living arrangements for good. She was willing to bide her time.

feel torn between loyalty to a new spouse and loyalty to children from a prior marriage. Because of the new mixing of people and the more complicated structures involves in stepfamilies such loyalty conflicts are understandably common occurrences.

A social worker faced with these issues needs to help make the family understand that people don't have limited quantities of love which must be divided between some finite number of people. Rather, love can be shared and expressed in many ways. It might be the task of the practitioner to help family members establish ways of displaying love and affection differently and more effectively than they have in the past.

Boundary problems make up the sixth area important to monitor in stepfamilies (Visher & Visher, 1988, p. 232). As we've discussed, appropriate boundaries are important to maintain in any family. For instance, the spouse system needs to maintain its special, unique status. However, in stepfamilies boundaries may easily become vague or confused because of the complex nature of relationships.

The seventh potential problem area in stepfamilies involves *discrepant life cycles* (Visher & Visher, 1988, p. 232). When two twenty-five-year-olds marry and start out together, their life cycles are synchronized. They're progressing through their life stages at the same pace and are experiencing major life events more or less coincidentally. However, when remarriage is involved, other variables often come into play. There may be a substantial age difference between spouses. One's children may be preschoolers and the other's in high school. One may not have children at all.

An issue which commonly surfaces is that of whether or not to have children together in this new family. There is no ideal decision to make about this. Each individual couple needs to examine the pros and cons of each choice, including how strongly each feels about the issue. As with other issues addressed in families, generalist practitioners can facilitate family members in making such decisions.

Intervention with stepfamilies is similar to that of intact families. Of course, some attention needs to be directed to the special issues we've described in addition to problems common in intact families. However, many of the same techniques can be used in stepfamilies to achieve similar ends.

Chapter Summary

This chapter provided a foundation for understanding and working with families. Family communication was discussed. Verbal and nonverbal communication within families was explored. Various avenues of communication were identified. The significance of assessing family structure and the family life cycle was explained.

Family conflict including marital difficulties, parent-child relationships, individual personal problems, and external environmental stresses were explored. Variations in family structure including single-parent families and stepfamilies were examined.

10 Working with Families

Focusing on the family

Donna didn't know what to do. She was thirty-six years old and divorced. She had a five-year-old son from her prior marriage. Donna was an attractive woman with fiery red hair and penetrating bright blue eyes. She was tremendously proud of being a junior in college. She had worked very hard raising her son with no child support payments from his father who was pretty much "out of the picture." Donna's grades were excellent, and she looked forward to a bright professional future.

All these things had little or nothing to do with the problem upon which she was so intent. After dating a number of men steadily and some not so steadily, she had finally found a man with whom she'd like to spend the remainder of her life. John, age forty, was also divorced. Donna and he were deeply in love and were planning to marry within a few months.

Now we're approaching the problem.

John also had a child from his prior marriage. His daughter Josie had just turned eighteen. Here was the problem: Josie had become pregnant while still age seventeen and single. Her daughter, Dawn, was born just two weeks after Josie turned eighteen. Josie, therefore, was considered an adult who was supposed to be a responsible guardian for Dawn. The alleged father denied his paternity and wanted nothing to do with either of them.

However, Josie had a number of problems which interfered with her ability to be the responsible adult she was supposed to be. For one thing, Josie was a coke addict. For another, she experienced radical swings in her feelings toward Dawn. One minute Josie would hold Dawn lovingly, and the next, she'd throw her down on the couch, run out the door, and leave Dawn alone screaming wildly in their tiny, sparsely furnished apartment.

Once Josie got so frustrated that she screamed she couldn't stand it anymore ("it" being the burdensome responsibility of parenthood, Dawn's cryin and the infant's constant demands for attention). She then picked Dawn up, ran down the hall of her apartment building, stopped at the first door she heard music emanating from, and knocked on the door. She had no idea who the apartment's residents were. Nonetheless, she almost threw Dawn at the woman who answered and loudly stated the woman had to take care of her baby. Josie said she had something she had to do and would be right back. Josie didn't return to the apartment to pick up her six-week-old infant for two full days.

Donna was terribly worried about Dawn. Soon, Donna would become Dawn's step-grandmother. Donna would be an integral part of the family and would thus be one of the owners of the problem. Donna didn't think Josie really wanted to keep Dawn, yet Josie was terrified of giving Dawn up.

CHAPTER TEN

Donna felt Josie was abusing and neglecting Dawn. What should Donna do? Should she call Protective Services and tell them about what's been happening? What would Josie think of Donna then? Dawn is now two months old. How much longer can she stay in such an environment with Josie and not be seriously damaged? Should Dawn be placed in foster care? But even then, how could Donna be certain that the foster care placement would be a good one?

Donna did have an idea. She had an aunt who lived in a state two thousand miles away. Her aunt was thirty-eight years old, married, and infertile. Donna felt her aunt would give virtually anything to have a baby of her own. Her aunt had difficulties applying for an adoptive child for a number of reasons, including being in her late thirties. On the other hand, Donna's aunt was doing well in the business she and her husband owned. They were financially well off.

Donna wondered if she should call her aunt and tell her about Dawn. Would her aunt be interested? What if her aunt would pay Josie, perhaps, twenty-thousand dollars to cover "adoption costs?" Josie was broke and would really like the cash.

But what were the legal ramifications? Was such an adoption possible? Would Josie "go for it?" If Donna called her aunt, would she just be raising her aunt's hopes for nothing? What if Josie bluntly refused any such idea? Then, there is still Dawn, poor, precious Dawn, crying all the time.

Donna didn't know what to do.

Introduction

The story described above is true. No answer has yet been found. It illustrates some of the infinite issues and problems that can confront families. Working with families can be phenomenally complex, monumentally frustrating, and yet fantastically fascinating. When the story left off, Donna was in the process of contacting a social worker to help her with some of her issues and questions. The problem obviously is difficult. Yet those with the most difficult problems can use the most help.

This chapter will examine how to work with families in generalist social work practice. Based on the content in chapter 9, this chapter will explore specific approaches and techniques for helping families solve their problems.

Specifically, this chapter will:

- Relate generalist practice skills to working with families;
- Discuss beginnings with families and propose a range of intervention techniques including reframing, family sculpting, role playing, videotaping, and homework assignments;
- Explore issues involved in working with gay/lesbian and African American families;
- Address work with multiproblem families;
- Describe family preservation;
- Appraise the current status of family services;
- Examine macro practice with families.

Generalist Practice with Families

Many of the same skills that apply to any other type of intervention in social work practice also apply here to families. Working with families is built upon understanding the relationship-building and interviewing skills discussed in chapter 2. These skills are the basic ones necessary for generalist micro practice. Families are made up of individuals who communicate with each other. Problem-solving is based on communication. Therefore, many of the same skills are used when working with families. These include: monitoring your own and your clients' nonverbal and verbal behavior; maximizing warmth, empathy, and genuineness; using verbal responses and initiators such as clarification, interpretation, and summarization as part of the problem-solving process; and overcoming issues and hurdles such as clients who insist on not saying anything or on voicing extreme hostility.

Working with families also requires the skills discussed in chapter 3, which we refer to as mezzo skills. These, of course, involve working with groups. Since a family is a special kind of group, these skills also apply. Group dynamics, decision-making strategies, and roles are concepts which also apply to families. Making assessments, formulating plans, and leading the family through the intervention process occurs in families much as it takes place in other types of groups.

Finally, working with families often requires those skills discussed in chapter 4, which emphasize working in and with agencies and systems. Policies regarding how families are treated may be unfair. Families may not have access to the resources they desperately need.

Additionally, there are a number of more specific techniques which apply primarily or only to families. The main focus of this chapter will be the special approaches for working with families in view of the issues confronting them. As with any other generalist intervention, we will apply a problem-solving approach.

Family Treatment and the Problem-Solving Process

Working with or treating families follows the Generalist Intervention Model, just as any other type of social work intervention would. First, the family needs to be *assessed* by examining its micro, mezzo, and macro facets. Next, just as in any other type of intervention, a *plan* needs to be formulated. Some of the family's micro, mezzo, and macro aspects will be targeted for a change. The next stage involves the *intervention* or actual carrying out of the plan. Following this the intervention needs to be *eval-*

uated to determine its effectiveness. Finally, *termination* and *follow-up* need to occur.

Planning for Family Intervention: Do You Always Have to See the Entire Family?

As we know, a family is a system. Every single part of a system is important because what affects any *part* of the system affects the *whole* system. It follows logically, then, that since each family member is an important part of the family system, they all need to be involved in the intervention process. The term "conjoint" family treatment refers to meetings involving at least two family members (Janzen & Harris, 1986, p. 57).

There are at least three advantages to seeing the entire family together. First, being able to observe the entire family in interaction can give great insight to understanding its dynamics (Sherman, 1977; Janzen & Harris, 1986). When family members are missing, part of the family's interactional patterns are also lacking. For example, a single-parent mother and her twelve-year-old daughter might consistently complain together about the sixteen-year-old son/brother in the family. They say he's "no good." He fights with them all the time, lies, steals, and is generally impossible to live with. Without being able to observe the mother's and daughter's interaction with this boy, the worker doesn't really know what's going on in the family. The worker can see neither the boy's behavior nor the family's problems from the boy's perspective. Perhaps the mother clearly favors her daughter and regularly criticizes her son. Maybe his acting out is his way of expressing his anger at the situation and demanding some attention.

This leads us to the second advantage of seeing the whole family together. It enhances the worker's ability to be fair and objective. In other words, the worker is better able to assess and understand the problem from the perspective of all family members. The worker is thus less likely to take sides on the part of one person or the other. Bandler, Grinder, and Satir (1976) emphasize that a person working with the family "must be careful not to assume any one member of the family is a spokesperson for the rest of the family" (p. 15).

A third advantage to seeing the entire family involves the opportunity to see communication patterns. As Sherman (1977) indicates, "Communication patterns within the family become the first and major focus of observation and response by the worker" (p. 438). It is much easier to assess what you can observe right in front of you than to hear about it secondhand. The difference between how family members *think* they communicate and how they really do communicate is often a major part of the family's problem.

However, stipulating that the entire family must be present during problem-solving sessions often presents problems. Sometimes there are family members who refuse to participate. Other times questions may be raised regarding the need for everyone to be there. For example, if the parents are having sexual difficulties, is it appropriate for their four children, ranging in age from eight to eighteen, to be present during the meetings? At yet other times, scheduling everyone together may be impossible or nearly impossible. For instance, parents may work opposite shifts and are only available on weekends when you don't want to work. Sometimes, family members live out of town. Finally, is it really necessary to solving the designated problems that all family members expend the time and energy to be present all the time?

Janzen and Harris (1986) conclude that "family treatment ... is any treatment that changes the family" (p. 58). In other words, the important thing is to help solve the family's problems. Although family treatment means that the end result should benefit the entire family unit, how this is accomplished is variable.

It may be more advantageous to see one or two individuals, on the one hand. On the other, it may be necessary to work with the entire family in order to effect the changes that are needed. The critical thing is that the family benefits from the change effort.

Bandler et al. (1976) indicate that it is important to see all family members at least once. This can be done on an individual basis. It may be that only one person is available at a time. The purpose is to assure that the worker does not assume what one or two family members say accurately represents how all family members feel.

Perhaps the best rule of thumb is to see the entire family together at least once if it is at all possible. From there, arbitrarily determine which subsystems are needed to work on which problems. If it's not possible to get everyone together, then do the best you can. Get as many together as is possible and reasonable. As we've emphasized many times, social workers must be flexible. They need to do the best they have with what they have. Situations are rarely ideal. The important thing is to help effect change and solve problems.

I once had the opportunity to view a videotape of a nationally famous "family therapist" in the process of doing therapy. He, incidentally, was not a social worker by profession. He was beginning treatment with a family consisting of a mother, a father, a sixteen-year-old daughter, and a nineteen-year-old son. The identified problem was the son, who was extremely depressed. The identified problem, by the way, is the reason the family stated it came in for treatment. The real problem was something quite different.

This therapist was of the school of thought that the entire family must be present in order for the therapeutic process to do any good. He felt treatment was useless unless all family members were involved.

As the interview progressed, it surfaced that the son was gay. He was having a terrible time coping with the ramifications of the fact. These included the homophobic responses of other people and the realities of living outside of the heterosexual mainstream. He also had difficulties accepting himself for what he was, namely, a worthwhile human being.

The young man's father stated adamantly that homosexuality was bad and wrong. The father refused to discuss it during that interview or at any time in the future. He stated that he would not attend any more therapy sessions until the son stopped being gay. This, of course, devastated his son who, teary-eyed, was pleading for his father's acceptance.

After going around and around on the issue, the famous therapist responded that if the whole family didn't attend therapy sessions, he would not continue therapy. That was that. This was despite the fact that both mother and daughter expressed serious concern for their son/brother and commitment to the therapeutic process.

Perhaps, the therapist was trying to force the father into participating in the treatment sessions. Or, maybe, the therapist sincerely felt it was useless to work with the incomplete family system and that nothing could be achieved under such conditions. At any rate, the young man hanged himself the following week.

As a generalist practitioner, what would you have done with this family? What other alternatives might have been available? The therapist involved assumed a unilateral approach. He considered no other options. As a generalist practitioner in this situation, you might have considered seeing only those family members who were available and doing what you could within those limitations. Another possibility was to refer the young man to someone who could work with him individually. Still another option included referral to a gay support network or group.

It surely wasn't the therapist's fault that the young man killed himself. Each of us ultimately is responsible for our own life. However, the problem lay in the lack of options presented to the clients. The family was cut off because of one member's unwillingness to comply with the therapist's rules. The young man may have killed himself anyway. No one will ever know. However, perhaps a more compassionate approach would have helped. Maybe providing him with some other options may have made the young man feel as though someone cared. At any rate, I was thankful it was not me who turned the family away.

Beginnings with Families

Janzen and Harris (1986) cite three primary goals when beginning the intervention process with families. First, the worker needs to get a clear picture of the family's interaction, the problem itself, and how the family's interaction serves to maintain the problem. Second, the worker must gain the family's consent to begin treatment and their commitment to participate. This may not be an easy task. Some or all family members may deny that the problem even exists. They may insist that a certain family member or members are really to blame for the problem and, therefore, really should be the target of intervention. They may not even feel that anyone but the person with the identified problem should participate in treatment. The third initial goal when beginning an intervention with families is "to set procedures for change in motion. Family members should be able to leave with beginning confidence that they have been understood, that something new is being offered, and that something positive can happen as a result of agency contact" (p. 68).

Janzen and Harris (1986) continue that there are five phases to beginning treatment. These are stated below.

Phase 1: Alleviate or at Least Minimize Early Apprehension

The first thing the worker can do is begin making each family member comfortable about being there in the interview. The most effective way is probably to ask each person to describe his or her thoughts and feelings about being there. It's important to think how clients might be feeling as they enter this probably unknown situation. Will this social worker ask very personal questions in front of everybody else? Will she cut me down to nothing? Will everyone have to lie down on couches? Do they still perform labotomies? Thus, it's important to alleviate unsubstantiated fears and begin talking about the realities of family intervention.

Many of the introductory techniques resemble those described in chapter 2 on micro practice. However, there are two major differences between initial individual and initial family interviews. First, you as the worker have more than one person to interact with and observe. Second, you need to make certain that each individual has the opportunity to voice his or her opinions. Each individual needs to feel that she's important right from the very beginning.

Specific questions you might ask include:

"What kinds of things did you expect when you first walked in? Is this anything like you thought it would be?"

"Did you have a chance to discuss our meeting beforehand? If so, what kinds of things did you talk about?"

"I know this is a new experience for you. How do you feel about being here?"

Phase 2: Ask Family Members to Explain What's Wrong

The second phase in initial family intervention involves asking each family member to specify what he or she thinks the problem involves. There will likely be a wide variety of different perceptions. Doing this also allows the worker to observe family members' reactions to each others' definitions. It should be empha-

sized that this is not the time to start solving the problem. This is a time for observation. The problem must be clearly understood before the change process begins.

Frequently, family members will point their fingers at one person and blame him or her for the problem. It may be tempting for the worker to confront this blaming behavior and start talking about how the problem belongs to the entire family. However, it's important to allow the family to act as "naturally" as possible at this point. The worker wants to set the groundwork for change. The important thing here is to observe interactions, understand the problems, and target the most appropriate things for change.

Other issues may emerge. For instance, some family members may find it difficult to restrain themselves from talking and wait their turn. They may burst in and interrupt. For example, parents may find it difficult to be patient and allow their teenage daughter, the identified problem in their eyes, a chance to tell her side of the story. Old interactional patterns may kick in. The parents may immediately think how they've heard all this before and turn themselves off to it. Here the worker needs to establish one of the rules for the sessions. Namely, no one is to interrupt another when he or she is talking. All family members must feel their opinions are important. However, in the above case, it is relevant for the worker to note the interaction between parents and child. It probably dramatizes what typically occurs in their daily living situations.

At other times, there may be family members who won't say anything. The worker may then attempt to draw them out. For instance, the worker might say, "You're being awfully quiet right now. What are your feelings about the problem?" The important thing is to let the quiet person know that his or her feelings are also valued. For example, the worker might say, "Your ideas are important. I'd really like to hear them whenever you're ready." The client should know that his or her input will be welcomed when s/he feels comfortable enough to give it.

Phase 3: Establish Agreement about What's Wrong

After problem definitions have been elicited from all family members, the trick is to come to some agreement about what problem or problems should be worked on. Problems are usually very complex. Reid (1985) highlights how difficult it is to determine the "real" problem (p. 31). In any family it would be nice to have a clear, concisely agreed upon definition of the problem. He emphasizes "that all problems are 'real' to someone. It is usually impossible and fruitless to search for the one problem that has some quintessential reality [that is, the essence of the problem in its clearest, purest form] that others lack." In other words, there is no crystal clear, absolute problem.

Perhaps a more useful perspective is to think of most stated problems in terms of their "representativeness" (Reid, 1985, p. 31). Many families will verbalize superficial issues that are related to underlying problems. For example, a teenage son will state that his mother "nags" him about "everything all the time." His mother, on the other hand, says the problem is that her son will neither clean up his room like he's supposed to nor obey her curfew limitations concerning when he gets in at night. These perceptions are significant and important in the pair's day-to-day lives. However, a more pertinent issue involves the struggle for control between mother and son. The stated issues are really symptoms of the difficulties in the overall interaction.

Bandler et al. (1976) emphasize the usefulness of focusing "not on the problems and content, but on the processes of coping and communicating. This allows him to select useful information from the perspective of process,

instead of being overwhelmed by detail. Transforming the system will entail change at the coping level, not at the content level" (p. 138). In other words, work with families often involves changing how family members interact and communicate. The end result is teaching them different means of problem-solving than those they've used unsuccessfully in the past. Changing family processes enables the family to solve a wide range of problems, instead of the relatively limited ones they initially verbalize.

Let's return briefly to the example of mother and son cited above. The son probably will not agree that he is to blame for the real problem, because he neither cleans up his room nor gets in on time. Nor will the mother probably agree that the real problem is her fault. Namely, she criticizes and badgers her son excessively. However, a worker might get them to agree that the conflict occurring regularly between the two is a problem for both of them.

Reid (1985) suggests several techniques for engineering a problem consensus. The initial two summarize much of what we've already discussed. First, attempt to focus on a problem or some aspect of a problem over which the family will concur. Second, "recast problems expressed in individual terms as problems of interactions between family members or as problems of the family as a whole" (Reid, 1985, p. 35). This is one illustration of "reframing," a technique we will discuss more thoroughly later on in the chapter. Reframing "gives family members a different definition of the situation, one that may help them see the problem in a new light" (Reid, 1985, p. 36).

Third, help the family to articulate problems you observe in their interaction during the interview, but which they aren't able to express verbally themselves. For instance, take a family where each member actively criticizes each other family member during the interview. However, they don't define the problem as involving excessive criticism. Rather, each family member states that the real problem involves the behavior of other family members. For example, verbalized problems might include drinking excessively, running away, not being able to hold a job, or poor housekeeping. Each problem is expressed as being someone else's fault. The worker might assume a totally different perspective. Intervention may focus on defining the family's hostile, confrontational communication instead.

There is a fourth technique for establishing agreement about a problem. If several problems have surfaced, present them to the family in the order you consider them important. Ask each family member to rank the problems in the order she or he feels they're important. Then compare and contrast the results. Generally, problems which are considered more important by the most family members would be given higher priority. If there seems to be a tie between problems for top places, you as the worker can choose which you feel is the easiest to solve. It's important for the family to achieve some success in its treatment as soon as possible.

The fifth technique for gaining problem consensus within a family must be used especially carefully. It involves preventing family members from pointing their fingers at some individual and making that person the family scapegoat, at least during the process of coming to a consensus.[1] This might be done by labeling the scapegoating as it occurs. Such feedback can help family members begin to identify their behavior and patterns of interaction. Another subsequent approach is to ask family members to stop the scapegoating in order to continue their progress toward a problem consensus.

Practitioners may also ask scapegoats to share their perspectives of the family problems.

Likewise, scapegoats can be asked how they feel about being targets of blame. Soliciting scapegoats' feelings can serve to enhance empathy among family members. Additionally, such encouragement serves to tell scapegoats that their feelings are important, too. No one should be made to feel the lonely target of blame. Finally, encouraging such participation demonstrates how each family member's input is important. All family members should be asked at some point their personal perspectives concerning family problems. The family's problem concerns all family members. The practitioner can emphasize this principle to the family. Each person is involved and, therefore, somewhat to blame. It is the worker's task to help the family develop this perspective.

Reid (1985) gives three additional suggestions for targeting the family's problems. The first is to limit the initial list of problems to three. The list can always be changed and modified at a later time. The second suggestion is that even a vague problem about which the family has a consensus is better than a list of minor, very specific complaints. For instance, "improving family communication," although vague and global, would be more desirable than a list like "talks on the phone too long," "wears same socks for five days in a row," and "is sarcastic whenever asked a question," where there is no consensus.

Phase 4: Concentrate on How Family Members Relate to Each Other

Focusing on how family members relate to and communicate with each other is the fourth phase in beginning family treatment. This phase follows establishment of a problem consensus with the family. Typically, during this step the worker orchestrates discussion of the problem by family members. There are three structured ways of doing this.

The first way involves communication be-

---

1. At other times during the problem-solving process, scapegoating might be allowed. For example, at some time during assessment, the practitioner will probably want to observe the family's genuine interactions in order to plan for effective changes. Practitioners must first observe problem behaviors before targeting them for change.

tween the worker and individual family members. The worker directs questions to members which further explore the problems. Reid (1985) notes four major aspects of the target problem which can be explored. These include: how long the problem has existed and major events related to the problem since it began; the problem's intensity and incidence for the week or two prior to the interview; what family members have done to try to solve the problem in the past; and what barriers have been operating both inside and outside the family, which have prevented the problem's solution until now. Highlight 10.1 provides an example of how a target problem can be explored.

Hearing how each family member talks about the problem provides the worker with much information. She or he can find out how the problem evolved and how it's been intertwined in the family's interpersonal dynamics.

A second way the worker can structure how family members talk about a problem is through a discussion in which all family members participate. The worker instructs the family members to talk to each other about the problem. At the same time, the family is instructed not to direct any communication to the worker. In this way the worker can observe how family members participate in problem-solving together and what some of the obstructions in communication are.

Janzen and Harris (1986) note some of the communication difficulties which can be observed in families. They state, "Communications may be unclear; topics may be changed before issues are resolved, statements interrupted, blame affixed, support offered. Statements may be addressed to nobody in particular, and some individuals may attempt to speak for others" (p. 78). Additionally, family members may vie for power, initiate conflicts, form liaisons, or give support to each other. All this the worker can observe and later use to help the family target ineffective interactions for change.

The third way a worker can structure a family's discussion of problems is to instruct only two family members to talk about how to solve the problem with each other. At any point the worker can establish parameters about how communication will occur (Janzen & Harris, 1986). For example, the worker can specify that one person may not interrupt another, discussion should not stray far from the targeted topic, and that speakers will take responsibility for their own feelings and avoid speaking for other people.

Any of these three approaches provides the worker with a small sample of the family's real-life interaction. In effect, a small laboratory is created. Working with families is difficult. There are so many dimensions and nuances involved. Sometimes a worker can find out a lot about a family very early on. At other times, it takes much longer. At the very least, however, structuring such communication at the beginning of family treatment shows the family the types of things that can go on in family intervention and prepares them somewhat for future work.

Phase 5: Establish Commitment to a Plan of Action

Establishing an agreement regarding what is to be done and who is to do it is an important aspect of planning. In other words, we establish a contract with clients. This is a major step in the problem-solving process of the Generalist Intervention Model. The information in chapter 5 on planning relates to contracting with families just as it relates to contracting with individuals, groups, organizations, and communities. The contract becomes both a map or guide for the intervention process, and a seal of commitment by both family and worker. It reflects the primary problems to be worked on and the work assignments involved.

HIGHLIGHT 10.1

Four Ways of Exploring a Target Problem

The Situation

Rosie, age fifty-eight, works part-time as a salesperson at a small shoe store. She is married to Bob, age sixty-one, who is a retired luggage department manager for Sears. Their three children, Sean, Shane, and Sher, are married and live in other states. The problem is Bob's mother, Yetta, age eighty-seven, whose health has seriously declined. She has difficulty walking. Her sight is failing. She is becoming increasingly forgetful. Yetta has been living in the same urban flat since her husband died forty years ago. Rosie and Bob live in another area of the same city. Yetta has one other son who lives in another state and who rarely comes to visit her.

Yetta receives Meals on Wheels every day. This supportive service delivers daily noon meals to elderly persons in their own homes for relatively reasonable fees. One day, the delivery person finds Yetta disoriented and babbling. Yetta mumbles that she fell and hit her head.

The Meals on Wheels delivery person calls for an ambulance, and Yetta is taken to the hospital. She remains in the hospital for several days to evaluate her condition. Medical staff raise questions regarding whether Yetta is capable of living alone in her own home anymore. The case is referred to the hospital social worker.

Exploration of the Problem

The hospital social worker arranges a meeting with Bob, Rosie, and Yetta to discuss Yetta's situation. Yetta is no longer disoriented, so is able to share her feelings. The worker proceeds to explore the problem by pursuing four major dimensions involving the following questions; she receives the information that is recorded after each:

1. *How long has the problem existed, and what were the major events related to the problem since it began?* Yetta's health has been gradually failing over the past three years. However, she has fallen only once prior to about a month ago. Until now she has never really hurt herself.

2. *How intense has the problem become in the past two weeks?* Yetta admits that she has fallen several times during the past two weeks. However, she emphasizes that she has never really gotten hurt until now. Bob and Rosie were unaware of any of the other falls.

3. *What have family members done to solve the problem in the past?* Bob has tried to talk to Rosie about the possibility of Yetta moving in with them several times since Yetta's health began to fail. Rosie, however, has consistently refused to talk about it. She would typically "cut Bob off" and state that they should just "leave well enough alone." Yetta has never raised the issue of moving to either of them.

4. *What barriers have been operating both inside and outside the family that have prevented the problem's solution until now?* Yetta has adamantly maintained that she does not want to move from her home. She is determined not to enter a nursing home.

Rosie has never gotten along very well with Yetta. Rosie feels Yetta is stubborn and overly talkative. She feels she's been good to Yetta and cares about her well-being. However, Rosie has consistently avoided discussing the possibility of letting Yetta live with her and Bob. Rosie has been enjoying her time and relative freedom since her children have left. She dreads having to give these up to care for Yetta. Rosie doesn't feel it's fair to become a "full-time nurse" at her age.

Bob worries intensely about his mother. Whenever he has tried to talk to Rosie about his concerns, she has abruptly refused. He feels Yetta should leave her flat and come to live with him and Rosie. He feels he has a responsibility to take care of his mother. He wishes Rosie felt the same way. However, he also worries about how Rosie and Yetta would get along. He doesn't want to live on a battleground.

The family has no information about the nursing homes in the city. Nor do they know how to go about getting it.

Several external barriers have been working to maintain Yetta in her own home. Thus, the problem of Yetta's failing health has not been addressed. First, Meals on Wheels has provided one hot meal a day, so Yetta has been getting adequate nutrition. Second, a concerned friend from Yetta's church named Alice Dicks looks in on Yetta almost every other day. Additionally, Alice, who is twenty years Yetta's junior, takes her to church activities when Yetta feels up to it. Yetta's minister also visits her regularly. Finally, Bob and Rosie call Yetta at least twice a week, frequently take her on outings, invite her for dinner, and help her with laundry and shopping.

Summary

The intent of this brief vignette involving Yetta and her family is to provide an example of how a social worker might begin to explore at least four dimensions of a target problem. This problem situation has many other facets that are beyond the scope of this abbreviated description. In real life, many other questions could be asked and other issues examined.

So What Happens?

We won't take the time here to explain how all the specific steps in the Generalist Intervention Model are applied. However, we will tell you what happens.

Because Yetta remains insistent upon staying in her own home, she does so, at least temporarily. The social worker obtains some additional supportive equipment for her. This includes a walker (that is, a device made up several hollow aluminum legs which Yetta can lean on for balance as she walks) and a "beeper" (that is, a device she constantly wears around her neck which will notify the hospital immediately if pressed when she has trouble and needs help).

For four months Yetta continues to receive support from family, friends, minister, and Meals on Wheels. However, she eventually falls again and breaks her arm. She, together with Bob and Rosie, then make the decision that she will move in with them. Rosie does her best to take care of Yetta. One year later, Yetta becomes extremely disoriented. Several times she wanders out of the house for no apparent reason and gets lost. Finally, she can no longer retain her bodily discharges such as urine.

Bob and Rosie go to the County Department of Social Services and ask how to go about finding a "good" nursing home placement for Yetta. There they are referred to the appropriate social worker. They explore a variety of nursing homes, evaluate the respective pros and cons of each, and eventually place Yetta in the one they consider best for her.

Problems don't always have one best solution. Often, there are a number of possible solutions. Sometimes, as in Yetta's case, the solutions are progressive.

Techniques of Family Intervention

For our purposes, the family is considered a mezzo system. It is a small group, yet a unit unto itself. Micro aspects of intervention apply to families because of the importance of interpersonal communication and relationships. Macro aspects of intervention also apply to families. Both individual family members or whole family units may need changes in policies or services in order to get what they need. Advocacy and brokering skills are often vital to serving families. These skills will be discussed more thoroughly in later chapters.

Here we will focus on those techniques which are especially useful for enhancing both a family's interaction and problem-solving capabilities. The core of each technique is communication. They include reframing, family sculpting, role playing, videotaping, and giving homework assignments.

Reframing

Reframing means helping family members view a problem or an issue with a different outlook or understand it in a new way. It's also referred to as "relabeling or redefining" (Sheafor et al., 1988, p. 345). "Within the family treatment context, this usually means helping one family member change negative thinking about another family member to a new, more positive perspective. Reframing often helps one person better empathize with another person or understand content more clearly from that person's perspective.

Below are some examples of a client's statement followed by a worker's reframing of the client's thought:

Client's Statement: "Johnny hates me. All he does is scream at me. I don't even want to go near him anymore."

Worker's Reframing: "You sound upset and hurt at how Johnny yells at you so much. Maybe he's upset and hurt, too. Maybe he feels you're avoiding him. If he didn't care about you, he probably wouldn't expend so much energy yelling at you and trying to get your attention."

Client's Statement: "My dad says I'm much too close to my grandmother. He says it's a sick relationship, that all she does is manipulate me."

Worker's Reframing: "It's interesting that he's so concerned about that relationship. Maybe he's jealous that you two are so close. Maybe he'd like to feel closer to you, too. After all, you visit your grandmother whenever you have the chance. Yet, you never visit him. Also, you've told me how he resents his own mother and how she tried to manipulate him when he was small. Maybe that has something to do with it."

Client's Statement: "All my parents do is try to control me. They're like two little dictators. They ask me who I'm going out with every second I'm gone. They tell me I'm supposed to have a 10:00 P.M. curfew. If I'm two seconds late, they're waiting for me at the door to ask me where I've been. They're driving me crazy."

Worker's Reframing: "You sound like you're feeling suffocated by your parents. It sounds to me like they're very concerned about you. If they didn't really care what happened to you, they wouldn't care what you did. Maybe they don't see their behavior as controlling. Maybe they see it as being good parents and trying to keep you out of trouble."

Family Sculpting

According to Sheafor et al. (1988), "Family sculpting is a technique designed to help an individual client and/or a client family reenact and thus relive some important aspects of their family's behavior. It is a tool for assessment, as well as treatment" (p. 347). Each family member is given a turn at positioning the other members of the family. It provides a nonverbal means for communicating how the sculptor feels about the family and its interactions. The sculptor can place family members as close or as distant as s/he wants. Likewise, the sculptor can ask them to adopt certain positions. After the sculptor finishes arranging the others, he or she also places him- or herself within the sculpture. Subsequently, the sculptor is asked to explain reasons for where and how he placed other family members. Other family members are then asked to discuss their feelings and reactions to the sculpting placements.

This technique can provide an interesting visual display of family relationships. For example, take Janice, who's jealous of the attention another sister, Delia, gets from their parents. The worker asks Janice to be the sculptor. First, Janice asks her parents to stand up and places them together on one side of the room. Janice then takes Delia by the hand and places her smack up against the parents. Janice, however, places herself at the opposite side of the room. This communicates nonverbally how Janice feels about her parents' treatment both of herself and Delia. Janice obviously feels very distant and detached from her parents. At the same time, she feels that Delia is overly close to them.

The worker then asks Janice to talk about her feelings and encourages her to elaborate on the reasons for her jealousy. How specifically did Janice's parents treat Delia differently? In what instances did she feel she was not getting enough attention? Subsequently, the worker asks the other family members to respond. How did each of them feel about Janice's resentment and jealousy? Did they feel it was valid? Why or why not?

Thorman (1982) expresses the possible variations which can be expressed by using family sculpting, "Some [sculptors] indicate that they feel 'isolated' or 'left out' while other family members respond that they feel 'smothered' or 'hemmed in.' Still others express satisfaction because they are protected by other family members or because they have a privileged position within the family system" (pp. 161–62). Thus, family sculpting presents an interesting assessment and treatment alternative.

Role Playing

Role playing refers to having a person assume a different role or part than s/he normally would. It usually involves one of two scenarios. First, within the family treatment context the worker directs one family member to assume the role or character of another. The major requirement is that "the role player must try to act and feel the way he thinks the person does" in real life (Perez, 1979, p. 104). Role playing allows family members to understand more clearly how other family members feel from their own unique perspectives. Frequently, a technique called "role reversal" is used where two family members are asked to exchange and act out each other's roles. The intent is usually to help people see how they each perceive each other.

An example concerns a father and "uncontrollable" fourteen-year-old daughter who are asked to reverse roles. The father portrays his daughter by walking around in a huff, swearing at his role play "father," and threatening to break things. On the other hand, the daughter acts out her father by screaming at her role play "daughter," telling her she's grounded, and savagely raises her fist as if ready to strike.

The practitioner would then help the client to begin talking about how each perceived the situation and how each felt. One intent of such discussion is to enhance their empathy toward each other.

The fourteen-year-old then describes to her father how she feels about her situation and how this was demonstrated by her role-play actions. She does not have a very positive self-concept. She feels it's difficult for her to make friends, so she "hangs out" with those who will accept her. She doesn't care if they shave half their heads and dye their hair in purple and orange streaks. She's caught in a no-win situation when her father tells her she can't associate with them anymore. She feels she has no choice. If she doesn't associate with the friends she's got, she'll have no one.

Her father also explains his feelings and why he acted the way he did. In reality, he stresses, he feels worried and frustrated. He feels his daughter won't listen to him as children *should* respond to their parents. To him she looks like "a mental case" by the way she dresses. He's feeling like a failure as a parent because nothing he tries helps him get control over the situation. He's desperately worried that belonging to such a "wrong crowd" will only result in drug use, sex, and who knows what else.

Having these two people reverse roles and interact with each other may provide some interesting insights into their own behavior. When father walks around in a huff, swears at daughter, and threatens to break things, daughter sees how she looks to people outside of herself. On the other hand, when daughter screams at father telling him he's grounded and raises her hand to strike him, father may get some insight into his own actions. He may never have had any idea regarding how his behavior looked to anyone else.

Of course, family members will probably not get instantaneous revelations and have their problems miraculously cured by doing role re-versal. However, there is potential for them to increase their empathy for others, broaden their view of problem situations, and become aware of alternatives never thought of before.

The second kind of role playing involves having people remain themselves but act differently than they normally would in some defined situation. This allows them to try out and practice new ways of behaving in fabricated situations, without taking the risks those new behaviors might pose in real life.

For instance, take a woman who is afraid to share her true feelings with her husband. She feels he is a domineering man and wouldn't listen to her anyway. Via role playing, she can practice what to say and how to say it before ever really confronting him. This allows her to gain confidence in how to act. It also lets her think through ahead of time how she might respond to a variety of his possible reactions.

The bad thing about role playing is that the situation is obviously not a real one. Sometimes it seems "fake" to participants. However, the very good thing is that it allows people to plan what to do and practice before the actual situation takes place. Risk is minimal.

Videotaping

"I hate watching myself on videotape" is a frequent comment of students who are forced to videotape themselves for their social work practice courses. They don't like the grating tone or the soft mumbling of their voices. They hate to see how they jiggle their feet or slump in their chairs. They think they look too fat or too lanky.

What videotaping does is make people observe themselves as others see them. It makes them confront the effectiveness and appropriateness of their various verbal and nonverbal behaviors. So it also is with families.

When viewing tapes of their interaction,

family members can be made to see themselves as others see them. When a mother tells her delinquent son, "I love you," she can see the scowl on her face and hear the angry, harsh tone of her voice. Videotaping can be very useful for pointing out double messages such as this. The mother was saying one thing verbally, but communicating quite another thing nonverbally.

Videotapes can be used to demonstrate family alliances. For example, a mother may observe herself sitting next to her young daughter and patting her daughter's arm lovingly and frequently during an earlier interview. Videotaping can also dramatize conflicts. For instance, a husband and wife can watch themselves both talking at the same time, trying to cut each other off, and struggling to be heard.

There is one note of caution, however. Workers should use discretion regarding how much of a family session to play back. Time, of course, is valuable. Segments of family interviews should be selected to illustrate specific points related to target problems.

One other point to keep in mind is the fact that some families may initially feel uncomfortable or self-conscious when videotaped. This, however, usually passes with time. Most soon become accustomed to the equipment being there and essentially forget about it. Videotaping should never be used, of course, without each family member's clearly expressed permission.

Homework Assignments

Homework assignments are tasks given to clients to be completed at home outside of the interview. They can be given to individuals or entire families, depending on the assignment. The important thing is that they are very clearly specified. They should incorporate at least one of the following elements (Shelton & Ackerman, 1974; Sheafor et al., 1988):

1. Directions regarding specifically what is to be done (for example, talk about a specified issue, study this handout, or rehearse a specified activity);
2. Specification regarding frequency or amount of times the homework should be done (for instance, do the homework two times each day or during three evenings next week);
3. Specification of how the homework is to be counted or kept track of (for example, each time the specified homework is done, mark it down on a progress sheet);
4. Directions regarding what is to be brought to the next interview or meeting (for instance, bring your behavioral chart or a list of your partner's strengths);
5. Indications of what will happen under specified circumstance (for example, you will earn thirty minutes of free time, gain one additional point, or place one dollar in the treatment account each time you participate in the specified behavior).

In other words, homework assignments should follow our general guidelines for specificity. Family members should understand the assignment's purpose. They should know who should do what and how by when. Finally, they should clearly understand the results of these actions.

Social workers are not required to give homework assignments to families. Sometimes there are none which are appropriate. Other times families are not willing to cooperate. However, such assignments do provide a viable option for enhancing family treatment time. That is, time to work on problem-solving is expanded because some of it is used outside of the session. Assignments also provide opportunities for families to apply what they've learned in treatment sessions to what they do in their real lives outside of treatment. In other words, they can practice new behavior and skills outside of the interview situation.

Multiproblem Families

Many families that come to you for help will be overwhelmed with a hoard of mammoth problems. For instance, one family of five may have the following problems affecting one or more of its members: poverty; physical disability; delinquency; alcoholism; developmental disability; marital discord; inadequate housing; and unemployment. Families often will come to you because they have nowhere else to turn. They will probably be desperate. A state of crisis is likely (crisis intervention was discussed in chapter 7).

What will you do? Where will you start? How will you begin to sort out the problems and plan strategies to solve them?

Thorman (1982) relates how "one of the most successful approaches to helping the multiproblem family is a problem-solving model that enables the family to untangle the web of problems it confronts to establish specific goals to be achieved, and develop the skills needed to solve their problems" (p. 112).

When you work with problems having such multiple levels, there are five primary points to remember:

1. *Do not get overwhelmed yourself.* Stay calm. Try to remain objective. Avoid getting emotionally involved with a series of small crises. You can be of no help to the family unless you retain your professional objectivity and judgment.
2. *Follow the problem-solving process as you would with any other problem situation in micro, mezzo, or macro practice.* Keep on track. Assess, plan, intervene, evaluate, terminate, and follow up. Clarify for yourself where you are in the problem-solving process at all times.
3. *Partialize and prioritize the problems involved.* Partialize or divide the problems up. Define what each problem involves and specify the family member(s) it most

affects. Next, prioritize the problems as you would prioritize them for any other case situation. Which are felt to be most important by all family members? Which are most critical? For which do you have a good potential for achieving solutions?

4. *Determine which, if any, problems you can work on yourself.* Part of planning for intervention involves translating client problems into needs. The next logical step is to review what services are available to satisfy these needs. What intervention possibilities fall within your own skill level and job description? Which are services that your agency readily provides? Which are possible to accomplish within your caseload responsibilities and time constraint? It's usually humanly impossible for one practitioner to meet all the needs evident in a multiproblem family.
5. *Identify and use relevant community resources.* Which client needs demand resources and services that can best be supplied by your agency's staff other than yourself or by other agencies entirely? This necessitates your need to know about the resources available in your community. Chapter 15 stresses and explains the importance of brokering and case management for a wide range of interventions including those targeting multiproblem families.

Family Preservation

The concept of *family preservation* is relatively new in the realm of family-based services. However, it has come to be a major thrust in agencies throughout the country. It involves doing everything possible to keep the child in the home and provide treatment for the family.

In past decades, working with families usually involved focusing on protecting the child.

This, in turn, often meant removing the child from the home. Services were then provided in a segmented manner by a variety of workers. For example, take an alleged case of child abuse. One protective services intake worker would gather the initial intake data when the child is initially referred. Another outreach protective services worker might provide services to the family. Still another would work with the foster family if the child had been placed there. And so it goes.

Family preservation, on the other hand, emphasizes providing services to the family unit in a more coordinated fashion. For instance, one worker might do the majority of the assessment, planning, intervention, evaluation, termination, and follow-up process. The child would be likely to remain in the home. All services would be provided or coordinated by a designated worker with the intent being to help the intact family solve its range of problems.

An extensive example of a program based on family preservation principles was provided in chapter 7. It concerned applying risk management to combat child maltreatment.

Major Themes in Family Preservation

Maluccio (1990, pp. 23–25) identifies eleven concepts which tend to characterize family preservation programs. They include:

1. *Crisis orientation.* Family preservation is based on intervention when a crisis is taking place within the home. Workers can then take advantage of the family's motivation to alleviate the stress it's experiencing.
2. *Focus on family.* The family is all-important. The family is considered the optimum place for children to remain. All intervention emphasis is directed toward keeping the family together and strengthening its members.
3. *Home-based services.* Services are provided in the home whenever possible. The ongoing thrust is improving the home environment.
4. *Time limits.* Since family preservation workers intervene during times of crisis, they work quickly. The intervention process in most models ranges from four to twelve weeks, although some extend longer than that. Setting time limits helps workers and their clients evaluate progress regularly.
5. *Limited, focused objectives.* All intervention objectives are clearly specified. The primary goal is to alleviate the crisis situation and strengthen the family unit so that a crisis is less likely to erupt again.
6. *Intensive, comprehensive services.* Workers' time and attention is concentrated on the families and their progress. Workers may spend as much as twenty to twenty-five hours each week arranging for resources and providing services themselves (such as problem-solving counseling and parenting skills education).
7. *Emphasis on education and skill building.* The family preservation approach is a positive one. The assumption is that people can improve if they are provided with the appropriate information and support.
8. *Coordination.* Because intervention is intensive and numerous resources often are involved, coordination is very important. Frequently, a practitioner will assume a case-management role.
9. *Flexibility.* Each family is different, having varying problems and needs. Flexibility enables practitioners to match a wide range of services and resources with the individual family's needs.
10. *Accessibility.* Workers in family preservation must be readily accessible to families in crisis. Their work is intensive and time limited. Workers' caseloads typically are

---

HIGHLIGHT 10.2
Confronting Homophobia

Lesbian and gay people live in a heterosexual world. To help understand what it's like to be gay or lesbian, it's useful to view the world from their perspective. Assuming that you're heterosexual, what would it be like if you lived in a world where the mainstream of society was gay? Consider the following questions.

1. What do you think caused your heterosexuality?
2. Have you ever been attracted to someone of your same gender?
3. Do your parents know that you're heterosexual?
4. Aren't you worried that your children may turn out to be heterosexual also?
5. Do you ever suffer any discrimination because of your heterosexuality?
6. Why don't you try homosexuality? You might like it.
7. Wouldn't you rather fit in with everybody else in our homosexual society?
8. In view of the fact that there is such a high divorce rate even among persons of the same gender, isn't it even more difficult to share a life with someone of the opposite gender?

---

very small so that they can concentrate their efforts.

11. *Accountability.* Accountability is considered very important. The emphasis on focused objectives and time-limited interventions enhance workers' ability to evaluate their effectiveness.

Diversity and Families

No two families are alike. We've been discussing some of the general techniques that can be applied in a broad range of work with families. Now we will discuss two subgroups of the total pie of families, namely, gay/lesbian families and African American families.

Lesbian and Gay Families

Many of the issues faced in families where parents are gay or lesbian closely resemble those addressed in families with heterosexual parents. However, generalist practitioners need to be aware of some special issues affecting lesbian

and gay families. The five which we will address here are the impacts of homophobia, lesbians and gay men as parents, coming out to children, special custody issues, and special environmental issues in gay relationships.

Homophobia

Homophobia is the irrational "hostility and fear that many people have toward homosexuality" (Masters et al., 1988, p. 422). Whitham and Mathy (1986) potently describe the extent of homophobia:

"Not only are homosexuals criminalized, victimized, and labeled pathological, they are also regarded by some religious groups as sinners deserving to be put to death, a view reminiscent of the Inquisition. There are very few, if any, groups in American society which evoke more hostility than homosexuals" (p. 180).

Lesbian and gay people are people who are oriented toward having sexual relations with the same gender. They cannot legally join the FBI, the CIA, or the military. The Roman Catholic Church has decried homosexual behavior as sinful. In many Protestant churches (although not all denominations) lesbian and gay people are not allowed to join the clergy. Lesbian and gay people have been denied or lost jobs and housing purely on the basis of their sexual orientation. Violence against lesbian and gay people has risen dramatically in the past few years.

Generalist practitioners need to examine homophobia from two perspectives. First, they need to explore and cope with their own homophobia. Second, they must be aware of the oppressive impacts homophobia wreaks on the families of lesbian and gay clients.

Confronting your own homophobia may be very difficult. It may involve serious soul-searching to identify and evaluate your own personal values. A possible consequence may be making some hard distinctions between your own personal opinions and professional values. Some people have expressed serious religious convictions that condemn homosexuality. On the other hand, the professional social work Code of Ethics emphasizes individual clients' rights to make choices about their own lives. As a professional social worker, it's your job to assist people in solving their problems. It is not your job to tell clients what to do or how to act.

The second perspective concerning homophobia involves the oppression lesbian and gay people and their families suffer. We've already noted some aspects of discrimination. Gay people may be denied access to certain jobs and residences. They may be ostracized socially. They may live in constant fear that they will be fired from their jobs if found out. You may need to address the additional problems generated by homophobia just as any other problems your clients may have.

Lesbians and Gay Men as Parents

It is estimated that at least one third of lesbians and about 10 percent of gay men have children, although not all of their children live with these parents (Moses & Hawkins, 1982; Riddle, 1977). It's important to realize that myths prevail about gay and lesbian parents with respect to their children. For example, one involves the idea that gay people will goad their children into being gay. This is not the case. Children raised by gay or lesbian parents are no more likely to "become gay" than children raised by heterosexual parents (Harry, 1988; Moses & Hawkins, 1982). Looking at it in another way, perhaps children with gay parents are raised to be more aware and acceptant of individual human differences in general. Sexual orientation is only one of many ways in which human beings differ from one another.

Coming Out to Children

"Coming out" refers to "the process of self-identification as a lesbian woman or gay man, followed by revelations of one's sexual orientation to others" (Barker, 1987, p. 28). Coming out to their children is an issue with which many gay/lesbian parents must deal. It is recommended that gay/lesbian people come out to their children at the earliest opportune time (Berzon, 1978; Moses & Hawkins, 1982). Moses and Hawkins (1982) cite at least four reasons for this. First, hiding one's homosexualtiy creates an atmosphere of secrecy. It can give children the impression that sexuality is something to be ashamed of. Second, evading the issue hinders positive, straightforward communication between parents and children. Children may get the idea that they can't talk to their parents openly about other issues in the same way they can't talk about their parents' relationships and sexuality. Third, avoidance of the issue runs the risk that children may be informed about their parents' homosexuality from others. Such information may be conveyed in a negative and critical manner. This may only validate for children the homophobic idea that being gay/lesbian is bad. Fourth, the effort it takes to maintain such secrecy may put pressure on family relationships. Problems such as resentment, anger, rebelliousness, or communication lapses may result.

Social workers may be placed in the position of helping gay/lesbian parents come out to their children. Moses and Hawkins (1982) suggest a number of ways in which social workers can help parents do this. First, gay/lesbian parents need to be comfortable with the fact that they are gay or lesbian. The parent may express resistance and voice concern about coming out to children. In this case, the social worker can help the parent explore reasons for these feelings. Are these reasons valid? Or is the parent painting an exceptionally dark picture? The parent needs to understand that the children eventually will find out anyway. A social worker can help parents evaluate the possible results and repercussions if they tell the children themselves versus if the children find out from some other source. A social worker can help gay/lesbian parents explore the contrast between explaining their sexual orientation as a positive aspect of life as opposed to finding out about it as a surprise in a possibly negative way.

Second, gay/lesbian parents need to plan exactly what to tell their children about sexual orientation. A social worker can help them think through what they want to say and how they want to say it. A social worker can assist them in role playing the scenario before it actually occurs. Parents can also be helped to prepare themselves for the potential negative responses of their children. As a social worker, you can suggest ways in which parents can react to and cope with such less than desirable reactions.

Counseling can be of great value to same-sex parents, particularly in a homophobic community. In addition, legal counseling may be necessary. These two parents—one a certified family law specialist—have raised four children from infancy and are currently raising a three-year-old grandson.

Thinking through the entire situation ahead of time can decrease parents' anxiety and help them to feel they're in greater control.

The third suggestion for helping gay/lesbian parents come out to their children involves timing. If possible, it's probably least difficult to come out to children who are very young. Becoming familiar and comfortable with an environment in which differences in sexual orientation are considered "normal" helps children incorporate the concept as just another part of life. Sexual orientation then becomes nothing out of the ordinary with which they need to become concerned.

It is important to note that very young children may not be able to hide the fact of sexual orientation from others very well. They may not be able to discriminate between when it's appropriate and inappropriate to share this information. Children are not sophisticated enough to analyze the effects of telling someone they have parents who are gay or lesbian. Therefore, gay/lesbian parents who come out to very young children need to be prepared to come out to everyone, even if they would choose not to.

An example comes to mind. Take Tabitha, the six-year-old daughter of a lesbian mother living with her lifetime lover and partner. Tabitha's teacher was talking to Tabitha's first grade class about the upcoming parent/teacher conferences. Her teacher was saying that she hoped both mothers and fathers would be able to attend. Tabitha raised her hand and, when called upon, blurted out, "I don't have a dad, but both my moms are coming. They sleep together." One's response might be, "So much for subtlety."

Telling older children about being lesbian or gay involves some different issues. Although older children have greater understanding of personal relationships and of life in general, they may also be more sophisticated regarding their concerns. Moses and Hawkins (1982) discuss this possibility by reflecting how older children "may be embarrassed by their gay parent(s) in public, and may worry that their friends will find out" (p. 206–207). They continue, however, that "these worries usually subside after an initial period of time, but they are worth anticipating. An atmosphere of openness and trust will make it easier for children to communicate their reactions directly" (p. 207).

Wolf (1979) found that lesbian mothers encouraged their children to be wary of to whom and under what circumstances they reveal their mother's lesbianism. Likewise, Bozett (1980) found that gay fathers encouraged their children to be cautious regarding disclosing information about their father's homosexuality. For instance, take the situation where a father's partner lives with the family and functions as an integral part of it. In this case he might be alluded to as an "uncle" before people who are not family members (Harry, 1988, p. 109).

Bozett (1985) also found that children with gay fathers frequently used "impression management" to control intimidation and criticism by others (Harry, 1988, p. 110). For example, these children closely scrutinized how they phrased things about their family. Likewise, they would avoid being seen by their friends when with both their father and his lover.

Wolf (1979) encourages gay/lesbian parents to teach children "situational ethics" (p. 155). In other words, children can be taught to evaluate each situation and the potential reactions of specific individuals involved. They can learn to formulate questions in their heads. For example, does this person seem like one who might be open to homosexuality? What might the negative results be if this person were told? On the other hand, what might the positive results be? Might it be best simply to remain silent?

Lesbian and Gay Parents and Child-Custody Issues

Child-custody issues often become a major concern for gay/lesbian parents. Therefore, this may be an issue over which gay/lesbian parents may come to you as a social worker for help. Gay parents have only half as good a chance as heterosexual parents in winning a court battle for custody of their children (Moses & Hawkins, 1982). Gay fathers are at even a greater disadvantage than lesbian mothers in that they usually must fight for the right to see their children at all (Hitchens, 1979–80). These are not very good odds.

Cases have been cited in which a lesbian mother must abide by personal restrictions imposed by the courts even when she's received custody of her child. One good example is provided by a San Francisco mother who was awarded custody of her three children (Lewis, 1980). The court mandated that as a condition for custody the mother see her female lover only at specified times. These times included when her children were at school or when they visited their father. The question must be raised whether such conditions would have been imposed had her lover been a male.

Judges presiding over custody disputes can make arbitrary judgments concerning what is in a child's best interest (Moses & Hawkins, 1982). Some judges may have homophobic ideas, which have the potential of influencing their decisions. For instance, one lesbian mother felt forced to move from one state to another. She moved from a state where judges were known to make oppressive decisions concerning gay/lesbian people to another having more liberal legislation and judicial precedents on the part of gay/lesbian parents. The move was triggered by her fear that her ex-husband would attempt to regain custody of their three children if he found out she was a lesbian. This was despite the fact that he had not seen his children for over five years. Additionally, when her family lived with him in the past, he had been physically abusive both to her and to the children. She moved because her chances of winning a potential custody battle were poor in the former state and much improved in the latter.

Gay people are slowly making progress in attaining more positive custody decisions (Green, 1978; Hitchens, 1979–80). Social workers can help gay/lesbian parents fight and win these battles in several ways (Moses & Hawkins, 1982). First, the parent must realize that although progress has been made, the odds for gaining custody are still not very good. The parent needs to realize that such cases usually take considerable time and energy. Court cases also frequently cause burdensome stress for both parent and children, in addition to being expensive. Teaching the client such skills as assertiveness, stress management, and problem solving are frequently useful. Another suggestion is to make certain to get a highly competent attorney. Referring the gay parent to support groups is also helpful. Finally, educating the gay parent by providing reading material is often beneficial.

Social and Economic Oppression of Lesbian and Gay People

There are a number of special environmental circumstances characterizing gay relationships. Social workers need to be aware of these special conditions in order to help gay/lesbian families cope with them. First, in no state in the nation can gay people legally marry. Heterosexual unions are characterized by, hopefully, much celebration and legal support. Families and friends hold wedding showers, give gifts, and make the wedding itself a major social event. Gay people, however, do not have this legal alternative. "Partners" can't be included in health insurance policies. Nor can partners file joint tax returns.

If a gay person becomes critically ill and needs hospitalization, his or her partner may be denied visiting privileges. A gay lover and partner has no legal rights because he or she does not fall under the legal definition of family. Gay people are encouraged, therefore, to draw up a legal document involving the medical power of attorney; these may address "visitation rights, the right to be consulted and to give or withhold consent about medical decisions, and in case of death, the right to personal effects and the right to dispose of the body" (Schwaber, 1985, p. 92).

Wills and the exercising of their instructions are another source of difficulty for many gay people. Gay partners have no rights at all to any inheritance if there is no will. All inheritance will be given to legal family members. Therefore, gay people are strongly encouraged to have a will made. Wills may clearly specify what possessions will go to which people.

Even with a will, however, relatives may still challenge it under the concept of "undue influence" (Peters, 1982, p. 24). This principle implies that unfair manipulation has occurred on the part of the gay partner to influence the dictates of a will. Gay people are therefore encouraged to update the contents of the will from time to time. Each time they should ascertain that the will accurately reflects their current assets and that all is well documented.

It's important for social workers to be sensitive to the unfairness and oppression suffered by gay and lesbian people. Plans and interventions can target not only improving an individual gay or lesbian person's situation, but also at changing larger systems. At the macro level, practitioners can advocate for new laws that forbid discrimination on the basis of sexual orientation. Likewise, workers can exert pressure for the dissolution of old laws and policies that oppress gay and lesbian people.

Working with African American Families

It is a necessity for generalist social work practitioners to understand the cultural expectations, economic conditions, and social realities of the various minority groups with whom they work. Lloyd and Bryce (1984) stress that workers "must understand the family's culture

and values if they are to be effective helpers. Worker insensitivity to cultural values can result in unintended and unrealized attacks on any area of a family's life—language, appearance, relationship patterns, aspirations" (p. 25).

Chapter 12 addresses ethnically and racially sensitive generalist practice. Many social workers are white and have a middle-class background. However, their practice is likely to involve African American families steeped in poverty. Thus, understanding family dynamics common to African American families in addition to their more subtle strengths is very important.

The Many Strengths of African American Families

Highlight 10.3 emphasizes the importance of African American history in terms of recognizing the oppression African Americans have suffered. It is just as important to develop an appreciation of the many strengths African American families have evolved in response to this oppression. First, African American families tend to have "strong kinship bonds among a variety of households" (Ho, 1987, p. 180). There is a strong support network developed beyond the simple nuclear family. It's easy for workers coming from a white mainstream orientation to view this family structure as inferior and inadequate.

For instance, one practitioner worked for a day treatment center which offered both special education and therapy for adolescents with behavioral and emotional problems. One twelve-year-old African American client at the center was the source of unending frustration to the social worker and the other staff. The boy seemed to change his place of residence on a weekly or biweekly basis. This required repeated updating of the bus route responsible for picking him up every day. Additionally, it made it very difficult for the boy's social worker to work with the boy's family. For one thing, it was difficult to tell who the primary caretakers were because there were so many people involved. For another thing, that kind of extended family structure simply did not fit into the family counseling model to which the worker was accustomed. The worker, by the way, was white and middle-class. She had been trained to work within the context of a nuclear family where the child's two parents were supposed to take total responsibility for the child's welfare.

In this case the worker could have assumed a more appropriate and effective perspective. She could have looked at the substantial extended family network as a strength rather than a deficit. There were many caring, involved resources and role models available to this boy instead of the one or two provided by parents.

A second strength often available to African American families is the flexibility of family roles (Ho, 1987). Contrary to traditional gender stereotypes, both men and women can assume either emotionally expressive or economically supportive roles. This allows greater flexibility in terms of improving family functioning. It follows that in a family where both parents are present, a worker should not assume a matriarchal structure just because the mother/spouse makes her points strongly. Marital relationships

---

HIGHLIGHT 10.3

The Impacts of History and Oppression on African American Families

This text is a practice text which describes practice skills. However, it is important to examine the historical and current social context in which African American families live in order to best apply these skills.

McAdoo (1987) relates some of the major historical conditions impacting African American families. Initially, of course, African Americans as slaves were often "forced to live polygamously," "were bred as animals," and saw "a domestic pattern of mother-child units" evolving as the result of plantation life (p. 196). Families had little control over their destiny. Couples were torn apart at the whim of their owners.

Later, during Reconstruction, McAdoo continues, individuals striving to gain and maintain power and white supremacy (for example, the Ku Klux Klan) worked to make life as restricted as possible for African American people. Many African Americans were forced to move west, leaving extended family behind. Later in the 1930s, African American families also migrated to the hubs of industrialization in the North. There they could find jobs, despite, once again, leaving much of their extended family network behind.

McAdoo (1987) stresses that "since the mid-1970s, [African Americans] have faced another form of disruption—increased levels of impoverishment and deteriorating social conditions which have led to further economic and structural changes in their families" (p. 196). She cites a number of facts which have led to such changes; these include "lower marital fertility, increases in the rates of divorce and separation, the earlier sexual activity of [African American] youths, the reluctance to give children up for adoption outside the familial networks, delays in marriage, the imbalance in the ratio of men to women, and the high unemployment rate of young [African American] men" (p. 198). African American people are much more likely to be poor than whites (U.S. Bureau of the Census, 1985). They receive an inferior education at the primary and secondary levels to that of whites (McAdoo, 1987, p. 199). Because of deficient conditions, "African Americans have more health problems than do whites" (McAdoo, 1987, p. 202), in addition to a higher death rate (McAdoo, 1987).

Thus, prevalent values in African American families have resulted both from the history of slavery and from the ongoing oppression suffered since those times. Social work practice with African American families needs to proceed within the context of the resulting social and economic conditions.

in African American families are egalitarian or equal by nature.

A third strength often apparent in African American families involves "the strong education and work achievement orientation" (Ho, 1987, p. 181). Hill (1972) cites how this emphasis on achievement is evidenced by the high proportion of African American youth attending college whose parents never had that opportunity themselves. The implication is that people realize how important education is for one's future potential and encourage their children to strive for a better life.

A fourth strength often inherent in African American families is their dedication to religious values and serious involvement in their churches (Ho, 1987; McAdoo, 1987). African American churches provide a massive resource for hope and spiritual growth, social support, and a range of services to meet members' needs. Such services may include "senior citizen activities, child care, educational groups, parenting groups, and housing development" (Ho, 1987, p. 182).

Social Work Practice with African American Families

McAdoo (1987) identifies three major roles for social workers to assume when helping African American families. First, the worker needs to develop empathy for the cultural context saturated with the oppression in which African American families must live. Second, the worker must maximize the use of practice skills and available resources to improve the social and economic conditions of African American families. Third, the practitioner must advocate on the behalf of African American families to change the policies, regulations, and expectations that act to discriminate against African Americans.

Additionally, Ho cites at least four major approaches that are useful when working with African American families (1987):

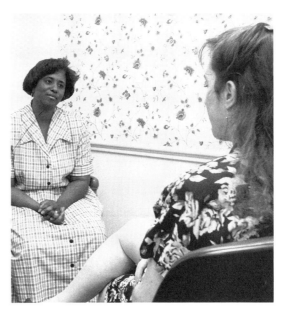

Counselors must be sensitive to racial and ethnic differences.

1. Engage the client/family

Regardless of race, it's important to empathize with a family and its situation. The referral process may have been tedious or confusing. Family members may have had bad experiences with agencies in the past, which can eat away at trust.

It's also important to understand the initial silence and apparent lack of communication often posed by African American family members. This may convey their lack of faith and confidence either in your ability to help them while in the role of worker or in the agency's commitment in and ability to do so. Family members may be experiencing their own anger at how they've been treated by white society. Their resentment may indirectly be projected onto you.

Reasons for communication blocks need to be addressed just like any other issues raised in the problem-solving process. If you are not African American and especially if you're white, you may want to discuss straightforwardly any racial tensions you may perceive. Don't be defensive if family members express anger. It's logical for them, if they have negative feelings, to vent them at you just because you're there. These feelings must be addressed and placed within perspectives before the problem-solving process can proceed.

On the one hand, be understanding. However, on the other, also be strong and assertive. Most African American families will expect the worker to competently and straightforwardly lead the intervention process.

Finally, realize that most African American families will react most positively to an intervention process with clearly identified goals and with constraints on how long it will take to get results. In other words, telling an African American family that the change process will take an indeterminable amount of time will probably not be well received.

2. Assess the family in past and present

Understanding dynamics in African American families is as critical as it is in other families. Most African American families are more interested in what's going on in the present than in the past. Therefore, the reasons for soliciting information about more historical issues (for example, how parents themselves were raised by grandparents, or what family incidents occurred several years ago that had serious impact on the family) need clear explanation regarding why they're important.

3. Set mutual goals

Goal setting is just as important when working with African American families as any other families. It's often likely that the African American family will be plagued by a number of concurrent problems. Therefore, the worker must both be problem-oriented and maintain a focus on how circumstances outside of the family fuel the problem. An African American family would probably consider solving an economically related problem (like unemployment) much more important than resolving interpersonal conflicts (for example, a disagreement between marital partners). The family's top priorities need to be addressed first. Additionally, the faster a problem can be solved, the more cooperative family members will probably become.

4. Identify the target system for change

As with any other family, the worker needs to identify the systems in need of change. This should be done in a prioritized order. Sometimes the problem can best be solved by targeting some external system like the schools or the health care system. Other times the system in need of attention and change is some aspect of the extended family system. For instance, interference and involvement of extended family members has been shown to disrupt the marital relationship (McAdoo, 1977). At still other times, interpersonal changes are needed within the African American family system.

The Current Status of Family Services

Family services are those "provided by social science service agencies that emphasize a concern for families in their mission or statement of purpose" (Erickson, 1987, p. 589). In other words, a broad array of agencies can provide services to families as long as these agencies clearly state that families are to be the primary recipients of service. One survey of North American Family Service agencies (Family Service America, 1984) found that "the major concerns of families are unemployment, single-parenthood, increased family violence, incest, blurred sex roles, depression and loneliness, and alcohol and drug abuse" (Erickson, 1987, p. 593). Erickson (1987) continues that programs include: various types of counseling; "educational programs; financial assistance programs; employee assistance programs; and programs geared toward effecting social or institutional change" (p. 593).

The types of family services available in any particular community depend on what the community needs, on the one hand, and what it can afford to pay for, on the other. Thus, the services available to families vary drastically from one area to another.

Most family service agencies provide services directly to individuals, groups of individuals facing similar problems, and the families themselves. For example, they might provide individual counseling for depressed family members, support groups for battered women, or family counseling for entire families.

However, there is also a definite macro practice aspect to the family service agency. It typically addresses problems held by a number of people in the community. In the event that services are not available, the generalist practitioner may need to assess the community's needs. For instance, the worker may determine that alcohol and other drug abuse (AODA) treatment services are inadequate to meet the needs of families within the community. That worker may then proceed to gather data to document that the need truly exists and subsequently to advocate for the expansion of current programs.

In another situation, the worker may discover that AODA services are available but are not getting to the people who really need them. In this case, the worker may investigate what's causing this blockage and try to remedy the problem. For instance, are available treatment programs not being publicized adequately? Is the "red tape" so thick that it's difficult for people to cut through it and get services? Or, for some reason, are agency policies making the neediest people ineligible?

Whatever the reason, family service agencies can provide effective and flexible resources to help satisfy community families' real needs. Generalist social workers may not only be called upon to serve individuals, families, and groups, but also to advocate for changes in agency poli-

cies, governmental legislation regarding how resources are distributed, and expansion of services that are already there.

Erickson (1987) emphasizes the importance of "empowering" people via family service agencies; in other words, he stresses "helping people to help themselves" (p. 592). One aspect of the generalist social worker's macro role is to help people join and work together in order to bring about their own changes.

Macro Practice with Families: Promoting Social and Economic Justice

Thorman (1982) cites insufficient income, inadequate housing, lack of job opportunities, and deficient services both for transportation and recreation as being primary problems among the families who turn to family based service agencies for help. He continues that "our nation's professed belief that the family is the cornerstone of our society is not matched by public policy. We have not really addressed the question of how to guarantee all families the conditions necessary for family support" (p. 91). Unavailability of health insurance, lack of supportive day care services for the children of parents who work, and a dearth of strategies to train workers for skilled vocations where jobs are available are among the myriad of problems confronting America's families.

Generalist practitioners in agency positions often feel frustrated and overwhelmed at the concept of "changing the system" because it isn't working right. They often feel they have enough to do with their daily micro and mezzo practice concerns. However, the roots of clients' problems should always be kept in mind. Sometime there might be an opportunity to amend an agency policy, even a relatively minor one, so that clients are better served. A worker may be able to assist in a political campaign to elect an official who's more sensitive to families and their needs. Or, a worker might be able to advocate for clients, prove the need for some service, and succeed in making that service available to people who really need it.

The Generalist Intervention Model emphasizes constant awareness of the impacts of macro systems. The potential to make improvements in agencies, organizations, and systems should never be forgotten as one means of effecting positive change for clients.

The Carnegie Council on Children emphasizes that poverty is a major stumbling block obstructing the progress of multitudes of American children (Keniston, 1977), and, in effect, their families. The Carnegie Report stresses that a different configuration of services could be made available to American families if policies geared toward families were improved. Generalist practitioners should best keep these concepts in mind when considering intervention alternatives. Sometimes macro level changes may be possible. Improved family service policies would follow a number of principles.

First, all families should have access to the services they need regardless of their income bracket. Second, services should be distributed neither along racial nor economic lines. In other words, the same quality of services should be available to everyone. Agencies providing family services would have a mixture of races and economic levels characterizing its clientele. Third, services should be convenient for everyone. All families should have access to coordinating referral and appointment centers which they could contact. Fourth, families should

have as many options as possible so that they could select the service of their preference. Fifth, parents should be given significant input into the agencies and their policies serving families. Sixth, more volunteers and paraprofessionals should be used to aid in service delivery. Using such people to perform less specialized tasks would minimize the cost of expensive specialists. Finally, seventh, more resources should be devoted to preventing problems before they occur rather than applying Band-aids after the problems already exist. A more superficial view sees prevention as an extravagance that isn't absolutely necessary. Therefore, the programs and services that could prevent and minimize problems often rest at the bottom of priority lists. Money runs out and programs aimed at prevention are frequently among those first cut.

Chapter Summary

A wide range of generalist practice skills was related to working with families. A variety of techniques for family intervention were examined. These included beginning work with families, planning, reframing, family sculpting, role playing, videotaping, and giving homework assignments. Multiproblem families were discussed and family preservation described.

Diversity in families was explored by discussing issues involved in working with gay/lesbian families and African American families. Finally, the current status of family services was appraised and the relationship between macro practice and working with families explored.

11 Making Ethical Decisions

by Lloyd G. Sinclair, A.C.S.W.[1]

Confidentiality

1. Lloyd G. Sinclair, MSSW, ACSW, AASECT Certified Sex Therapist, Educator, and Supervisor, is a psychotherapist at Midwest Psychotherapy Center, Madison, WI.

At the very core of the theory and practice of social work lie ethics—the principles of moral conduct that govern social workers' interactions with others, whether they be individual clients or entire communities. As discussed in chapter 1, ethics involve principles that specify what is good and what is bad, a moral creed for behavior. Ethics are based on underlying values that define what is good and desirable. It is upon that foundation of values that the social worker makes ethical decisions about how to practice professionally.

CHAPTER ELEVEN

Beth, a social worker, received a telephone call from an architect, Robert, who was very concerned about his nineteen-year-old son, Daniel. Robert had learned his son, while working as a camp counselor, had exposed himself to youthful campers. Additionally, he had vaguely invited one camper to engage in sexual activity with him. These incidents came to light after the campers returned home, and one told his mother about it. The mother relayed this information to the camp director, emphatically stating she wanted to cause no trouble. This church-affiliated camp had served boys and girls for generations.

Beth immediately asked Robert if the camp director, or anyone else, had reported these incidents to the local police or social service department. She knew that professionals were legally required to report suspected child abuse—physical or sexual—and wanted to ensure such a report had been made. Robert indicated the camp had performed its own investigation, which determined the incidents were isolated and involved no actual physical touching. Furthermore, they had immediately asked the nineteen-year-old counselor, Daniel, to leave, which he did. The campers have since all returned home, with apparently no ill effects.

The camp's board of directors met with their attorney. She examined the state child-abuse reporting statute and determined they were not legally required to report these incidents. They were a religious organization, not licensed professionals. The board of directors decided reporting this matter would cause them more harm than good. Reporting might put all campers through unnecessary and embarrassing interviews and needlessly damage the camp's fine reputation.

Robert heartily endorsed this decision. As a father, he did not want his son to risk being labeled a sex offender, thereby compromising his family's excellent standing in the community. He wanted no coverup; he simply wanted Daniel to receive whatever professional help he required.

This placed Beth on the horns of a dilemma. She knew that as a certified professional, *she* was required to report child abuse. However, she need only report if she learned of such an allegation via her work with a victim. In this case, she had become aware of these incidents through the concerned father of the admitted perpetrator of the abuse. Therefore, Beth had no legal requirement to report this matter to other professionals.

Beth felt both sincerity and fear in Robert's voice, believing he was truly concerned and supportive of his son. Daniel was no longer with the campers, thus they were in no danger from him. Although it was more than a hundred miles north of where she lived, Beth was aware of the camp. Her own friend's children had benefitted from the camp's outstanding work with youth. A scandal that could grow from the public learning of this matter might unnecessarily wound the camp's programs for hundreds of youths. It would potentially prohibit these children from gaining many future benefits. Beth reminded herself that Daniel apparently did not sexually touch any children. Perhaps her concerns were an overreaction because she did witness so much abuse in her professional work.

But what if Daniel had engaged in more sexual activity than had been reported? Beth knew boys were typically very poor reporters of sexual abuse; they generally chose to suffer in silence and self-blame (Bolton et al., 1989). The camp's internal investigation was perhaps biased by their understandable desire to minimize risking their reputation. They would logically try to ward off any potential damage.

Beth knew most sex offenders began their offenses as adolescents or early adults (Abel, 1988). Furthermore, histories of indecent exposure are associated with the development of more invasive sexual assaults (Romero & Williams, 1985). Additionally, Beth knew sex offenders frequently understate the extent of their problems. They also tend to drop out of treatment prematurely unless they are compelled by an outside authority (such as a probation agent) to resolve their problems fully (Salter, 1988).

Therefore, if Beth did not report these incidents to social services or the police, would she be acting ethically? Would she be contributing to the problem by inhibiting victims from getting help? Would Beth be enabling a sex offender in avoiding appropriate treatment? Even worse, would she be helping create future victims?

Bennett, an executive, came to see Frank, a social worker who worked as a mental health counselor. Bennett complained of increasing depression and a general lack of interest in most areas of his life. Frank learned that Bennett was forty-two years old, had been married for seventeen years, and had three children. He worked as an executive director of an organization that represented the interests of large building contractors. Bennett stated he was generally content with his marriage although it was less satisfying to him lately. He indicated that he enjoyed his children but found himself increasingly impatient with them. He added that he was quite comfortable in his job.

Several sessions of counseling and a physical examination revealed no apparent basis for Bennett's depression. After he felt considerable trust in and rapport with Frank, he began to discuss his occupational concerns more candidly and concretely. He revealed that his job was to present favorably (both to the public and in legislative arenas), the large building contractors who were voluntary members of his employing organization. He was, therefore, a lobbyist and spokesperson for this industry. Most of the member companies engaged in large public works projects (that is, building projects for the government).

Bennett had learned some time ago that the heads of these companies were in the habit of secretly meeting to discuss financial bids when the government solicited competitive bids for projects they were funding. In other words, the companies were illegally circumventing the competitive bidding process. They would agree among themselves which company would be awarded which project. They artificially inflated all the bids to ensure large profits. They rigged the outcome by having the company they agreed would get the contract submit a slightly lower bid. This gave the appearance of the government getting the best value, but the government was, in fact, being cheated.

Bennett revealed to Frank that he was uncomfortable with this practice, knowing it was morally wrong, illegal, and punitive to the taxpaying public. However, he had not participated in this bid rigging directly. He had simply worked for the organization to which these contractors belonged. He was never directly involved with any government contract work.

Bennett had many fears. Personally, he was well aware that his professional position was the culmination of many years of diligent and painstaking work. He knew his career would be destroyed if he did not continue to participate passively in this fraud. If he lost his job from his "whistle-blowing," he might never get another job in his profession. Prospective employers would fear he would similarly betray their trade secrets. He was worried what consequences would inevitably befall his family if he could no longer draw his substantial salary. Their life-style demanded a comfortable income, and his oldest daughter would soon be attending college.

Bennett's deepest fear was even more basic, however. He had heard stories of the untimely deaths of persons who had revealed fraud in the construction industry, and the possible cover-up by members of the government from fear or personal gain. He could not bear to face the possibility of physical harm to himself or a member of his family.

Frank and Bennett agreed that the major source of Bennett's depression was his pervasive helplessness in the face of this troubling matter. Both agreed further that the *right* thing to do was to report this fraud to a government agency that would have the power and ethics to end it. Bennett felt that the risk was just too great to do that, however.

Frank was extremely troubled by this knowledge. He respected his client's right to self-determination. Yet this situation involved so much more than simply his client. Did he have a responsibility to the community which superseded his contract with his client? Should Frank report this illegal behavior? Would such reporting protect Bennett from harm, or might it cause his organization to collapse? The outcome of reporting would be impossible to predict accurately. Should Frank exert pressure on Bennett to report this fraud, or would this be imposing his own agenda onto him? Could Frank effectively help Bennett resolve his depression while knowing the probable cause was something neither was willing to address? What was the most ethical way to proceed?

Nadine is a social worker who is employed by a federally funded family planning clinic. The government has decreed, and the Supreme Court has upheld, its moral opposition to abortion. Therefore, counselors at such clinics are not allowed to discuss termination of pregnancy. The only exceptions are in cases where two independent physicians determine that carrying the particular pregnancy to childbirth would almost certainly result in severe physical injury or death to the mother.

Jennifer enters the clinic's doors. She appears scared, unkempt, and more like a small child than even a teenager. She describes her situation. She believes she might be pregnant after her father forced her to have intercourse with him on numerous occasions. Nadine arranged for Jennifer to have a pregnancy test, and her worst suspicions are confirmed. She is indeed in her first three months of pregnancy.

Nadine has seen many immature young people in her relatively brief employment at the clinic, but never before has she seen a more compromised, defeated, and terrified young client. The effects of economic deprivation, abuse, and community hopelessness bear their scars deeply on Jennifer. Frighteningly, soon this child may be having her own child.

Nadine abhors abortion, which ordinarily makes operating under the clinic guidelines comfortable for her. Her experience had consistently been that few clients opted to terminate their pregnancies. While clients might be attracted to the seemingly simplest resolution of an unintended pregnancy—abortion—most chose other alternatives. They either carried the pregnancy to term and raised the child, turned the child over to a relative to raise, or placed the child up for adoption. However, Jennifer's situation was so pitiful. Would Nadine be supportive of her if she required Jennifer to give birth to a child conceived from incest with her father? Her shame and self-loathing were so profound. She obviously felt the options for her future were closed to her.

Nadine knew where Jennifer could get funding for a safe, legal abortion, one that carried less physical risk for her young body than having a baby. If Nadine did not tell Jennifer of this option, might Jennifer attempt to perform the abortion herself? Or, might she become so despondent that she would end her life? Discussing abortion with Jennifer would be a blatant violation of clinic policy. The violation was so severe that it carried with it the possibility of actually closing the clinic. Even if this client would be well-served by such a discussion, what about the present and future needs of all the other hundreds of clients whom the clinic serves? If the clinic closed, they would all be deprived of help.

Introduction

We have examined throughout this text many aspects of generalist social work practice, as well as discussing specific skills for intervention in a variety of social work situations and settings. This chapter will address social work values, the ethics that grow from those values, and how social workers can utilize ethical principles in their everyday professional lives.

When asked, most social work students say they chose this field because of a deep desire to help other people. Thus the profession is comprised of a self-selected group of persons who subscribe to altruistic values—having an unselfish interest in and care for the welfare of others. What a rich human resource this is! As a group, social workers have a legacy of helping those in need, whether they be individuals with a specific difficulty or an entire community or subculture. Beginning social workers are excited to harness this combination of goodwill and newly acquired skills. They go forth and serve their clients, flush with the potential for good works.

Very soon, however, this energetic naiveté confronts situations where it is terribly unclear how to "do good." Well-intentioned but less than careful intervention can result in harm. While this ensures social work will never become boring or rote, it presents a challenge to professionals to stay ever vigilant and self-aware, remaining true to their original intent— to help others. This self-examination promotes growth for individual social workers and guides the development of the entire field. Social work values provide the home base to which social workers can return again and again. Social work ethics are likewise parents whom social workers can always trust and go to for help.

Specifically, this chapter will:

- Examine the chief document of social work values, the Code of Ethics of the National Association of Social Workers;
- Discuss the most widely accepted theories of moral development, understanding how people develop the capacity to exercise moral decisions;
- Address some of the special problems of-

ten presenting ethical dilemmas for social workers, such as balancing clients' privacy against public safety, or allocating scarce resources among people whose needs exceed those resources through the thoughtful scrutinizing of case examples and practice vignettes.
- Develop a model social workers can utilize to guide them toward sound, ethical decision-making.

The Code of Ethics of the National Association of Social Workers

Attempts have been made in recent history to formulate codes of ethics for the social work profession, thereby documenting a creed of principles as well as rules for sound professional practice. The first such code to be formally adopted by a large social work organization came in 1947. At that time, the largest social work association—the American Association of Social Workers—ratified their first code of ethics. Since then, other social work groups, such as the National Association of Black Social Workers, have developed codes of ethics.

The National Association of Social Workers (NASW) adopted its first code of ethics in 1960, which since has undergone several revisions and expansions to address evolving issues in social-work practice. The earliest code consisted essentially of a list of proclamations or promises the social worker was supposed to make and subscribe to. These highlighted the general core values the profession represented, such as giving precedence to professional responsibility over personal interests.

An example of an addition to the code of ethics which responded to the evolving values of the profession (as well as the society at large) was the inclusion of a principle of nondiscrimination, enacted in 1967. From our present-day perspective, it seems shameful that this principle wasn't an integral part of any first code.

Figure 11.1: National Association of Social Workers' Code of Ethics (As adopted by the 1979 NASW Delegate Assembly, Effective July 1, 1980.)

Summary of Major Principles*

I. The Social Worker's Conduct and Comportment as a Social Worker

A. Propriety
The social worker should maintain high standards of personal conduct in the capacity or identity as social worker.

B. Competence and Professional Development
The social worker should strive to become and remain proficient in professional practice and the performance of professional functions.

C. Service
The social worker should regard as primary the service obligation of the social work profession.

D. Integrity
The social worker should act in accordance with the highest standards of professional integrity.

E. Scholarship and Research
The social worker engaged in study and research should be guided by the conventions of scholarly inquiry.

II. The Social Worker's Ethical Responsibility to Clients

F. Primacy of Clients' Interests
The social worker's primary responsibility is to clients.

G. Rights and Prerogatives of Clients
The social worker should make every effort to foster maximum self-determination on the part of clients.

H. Confidentiality and Privacy
The social worker should respect the privacy of clients and hold in confidence all information obtained in the course of professional service.

I. Fees
When setting fees, the social worker should ensure that they are fair, reasonable, considerate, and commensurate with the service performed and with due regard for the clients' ability to pay.

III. The Social Worker's Ethical Responsibility to Colleagues

J. Respect, Fairness, and Courtesy
The social worker should treat colleagues with respect, courtesy, fairness, and good faith.

K. Dealing with Colleagues' Clients
The social worker has the responsibility to relate to the clients of colleagues with full professional consideration.

IV. The Social Worker's Ethical Responsibility to Employers and Employing Organizations

L. Commitments to Employing Organizations
The social worker should adhere to commitments made to the employing organizations.

V. The Social Worker's Ethical Responsibility to the Social Work Profession

M. Maintaining the Integrity of the Profession
The social worker should uphold and advance the values, ethics, knowledge, and mission of the profession.

N. Community Service
The social worker should assist the profession in making social services available to the general public.

O. Development of Knowledge
The social worker should take responsibility for identifying, developing, and fully utilizing knowledge for professional practice.

VI. The Social Worker's Ethical Responsibility to Society

P. Promoting the General Welfare.
The social worker should promote the general welfare of society.

*Constitutes a summary of the Code of Ethics effective July 1, 1980, as adopted by the 1979 NASW Delegate Assembly. The complete text, including preamble and expanded definition of principles, is available upon request.

NASW members soon found the code of ethics to be overly vague in guiding them in specific situations. Additionally, it lacked specific methods for recourse against those who did not uphold elements in the code. Thus, a new code of ethics was adopted in 1979, expanding the provisions of the previous code and adding new material. It is the 1979 document which forms the foundation for the most recent revision, adopted by NASW in 1990. The preamble to the code of ethics explains its function; it states the code is "a guide to the everyday conduct of members of the social work profession and . . . a basis for the adjudication of issues in ethics when the conduct of social workers is alleged to deviate from the standards expressed or implied in this code" (National Association of Social Workers, 1990). The preamble continues to explain that the code is founded in the fundamental values of the profession. These include "the worth, dignity and uniqueness of all persons as well as their rights and opportunities" (National Association of Social Workers, 1990).

In utilizing the code of ethics, social workers are expected to weigh each ethical dilemma they encounter against the many tenets of the code. They then choose a course of action which represents their best judgment. This judgment is necessary because no code of ethics could ever be so specific or inclusive that all complex situations could be addressed. Instead, "the code offers general principles to guide conduct, and the judicious appraisal of conduct, in situations that have ethical implications" (National Association of Social Workers, 1990).

The ultimate decision made in any practice situation will probably be that of the individual social worker involved. However, it will be against the backdrop of the social work profession that the decision will be judged, often by the social worker's peers. The social worker thus understands that ethical decision making and behavior involves clients, the social worker, colleagues, the profession, and ultimately the larger society. While this may seem like an awesomely heavy responsibility, it can best be viewed as an entire network of people guiding the social worker to perform in the most noble fashion.

The final issue in the preamble to the NASW code of ethics implores social workers to discourage, expose and correct unethical conduct as well as assist colleagues who may be unjustly accused of unethical conduct. This underscores the social worker's obligation to uphold high standards of practice while supporting deserving colleagues. The summary of the major principles of the *Code of Ethics* of the National Association of Social Workers is included in Figure 11.1.

The NASW Code of Ethics describes general rules for professional behavior, which stem from the values of the social work profession. Occasionally, an issue can be so straightforward that a specific guideline or prohibition is stated. An example of this is the prohibition against social workers taking anything of value (like money) for making a referral. But, ethical issues rarely present themselves in such a discrete and simple form. Instead, ethical dilemmas involve the conflict of several important principles, requiring the careful weighing of various factors to determine the most ethical course of action. As with most complex situations, there are often many points of view and many defensible courses of action. Even after a decision has been made, frequently it is followed by some self-doubt and review.

The Social Worker's Conduct and Comportment as a Social Worker

Let us examine the major points in the NASW Code of Ethics:

- The code indicates that social workers should conduct themselves according to high professional standards. They are entitled to the same freedom of personal conduct as anyone, except as it might affect their professional roles. Social workers should not engage in dishonest behavior. They have a responsibility to indicate when they are representing their profession and when they are acting as private citizens.

- Social workers should strive for proficiency.
- Social workers should only work within their areas of competence, and never misrepresent their qualifications.
- The primary obligation of the social work profession is to serve others. It is the social worker's responsibility to provide high-quality services and avoid inhumane or discriminatory practices against anyone or any group of people.
- Social workers should exhibit honesty and impartiality.
- Social workers should be careful not to exploit their professional roles for personal gain.
- Social workers who perform research should always respect the rights of people they may be studying, including obtaining their voluntary and informed consent.
- Social workers should ensure research participants are not subjected to physical or mental discomfort.
- Social workers should be vigilant in protecting the privacy of study participants.
- Social workers should assume credit only for their own work, being careful to accurately credit the work of others.

The Social Worker's Ethical Responsibilities to Clients

- Social workers have as their greatest responsibility their relationships to clients.
- Social workers should serve their clients with a high level of competence and never exploit them or discriminate against them.
- Social workers should guard against conflict of interests when serving clients.
- Social workers should never have sexual interactions with clients.
- Social workers have a responsibility to explain to clients what can be offered to them, and what opportunities and obligations they face.
- Social workers should consult with other professionals when this might be helpful.
- Social workers must end their professional relationships with clients when their work is no longer helpful, but not sever their relationships abruptly or without warning.
- Social workers should help clients determine their own destiny. When a client is not competent to safeguard her/his own interests, social workers should take care to do so, exercising care not to violate the client's civil rights.
- Social workers must take great care to protect the privacy of clients, revealing confidential information only when given permission to do so by clients or in extremely unusual (such as life-threatening) circumstances.
- Social workers should inform clients of the limits of confidentiality.
- Social workers should set their professional fees fairly and consider their clients' ability to pay.

The Social Worker's Ethical Responsibility to Colleagues

- Social workers should cooperate with and respect colleagues.
- Social workers should promote ethics and competence in colleagues.

- Social workers should utilize appropriate conflict resolution when differences arise with colleagues, and not exploit such differences for personal gain.
- Social workers who employ or supervise others should be clear about the expectations of their relationships with colleagues, fair in their dealings, and open about their evaluations of others' performance to the colleague.
- Social workers should not work with a colleague's clients without consultation with that colleague.
- When substituting for a colleague, social workers should serve the colleague's clients as any other client.

The Social Worker's Ethical Responsibility to Employers and Employing Organizations

- Social workers should honor commitments made to employers.
- Social workers have an obligation to improve the efficiency and effectiveness of their employing agency.
- Social workers should avoid working for or supervising students in agencies sanctioned by NASW for violations.
- Social workers should prevent discrimination in the workplace.
- Social workers should respect the property of their employing organizations, using it only for its intended purpose.

The Social Worker's Ethical Responsibility to the Social Work Profession

- Social workers should uphold and promote the values, ethics, knowledge, and purpose of the profession.
- Social workers should respect their profession, constructively criticizing it where appropriate.
- Social workers should act against unethical conduct by other social workers and unqualified practice of social work.
- Social workers must use care not to falsely advertise their competence or the outcome clients will achieve.
- Social workers should give of themselves to promote the availability of social services to clients.
- Social workers should use the relevant knowledge of the profession, and contribute to that knowledge.

The Social Worker's Ethical Responsibility to Society

- Social workers should promote society's general welfare.
- Social workers should prevent all forms of discrimination, including that of race, gender, sexual orientation, age, marital status, beliefs, mental or physical limitation, or any other characteristic or status.
- Social workers should promote all persons having access to the resources and opportunities which would be beneficial to them.
- Social workers should work to expand opportunities for people, especially for members of disadvantaged groups.
- Social workers should respect and embrace the diversity of cultures present in the United States.
- Social workers should provide their services in public emergencies.
- Social workers should support legislative activity to improve social conditions and justice.
- Social workers should encourage public involvement in the shaping of social policies.

Moral Development

Before we turn our attention to the resolution of ethical dilemmas that commonly face professional social workers, let us first look at the development of moral reasoning in general. Developmental theory suggests that, unlike lower animals who rely almost exclusively on instinct, human beings possess the capacity for extraordinarily complex reasoning and the potential for the belief in a "higher" good. This higher good may be codified in religious beliefs or more personally be integrated into something we might identify as *conscience*. We know these beliefs, and the conduct which grows from these beliefs, is not innate but learned. Only the capacity for their development is inborn. Thus, babies are selfish, demonstrating complete lack of concern (to the chagrin of their parents at 4:00 A.M.) for the rights, needs, or wishes of those around them. They respond exclusively to pleasure and pain, and in their primitive communication, are remarkably effective in conveying those feelings to their care givers. This is a requirement for survival at this stage of life. Without such self-concerned behavior on the part of the child, the human race wouldn't survive.

But the reciprocal role, that of the care giver, requires considerable selflessness and remarkable sacrifice of her or his personal needs. How does it happen that in two decades of life, persons evolve from complete neediness to a high degree of selflessness?

Developmental theorists, including Piaget (1970), Kohlberg and Gilligan (1971), Loevinger (1976), Selman (1976), and Gilligan (1982), teach us that human development progresses through definable stages. Each stage builds upon the previous, more primitive one. John Dewey (1963) first posited the idea that children and adolescents move through stages of development. He taught that children were not miniature adults, but rather people who developed through qualitatively distinct stages. Each stage is unique, possessing its own special way of organizing thoughts and interpretations of the world. The developing young person must travel through each stage successfully. Each stage depends on the successful learning which occurred in the previous stage. Further, once people achieve a particular stage of development, they cannot backslide or reverse direction; remaining in that stage or preceeding to the next higher stage are the only options.

The progress from one stage of development to the next is entirely determined by interactions with the environment, thereby differentiating humans from lower animals. Humans learn and animals are driven by instinct. Growth does not take place automatically or magically. Rather, it occurs as a result of each person undergoing significant experiences in the environment. Most of this growth occurs between infancy and late adolescence.

Jean Piaget (1970) outlined stages of cognitive development (that is, the way people think). For example, he identified that adolescents can conceive of possibilities and probabilities in ways young children cannot. This is not a matter of what people think, which can be simple memorization, but rather how they think, such as their ability to change their beliefs on the basis of new information.

Lawrence Kohlberg expanded on Piaget's theories of cognitive development to address moral thinking (Kohlberg, 1969). He examined how people conceived of issues related to social justice—morals, principles, and ethics. Kohlberg, like Piaget and other developmental theorists, believed persons travel through distinct stages. This stage development can be identified in guiding moral reasoning. He identified six stages of moral development, as described in Figure 11.2.

The first level, the "preconventional" or premoral level, is characterized by giving precedence to self-interest. People usually experience this level during ages four to ten years. Moral decisions are based on external standards.

Behavior is governed by whether a child will receive a reward or a punishment. The first stage in this level, "the punishment and obedience orientation," is based on avoiding punishment. Children do what they are told in order to avoid negative consequences. The second stage in Level I, "naive instrumental hedonism," focuses on rewards instead of punishment. In other words, children do the "right" thing in order to receive a reward or compensation. Sometimes this involves an exchange of favors, a form of "I'll scratch your back if you'll scratch mine."

Level II of Kohlberg's theory is the "con-ventional" level, where moral thought is based on conforming to conventional roles. Frequently, this level occurs during ages ten to thirteen. There is a strong desire to please others and to receive social approval. Although moral standards have begun to be internalized, they are still based on what others dictate, rather than on what is personally decided.

Within Level II, Stage 3 or "good boy/girl morality" focuses on gaining the approval of others. Good relationships become very important. Stage 4, "authority-maintaining morality," emphasizes the need to adhere to law. Higher authorities are generally respected.

Figure 11.2: Kohlberg's Theory of Moral Development

Kohlberg's Six Stages of Moral Development are summarized below:

Level	Description
Level I: Preconventional (Conventional role conformity)	Controls are external. Behavior is governed by receiving rewards or punishments
Stage 1: Punishment and obedience orientation	Decisions concerning what is good and bad are made in order to avoid receiving punishment
Stage 2: Naive instrumental hedonism	Rules are obeyed in order to receive rewards. Often favors are exchanged.
Level II: Conventional (Role conformity)	The opinions of others become important. Behavior is governed by conforming to social expectations.
Stage 3: "Good boy/girl morality"	Good behavior is considered what pleases others. There is a strong desire to please and gain the approval of others.
Stage 4: Authority-maintaining morality	The belief in "law and order" is strong. Behavior conforms to law and higher authority. Social order is important.
Level III: Post-conventional (Self-accepted moral principles)	Moral decisions are finally internally controlled. Morality involves higher level principles beyond law and even beyond self-interest.
Stage 5: Morality of contract, of individual rights, and of democratically accepted law	Laws are considered necessary. However, they are subject to rational thought and interpretation. Community welfare is important.
Stage 6: Morality of individual principles and conscience	Behavior is based on internal ethical principles. Decisions are made according to what is right rather than what is written into law.

At Level III of Kohlberg's theory of moral development, people contemplate laws and expectations and decide on their own what is right or wrong. The pedestrians here watch as police respond to a traffic accident.

"Law and order" are considered necessary in order to maintain the social order.

Level III, the "postconventional" level, concerns developing a moral conscience that goes beyond purely what others say. People contemplate laws and expectations, and decide on their own what is right and what is wrong. They become autonomous, independent thinkers. Behavior is based on principles instead of laws. This level progresses beyond selfish concerns. The needs and well-being of others become very important in addition to one's own. At this level, true morality is achieved.

Within Level III, Stage 5 or "the morality of contract, of individual rights, and of democratically accepted law" involves adhering to socially accepted laws and principles. Law is considered good for the general public welfare. However, laws are subject to interpretation and change. Stage 6, the "morality of individual decisions and conscience," is the ultimate attainment. During this stage, one becomes free of the thoughts and opinions expressed by others. Morality is completely internalized. Decisions are based on one's personal conscience, transcendent of meager laws and regulations.

From Kohlberg's perspective, early-stage thinking focuses on both escaping pain by avoiding being punished by authority figures and selfishness. Later-stage thinking, on the other hand, considers the rights of others and that actions affect the larger society. Successful upbringing includes the promotion of high levels of moral development. This facilitates the entry of a person into an organized and interdependent society.

Carol Gilligan (1982) and others noted that women tend to view moral decisions in terms of personal situations rather than societal ones. This may be because women are raised with an ethic which endorses sacrificing one's own well-being for the good of others. Thus, men may view moral decision-making in a more global context of truths, whereas women tend to view such decision-making in terms of their close interpersonal relationships. Gilligan found that women tend to view morality "in terms of selfishness and responsibility, as an obligation to exercise care and avoid hurt. People who care for each other are the most responsible, whereas those who hurt someone else are selfish and immoral. While men think more in terms of justice and fairness, women think more about specific people" (Papalia & Olds, 1981, p. 416).

HIGHLIGHT 11.1
Gilligan's Levels of Moral Development

Level 1: Orientation to Personal Survival

This level focuses purely on the woman's self-interest. Her needs are salient. The needs and well-being of others are not really considered. At this level, a woman focuses first on personal survival. What is practical and best for her is most important.

Transition 1: Transition from Personal Selfishness to Responsibility

This first transition involves a movement in moral thought from consideration only of self to some consideration of others involved. During this transition, a woman comes to acknowledge the fact that she is responsible not only for herself but also for others, including the unborn. In other words, she begins to acknowledge that her choice will impact others in addition to herself.

Level 2: Goodness as Self-Sacrifice

Level 2 involves putting aside one's own needs and wishes. Rather, the well-being of other people becomes important. The "good" thing to do is sacrifice herself so that others may benefit. A woman at this level feels dependent on what other people think. Often a conflict occurs between taking responsibility for her own actions and feeling pressure from others to make her decisions.

Transition 2: From Goodness to Reality

During this transitional period, women begin to examine their situations more objectively. They draw away from their dependence on others to tell them what they should do. Instead, they begin to take into account the well-being of everyone concerned, including themselves. Some of the concern for personal survival apparent in Level 1 returns, but in a more objective manner.

Level 3: The Morality of Nonviolent Responsibility

Level 3 involves women thinking in terms of the repercussions of their decisions and actions. At this level, a woman's thinking has progressed beyond mere concern for what others will "think" about what she does. Rather, it involves her accepting her responsibility for making her own judgments and decisions. She places herself on an equal plane with others, weighs the various consequences of her potential actions, and accepts the fact that she will be responsible for these consequences. The important principle operating here is that of minimizing hurt, both to herself and others.

Gilligan identified three levels of moral development for women, and two primary transitions. Her theory is summarized in Highlight 11.1 (Gilligan, 1982).

The differences between the theories of Kohlberg and Gilligan highlight the importance of being sensitive to gender. One might assume an area such as moral reasoning would not be influenced by one's sex. However, our experiences as females or males are woven into the fabric of almost all the ways we think and behave. Those different life experiences can enhance our appreciation for the diversity of human beings, and promote a broader view of moral thinking and behavior.

Obviously, not all adults achieve higher levels of moral development. This necessitates the imposition of social controls (laws and punishment for breaking them) on those who do not conform their behavior to positive social values.

Social workers generally rise to the highest levels of moral development. Their decisions are not governed principally by avoiding punishment. Rather, they conduct themselves out of their set of values which include, among others, the following beliefs:

- Each person is entitled to equal opportunity.
- Each person has inherent worth and dignity.
- Each person is entitled to adequate resources to meet his/her needs for nutrition, housing, medical care and to avoid discrimination.
- Each person is responsible for herself/himself.
- Each person is entitled to realize her/his fullest potential.
- Each person benefits from interaction with others.
- Each person shares needs common to all people, but is also unique.
- This uniqueness and diversity should be celebrated, not compromised.

Acting ethically means dynamically applying these underlying beliefs in everyday decision making. However, sometimes decisions superficially appear to be ethical, but really have nothing to do with an ethical decision-making *process*. In other words, people may come to ethical decisions by a not so ethical process. For example, a social worker might advocate for a client because she is afraid she will lose her job is she doesn't do so. This is very different in intent from advocating because she believes deeply in advocacy for disadvantaged persons. The outcome might be the same in either case. However, the process of decision making reveals two very different motivators and, therefore, separate levels of moral development.

Ethical Issues Commonly Presented in Social Work Practice

The very nature of social work practice frequently presents ethical dilemmas to which practitioners must respond. While no text can address all categories of potential ethical dilemmas, social work professionals find these challenges most often fall into the following eight areas:

1. Confidentiality and privileged information versus public protection;
2. Informed consent;
3. Truth telling;
4. Paternalism and self-determination;
5. Laws, policies, and regulations;
6. Whistle blowing;
7. Distributing limited resources; and
8. Personal and professional values.

Client Confidentiality versus Public Protection

Confidentiality is "a principle of ethics according to which the social worker or other professional may not disclose information about a client without the client's consent. This information includes the identity of the client, content of overt verbalizations, professional opinions about the client, and material from records" (Barker, 1991, p. 46). The principle of client confidentiality is central to the social work profession. Quite rightly, we assume clients will benefit from a relationship of trust with social workers. At the core of that trust is the belief that clients can (and should) reveal extremely personal and private material which would be entirely inappropriate to reveal in another setting. For instance, clients might openly reveal their critical financial problems to a social worker in the process of trying to solve them. However, these same clients might cling doggedly to secrecy in order to withhold that same information from friends, family and neighbors. Indeed, the failure of clients to reveal this sensitive information may preclude them from receiving the assistance necessary to resolve significant problems.

As indicated earlier, the NASW Code of Ethics embraces this principle by devoting an entire heading to confidentiality and privacy, explaining, "The social worker should respect the privacy of clients and hold in confidence all information obtained in the course of professional service" (National Association of Social Workers, 1990). However, the Code immediately goes on to address exceptions to this general principle. It is these possible exceptions which present ethical dilemmas for social workers.

Social workers learn early in their education to determine who their client system is. This is often a simple determination, as when an individual comes to you seeking assistance. Or, is this so simple? Systems training has taught us that no person is an isolated entity. Thus, our primary client may be the person seeking help but the client system may be the individual's entire family.

What happens if this individual client re-

veals he has done something, or might do something, to harm another person? Do you as a social worker have your primary responsibility to this "client," perhaps someone you have never even heard of before? Of course you do. However, it is the weighing of the rights and responsibilities of these various "clients" that can be so difficult. Consequences are potentially tragic if the wrong decision is made.

Privileged Communication

The matter of confidentiality is of such importance that there is considerable legislation and case law governing it. Confidentiality, when discussed in legal terms, is referred to as *privileged communication* or *client-professional privilege*. Privileged communication is "the premise and understanding between a professional and client that the information revealed by the client will not be divulged to others without express permission" (Barker, 1991, p. 182).

While psychiatrists, attorneys, and clergy enjoy the benefit of a legal right to withhold information derived in professional contacts with clients, social workers often do not. This varies from state to state, and frequently is influenced by professional licensing. Therefore, a client may meet with both psychiatrists and social workers. If social workers do not have the protection of privileged communication, their records are available to be subpoenaed in court. However, those of the psychiatrists will likely not be.

This is a critical matter for social workers to understand. Case records can have considerable bearing on legal dispositions, such as child custody decisions. It is important to understand that client-professional privilege belongs to the client, not the professional. That is, clients have the right to waive their rights to this confidential information. The professional cannot do so without the client's express permission.

There are numerous situations where privileged communication is superseded by more compelling concerns. For example, take situations where clients demonstrate substantial potential harm to themselves or others, or when they have already significantly hurt themselves. Here social workers have the ethical (and legal) duty to override confidentiality. They need to ensure that necessary interventions are made either to prevent harm or to find treatment for those already harmed.

The following are generally accepted as *universal exceptions to privilege/confidentiality* for social workers (adopted from Huber & Baruth, 1987).

- When a social worker is court-appointed, such as to evaluate a client;
- When a social worker judges a foreseeable suicide risk;
- When a client initiates a lawsuit against a social worker, as in malpractice litigation;
- When a client introduced "mental condition" as a claim or defense in a civil court action (for example, if a client is being sued for harming another person and the client states he was not responsible due to his mental condition;
- When a client is a minor and the social worker suspects the child is being victimized physically, emotionally, or sexually;
- When a social worker believes the client's symptoms are sufficiently severe to merit psychiatric hospitalization (for example, when a client is so severely neglecting herself that she risks starving to death);
- When criminal activity is involved (for example, when a client reveals he has committed a felony);
- When otherwise privileged information is made an issue in a court action;
- When a client reveals an intent to commit a crime, harm another person or herself/himself, or behavior is sufficiently dangerous that the potential for such harm exists.

The courts in the United States have addressed difficult issues of client-professional privilege. Perhaps, nowhere has this been more heatedly debated than in matters of professionals' duty to warn those who might be harmed by a client.

One groundbreaking case which illustrates the helping professional's responsibility in this arena is *Tarasoff v. Regents of the University of California* (1974). This situation involved a university student who informed his psychiatrist of his intent to kill his girlfriend when she returned to the campus area. The psychiatrist notified the campus police and asked them to take appropriate action. The psychiatrist did not warn the potential victim or her parents. Although the client was apprehended by the campus police, they released him because he "appeared rational." He then murdered his girlfriend.

The girlfriend's parents sued the psychiatrist and won. The court ruled that the psychiatrist had a legal obligation to give a warning to avert danger not only to the police but to the intended victim. The court concluded, "The protective privilege ends where the public peril begins" (*Tarasoff v. Regents of the University of California*, 1974).

This case clearly underscores the social worker's proactive responsibility to warn victims of grave and potentially mortal danger. However, cases involving less serious crimes, such as theft or property damage, are much less clear. They have been dealt with by the courts less consistently. Therefore, once again, a social worker must weigh the various rights and responsibilities against the potential harms when determining the most ethical course of action.

Confidentiality is breached by helping professionals to an alarming extent. In one recent study, Baker and Patterson (1990) found that while only eight percent of therapists from several disciplines reported that they discuss their clients by name with friends, more than 75 percent stated they discussed their clients among friends anonymously.

Study respondents were even more likely to violate clients' confidentiality with their family members. To some extent it's understandable that social workers are tempted to share their work experiences with people who are close to them. Many aspects of social work are filled with emotion and crisis. Nonetheless, violating confidentiality is a clear violation of the *NASW Code of Ethics*, and may be a violation of the law. Clients' rights to privacy should never be compromised in such an unprofessional manner.

Limits of Confidentiality

Just as it is social workers' ethical responsibility to respect strict rules of client confidentiality, it is equally their responsibility to inform clients of the limits of such confidentiality. This information should come early in the development of a social worker-client relationship. Thereby, clients are protected from assumptions about privacy they might make that cannot be assured.

This need not be a cumbersome requirement in actual practice. It can be dispatched with a few simple sentences. For example, the social worker can state to the client, "Ordinarily, whatever we discuss will remain between you and me. There are only a few exceptions. One involves my regular consultations with my supervisor. Another requires me to reveal information about children being abused. The other exception is if you seemed like you were going to seriously harm yourself or someone else."

If social workers' records were likely to become the subject of subpoena, or their testimony might be required in court, the client should be so warned.[2] As these are unlikely events in most social work interactions, we won't spend time discussing them.

Perhaps the most effective method to convey information about limitations of confidentiality to a client is to develop a "bill of rights" for all clients in each agency. Such a document explains in writing to all clients their rights. These rights might entail, for example, the right to receive prompt and adequate treatment, to refuse being videotaped or audiotaped without consent (additionally they should not suffer penalty for such a refusal), and to bring legal action for damages against agency staff who might violate their rights. To ensure that each client has received this information, many agencies require staff to obtain clients' signatures indicating their receipt of this outline of their rights.

Informed Consent

A corollary issue to confidentiality is the concept of informed consent. Informed consent involves "the client's granting of permission to the social worker and agency or other professional person to use specific intervention procedures, including diagnosis, treatment, follow-up, and research" (Barker, 1991, p. 114). Clients cannot give true consent to social workers to break confidentiality, or even provide them with treatment, unless they fully understand their rights, prognoses, and so forth.

The matter becomes less clear when the client is under some pressure to be cooperative. For example, take a prison inmate who may be seeking parole. Informed consent requires knowledge, voluntariness, and the competence to make appropriate decisions. It can be argued that clients lack the potential to give informed consent. For instance, consider clients who reside in institutions, are affected by prescription medications, are intellectually compromised, or are mentally ill.

2. For an excellent discussion of privacy in social work record keeping, see J. D. Kagle, (1991), pp. 164–90.

Truth Telling

The full text of the *NASW Code of Ethics* contains the statement, "The social worker should afford clients reasonable access to any official social work records concerning them" (National Association of Social Workers, 1990). Social workers generally believe apprising clients of all aspects of their care and the prognosis for improvement likely to result from social work interventions is consistent with respecting the rights of clients. However, some social workers argue there might be instances where withholding information from clients would be in clients' best interests. For example, to fully reveal the findings of an evaluation of a client to that person may be emotionally overwhelming. This could result in unnecessary discouragement, fear, and voluntary withdrawal from receiving necessary services. This dilemma is most difficult to resolve in the cases of clients who are children or adults who are intellectually impaired.

Paternalism and Self-Determination

Social workers advocate for the rights of their clients and attempt to protect them from harm. In doing so, they risk overstepping their proper role and compromising the rights of their clients. A fundamental value in social work is to "make every effort to foster maximum self-determination on the part of clients," (National Association of Social Workers, 1990). However, fostering self-determination may have the unintended result of lowering clients' standard of living or ability to function effectively. Ethical dilemmas arise in such situations, where protecting clients may require intervening against their immediate wishes. This results in coercive intervention.

Laws, Policies, and Regulations

As Steven's example in Highlight 11.2 illustrates, the conduct of social workers and other professionals is frequently governed by legal regulations. These regulations are almost always consistent with sound social work practice. However, as we have seen, these laws or agency policies can occasionally enable clients to be harmed. For example, a social worker might refuse to divulge information in court she believed would expose her client to assault. Likewise, a social worker might choose to violate an agency policy which promotes the general welfare but inhibits the self-determination of his client. These are extremely difficult dilemmas, requiring exhaustive examination of potential outcomes and often painful moral choices.

Whistle Blowing

The NASW Code of Ethics implores social workers to "create and maintain conditions of practice that facilitate ethical and competent professional performance by colleagues," and to "take action . . . against unethical conduct by any other member of the profession" (National Association of Social Workers, 1990). This requires social workers to police each other, an inherently uncomfortable role for people who respect their colleagues. Practically speaking, social workers generally know that to report unethical conduct or rule violations can have enormous unintended consequences. Included among these can be: humiliation to the alleged violator; embarrassment to professionals associated with the agency; a diminishing of the stature of the agency in the community and a resultant compromise of the agency's effectiveness; a reduction in its funding; and repercussions to the "whistle blower." Ethical dilemmas most often arise in this area when the rule violation seems defensible, or the conduct of the social work colleague is substandard but not grossly unethical. Weighing the larger good against human failings and frailties, with an understandable desire to protect one's self-interests, can pose a very difficult ethical dilemma.

Distributing Limited Resources

In chapter 1, we were introduced to an ethical dilemma where a social worker had to decide where to allocate money for services among ten very deserving persons. This is a simplified version of the judgments made by social workers every day. By definition, social work clients are

---

HIGHLIGHT 11.2

Ethical Dilemmas and the Mentally Ill: A Case Example

When a conflict arises between not interfering with a client's freedom and the obligation to provide professional help to improve the client's welfare and functioning, social workers struggle with deep philosophical and ethical issues. This dilemma frequently presents itself when working with mentally ill adults. The following case vignette illustrates such an ethical quandary:

Since Steven entered adolescence, his behavior varied between erratically bizarre and normal for a teenage boy. While he generally got along well with his peers and family members, he would occasionally erupt with extreme outbursts of anger accompanied by destruction of his property. His parents finally sought professional help. Professional opinions, however, proved to be as varied as Steven's behavioral repertoire. By the time he was sixteen years old, mental-health practitioners began to agree that Steven was schizophrenic.

Schizophrenia is a form of psychosis that is probably not physical in origin.* Symptoms typically include thought disturbances (often including misinterpretation of reality, misperceptions, loose associations, delusions or hallucinations); mood changes (inappropriate effects, blunted emotions, inability to empathize and ambivalence); communication problems (incoherence or poverty of speech content); and behavior patterns that may be bizarre, regressive, or withdrawn (Barker, 1991, p. 207).

Schizophrenic patients frequently benefit from medication. Thus, Steven's parents were told to administer drugs to him. Steven refused to take them. As the law forbade anyone from forcing medication on Steven, he went without.

The next few years witnessed Steven's severe deterioration. He exhibited behavior that demonstrated he was out of touch with the reality most people perceive. He disappeared for weeks at a time, and suffered from malnutrition. He needed supervised care, but since he did not meet the threshold of being a danger to himself or others, he could not be involuntarily committed to a hospital.

Steven's parents became desperate. They implored the social workers and health-care professionals to rescue their son. However, the law prohibited them from intervening with Steven without his permission.

When his malnutrition and lack of shelter from the cold finally became life-threatening, Steven was hospitalized briefly and administered medications. He responded exceptionally well, considerably reducing his bizarre behavior and gaining weight. This improvement resulted in his being declared capable of making his own decisions. He decided to refuse further medication.

Predictably, Steven rapidly lost his recent gains. He drifted back into bizarre behavior with angry outbursts, physical deprivation, and social isolation. The system designed to help Steven was only able to respond to him when he was totally out of control and risking grave consequences. As a result, he will likely never be cured of his schizophrenia.

In such a case, should the social worker adhere strictly to the law protecting Steven's civil rights (and therefore his right to destroy himself)? Or does a social worker have some moral obligation to compromise Steven's self-determination and intervene against his will? The deeply held value of clients' rights to self-determination can collide with the deeply held value to promote clients' welfare.

---

*Psychosis involves "a group of serious and frequently incapacitating mental disorders" (Barker, 1991, p. 188).

persons in need. There have never been adequate resources for all persons in our society. With resources continuing to shrink, there certainly will not be enough in our lifetimes. Thus, resources are strained among many competing persons and groups, whether those resources involve money or services (such as foster home care). The following two examples illustrate this type of ethical dilemma.

Case Example 1

It had been a time of fiscal belt-tightening. In spite of a growing list of clients, the protective services agency was forced to curtail services. Funds allocated by the county board and the state had been drastically reduced from the previous year's allocation. To exacerbate this seemingly impossible situation, there was a constant shortage of foster parents who were capable and willing to provide temporary parental care to children in need.

The police contacted the protective services social worker regarding an adolescent boy who had had a serious battle with his parents the previous evening. He grabbed a knife in the kitchen where they argued, and threatened to kill them. No one was certain what he might have done had his parents provoked him further. The police stated they could confine him for a few days, but preferred not to. He had no previous juvenile record, and the police officer believed he was more in need of a supervised "cooling off" period away from his parents. The social worker was faced with the question of whether a temporary placement could be established. Only then could the family become composed enough to begin family therapy.

The social worker was exhausted from working overtime. Just last evening, she had been up almost all night investigating a reported child-abuse case at the height of its crisis. Staff cutbacks meant she was handling more responsibilities than ever before. The pressure was tak-

ing its toll. She had struggled to recruit an adequate number of foster parents, but there were never enough.

She knew of one family who would probably take this boy. However, these foster parents were already overtaxed. They had two adolescent foster children in addition to their own two children. The social worker had learned from previous experience that placing too many demands on foster parents decreased their effectiveness or, worse yet, so burned them out that they refused to continue to accept these needy young people.

Was this situation sufficiently serious to risk compromising the care of children already in placement? Was it worth asking a "favor" of these generous people to take yet another troubled boy into their home? If they were told about the boy's brandishing a knife in the midst of the argument with his parents the previous evening, would they be too frightened of this young person to consider caring for him?

Was this really a matter for the police to deal with? Should the social worker simply recommend placement of the boy in juvenile detention and end the matter, at least for today? She knew juvenile detention could be used only for a maximum of three days. Thus, without foster placement, the boy would soon be returned to his home. Was that a safe plan given the explosive situation present in the boy's home?

Case Example 2

Melissa, a school social worker, enjoyed her job in a small rural school district. Her responsibilities included identifying students who had special needs which could interfere with their academic potential, and helping these students get services to address those needs. She nurtured her excellent relationships with teachers, administrators, students, and their parents. She concentrated her time on the relatively few students who needed her most. The majority of students progressed through grade school with no major difficulties.

One student for whom she felt a special commitment was a bright boy named Henry. He had suffered from a farm accident as a five-year-old, resulting in a spinal-cord injury. Henry, now age nine, was unable to walk, but functioned quite independently in his wheelchair.

The social worker was aware of state laws that required equal, barrier-free access to educational opportunities for all students. The older school building where she worked and Henry attended classes had many levels. Access to these levels could be gained only by going up and down stairs, which Henry obviously couldn't do. The school administration had arranged Henry's schedule to accommodate his physical limitations, enabling him to remain in the same classroom all day. However, this still meant he could not participate in music and art classes.

Henry's parents were not aware of the legislation requiring barrier-free access. Thus, they accepted the school district's accommodation to their son's physical limitations.

The school district could install an elevator in the grade school. However, engineering and architectural quotes indicated the cost of such an addition was approximately ninety thousand dollars. While the law could force the district to make such a building improvement, the money would substantially affect the system's budget. The end result would be inevitable cutbacks in staff and programs which benefit all students. Melissa knew if she did not raise this legal right with Henry's parents, their son would progress through grade school with some academic compromises. Additionally, Henry's isolation from other students would be intensified. Henry's experiences would be all the more unmatched and unequal to those of his peers at school.

Was this fair to Henry? By serving his needs for equal physical access to education and social opportunities, was it reasonable to compromise the education of all students? The conse-quences of making the school more accessible to physically disabled students might negatively affect Henry to some extent. Along with his peers, he would be deprived of services which could no longer be provided due to budget cutbacks. Would notifying Henry's parents of their rights unfairly burden them by forcing them to advocate for Henry, or feel they are abandoning his interests? Would they suffer the ire of many other parents? Would the potential ill will result in Henry's being discriminated against or shunned by the sons and daughters of the parents who disagreed with the merits of barrier-free access in this situation?

Personal and Professional Values

Social workers bring to their work an accumulation of life experiences and values. These values have been forged from family, social, religious, and personal beliefs, and by adulthood, they are well developed and deeply held. Indeed, it is often this set of values that attract social workers to the profession.

However, occasionally these personal beliefs are in conflict with the values of the social-work profession. Likewise, they may be at odds with the equally deeply held beliefs of clients. For example, take a social worker who strongly believes in equality between women and men. He finds himself in the situation of counseling a couple whose value is for the husband to be extremely dominant in the household. This includes prohibiting the wife from working outside the home. The social worker might believe this woman's failure to reach her full potential contributes significantly to the couple's marital problems. However, challenging this mutually held belief system may be disrespectful of the clients' values. The social worker may find himself disliking this man because of his dominant nature. The social worker must successfully resolve this dilemma in order to serve these clients fully.

The potential conflict between personal and professional values occurs most frequently, and is felt most profoundly, in matters of life, health care, and death. The morality of abortion is argued in the political, legal, social, and social work arenas. Trying to help a child who is being prohibited from receiving conventional medical care due to his parents' religious beliefs challenges social workers in the most profound ethical sense. Allowing a terminally ill patient to be taken off life-sustaining interventions reaches to the core of social workers' values, which may or may not be consistent with the values of the patient's family or the ethics of the profession. As with all ethical dilemmas, social workers must weigh every facet of the question thoroughly, exercising great care to avoid imposing their personal values inappropriately.

Guidelines for Ethical Decision-Making

A central function of social work is to mediate between individuals and their society. In an ideal world, what is good for society is also good for the individual, and vice versa. When that luxury presents itself, there are no opposing forces. However, all too often hard choices need to be made and priorities need to be formulated in order to respect the needs of individuals as well as the needs of the larger society. As was illustrated in previous examples, what is good for the individual may deprive the larger group.

A dilemma is a predicament in which a decision maker must choose between two or more similarly attractive (or unattractive) options. An ethical dilemma inevitably arises when a social worker is faced with two or more competing values. These might be justice and equality, civil rights and self-determination, or fairness and conformity to law. There is general agreement among social workers on basic values. However, there is considerable disagreement about what should be done when these values seriously compete with each other.

When faced with an ethical dilemma, social workers benefit from following the guidelines described below. As previously indicated, there is no prescribed outcome for all dilemmas, just as there are no absolute rules for arriving at the "right" choice or compromise. By definition, an ethical dilemma affords the possibility of several "right" choices. The best choice always depends on the careful weighing of significant facts and anticipated outcomes.

Complex decision making is a multistage process. Thoughtful decisions require the following: considerable deliberation, the examination of the potential interactions of many variables, frequent consultation with others, projecting intended and unintended consequences of various alternatives, and ongoing evaluation. Thus, we offer the following multistage plan to guide social workers toward making ethical decisions. It is important to understand this is a fluid process. Effective decision-making requires returning to previous steps and ongoing review, rather than proceeding in a stepwise fashion without looking back.

1. *Gather information.* The first step in any complex decision-making process is to acquire information. This is required to assure that your ultimate decision is based on as many facts as possible. Obviously, faulty decision-making would inevitably result from a failure to understand the underlying facts in a situation.

   The adage "There are two sides to every story" operates here. In fact, there are many sides to most stories. Seldom is one source of information sufficient. Social workers should exercise patience and thoroughness in acquiring all relevant information before taking the next step. The alternative would be to risk a hasty, ill-advised decision.

2. *Determine if an ethical dilemma exists.*

Often by completing step one thoroughly, the gathering of complete information reveals that an ethical dilemma does not, in fact, exist. Only when two or more values of relatively equal significance conflict do you have an ethical dilemma.

3. *Determine your role.* Now that you have established your awareness of an ethical dilemma, examine what your proper professional role may be in responding. Are you the person who is principally responsible for determining and implementing a course of action to resolve this matter? Is it more properly the responsibility of someone else? Is this a matter which requires shared responsibility (for example, with your supervisor, or another worker involved)? A careful examination of the boundaries of your required intervention is in order here. Perhaps you will need to reflect on your job description as well as your commitment to the principles of social work.

4. *Prioritize.* The successful resolution of a dilemma is often facilitated by prioritizing

All too often, hard choices need to be made and priorities formulated in order to balance the needs of individuals against those of the larger society.

the needs, goals, and objectives of competing forces. For example, when the needs of a client can be substantially met at very little cost to society, the client's needs may take obvious precedence. Thus, the dilemma might be resolved with relative ease. The most difficult dilemmas involve competing forces of equal gravity.

These guidelines will be continued below, but first, an examination of the codification of social-work values, the *NASW Code of Ethics*, is appropriate here. Social workers do well to return to this document and review the values of the profession for guidance. This may be especially helpful when personal and professional values conflict. The *NASW Code of Ethics* is a carefully crafted document which guides the profession. When social workers' personal values erode their professional commitments, the *Code of Ethics* can remind them of their professional mission.

Nonetheless, the NASW Code of Ethics does not rank order ethical priorities. Social workers Frank Loewenberg and Ralph Dolgoff (1988) developed a priority list of ethical obligations for this purpose.

They suggest that practitioners can use the values prioritized below to make ethical decisions. In other words, in the event that two values are competing, you should abide by the one higher in the order. For instance, if you are debating between value number one (life protection) and value number two (autonomy, independence, and freedom), you should act on the behalf of value number one. Likewise, value number two should take precedence over values number three through number seven, and so on.

The prioritized values are as follows:

1. Protect life—basic survival needs of individuals and/or society;
2. Maintain autonomy, independence, and freedom;
3. Foster equality of opportunity and equality of access;
4. Promote a better quality of life;
5. Strengthen every person's right to privacy/confidentiality;
6. Speak the truth and fully disclose all relevant information;
7. Practice in accord with rules and regulations voluntarily accepted (Loewenberg & Dolgoff, 1988, p. 122).

This scale can guide social workers in prioritizing competing needs and interests. To continue the guidelines for ethical decision making:

5. *When possible, share it.* Another adage, "Two heads are better than one," is highly applicable here. We often benefit from another person's point of view. This is especially true when that other person has more experience or represents a different vantage point. Concerns about confidentiality are, of course, important here. However, most social workers are supervised by a more experienced professional. Supervisory consultations are known exceptions to client-social worker privilege. The potential benefit from discussing an ethical dilemma with another professional cannot be emphasized enough.

6. *Examine the dilemma from a high level of moral reasoning.* Here we return to the work of Kohlberg (1969) and Gilligan (1977). The highest levels or stages of moral reasoning, Kohlberg's Stage 6 and Gilligan's Level 3, promote our making the most ethical decisions. Use these models as guides, not in what to think, but in how to think about these complex matters.

7. *Explore alternatives.* The concept of "brainstorming" is helpful as a next step. This involves entertaining multiple possible options without prioritizing them. It is best to generate as many alternatives and strategies as possible. It may be help-

ful to write them down to assist your memory in the next step.

8. *Weigh alternatives.* Carefully examine each alternative generated in Step 7 above. Rank order the ethical principles involved in each option. Discard those options that are unacceptable. Narrow the range of possible decisions.

9. *Examine potential outcomes and consequences.* Carefully project desirable and undesirable outcomes that are likely to result from the alternatives you are considering. Remember to include outcomes that might affect clients, relatives, the larger society, yourself, your agency, the profession of social work, your colleagues, and others. Thus, a thorough assessment is in order.

10. *Determine a tentative resolution.* The foregoing steps have guided you toward a sound decision. Make your best decision and formulate your plan.

11. *Self-examine your proposed decision in the "court of professional opinion."* Most social work ethical dilemmas are intensely private matters; confidentiality requires that they be so. Social workers often have a remarkably clear sense of how an unbiased group of social work or other colleagues would judge their decision and behavior. Imagine the decision you are proposing suddenly became known to all your professional colleagues. Is it one you would stand by proudly, or would you shrink away in fear of their appraisal? Remember, we like to view ourselves based on our most noble acts. However, others often judge us based on our least ethical act.

12. *Consolidate.* The thorough process described above has led you to your decision. Review any necessary steps (particularly consulting another professional if appropriate) and form your final decision.

13. *Act.* It has often been observed that not to act is really to act. In other words,

events progress with or without intervention. By doing nothing, you make a decision to follow a course of action—namely, that of doing nothing. Favorable outcomes are rarely enhanced by passively standing by. You have wrestled painstakingly with a dilemma. Now it is important to put your decision into action. Without intervention, events can evolve in a haphazard way. Sound decisions are a far better guide than change.

14. *Evaluate the results of your actions.* Monitor the effects of your decision on all involved parties. When necessary, alter your behavior to minimize unintended, negative consequences. Compare the actual outcomes with your earlier projected outcomes, and see what you can learn from any errors you made in your expectations.

Chapter Summary

The practice of social work is guided by professional values that have evolved over many decades. Professional ethics deal with questions about what actions are morally right and how practitioners should proceed. The *Code of Ethics* of the National Association of Social Workers documents social workers' responsibilities to live by the profession's values.

Professional ethics were examined. Current theories of moral development were reviewed in an attempt to understand why people view moral issues in various ways. Several areas of social work practice where ethical dilemmas frequently arise were addressed. Finally, a model for sound, ethical decision making which is applicable to a variety of situations was explored.

Regardless of their particular professional role, social workers operate on the basis of ethical principles in most of what they do. This is a proud tradition and one that supports the mission of the profession.

12 *Ethnically and Racially Sensitive Social Work Practice*

The ethnic gourmet

Janis England was mystified. In talking with Lana Black Bear, mother of a family on her caseload, she learned that Mr. Black Bear's two nephews were coming to live with the family for a while. The Black Bear family already had great trouble getting by on their meager income from the sawmill. How could they afford to care for two more children? In addition, Lana Black Bear had serious medical problems stemming from a car accident two years ago. Why would she want to take on this extra burden on top of raising her own three children? "It seems crazy," Janis thought to herself. "I guess I'll have to talk to the Black Bears about this."

John Martin, social worker for the Dinh Phuc Van family, had just walked into the waiting room of the human services department. This was to be his first meeting with the family, recently referred to him by the Salvation Army social worker. The couple were Vietnamese refugees and had just arrived in the city. "Hello, Dinh, how are you today?" He smiled and shook Dinh Phuc Van's hand. He greeted the wife similarly, shaking her hand and motioning them both toward his office.

Although John expected the family to be somewhat hesitant in asking for help, he was very surprised when the couple seemed both distant and uncommunicative. During the brief interview, John learned nothing that would help him decide how to help the family. The interview concluded when the husband apologized for bothering John and said they had to leave.

CHAPTER TWELVE

Introduction

The United States is a pluralistic nation composed of, except for Native Americans, immigrants or the descendants of immigrants. With a total population of over 245 million, the United States is an extremely diverse society. Over 30.2 million people are of African American heritage, 6.5 million are from Asian American backgrounds, and 19.8 million are of Hispanic or Latino extraction. An addition 1.7 million are Native Americans (U.S. Department of Commerce, 1990).

The white population is a similarly diverse amalgam of peoples from Western and Eastern Europe, sometimes representing cultures with long histories of enmity and conflict. The differences and animosities which many people from many countries felt toward each other became submerged in what Americans like to call the *melting pot*. The melting pot idea is used repeatedly to suggest that all peoples who come to America somehow get stirred into a giant pot and come out looking, thinking, and acting alike. As a concept, it was an attractive way for a nation to see itself—a country where all people could go and become as one.

Yet the reality of America is vastly different from the image of the melting pot, as we will discuss in this chapter. For example, we will look at the two cases that opened this chapter, identifying problems caused by social workers who lacked a multicultural perspective on human behavior. In addressing the reality of social work practice in a diverse society this chapter will:

- Explore the general experiences of minorities in the United States;
- Examine the ways in which various forms of racism affect social work practice with people of color;
- Propose practice skills which can be effective tools for working with ethnically and racially different groups;
- Formulate assessment strategies for culturally diverse groups;
- Evaluate ways in which social work institutions can be more effective in delivering service to peoples of color.

Diversity in the United States

In the introduction to this chapter we noted that the United States is an enormously diverse society. Over 23 percent of our current population is descended from people who did not come from the European backgrounds that characterized immigrants in the eighteenth, nineteenth, and first half of the twentieth century. The melting pot concept is not applicable to the experiences of these people of color. It does not even adequately address the history of white immigrants to America who often maintained their values, beliefs, traditions, and behavior through successive generations. The melting pot idea is a narrow theory that ignores enormous diversity within Anglo (white) culture. It completely fails to address the experiences of people of color. Unfortunately, it has been a popular notion and still has vestiges of support. This support compounds the difficulties already experienced by racial and ethnic groups in our society.

This chapter approaches the topic of ethnicity- and race-sensitive social work practice assuming that most of the readers are not people of color. This assumption is based on the fact that most of the students in social work programs are not minorities and likely lack substantial experience with different cultures (Spaulding, 1991).

Historic and Current Discrimination

That there are major difficulties experienced by people of color is evident. From historic accounts of inhuman treatment of Native

Americans, African Americans, and Asian Americans to current reports of police brutality of minority populations, there is substantial evidence of systematic discrimination in our society. Most racial minorities in the United States have encountered some level of prejudice and discrimination in dealing with various societal institutions including social service agencies.

Moreover, the United States has historically discriminated against minorities and people of color. Europeans who colonized this country brought racism with them. This was evident in the wholesale genocide practiced on the indigenous Native American population. Although our government is predicated upon the primacy of dignity, freedom, equality, and human rights, our economy before the Civil War depended heavily upon slavery. The period between the Civil War and World War II saw many examples of racist behavior toward Native Americans, Asians, and Hispanics. Institutional racism within education was the law of the land until 1954, when the U.S. Supreme Court overturned separate-but-equal educational systems. Despite this ruling, de facto (actual) segregation of school systems still exists in hundreds of school districts throughout the United States.

In the 1960s, minorities won rights both to attend the colleges and universities of their choice, and to vote without harassment. Of course, these were rights that white Americans enjoyed for almost two centuries. Actually, they were rights enjoyed specifically (and only) by white males until 1920, when white women gained the right to vote.

In the 1960s, 1970s, and 1980s, minority

┌ HIGHLIGHT 12.1
Common Terminology

Institutional racism: "Those policies, practices, or procedures that systematically exclude individuals or groups on the basis of race or ethnicity with the intentional or unintentional support of the entire culture" (Barker, 1991, p. 116). For example, college admission standards which admit only students receiving extremely high scores on the Scholastic Aptitude Test (SAT) or other similar tests systematically exclude many minorities who, as a group, may not do as well on such tests.

Individual racism: "The negative attitudes one person has about all members of a racial or ethnic group, often resulting in overt acts such as name-calling, social exclusion, or violence" (Barker, 1991, p. 113). Often, racism rests on an assumption of racial superiority. It is difficult, though not impossible, for individual racism to flourish without legitimation by institutionalized racism (Osborne, Pinkleton, Carter & Richards, 1983).

Minority: "A group, or a member of a group, of people of a distinct racial, religious, ethnic, or political identity that is smaller or less powerful than the community's controlling group" (Barker, 1991, p. 145).

People of Color: People whose skin color differs from that of the community's predominant group. Typically this includes Native Americans, Asian Americans, African Americans, and some other groups. The term may be used synonymously with *minority* when people of color are also smaller in number or less powerful than the community's controlling group.

Ethnocentrism: "An orientation or set of beliefs that hold that one's own culture, ethnic or racial group, or nation is superior to others" (Barker, 1991, p. 77). This belief, epitomized in Hitler's belief in a "master race," led to the extermination of millions of Jews during and prior to World War II. It is also characteristic of apartheid in South Africa and of the extremist views of such groups as the Ku Klux Klan.

groups made continued efforts to improve economic opportunities for people of color (Garvin & Cox, 1987). In the 1980s, a conservative, anti-government series of political administrations systematically eliminated or reduced the role of the federal government in helping assure equality and economic justice to ethnic minorities.

The picture for people of color during the early 1990s is dismal. Black families continue to be more likely to fall below the poverty level. Inner-city minority groups experience increasingly high levels of gang and drug-related violence. Medical and health problems affect minority group members disproportionately. Economic disadvantage affects almost all people of color.

The level of disadvantage, combined with reduced federal and state social service programs and a corresponding increase in the poverty level, makes it difficult to ignore the link between governmental policy and economic deprivation. Institutional racism remains a fact of life for a large portion of the minority population in the United States.

Minorities of color must deal with experiences that many white families do not confront, such as educational and employment discrimination. In addition, most white families have no need to help their children understand and cope with racism and its negative effects on self-image.

Most minority groups have been victims of discrimination at the hands of almost every major social institution in our society including schools, the justice system, health care providers, even the social welfare system. As a consequence, they may be more likely to view such institutions with distrust and suspicion. Unfortunately, social work itself has too long focused on blaming-the-victim psychological change strategies. These strategies assume that the victims have brought upon themselves the problems they experience. For example, it is easy to assume that an unemployed father is simply lazy or chooses not to work rather than understanding the role of racism and cyclical un-

employment in an economic system based on capitalism. Thus, it is not unusual that people of color may doubt whether social workers have the skill or motivation to help solve basic institutional problems. Many problems of minority clients are, in fact, intertwined with the behavior of oppressive institutions with which they interface.

Barriers to Effective Multicultural Social Work

Being an effective social worker in a multicultural society requires that we be aware of the many barriers that impede our ability to function. For example, continued acceptance of the myth of the melting pot is a barrier. It uses an inappropriate and inadequate theory that often blames people of color for failing to "melt."

Another barrier is the assumption that all who come to our country will be overjoyed to be here. Some may be; others may be depressed or unhappy over leaving their homeland, loss of family members and loved ones, and the enormous burden of surviving in a strange land. Some may be anxious and fear the unknown. Expecting every new immigrant to be delighted is unrealistic.

A third barrier is the tendency to explain a person's behavior by reference to their culture. Certainly, many people of the same culture share life experiences. Yet this shared experience does not explain all or even most of a person's behavior. Instead, it ignores the enormous diversity that always exists within a given culture. All minority groups are heterogenous. They are as different individually as any group of whites.

Similarly, it would be a mistake to lump all people of any one race together. For example, despite their enormous poverty and multiple problems as a group, most adult African Americans are employed, not on welfare, and not involved in the criminal justice system.

A fourth barrier is an attempt to be color-blind. Color-blindness occurs when a person decides to "treat everybody alike" and pretends that culture and experience have no role in determining behavior. As with the third barrier, this is an extreme position and equally troublesome.

A fifth barrier is our tendency to assume that words mean the same thing to everyone. A client who talks of going home to her "man" may or may not be referring to her husband. Another client who says she "whips" her children may not be admitting child abuse. Language differences can be a source of confusion to social workers and other helpers.

A sixth barrier is assuming that clients think as you do. Two people from different cultures can look at the same situation and come to totally different conclusions about what happened, who was at fault, and what should be done. Even eye witnesses to events do not report similar enough accounts to be trusted in court. We tend to see life experiences in relation to our frame of reference. Expect that clients may think differently than you do. Take the case of a youngster sent to the principal because he was talking in class and got out of his seat. According to the teacher, his behavior was inappropriate to an academic setting and shows he was not paying attention. According to the child, he did not hear what the teacher said and, wanting to understand the assignment, got up to ask a friend in another aisle.

A seventh barrier is expecting that clients will understand the social worker's role. It is perhaps just as likely that some clients will make erroneous conclusions about you based on their experience with other social workers they may have encountered. Clients may need to be told about confidentiality, what is expected of them, and what occurs in a social worker-client relationship. This will be especially important with cultures that are hesitant to share personal information with nonfamily members. For example, in many Asian cultures, admitting a problem to someone outside the family is to lose face. This brings shame upon oneself and one's family, and is usually avoided, if possible.

An eighth barrier is insufficient self-awareness. By this we mean a lack of understanding of your own culture (including ethnic heritage, values, beliefs, expectations, and behavior). We also may have a lack of sensitivity to our own biases. All of us grow up exposed to a variety of beliefs about other groups and interpretations of what is "good" or "right." This is part of what makes us a product of our culture. It is also what often makes us ethnocentric. We may conclude that things are "crazy," "odd," or "different" because they are not what we are used to. Thus, we tend to see life through a set of cultural sunglasses that colors all we experience, personally and professionally.

A ninth barrier is the absence of a repertoire of effective multicultural intervention techniques. This includes both those that are likely to be effective across various groups and those specific to a single ethnic or racial group. Much of the remainder of this chapter will address such intervention skills.

A tenth barrier is lack of knowledge of the culture and experiences of specific groups with whom you are likely to work. Practically speaking, it is probably unlikely that you will become an expert in working with every racial or ethnic group. Rather, it is expected that you will take the additional time to learn about the cultural and life experiences of those unique groups that comprise your caseload or that live in your geographical area.

Practical Knowledge and Skills

The intent of this section is not to make you an expert on working with people of color. Instead, we expect that you will begin to develop an understanding of the experiences of many people of color. We also intend to provide you with specific skills that are generally effective with specific groups. The last portion of this section will focus on some principles that are useful across multiple groups.

Practice Knowledge and Skills— Native Americans

Intervening effectively with Native Americans requires understanding the unique history of this culture in North and South America. Unlike all the other groups who eventually populated these regions, Native Americans were here first. Their cultures ranged from highly sophisticated social systems (such as the Aztecs, Mayas, and Incas) to the more simple organizations (such as Paiute). Most Native Americans were farmers and fishermen living in villages and communities (Kitano, 1991). Though they numbered in the millions, they were no match for the military societies of Europe. Slowly, inexorably driven off their land, they were murdered and subjected to all manners of individual and institutional racism. At various times it was federal government policy to exterminate, erase, or otherwise rid the continent of Native Americans. Military force was used to destroy tribal communities that refused to obey federal orders to move from their homeland. Tribal leaders were killed by white soldiers or by other Native Americans working for the U.S. Army. Using the melting pot myth, later efforts attempted to assimilate or acculturate Indians with the ultimate goal of destroying forever the culture of this race.

In this century, the federal government has attempted to eliminate tribes by disposing of the reservations where they live. Massive efforts were undertaken to teach Native American youth the "white man's way." By removing children from their reservation homes and sending them to Bureau of Indian Affairs boarding schools, the federal government managed to destroy the family life of millions of Native Americans. In addition, they prevented many children from learning the traditional (and usually non-punitive) child-rearing approaches used by Native Americans. Rather, the bureau's actions exposed them to the indifferent (and often brutal) discipline used at the boarding schools. Child abuse among Native Americans was relatively unknown until recently because corporal punishment (administering physical pain such as spanking) was rare. Boarding-school personnel used beatings, head shavings, and other indignities to punish Native American children for such crimes as speaking their native language, observing their religion, or running away from the boarding home. Many of the poor parenting skills noted among Native American adults can be traced to these experiences.

Traditional cultural styles of Native Americans are significantly different from most European cultures. Knowing those differences is often important for social workers. Applying culturally irrelevant or inappropriate interventions can be prevented with a basic knowledge of the culture of the client with whom we are working. Let's look at a few areas where Native American cultural values and approaches can influence social work effectiveness.

The Value of Time

Compared to Native American culture, white Americans are often said to be in a hurry (Green, 1982). Most of us maintain calendars to keep track of our busy schedules. We frequently violate speed limits as we hurry to get to our destinations. We talk of not wasting time or of ways to "save time," although no one has yet found a way to accumulate the time we have saved and use it later.

Traditional Native Americans do not share this near obsession with time. Instead, they have several values that supersede time—values like spending time with people or of not intruding on the life space of others. Practically speaking, this means that Native Americans are not married to the clock. Their approach to time is more flexible and relaxed. Consequently, they are less rigid when it comes to the starting time for meetings or being on time for appointments. For example, let's say you have an appointment at 10:00 A.M. with a Native American client. If a friend stops by to chat with your client just before your appointment, spending time with that friend is likely to take precedence over getting to the appointment on time.

Similarly, we frequently advocate that meetings start on time and that latecomers simply experience the consequences of their untimely arrival. Native Americans are much more likely to wait until all the important people are present, even if this means others must wait. The lack of a time focus is really part of a people-focused perspective on the world. Thus, it is advisable to expect longer periods to develop relationships and to settle on mutually agreeable goals. Reaching those goals also will take longer. The idea of focusing on people instead of other issues is very compatible with the values of the social work profession.

Native American Noninterference

We mentioned that Native Americans object to intruding in the lives of others. Native American noninterference could be considered a logical extension of social work's value of client self-determination. Within the culture, it is typical for Native Americans to resent workers who try to rush into the interview or rush into contacting. Indian clients need time to get to know (and trust) the worker and to become comfortable in the social worker-client relationship (Good Tracks, 1973). This value also means that intrusive, aggressive styles of probing for information are likely to be ineffective. Participatory, self-directed relationships have greater value.

In group settings, the value of noninterference may manifest itself in other ways. Silence and lack of peer pressure are common. Peer pressure is just another way of intruding on others and is unacceptable. In task group situations,

this value is apt to mean that decision making will emerge from consensus instead of majority-rule. Group decisions are also more likely to take precedence over individual decisions. This means that the will of the group may overrule individual preferences of group members. Members thus defer to the decision of the group. When designing programs to benefit an entire community, maximum involvement of the people to be affected is important. Participatory decision making is critical.

Communication Patterns

We have mentioned the quietness of Native Americans. Indian communication usually is considered to be more nonverbal than in white culture. It is not a loud culture. Indian children who are quiet in school may be viewed as problems by teachers. Such teachers may be ignorant of the value Native American culture places on deference to authority and individual dignity (Richardson, 1981; Baruth & Manning, 1991).

Native Americans also do not self-disclose readily (Lewis & Ho, 1975), nor do they share information that might discredit their family. Family loyalty is important to Native Americans. Children are less likely to brag about their accomplishments, a behavior which would seem to place them above others. Conversely, it is important not to praise them in front of others. Praise that might be viewed positively by others embarrasses Native Americans.

Fatalism

Other Indian values are also important to social work practice. For example, Native Americans show greater acceptance of fatalism (a trait they share with Hispanics). Fatalism involves an attitude "that events are fixed in advance for all time in such a manner that human beings are powerless to change them" (Mish, 1991, p. 451). The attitude that "what will be, will be" is anathema (intensely disliked) to social workers taught to believe that things in life can be changed. Taken to an extreme, Indians are sometimes criticized as "lazy." This occurs when those ignorant of Native American culture misinterpret this more relaxed, "laid back," life-style as being negative. Rather, such Native American behavior is rooted in their greater cultural acceptance of fatalism (Miller, 1982).

Sharing and Acquiring

A corollary is that many Native Americans do not possess the white value of acquisition for acquisition's sake. In Indian culture it is more important to share than to acquire for oneself. This often means that Native Americans will share their home, food, and resources with others though it places a strain on their own lives. If you think back to the case that opened this chapter, you will recall the upset social worker wondering how the Black Bear family would take on responsibility for children of relatives when their own situation was so tenuous. Caring for and sharing with others, especially family, is more important than hoarding your own resources. It should be emphasized that this value of sharing is not universal within Native American culture. For example, it is more important in the Sioux culture than in the Chippewa (Locke, 1973). However, the value of generosity transcends tribal culture.

Attending Skills

Attending skills may have to be modified when working with Native Americans. For example, we frequently demonstrate the nonverbal behavior of leaning forward toward the client and maintaining eye contact in order to demonstrate our attentiveness. However, both behaviors are inappropriate. Leaning forward may be seen as intruding into the life space of another.

Likewise, Native American children who do not make eye contact with the teacher, or look away when the teacher looks at them, sometimes give the impression they're not paying attention. These children adopt such behavior because sustained eye contact is considered rude in Native American culture. As a social worker, you will need to adjust your attending behavior to avoid violating these cultural taboos.

Intervention Styles

Adapting one's intervention style to the culture of the client is a challenge for the social worker. Sometimes a portion of the approaches we normally use will work well. For example, techniques such as restatement, clarification, summarization, reflection, and empathy can be useful with Native American clients. Similarly, clients' confidence in you as the social worker will increase to the extent that they believe in your ability, trust you, and know you understand their culture.

Dillard (1983) suggests that client-centered strategies are less likely to work with Native Americans, who may appear more passive. He believes that more directive approaches will be effective. Thus, it may be appropriate to consider using elements of both approaches. For example, the positive regard, honesty, authenticity, and sensitivity to feelings that characterize the client-centered approach might be used along with behavioral or cognitive-behavioral interventions. This combines the low-key, nonintrusive benefits of the first approach with the confidence-inspiring characteristics of the latter.

One way of increasing client trust in you is through your involvement in other aspects of the client's life. Home visits, participation in tribal activities such as powwows (community social gathering), and an evident appreciation for the culture are useful. Additionally, your office should contain some evidence of your interest in Native American life. This might include paintings, artifacts, or books related to Native American culture.

Caveats

There are over two hundred American Indian tribes in the United States (Thompson, Smith, Blueye, & Walker, 1983). Though almost all have experienced varying degrees of institutionalized and individual racism and discrimination, their histories and tribal experiences are often quite different. The result is that individual clients may be different in perception, expectations, and behavior. You cannot expect to be an expert on every group. There is no shame in admitting ignorance of aspects of a culture or of a specific meaning or event in a client's life.

A sensitivity to cultural influences and a willingness to learn about clients' experiences is essential to work with Native American and other cultures.

Practice Knowledge and Skills—Hispanics

Hispanics are one of the fastest growing minority groups in the United States (Lum, 1992). Hispanic culture is often an amalgam of European, Indian, and African traditions and values. Even the term *Hispanic* covers such a wide group of nations as to be somewhat overbroad. For example, Hispanic covers people of Puerto Rican, Cuban, Mexican, and Central–South

Hispanics include people of Puetro Rican, Cuban, Mexican, and Central and South American origin. They are just one of many groups to whom a generalist practitioner must be sensitive.

American origin (Lum, 1992). While the term Hispanic often is preferred on the East Coast, the word Latino is used more on the West Coast. *Chicano*, a term used on the West Coast, refers to Mexican-Americans and persons of Mexican lineage born in the United States (Bernal, Martinez, Santisteban, Bernal, & Olmedo, 1983).

Most of the groups covered by the term *Hispanic* came to the United States as immigrants. Yet many Mexican-Americans can trace their lineage to ancestors who were residents of Texas, New Mexico, California, and Arizona when those territories were "purchased" by the United States. Consequently, they are not direct descendants of immigrants, and share the same claim to birth rights as Native Americans. Like Native Americans, they also share a legacy of institutionalized racism and discrimination focused on genocide and acquisition of their territory (Kitano, 1991). Institutional racism, you may recall, "systematically excludes individuals or groups on the basis of race or ethnicity . . ." (Barker, 1991, p. 116). The history of the United States reflects a consistent devaluing of people of color. This pattern has implications for our current efforts to understand and work with all groups, including Hispanics.

Hispanic culture, like that of Native Americans, has vastly different values, beliefs, and practices from Anglo culture. The term *Anglo* refers to "Caucasian inhabitant[s] of the U.S. of non-Latin extraction" (Mish, 1991, p. 86). In the next sections, we will look at how some of these differences impact social work practice.

Family Centering

The typical Anglo value of *individualism* is at odds with the Hispanic family-centered cultural approach. The Hispanic family represents the one solid refuge from a difficult world (Bernal et al., 1983). The "family" may really be a combination of both nuclear and extended relatives and other networks such as friends and neighbors.

The family is central to Hispanic culture and it is hierarchical in structure. That is, the father is the primary authority figure (Dieppe & Montiel, 1978). Children owe respect to their parents, but especially to their father. Thus, it is not uncommon for children to remain in the home until they marry. This occurs in part because children owe a debt to the family that they can never repay. Contrast this with the common Anglo idea that parents should do everything possible to help their children.

The closeness of the Hispanic family may be seen as problematic by those assessing the family using typical Anglo approaches. For example, the interdependence expected of, and seen among, family members may be viewed as enmeshment. An enmeshed family is one demonstrating "an unhealthy family relationship pattern in which the role boundaries between various family members are so vague or diffuse that there is little opportunity for independent functioning (Barker, 1991, p. 75). In other words, the family may be viewed as much too close. This is not to say that the Hispanics believe individualism is bad, but rather that individualism must occur within the context of the family and traditional Hispanic values. Consequently, efforts to increase the independence (or reduce the dependency) of individual family members may be culturally inappropriate (Bernal et al., 1983).

Parental Roles

Many Hispanic fathers appear somewhat aloof from the family, especially the children. Commonly, the father is less likely to express emotional support. The father's role is to pursue instrumental roles such as earning a living, thus he may appear more distant. He may not consult the mother in making decisions, yet he expects to be obeyed. The mother's role typically is to balance the father's (Lum, 1986; Baruth &

Manning, 1991; Kitano, 1991). Mothers receive help in fulfilling this role from other members of the extended family. When intervening in Hispanic families, it may be necessary to include other family members who play crucial roles in the family constellation.

Similarly, even when the problem seems restricted to a single family member, it is often wise to encourage other family involvement whenever possible. Even if the client does not mention family members, it is appropriate to ask about them. This shows interest and an awareness of the importance of family members to the client. Sometimes these casual questions will lead to disclosures of problem areas or strengths and can set the stage for further interventions. For example, asking about a daughter may elicit parental concern that she is becoming "too independent" of their control. Asking for further clarification from the parents will help the worker know whether the situation reflects normal parent-child tension associated with adolescent independence, potential delinquent behavior, or other problems needing help.

Communication Patterns

Like Native Americans, Hispanic communication patterns have a strong nonverbal tradition. Thus, the worker must be alert to facial expressions that often provide more clues to feelings than verbal comments. Verbal expressions of feelings are much less common than among white clients. This often means that you should expect to spend more time in building a relationship and in assessing the situation than would normally be the case. It is essential that the client become comfortable with you and trust your skills as a worker.

Interviews should typically begin with a period of small talk reflecting the informality valued by Hispanics. Jumping right in would be considered rude. Like Native Americans, Hispanics dislike being singled out and are apt to

avoid competition. Hispanic culture emphasizes being personal and informal in contrast to the Anglo focus on efficiency and impersonality. Thus, Hispanics may appear passive and inappropriately nonaggressive when compared to the Anglo emphasis on competitiveness and quest for achievement.

Fatalism

As with Native Americans, fatalism plays a major role in the Hispanic outlook on the future. Consequently, Hispanics may disregard ideas that seem out of their control. Future-oriented approaches may be of less importance than concrete services offered right now. Thus, it may be more important to help the family work on a current problem and demonstrate that you and they do have the ability to effect change. This might mean arranging temporary day care for an elderly family member with Alzheimer's disease while postponing discussion of a son's future college degree. The parents may not believe that they have much control over the latter.

Bilingualism

Learning to speak Spanish clearly facilitates the efforts of a social worker serving large numbers of Hispanic clients. Social work students with ability in language might seriously consider learning Spanish. The shortage of bilingual workers will continue to stymie efforts to serve large groups of Hispanic clients. For example, there are continual problems in getting Hispanics to use community mental health facilities. Bilingual social workers could help confront this problem.

At the same time, the efforts of Hispanic children to learn two languages (English and Spanish) may be a source of stress for them. Learning Spanish at home and English at school may subtly communicate that their native language is not highly valued.

Intervention Styles

Being bilingual, however, will not help if the worker continues to use interventions that are appropriate primarily to Anglos. Fortunately, the usual approaches associated with good interpersonal interventions will be effective with many Hispanic clients. In other words, empathy, genuineness, warmth, and positive regard toward the client will be helpful. Hispanics value respect and dignity of the person. They may appear submissive when first seen because of their emphasis on not being rude. Attempting to teach skills such as assertiveness may be somewhat difficult. This is especially true for Hispanic women, in view of the patriarchal nature of the culture. It may be appropriate to teach such women to be more assertive and recognize that others' needs don't always have to come first. Workers should remember, however, that doing this may place the client at odds with her own culture.

A more directive approach using fewer reflective techniques may be useful when combined with the characteristics described in the above paragraph. For example, the worker may need to suggest specific actions which the client may wish to take to manage a particular problem. This can be done in such a way that the worker is seen as providing direct consultation or advice which the client is free to follow. As always, giving advice to clients carries some risk.

Caveats

We have described how the term *Hispanic* applies to people whose heritage derives from any of several countries. Each of these countries has its own individualistic history, which influences how citizens experience the world. Knowing something about this history can help with individual clients. However, even immigrants from the same country are likely to have differences in expectations, social class, and life experiences. Each of these factors has implications for individual adjustment.

In addition, ethnicity is not immutable (unchangeable). People can select aspects or elements of their ethnicity which they wish to observe. Despite the enormous influence culture has on most people, none of us are automatically doomed to accept all the values and beliefs of our culture, whether it be Anglo or Hispanic. We may choose to value certain aspects of our cultural heritage and de-emphasize others. Never assume that a Hispanic client (or any other client, for that matter) is controlled by cultural, ethnic, or racial experience. Human beings continue to confound those who would predict and control their behavior.

Practice Knowledge and Skills— African Americans

Of all the other ethnic and racial groups which comprise the United States, only one, African Americans, came here as slaves. That background and an almost continuous history of maltreatment have combined to produce one of the saddest stories in the annals of the United States.

African Americans have been the victims of both institutional and individual racism in ways that have left almost indelible imprints on every man, woman, and child. By all the usual measures of success (economic, educational, and occupational) African Americans have suffered at the hands of a predominantly white nation. African Americans have a substantially lower per-capita income, despite their level of education. As a group they are much less likely to attain the educational qualifications needed for advancement in a technologically-oriented society. The jobs that are open are more likely to be lower paying and offer the least opportunity for advancement. They experience discrimination in employment, housing, health care, and education.

As a nation, we have had great difficulty confronting the multiple problems experienced by African Americans. Even well-intentioned programs that grew out of the 1960s War on Poverty (Job Corps, Head Start, VISTA) were seriously underfunded and opposed by those who benefited from the status quo. During the past ten years, conservative political administrations have systematically dismantled programs benefiting the poor (African Americans included), producing dramatic results. Instead of having fewer people in poverty, a trend that began in the 1960s and continued into the 1970s, we now have more. We also have more homeless people, more street people, and a larger proportion of untreated chronically mentally ill people (Conference on Poverty, 1987; Dekoven, Waxman, & Reyes, 1987). This government indifference and neglect has disproportionately affected African Americans (Kitano, 1991). Government attempts to gut affirmative-action programs (programs designed by employers to encourage hiring of minority workers) have similarly hurt African Americans and other minorities.

Even our attempts to describe African Americans have been problematic. The term *colored people* gave way to *negro*, which was supplanted in turn by *Black*. Although some would argue that the words we use are unimportant, words do convey a variety of messages. The term *Black*, for instance, is simply a variant of *negro*. (*Negro* is from the Latin word *niger*, which means black.) Historically, the color black has been associated with ignorance, evil, and darkness. White is associated with light, goodness, purity, all positive connotations. While the term *Black* may have had value during the 1960s and 1970s (primarily through its association with Black Power) it still has significant limitations (Osborne, Pinkleton, Carter, & Richards, 1983). We have given up references to Asians as *yellow*, and it is rare that anyone speaks about the *red man*. It is time to stop referring to people by the color of their skin. It makes more sense to use terms that lack negative connotations and are consistent with the primary geographical origins of most African Americans (namely, Africa).

Communication Patterns

You may hear frequent references to the term "Black Vernacular" or "Black English" (Dodson, 1983, p. 136). Frequently, the term is an attempt to describe a pattern of word usage and sentence structure used by many African Americans. The connotation, of course, is that *Black* English is a substandard variant of ordinary English. Actually, the language patterns of many African Americans follow a set of rules as complex and understandable as standard English. For a more detailed description of some of the rules, see Dillard (1983). It is far more appropriate to accept this language and focus our efforts on understanding African American clients than to worry about whether the words they use are correct according to Anglo standards. If you don't understand what a word used by the client means, ask. Moreover, it is most inappropriate for you, the social worker, to try to use slang or adopt language with which you are not comfortable.

More important than *how* African American clients communicate is *what* they communicate. Clients may be reluctant to reveal personal weaknesses because they don't know how the social worker will react. Consequently, clients can appear suspicious of or reserved toward persons in positions of power or authority. A logical question in assessment is how past interactions with other social systems have reinforced or extinguished certain behaviors. How have they influenced the person's self-esteem? For example, has the client experienced racism or discrimination that has left her feeling inferior or put down? Recognize that the minority experience may lead to feelings of powerlessness and despair. It may manifest itself in nonverbal, resistive, or even hostile, defensive behavior. Sensitivity to the possible influence of these experiences may help you understand the communication patterns of African American clients.

Family Experiences

Religion plays a very important role in the family lives of most African American and other minority groups (Netting, Thibault, & Ellor, 1990; Haber, 1984; Tayler & Chatters, 1986; Delgado & Humm-Delgado, 1982; Gibson, 1980; Coughlin, 1965). The church serves as a source of inspiration and support as well as a meeting place. African American churches have played an important part in the history of the civil rights movement (Netting, Thibault, & Ellor, 1990). Thus, when working with African American families, it is important to assess the significance of religious values and experiences for family members. It is also important to figure out whether the church is a resource for the family. For example, the church should be considered "a significant other" (for example, like a family member, loved one, or otherwise important person) when determining family strengths and problems. As with Native Americans, attention should be paid to extended family members who may play an important role in family decisions. Even single-parent households may have others who are playing one or more significant roles in the accomplishment of family tasks. These individuals could be related by blood, marriage, or friendship. Understanding and using these resources can be very helpful in the assessment and intervention stages (Haber, 1984; Tayler & Chatters, 1986).

Intervention Styles

We have discussed before the importance of showing respect for clients by using their formal names and titles. This advice remains salient for African American clients. Don't use nicknames, first names, or other signs of informality unless invited to do so. In other words,

When appropriate, interventions with clients should be based on a goal of their reaching empowerment.

use Mr. or Ms. to convey respect. You might ask the clients if they prefer "Mrs." and, if they do, use it. Although many consider it a sexist term, it is the client's right to be referred to as she pleases. This also will help ensure that the client knows you are seeking a relationship based on mutual respect and sharing of information, instead of the superior-inferior relationship that characterizes many professional-client relationships (such as doctor-patient or lawyer-client). We must communicate respect by recognizing and building upon clients' strengths.

We have also discussed the importance of learning about the culture with which you will be working. For example, it may be wise to study African American literature and music to get a sense of how life experiences affect how the world is perceived. For example, many African American writers and poets paint a portrait in words of what it is like to be a person of color in a white society. Through their eyes you may become aware of events and behaviors which are perceived as negative (for example, how celebrating Columbus's arrival is not perceived positively by many Native Americans). Similarly, it is helpful to read minority newspapers. These typically reflect the interests and perspectives of minority-group members and give additional insight into their world.

In some situations, there may be value in acknowledging the differences in culture and experiences between you and your clients. This is especially true if these differences appear to be problematic. For example, clients who raise questions about whether you can understand their situation should be answered frankly. Most of us don't have to be hit with a brick to know it will hurt. Yet some clients doubt whether you can understand their feelings if you have not gone through the same experience. Discussing this openly and honestly will likely lead to a more productive relationship with your client.

Clients often expect those in power to be reluctant or hesitant to act on their behalf. With African Americans there is genuine value in moving aggressively to confront the environmental obstacles with which they are struggling. Providing concrete services and connecting clients to these services through brokering are important. Avoid vague discussions about what might be done and concentrate on achievements which show your commitment to helping solve the client's problems. To the extent possible, our interventions should be based on a goal of empowering our clients. Empowerment is the "process of helping individuals, families, groups, and communities increase their personal, interpersonal, socioeconomic, and political strength and influence toward improving their circumstances" (Barker, 1991, p. 74). Thus we need to be seen as a peer who helps people develop confidence in their ability to cause change in their lives. The social worker becomes a resource instead of an expert in this process.

We also need to assess whether race or ethnicity is a factor within the institutional or organizational environment in which the client must operate. For example, some clients will blame themselves for situations that arise from subtle racism in work or school environments. While not all problems can be traced to macro system or environmental causes, the possibility should be considered whenever dealing with people of color. This is especially true when the client is having trouble with other social systems such as being denied service, given the runaround, or otherwise mistreated.

Macro Level Approaches to Intervention

Finally, we must look at our own agencies and environments to decide whether they are sensitive and responsive to the situations of African Americans and other minorities. Does our agency provide outreach services, or do we wait for minority clients to come to us? Do we recruit and hire people of color to work directly with clients, or only for clerical and less powerful roles? Does the agency's environment reflect the cultural diversity of society? Do we contribute to clients' unhappiness with the system? Are we part of the problem, or part of the solution?

Caveats

Here, we would simply remind you that no one's behavior or problems can be explained solely by their race. Be as cognizant of this idea with African American clients as you will be with other people of color.

Practice Knowledge and Skills—Asian American and Pacific Islanders

There is enormous variation within Asian culture. Among these groups are Japanese, Filipinos, Koreans, Burmese, Indonesians, Guamanians, Hmong, Samoans, South Vietnamese, and Thais, to name only a few. Contrary to popular belief, Asians are not homogeneous. Each group has its own language, history, religion, and culture. The groups differ in terms of group cohesion, socioeconomic status, and level of education. For example, the level of education and socioeconomic status of Japanese Americans approaches that of the dominant white majority, while for Samoan Americans, both are lower.

In addition, we have both "between-group differences and within-group differences" (Wong, Kim, Lim, & Morishima, 1983, p. 27). Wong, Kim, Lim, and Morishima (1983) provide a list of possible factors capable of producing differences within a single group. These factors appear in Highlight 12.2

As you can see from Highlight 12.2, there are many factors that can impact on the Asian American client and produce differences even within peoples from the same national background. Yet similarities do exist. In particular, *filial piety* and respect for authority are common to all these groups. Filial piety means a devotion to and compliance with parental and familial authority, to the point of sacrificing individual desires and ambitions. It is the duty of Asian children to listen to and obey their parents. Because of this respect for and obedience to the family, Asians generally seek to enhance the family name. This may be accomplished, for example, through occupational or academic success. On the other hand, they are apt to experience a sense of guilt or shame in seeking social services. They may believe that having personal

---

HIGHLIGHT 12.2
Within-Group Differences

Within-group differences include those factors that produce different expectations, experiences, aspirations, and reactions of Asian Americans (and other groups) of similar national origin. For example, any of these factors might explain why two people of Japanese extraction are so different culturally. While the emotions in various groups may differ little, the life experiences, sense of priorities, and intensity of reactions may vary dramatically. Within-group differences may include:

- Area of residence;
- Generational status, that is, first, second, third generation (For example, elderly Asians in this country may feel at a loss without the strong familial reference normally shown to aged Asians in the old country);
- Degree of acculturation (or how well the person has learned about, and adapted to, a new culture);
- Degree of fluency with one's native language;
- Degree of identification with one's home country, or region within one's country;

- Education (including both education in the United States and outside);
- Age;
- Family composition and degree of intactness;
- Degree to which group is embedded in formal and informal networks (such as family association, churches);
- Religious beliefs and value orientation;
- Economic status and financial situation;
- Comfort and competence with English language;
- Whether one or both parents in any family are from the same nation.

Source: Adapted from pages 27 and 28 of *Mental Health and People of Color: Curriculum Development and Change* edited by Jay C. Chunn, II, Patricia J. Dunston, and Fariyal Ross-Sheriff. Copyright 1983 by the Howard University School of Social Work and Howard University Press. Reprinted by permission of Howard University Press.

or social problem reflects negatively on their family.

Family Centering

The devotion to the family also means that clients are likely to be reluctant to discuss personal or psychological problems with non-family members. To do so is to bring shame on themselves and their families. The stigma of accepting service arises from the value placed on pride and dignity, and the desire to keep difficulties within the home. There is an expectation that the family should take care of its own needs.

The father's role is that of head of the family. Individual achievement of family members is encouraged only if it brings recognition to the family (Jung, 1976). Whenever possible, you should attempt to work through the father when planning interventions involving the family or other family members.

In addition, family experiences may be different depending upon whether we are working with people who have been in the United States for extended periods (fifty or more years), are recent arrivals, or were born here. For example, recent and older immigrants may request specific services, such as advocacy or brokering (Kuramoto, Munoz, Morales, & Murase, 1983). American-born Asians are more likely to accept counseling and interpersonal interventions.

Clients seen in family settings may appear uncaring or cold to outsiders. This is because Asian Americans are less likely to show much feeling in interactions with their children, especially in the presence of strangers.

Communication Patterns

We have mentioned that many cultures employ nonverbal communication to a much greater extent than verbal communication. This is also true in Asian American cultures. Looks and gestures may convey more than words can ever tell. Therefore, you must be alert to this form of communication. In addition, some gestures may be confusing to the novice. For example, a Japanese person may nod his head to show he is following your conversation. The uninitiated may notice this gesture and mistakenly conclude the client is in agreement.

Similar to Native Americans, it is easy to confuse respect for authority with passiveness or refusal to express feelings. Tactfully encouraging clients to self-disclose may help them become more comfortable with the expectations of the social work experience. For example, saying to a mother and father that "It must be very difficult to raise children to respect the old ways" acknowledges how such influences as peer pressure, drugs, or violence in neighborhood schools and urban gangs can undercut the best efforts of the parents.

It is also important to show respect by learning the client's name. For example, in Vietnamese, a person typically has a three-word name. The first word is the family name, the second is the middle name, and the third is a given name. Since formalities are observed, a stranger would call Dinh Phuc Van, "Mr. Van." A close friend would call him "Van." If you recall, the social worker in the vignette at the start of this chapter called the client "Dinh," as if it were an American first name. Not only did he use the wrong name as if he were on a first-name basis, but he didn't use the "Mr." which is a title of respect.

Attending Skills

Attending skills are just as important when working with Asian Americans as with other groups. Like Native Americans, avoidance of eye contact is typical among some Asians. For example, the Vietnamese find eye contact more problematic than do whites. There is also a protocol to the introductions of many Asian Americans. For example, handshakes are generally a part of our life-style. We extend our hand to almost everyone. Within Vietnamese culture, however, it is an insult for an adult male to shake the hand of, or touch, adult females. Similarly, it is important to avoid being in a closed room with females over twelve years of age. You may remember that John Martin, the social worker greeting the family of Dinh Phuc Van, shook Ms. Van's hand. The combination of failing to show respect by proper use of the man's name, failing to use the term "Mr.," and touching Ms. Van helped contribute to the premature end of this interview.

Intervention Skills

It is important that clients have confidence in you. You should attempt to project a calm, dignified image and have a clear sense of where you are going with the relationship. If you look like you're floundering, clients will lose confidence in you. Thus, a more direct, goal-oriented, approach is often preferable. Counselors are expected to be directive, like other authority figures, including teachers. Similarly, you should strive to be reliable and dependable. Both are virtues in the Asian culture.

Self-disclosure may be useful to a degree if it helps engender client trust in the worker. But, as always, the purpose of self-disclosure is to help the client, not address the needs of the social worker. This means that disclosing some of your own experiences is appropriate when it relates directly to what the client is saying, and when doing so will probably show the client that you understand their experience. It should not be done simply because you feel like sharing information or because you want to talk about your experience.

Paraphrasing is a skill that probably should be used less than in most practice situations. This is because it may seem unnatural to the client. That is, clients may perceive that you don't have confidence in (or you doubt) what they've said.

Questioning should be used carefully and sparingly. It is easy to overwhelm clients or appear to be bombarding them. Questioning often gives the impression that when all the answers are provided, the worker will give the client a decision or recommendation. It is possible that what the client needs is not a "solution" but a forum to talk about ideas and discover his/her own individual solution. Also, asking specific questions about topics such as illnesses or sexual behavior may be considered extremely rude or intrusive (Lum, 1986). When a client considers some problems private, asking about them may make the social worker appear pushy. It takes time and patience to overcome this hesitancy.

Speaking of time, some Asian American groups (for instance, the Vietnamese) have values about time similar to Native Americans. They view time as elastic, not static. Specific limited units of time are unimportant. They are often more patient and relaxed about time and work than many Anglos. Awareness of this value can make it easier, for example, to understand some Vietnamese behavior and view it within a cultural context.

Community-based services are more likely to be accepted and used in the Asian American community. This is especially true of those located physically close to the population to be served. These agencies are more likely to develop close ties to the community, enhancing their utility to the clients.

Group situations can be difficult for Asian Americans, especially if they must open up in front of strangers. In group situations, it is important to avoid using confrontative tactics with Asian American clients. Conflict is generally considered disharmonious. The loss of face that confrontation produces can undermine anything previously accomplished. Yet, assertiveness and considerable structure are appropriate, especially in the early phases of group interventions. Also in group situations, don't expect Asian Americans to compete with one another. Mutual aid and reciprocity are more valued than competition.

Individual approaches that are more useful with Asian Americans include advice giving, warning clients about the consequences of particular course of action, and "direct cognitive appeal" (Dillard, 1983, p. 193). For example, with an Asian American client who is thinking about dropping out of college in mid-semester, you might say "Dropping out of school before the end of the semester is likely to affect your financial aid, your ability to remain in the dormitory, and your ability to take classes next semester." Clients need to be completely aware of possible consequences to make an informed decision about their options.

The value of cognitive approaches stems from the fact that Asian Americans are often unwilling or unable to talk about their feelings. Cognitive approaches such as appeals to logic and clarifying the client's thinking may be acceptable alternatives to discussing feelings. Dillard even suggests appealing to shame and guilt, both of which are culturally relevant reasons for behaving in specific ways. Focusing on willpower and self-control approaches also fit in nicely with the Asian culture's belief system. For example, you might stress to the Asian American client described above that she is the one who decides whether she achieves her goals, and that she must make the decision to stay in school. This emphasizes the client's responsibility for her actions and her control over her future. Additionally, you may teach clients assertiveness skills, but you must do this carefully. A skill useful for navigating American society may be problematic in an Asian culture. For example, a traditional Asian American wife who suddenly becomes more assertive with her husband can provoke marital problems which did not previously exist.

Like many other cultures, Asian Americans are more likely to recognize the value of indigenous healing approaches. The use of acupuncture, massage, natural medications, and herbs should not be discouraged simply because the worker does not recognize or use these treatments. Asian use of these approaches typically stems from cultural explanations of mental or physical problems. Problems are thought to be caused by the mystical (supernatural) or to be punishment for failing to abide by cultural norms. In some instances, the problem also may be attributed to bad luck (Dillard, 1983). Often, it is possible to convince the client to use both these natural approaches and to consult a physician. You can thus assure the benefits of both cultures' wisdom.

Empowerment is a goal to which we should strive with all groups that have been historically exposed to and are presently experiencing discrimination and prejudice. Clients who are trying to live between two cultures, often with conflicting values, may experience social or emotional problems. Coming to the United States was a major culture shock for many Asian Americans. For example, problems with low self-respect may be common to groups which, after coming to America, have to accept welfare or low status employment. They need help to understand and negotiate the systems that are causing or contributing to the problems.

Another way of showing respect for clients whose native language is other than English is through the skillful use of interpreters. However, children should never be used as translators for adults. Such juxtaposing of family roles causes embarrassment for both child and parent. When an interpreter is used, it should be another adult, preferably one already trusted by the client. You should address your questions to the client by looking at the client, instead of talking to the interpreter. Some translated interviews look like the client is invisible because the worker talks only to the interpreter. This is a mistake.

Finally, it is appropriate to focus efforts on providing concrete services such as referrals, housing resources, and economic assistance in an atmosphere of respect for the client and his values (Ho, 1983). Concrete services show the efficacy of the social worker and the ability to help the client meet identified needs. This, in turn, increases the client's confidence in the worker, and can open the way to the client seeking help in additional areas.

Caveats

Clearly, there are both similarities and dissimilarities among the various cultural groups with which you may come in contact. Asian Americans and Pacific Islanders are an extremely diverse group. It is logical to want to adopt strategies which will work with all the groups subsumed under this title. To do so would likely be a mistake. In the following section we will look at some techniques that generally can be used with a wide range of Asian and other people of color. However, alert social workers must constantly guard against generalizations which don't apply to the particular clients with whom they're working.

Developing Effective Cross-Cultural Interventions

Effective cross-cultural social work requires skills in several areas: attending, assessment, and intervention. Highlight 12.3 provides several recommendations important in cross-cultural assessment.

Green (1982) discusses the attributes of a culturally responsive social worker. She believes workers should think about clients in terms of both group strengths and limitations in addition to individual problems. In other words, you should be able to use knowledge about clients' racial or ethnic group in the assessment process. Simultaneously, you must remember that membership in a particular ethnic group does not automatically explain a person's behavior.

Other characteristics of a culturally responsive social worker include recognizing one's own cultural limitations and appreciating cultural differences. Our own biases and anxieties

when working with minorities can become a problem. Anxiety or guilt can get in the way of being empathic. Moreover, we may tend to transfer our reactions to situations to clients assuming they will react, feel, and think as we do. A willingness and eagerness to learn about a client's culture will go a long way toward building better cross-cultural relationships.

Dillard (1983) has summarized his recommendations for effective cross-cultural interventions, focusing largely on interpersonal dimensions and attending skills. These include:

1. Maintain awareness that nonverbal communication probably constitutes more of the communication in a counseling relationship with people of color than does the verbal component.
2. Recognize that eye contact can be a problem for many ethnic groups.
3. Use both open-ended and closed-ended questions. They are almost universally acceptable.
4. Remember that reflection of feelings works with many cultures, but not with all (in many cultures reaching for feelings should be used carefully and slowly).
5. Recall that paraphrasing generally is an acceptable technique in most cultures.
6. Utilize self-disclosure judiciously.
7. Give interpretations and advice in cultures expecting a directive helper.
8. Summarize from time to time.
9. Use confrontation appropriately and carefully with certain racial groups.
10. Remember that openness, authenticity, and genuineness are respected in all cultures.

Dillard concludes that using approaches that are not culturally sensitive is a form of ethnocentrism, a perpetuation of racism, and an imposition of one group's ideas on another.

Green (1982) argues that it is important to explore how clients and their respective reference group see a particular problem. The way we define or view a problem is often affected by one's culture. It is usually important to find out the views of important members of the client's family including extended family members and nonmembers who have family status, such as godparents.

Whenever possible, we should focus on the specific problems for which the client sought help before getting into areas where the client

---

HIGHLIGHT 12.3
Strategies for Cultural Assessment

Miller (1982) has provided a sound list of strategies that can be used across all cultural groups when doing assessments.

1. Consider all clients as individuals first, as members of minority status next, and then as members of a specific ethnic group. This will help prevent overgeneralizing and making erroneous assumptions.

2. Never assume that a person's ethnic identity tells you anything about his or her cultural values or patterns of behavior. Remember that within-culture differences are often substantial and that two clients from the same culture may have vastly different life experiences.

3. Treat all "facts" you have ever heard or read about cultural values and traits as hypotheses, to be tested anew with each client. Turn "facts" into questions.

4. Remember that all minority groups in this society are at least bicultural. That is, they all live in at least two cultures, their own and the majority culture. The percentage may be 90 to 10 in either direction, but they still have had the task of integrating two value systems that are often in conflict. The conflicts involved in being bicultural may override any specific cultural content. That is, the difficulty of surviving in a bicultural environment may be of greater importance that the fact a person is from a particular racial group.

5. Remember that some aspects of a client's cultural history, values, and life-style are relevant to your work with the client. Others may be simply interesting to you as a professional. Do not prejudge what areas are relevant. Only the client can identify those factors which are important.

6. Identify strengths in the client's cultural orientation you can build upon. Help the client in identifying areas that create social or psychological conflict related to biculturalism, and seek to reduce dissonance in those areas. For example, you might help the client understand that it is appropriate to adopt some Anglo behaviors needed for survival in the business world (such as assertiveness) but not to use them within her traditional family, where they might be considered improper. By doing this, she is adapting to the larger culture where necessary but not abandoning her traditional values.

7. Be aware of your own attitude about cultural pluralism. Know whether you tend to promote assimilation into the dominant society or whether you stress the maintenance of traditional cultural beliefs and practices. Your own biases and perspectives are important, and can affect your work with clients.

8. Engage your client actively in the process of learning what cultural content should be considered. This means you must ask clearly about clients' experiences, beliefs, and values.

9. Keep in mind that there are no substitutes for good clinical skills, empathy, caring, and a sense of humor.

Source: From Nancy Brown Miller, "Social Work Services to Urban Indians," in *Cultural Awareness in the Human Services,* James W. Green ed., 1982, p. 182. Adapted by permission of Prentice-Hall, Englewood Cliffs, New Jersey.

has not yet seen a problem. For example, it may be clear to us from an initial session with a client that he is showing signs of serious problems in his marriage. However, the client has sought help for problems with his oldest son. Thus, we should first focus our attention on this area.

As a corollary, you should use the client's definition of a successful intervention, not just your own. Sometimes the client defines a problem as "solved" although the social worker will recognize additional areas where work could still be done. Self-determination is especially important in work with people of color. Likewise, demonstrating respect for the client's worth and dignity will be effective in all cultures.

Openness to the use of indigenous (natural) helpers is also recommended by Green (1982). For example, many cultures value natural helpers (such as curanderos, medicine men) and other paraprofessionals. When clients have faith in the work of these auxiliary helpers, we should not discourage their utilization. Using both clients' cultural resources and those of their community are appropriate helping activities.

In some situations, there really is no easy or simple solution to be found. For example, clients have realistic problems (such as getting along on an Aid to Families with Dependent Children budget). No amount of counseling will eliminate this problem. Providing empathy and helping clients find creative ways to stretch their budgets have their place but also their limits. Ultimately, political stances strongly supporting adequate resources for human service programs probably would be more helpful. This includes writing and calling your political representatives, lobbying for increased budgets, and working with NASW and other organizations. In addition, social workers must become active in the political process. It is the only way to ensure that elected officials from the school board, city council, legislature, Congress, governor's office and White House are sensitive to ethnic diversity and the specific needs of people of color.

Moreover, social workers need to continue to focus efforts on political and social action to create changes which benefit those who have been historic victims of discrimination. For example, health care should be available to all citizens and not be dependent solely on the beneficence (goodwill) of an employer. Recently many companies and businesses have strived to hire part-time employees. Doing this allows them to avoid paying the health and other benefits available to full-time employees. Such policies affect people of color and women adversely and disproportionately.

In addition, we need to encourage research that tests various approaches to understanding and intervening in problems experienced by people of color. We should know which interventions work best with which groups and why. Our level of understanding in this area remains rudimentary at best.

Chapter Summary

This chapter has introduced the topic of ethnically and racially sensitive social work practice. The United States is a pluralistic nation that includes a variety of ethnic and racial groupings. It has also been a nation struggling with racism and discrimination against people of color. The chapter discussed some barriers to effective multicultural social work facing the social worker today.

In addition, the chapter examined in greater detail elements of the practice, knowledge, and skills needed by social workers in a heterogenous culture. Specifically, the chapter focused on knowledge and skill for work with Native Americans, Hispanics, African Americans, and Asian Americans. Among the topics mentioned under each of these groups were communication patterns, family issues, and intervention styles. The chapter concluded with a review of interventions that appear to be useful across most cultural groups.

13 *Gender Sensitive Social Work Practice*

The fairness factor

Julia, age twenty-three, and her four young children are homeless. All the shelters are filled. She had married at age seventeen and had never worked outside of the home. She and her children had always been poor, her husband jumping from one low-paying job to another. Last month her husband told her he was sick of her and all of his responsibility, and abruptly left without telling her where he was going. Julia has no money and desperately needs food and clothing for her family. She has no access to relatives or other personal support systems who could help her. Also, to remove herself from her homeless situation permanently, she needs job training along with concurrent day care.

Jeannette, age twenty-nine, was raped fourteen months ago and now has discovered she has AIDS. Her assailant has been apprehended and she has learned he is HIV positive. Thus, she thinks he was the one who contaminated her. Her health has deteriorated rapidly. She desperately needs expensive health care, including expensive drugs which could help her keep at least some of the more severe diseases at bay. She had been a secretary but her health problems no longer allow her to work. She does not have any health insurance and her savings are completely depleted.

Danielle, age fifteen, has been on the streets for two years. She thinks she is cocaine and alcohol addicted. She ran away from home because her stepfather had been sexually abusing her since she was eleven and she couldn't stand it anymore. She needs both a home and an expensive rehabilitation program to survive.

Gertie, age thirty-seven, is a battered woman. The beatings are getting worse. She doesn't know how long she literally can live in her environment. She is only one of about 150 battered women identified in her small midwestern town. Counseling, day care, legal aid, and a place of respite for these women are desperately needed. However, a minimum of twenty thousand dollars is required to keep the shelter for them open another three months.

Ruth, age fifty-seven, has been divorced for twenty-three months. Her ex-husband, a businessman two years her senior, left her to run off with a twenty-six-year-old woman. He got an expensive lawyer and manipulated most of their assets so that they were unavailable to her. She received half of the money from their house and $230 a month in alimony for two years. Their house was beautiful, but their equity in it was relatively small. As a result, Ruth now has almost no money left and her alimony is about to stop. Her ex-husband has spent thirty-five years establishing a career for himself. He is well-off. Ruth, however, has spent her life taking care of his home, entertaining his associates, and doing charity work for her community. She has no experience working outside of the home other than the minimum-wage job she has managed to get at a local frozen yogurt store. Her reserve of cash is almost gone. What she earns now will barely pay for her rent, let alone for her food, health care, and other needs. She has no idea about what she will do.

Introduction

All of the preceding situations involve women. All portray situations and conditions either unique to women or more likely to characterize women than men. The core issues for most of the examples are poverty and violence, two widespread problems which "directly or indirectly threaten the well-being of all women" (Jones, 1987, p. 880). This chapter explores the special approaches to intervention with women and their special environmental circumstances. These circumstances are very different from those which characterize the world of men.

Specifically, this chapter will:

- Demonstrate the importance of gender sensitivity;
- Formulate a feminist perspective on micro, mezzo, and macro aspects of generalist practice;
- Present a definition of feminism for practitioners;
- Explore micro practice with women by describing common problems and proposing techniques for working with women;
- Demonstrate how assertiveness training can be used to help women;
- Recognize the importance of a feminist approach to macro practice;
- Examine the issues of sexual assault, the physical abuse of women, and the feminization of poverty, and;

- Propose micro, mezzo, and macro intervention approaches to correct them.

Gender Sensitivity

As we begin to explore the special sphere of women, it's important to be familiar with a number of terms. They are:

Sexism: "Prejudice or discrimination based on sex, especially discrimination against women" that involves "behavior, conditions, or attitudes that foster stereotypes of social roles based on sex" (*Webster's Ninth New Collegiate Dictionary*, 1991, p. 1079).

Sex (or Gender) Role Stereotypes: Expectations about how people should behave based upon their gender. Female stereotypes include having "warmth," "expressiveness," "emotionality," and a "lack of competitiveness." Additionally, a 'feminine' woman should be sexually attractive to men and, in turn, to be attracted to them" (Hyde, 1990, p. 370). Men, on the other hand, are supposed to be "aggressive, athletic, successful, unemotional, brave, and instantly aroused by attractive women" (Hyde, 1990, p. 373).

Oppression: "The social act of placing severe restrictions on a group or institution. Typically, a government or political organization that is in power places these restrictions formally or covertly on oppressed groups [such as women] so that they may be exploited and less able to compete with other social groups" (Barker, 1987, p. 112).

Sex Discrimination: "Treating people differently based on their sex. Usually the term refers to favorable treatment of males and relegation of females to subordinate positions. Sex discrimination is manifested in such activities as promoting men over women and paying male employees more than female employees for comparable work" (Barker, 1987, p. 148).

Many people are initially "turned off" by the concept of sexism. They find it very difficult to consciously recognize and accept the possibility that this is an imperfect, sexist world. They think things are supposed to be fair and they shouldn't have to waste their time and energy battling such problems as sexism. For many women, it's easier to adopt an "out of sight, out of mind" philosophy. In other words, if one doesn't think about a problem, then it doesn't really exist. Why make up and dwell on problems which are nonexistent or insignificant?

Here are some facts:

- Women who work full-time earn 65 percent of what men earn full-time (Blau & Winkler, 1989).
- 72.7 percent of all women work outside of the home; 38 percent of all women having children within the past year are in the paid labor force (Ginsberg, 1990).
- 80 percent of women work in only one quarter of all possible occupations: "librarians, secretaries, retail clerks, household workers, nurses, and teachers," all of which "pay less and offer fewer opportunities for advancement than do those occupations filled predominantly by men" (Jones, 1987, p. 876).
- Women are twice as likely as men to be poor within their lifetimes (Shortridge, 1989).
- Slightly over one third of all single female-headed households are poor; families headed by single African American or Hispanic women are significantly more likely to be poor than families headed by white women (U.S. Bureau of the Census, 1985).
- In 1987 there were over 91,000 reported rapes in the United States (Hyde, 1990, p. 474). However, only one in five stranger rapes and, even more strikingly, 2 percent of acquaintance and date rapes are reported (Koss, Dinero, Siebel & Cox, 1988).

- Every woman has a 26 percent chance of being raped during her lifetime (Russell & Howell, 1983).
- Studies indicate that between 21 percent (Schulman, 1979) and almost 28 percent (Straus, Gelles & Steinmetz, 1980) of all husbands act violently against their wives at some time during their marriage. In view of the tendency not to report incidents, the real rate of violence against wives may be 50 to 60 percent of all couples (Star, 1987; Straus, 1978).
- Extremely severe, repeated violence occurs against women in almost 7 percent of all marriages (Dutton, 1988).

As a generalist practitioner, you will be called upon to work with women. Women are more likely than men to be poor. Additionally, women are victims of specific kinds of violence rarely suffered by men. Therefore, it is critically important that you understand the issues, interpersonal dynamics, and most effective intervention techniques involved in helping women.

A Feminist Perspective on Micro, Mezzo, and Macro Aspects of Generalist Practice

Before we review specific intervention techniques for working with women, we need to set the stage. You need to understand the basis for why working with women is different than working with men. A brief discussion of feminist social work practice will help to achieve this.

The Social Work Dictionary (Barker, 1987) defines feminism very simply as "the social movement and doctrine advocating legal and socioeconomic equality for women" (p. 56). Superficially, this may seem quite simple. However, in reality the issues are very complicated.

Van Den Bergh and Cooper (1987) elaborate on the principles of feminist social work.

┌─ HIGHLIGHT 13.1 ───

Are You a Feminist?

Do you believe that women should have the same rights as men?

Do you believe that women should be able to have the same access to jobs and social status as men?

Do you believe that women should *not* be discriminated against or *denied* opportunities and choices on the basis of their gender?

Do you believe that ideally people's attitudes and behavior should reflect the equal treatment of women?

Do you think that many people need to become more educated about women's issues?

Would you be willing to advocate on the behalf of women (for instance, for poor women or women who have been raped)?

Do you believe that both men and women have the right to their own individual differences (that is, of course, differences which don't harm other people)?

Do you think that our society is generally structured legally, socially, and economically by and for men instead of women? (This last question is probably the most difficult and perhaps, the most painful, to answer.)

If you've answered "yes" to all or most of these questions, according to our definition which will be discussed later, there's a good chance that you are a feminist.

└──

They state that in many ways feminist social work conforms well with the principles and values of traditional social work practice. For example, both stress the importance of individuals' interactions with their surrounding environments and communities. Additionally, both emphasize the significance of being concerned with "human dignity and the rights of self-determination" (Van Den Bergh & Cooper, 1986, p. 3).

A feminist perspective on micro practice with women targets women's inner feelings and access to personal power. For instance, women "tend to have lower self-esteem and less confidence in their own abilities to succeed at future tasks" than do men (Hyde, 1990, p. 378). Lott (1987) cites a number of studies which "report a general tendency for women to state lower self-expectancies than men, to underestimate their performance on a variety of tasks, and to express less self-confidence than men" (p. 247).

Women also tend to be less aggressive than men; this is true essentially for all types of aggression including both physical and verbal (Hyde, 1984). This frequently causes problems for women who not only aren't aggressive, but don't appropriately stand up for their own rights. Self-esteem may be related to aggression in that women who don't value themselves may not feel capable of asserting themselves.

Later in the chapter, we will discuss the continuum of aggression, assertiveness, and passivity. We will also provide some intervention suggestions for helping women become more appropriately assertive.

A feminist perspective on mezzo practice focuses on women's relationships with others around them. This involves both personal relationships and interactions in their world of work. If women tend to have lower levels of self-esteem and aggression, how does this impact their relationships? This again may involve having difficulty in feeling good enough about themselves to be appropriately assertive.

The micro and mezzo levels of a feminist practice perspective are intimately intertwined. It's difficult to classify which aspect of working with women falls clearly within micro practice and which falls within mezzo practice. Likewise, the feminist macro practice perspective is intimately related to what occurs in women's personal, interpersonal, and work lives.

We've already presented some facts which reflect how women are oppressed. On the one hand, many women need to enhance their own self-esteem to better advocate for themselves. On the other hand, there are obvious impediments and hazards which women must endure that don't impact men's lives at all or nearly as much. For example, what structural barriers confront women in our society which lead them to earn significantly less than men? Why is it likely that more than one in four women will be sexually assaulted at some time in their lives? How does this fact restrict women's behavior? Should they not go to the library at night to study because it's dangerous to walk home? How does this affect their ability to compete with men who don't have such fears and restrictions? In other words, feminists view our world as being one primarily built by and for men. The special needs of women frequently remain unmet.

A feminist perspective on macro practice then looks at the social policies and political structures which act to hamper women in leading free and productive lives. You as a generalist practitioner need to be aware of oppression. You also need to be willing to advocate for and sometimes fight on behalf of people who are oppressed. This chapter assumes a feminist perspective for generalist social work practice.

A Definition of Feminism for Practitioners

Feminism is a complex concept which is difficult to define concisely. It involves "the theory of the political, economic, and social equality of the sexes," in addition to "the organized activity on behalf of women's rights and inter-

ests" (*Webster's New Collegiate Dictionary*, 1977, p. 422). Van Den Bergh and Cooper elaborate on the relationship of feminism to social work practice by emphasizing its "commitment to altering the process and manner in which private and public lives are organized and conducted." They state that "basically, feminism is concerned with ending domination and resisting oppression" (1986, pp. 1–2).

Some people have extremely negative reactions to the word "feminism." The emotional barriers they forge and the resulting resistance they foster makes it very difficult even to approach the concept with them. Others consider feminism a radical ideology which emphasizes separatism and fanaticism. In other words, they think feminism involves the philosophy adopted by women who spurn men, resent past inequities, and strive violently to overthrow male supremacists. Still, others think of feminism as an outmoded tradition that is no longer relevant.

The definition of feminism presented here is designed to relate to basic concepts involving the daily lives of people like you (Kirst-Ashman, 1991). It involves readily understandable concepts. Many people have failed to develop a sensitivity to the sexist barriers surrounding them. For one thing, it's painful to acknowledge such unfairness. For another, it's easy to assume that "that's the way things are" simply because people haven't thought about other, better ways of doing things.

For our purposes here, feminism is defined as the *philosophy of equality* between women and men that involves *both attitudes and actions*, which infiltrates virtually *all aspects of life*, which often necessitates providing *education and advocacy* on the behalf of women, and which appreciates the existence of *individual differences* and personal accomplishments regardless of gender. There are five major components within this definition which relate directly to the core of professional social work practice.

The first component is equality. Equality

does not mean that women are trying to shed their female identities and become clones of men. Nor does it mean that women should seek to adopt behaviors which are typically "masculine." Feminism does involve equal or identical rights to opportunities and choices. It relates to women's and men's rights not to be discriminated against nor denied opportunities and choices on the basis of gender.

The second major component inherent in feminism is the fact that it embodies both attitudes and actions. Attitudes concern how we look at the world and perceive other people. Feminism involves viewing other people from a fair and objective perspective and avoiding stereotypes.

For example, take a social services supervisor who firmly states she is a feminist. However, she ignores one of her male supervisees who consistently makes sexist comments about his female colleagues. The worker frequently tells sexist jokes about breast size. He also likes to tell his colleagues how women just get too emotionally involved with their clients and aren't able to be objective enough to formulate effective intervention plans. This man's behavior is a form of sexual harassment. His supervisor is legally responsible to see that such obtrusive behavior does not occur in the work environment. However, that's the beginning of another story. The point is that although this supervisor may be a feminist in terms of attitude, she is not a feminist in terms of action. A feminist supervisor would confront her supervisee about his specific inappropriate, sexist remarks. Feminism involves acting on one's beliefs on behalf of gender equality.

The third critical component of feminism

HIGHLIGHT 13.2
Principles of Feminist Counseling

Van Den Bergh and Cooper (1987) propose seven principles of feminist intervention. These principles provide lenses with which to view women and their problems. They involve assumptions about the causes of many problems. Therefore, they're like molds with which social workers can shape their interventions. These principles provide clues and guidelines for how to proceed. The principles are:

1. A client's problems should be viewed "within a sociopolitical framework" (p. 613). These problems are often rooted in a sexist social and political structure and cannot be considered simply personal or individual. Another way of putting this is that for women, "personal is political" (p. 613).

2. Clients need encouragement to free themselves from traditional gender role bonds. They need encouragement to make free choices and pursue the tasks and achievements they choose. Tasks and goals should not be limited to those allocated primarily to women. They should include those traditionally offered primarily to men.

3. Intervention should focus on the identification and enhancement of clients' strengths rather than on pathologies. Strengths provide a foundation upon which to build. Women need to be empowered so they "can increase their ability to control their environments to get what they need" (p. 613).

4. Women should be encouraged to develop "an independent identity that is not defined by one's relationships with others" (p. 613). In other words, women's identities should not be determined by whom they're married to or whom they're dating. Rather, their identity should be solidly based on their own strengths, achievement, and individuality.

5. Other women are considered valuable and important. In a society which devalues women in general, it is easy even for women (who, of course, are also part of that society) to see other women as being insignificant. Feminist

is the idea that it concerns all aspects of life. Equality does not only apply to an equal unhindered chance at getting a specific job or promotion. It also involves the right to have personal opinions about political issues and the right to make decisions within personal relationships. It entails a woman's right to make a decision about what to do on a Friday night date, as well as her right to choose whether or not to have a sexual encounter. Essentially, this step includes the acknowledgment that our social, legal, and political structure is oriented toward men, not women.

A fourth important aspect of feminism is the frequent need to provide education and advocacy on behalf of women. We've established that feminism involves values. Values provide the basis for decisions about how a person behaves. If a person sees things oc-

curring which are contrary to her values, in this case to feminist values, steps may be necessary to help remedy the situation. Many times people need information about women's issues. The male worker mentioned earlier who is sexually harassing female colleagues may need information about what sexual harassment is and how it negatively affects women. He may be ignorant of these effects. A feminist will share and provide information to others to initiate positive changes in their attitudes and behavior.

Sometimes there will be a need for even greater effort and advocacy may be called for. An advocate is "one who pleads the cause of another" (*Webster's New Collegiate Dictionary*, 1977, p. 18). This often involves initiating change or going out of one's way to provide help. Feminism focuses on helping women

---

intervention urges clients to reevaluate their relationships with other women. This principle of feminist intervention emphasizes how valuable other women can be to clients. This is related to the concept of networking, which is "the social worker's therapeutic efforts to enhance and develop the social linkages that might exist between the client and those relevant to the client; other women can serve as "effective resources in helping to achieve the client's goals" (Barker, 1987, p. 107). They can share their experiences and solutions they've found to similar problems. Additionally, they can provide nurturance and emotional support.

6. Feminist intervention emphasizes finding a balance between work and personal relationships. A corollary of this is that men and women are encouraged to share in both the nurturant aspects of their lives and in providing economic resources.

7. "Whenever possible, the personal power between . . . [practitioner] and client approaches

equality. This means that feminist . . . [practitioners] do not view themselves as experts on clients' problems; rather, they act as catalysts for helping clients empower themselves. This reconceptualization of the . . . [practitioner-client] relationship is based on the feminist concern with eliminating dominant-submissive relationships" (Van Den Bergh & Cooper, 1987, p. 613).

Feminist intervention fits well with our generalist problem-solving model. It emphasizes focusing on clients' strengths and is oriented toward viewing the individual as a dynamic micro system interacting with the many mezzo and macro systems in her environment. Emphasizing the significance of the environment in which people live easily sets the stage for advocacy and macro practice change. You need to focus your attention on "the system" to find out what's wrong with it and then structure your interventions so that they work for positive change.

achieve greater equality and opportunity. Feminist advocacy involves speaking out for others who need help. A natural part of advocacy is helping those in positions of lesser power and opportunity.

The fifth major concept involved in the definition of feminism is the appreciation of individual differences. The feminist perspective lauds the concept of empowering women by emphasizing individual strengths and qualities. Feminism stresses freedom and the right to make choices about one's own life.

Van Den Bergh and Cooper (1987) emphasize the relevance of a feminist perspective in social work practice. They refer to such practice as "a model of activism and sensitivity, of growth and change, of challenge and risk"; they conclude "a feminist social work practice is a viable way to accomplish the unique mission of social work, to improve the quality of life by facilitating social change" (p. 617).

Micro Practice with Women: Common Problems

The issues women often bring to counseling situations are related to traditional gender roles and to the situations in which women often find themselves. It's not that men never suffer from any of these needs. Rather, it's that women are more likely to have these needs because of their gender role socialization. These problems are clustered in two major categories, stressful life events and personal issues.

Stressful Life Events

Collier (1982) cites at least two groups of events which can be very stressful to women and provides a number of examples. The first group involves happenings in women's personal lives, such as separation and divorce. For many women, the natural aging process can also cause undue stress. Accepting the inevitable fact that one will lose both youth and beauty can be difficult, especially in a society that stresses their importance, particularly for women. Accepting the death of someone close can also be very difficult. Finally, many women are forced to move from familiar surroundings to new, unknown environments due to a job change or out of economic necessity. Such changes and forced readjustments can be very stressful.

The other group of events that can cause women substantial stress concerns work and financial status. Women may have low self-esteem and worry about the adequacy of their job performance. Or they may be overburdened with employment, home, and child care responsibilities. With or without jobs, women have a high likelihood of being poor and experiencing the resultant stresses and strains.

Finally, women may suffer from blatant sex discrimination at work. Collier (1982) describes a common scenario:

> Because most women are taught to discriminate against themselves, they are often unaware that their low status and high frustration on the job is due to the pervasiveness of sex discrimination; they therefore tend to blame themselves as if for personal failings. Discrimination is not less blatant but just as pervasive and, if a woman does recognize its presence, she may become frustrated and collapse into unproductive anger, potentially stifling her own efforts (p. 51).

For instance, take a woman who is hired at the same time as a man for identical jobs. Both have similar levels of education, experience, and skills. The woman, however, is hired at 80 percent of the man's salary. Women are unfairly socialized to blame themselves, however, and the woman in this example is likely to feel that there is something wrong with *her*, which results in her lower salary. She is likely to accept the situation as it stands (after all, it must be her fault) instead of fighting for what she rightly deserves.

Personal Issues

Collier (1982, pp. 57–77) describes eight problems that women frequently bring to counseling situations. They are:

Powerlessness: Women who have been taught to be deferent and dependent often don't feel they can take control of their lives. They feel no matter what they do, it won't change anything. Because of lack of practice in being assertive and making decisions, they don't feel they have the potential to do so.

Limited Behavioral and Emotional Options: Because of being herded down certain gender-role related paths, women don't often see the variety of alternatives which may be open to them. For instance, it may not even occur to a divorced woman who has never worked outside of the home that she may be able to establish a career for herself. Or a battered woman may be so cowed by her perpetrator that she might not even think leaving him is an option.

Anger: Women often come to counseling harboring deep feelings of anger. They may be angry at the condescending treatment they've been receiving in their workplaces or in their homes. They may be angry that they're trying to be supermoms, superworkers, and superwives all at the same time, and they just can't do it. Or they may be angry that their perceived expectations of how they should be (gentle, nurturant, passive) are conflicting with how they really want to be. Instead of targeting the real cause of the anger, the woman often becomes angry at herself, which results in depression.

Inadequate Communication Skills: Women who come to counseling may not have the words to clearly express what they mean. Additionally, they may not feel that they have the right to say what they think. Opportunities to discriminate between nonassertion, aggression, and appropriate assertion may never have been available to them.

Failure to Nurture Self: Women who have devoted themselves to nurturing and caring for others may feel their own identities are lost. They may be searching for who they are and what they can do for themselves. They may have sacrificed so much for others that they no longer know what they as independent individuals need or want.

Balancing Independence with Interdependence: Being dependent involves relying on someone else for support and probably being subordinate to that person. Being independent, on the other hand, entails being able to function well on your own without having to rely on anyone. Collier (1982) articulates a woman's dilemma:

The normal woman finds it difficult to establish her autonomy. The feminine sex-role stereotype encourages her to create her existence not by doing but by accompanying others who do. Her role is to listen, to tend, to care, to understand, and to prohibit herself from expressing what she needs, wants, thinks, and feels at the expense of others (pp. 68–69).

One of your tasks as a social worker focusing on a woman's inner emotional needs and development is to help her establish the difference between being too dependent and being completely independent (that is, needing no one else for anything, including emotional support). The term for such a balance is interdependence. This involves feeling confident enough to function autonomously, yet acknowledging that you are a social entity whose interactions with other people are important to you.

Lack of Trust in Self-Direction: If a woman has low self-esteem and, for a variety of reasons, little experience in independent action, it's logical that she will have difficulty trusting her own judgment for how to proceed. Take, for example, my neighbor. She is a professional woman in her early forties who has no children and is recently divorced. She is taking it upon herself to build her own house. It's a custom-built contemporary home with steeply descending areas of roof and bold lines. Whenever I speak with my neighbor, her statements about the house seem to end with question marks. For instance, she might say, "It certainly is contemporary. I wonder if it's too drastic." Or, "I'm finishing the cabinets myself; I hope they're not too light colored and the coating isn't too rough."

I am not criticizing her. It is quite a task to build a home and make the hundreds of choices required ranging from what color the living room rug should be to where to place the electrical outlets. However, I regularly note how "insecure" she appears, trying to assure herself that she's made an adequate choice. I find myself slipping into "nurturance mode" and saying things like, "Why, it's beautiful; I'm sure you'll love it when it's done." What I really want to say to her (and don't because she's not a client, but a neighbor whom I don't know very well) is, "I wish you'd have more confidence

in your own decisions. You've given each one a lot of thought and done the best you can. Good for you!" I can't picture a man reacting in the same insecure way that she is. But then traditional male stereotypes dictate that men are supposed to be decisive and never expose any sign of emotion or self-doubt.

Many times, your task as a social worker will be to realistically bolster your female client's self-esteem. Additionally, you often will need to help her identify her various alternatives, evaluate the pros and cons of each, and then make a decision to the best of her ability.

Old Rules and Expectations: The old cliché "times change and so do people" comes to mind. In organizing our lives, most of us establish certain ways of doing things. We *expect* things to be a certain way and formate *rules* for our behavior based on these expectations. Sometimes, however, we're forced to face major transitions. For instance, suddenly we face a divorce after six years of being a wife, mother, and homemaker who was not employed outside the home. Or other times, old rules and expectations no longer work well. For example, take the wife who gets a new job which requires her to travel around the country at least two weeks each month. This forces major changes in her relationship with her husband. Although they always "shared" tasks before, each spouse tended to undertake different household jobs. Now even taking out the garbage becomes an issue requiring new procedures and communication.

Helping Women in Micro Practice

We will address three major aspects of working with women on a one-to-one level: increasing empowerment, expanding the number and quality of options available to them, and establishing new rules and expectations for their behavior (Collier, 1982).

Empowering Women

You as a social worker can help a woman client regain her sense of power and control over her own life. Lott (1987) asserts that the "personal traits that have clearly been shown to relate positively to measures of self-esteem or subjective well-being are the same for women as for men; and include assertiveness, independence, self-responsibility, and efficacy, characteristics typically included in the stereotype of masculinity" (p. 277).

Enhancing Self-Esteem

Self-confidence and self-esteem are essential for empowerment. There are a number of tactics you can use to address this issue. First, you can help your client *explore* how she feels about herself. Ask her for positive and negative adjectives that she feels best describe her. Have her describe her strengths and weaknesses. Then help her to summarize how she perceives her self-esteem. Does she feel good about herself or does she criticize herself every chance she gets?

Second, you can give your client *feedback* about her responses. Is it difficult for her to think of strengths? You can share with her your perceptions about her strengths. Emphasizing

Social workers can help female clients regain their sense of having power and of being in control of their own lives.

strengths was illustrated more thoroughly in earlier chapters. Strengths may include virtually anything—personal qualities, being a hard worker, being motivated for change, being caring or articulate.

Third, help your client look more realistically at those areas where she is experiencing *guilt* (Chaplin, 1988). There is some tendency for women with low self-esteem to blame themselves for everything that's wrong. The battered woman typically blames herself for being battered. She had supper on the table one and a half minutes too late. Or perhaps your client blames herself for any unhappiness other family members experience. She feels she could have been more supportive or should have anticipated the problem. You can help your client distinguish between the point at which her responsibility ends and other individuals' begin.

Fourth, you can help your client accept the fact that most aspects of life have both *positive and negative* sides. It's easy for people with low self-esteem to categorize themselves as essentially bad in comparison to other people who are essentially good. It's important for clients to look realistically at themselves and the world around them. A good approach is to view the world in terms of having both strengths and weakness, highs and lows, happinesses and sadnesses. Acknowledging the negative does not mean you have to dwell on them. However, admitting to yourself that they exist can save a lot of energy trying to hide or fight them. Even winning twenty million dollars in the lottery might have its disadvantages. How many of your friends and relatives will expect you to dole out money to them? What's the matter with you? Can't you share? Or might some criminal kidnap your child or baby sister or mother in order to get a big ransom? And then, there's always the next tax audit to worry about.

The other side of this strength/weakness coin is acknowledging, appreciating, and using strengths. You can help your clients appreciate the positive while acknowledging the negative.

For example, a single mother of five children may hate having to receive public assistance. Yet a strength in this situation is that she is able to care for her children full-time. That is, it's a strength if the public assistance system doesn't force her to work outside the home.

The fifth thing you can do to enhance self-esteem is help clients target those areas in which they want to see *improvements*. You can assist them to pinpoint where they're exceptionally self-critical or on what aspect they want to work at feeling better about themselves. You can help them examine what qualities people with higher self-esteem have (Apgar & Callahan, 1980) and then help them work out how they might apply those characteristics to themselves.

Increasing Assertiveness

Social workers can teach women about assertiveness and how to develop assertiveness skills. They can provide practice situations and guide their female clients through more effective ways of handling difficult or uncomfortable situations. Assertiveness improves personal interactions, which in turn builds confidence.

Assertiveness involves verbal or nonverbal behavior which is straightforward but not offensive. Assertiveness involves taking into account both your own rights and the rights of others.

It sounds simple, but for many people appropriate assertiveness is difficult to master. For instance, take the situation where you are patiently waiting in line at the grocery store. A man hurriedly steps in front of you, slams his six pack of beer on the counter, and throws a ten dollar bill at the clerk. He is big, threatening, and obviously rude. Do you shyly allow him to continue because you'll be glad to see him leave as soon as possible? Do you brashly step in front of him and shout, "You turkey, I was in line first!" Or, do you calmly and straightforwardly say to the clerk, "Excuse me, I was in line first. Here are my groceries."

Many times it's difficult to look at a situation objectively and take the feelings and needs of all concerned into account. It's often especially difficult for women who have been taught to be sensitive to others' needs, are frequently critical of themselves because of low self-esteem, and are not accustomed to assuming a strong leadership role.

Assertiveness involves specific skills which can be taught. This, of course, is referred to as assertiveness training. Here we will discuss in more depth the meaning of assertiveness and some concepts involved in assertiveness training.

The Meaning of Assertiveness

Do you have trouble telling someone when you're annoyed? Do you hate arguments and avoid them at all cost? Do you feel uncomfortable asking people for favors even when you're in desperate situations? Do you feel that your views are not quite as important as the next person's? If you answer "yes" to any of these questions, you may be having difficulty being assertive enough.

It should be noted that women are not the only people who sometimes have trouble with assertiveness. However, as we've discussed, traditional gender role stereotypes and expectations may make it harder for many women to develop assertiveness skills. Many of your female clients will have difficulty being appropriately assertive. They will come to you with problems involving poverty, jobs, domestic violence, relationships, or sexual assault. Many of them would benefit greatly by developing assertiveness skills to address their respective problematic situations.

Assertiveness can be perceived as the center of a continuum ranging from aggression to passivity. Alberti and Emmons (1975) describe typical behavior evident in each of these three styles:

In the nonassertive style, you are likely to hesitate, speak softly, look away, avoid the issue, agree regardless of your own feelings, not express opinions, value yourself "below" others, and hurt yourself to avoid any chance of hurting others.

In the aggressive style, you typically answer before the other person is through talking, speak loudly and abusively, glare at the other person, speak "past" the issue (accusing, blaming, demeaning), vehemently expound your feelings and opinions, value yourself "above" others, and hurt others to avoid hurting yourself.

In the assertive style, you will answer spontaneously; speak with a conversational tone and volume, and look at the other person, speak to the issue, openly express your personal feelings and opinions (anger, love, disagreement, sorrow), value yourself equally to others, and hurt neither yourself nor others (p. 24).

Apgar and Callahan (1980, pp. 43–44) characterize the three styles respectively as the "martyr," the "persecutor," and the "balancer." A *martyr* is a nonassertive, passive person whose primary aim is to keep others happy. She will put aside her own needs and wants in deference to the wants of others. In essence, the martyr thinks of herself as not being very important.

The *persecutor*, on the other hand, thinks only of herself as being important. Other people don't really matter. The persecutor will insist upon getting her own way. She is aggressive. She "gets what she wants by dominating, manipulating, and humiliating others" (p. 43). Frequently, she is hostile in her interactions or ignores other people altogether.

The *balancer* does just that. She balances both her needs and the needs of others. Appropriate assertiveness involves consideration of both yourself and others.

Consider a situation where you are involved in a deep conversation with a good friend. Another mutual acquaintance walks up, rudely interrupts, and begins to talk about how he recently received the highest grade in the class on his last exam. The following illustrates possible responses:

The *unassertive martyr* says and does nothing.

The *aggressive persecutor* loudly screams, "Shut up, you lowlife dirtball! Can't you see we were talking? Go away."

The *assertive balancer* calmly states, "Excuse me. You interrupted an important conversation. Maybe we can talk to you later."

Assertiveness Training

Assertiveness training helps people distinguish among assertive, aggressive, and nonassertive responses. It gradually helps people to shape their behavior so that they become consciously more assertive. It helps them gain control of their emotions and their lives.

As we know, social work is practical. Therefore, you can use the suggestions provided to enhance both your client's assertiveness and your own. Alberti and Emmons (1976) developed the following thirteen steps to help establish assertive behavior:

1. Help your client scrutinize her own actions. How does she behave in situations requiring assertiveness? Does she think she tends to be nonassertive, assertive, or aggressive in most of her communications?

2. Ask your client to make a record of those situations where she feels she lacked assertiveness. How could she have behaved more effectively, either more assertively or less aggressively?

3. Help your client select and focus on some specific instance where she feels she could have been more assertive. Encourage her to visualize the specific details. What exactly did she say? How did she feel?

4. Help your client analyze how she reacted. Examine closely her verbal and nonverbal behavior. Alberti & Emmons (1975, pp. 31–32) cite the following seven aspects of behavior that are important to monitor during assertiveness training. They include:

a. *Eye contact.* Did your client look the person in the eye? Or, were her eyes downcast? Did she find herself avoiding eye contact when she was uncomfortable?

b. Body posture. Was she standing up straight or was she slouching? Was she sheepishly leaning away from the person? Was she holding her head high as she looked the person in the eye?

c. *Gestures.* Were her hand gestures fitting for the situation? Did she feel at ease? Was she tapping her foot or cracking her knuckles? In the beginning of his term, people often criticized President George Bush for flailing his arms and hands around during his public speeches. This tended to give the public the impression that he was frantic. Professional coaches helped him gain control of this behavior and present a calmer public image.

d. *Facial expressions.* Did she have a serious expression on her face? Was she smiling or giggling uncomfortably, thereby giving the impression that she was not really serious?

e. *Voice tone, inflection, volume.* Did she speak in a normal voice tone? Did she whisper timidly? Did she raise her voice to the point of stressful screeching? Did she sound as if she was whining?

f. *Timing.* It is best to make an appropriately assertive response right after a remark is made or an incident happens. It is also important to consider whether a particular situation really requires assertiveness. At times it might be best just to remain silent and "let it go." For example, it might not be wise to tell a prospective employer that he

HIGHLIGHT 13.3
Each of Us Has Certain Assertive Rights

Part of becoming assertive involves clearly figuring out and believing that we are valuable and worthwhile people. It's easy to criticize ourselves for our mistakes and imperfections. It's easy to hold our feelings in because we're afraid that we will hurt someone else's feelings or that someone will reject us. Sometimes feelings that are held in too long will burst out in an aggressive tirade. This applies to any of us, including our clients.

For example, let's say some close friends from a distant state come to visit with their sixteen-month-old baby, Robert. They obviously adore Robert. They also feel that Robert "has a mind of his own" and allow Robert to do more-or-less exactly what he wants. First, he plays with all your magazines and casually throws them all over the floor. You find this mildly annoying, but don't get too upset because you rarely get to see your friends and what harm can Robert do to magazines anyway. They then feed Robert some crackers and later some sticky candy. Robert smears the food all over himself, the furniture, and the rug. His parents don't seem to notice. You find this annoying, but think that the furniture, the rug, and probably Robert can all be cleaned up later.

Robert then spied your prized collection of compact discs and heads directly for them. His mother calmly remarks, "Oh, look, Robert's found the compact discs. It's funny he hasn't noticed them before this." She smiles lovingly at him as he pulls the first one out of the case. This, you think, is too much, and try to calmly say, "Let's go into the kitchen and round up some lunch." Finally, back in the living room, Robert breaks a lamp. His parents say they're sorry. By this time all you're beginning to focus on is your anger. You muster up the stamina and say, "Oh, that's all right. It was an old lamp anyway." You retreat to the kitchen to take several deep breaths and regain control. You return to the living room with some drinks. Robert's father comes up to you and timidly says, "Well, Robert really ruined your picture." Earlier you had shown your friends a picture of your family given you by your grandmother. It was sentimentally invaluable to you and also irreplaceable.

This was it. The room turns red. Your blood feels like it's boiling in your veins. You turn to your friends and say, "Get out! Get out! Take that devil-monster with you and never come back!"

This final cataclysm could have been avoided if early on in the process you had acknowledged that you, too, had rights.

The following are eight of your and your clients' assertive rights.

1. You have the right to express your ideas and opinions openly and honestly.
2. You have the right to be wrong. Everyone makes mistakes.
3. You have the right to direct and govern your own life. In other words, you have the right to be responsible for yourself.
4. You have the right to stand up for yourself without unwarranted anxiety and make choices that are good for you.
5. You have the right *not* to be liked by everyone (Do you like *everyone* you know?)
6. You have the right, on the one hand, to make requests and, on the other hand, to refuse them without feeling guilty.
7. You have the right to ask for information if you need it.
8. Finally, you have the right to decide not to exercise your assertive rights. In other words, you can choose not to be assertive if you don't want to.

Source: Most of these rights have been adapted from those identified in *The New Assertive Woman* by L. Z. Bloom, K. Coburn, and J. Perlman (New York: Dell, 1976) and in *Four One-Day Workshops* by K. Apgar and B. N. Callahan (Boston: Resource Communications Inc. and Family Service Association of Greater Boston, 1980).

has horrendously offensive breath during a job interview with him.

   g. *Content*. What she says in her assertive response is obviously important. Did she choose her words carefully? Did her response have the impact she wanted it to have? Why or why not?

5. Help your client identify a role model and examine how that person handled a situation requiring assertiveness. What exactly happened during the incident? What words did the role model use that were particularly effective? What aspects of her nonverbal behavior helped to get her points across?

6. Assist your client in identifying a range of other new responses for situations where she lacks assertiveness. In the future, what other words could she use? What nonverbal behaviors might be more effective?

7. Ask your client to picture herself in the identified problematic situation. It often helps for her to close her eyes and concentrate. Step by step, tell her to imagine how she could handle the situation more assertively.

8. Help your client practice the way she has envisioned herself being more assertive. Ask her to target a real-life situation that remains unresolved. For example, perhaps the person she lives with always leaves dirty socks lying around the living room, or drinks all her cola and forgets to tell her when the refrigerator is bare. You can also help your client role play the situation. Role playing provides effective mechanisms for practicing responses before clients have to use them spontaneously in real life.

9. Once again, review her new assertive responses. Help her to emphasize her strong points and try to remedy her flaws.

10. Continue practicing steps 7, 8, and 9 un-

til her newly developed assertive approach feels comfortable and natural to her.

11. Direct your client to try out her new assertiveness approach in a real-life situation.

12. Encourage your client to continue to expand her assertiveness repertoire until such behavior becomes part of her personal interactive style. She can review the earlier steps and try them out with an increasingly wider range of problematic situations.

13. Reinforce your client for her achievements in becoming more assertive. It is not easy to change long-standing patterns of behavior. Encourage her to focus on and revel in the good feelings she experiences as a result of her successes.

Other Positive Intervention Approaches for Women Clients

Earlier, we cited anger as one of the problems women often bring to a counseling situation. You as a social worker can encourage a woman to express her anger instead of holding it in. The real causes and targets of the anger can be identified. Once causes are recognized, you can "help the client learn to deal with anger directly through verbal and nonverbal communication styles, negotiation, confrontation, alliances and networks, compromise and resoluteness" (Collier, 1982, p. 277). You can help women to address the situations which cause their anger. If a woman is angry with her spouse, she can be taught how to express her feelings effectively so that whatever is happening to cause the anger can be changed.

Additionally, you as a social worker can encourage a female client to take care of herself. The qualities that she likes about herself can be nurtured. A woman can learn that she has the right to time for herself to participate in activities she enjoys.

All of these suggestions including those concerning enhancing self-esteem and increasing assertiveness are related to each other. Each one enhances the accomplishments of the others. Becoming more assertive enhances one's sense of control. An increased sense of control improves self-esteem. Greater self-esteem increases one's confidence in being assertive. The overall intent is to establish a confident, competent sense of self, which is every person's right.

Expanding Options

In addition to enhancing self-esteem, you can help women recognize the various alternatives available to them and evaluate the pros and cons of each. In other words, you can teach them how to make decisions and solve problems. Success at using such skills breeds more success. Once women have learned the process of making their own decisions and solving their own problems, they can apply these skills to more decisions and more problems. This can help to build their feelings of being in control.

Changing Rules and Expectations

Female clients often not only need to change how they view themselves and the world, but also their expectations for what is appropriate, effective behavior. This includes both their own behavior and that of others. For instance, perhaps in the past a client felt she should be agreeable with and obedient to her spouse regardless of the issue. In view of her enhanced self-esteem and increased assertiveness, she no longer assumes this consistently deferent approach. Rather, she assertively shares her own feelings about issues and aims to get her own needs met in addition to those of her spouse. In other words, as part of the micro intervention process, clients will integrate what they've learned about themselves and their values about how things "should" be will change.

Common Circumstances Facing Women

It's important to understand the special, internal dynamics of women at the micro level before proceeding to the mezzo and macro levels of intervention. Here we will arbitrarily examine three common circumstances facing women. They are sexual assault, domestic violence, and poverty.

For each, background information will first be provided so that you better understand the issue. Next, intervention strategies at the micro and mezzo levels will be proposed. Frequently, it's difficult to clearly separate out the micro level from the mezzo level of intervention because the personal and the interpersonal are so integrally related. Thus, we will discuss these strategies together. Finally, we will examine the macro aspects of each issue and propose macro methods of intervention.

Women as Survivors of Sexual Assault

We've already established the following facts. In 1987 there were over 91,000 reported rapes in the United States (Hyde, 1990, p. 474). Only one in five stranger rapes is reported and, even more strikingly, only 2 percent of acquaintance and date rapes are reported (Koss et al., 1988). Every woman has a 26 percent chance of being raped during her lifetime (Russell & Howell, 1983). Hence, sexual assaults upon women are very common. How can this be? Why are women in our society so terribly vulnerable?

This section will examine the feminist perspective on sexual assault, typical reactions of rape survivors, and suggestions for counseling. Finally, a macro practice perspective on the problem will be explored.

First, we need to define our terms. The most intimate violation of a person's privacy and dignity is sexual assault. Sexual assaults in-

┌ HIGHLIGHT 13.4 ───────────

A Feminist Approach to Macro Practice

We've established that, in many ways, a feminist perspective corresponds well with the basic principles of generalist macro practice. Brandwein (1987) conceptualized at least four aspects of feminist macro practice and applies the feminist approach to policy making, community organization, and administration.

First, feminist macro practice values the process of how things are accomplished as much as the final result of the process. For example, policies, of course, are important. However, a feminist perspective emphasizes that how well a policy is implemented is just as important as what the policy says. Take an agency policy which states that both men and women should be treated equally in terms of receiving annual raises in salary. The policy is clearly stated on the books. However, if women typically receive significantly fewer raises than men, then the policy is not working. Feminist macro practice then focuses in an ongoing manner on how well things are accomplished.

Second, feminist macro practice adopts a "win-win" rather than a "win-lose" philosophy (p. 889). Brandwein articulates that a feminist view of power "is not necessarily power over others, but self-empowerment." In feminist macro practice, you don't have to crush the enemy. Rather, you work things out with those in disagreement. Power is not something available only in limited, finite quantities to be doled out to a select few. It can be shared and compromises can be made. Feminist macro practice espouses a collaboratory style of decision-making in which a group of equals comes together and works toward a mutually satisfactory decision. There is no strict hierarchy where each participant has a quantifiable amount of power either more or less than every other participant.

A third principle of feminist macro practice emphasizes the importance of interpersonal relationships. A non-feminist approach might emphasize forming relationships temporarily to complete some specified task. Feminist practice, on the other hand, values the establishment of relationships on an ongoing basis. The focus is not on the completion of any small or even large task. Rather, it's important that all participants in the system continue working together productively.

The fourth principle involved in feminist macro practice is the high value placed on human diversity. Differences are applauded and appreciated rather than denied. All participants in a process are considered equal. There is no concept of one person being better than another for some reason.

So how does all this apply to the actual practice of generalist social work? First, the emphasis on diversity helps to sensitize feminist practitioners to the existence of inequality and oppression. Feminist practitioners then are more likely to turn to macro interventions to change the systems which cause the oppression.

Second, the high value placed on the process of how things are accomplished orients practitioners to focus on policy. Policies, of course, provide the rules for what you as a social worker can and cannot do. Feminist practitioners are very concerned with policies because they control the ongoing processes of how things are done.

The third application to macro practice involves community organization. The feminist's concern with equality and collaborative decision-making fits well with the idea of getting as many community people involved as possible. The emphasis on equality frames each participant's view as important.

A fourth application of feminist macro practice concerns administration. Feminists emphasize the value of employee input. Since employees are seen as significant participants, development of their skills is important. Attention is given "both to process and interpersonal relationships." This "would not be at the expense of accomplishing tasks, but would enhance the results" (Brandwein, 1987, p. 890).

volve any unwanted sexual contact where verbal or physical force is used. A commonly used legal definition of rape involves a sexual assault where penile penetration of the vagina occurs without mutual consent (Masters et al., 1988). Now, we need to explore why sexual assault is such a major problem.

The Feminist Perspective on Sexual Assault

The feminist perspective emphasizes that rape is the logical reaction of men who are socialized to dominate women. Rape is seen as a manifestation of men's need to aggressively maintain power over women. It has little to do with sexuality. Sexuality only provides a clear-cut means for exercising power. Rape is seen as a consequence of attitudes toward women that are intimately intertwined throughout the culture. The feminist perspective views rape as a societal problem, rather than only an individual one.

Herman (1984) elaborates on this view. She points out that both aggressors and victims are brought up to believe that sexual aggression is natural. As a result, victims often blame themselves for the assault. The rationale is that they should have expected to be raped and should have been prepared or have done something to prevent it.

An analogous situation concerning self-blame is the example of a woman who has her purse snatched while shopping on a Saturday afternoon. If the self-blame concept were applied, it would follow that the woman would blame herself for the incident. She would chastise herself by saying it was her fault. She never should have taken her purse with her to shop in the first place. Maybe she should only shop by catalog from now on. Of course, taking that course of action would be absurd. It was not the woman's fault. It was the purse snatcher who broke the law and he is the one who should be held responsible.

Blaming oneself for being raped is inappropriate. The feminist view holds that society is wrong for socializing people to assume that male sexual aggression is natural. Socializing women to consider themselves weak and nurturant also contributes to the problem. It helps to develop a victim mentality, that is, an expectation that it's natural for women to be victims. The feminist perspective emphasizes that these attitudes need to be changed. Only then can rape as a social problem disappear.

The term *victim* implies weakness and powerlessness. From here on, therefore, we will use the term rape *survivor* instead. Survivor implies strength and is oriented toward the future. It coincides with the suggestions for counseling, which emphasize helping rape survivors regain confidence and control of their lives.

Reactions to Rape

Burgess and Holmstrom (1974[a], 1974[b]), studying the reactions of ninety-two rape survivors, found that women can experience serious psychological effects that can persist for a half-year or more following a rape. They call these emotional changes the *rape trauma syndrome*. The syndrome has two basic phases. The first is the acute phase, which involves the woman's emotional reactions immediately following the rape and up to several weeks thereafter. The second involves a long-term reorganization phase.

The Acute Phase

Immediately following a rape, the survivor usually reacts in one of two ways. She may show her emotions by crying, expressing anger, or demonstrating fear. On the other hand, she may try to control these intense emotions and hide them from view. Emotions experienced during the acute phase range from humiliation and guilt to shock, anger, and desire for revenge.

Additionally, during this phase women will often experience physical problems including difficulties related directly to the rape. For instance, a woman may suffer irritation of the genitals, or rectal bleeding from an anal rape. Physical problems also include stress-related discomforts such as headaches, stomach difficulties, or inability to sleep.

The two primary emotions experienced during the acute phase are fear and self-blame. Fear results from the violence of the experience. Many rape survivors report that during the attack they felt their life had come to an end. They had no control over what the attacker would do to them and were terrified. Such fear can linger. Oftentimes, survivors are afraid that rape can easily happen again. The second emotion, self-blame, results from society's tendency to blame the survivor instead of the perpetrator (that is, the rapist) for the crime.

Women fail to report being raped for many reasons. Victims whose bodies have been brutally violated often desperately want to forget that the horror ever happened. To report the rape means dwelling on the details and going over the event again and again in their minds. Other victims fear retribution from the rapist. If they call public attention to him, he might do it again to punish them. No police officer will be available all of the time for protection. Other victims feel that people around them will think less of them because they've been raped. It's almost as if a part of them has been spoiled, a part which they would prefer to hide from other people. Rape is an ugly crisis which takes a great amount of courage to face.

One young woman's reactions illustrate some of these points. A student, age twenty-two, entered my office and sat down. She had a stern look on her face. She could have been there for any number of reasons. Perhaps she needed feedback on her research assignment or wanted me to double check that she had fulfilled all her requirements for her upcoming graduation. I asked her what she needed. Spon-taneously, she began to cry almost uncontrollably. She said she had been at a party the past Saturday night (it was now Tuesday afternoon). The party was held at the home of a young lawyer who was a mutual friend of a group of her best friends. She described the party as being "typical," meaning a big crowd, lot of beer, some drugs, and loud music. She said that she found herself sitting on a bed with the young lawyer who lived in the apartment. (To me the scene resembled a common pre-dating ritual where a couple meets and decides if there is some "spark" there.) Suddenly, he got up, closed the bedroom door, locked it, threw her down on the bed, and raped her. She was stunned. How could this be? He was a good friend of her friends. He was a lawyer!

So, we returned to the present. It turned out that her primary fear was that her friends would find out about the rape. We talked about how it was the rapist's fault, not her fault. We discussed how he had taken total control from her by virtue of a surprise attack. She never would have suspected that a lawyer would commit such a crime. I also commended her for surviving. In a crisis situation like that, a woman can have no idea what a perpetrator will do. He could kill her, for all she knew.

Finally, we discussed her friends. What true friends would condone such violence? She began to look at the experience more objectively. She began to get in touch with her intense anger at the lawyer for what he'd done to her. She started to regain some of her sense of self-confidence. We also talked about pregnancy, but she felt the risk was minimal since she was taking birth control pills. We spoke of the alternatives available to her. I called a local rape crisis center and made a referral that she said she'd follow up on. We talked about reporting the rapist. It was too late to prosecute successfully. However, she could report his name to the local authorities and said she wanted to do so. Finally, she said she was going to tell her friends about the whole experience. She felt they needed to know what this man was really like.

In summary, we couldn't erase the horror. The incident had happened. However, the young woman was able to begin dealing with her feelings and gaining control. Techniques for helping rape survivors will be discussed more thoroughly in a later section of this chapter.

The Long-Term Reorganization Phase

The second stage of the rape trauma syndrome is the long-term reorganization and recovery phase; the emotional changes and reactions of this phase may linger on for years. Nadelson et al. (1982) found that three-fourths of rape victims felt that the rape had changed their lives in one way or another. Reported reactions included fear of being alone, depression, sleeplessness, and, most frequently, an attitude of suspicion toward other people. Other long-term changes that sometimes occur include avoiding involvement with men (Masters, Johnson & Kolodny, 1985, p. 474) and suffering various sexual dysfunctions such as lack of sexual desire, aversion to sexual contact, or difficulty in having orgasms (Kolodny et al., 1979).

It is very important for survivors of rape to deal with even the most negative feelings and get on with their lives. In some ways rape might be compared to accepting the death of a loved one. The fact that either has occurred cannot be changed. Survivors must learn to cope. Life continues.

Suggestions for Counseling Survivors of Sexual Assault

Three basic issues are involved in working with a woman who has survived a rape. First, she is most likely in a state of emotional upheaval. Her self-concept is probably seriously shaken. Various suggestions for helping a rape survivor in such a traumatic emotional state will be provided. Second, the rape survivor must decide whether to call the police and press charges. Third, the rape survivor must assess her medical status following the rape, including injuries, disease, or potential pregnancy.

Emotional Issues

Collier (1982) suggests that helping women who have been sexually assaulted involves three major stages. First, you as a social worker need to provide the rape survivor with immediate warmth and support. The survivor must feel safe and free to talk. She needs to ventilate and acknowledge her feelings before she can begin to deal with them. To the extent possible, help

A sexual-assault survivor should be provided with warmth and support while she experiences the emotional effects of the assault.

the survivor to know she is now in control of her situation. Don't pressure her to talk. Rather, encourage her to share her feelings, even the worst ones, with you.

Although it is important for the victim to talk freely, it is also important that she not be grilled with intimate, detailed questions. She will have enough of those to deal with if she chooses to report the assault to the police.

Frequently, the survivor will dwell on what she could or should have done. It is helpful to emphasize what she did *right*. After all, she is alive, safe, and not severely physically harmed. She managed to survive a terrifying and dangerous experience. It is also helpful to talk about how she reacted normally, as anyone else in her situation would most probably have reacted. This does not mean minimizing the incident. It does mean objectively talking about how traumatizing and potentially dangerous the incident was. One other helpful suggestion for dealing with a rape survivor is to help her place the blame where it belongs, namely on the rapist. He chose to rape her. It was not her doing. Research bears out the fact that the majority of rapes have absolutely nothing to do with the behavior of the survivor (Amir, 1971).

The second stage of counseling, according to Collier (1982), involves creating support from others. This support may include that of professional resources such as a local rape crisis center, as well as support from people who are emotionally close to the survivor. Sometimes, you will need to educate those close to the survivor. They must find out that what the survivor needs is warmth and support and to feel loved. Avoid questions which emphasize her feelings of self-blame such as why she didn't fight back or why she was wearing a low-cut blouse.

An anecdote illustrates the importance of educating people close to the survivor. I was sitting in my office late one afternoon finishing up some extremely dull paperwork. The University halls were empty and desolate as they get in late afternoons. I suddenly heard a knock at my door and looked up. There stood an extremely tall, red-headed, handsome young man of about age twenty-four or twenty-five. I knew at once that he didn't look familiar. He then asked if I was so-and-so who had just been quoted in the university newspaper about some information on sexual assault. I replied that I was. Meanwhile, I thought to myself, "Now this guy could *not* have been raped . . . although you never know." I also became aware of how big he was and how alone I was.

At any rate, he sat down and told me his story. His girlfriend had recently shared with him how she had been brutally raped by one of their mutual acquaintances last year. He said he loved this young woman dearly and planned to marry her. However, he couldn't bear even to think about the horrible incident. He said she had been trying to talk to him about it because it still disturbed her, but each time she tried, he'd cut her off. His anger at the rapist was so overwhelming he feared he couldn't control it.

We sat for over two hours and discussed his situation and his options. We talked about the emotions survivors of sexual assault typically experience. What were the consequences of not allowing her to talk to him about the assault? Perhaps she would feel that he was blaming her for some part in the assault. Maybe she would feel dirty or permanently violated. Or, at the very least, he was probably communicating to her that she would be unable to talk to him about things such as this which were critically important to her.

On the other hand, what if he could acknowledge and gain control of his anger? What would he be communicating to her if he encouraged her to talk to him about something as painful as this? He came to realize that taking this route would probably communicate to her how much he loved her. She would see that he truly cared how she felt and was trying desperately to understand. It would also probably destroy any feelings she had that he felt she was damaged or to blame. Finally, it would communicate to the young woman that she would be able to share virtually anything with him, even something this difficult. He decided that he definitely needed to listen to his girlfriend and break through his own defenses and help her as much as he could.

The young man left my office with a number of handouts supplying information similar to that presented here. Although I never heard from him again, I sincerely hope that he was able to help his girlfriend work through the aftermath of that nightmarish experience. I also romantically like to think of them still living happily together.

Collier's (1982) third stage of counseling involves rebuilding the victim's trust in herself, in the environment around her, and in her other personal relationships. Rape weakens a woman. It destroys her trust in herself and in others. During this stage of counseling, you need to focus on the survivor's objective evaluation of herself and her situation. You need to clarify and emphasize her strong points so that she may gain confidence in herself.

The survivor also needs to look objectively at her surrounding environment. She cannot remain cooped up in her apartment for the rest of her life. She can take precautions against being raped, but needs to continue living a normal life.

Finally, you can help the survivor assess her other personal relationships objectively. Just because she was intimately violated by one aggressor, this has nothing to do with the other people in her life. She needs to concentrate on the positive aspects of her other relationships. She must not allow the fear and terror she experienced during that one unfortunate incident to taint other interactions. She must clearly distinguish the rape and rapist from her other relationships.

A woman who has been raped may initially want to talk with another woman. However, it might also be important to talk to men, including those close to her. It is important for the survivor to realize that not all men are rapists.

Sometimes there is a male partner and his willingness to let the victim express her feelings, and, in return, offer support and empathy, is very important (Masters et al., 1985).

Reporting to the Police

The initial reaction to being raped might be to call the police and report the incident. However, many survivors choose not to do this. Masters et al. (1985) list numerous reasons why this is so, including fear that the rapist will try to get revenge, fear of public embarrassment and derogation, an attitude that it won't matter anyway because most rapists get off free, and fear of the legal process. It's financially expensive and emotionally draining to take a rape case to court (Herman, 1984). Even then, few rapists are actually convicted.

Some positive changes are occurring in police investigation of rape cases (Moody & Hayes, 1980) and their legal handling (Lasater, 1980). Many police departments are trying to deal with rape survivors more sensitively. Some departments in larger cities have special teams trained specifically for dealing with survivors. In many states, information about the survivor's past sexual history is no longer permissible for use in court because it can serve to humiliate and discredit the survivor.

Some states have more progressive laws. Wisconsin,[1] for example, has established four degrees of sexual assault, in addition to forbidding the use of the survivor's past sexual conduct in court. According to Wisconsin law, the severity of the crime and the corresponding severity of punishment is based on the amount of force used by the rapist and on the amount of harm done to the survivor. A wife is also able to prosecute her husband for sexual assault when he forces sexual relations upon her.

Despite the potential difficulties in reporting a rape, the fact remains that if the survi-

---

1. *See* Wisconsin State statute 940.225.

vor does not report it, the rapist will not be held responsible for his actions. A rape survivor needs to think through her various alternatives and weigh their respective positive and negative consequences in order to come to this often difficult decision.

In the event that a survivor decides to report, she should not take a shower. Washing will remove vital evidence. However, survivors often feel defiled and dirty. It is a logical initial reaction to try to cleanse themselves and forget that the incident ever occurred. You need to emphasize to a client who has been raped that she should not wash, despite how much she would like to.

Reporting a rape should be done within forty-eight hours at the absolute most. The sooner the rape is reported and the evidence gathered, the better the chance of being able to get a conviction.

Medical Status of the Survivor

In addition to emotional issues and the decision whether or not to report the incident, a third major issue, medical status, merits attention. At some point, the survivor needs to attend to the possibility of pregnancy. She should be asked about this issue at an appropriate time and in a gentle manner. She should be encouraged to seek medical help both for this possibility and for screening sexually transmitted diseases. The negative possibilities should not be emphasized, but the survivor needs to attend to these issues at some point. Of course, you should also urge the survivor to seek immediate medical care if she has any physical injury.

A Macro Practice Perspective on Sexual Assault

We've been primarily discussing the micro and mezzo aspects of intervention with survivors of sexual assault. The micro aspects focus attention on a woman's inner sense of self. The mezzo facets involve the survivor's relationships with others around her. The macro perspective on sexual assault is just as significant. It involves the way society perceives of rape survivors, how they are treated, and what services are available to them. Toomey (1987) describes and examines a number of macro perspectives on sexual assault. They include the significance of general societal responses and the evaluation of current services.

General Societal Responses

How society views rape survivors is critically important to what services are made available. Resources are generally scarce. Therefore, decisions must be made about what's important enough to expend them on and what's not. Herman articulates the problem well (1989):

> In cases of rape, judges, juries, police, prosecutors, and the general public frequently attribute blame and responsibility to the victim for her own victimization. Unfortunately, these negative responses are often compounded by reactions from family and friends. Encounters with parents, relatives, friends, and spouses many times involves either anger at the victim for being foolish enough to get raped or expressions of embarrassment and shame that family members will suffer as a result of the attack (p. 37).

Therefore, if society and the general population consider rape to be a woman's own fault, they are less likely to support her with resources and services. One potential thrust then of macro practice in this area is to educate both the general public and, more specifically, those most likely to deal directly with rape survivors. This might involve using your macro practice skills to disseminate information, set up educational task forces, or mobilize community groups.

One specific group needing education includes hospital staff in emergency rooms. They need to know how to deal with survivors emotionally "while preserving evidence for criminal prosecution" (Toomey, 1987, p. 570).

Police and other legal staff involved in prosecution make up other groups needing education. Initiatives have included "changing the attitudes of law enforcement officers, increasing the participation of female officers, and encouraging victim/witness support program in prosecutors' offices" (Toomey, 1987, p. 570).

"Rapist control" provides another legal approach to enhancing survivors' situations (Toomey, 1987, p. 571). This involves the extent to which perpetrators are reported, sought, charged, convicted, and imprisoned.

Women in the general population themselves also need education. They need to minimize their vulnerability. This not only means learning self-defense techniques and following suggestions to prevent sexual assault, but also enhancing their self-concepts and gaining a greater sense of control.

Current Services

Toomey (1987) summarizes the following trends in services for sexual assault providers:

1. Continuance of twenty-four hour "hot lines," as well as support and advocacy assistance.
2. Short-term "counseling" for victims in either individual or group situations.
3. Long-term work with victims (one year or more after the assault).
4. Couples and group work with victims and significant others.
5. Group work with families, especially around an assault situation within the family.
6. Special focus on adolescent victims.
7. Counseling for mothers of children who are victims.
8. Individual and group counseling with

women who were victims of rape or incest in the past (p. 572).

Such services may or may not be available in the area in which you'll work. Resources and services vary drastically from one community to another. You may need to use your macro practice perspective to assess needs and advocate for service provision.

Jones (1987) proposes the following:

One way to assess the deficiencies in the programs and services for women of the traditional social agencies is to compare such programs to those of the many alternative agencies that have been founded in the past ten to fifteen years. Typically guided by feminist values, principles, and methods in their structure and operation, organizations such as rape crisis centers, shelters and programs for battered women and their children, nontraditional employment, training and educational programs, and women's counseling and health centers have provided services to individuals in addition to advocating for institutional and policy changes. Social workers should examine the work of these agencies to learn about the gaps in traditional services and successful methods for effecting positive changes in women's lives (p. 880).

Additionally, in making determinations about service provision, it's helpful to address a number of questions (Toomey, 1987). How much effort can you afford to expend on macro practice efforts such as public education and advocacy, and how much on direct service provision? Even if services are available, how effective are they? Can they be improved, and, if so, in what ways? Are they accessible to all groups in the community or limited to only a privileged few?

Battered Women

Battered women is the second issue we will address from the micro, mezzo, and macro intervention perspectives. Terms associated with wife beating include domestic violence, family violence, spouse abuse, and battered women. Strong (1983) describe battering as a catch-all term that includes, but is not limited to, the practices of slapping, punching, knocking down, choking, kicking, hitting with objects, threatening with weapons, stabbing, and shooting. The battered-woman syndrome implies the systematic and repeated use of one or more of these practices against a woman by her husband or lover.

Some of the myths about battered women include the following (Cultural Information Service, 1984):

- Battered women aren't really hurt that badly.
- Beatings and other abuses just happen; they aren't a regular occurrence.
- Women who stay in such homes must really enjoy the beatings they get; otherwise they would leave.
- Wife-battering only occurs in lower-class families.

Studies indicate that between 21 percent (Shulman, 1979) and almost 28 percent (Straus, Gelles, & Steinmetz, 1980) of all husbands violently act against their wives at some time in their marriage. In view of the tendency not to report incidents, the real rate of husbands' violence against their wives may be 50 to 60 percent of all couples (Star, 1987; Straus, 1978). Extremely severe, repeated violence occurs against women in almost 7 percent of all marriages (Dutton, 1988). Although there is some mention in the media of battered husbands, the overwhelming majority of domestic violence victims are women (Gelles, 1979).

Battery victims don't like to be beaten. Women go to domestic-violence programs for help to stop the beatings and maintain their marriages (Norman & Mancuso, 1980). They don't enjoy the pain and suffering, but for

reasons that will be discussed later, they tolerate it.

Wife battering is not limited to poor families, minorities, people in blue-collar occupations, or families of lower socioeconomic status (Gelles, 1974). Battered wives come from virtually every socioeconomic level. It's more likely for wife-battering to be reported to police, public agencies, and hospitals when it happens in lower-class families (Stark & McEvoy, 1970). Middle- and upper-class families have more resources available to them either to deal with battering in other ways or to keep it hidden from public scrutiny.

This section will provide a profile of the battered woman, a description of an abusive husband, an analysis of the battering cycle, and exploration into why so many battered women opt to remain in their abusive environments. Counseling strategies will be explained to help a woman address her situation from the micro and mezzo perspectives. Finally, implications for macro practice intervention on the part of battered women will be formulated.

A Profile of a Battered Woman

Walker (1979) describes the battered woman as tending to have certain characteristics such as very low self-esteem. Social workers who counsel battered women indicate that psychological abuse is frequently involved. Battering husbands tend to criticize their wives and make derogatory remarks. They also tend to emphasize how their wives couldn't possibly survive without them. Over an extended period of time, their wives start to believe them.

A second characteristic of battered women is their tendency to believe in the common myths about battering. These women are especially likely to believe that the battering is somehow their fault. The typical battered woman believes that it is her responsibility to nurture and maintain the marriage; she will often blame herself completely for a bad marriage (Martin, 1976).

A third characteristic is the battered woman's traditional beliefs concerning gender roles. She tends to believe in men being the dominant decision-makers and leaders in the family and feels she should be submissive and obedient. Perhaps she feels she deserves to be beaten for not adequately obeying her husband and doing what she was told. Walker (1979) refers to a sense of learned helplessness and states, "Women are systematically taught that their personal worth, survival, and autonomy do not depend on effective and creative responses to life situations, but rather on their physical beauty and an appeal to men. They learn that they have no control over the circumstances of their lives." The more a woman is battered, the more helpless she feels and the less she is able to see her way out of her plight.

The Abusive Husband

Strong et al. (1983) propose a series of traits that tend to characterize men who batter their wives. Many of their attitudes and beliefs resemble those of their wives. For instance, they tend to have low self-esteem, believe in the common myths about battering, and firmly maintain traditional gender-role stereotypes. Also, men who batter women are frequently emotionally immature and tend to use wife beating as a means of alleviating stress. Abusive men, in their personal insecurity, frequently become very jealous and possessive of their wives. Much of the research about the battered-woman syndrome suggests that alcohol is frequently involved (Norman & Mancuso, 1980).

Some evidence suggests that men who batter have learned from their own parents to use aggressive behavior as a coping mechanism (Gelles, 1976; Marsden & Owens, 1975; Straus, 1974). For instance, a male child can learn abusive behavior by observing the behavior modeled by his own father. As an adult the man learns he can gain satisfaction by battering as it gives him control over something in his life.

The Battering Cycle

Walker (1979) has described a cycle of battering and indicates that wife abuse tends to occur in three basic phases. The first phase involves the building up of stress and tension. The wife tries to "make things okay" and avoid confrontations. There may be a few minor abusive incidents, but this phase is primarily characterized by the build-up of excessive tension.

The second phase in the battering cycle is the explosion. This is where the tension breaks, the batterer loses control, and the battering occurs. Although this is the shortest of the three phases, it may last for a few hours to several days.

The third phase involves making up and being in love again. Since his tension has been released, the batterer now adamantly states that he is truly sorry for what he has done and swears he will never do it again. The battered woman relents and believes him. He is forgiven and all seems well, that is, until the cycle of violence begins again.

Why Does She Stay?

One of the most frequently asked questions about domestic violence concerns why the battered woman remains in the home and in the relationship. Approximately 60 to 70 percent of women who seek help from shelters and even those who initiate separation through the courts eventually return to their abusive home situations (Norman & Mancuso, 1980, p. 120). In actuality there are many reasons why these women return, including lack of self-confidence, traditional beliefs, guilt, economic dependence, fear of the abuser, fear of isolation, fear for her children, and love.

Lack of Self-Confidence

It's already been established that battered women frequently have low levels of self-esteem. It takes initiative and courage to leave a situation that is known to them—even one which is painful—and strike out for the unknown. The unknown is frightening. At least if she stays in the home, she knows she has a place to stay and what to expect.

Adherence to Traditional Beliefs

Battered women also tend to believe in traditional gender-role stereotypes. They believe in their husbands as caretakers and providers and dislike the alternatives of being separated or divorced. It's often difficult for them to imagine what they could possibly do alone.

Guilt

Another motivating force keeping battered women in their abusive homes is guilt. As we've already discussed, many feel that it is their own fault that they are abused. To some extent this may be due to their husbands telling them that they're to blame for causing trouble. Perhaps because of their low levels of self-esteem it's easy for them to be critical of themselves. Their belief in traditional gender-role stereotypes may cause them to wonder how they have failed in their submissive, nurturant role of wife.

Economic Dependence

Economic dependence upon their husbands may be one of the most motivating reasons for battered women to remain in their homes. Many battered women are not financially secure in their own right. Even those who are may not feel confident in their ability to handle financial matters on their own. Many might not have the skills and training necessary to obtain jobs where they could maintain their current standard of living. When children are involved there is the additional problem of who would care for them if their mother had to increase the amount of time she spent outside of the home in order to earn a living.

Fear of the Abuser

It might be logical for a battered woman to fear brutal retaliation by her husband if she leaves him. A person who has dealt with stress by physical brutality before might do so again when it is initiated by the stress of his wife leaving him. The battered woman might even fear being murdered by an abandoned husband.

Fear of Isolation

Battered women often try to keep the facts of their abuse a secret for many of the reasons already presented. They may feel isolated from friends and family. They may indeed actually be isolated by the time their battery reaches such crisis proportions. Many times "familial ties have been strained over the years, and closeness is lacking" (Norman & Mancuso, 1980, p. 120).

Fear for Her Children

The battered woman might also fear for the safety of her children. First, she might be worried about her ability to support them financially without her husband. Second, she may firmly believe the traditional idea that children need a father. She may feel that a father who abuses his wife is better than no father at all. Third, she may even fear that she may lose custody of her children. Her husband may threaten to take them. She may have little knowledge of the complicated legal system. She may believe that he can and will do it.

Love

One other reason why battered women don't leave their abusive spouses is that they still love them. Most abused women who seek help still would prefer to remain in their marriages if the battering could be stopped (Geller, 1978). Walker (1979) cites one elderly woman's reactions to her husband's death. The woman, a university professor, had been married for fifty-three years to a man who battered her throughout their relationship. The woman states, "We did everything together. . . . I loved him; you know, even when he was brutal and mean. . . . I'm sorry he's dead, although there were days when I wished he would die. . . . He was my best friend. . . . He beat me right up to the end. . . . It was a good life and I really do miss him."

Counseling Battered Women

Despite the difficulties in dealing with domestic violence, there are definite intervention strategies that can be undertaken. They involve police departments, shelters, and specific counseling approaches (Hutchins & Baxter, 1980).

The Police and Battered Women

It is likely that police officers will be the first outside means of intervention involved in episodes of domestic abuse (Hutchins & Baxter 1980, p. 201). It's already been established that this is a physically dangerous role for them because of the high incidence of violence and injury. However, there is evidence that police departments are taking an increasingly active interest in addressing the issue of family violence (Hutchins & Baxter, 1980, p. 203). Because of the seriousness of the issue and the high potential for injury and fatality, they are acknowledging that something must be done. For example, training programs targeting domestic violence are being developed for police personnel (Bard & Zacker, 1971). One thrust of these programs is the development of specialized interpersonal skills for dealing with domestic violence. There is also a growing awareness that female officers may play a special beneficial role in the intervention process (Hutchins & Baxter, 1980, p. 203).

Shelters for Battered Women

The most immediate need of a woman who has been seriously battered is a place to go. For this purpose, shelters have been developed around the country. This is a relatively recent occurrence. The first American shelter for battered women, the Rainbow Retreat in Phoenix, Arizona, opened in 1973 (Hutchins & Baxter, 1980, p. 206).

The one thing that all such programs have in common is the provision of a safe place where battered women can go to obtain temporary shelter. Beyond this commonality, Hutchins and Baxter (1980) conceptualize the range in philosophies adopted by shelters. On one end of the continuum are the more traditionally oriented agencies that emphasize the conventional values of keeping the family together and orient themselves toward helping women resolve their problems with their mates, stopping the battering, and enabling these women to safely return home.

Neiding and Friedman (1984) describe a treatment program for couples oriented toward achieving similar goals. Since most battered women report that they would prefer to return home, the program focuses on situational and relationship variables and teaches both members of the couple such skills as "coping strategies, stress management, and relationship enhancement" (p. 3).

On the other side of the philosophical continuum of battered-women shelters are those adopting a purely feminist perspective. For these, "wife abuse is seen as a social problem, rooted in sexism and manifested in the suffering of countless individual women. The women are regarded as victims in need of immediate protection and long-term life change. Some of the shelters with this philosophy actively encourage permanent separation of the couple" (Hutchins & Baxter, 1980, p. 207). Here the idea is that women need not be dependent on men, especially those who have been cruelly abusive to them. Rather, such abused women need to nurture confidence in themselves and develop their own alternatives.

Many shelters, however, adopt philosophies somewhere in between the purely traditional and the purely feminist. These shelters encourage women to think through their individual situations, evaluate their alternatives, and make their own decisions concerning what they feel is best for them.

Counseling Strategies

The following are some basic suggestions gathered from a range of sources regarding how social workers and counselors can help battered women:

Offer Support

A battered woman has probably been weakened both physically and emotionally. She needs someone to empathize with her and express genuine concern. She needs some time to sit back, experience some relief, and think.

Review Alternatives

A battered woman may feel trapped. She may be so overwhelmed that alternatives other than surviving in her abusive situation may not even have occurred to her. Her alternatives may include returning to the marriage, getting counseling for both herself and her husband, temporarily separating from her husband, establishing other means of financial support and independent living conditions for herself, or filing for divorce.

Furnish Information

Most victims probably don't have much information about how they can be helped. Information about available legal, medical, and social services may open up alternatives to better enable them to help themselves (Resnick, 1976).

Advocate

An advocate can seek out information for a victim and provide the victim with encouragement. An advocate can also help the victim get in touch with legal, medical, and social service resources and help the victim find her way through bureaucratic processes. Advocacy involves expending extra energy, "going that extra mile," on the victim's behalf.

Resnick (1976) has developed a training manual for counselors of battered women. She makes some excellent and specific suggestions regarding, among others, the following counseling issues: the initial interview, the range of the victim's emotional reactions, and specific counseling techniques.

The Initial Interview

A battered woman will probably be filled with anxiety during her initial meeting with you as a social worker. She may be worried about what to say to you. Therefore, you should try to make the woman as comfortable as possible and emphasize that she doesn't have to talk about anything if she doesn't want to.

The battered woman may also anticipate that you will be judgmental and critical of her. Resnick emphasizes that it's important that you put personal feelings aside and not pressure the battered woman into any particular course of action. This may be especially difficult when you have some strong personal feelings that the woman should leave the abusive situation. A basic principle is that it's the woman's decision regarding what she will choose to do. In those cases where the battered woman chooses to return home, it may be helpful for the counselor to help her clarify the reasons behind this decision.

Confidentiality may also be an issue for the battered woman. She may be especially fearful of the abuser finding out she's seeking help and of his possible retaliation. You need to assure her that no information will be given to anyone unless she wants it to. In the event that she does need a place to go, make it clear to her that the shelter is available.

The woman may show some embarrassment at being a "battered woman." The label may make her feel uncomfortable. Therefore, you should make efforts to disperse any embarrassment by emphasizing that she is a victim. The abuser is to blame for his own violent behavior. This problem has nothing to do with her character or with her intrinsic human value.

Emotional Reactions

Many battered women will display a range of emotional reactions. These include helplessness, fear, anger, guilt, embarrassment, and even doubts about her sanity. You need to encourage her to get all of these emotions out in the open because only then will she be able to deal with them. You now can help her look objectively at various aspects of her situation and help get control of her own life.

Specific Counseling Techniques

Resnick emphasizes that the foundation of good counseling is good listening ability. The battered woman needs to know that she can talk freely to a social worker and that what she says will have meaning.

A battered woman is often overwhelmed and confused. One of the most helpful things you can do is to help her sort through her various problems. She can't do everything at once, but she can begin getting control of her life by addressing one issue at a time and making decisions step by step.

There is one aspect of counseling which is frequently very easy to forget in the wake of the multitude of problems. It involves focusing on the woman's strengths. A battered woman will

probably be suffering from low self-esteem. She probably will need help in identifying her positive characteristics, which might include the fact that she is bright, a terrific mother, a hard worker, or that she has established some good coping skills in dealing with crises in the past.

One other important counseling technique is helping the woman establish a plan of action. She needs to clearly understand and define what she chooses to do. This may include formulating major goals such as divorcing her husband. It may involve setting smaller subgoals such as developing a list of existing daycare centers she can call to find out available child care options.

In summary, battered women need to strengthen their self-esteem and define more objectively the alternatives available to them. They need a chance to vent their feelings and to have someone there to listen to them. They need to have a place of refuge until they can think through their situations and hopefully make decisive plans of action for the future.

Suggestions for Macro Practice on Behalf of Battered Women

Most unfortunately, there is no national legislation which mandates that the rights of battered women be upheld and helpful services provided to them. The result is that states and localities have to orchestrate their own responses to the problem. Another result is inconsistency from area to area in terms of available services. In many areas there are broad gaps of services. You, as a generalist practitioner, may be employed in an area rich with related services. For example, most large cities have shelters and crisis hotlines for referrals. On the other hand, there may be a striking scarcity of resources in your area. In this latter case, you may choose to put your macro practice skills to work.

Research thus far has targeted strengthening the legal and criminal justice systems in order to curtail domestic violence (Fagan, Fried-man, & Wexler, 1984). In other words, areas where interventions and referrals are done in alliance with police help diminish the number of multiple battering complaints made to police departments. Star (1987) explains that "an active arrest policy and prosecution proved to be the most effective deterrent to further violence, especially in more severe cases" (p. 473).

In view of this evidence, one avenue of macro intervention is to lobby actively for better legislation at the national and possibly the state level. Strong national legislation that would require service provision to battered women and uphold their rights would be ideal.

Another aspect of macro practice is to advocate for the establishment of services within your community. Once again, informing the community of the need and organizing potentially interested community groups to help in the task is a possibility. Star (1987) articulates the need for "comprehensiveness, continuity,

and coordination of services" among various social work agencies and other disciplines in order to combat domestic violence (p. 474).

Star (1987) makes some additional suggestions for what you can do at the agency level. She states that "social work agencies can upgrade their professional staff's knowledge base and skills regarding the dynamics of and intervention in family violence through in-service training; establishing a legal aide position to keep staff apprised of court rulings and clients aware of their legal rights; offering support groups and family life education programs to clients; and maintaining positive relationships with community agencies to ensure timely and coordinated referrals" (pp. 473–74).

The Feminization of Poverty

The term *feminization of poverty* has been coined to reflect the fact that women as a

---

┌─ HIGHLIGHT 13.5 ─────────────────────────────

Women of Color Are "Doubly Disadvantaged"*

Consider the following facts:

- From 1975 to 1987, African American women's income declined from 96 to 91 percent of white women's income (Blau & Winkler, 1989).
- Whereas 20 percent of all American families with minor children are female-headed, 48 percent of all African American and 25 percent of all Hispanic families with children were headed by women (U.S. Bureau of the Census, 1988a).
- Nonwhite women can expect to live until age sixty-nine, while white women can expect to live to be age seventy-six (U.S. Bureau of the Census, 1987).
- Among white families headed by women, 40 percent live in poverty. Only 8 percent of

white families with a male parent involved are poor. 58 percent of African American families headed by women are poor, while 13 percent of African American families with a male parent involved fall below the poverty line. Finally, 60 percent of Hispanic families headed by women are poor, while 20 percent of Hispanic families with a male parent involved live in poverty (U.S. Bureau of the Census, 1987).

---

*This term is taken from "The Doubly Disadvantaged: Women of Color in the U.S. Labor Force" in *Women Working*, 2nd ed. by A. H. Stromberg and S. Harkess, eds., (Mountain View, CA: Mayfield, 1988), pp. 61–80.

group are more and more likely to be poor than are men. We've already established that women are twice as likely to be poor within their lifetimes as are men (Shortridge, 1989). Additionally, slightly over one-third of all single female-headed households are poor; families headed by single African American or Hispanic women are significantly more likely to be poor than families headed by white women (U.S. Bureau of the Census, 1985).

Women who work full-time earn 65 percent of what men earn full-time (Blau & Winkler, 1989). 72.7 percent of all women are working outside of the home; 38 percent of all women having children within the past year are in the paid labor force (Ginsberg, 1990). 80 percent of women work in only one quarter of all possible occupations which include being "librarians, secretaries, retail clerks, household workers, nurses, and teachers," all of which "pay less and offer fewer opportunities for advancement than do those occupations filled predominantly by men" (Jones, 1987, p. 876).

Micro and Mezzo Perspectives on Women in Poverty

People living in poverty are subject to a number of stereotyped, judgmental, negative perceptions by much of the public at large. Collier (1982) speaks of how we foster an independent, anyone-can-be-president image in this country. This image conflicts with the fact that permanently poor people exist here. Why are these people poor in a nation where, theoretically, anyone can become rich? She continues:

> We see them as not only poor but also immoral, as associated with crime, violence, alcohol and drug addiction, prostitution, and (the worst sin of all) lack of willpower.... Our judgments about the lower class tend to be more moralistic than sensible. If we see a prostitute, we see an immoral woman rather than one who lacks job

skills and wants money.... We assume that people are poor because they do not want to be otherwise, though the reality is the opposite (pp. 229–31).

Contrast the situation of the middle class with that of the lower class. How does education in the inner cities compare with that in the much richer suburbs? How well are lower-class people prepared educationally to compete for college entrance, vocational training programs, or jobs compared with middle-class people? In terms of prioritizing need, where will a poor, single mother find enough additional money to pay for daycare for her children, transportation to and from work, and the appropriate clothing to get and keep a job? Her main concern is to keep her family solvent from day to day with enough food and shelter to live. The point is that the same options are simply not available to poor people that are to middle- and upper-class people (Collier, 1982).

I will never forget a client who taught me about the futility encompassing poverty. She was a fifteen-year-old female client named Marcia. Her mother had never been married and had given birth to Marcia when she was just sixteen.

Marcia attended a day treatment facility where she received special education and therapy, yet still returned to her home each evening. She had a lengthy history of self-abuse including drug abuse, truancy, running away, and promiscuity (it's interesting how this latter term is not used to characterize boys). Marcia was assigned to my social work caseload for counseling.

Marcia was obviously bright. She grasped ideas quickly and articulated her thoughts well. At times, she showed interest in areas such as photography and nature, which contrasted starkly with what was available in her home environment. Although she was still behind in school, she was making significant strides and demonstrated excellent potential for being a good student.

At one point, I asked Marcia if she had ever considered going to college. She looked at me as if I had just developed hundreds of huge purple spots all over my body. "Where would somebody like me ever get the money to go to college? Are you nuts?" she asked.

The interesting thing was that I couldn't think of a rational response. "Yep," I thought to myself, "Where would she get the money?" She wouldn't get it from a scholarship because she essentially had no grade point at her special therapeutic school. Her mother and everyone else she knew except for staff at the treatment center were devastatingly poor.

It would be difficult to work her way through college because any job she'd be able to get would barely cover the cost of food, clothing, and rent. Worse yet, where would she get the confidence to go on to college, assuming that she could even obtain her high school equivalency through our program? Where would she find out how to apply to schools? Where would she learn how to act and how to study? She was used to the streets and special treatment programs. Nobody she knew at home ever went to college. In fact, few even completed high school. There was no one to serve as a model or to encourage her. My involvement with her would only last a few months. Then what?

The hurdles this young woman would have to overcome were awesome. Her realistic alternatives were severely limited. I certainly had no magic answers.

Several years later long after I left my job, I ran into another staff member. We began talking about old times and Marcia's name came up. I found out she had gotten pregnant when she was seventeen, quit school, and lived with a series of men after that.

Marcia's environment was restrictive. Her resources were limited and she simply was not prepared to compete in a middle-class world. That is why when we talk about women and poverty, we will emphasize the macro approaches for change. The "system" as it exists provides her with few, restricted options. Therefore, it's logical that it is the system and not Marcia who needs to change.

Of course some individuals can fight against amazing odds and eventually get a good job or receive vocational training or even a college degree. But the chances of success for the vast majority of these individuals are slim.

At the micro and mezzo levels of intervention you can essentially do five things. First, you can work to enhance your client's self-confidence. Second, you can help your client to define and evaluate the realistic opportunities available to her. Third, you can educate her regarding the resources that are available and help her get involved with them. Fourth, you can do "outreach" to clients yourself (Collier, 1982). This involves going out into the community and your clients' homes, asking questions, educating them about how to deal with the system, and going far beyond your call of duty in helping them to do so. Finally, you can teach and encourage your client how to work with the system to her advantage (Collier, 1982).

Macro Perspectives on Women and Poverty

You know about macro practice. You know how difficult it can be to make even minor changes in mammoth bureaucratic systems. However, this is such a major issue that it's important as a generalist practitioner to evaluate the possibility of macro changes whenever you can. We will discuss three potential approaches: reforming society's ideas about women's life experiences involving employment and family responsibilities, bettering conditions and resources in the workplace, and improving legislation providing for equality. The first two are closely related to changes in legislation, as incentives for such changes are essential.

Reforming Society's Perspective

Gottlieb (1987) describes the difficulty we face in trying to change a system that places women "in a disadvantageous power position" which "results in serious social, economic, and political consequences for women as a group" (p. 562). She states that "long-standing systems of belief are difficult to change, and entrenched power resists dislodging. Although affirmative action and antidiscrimination laws and policies have had an impact, they have not replaced the tenaciously held view of men and women. The restrictive role society imposes on women and the power differential between men and women continue to foster a range of discriminatory practices" (p. 568).

Although it is depressing, this situation cannot be ignored. It is a generalist practitioner's responsibility to be aware of this oppression so that she can work to educate others and effect change.

Society's perspective on women's family and work responsibilities is an enormous problem. On the one hand, society has traditionally viewed a woman in terms of her family role and she is considered the nurturant, giving maintainer of the home whose primary responsibility is to keep her family healthy and together (Lott, 1987).

Women who are married have poor odds of being able to fulfill this primary role without assuming economic responsibility for their families. About one in two marriages end in divorce (U.S. Bureau of the Census, 1988b). Women suffer an instant 73 percent drop in their standard of living following a divorce, whereas a divorced man enjoys an average increase of 42 percent (Weitzman, 1985).

There are over ten million female-headed families in this country, almost half of whom are poor; within this statistic, more than half of African American and Hispanic female-headed households are poor (Shortridge, 1989). It is a significant problem. A multitude of women have primary responsibility both for their family's caretaking and for its economic support.

Many poor women and their children receive public assistance, but no state provides enough assistance to bring families above the poverty level. Alabama provides the lowest proportion of assistance at 16 percent of the poverty level and California the highest at 85 percent (Burke, 1987). Public assistance's "eligibility requirements now center on a mother's willingness to work, although available training programs continue to pigeonhole women into sex-segregated occupations" (Gottlieb, 1987, p. 566). Additionally, public assistance recipients have been tormented with judgmental innuendoes regarding their sexual behavior and inability to access pay equal to that of men (Gottlieb, 1987).

Pierce (1989) elaborates upon the problems in society's philosophy regarding women, work, and public assistance:

1. The obsession with 'put them to work' results in women taking jobs with income or benefits (particularly health insurance) that are insufficient for their families' needs.
2. Training available . . . has too often been for traditionally female jobs (e.g., cafeteria worker) that pay poverty-level wages. Such 'opportunities' thus reinforce the occupational segregation and ghettoization of women and the poverty that results. [Public assistance recipients are allowed to attend two-year vocational programs. However, they can't get support to attend four-year colleges which would lead to substantially greater economic opportunity.]
3. Even in training programs, often no provision is made for child care, although half the mothers receiving welfare have a child under age six (p. 502).

Society is telling women that they must assume responsibility for their children, both as primary caretakers and as economic providers, but it does not provide the minimal essential resources to do so. Even women who pursue such job "opportunities" often can't afford to continue because of day care unavailability, lack of health insurance, or because such jobs are in "marginal, unstable industries" (Pierce, 1989, p. 502).

The link between women's family responsibilities, poverty, and their access to adequate working opportunities is becoming clearer. If we expect women to both care for their families and support themselves, more resources must be provided. Women need to have greater accessibility to adequate jobs. Their work environments need to be more supportive and supplementary resources for their children must be made more available. The final sections of this chapter address these issues.

Improving Conditions in the Workplace

As a generalist practitioner, you need to be aware of intimidating conditions for women in the workplace so that you may use your macro skills to alleviate them. Lott (1987) cites at least six conditions that make it particularly difficult for women to perform effectively in the workplace. The first involves the *numerous family responsibilities and the many roles women are expected to perform in their work and personal worlds.* Additionally, employed women who are in relationships with men still maintain primary responsibility for most of the in-home work. Consider the following facts:

- Women employed outside of the home assume as much responsibility for household tasks as those who work as full-time homemakers (Hammond & Mahoney, 1983; Lott, 1987; Pyke & Kahill, 1983; Radloff, 1975).
- Women spend significantly more time and expend significantly more energy caring for their homes and children than men do; women are also much more likely than men to accomodate themselves to what other family members need and want. (Lott, 1987). For example, women are much more likely than men to use their employment "sick days" to stay home and take care of sick children or attend to other matters involving their children (Englander-Golden & Barton, 1983); this was despite the fact that both men and women took similar total amounts of sick leave.
- Women employed full-time do significantly more housework than their husbands who are also employed full-time (Bryson, Bryson, Licht, & Licht, 1976; Gilbert, 1985).

What can you as a generalist practitioner do about these problems? You can work to influence employers to provide assistance to working women. Four strategies are possible. First, child care could be provided (Harkess, 1988). It could be considered one of a series of possible benefit choices from which employees might choose. For instance, if one spouse has medical coverage at her full-time job, the other might opt for child care at his full-time job instead of duplicating health-care coverage.

A second thing you can advocate for employers to do is to offer flexible working hours (Harkess, 1988). The strictly enforced nine to five working day is not carved in stone. It may be easier to arrange for alternative day care or to be home when the children arrive from school if a parent is allowed to work from 7:00 A.M. to 3:00 P.M. instead.

A third suggestion for employers is to provide better part-time work for women (Harkess, 1988). Wages and benefits should both be equal to those provided full-time workers.

The final suggestion for employers is to provide adequate mandatory parental child-care leaves (Lott, 1987) at full or partial salary. Return to the same job should be guaranteed and a woman's seniority should not be sacrificed because of her leave.

HIGHLIGHT 13.6

Women's Salaries in Social Work*

In 1987 the National Association of Social Work (NASW) made a survey of its members' salaries. The average salary for BSW respondents was $22,900, for MSW's $27,700, and for DSW's or Ph.D.'s $35,500 (Williams & Hopps, 1990). Women made up 71 percent of the respondents.

The overall average salary for all degree levels was $27,800. The average salary of all women respondents was $25,900 and the average salary for men was $37,500. In summary, women social workers earned 69.5 cents for every dollar earned by men social workers.

Some of this difference might be due to women's greater likelihood of working part-time instead of full-time. However, the summary report states, "The marked gap in income between males and females cannot be attributed to the part-time employment factor alone. The gap exists at all income levels and seems to reflect the income gender gap in the society at large" (NASW, 1987, p. 4).

---

*This information is taken from an article entitled "The Social Work Labor Force: Current Perspectives and Future Trends" by Leon F. Williams and June G. Hopps in the *Encyclopedia of Social Work*, 18th Edition, 1990 Supplement, published by the National Association of Social Workers, Silver Spring, MD.

In addition to multiple roles, a second condition confronting women in the workplace is one we've already established. Namely, *jobs are segregated by gender*. Attending to this issue involves encouraging women to pursue fields and careers traditionally sought primarily by men. Examples include math, science, engineering, and skilled trades such as carpentry. Similarly, it means encouraging men to seek jobs traditionally held by women, such as child-care work, teaching, and nursing. Employers can be pressured to recruit women into nontraditional fields more actively (Harkess, 1988).

A third problem women encounter in the workplace involves a *lack of positive female role models holding powerful positions*. Although "some women have, in recent years, moved into important decision-making positions, recognition of this has been slow and hampered by continued portrayal of stereotypes in media advertisements" (Lott, 1987, p. 223). When you watch television, read the newspaper, or browse through your favorite magazine, watch for how women are portrayed in comparison to men. Who is portrayed as strong and who is meek?

How much emphasis is placed on women's beauty? Who is pictured concerning topics such as governmental leadership and high finance? These images convey subtle and not so subtle information about how men and women are supposed to be.

In effect, few women have made it to powerful, highly visible positions. For example, in 1986 there were two women governors, one woman in the president's cabinet, twenty-three women out of 435 members in the U.S. House of Representatives, and two women out of 100 U.S. senators. Only two of seventy-five astronauts were women ("Poll: Women" 1986).

What can you do to remedy this? For one thing, be sensitive to the composition of any particular group. Is there gender balance? If women are lacking, encourage their inclusion. Evaluate political candidates concerning their views on women and women's issues. Strongly support female candidates whose views coincide with yours. Educate other people to become more gender sensitive. When you see things in the media that you find gender insensitive or offensive, write and complain. Encourage and support women to assume important positions. If you are a woman, consider aiming for important positions yourself.

A fourth barrier to women in the workplace concerns *salary discrimination*. We've already indicated that women earn approximately sixty-five cents for every dollar earned by men. Several factors contribute to this. For one thing, women are significantly more likely to experience a work interruption lasting at least six months at some time over their working career (U.S. Bureau of the Census, 1987) because of having children, or, perhaps, caring for aging parents.

A second factor contributing to the wage differential involves occupational discrimination by sex. We've discussed how women tend to be clustered in a few occupations with relatively low pay. However, even if we break this down, there are some gaps that are difficult to explain. Consider men and women in the same occupation. Women earn these percentages of what men earn in the following professions: bookkeeping, 73 percent; clerical workers, 68 percent; computer programmers, 80 percent; cooks, 76 percent; lawyers, 75 percent; and office managers, 61 percent (Schreiner, 1984). See Highlight 13.6 for how women's salaries compare to men's in social work.

Like the other impediments to women in the workplace, the salary one is not easy to solve.

HIGHLIGHT 13.7

Confronting Sexual Harassment

Victims of sexual harassment have several alternative routes available to them. Each has its own potential positive and negative consequences. Alternatives include ignoring the harassing behavior, avoiding the harasser, or confronting the harasser and asking him to stop (Martin, 1984). One study (MSPB, 1981) found that ignoring the behavior had virtually no effect. Asking the harasser to stop, however, effectively terminated the harassment in half of the cases.

Avoiding the harasser is another option. A severe shortcoming of this approach is that the victim is the one who must expend the effort in avoidance behavior. The ultimate avoidance is actually quitting the job or dropping the class in order to avoid contact with a sexual harasser. This is the least fair (and potentially most damaging) alternative for the victim.

There are, however, several other suggestions to help victims confront sexual harassment. In many cases using these strategies will stop harassment. First, a victim needs to know her or his rights. A call to the Equal Employment Opportunity Commission (EEOC), the federal agency designated to address the issue of sexual harassment, is helpful. Many women can obtain necessary information about their rights and the appropriate procedures to follow for filing a formal complaint.

Sexual harassment is illegal at the national level. Many states also have laws that specify what can be done to combat it and often have agencies or offices that victims may call for help and information. For example, Wisconsin has the Wisconsin Equal Rights Division to address such issues. Additionally, organizations and agencies have specific policies against sexual harassment. Filing a formal complaint through established procedures is often a viable option.

Most victims, however, choose not to pursue the formal complaint route because they fear reprisal or retaliation (Martin, 1984; MSPB, 1981). Others don't want to be labeled "troublemakers." Still others choose not to expend the time and effort necessary to carry out a formal process. Most victims simply want the harassment to end so that they can do their work peacefully and productively.

In addition to knowing your rights, the following suggestions can be applied to most situations where sexual harassment is occurring:

1. *Confront your harasser.* Tell the harasser which specific behaviors are unwanted and

However, once inequities are identified, you can fight to have them obliterated. You can use your macro skills to apply pressure for change. In some instances, conflict in terms of legal action may be necessary.

A fifth factor contributing to a problematic work environment involves *discrimination in benefits and job loss*. This may be due to a woman finding "that her request for maternity leave is reacted to negatively by her employer, that she is without a pension after years in the work force, or that she is among the first to lose her job during slow periods in the economy" (Lott, 1987, p. 226). It is beyond the scope of this text to elaborate on the extensive research in support of such inequities. Let it suffice that you as a generalist practitioner are encouraged to be aware of such potential discrimination and combat it where it exists.

Establishing labor unions is one method to confront and change inequitable practices (Harkess, 1988; Lott, 1987). A strong union with numerous members can exert substantial pressure on an employer. Women must have significant clout within a union's membership for it to work on their behalf. A variety of macro skills for organizing could be useful here.

A sixth factor working against employed women on their jobs is *sexual harassment*. Sexual harassment involves unwelcome sexual ad-

---

unacceptable. If you feel you cannot handle a direct confrontation, write the harasser a letter. It is helpful to criticize the harasser's behavior rather than the harasser as a person. The intent is to stop the harassment and maintain a pleasant, productive work environment. There is also the chance that the harasser was not aware that his or her behavior was offensive. In these cases, giving specific feedback is frequently effective.

2. *Be assertive.* When giving the harasser feedback, look him or her directly in the eye and assume an assertive stance. Don't smile or giggle even though you may be uncomfortable. Look the harasser directly in the eye, stand up straight, adopt a serious expression, and calmly state, "Please stop touching me by putting your arms around me and rubbing my neck. I don't like it." This is a serious matter and you need to get your point across.

3. *Document your situation.* (Farley, 1978). Record every incident that occurs. Note when, where, who, what was said or done, what you were wearing, and any available witnesses. Be as accurate as possible. Documentation does not have to be elaborate or fancy. Simple handwritten notes including the facts will suffice. It is also a good idea to keep copies of your notes in another location.

4. *Talk to other people about the problem.* Get support from friends and colleagues. Sexual harassment often erodes self-confidence. Victims do not feel they are in control of the situation. Emotional support from others can bolster self-confidence and give victims the strength needed to confront sexual harassment. Frequently sharing these problems with others will also allow victims to discover they're not alone. Corroboration with other victims will not only provide emotional support, but it will also strengthen a formal complaint if that option needs to be taken sometime in the future.

5. *Get witnesses.* Look around when the sexual harassment is occurring and note who else can observe it. Talk to these people and solicit their support. Try to make arrangements for others to be around you when you anticipate that sexual harassment is likely to occur.

vances, requests for sexual favors, and other verbal or physical conduct of a sexual nature where the following results. First, submission to such conduct is required as a condition of employment or education. Second, submission to such conduct is used as a basis for decisions that affect an individual's employment or academic achievement. Third, such conduct results in a hostile, intimidating, or anxiety-producing work or educational environment.[2]

Sexual harassment includes not only sexual solicitations and physical attacks, but also any type of behavior that makes a work setting uncomfortable, unproductive, or hostile. This includes gender biased remarks, crude sexist jokes, and unfair treatment on the basis of gender.

An accurate, specific profile of when, where, how, and to whom sexual harassment occurs does not exist. However, some recent surveys suggest that it is quite prevalent in a variety of settings (Maypole & Skaine, 1983; Safran, 1976; U.S. Merit Systems Protection Board, 1981).

Improving Legislation for Equality

In chapter 4 we talked about specific skills for influencing decision makers. Those same skills apply here regarding the improvement of pro-equality legislation. We will, therefore, discuss three of the issues which need legislative attention: pressing for antidiscrimination legislation and initiating lawsuits when unfairnesses surface (Lott, 1987); bolstering affirmative action activities (Gottlieb, 1987); and actively supporting the comparable worth movement (Gottlieb, 1987; Lott, 1987).

---

2. The definition of sexual harassment is taken from Resolution #2384 of the Board of Regents of the University of Wisconsin System dated May 8, 1981. The Equal Employment Opportunity Commission has published a similar definition of sexual harassment in "Guidelines on Discrimination Because of Sex, Title VII, Sec. 703," *Federal Register,* 45 (April 11, 1980).

Antidiscrimination Legislation

A number of bills have been passed since 1963 that prohibit discrimination on the basis of gender (for example, the Equal Pay Act of 1963 and Title VII of the Civil Rights Act of 1964). Lott (1987) identifies a primary problem with implementing the legislation by stating, "Machinery to counter sex discrimination in employment exists, but working through it is cumbersome, time-consuming, frustrating, painfully slow, and typically drains the complainant(s) of energy, money, and self-confidence" (p. 234). However, such legislation at least opens the door a crack in combating gender discrimination. It should be considered as one of the options available to pursue in generating positive change. There is some indication that class-action suits have exerted more pressure and had greater possibilities of success than those initiated by individuals (Lott, 1987).

Affirmative Action

Affirmative action involves "positive steps taken by an organization to remedy imbalances in minority [and women's] employment, promotions, and other opportunities" (Barker, 1987, p. 5). You can use affirmative action to pursue three positive thrusts on the behalf of women (Gottlieb, 1987). First, affirmative action can be used to monitor the proportion of women in any particular job category. Employment of women in an agency or organization should approach that proportion. For example, if 14 percent of all skilled bricklayers in the country are women, then at least 14 percent of the bricklayers employed by every construction company should be women.

A second manner in which affirmative action can be used involves "identifying areas in which women are poorly represented, setting goals for improvement, and monitoring those goals" (Gottlieb, 1987, p. 565). Affirmative action provides a rationale and mechanism for addressing these inequities.

The third way in which affirmative action

can be helpful involves wiping out discriminatory policies and practices. For example, advertising a job position for a social worker who must be a male violates affirmative action principles.

Comparable Worth

We've established several facts. First, most women work outside of the home. Second, women tend to be clustered in an extremely small number of relatively low-paying occupations. Third, women have significantly less political power in terms of the actual number of political offices they hold.

The principle of comparable worth may be defined as "calling for equal pay for males and females doing work requiring comparable skill, effort, and responsibility under similar working conditions" (Bellak, 1984, p. 75). Comparable worth does not refer to jobs that are identical, but rather that are similar or comparable. For example, a male janitor might receive a substantially higher salary than a female secretary, even though both jobs might require similar *levels*, not types, of training and experience.

Bellak (1984) describes the comparable worth situation. Although many state laws refer to the concept of comparable worth either directly or indirectly, they tend not to be very specific about what should be done, if anything, to remedy problematic situations. Currently, only the state governments, not private businesses and corporations, have even attempted to address the issue.

Although it is not clearly specified as law at this time, comparable worth is being used as a basis for an increasing number of pay-discrimination suits. You as a generalist practitioner can support the concept and work on its behalf.

There are two basic suggestions for how the doctrine of comparable worth might be attained. First, a system of "job evaluation" must be developed. Job evaluation would involve evaluating each job in an organization on the basis of "skill requirements, effort, responsibility, and working conditions" (Schwab, 1984, p. 86). A system would have to be worked out whereby these job aspects could be analyzed, compared, and rated on a certain scale. The end result would be *comparable* job classifications with *comparable* salaries.

The second recommendation for implementing the doctrine of comparable worth would be to establish legislation to mandate compliance. Laws need to be created to require both governmental and private business organizations to abide by comparable worth. This would require the development of job evaluation systems. It would also necessitate careful monitoring of organizations to make certain that they comply with or obey the rules.

Chapter Summary

This chapter explored generalist social work practice with women from a feminist perspective. Feminism was defined and principles of feminist counseling identified.

Micro practice with women was examined. Common problems of women including stressful life events and personal issues were discussed. Empowering women through enhancing self-esteem, increasing assertiveness, and other positive approaches was described. Expanding options and changing rules and expectations were other intervention alternatives provided.

Common circumstances facing women were identified and examined. These included women as survivors of sexual assault, battered women, and the feminization of poverty. Multi-level intervention approaches for each were proposed.

14 Advocacy

The art of accessing resources

Sharon McManus ran into a brick wall. Trying desperately to find housing for her homeless client, Sharon had finally located a house which met the family's needs. The house was large enough to accommodate Mr. Vue and his four children, and would eliminate the need for the family to continue sleeping in their car. (Mr. Vue was a Hmong who had immigrated from Vietnam with his family.) The only problem was that the house had to be approved by the Indian Falls City Housing Authority if Mr. Vue was to receive a housing subsidy. The subsidy was a monthly payment from the housing authority which would help Mr. Vue pay the rent on this house.

When Sharon called the housing authority requesting approval of the house, she learned that it would be several weeks before the home could be inspected and certified for inclusion in the housing subsidy program. Sharon knew that Mr. Vue did not have several weeks. His children were not in school, he lacked food, and the family could not be expected to continue living out of his car. Frustrated, Sharon decided it was time to try a different approach. Assuming the advocate role, Sharon contacted Barbara Soderholm, her representative on the Indian Falls City Council. She explained the situation to Councilwoman Soderholm and asked if there was anything she could do to speed up the process. Within the day, Sharon received a call from the housing authority. Councilwoman Soderholm had called an official she knew at the housing authority and exercised her influence to speed up the process. The housing authority representative would inspect the house the following day.

Sharon was elated. She arranged for the house to be cleaned before the visit by the housing authority, and notified Mr. Vue of the good news. Following the visit, the house passed inspection and the Vue family finally had a home. Sharon then helped Mr. Vue enroll his children in school. She maintained contact with him for the next few months to ensure that his transition to his new home was proceeding satisfactorily.

CHAPTER FOURTEEN

Introduction

In this chapter we will place the preceding example within the context of the social work role known as advocacy. Specifically, this chapter will:

- Define advocacy and discuss its relationship to the profession of social work;
- Discuss the assumptions associated with advocacy;
- Explore various assumptions about power, organizations, clients, and various approaches to advocacy;
- Review the knowledge and skills required of advocates;
- Review the assessment process used in advocacy situations;
- Describe strategies and tactics used by the advocate;
- Discuss different models of advocacy.

Defining Advocacy

One of the most important objectives of social work is to help people obtain needed resources. Often this occurs through the brokering role explained in chapter 15. The broker role requires that the social worker help clients by connecting them to appropriate agencies or services. Sometimes the worker must act as a mediator between the client and a resource. This might be required, for example, when a client has been refused service or benefits through a misunderstanding or confusion about whether the client was eligible for the service.

In other situations, the worker must assume yet another role, namely that of the advocate. Barker (1991, p. 7) defines advocacy as the "act of directly representing or defending others; in social work championing the rights of individuals or communities through direct intervention or through empowerment. According to the NASW Code of Ethics, it is a basic obligation to

the profession and its members." Briar (1967) was one of the first to argue that case advocacy should be considered a natural part of the professional social work role. Briar (1967, p. 28) said the advocate is the client's supporter, advisor, champion, and representative in "dealings with the court, the police, the social agency and other organizations." Social workers use their positions and professional skills to "exercise leverage for needed services on behalf" of individuals and groups (Brown, 1991, p. 212). As part of the social work profession's obligation to serve the most vulnerable populations, we must expect that many clients will need our assistance. Isolated clients, the disabled, de-institutionalized clients, and children are examples of those on whose behalf advocacy may be essential. Many organizations exist specifically to advocate for certain categories of clients. Examples include Mothers Against Drunk Drivers (MADD), the Alliance for the Mentally Ill, and the Gray Panthers.

Advocacy is "a concept borrowed from the legal profession" according to Mailick and Ashley (1989, p. 625). They view the advocate as an "unequivocal partisan serving the interests of the client, even, in the extreme, in opposition to the policies of his or her own agency" (p. 625). Sheafor, Horejsi, and Horejsi (1991, p. 357) say the advocate "speaks, argues, manipulates, bargains, and negotiates on behalf of the client." Sosin and Caulum (1989, p. 533) argue that advocacy is a core activity of social work that sets us apart from others in the helping professions. In their view, advocacy grows out of social work's emphasis on understanding people within their environment. It is also rooted in the profession's awareness of how that environment can influence clients' well-being.

Case Advocacy

Case advocacy, as the name implies, refers to activity on behalf of a single case. It is usually employed in situations where the individual is in conflict with an organization, perhaps over benefits that have been denied. As we described earlier in chapter 4, the "case" may be an individual, a family, or a small group.

Effective case advocacy requires several types of knowledge:

- Knowledge of the agency's policies, regulations, and administrative structure;
- Knowledge of the agency's appeal procedures;
- Knowledge of available legal remedies;
- Knowledge of the agency's formal and informal power structure;
- Knowledge of external forces to which the organization responds;
- Knowledge of the consequences (for both client and others) of escalating issues (Anderson, 1981, p. 44).

The reader may be wondering at what point case advocacy becomes cause or class advocacy. The line between advocating for a single client and engaging in macro practice (working on the behalf of whole groups or populations of clients) can become somewhat blurry. For example, a successful appeal of an adversary's decision in the case of a single client may result in a new interpretation of old rules benefiting all clients in similar situations. Yet a discouraging reality of case advocacy is that while the advocate may successfully challenge the agency on behalf of a specific client, no long-term change in agency policy is guaranteed. Consequently, other clients face the same hurdles in their interactions with the agency.

While there are similarities between the two approaches, case advocacy generally involves strategies and tactics different from those employed for cause advocacy. This is especially true when we look at legislative advocacy, a form of cause advocacy which will be discussed later in the chapter.

Cause Advocacy

Cause advocacy involves social workers' efforts to address an issue of overriding importance to some client group. The emphasis on *cause* means that this type of advocacy affects multiple groups of clients or potential clients. It is also sometimes called class advocacy.

For example, early social workers were active in efforts to develop kindergartens, to create laws prohibiting child labor, and to require education for physically disabled persons. The intended and actual beneficiaries of these efforts were not individual clients, but entire categories of persons. A more current example might involve a social worker advocating to serve a category of clients more effectively within his or her own agency. Perhaps the location and office hours of an agency make it difficult for low-income clients to use the agency's services. A worker might attempt to get the agency to open an office in a different, more accessible, location or to expand agency office hours further into the evening.

Let's re-examine the case involving a social worker named Glen, which was described in chapter 4. You may recall that Glen's supervisor wanted prospective foster parents to come in during the day for their appointments even if it meant taking time off from their work. In this case Glen used cause advocacy. He advocated for all prospective foster parents as a large group and tried to convince his supervisor that the agency should be more flexible. He argued that the agency should expand its hours in the evening so more foster parent candidates could have access to its services.

The need for class advocacy may become more obvious after repeated cases arise having similar characteristics. You may notice patterns in case records or observe striking similarities in the types of problems clients are having.

At the agency level, individual social workers may conduct cause advocacy working alone.

Beyond the agency level advocates are much more likely to involve themselves in coalitions with other workers and agencies because some forms of advocacy require major effort. Consider a new state law that requires community agencies to serve formerly institutionalized clients but does not provide any funding for such services. Since the problem is at a level far above the individual agency, it will take many groups working in concert if a change in this law is to be achieved.

Cause advocacy often involves resistance because it requires significant change in the status quo. You may have to use tactics involving conflict to overcome this resistance. We've established that people in power usually do not want to give it up.

Let's refer back to Glen's case. Pressuring his agency to expand its hours has implications and repercussions. More hours requires spending more money to staff the agency longer. Agency administrators may resent being pressured to "dig up" more funding or to allow workers to accrue compensatory time. They might resist any change in the status quo. People in administration also tend to resist being told or pressured regarding what to do. This is especially the case when it involves employees under their theoretical control.

Some cause advocacy has resulted in lawsuits challenging official regulations and governmental inaction. Sheafor et al. (1991, p. 490) observe that " . . . within the past twenty years, most of the reforms in the areas of mental health and mental retardation grew out of lawsuits." Lawsuits can be extremely threatening to an agency's or organization's administration. They usually involve potentially significant conflict. Lawsuits make problems public. They are also expensive. For both reasons, administrators will frequently avoid them like the plague.

Cause advocacy then often involves risks, both to the agency and to the worker initiating it. This is why advocacy requires such sensitivity, tact, and skill. You, as an advocate, want to facilitate change for the well-being of your clients. However, you probably do not want to get fired.

Useful Skills in Cause Advocacy

The effective advocate will need to know *how to use government documents and other data sources.* Often, it will be necessary to document the existence of a problem. You may need to know where to get facts, information, and official statistics.

Comfort with and ability to use the political process are also important. Most of the rules, regulations, and funding for human service programs are derived from laws passed at the state or federal level. Changing laws requires that you know how the political process works, and are able to use this process to achieve social work goals.

Whether the target is an agency supervisor, a board of directors, or a legislative committee, the advocate must *be comfortable speaking in public.* For example, you may find yourself needing to present arguments or ideas to groups such as legislators or members of an agency board of directors. Public speaking skills will make it easier to do this.

A level of *tolerance for conflict* is also important. Change is often difficult for others and resistance is common. You must be comfortable in situations where people disagree with you or your ideas.

The Goals of Advocacy

The advocate (either alone, or in consort with others) is attempting to "influence another individual or group to make a decision that would not have been made otherwise and that concerns the welfare or interests of a third party" (Sosin & Caulum, 1989, p. 534). We have emphasized throughout this text the problem-solving framework used by social workers. Our position is similar to Green's (1982) that advocacy is simply a more radical approach to problem solving. The purpose of client advocacy is "to secure services that the client is entitled to but unable to obtain on his or her own" (Sheafor et al., 1991, p. 357). The nature of this task is such that advocacy is more likely to involve confrontation than most other approaches to intervention (Sheafor et al., 1991).

Connaway and Gentry (1988) argued that it is important to make a distinction between two aspects of advocacy. On the one hand, advocacy involves making certain that clients have access to *existing* rights and entitlements. On the other hand, advocacy also concerns *social action* to secure new rights and entitlements. We have discussed social action in previous chapters and will revisit this topic again when we look at cause and legislative advocacy. Essentially, the advocate is working to help clients reach goals they have defined as desirable. Those goals usually require some action on the part of a decision maker. That decision maker may have to change a previous decision, reinterpret rules or modify procedures to benefit the client, or abide by and enforce existing rules or regulations. In the case opening this chapter, the goal was to influence the decision maker (representative from the housing authority) to act immediately in a crisis rather than following the usual procedures of first-come, first-served.

The advocacy task of securing services to which the client is entitled but unable to obtain without help is more likely to involve confrontation than other intervention approaches.

┌─ **HIGHLIGHT 14.1** ─────────────────────

Indications for Advocacy

Advocacy is likely to be the role of choice in any of the following sets of circumstances:

1. when an agency or staff person refuses to deliver all services or benefits to which a client is entitled
2. when services are delivered in a dehumanizing manner (e.g., when rape victims are humiliated)
3. when clients are discriminated against because of race, religion, creed, or other factors
4. when gaps in services and benefits cause hardship or contribute to dysfunction
5. when the government or agency policies adversely affect people in need of resources and benefits

6. when clients are unable to act effectively on their own behalf
7. when many people have common needs for which resources are not available
8. when clients have unusual needs for immediate service or benefits because of a crisis (e.g., migrants who are seriously ill or have acute financial needs)
9. when clients are denied civil or legal rights
10. when procedures or facilities of organizations adversely affect clients.

───────

Source: Reprinted from D.H. Hepworth and J. Larsen, *Direct Social Work Practice: Theory and Skills*, 3rd ed., by permission of Wadsworth Publishing Company, Belmont, CA 94002.

Targets of Advocacy

Targets of advocacy may include individuals, groups or organizations, elected or appointed officials, public and private human service agencies, legislative bodies, court systems or governmental entities (such as the housing authority). Any of the persons or organizations listed above may impede client access to service or treat clients inhumanely. By doing so, they become potential targets of advocacy because as social workers, we adhere to several principles.

First, we work to increase *accessibility* of social services to clients. Not only should needed services exist, but clients should be able to use them without undue difficulty. For example, clients for whom English is not their primary language will have difficulty completing lengthy forms written in that language. If they can't complete the forms, they won't receive the services.

Sometimes the services themselves are satisfactory, but other problems prevent clients from using them. For example, services may be available only during the day when clients work. Or there may be long waiting periods before services can be received. Another problem entails services offered at locations that are inaccessible to clients. This might occur when a building is not accessible to the disabled, or when services are offered at sites far from clients' homes.

A second principle for us as social work advocates is that we promote *service delivery that does not detract from clients' dignity*. In other words, clients should not be put in humiliating or embarrassing situations in order to receive services. For instance, consider a situation where clients must wait in a filthy, crowded waiting room for hours in order to receive the public assistance they need. It is appropriate to advocate that such conditions be changed because they are an affront to the clients' dignity.

Sometimes services are provided in a fashion that is demeaning to clients. For example, one large county social services agency provided workers with desks located within a giant facility which resembled a remodeled warehouse. There were no walls or partitions between workers' desks. Thus, anyone within sight or hearing of the desks could easily find out what the client and the worker were talking about. Privacy was almost non-existent.

A third principle to guide advocates involves working to assure *equal access to all who are eligible*. For example, when services are more accessible to white clients than to African American or Hispanic clients this kind of service delivery is unacceptable and needs to be changed.

Hepworth and Larsen (1990, p. 460) provide additional examples in Highlight 14.1 of situations where advocacy may be appropriate. As you will see from the examples, the targets of advocacy may vary depending upon the individual situation.

History of Advocacy in Social Work

McGowan (1987, p. 89) notes that although social workers have long acted as advocates for clients, the concept of advocacy is a somewhat recent addition to the profession's knowledge base. She also points out that there is some disagreement within social work over whether advocacy is a role, a function of social work, an activity, or a technique (p. 91). For purposes of this chapter, advocacy is considered a role encompassing a variety of activities and techniques.

Haynes and Mickelson (1991) take a historical perspective on advocacy. They note that the period from 1895 to 1915 is considered a progressive era in social work because of the supposed high level of social action and advocacy carried out by social workers. However, they note that "many social workers honored advocacy more with rhetoric than with practice" (p. 5). They point out that social workers of this era

were more likely to act as brokers or facilitators than as advocates. They note that the Charity Organization Society movement saw individual clients as dysfunctional and tried to change the clients. Meanwhile, the social settlement house workers tried to "reform the social environment that made people losers" (p. 5). The era saw both case advocacy (advocating for individual clients, families or groups) and class or cause advocacy (advocating for large groups of people sharing common characteristics, or advocating for social legislation).

Unfortunately, even the limited progressiveness of this era did not continue in the following years. Instead social work practice has experienced what appears to be cycles of advocacy. Following the earlier progressive era came a period in which social workers paid more attention to becoming professionals and adopting psychological treatment approaches than to solving client problems.

Later a resurgence of advocacy occurred during the period of the Great Depression. Then, social workers participated in many social programs designed to combat the unemployment and malaise of the 1930s. The period of the 1940s and 1950s appears in retrospect to mark another decline in social work focus on advocacy. The 1960s marked a resurgence of interest in advocating for both individual clients and for classes of people. Social workers contributed to many efforts to change organizations and institutions and make them more responsive to clients and oppressed groups. Advocates represented clients "against bulldozers of urban renewal, routes of proposed expressways, and intrusions of facilities into nearby areas" (Checkoway, 1987, p. 336). On the downswing, the 1970s and 1980s showed less advocacy for oppressed groups as the nation experienced a period of conservative political leadership. This period also saw the growth of advocacy-oriented, self-help groups dedicated to bringing better treatment and conditions to their members.

Clearly, advocacy today is an important role for social workers as they help clients negotiate the social environment. The political climate of the past twenty years has resulted in the erosion of services and benefits for some of our most vulnerable populations. Simultaneously, there is renewed interest in using the political process to create changes needed by these populations. Social workers today must use knowledge and a variety of skills to help clients. In the sections that follow we will look carefully at advocacy in social work practice.

Assumptions about Advocacy

The social worker playing the advocate role is operating under a different set of assumptions than is true in roles such as broker or facilitator. The assumptions cover three areas:

- Assumptions about power;
- Assumptions about organizations;
- Assumptions about clients.

Assumptions about Power

There are five assumptions about power that are helpful in understanding advocacy:

1. Those who hold power are generally reluctant to give up that power.
2. Those who hold power generally have greater access to resources than people with less power. For instance, those with more money have greater access to legal services, education and health care.
3. Resources in general, including power, are not distributed equally (Green, 1982). Some people simply have significantly more power than others.
4. Conflict between people and between people and institutions is inevitable, especially when those in power treat those

with less power unfairly. People don't want or like to be "underdogs." For example, Devore and Schlesinger, (1987, p. 136) see an inherent conflict in minority-majority group relations. They argue "dominant institutions dominate minority people, and advocacy identifies with clients who are subjects of domination."

5. You must have power in order to change existing organizations and institutions. Otherwise, large systems are very resistant to change. Change takes effort and work. Systems tend to cling to the stable state they're used to, whether or not that state is effective. Thus, it is necessary for the advocate to have access to sufficient power to influence the outcome of an intervention. Later in this chapter we will discuss ways in which workers can garner power to enhance their advocacy efforts.

Assumptions about Organizations

We've established that advocacy involves thinking about and manipulating power. Advocacy also entails working with organizations and their policies. Understanding organizations can help us to target them and their policies more effectively. Within the advocacy context, we have four major assumptions about organizations:

1. There are many reasons why organizations and institutions fail to meet client needs. Sometimes the system does not see a reason to respond to a need or even acknowledge that there is one (McMahon, 1990, p. 338). Often, agencies and organizations serve their own needs, not their clients' needs (McGowan, 1987, p. 89). Organizations may be experiencing a budget crisis. A top administrator may be more concerned about his own reputation than about serving clients' needs. Or

caseloads may be so great that clients can't be served adequately.

2. Agencies and organizations *do* have potential to change. Advocacy grows out of a philosophy that people have rights to social services and benefits provided by organizations. This is similar to how people are entitled to education or city streets, which are paid for by tax dollars contributed by all citizens. Checkoway (1987, pp. 335–36) notes that advocacy assumes "that existing institutions are capable of serving interests in society, that some interests mobilize more resources than others, and that practitioners can compensate for political imbalance by representing less powerful interests." To put it differently, the social worker believes that agencies and organizations can change or be changed to meet client needs. Influencing the organization to change requires that the worker mobilize resources on behalf of those who are less powerful. Of course, doing this is not often a simple task.

3. Many agency leaders would prefer that workers not advocate for changes in their organization. Agency board members and administrators usually find that it is easier to maintain the status quo if you don't have people urging you to change or expand services and resources. Therefore, attempts at change may be met with resistance. For example, the workers in a county human services agency wanted to provide each AFDC recipient with a booklet describing their rights and the benefits to which they were legally entitled. The booklets, developed by a client advocacy group, contained factually correct information that encouraged clients to get the benefits they needed. A request to include these booklets in the regular monthly mailing of benefit checks was denied by the agency administrator.

The administrator feared that clients might begin to assert rights that the agency was unwilling to recognize, which would invariably cost the agency more money. This increase, in turn, would raise the wrath of the county board. The administrator wanted to avoid this scenario at all costs. He adamantly refused to have anyone think he supported giving benefits to clients, other than those the agency was forced to provide.

4. Not only can agencies refuse to be helpful, but they may also subvert the rules or try to be secretive. As Austin, Kopp, and Smith (1986) point out, advocacy is needed because of the "attitude of human service agencies and institutions" (pp. 119–20). Agencies and organizations can deny clients services. Additionally, they can fail to follow rules or hide how their workers and supervisors are really performing. Similarly, they can keep clients ignorant of their rights. Sometimes the clients are too discouraged or powerless to stand up for themselves. Sometimes clients receive inappropriate treatment or mistreatment by the very agencies charged with responsibility to help them. Ultimately, the social worker must understand the dynamics of organizations and institutions. That understanding will be helpful at the point of assessing and planning for an intervention.

Assumptions about Clients

One of the most important assumptions about clients is derived from the social work conceptualization of the client in the environment. In this model, *clients are never seen as existing separate from their environment.* That is, clients both influence and are influenced by their environment. Whatever problems exist do so because of the dynamic interaction between the two.

In the past the emphasis was on how people deserved what they got. When applied to clients, this meant that the clients' problems were their own fault. We now can refer to this approach as "blaming the victim" and see that it's often the environment and how that environment influences clients that are really to blame for problems.

The second assumption concerning advocacy is that *clients should be helped to help themselves.* This means that workers should not act as advocates for clients when they can advocate for themselves. People tend to become dependent when we do things for them that they can do without us. Often, we can help people be advocates for themselves by teaching them to be assertive and modeling this ourselves.

A third assumption of advocacy is that it *should never be carried out without the full knowledge and consent of the client.* We will discuss the reasons for this caveat in the section on assessment of advocacy situations.

Knowledge Required by Advocates

Workers acting as advocates need to know many things. They need to know the *rights of clients* and the *avenues of redress (appeal)* available to clients. They also must know the *resources that can be mobilized* on behalf of the client. Finally, they must master *strategies and tactics* that are most likely to be effective.

Knowing the Rights of Clients

The effective client advocate needs to know the right of clients and their entitlements. "Rights are those protections and guarantees to which people or society have a just claim and cannot, in American society, be denied without due process of law" (Brill, 1990, p. 230).

There are two types of rights, *individual rights* and *societal rights.* Individual rights are those that you as an individual are guaranteed. Examples include the right to an education and freedom of speech. Societal rights, on the other hand, are the collective rights of the people as a whole that are considered more important than individual rights. For instance, you as a member of society have the right not to be murdered by another individual.

Sometimes individual and societal rights are in conflict. For example, it is possible for you to own land along a river and use that land as you see fit (individual rights). The river itself, however, cannot be modified by the landowner. You cannot forbid people to use the river, nor can you alter the river bank without permission (societal rights).

Another example of rights in conflict involves freedom of speech (an individual right). Saying whatever you want, however, does not allow you to shout "fire" in a theater when there really is no fire. Such exercising of freedom would threaten the safety of others (a societal right).

As you can see, there are limits even to the most basic rights we have as citizens. It is important to understand both the rights and the limitations of those rights. In view of societal rights, we cannot make unreasonable or illegal demands on agencies no matter how much clients want us to pursue their individual rights (Austin, Kopp & Smith, 1986, p. 121).

Avenues of Appeal

Challenging the actions of agency administrators or employees requires a thorough knowledge of the avenues of redress or appeal open to the client. For example, consider a decision that has been made by a line worker in the agency. To whom can this decision be appealed? Is the worker's supervisor the next step in the chain of command? Does the agency have an ombudsman (an individual designated to investigate charges and complaints) to whom complaints can be directed? Does the law provide for a fair hearing process in which clients can appeal decisions with which they do not agree?

Entitlements are "services, goods, or money due to an individual by virtue of a specific status" (Barker, 1987, p. 49). The nature of the entitlement may dictate the avenues of appeal available. Entitlements may be thought of as falling into three categories: those established by law, those based on organizational policy, and those based upon an interpretation of organizational policy (Connaway & Gentry, 1988, p. 80).

Knowing the source of the entitlement may help us decide what form our advocacy will take. For example, most entitlements guaranteed by law have specific appeal procedures built into the law. Agencies may or may not have identified appeal procedures for those who disagree with agency policy.

Frequently, appeal procedures appear in agency handbooks or regulations. Whenever possible, the established appeal procedures should be followed before considering other options. If you and the client have not exhausted the appeal system it is very easy for the agency to brush off your complaint. The agency can always say you have not followed proper procedures. This is why it is important to know specifically how to appeal different kinds of decisions.

Available Resources

Often social workers will seek the help of other resources in carrying out the role of advocate. Resources include both people and agencies/organizations that may help you and the client. One of the most important resources is assistance with legal questions. While it may not be possible to know everything about every client's rights, it is possible and advisable to have

access to those who do. Attorneys are important sources of information about certain kinds of rights such as those written into existing laws or guaranteed by the Constitution.

In addition, some organizations work actively to protect the rights of the individual citizen. For example, the American Civil Liberties Union exists to help ensure that individual rights are not abridged or limited, particularly by those elements of our society that are the most powerful (government and business). This organization may prove helpful to workers unsure about legal rights of a client.

Legal Aid is another organization providing pro bono (free) legal services. Sometimes the worker will know an attorney who will provide free service or help at nominal cost. Perhaps an organization like the Alliance for the Mentally Ill will be available to help. In the assessment section of this chapter, we will discuss other possible resources.

Tactics and Strategies of Intervention

The worker will need to be familiar with a variety of techniques and approaches useful in advocacy situations. Some of these strategies and tactics resemble those involved in other social work roles. Others are unique to the role of advocate. Much of the remainder of this chapter will be devoted to discussing strategies and tactics.

The successful advocate requires two types of skills. Required first are the generalist practice skills useful in virtually any type of intervention. These include skills in "interviewing, listening, observing, being empathic, supportive, confrontive . . ." (Hutchison, 1989, p. 409). The advocate also needs to understand group process—resistance to change, decision making in groups, nonverbal communication, and both formal and informal structures and procedures. It is also likely the advocate will need to know how to gather and present data.

476 ■ CHAPTER FOURTEEN

The second category of skills required by advocates includes those needed specifically for particular situations. For example, political or legislative advocacy requires skills somewhat different from those needed in advocating for an individual client. We will discuss these skills later in this chapter.

Assessment in Advocacy Situations

As in any assessment, there are several considerations you as an advocate need to take into account. On the one hand, examining your own position and potential ability to advocate is very important. On the other hand, you need to assess aspects of the potential advocacy situation outside yourself. These include the clients' resources and strengths, and characteristics of the adversary (that is, the person, organization, agency or policy that needs to change), and the resources, strategies and tactics available to cause change.

Self-Assessment

One of the first questions to address is the source of the advocate's sanction. In other words, who or what gives you the right to advocate? Does your job description include serving as an advocate for clients? Does the sanction come from the clients' clearly stated legal rights that are not being observed? Perhaps the primary source of sanction is the ethics of the social work profession as described in the *NASW Code of Ethics* (McGowan, 1987).

There are many barriers to successful advocacy. These include internal agency policies and external obstacles. For example, sometimes you will experience a lack of support from colleagues and superiors. Placing client interests above those of your own agency may cause conflict with peers and others (Mailick & Ashley, 1989, p. 626). The combination of barriers can make your job stressful. Workers must realistically assess their own vulnerability. What risks exist in serving as an advocate? Are the risks minor or great? What is the source of the risk? What means exist to counter the risk? Are the likely gains worth the risk? Do the tactics considered increase or decrease the risk?

Another factor is the ability of the worker to devote the necessary time to the change effort. Advocacy often takes more time because problems are more intractable (difficult to solve).

In addition, workers must deal with their own discomfort about being advocates. When dealing with people in power, the worker is in the uncomfortable position of asking for help instead of giving it. Often, the people targeted for change by the advocate have great experience in avoiding the issue. Because such people are frustrating to deal with, the worker may have to risk appearing aggressive or antagonistic to get anything done (Kadushin, 1990). The worker should be aware of this possibility and be prepared for it.

What Are Your Sources of Power?

What sources and kinds of power do you as an advocate have available to cause change? There are several different types of power according to French and Raven (1968). *Legitimate power* exists when person A believes person B has the "right" to influence him or her. The right often derives from a person's authority based on his or her position in an organization. For example, supervisors usually are perceived as having a legitimate right to direct the behavior of subordinates. Similarly, we usually step on the brake and pull over when we notice the police car with flashing red and blue lights in our rear view mirror. This action rests on our perception that the police have a legitimate right to direct us to stop (although we may argue with the officer for doing so).

Reward power is the ability to provide positive reinforcement to another person. Examples of rewards are salary increases, praise, promotions, and other things perceived by the receiver to be beneficial. Reward power may be lodged in any number of persons (for instance, parents, spouses, employers, friends).

Coercive power is the ability of someone to punish or otherwise use negative reinforcement on another individual. Here there is the real or potential threat that something bad will happen or something good will be taken away if you don't cooperate. In addition to their legitimate power, police officers have a certain amount of coercive power they can employ. The threat of a speeding ticket is supposed to coerce you to obey the speed limit.

What is experienced as coercive depends a great deal on the person being coerced. Because individuals vary so greatly, something considered coercive or unpleasant by one person may not be seen as bad by another. For example, sitting in a smoke-filled bar with extremely loud music playing might be a delight to one person and a noxious nightmare to another.

Referent power exists when one person allows himself or herself to be influenced by another person because of admiration for that individual. If you look up to someone, admire their values or ideas, or otherwise would like to emulate that person, you have accorded them referent power. Conversely, someone you find repulsive or unpleasant is not likely to have any referent power over you.

The final type of power is *expert power*. Expert power is available to those we consider to be an authority or especially proficient expert in some area. We generally accord physicians expert authority because we believe they know more than we do about the field of medicine.

Not infrequently, multiple sources of power exist in the same person or organization. For example, job supervisors may have legitimate power, coercive power, and reward power. Ideally the advocate should attempt to marshall as many types of power as possible. If the adver-

sary is vulnerable because he has broken the law, it's possible to use legitimate power to cause change. You may recall the case of the landlord who refused to fix up his slum apartments in violation of city law. Remember also in this case that tenants contacted the news media, which held the landlord up to public condemnation and ridicule, a coercive form of power.

Other Assessment Considerations

Three dimensions are important in assessment when contemplating advocacy. First is the nature of the problem situation. The second concerns the strengths, rights, and resources of the client. The third entails the characteristics of the adversary.

What Is the Nature of the Problem Situation?

Before beginning to advocate, you certainly need to understand the nature of the problem situation itself. For example, will the intervention take place at the level of the decision maker or does it require change in agency policy, administrative procedures or regulations, or social policy? Is the problem occurring because the client has a special need that is not being addressed? Or is it because there is a bad relationship between the target system and the client?

You will remember that the target system is "the individual, group, or community to be changed or influenced to achieve the social work goals" (Barker, 1987, p. 163). Is there a deficiency of some sort in the target system (either structural or in personnel)? Does the problem lie in dysfunctional social or agency policy (McGowan, 1987, p. 92)? Is the target system a worker, administrator, policy maker, or legislator who is not functioning the way you think she or he should? Is the target system external to, or part of, the worker's own agency? What types of relationships exist between the advocate and the target system? The answers to these questions suggest different strategies and tactics.

It is also important to keep an open mind about the situation and the target system, at least at first. For example, don't automatically presume that people or groups acting as barriers are malicious, deliberate, or mean-spirited. Often target system actions may be inadvertent or result from different perceptions of the situation. Initially assuming the worst may create a self-fulfilling prophesy. Highlight 14.2 shows an example of a problem in which several alternative hypotheses are possible.

Sometimes problems occur because of staff ignorance of client cultural values and beliefs or because the staff has not taken enough time to develop rapport with clients. Perhaps the client has not understood the necessity for certain information or misunderstood what was asked. Even the application forms clients must complete for specific entitlement programs (e.g., AFDC) may cause problems. Questions may be vague or call for answers the client does not

---

HIGHLIGHT 14.2
When the System Isn't Working

Nathan Washington and Ramon Vallejo owned a duplex together in the mid-sized college town of Fort Druid. They had lived there for almost seventeen years and were happy in their quiet, residential neighborhood.

One morning they were suddenly awakened by the eager "rap, rap, rap" of pounding hammers coming from the house immediately next door. The noise annoyed them. However, this was nothing compared to their annoyance and displeasure when they found the structure was being converted to tiny units of expensive student housing. They were infuriated. All they could envision was loud, pulsing music in wee morning hours and cases of empty beer cans strewn around the yard. Neither Nathan nor Ramon had been notified about this pending change.

It so happened that the city ordinance in Fort Druid is very clear regarding such structural changes. Any time there is a major change proposed in the use of a building or in its structure, residents within three hundred feet are to be notified. The city is required to send a letter describing the proposed action. For example, a request by a property owner to convert a single family home into an apartment must have the approval of the city planning commission. The commission must hold an open hearing (a meeting where anyone who wishes to come and speak can do so) and allow neighbors to present their views. The ordinance calls for notification of neighbors because changes in their neighborhood can have economic and quality of life significance for them.

If you were advocating on the behalf of Nathan and Ramon, three issues would confront you. First, it is possible the owners of the house had not obeyed the law, by seeking permission to modify their building. Second, if they had sought proper approval, the failure to notify residents as required by law may make the actions of the planning commission illegal. Therefore, their approval of the house conversion may be invalid.

Third, there is the question of why the problem occurred in the first place. Were the neighbors not notified because the required open meeting had never been held? Or had they failed to read the notice when it was mailed to their home? Was it a mistake by an individual staff person in city hall who simply forgot to mail the notices? Was it an attempt to keep the neighbors from exercising their legal rights to present their objections to the planning commission? Were the notices lost in the mail?

What actions an advocate might take are clearly dependent on the problem's cause. Assessment is critical to identify these numerous potential causes, explore their substance, and target the one that appears to be real.

have. One can wonder whether the use of confusing application forms exists to discourage clients from applying for help or simply reflects an agency's lack of sensitivity to clients.

Before advocating, you need to address a number of questions. First, is the goal to acquire new resources or improve existing ones, or reduce client system involvement with a dysfunctional system or policy (McGowan, 1987, p. 91)? How long has the problem existed? How serious is it? How many people are affected by it? Is there any history of advocacy efforts that would add information to the current assessment? If past efforts failed, what were the reasons for these failures? Has anything changed that would make the decision to advocate more likely to succeed?

The answers to all of these questions should lead you to believe you can influence the decision maker. Your assessment should convince that you can persuade or coerce the target system into acting as you wish. Otherwise, you are probably wasting your time and should consider other intervention options (Sosin & Caulum, 1989).

Assessing the Client

Clients must be closely involved in the decision to select advocacy strategies. *You need to assess their motivation to participate and their ability to do so.* There are at least five reasons for this. First, the chance for success is greatest if clients participate in planning the intervention. Second, clients are more likely to use and value resources they had a hand in developing. Third, resources are more likely to be appropriate when clients have helped develop or create them. Fourth, clients gain an important sense of efficacy (being effective) when they participate in actions designed to reach their goals. Fifth, working with others helps produce a sense of participation and involvement that may be important for clients lacking self-esteem and a support network.

You might ask yourself a number of questions. For instance, how important is the issue to the client? Is it an emergency or less pressing? Does the client have any ability to compromise, or is the issue too basic? Will this effort produce any problems for the client further down the line (Connaway & Gentry, 1988)? What resources does the client have (e.g., verbal skills, determination, leadership ability, social skills, intelligence)? Does the client have any other sources of power?

The answers to such questions will help us plan more carefully and wisely. For example, we can decide how quickly we need to act. We will also know whether compromises are possible, and what role may be played by the client.

Assessing the Adversary

It is critical to understand the adversary or target system well. "What are the power system's structure, channels, lines of authority, processes, rules of procedure? How are decisions made" (McMahon, 1990, p. 340)? What are the adversaries like? What do we know about their jobs, their titles, motivation, and capabilities?

Perhaps the first question to address is *how open to change is the adversary or target system?* Additionally, to what degree do you and the target system share the same views about client needs? We must know whether the target system (adversary) will be receptive to change. The target may be resistant, sympathetic, or indifferent to our efforts. Receptivity may be a function of the type of objective pursued. For example, if the objective is to increase access to already existing resources the target system might be more open to change. If, on the other hand, you're seeking changes in the basic policies or procedures of an agency, there may be less receptivity (and more resistance) to change (Brown, 1991).

We also want to know the *degree of vulnerability of the adversary.* Is the person violating agency policy (which is somewhat minor) or violating a law (which is much more serious)? Is the action taken permitted within the discretion normally granted the decision maker or has the person exceeded his or her authority?

Knowing *how this adversary handled complaints or challenges in the past* may be important. For example, does the person respond best to face-to-face meetings or are all decisions made by reviewing written materials (Connaway & Gentry, 1988)? Does the person usually make quick decisions or does she or he typically need time to think about requests?

Finally, it would be helpful to know the *values of the adversary*. What are the person's goals? Is this person likely to be more sympathetic to the client's viewpoint or to the worker's? Substantial differences in values and goals decrease the probability of quick solutions. The greater the divergence between values and goals of the client and adversary, the more power is required to change the situation. Determining the availability and potency of power is an important part of the assessment process.

Planning in Advocacy Situations

Planning in advocacy situations requires considering the knowledge gained from the assessment steps identified above and selecting the most appropriate interventions. The first step in planning is to consider the resources, strategies, and tactics that you will employ to bring about change.

Resources may include money, power, prestige, authority, commitment, and any other means we can muster to help reach our goal. You as an advocate, your client, or some aspect of the environment may be tapped for resources. Outcomes depend partly on the resources of the change agent and the receptivity of the target system. The most effective advocates use this information and adopt a variety of resources and techniques. Especially useful are communication skills (McGowan, 1974, p. 93).

Strategy concerns broad issues and your plan for approaching advocacy. For example, a strategy might entail the amount of conflict you plan to use in an advocacy effort. What strategies make the most sense given the available resources? McGown (1984) found that the choice of strategy depended on the problem, objective, sanction, change agent system and target system.

Tactics focus on the specifics of your plan such as how conflict is used and when (Sosin & Caulum, 1989, p. 539). For example, it might be important to confront the adversary immediately with an overwhelming show of support for your ideas. Remember the case mentioned in chapter 4 where the city council was intent on supporting a bypass highway around the city. By quickly confronting the city council with a petition signed by almost every business owner on the highway, the proposed bypass was rejected immediately.

One of the most important factors in the decision to advocate is the resources available to use in the intervention effort. Are there others who will join in to work on the problem? From whom can you expect support and opposition? Do you have some influence with the decision maker? Is some amount of money or power available to you?

The Ultimate Decision

Ultimately, the social worker must make a decision about when and when not to advocate. This decision is sometimes difficult. Fruitless efforts to change target systems are demoralizing to clients and workers. When the assessment phase points to the eventual failure of the intervention it is better to stop before committing further resources to the endeavor. In the words of the song, "The Gambler," sung by Kenny Rogers:

> You have to know when to hold 'em,
> know when to fold 'em,

know when to walk away,
know when to run.

Intervention: Advocacy Strategies and Tactics

Following assessment and planning, the worker and client must decide the appropriate strategy and tactics to use for a given advocacy situation. In this section we will look closely at the techniques that advocates often employ. They in-clude persuasion, fair hearings and legal appeals, political and community pressure, using the media, and petitioning. Some of these were discussed in chapter 4 and will only be addressed briefly here.

Persuasion

Persuading others to take certain actions can be simple or extremely difficult. It depends on several factors, including the nature of the

---

HIGHLIGHT 14.3

Guidelines for Advocacy

The following guidelines for advocacy are useful as a starting point in any attempt to serve as a client's advocate.

1. Be certain that your client wants you to serve as an advocate. Client's rights must be observed. Client self-determination is very important in advocacy situations.
2. Recognize that advocacy can be damaging to your relationships with other people. Also be aware that advocacy can affect your agency's relationship with other agencies.
3. Engage in advocacy only to help the client. Your motive to advocate should not be dislike of the adversary nor anything in your own personal agenda.
4. Be sure you have clear and accurate facts before confronting the adversary or others. Being wrong about facts, dates, or actions, can ruin your credibility and destroy your effectiveness as an advocate. Double check everything.
5. Prepare for your session with the target system by listing your concerns and your questions. Be clear about your complaint and about what you are requesting for your client.
6. Use interpersonal skills and empathy to understand the position of the target system. People you talk to will probably respond better if they feel you understand their own situation or position. Listen patiently to the opposing side. Treat your adversaries with respect and acceptance. Advocates should appear neither subservient nor unduly abrasive. This approach is consistent with other tenets of practice. It will help keep problematic matters from escalating or becoming more heated. Eventually, it will reduce the stress of all participants. Having a clear agenda, knowing the adversary, and showing interest in both increases the likelihood that you'll be effective; similarly, outcomes will probably be more satisfactory to both parties (Kadushin, 1990).
7. During your meetings with target systems write down the answers you are given and compare them with those provided by others.
8. If you are not successful in achieving your goal, find out who can overturn the decision. For example, can a supervisor, another administrator, or a board overrule the target system's decision. Indicate clearly to the target system that you intend to pursue this avenue.
9. Carefully document all appeals by recording exact details such as dates, times, and actions.

Source: Adapted from Bradford W. Sheafor, Charles R. Horejsi and Gloria A. Horejsi, *Techniques and Guidelines for Social Work Practice*, second edition. Copyright © 1991 by Allyn and Bacon. Reprinted with Permission.

problem, the degree of resistance experienced, the client's wishes, and the capabilities of the worker. Let's consider these factors.

Since advocacy work usually involves challenging the status quo, resistance will occur. We often select a strategy based on our perception of how difficult it will be to influence the adversary. Adversaries who share your views will probably require little persuasion. You may then need only to define the issue clearly and present your evidence that a problem exists which the adversary can resolve. In other words, persuasion is more likely to work when the target system understands the client's needs and values, accepts the worker's perspective, and shares the values of the worker (Toseland & Rivas, 1984). In these cases, collaborative strategies are possible and recommended. Collaborative strategies are synergistic. That is, working together gets more accomplished with less effort than people working alone. Collaboration involves giving and clarifying information. In a sense, advocates then can educate their adversaries. Joint problem solving is possible and both parties can begin working together on a solution.

Persuading the person usually entails four steps. First, clearly state the problem. Second, allow adequate time for discussion and answering questions. Third, identify exactly what needs to be done. Fourth, periodically summarize areas of agreement.

Austin et al. (1986, pp. 125–27) suggest several approaches to persuading adversaries.

1. Attempt to find a "common ground" between client and adversary. In other words, try to find some area where both parties are in agreement or have similar interests.
2. Be forthright and clear about what you think and want. It helps no one if you are vague or unclear about your request. State your position clearly.
3. Be candid about what you are going to

do if the problem is not remedied. Be aware that this conflictual approach will not always be successful.
4. "Be sincere and speak with conviction."
5. "Look the person in the eye." Eye contact is just as important in advocacy as in micro practice situations.
6. "Avoid negative appeals" that suggest the adversary is not interested in what you have to say. Assume they have as much interest in resolving this matter as you and the client.
7. Be careful not to filibuster or monopolize the conversation. Let the other person have a chance to speak. Listen empathetically.
8. "Control your emotions." Avoid showing "anger or irritation." People who blow up emotionally lose power during these encounters.[1]

In other situations we may choose different tactics. For example, we may try to negotiate with the adversary, bargaining or offering compromises to achieve as much of our goal as possible. This posture assumes, of course, that the matter of concern is one where compromise is possible and is sanctioned (supported) by the client.

When Persuasion Doesn't Work

Sometimes you may need to consider using confrontation and more conflictual approaches. These are usually used when the advocate has little influence over the decision maker (Sosin & Caulum, 1989, p. 536). This lack of influence suggests the need to take more drastic steps. Confrontal approaches involve three dimensions. First, you can *threaten* to disclose the ad-

---

1. From *Delivering Human Services: A Self-Instructional Approach*, 2nd ed., by Michael J. Austin, Judith Kopp, and Philip L. Smith, pp.125–27. Copyright © 1986 by Longman Publishing Group.

versary's failure to follow law or policy. Second, you can *actually disclose* the information, and allow the natural consequences to occur. Finally, you can appeal through *administrative hearings or the courts.*

The latter option is not employed routinely because of the cost involved. It may be appropriate only when other alternatives fail. Administrative appeals occur much more frequently because they are often the only way to cause changes in rules and regulations or decisions based on those rules and regulations.

Fair Hearings and Legal Appeals

Once you decide to use a conflictual strategy, choose your tactics carefully. Take, for example, the case where the adversary has improperly denied the client entitlements or other benefits in violation of standard rules and procedures. The tactic of choice may be filing a grievance. Sometimes called "fair hearings," such procedures exist to protect client rights.

Normally the clients notify agencies that they wish to have a fair hearing concerning the adversary's decision. This means that an outside person (usually a state employee) will be appointed to hear both sides of the argument. The fair hearing examiner may find the adversary has violated state or federal policies. Then the examiner may direct the adversary to comply with the rules and award the client his or her rightful benefits. Sometimes just the threat of using the formal appeal process will be enough to change an adversary's earlier decision. Other times the agency may have no policy for a fair hearing or appeal and other confrontational tactics can be employed. For example, it is often possible to seek advice and assistance from an attorney. Not infrequently, an attorney's letter presenting the possibility of legal action is sufficient to cause adversaries to change their position.

Political and Community Pressure

Consider the case discussed earlier regarding finding housing for a Hmong client. There a worker used an elected official (a city council member) to pressure a city agency to act in a responsive and timely fashion. Many political figures proudly tell their constituents of their efforts to combat bureaucracies at all levels on their constituents' behalf. For example, most members of the U.S. House of Representatives and Senate provide such help to constituents. The latter usually have expressed unhappiness about decisions or lack of action taken by the Social Security Administration and other federal agencies.

In other situations, pressure may be brought through community groups such as the Alliance for the Mentally Ill. Advocacy organizations exist to work for their membership. They often will intervene to help their members cope with uncooperative systems. Organizational pressures of this type depend, of course, on the existence and availability of such supportive associations.

Using the Media

Advocates may be able to use the media as a confrontive tactic to cause change. For example, some television stations conduct public service programs that respond to viewers' written complaints about agencies or organizations. A reporter will investigate the situation and discuss it on the evening news. Often this type of pressure will result in a favorable change for the client.

It should be noted that the problem does not have to involve a government bureaucracy. Clients who have received unsatisfactory responses from businesses have used these television programs to publicize their complaints.

Advocates can also use the media to publicize wrong doing. This, you may recall, was the tactic used by the apartment residents to embarrass the landlord. The landlord was unresponsive to both his own tenants and to the city's feeble enforcement efforts until the television stations reported the situation on the evening news. Chapter 4 has a more detailed discussion on using the media.

Petitioning

Another tactic you can employ as an advocate involves circulating petitions. We discussed this approach earlier in chapter 4. Petitions can be effective. However, many people will sign petitions without real commitment to the cause. Because signatures on petitions are generally easy to get, many officials discount their importance. Therefore, you should carefully consider their potential effectiveness before using them.

Selecting a Strategy for Advocacy

Sosin and Caulum (1989, p. 537) suggest that the advocate select the "strategy of least contest." This means that you should choose the approach requiring minimum effort and stress to achieve your desired goals. Their advice suggests that *nonconfrontal approaches should be used before confrontal ones*. For example, collaborative strategies should be applied before confrontive ones, if possible. Confrontation can be very wearing on you. It can siphon your energy away from your other job tasks.

A rule of thumb is to consider three conditions before deciding to exert pressure and cause a confrontation (Austin et al., 1986, p. 127). These include:

1. You've already tried less confrontational ways of instituting change. For example, you've tried to persuade your adversary. Nothing you've tried has worked.

2. You have enough proof that clients have been treated unfairly. You are absolutely certain that your grievance is consequential.
3. You determine that you have a good chance at succeeding by exerting pressure and initiating a confrontation. You don't want to waste your energy if the cause is hopeless.

Practitioners should determine if circulating petitions will be an effective means of creating political pressure in their community.

Whistle Blowing

Barker (1991, p. 250) defines whistle blowing as "alerting those in positions of higher authority in an organization about the existence of practices that are illegal, wasteful, dangerous, or otherwise contrary to the organization's stated policies." Some organizations such as the federal government provide means for whistle blowing to occur while maintaining the anonymity of the person reporting the problem. There are even laws designed to protect the whistle blower from retaliation of supervisory and administrative personnel whose positions are threatened by the revelations. These laws notwithstanding, whistle blowing carries a degree of risk that varies in direct proportion to the seriousness of the allegations. Whistle blowers have been fired, have been reassigned to insignificant responsibilities at remote locations, and have been harassed into quitting.

The purpose for providing this caveat is not to discourage social workers from advocating for clients with their own agencies or with others who are not acting in an appropriate manner. Rather, it is to assure that the decision to advocate is an informed one which has considered the risks involved.

Legislative Advocacy

Earlier in this chapter we discussed case advocacy and cause advocacy. In this section we will discuss a third type of advocacy called *legislative advocacy*. Legislative advocacy is similar to cause advocacy, in that the social worker is working for a broad category of clients or citizens. Legislative advocacy specifically entails efforts to change legislation to benefit some category of clients. In other words, it involves trying to get lawmakers to pass the laws you want.

Legislative advocacy also may embody efforts to defeat bills considered harmful in some way (Dear & Patti, 1987). For example, a pro-posed reduction in funding for the Headstart program would mean limiting or cutting off Headstart services previously available to clients. Headstart is a "federal program established in 1965 to provide preschool children of disadvantaged minority families with compensatory education to offset some of the effects of their social deprivation." (Barker, 1987, p. 69).

Another example of harmful legislation is a proposed bill to restrict access to reproductive health services such as Planned Parenthood. This agency provides information, contraception, counseling, and physical examinations, all directed at helping people (usually women) gain control over their own reproduction. Services are usually provided on a sliding fee scale. This means that fees are based on how much people can pay. Poorer people pay less than richer people.

Legislation limiting access might incorporate requirements such as forcing women under age eighteen to provide written parental permission before they can receive any services. Another inhibiting proposal might involve denying any state or federal funding if agency staff continue to discuss abortion as a possible alternative to unwanted pregnancy. Both of these examples limit available services. The first places restrictions on the basis of age. The second limits the potential for informing clients of the options available to them.

Responsibility for legislative advocacy is part of being a social worker. So many decisions affecting social work programs, social workers, and clients are made in the legislative arena that it is impossible *not* to be concerned about and involved in legislative advocacy.

Some social workers may feel a bit awed at the prospect of trying to get laws passed and programs funded. Fortunately, legislative advocacy has one unique feature that makes this effort less difficult than it seems. The primary rule of legislative advocacy is that getting elected and reelected is the most important activity of most legislators (Dear & Patti, 1987).

Consequently, this means that most legislators like to know what their constituents want and therefore are susceptible to their constituents' influence.

In addition, most legislators must make decisions about any particular proposed bill based on very limited information. Many bills are complex. This increases the likelihood that the legislator will need to depend on others for information. As a consequence, legislators may very well be influenced by a small number of advocates or by a particularly persuasive argument about a given bill. In other words, you are encouraged to tell your state and federal senators and representatives what you think should be done about bills and issues. You can also mobilize other workers or clients to write or call in what they think. This is one means of gaining at least some power over which laws are passed or defeated in the political process.

Simultaneously, there are realistic barriers that reduce the likelihood of getting new legislation passed. First, there is the fact that the majority of bills are not actually passed. Only about 20 percent of proposed bills eventually receive legislative approval and are signed by the governor or president to become law (Dear & Patti, 1981, p. 289). Moreover, most legislative sessions are somewhat short, lasting only a matter of months. The legislature might not even get to the bill you're interested in. This means that desired legislation may have to be reintroduced next year, which often involves starting the whole process of influence again from scratch.

Additionally, legislative bodies are unpredictable. Turnover in membership from session to session after elections, changes in control (for example, from Republican to Democratic leadership), economic news (for instance, lower than expected tax revenues resulting in less money available) make the entire legislative process more complicated. People in power also make unpredictable decisions that affect legislation. For example, in a recent race for governor, the incumbent ran for re-election based on his suc-

cess in increasing the economic growth and well-being of the state. He emphasized how well the state was doing financially because of his wonderful work and effort. Three weeks after winning the election, he announced that the state was experiencing a multi-million dollar shortfall in revenue because of economic conditions. In other words, the state had millions of dollars less than it had been expected to have. This required a freeze on hiring and a reduction in budgets for all state agencies including social services. As a result, many social workers who had supported that governor felt betrayed. Thus, the unpredictability of the legislative process means that the advocate must remain flexible and ready to change strategies as needed (Dear & Patti, 1987, p. 35).

Legislative advocates soon realize that a bill may not be passed just because it's a good bill. Patti and Dear (1975) note that even documented evidence strongly supporting a bill will not guarantee passage (p. 110). Other factors can easily defeat a bill. Economic conditions, political positions, lawmakers' personal values or life experiences, and legislative precedent may all override logic and compelling arguments. Besides, even when legislators support a bill it may be buried or defeated in a committee composed of a smaller group of legislators who evaluate the bill and prepare it for presentation to the entire legislature. Once on the floor of the legislature, a bill may be defeated or returned to committee. Finally, governors may veto bills for their own idiosyncratic reasons.

Factors Affecting Legislative Advocacy

Being successful as a legislative advocate requires that you understand some factors influencing whether or not a bill will be passed. For example, the fiscal (financial) consequences of a bill are extremely important to its chances for success. The cost of a proposed piece of legislation is perhaps the most important factor affecting its likelihood of becoming law. Logic might dictate that a bill's merit or usefulness is the most important aspect in making it pass, but this is not true in practice. Generally speaking, bills that ultimately require spending less money are more likely to pass.

The popularity of a bill also has some bearing on its potential success. The more popular a bill is, that is, the more support it has among constituents and legislators, the more likely it is to become law. Such bills are usually those that have very little impact on social change and require little or nothing from the public. In other words, bills which are popular and don't affect most people directly are more likely to pass. A bill to increase the penalty for selling drugs is a good example. It is likely to be popular with the general public because its impact will only be on a relatively small group of people, and it supports commonly held values about selling drugs.

Steps in Legislative Advocacy

There is a series of steps legislatures follow to pass new legislation; likewise there are coinciding steps a social worker can take to advocate for the passage of a new bill (Dear & Patti, 1981, p. 295). The steps for legislative advocacy include the following: developing a draft of the bill; figuring out who else will help you in support of the bill; getting specific legislators to sponsor the bill; asking your legislative sponsors to introduce the bill; educating the general public about the bill's worth and usefulness; trying to influence positively any legislative subcommittee members responsible for decision-making about the bill; and trying to influence other legislators who will be voting on the bill's passage.

Step 1: Developing and Revising the Draft Bill

Formulating an original piece of legislation can be a formidable task. It requires both knowl-edge of the law and familiarity with existing regulations, policies, and programs related to the proposed bill. Consequently, most proposals are sent to an already established unit (sometimes called a legislative reference bureau), which is responsible for writing the first draft of a bill. This body is usually an arm of the legislature. Its staff members often prepare a summary of the bill to help legislators understand its intent. Once in draft form, the bill needs to be refined. Often, clarifications and changes need to be made so that the bill reflects its supporters' intentions.

Step 2: Identifying, Obtaining and Maintaining the Bill's Supporters

Initially, it is important to identify those who are natural supporters of a bill. That is, who is naturally interested in the bill's topic or will obviously benefit from the bill. It is equally important to predict who will be neutral or opposed to a bill. If you hope to see this bill become law, you will need to know who is likely to dislike the bill. Knowing those who are initially neutral may give you a basis for later persuading them to support the bill. These people may include legislators, their staffs, external groups (for example, the National Association of Social Workers [NASW]), governmental agencies (for instance, the Department of Health and Social Services), and social service providers. It is important to iron out differences between factions supporting the bill. For example, it is common for people to support a bill for many different reasons. Each supporter may have ideas about how to improve the bill. One group may dislike a particular word or section in the bill. These differing perspectives must be reconciled if you are to reach an agreement on the final bill. It is important to keep supporters on board, and modifying the bill may be one cost of achieving this consensus.

It may be necessary to arrange face-to-face meetings and provide copies of the draft bill to potential allies and adversaries. This will allow these individuals a chance to explain their support (or opposition), and give you a chance to convince them to support the bill. This process also may result in changes in the bill as neutral or opposing groups come on board.

Attempt to get support from the governor and official state agencies affected by the bill. For example, a bill affecting who can be placed on probation would likely be of interest to the state bureau of corrections. State agencies are more likely to get bills they support through the legislature. Such agencies' opposition can be fatal to a bill. This is logical because state agencies are part of the arm of state government designed to administer bills passed by the legislature. Thus, they are considered to be experts on legislation affecting their respective areas of responsibility.

Step 3: Arrange for Sponsorship of the Bill

It is important to find legislators who are willing to introduce and work for a bill. Supporters who will do nothing to help a bill pass are not useful except to stay out of the way. If you are trying to get a bill passed, involve legislative staff members in discussions about the bill. Frequently, these staff (those who work for the legislator) have the greatest influence with the legislator. Making changes in the bill to gain their support can be especially important. For instance, they may be more likely to support a bill after you've made some compromises honoring their needs and wishes.

Past track records of legislators can be important as guides to how they will vote on any given bill. Have they supported similar bills in the past? Have they made public statements supporting the bill's intent? Or have they been critical of issues the bill addresses?

The "safety" of the legislator's seat also will be a factor. Those reelected by large margins or without opposition are often in stronger positions than legislators worrying that each vote may cost them the next election. Stronger positions may allow legislators to take greater risks.

For instance, they then may be more likely to support a bill that will require spending money if they believe in the merits of the bill.

Similarly, it is important to keep away from legislative extremists who will never compromise. Compromise is the currency of politics. Unwillingness to compromise on a bill is likely to lead to its defeat.

If possible, obtain support of legislators in the majority party. It's even better if you can gain support from members of both parties (bipartisan support). Obtain as many sponsors as possible for a bill because this will increase your support and the likelihood that the bill will pass.

Step 4: Introducing the Bill

Ask the legislative sponsors of your bill to introduce it before the legislative session or as early in the session as possible. This leaves more time for lobbying and modifying the bill to satisfy additional supporters. Bills introduced late in a session often do not become law because of time constraints. Lobbying involves seeking "direct access to lawmakers in order to influence legislation and public policy. The term originated in the tendency of some people to frequent the lobbies of legislative houses in order to meet lawmakers" (Barker, 1987, p. 90).

Step 5: Work with Interest Groups to Broaden Support for a Bill

Every bill has many potential supporters, some of whom never participate in the legislative process. Often potential supporters simply don't know that a bill has been introduced. Or they may not believe they can have much influence on the bill. Try to get as many potential supporters behind your bill as possible.

Step 6: Educate the Public

Educating the public is often difficult because frequently bills do not appear to be of interest to many people. One example of public education occurred in a state where NASW was attempting to pass a law for certifying social workers. Articles appeared in newspapers around the state describing situations where unethical social workers continued to practice without licensing. Social workers and others sent letters to, and wrote articles for, newspapers which stressed the importance of protecting the public from incompetent and unethical professionals. Such articles and letters served to educate the public about the issues and benefits of licensing social workers.

Step 7: Influence Legislative Committee Consideration

All bills introduced in a legislature are referred or assigned to one or more committees prior to being considered by the entire body. Legislatures thrive on committees. Committees are formed of smaller groups of legislators charged with analyzing, refining, and making recommendations about proposed legislation. Committees typically have jurisdiction over matters on a particular topic. So, for example, there may be a committee on agriculture, health and human services, another on judiciary and consumer affairs, and one on education, and so on. Legislators usually express an interest in serving on a particular committee. Committee appointments are normally made by the leadership of the respective legislative body. Thus, the Speaker of the House or the Senate President will have major influence over who gets on what committee.

In addition, subcommittees are formed within committees to investigate an even more narrowly defined area. For instance, the agriculture, health and human service committee mentioned above would probably have separate subcommittees on each of the three areas: agriculture, health, and human services.

Every bill must go through one or more committees or subcommittees. Committees can allow a bill to die by not acting on it and also can refuse to pass a bill that the sponsor won't agree to modify. Ultimately, if a bill is to go to the legislative body for a vote, it must have been approved by the respective committee to which it was assigned. Advocates must lobby committee members, ask for public hearings on a bill where a broad range of people can voice their views, and arrange for expert testimony at those hearings. Hearings increase the likelihood that a bill will pass and provide opportunities for further lobbying. They also offer chances to make compromises with opponents that will make the bill more satisfactory to a larger number of people.

Testimony at public hearings should be carefully planned to include who will speak, in what order, and what they will say. People who testify should provide a written copy of any testimony to the committee members before speaking. Not everyone who testifies needs to be an expert on a topic. The purpose of a hearing is to listen to all who wish to speak on the bill under consideration. Thus, both experts and interested parties are welcome to participate. There are a number of suggestions about how testimony should be structured and presented. These suggestions can apply to your own testimony or that of others you're helping to prepare for testimony.

First, the written statement should be able to stand on its own (that is, it should not need any additional verbal clarification). Additionally, it should be worded so that it's clear, straightforward, and readily understandable to any literate adult (Sharwell, 1982, p. 94). Jargon should be omitted. The statement should specifically explain why this law is important and what particular benefits it will have. Argue the case on its merits and never preach. Use factual material and cite its source (for example, census data, specific government studies or publications).

It is also permissible to use case examples

to illustrate the impact of a specific bill. However, use humor very carefully because it's important to be perceived as a serious professional person.

Avoid hostility and focus testimony on the proposed legislation. Be brief, show respect for committee members, and be ready to answer questions, including hostile ones. Finally, when you're finished thank the committee for the opportunity to speak.

Step 8: Influencing Action on the Floor

Bills may be amended or modified by legislators making motions from the floor. The advocate needs to anticipate this possibility and be ready to compromise in ways that won't destroy the bill. When a bill is on the legislative floor, only legislators can participate in what's done with it.

Outside of the actual legislative floor, you as a supporter can help by contracting uncommitted legislators and communicating your point of view. You can also help by seeking media coverage of the bill. Phone calls can be made to legislators within the forty-eight hours before voting commences. This time schedule helps ensure the legislator will remember the call when it is time to vote on the bill.

Keep track of supporters and opponents. Advocates for legislation should contact both those who support a bill and those who oppose it. All who will vote on the bill need to know constituents are supporting it. Lobbying cannot

---

┌ **HIGHLIGHT 14.4**
Writing Elected Officials

Social workers often have reason for writing to elected officials. It is important to use the correct form and address for such letters. Some common addresses and the accompanying salutation appear below.

Letters to the President
The President
The White House
1600 Pennsylvania Ave. NW
Washington, DC 20500

Salutation
Dear Mr./Ms. President:

Letters to U.S. Senators
The Honorable (insert full name)
United States Senate
Washington, DC 20510

Salutation
Dear Senator (insert last name):

Letters to members of the House of Representatives
The Honorable (insert full name)
U.S. House of Representatives
Washington, DC 20515

Salutation:
Dear Representative (insert last name):

Letters to Cabinet Secretaries:
The Honorable (insert full name)
Secretary of (insert name of Department)
Washington, DC (insert correct zip code)

Salutation
Dear Secretary (insert last name):

Note: Lists of your elected representatives can be acquired from the public library or by contacting your city hall. In addition, some states publish very detailed books listing all state officials. These may be found in your public library and often obtained for free from your state legislator.

be restricted to those already predisposed to the bill's passage.

Seek media coverage of the bill to reach and interest large numbers of constituents. You should plan to attend and be present for the debate on a bill. This will help you understand any opposition to the bill and you can then suggest to the legislator or his staff amendments or changes which might keep the bill on track. And when contacting legislators or the media you must be current regarding all the issues. Being present for the debate will help you in this regard.

It is important not to be discouraged by the amending process. Amended bills get through the legislature with much greater frequency than those without amendments.

Once a bill has received favorable action in one house of the legislature, the same eight steps are repeated in the other house. Generally, a bill may be introduced in either house first, although some constitutions require that certain types of bills must originate in one house or the other. The legislative process ends, hopefully, with the governor signing the bill into law.

One other aspect of legislative advocacy involves helping good legislators get elected. By "good" we mean people with values similar to our professional values. Helping a candidate win an election is an exhilarating experience. Because political campaigns require so many varied skills, it is always possible to find a role in a campaign. Possibilities include door-to-door campaigning; distributing flyers door-to-door

(called mail drops) or on campus; telephoning potential voters; soliciting or contributing money; transporting voters to the polls; putting up yard signs; placing a sign on your car; folding, stuffing, and sealing letters; and typing. The value of this work is clear. Elected officials remember who helped them and will be most sensitive to their helpers' views.

NASW founded PACE (Political Action for Candidate Election) to help elect candidates favorable to social work positions on issues. PACE is active in both national and state elections and provides financial support and other assistance to a wide range of campaigns. Becoming involved in PACE yourself gives you yet another way to become politically active.

Chapter Summary

This chapter discussed the topic of advocacy in depth. Defining advocacy and identifying its goals and targets was one specific focus. Assumptions about advocacy were explored including assumptions related to power, organizations, coercive strategies, and clients. Knowledge and skills needed by advocates were reviewed. The assessment process in advocacy was described, particularly as it affected the advocate, the client, the adversary, and advocacy strategies. Specific advocacy tactics were described. Finally, three types of advocacy including case, cause, and legislative advocacy were examined.

15 Brokering and Case Management

Connections

"Mary Ann Gibbons, please call the E.R." As she heard the hospital loudspeaker page her, Mary Ann tensed slightly. She knew that pages from the emergency room were always serious. Since she was already on first floor, Mary Ann walked briskly to the hospital's trauma center. The nurse on duty quickly explained the situation: Mr. B. Darwin arrived at the trauma center after suffering a heart attack on the interstate highway. Attempts to revive him failed and the emergency room physician was about to talk to his wife. The Darwins, both in their late sixties, had apparently been traveling through the state on the way to visit relatives.

Mary Ann accompanied the doctor to the trauma center waiting room where they met Mrs. Darwin. A petite woman, Mrs. Darwin looked very weary. The crumpled handkerchief in her hand was damp from tears. The doctor introduced herself and Mary Ann. Mary Ann then sat next to Mrs. Darwin.

"Is he dead?" Mrs. Darwin asked quietly. The doctor slowly nodded his head and responded, "Yes, he is."

Mrs. Darwin put her head in her hands and cried softly for a minute. She raised her head and asked, "What am I going to do now?"

Mary Ann said that she knew this must be a terrible time for Mrs. Darwin. She offered to do everything she could to help Mrs. Darwin and invited her to come to the social work office. As the doctor departed, Mary Ann reached out her hand and helped Mrs. Darwin to her feet. Together they took the elevator to Mary Ann's office.

Mary Ann again expressed her sensitivity to Mrs. Darwin's situation and asked her if there was anything that she (Mary Ann) could do. Slowly, Mrs. Darwin described the events of the day that preceded the death of her husband. In a few minutes Mary Ann discovered the following information:

The Darwins, who were residents of Wisconsin, were traveling through Minnesota to visit relatives in Iowa. They had car trouble about fifteen miles from the hospital. When Mr. Darwin got out to check on the car he fell to the ground. A passing trucker radioed a nearby highway patrol officer and together they attempted cardiopulmonary resuscitation. An ambulance arrived shortly and transported Mr. Darwin to the hospital. The highway patrol officer brought Mrs. Darwin to the hospital with their pet, a small dog. Mrs. Darwin said the car was still on the side of the highway and contained a large load of frozen meat in the trunk which was to be a gift to her daughter in Iowa. As they talked, Mary Ann began to make mental notes of the tasks ahead. She also learned some information about Mrs. Darwin that would prove helpful as they worked together to resolve the woman's concerns. Future tasks included:

CHAPTER FIFTEEN

1. Mrs. Darwin wanted to notify her daughter and son about the death of her husband.
2. Mrs. Darwin needed a place to stay for the evening (a place that would allow dogs).
3. The disabled car would have to be towed into town.
4. The frozen meat in the trunk would need to be cared for before it spoiled.
5. Mrs. Darwin would need to find transportation back to her home.
6. Mrs. Darwin would need to arrange the funeral and transportation of Mr. Darwin's body.

Mary Ann also tactfully asked whether this situation had created any critical financial problems for Mrs. Darwin. Did Mrs. Darwin have enough money to pay for lodging and meals? Could she depend on her daughter and son to be supportive in this time of grief? Did she know anyone in this area of the state?

Which of the problems/tasks above could Mrs. Darwin handle herself and which would need Mary Ann's intervention? As Mary Ann and Mrs. Darwin continued talking, the answers to each of these questions became clear. By the end of the day, each problem identified above, in addition to several others, had been resolved.

Introduction

Place yourself in Mary Ann's position. Would you know how to resolve each of these problems? In what order would you tackle them? Would you know what community resources might be appropriate to help Mrs. Darwin as she copes with this crisis? These are only a small sample of the many challenges facing a social worker. The ability to provide service to a client often requires knowing what resources are available. Brokering (connecting clients to appropriate resources) is the subject of the first portion of this chapter. With reference to brokering, this chapter will:

- Define brokering and explain the importance of the brokering role in generalist practice;
- Review some of the characteristics of an effective broker and the types of resources with which they must be familiar;
- Apply the problem solving process to the brokering role.

Case management is the focus of the second portion of the chapter. Case management goes beyond brokering and involves coordinating provision of a network of services. This chapter will also:

- Discuss the concept of case management and relate its usefulness to generalist practice;
- Apply the problem-solving process to case management with special emphasis on the intervention phase;
- Review factors influencing the delivery of case-management services;
- Discuss the effectiveness of case-management services.

A Definition of Brokering

Brokering is the linking of client systems to needed resources (Connaway & Gentry, 1988, p. 57). Such resources can target a broad range of client needs. Brokering might include helping a client get needed financial, legal, or medical assistance. It might involve helping a client find quality day care for children. Similarly, it might focus on helping to place a family member in a nursing home or a group home for developmentally disabled people.

By itself, the idea of brokering seems somewhat simple. A client has a particular problem and the worker tells the client about a resource that matches the client's problem. Of course, this is a great oversimplification of what really occurs in generalist social work practice. It is oversimplified because it assumes client needs can be met through existing services and resources. As discussed in earlier chapters, sometimes resources do not exist and must be created. These situations call for other social work roles including advocacy, a topic discussed earlier.

The role of the broker in social work has appeared in social work literature for at least fifty years (Hamilton, 1939). Social workers have long used directories of community resources to help clients. It has been taken for granted that social workers must know about community resources and services. The assumption has been that after assessing clients' needs, the worker then connects the client to available resources.

Importance of the Brokering Role in Generalist Practice

Sometimes a social worker's only role is that of broker. Other times the broker role is combined with other roles, depending on client need. For example, in addition to being a broker, the generalist social worker also might need to be an advocate for clients denied access to existing resources. For instance, a homeless person by definition has no address. A policy might require that an address is necessary in order for that person to receive financial aid. A worker might first have to advocate on the behalf of the client to change the policy before helping the client to actually receive the resources. We discussed the advocate role at greater length in chapter 14.

Additionally, the worker may play any of the roles described in previous chapters (for example, mediator or educator) either simultaneously or sequentially. Most simply, the generalist social worker plays the broker role by helping clients assess their needs and locating appropriate resources to meet those needs. Once a resource is *identified*, the worker connects the client to that resource through a *referral*. Finally, the worker evaluates with the client the effectiveness of the resource in meeting the client's needs. First, we'll discuss the importance of being familiar with various types of resources.

The Effective Broker

Becoming effective in the role of broker requires more than simply memorizing the names of available agencies. First, it requires knowledge of agency eligibility criteria (such as income or age limits). Second, it necessitates familiarity with many different kinds of resource systems (for example, emergency housing, food pantries, general assistance, Aid to Families with Dependent Children [AFDC]). Third, it requires that the worker develop a network of contact people to whom clients may be referred. In other words, you need to know specifically who to call. You must also know who can and will give your client the most help.

Maintaining familiarity with eligibility criteria is perhaps the most difficult of the tasks facing the worker because such criteria are constantly changing. New regulations, legislation, and evolving agency policies and procedures all affect eligibility criteria and complicate the job of the worker.

The Importance of Knowing Resources

A study of NASW members in Maryland (Rauch & Tivoli, 1989, p. 55) found that 52.8 percent did not know where to refer a person with a genetic concern. This involves situations in which couples or individuals fear the possibility of some inherited or other genetic defect in future offspring. Over 30 percent of workers did not even know if such a service existed within a thirty mile radius of the agency and forty-five percent did not know if genetic consultation was available to their agencies.

One of the most challenging aspects of beginning your professional life as a social worker is becoming familiar with the community or area in which you are practicing. Even social workers who grew up in a community may not know the myriad of agencies, services, and programs available in that area. The difficulty compounds if you have just moved and have little knowledge of your new community. New workers often develop their own resource lists which include information on each new agency or service they encounter. However, this method is not very systematic because the list contains only resources the new worker comes upon in a given period. We'll discuss more thoroughly this matter of identifying resources later in the chapter.

Eligibility Criteria of Resource Agencies

It is not realistic to believe that every social worker is going to become intimately familiar with all criteria for each program, agency, or resource available in a community. This would require an extraordinary memory for detail. Even if you could remember it all, the information would quickly become dated as criteria changed. It is appropriate, however, for you to become familiar with the broad categories of programs and to know generally the types of needs a program addresses.

For example, you might refer a family with no food to a free food pantry (operated by churches, hospitals, or other groups), the Salvation Army, or the local public assistance agency where the family could qualify for food stamps. Similarly, you might most appropriately refer a battered woman to a domestic-violence shelter. In each case, you need to know what types of resources are available and be able to discriminate which clients qualify for which programs.

Conversely, you must be capable of determining which resources are inappropriate. For instance, you wouldn't refer a sexual assault victim to a treatment group for sex offenders.

Because eligibility criteria do change, the worker will find it difficult to remain knowledgeable about specifics of each program. This problem can be alleviated somewhat by creating a homemade database. The database could be computerized, on alphabetized note cards, or any other system fitting your organizational style. The database should contain information such as types of problems for which referral is appropriate, names of contact persons, address and telephone numbers, and notes about eligibility criteria. For example, it is helpful to know that a given agency provides help only to those having incomes falling below a certain level. While this level may change periodically, at least you would know there is such a level and have some idea about where the cut-off line has been. Finally, if you have an ongoing system of agency contacts, you can simply call the likely agency contact person to figure out whether a client fits agency criteria.

Characteristics of the Resource Agency

Besides the criteria used by an agency in determining eligibility, you should be aware of a variety of agency characteristics (Connaway & Gentry, 1988). Such characteristics affect how well services will probably be delivered to your particular client. For example, is this an agency that is extremely formal and rule bound or does the agency have a flexible attitude toward solving client problems? What are the goals of the agency and the level of available resources? Does the agency provide assistance with fuel costs in the winter and, if so, what form does that assistance take? Will the food pantry allow a person to come every week or are there specified limits regarding the number of weeks food will be made available? How accessible is the building? Are ramps or elevators available to those with disabilities? Are there waiting periods before assistance can be given? Is there a long waiting list for certain kinds of service? What hours is the agency open? Is there any cost to the service and if so, how much? Is the service provided only seasonally (for example, at Christmas time)?

Such kinds of information can help the client and worker decide about the appropriateness of a given referral. It also can prevent clients from being referred to an agency that cannot meet their needs. When inappropriate referrals occur, clients may become discouraged and withdraw entirely from the helping process. Besides knowing the broad criteria and characteristics of various agencies, the worker should develop a network of contact persons within each agency. The reasons for this will be discussed in the next section.

Contact Persons in the Resource Agency

In larger communities, you can't be expected to learn the names of each person in every agency. We are, however, capable of remembering the names of an extraordinary number of people. It is not uncommon for a person to remember the names of well over one hundred people. If you doubt this, begin by writing down all the people in your family, nuclear and extended, add to the list all your friends, people in your class, faculty members, and teachers. Add university staff, doctors, dentists, store keepers, bartenders, etc. As you can see, the list gets longer and longer. With the names of agency contact people, the task is easier because you will be listing these people on your database of resource agencies.

When arriving in a new community it is helpful to spend some time visiting various agencies to become familiar with their programs and staff. It is especially important to learn the names of staff who handle intake since they may be the first person with whom your client will come in contact. Whenever you phone an agency make a point to jot down the name of the people you talked with and their areas of responsibility.

An advantage of having more than one contact person at an agency is that you can give a client other alternatives. This is helpful if the first person is not in when the client visits or calls the agency. Having alternative contacts increases the likelihood that the client will receive the desired service.

Finally, make a point to become involved in your community. Join a service club, participate in community meetings, sit in on city council meetings, or attend major community events (pancake day, fireman's chicken dinner, Fourth of July celebrations, etc.). These activities will increase your knowledge of community resources and enlarge the circle of people you can call upon in times of need. The smaller the community, the more important it is that you involve yourself in its life.

Types of Resources

The variety of resources in a community is almost limitless. One resource directory for three (mostly rural) Wisconsin counties turned up almost 400 different agencies (Hull & Zastrow, 1988). The challenge is to use the many available sources of information.

Community Resource Directories

Perhaps the most commonly used sources of information about community resources are published directories listing social or human services. These booklets are often put together by information and referral agencies, social service agencies, volunteer groups, or educational institutions. Ideally the directory should contain both an alphabetical index of agencies and services and a problem-focused index. You should not only be able to look up the agency's name, but also the type of problem you need to address. Highlight 15.1 shows a page from a single directory listing legal services, nursing homes, and nursing services. Under each topic is a list of specific agencies providing services that address these needs and the problems involved.

The listing for each agency in a directory should contain certain common items of information. These include the following:

- Name of the organization;
- Address and telephone number;

- Office hours;
- Executive Director or contact person;
- Services provided;
- Eligibility guidelines;
- Accessibility to the handicapped;
- Geographical boundaries of services;
- Source of funds.

Each directory should contain listings for various categories of services. These may in-

---

HIGHLIGHT 15.1

Community Resource Directory Index

Legal Services

Nursing Homes

Nursing Services

Source: Adapted from G. H. Hull and C. Zastrow, *Community Services Directory for Jefferson, Rock and Walworth Counties* (Whitewater, WI: University of Wisconsin-Whitewater, Department of Social Welfare, 1988).

HIGHLIGHT 15.2
Resource Directory Listing

Attorney General's Office
of Consumer Protection
123 W. Washington Avenue
Room 170
P.O. Box 7856
Madison, WI 53707
(608) 266-1852
(800) 362-8189 (toll free)

MILWAUKEE
819 N. 6th St.
Room 520
(414) 227-4949

Office Hours
Madison: 7:45 A.M.–4:45 P.M.
Milwaukee: 8:00 A.M.–5:00 P.M.

Services
Processes consumer complaints; enforces state consumer-fraud laws; may seek injunction to stop businesses or individuals from engaging in fraud and deception; may order businesses to pay restitution; uses computer data bank to analyze consumer problems; may enjoin public nuisance; provides consumer information/education materials upon request.

Serves
Wisconsin consumers

Accessibility to Handicapped
Office located on mezzanine; reach by stairs and elevators from West Washington Ave. entrance—*no stairs* from side entrance, Hamilton St.

Area Served
State of Wisconsin

Source of Funds
State tax supported

Beginnings Group Home
502 E. Holmes
P.O. Box 802
Janesville, WI 53547
(608) 756-4900

Office Hours
24 hours a day, 7 days a week

Director
Thomas Miles

Services
Individual and family counseling, crisis counseling, vocation exploration, instructive and corrective experiential living, educational planning, adventure-based recreation (Westbound Program), and behavior modification resident program

Serves
Status and delinquent youth between ages of thirteen to seventeen years.

Accessibility to Handicapped
Yes—ramp

Area Served
Rock County and surrounding counties

Sources of Funds
Rock County Department of Social Services and grants.

clude sources for emergency food, lodging, or clothing; financial help; and job and employment assistance. The directory should also list marital counseling or therapy; abortion and adoption agencies; services for categories of people such as the elderly, children, physically disabled, and chemically dependent; child-care services; correctional services; hospitals; educational and recreational services; and volunteer organizations. Highlight 15.2 shows a sample listing for two such agencies.

Telephone Books

Of course, resource directories are not the only source of information about community services. Most telephone books have listings for a variety of human services. Typically, these listings appear in the Yellow Pages under a range of headings. These may include:

- Alcoholism Information and Treatment Centers;
- Associations;
- Attorney Referral Service;
- Career and Vocational Counseling;
- Crisis Intervention Service;
- Drug Abuse and Addiction Information and Treatment;
- Hotline and Helping Lines;
- Human Service Organizations;
- Marriage, Family, Child and Individual Counselors;
- Mental Health Services;
- Psychologists;
- Rehabilitation Services;
- Social Service Organizations;
- Social Workers;
- Stress Management Services;
- Suicide Prevention Service.

These listings include not only formal social service agencies but also organizations and associations that may provide assistance for particular kinds of activities or events. Examples include:

- American Red Cross;
- Boy Scouts;
- Camp Fire, Inc.;
- Epilepsy Center;
- Girl Scouts;
- New Concepts for the Handicapped Foundation, Inc.;
- Special Olympics;
- YMCA;
- YWCA.

Information and Referral Services

Consulting established information and referral agencies or services provides another useful source of information about community resources. Public libraries and human service agencies often provide such a resource. One of your first steps as a new worker should be to find out which agency provides information and referral services for your community. Often a phone call is all you need to locate a particular service or resource.

Service Organizations and Clubs

Communities of every size have service clubs or organizations that offer a variety of resources. Examples of such organizations include:

- American Legion;
- Eagles Club;
- Elks;
- Exchange Club;
- JCs;
- Kiwanis;
- Knights of Columbus;
- League of Women Voters;
- Lions;
- Masonic Lodge;
- Moose;
- Rotary International;
- Shriners;
- United Way;
- Veterans of Foreign Wars (VFW).

The vast majority of these organizations provide specific services to their communities such as money to pay for special projects (for example, neighborhood parks, equipment for disabled persons, or medical treatment for specific handicaps). Others provide the labor needed to undertake and complete community projects. The Kiwanis, for example, donate money to help many community causes benefiting individuals, groups, and the community as a whole. Their members also donate hours of work for such projects as community beautification and building projects. The Lions have a particular interest in vision and eye-related problems. The Shriners operate a specialized hospital that treats burn victims.

Unless you know of such groups and understand what each sees as its mission in the community, it's likely you will miss an important resource. One social worker successfully approached two service organizations to fund a year of college for her client. For another client with serious respiratory problems, the same worker successfully approached a local service club and convinced members to donate a much needed air conditioner.

You can usually request listings of community organizations and service clubs from the local chamber of commerce or from the United Way. Once you receive a listing, you can make a point to learn more about these organizations. As your knowledge of these groups increases, they become yet another important resource for clients.

Other Resources

As a generalist practitioner, you can use limitless creativity in identifying and brokering resources. For instance, you may often identify and use informal or natural resource systems. Sometimes they may ultimately have more importance in the lives of your clients than more formal structured resources. Informal resource systems include groups or units with which clients are naturally involved (for example, relatives, friends, neighbors, or clergy). We sometimes refer to such systems as social networks. We will refer to more informal types of resources periodically throughout the rest of the chapter.

The Problem-Solving Process in Brokering

We have discussed the problem-solving process in greater depth in earlier chapters. This section will review briefly how that process applies to the role of broker, focusing primarily on the intervention phase.

Identifying and Assessing Client Needs

When clients come to us, or are brought to our attention, it is important to gain breadth and depth in understanding their needs. As part of the assessment process, we have the obligation to assess the urgency of client needs and the priority of need. Cultural characteristics and group identification also play roles in how clients request and accept help for specific needs. The client's attitude and reaction toward accepting help may be a barrier to providing that help. For example, a Hmong client may be reluctant to accept help because doing so violates cultural expectations that one should rely on family in times of need. Accepting help may also imply the client cannot manage his own affairs, which is also looked down upon within the Hmong culture.

Social work values play a clear role in the identification of need process. For example, the decision about which resource to use is always ultimately the client's. Client self-determination plays an important role in the assessment of needs. The social worker may believe that certain problems should have greater priority. Still, if the client will not acknowledge those problems or thinks them less important, there is little the worker can do. You, as a worker, can provide your client with alternatives. You can help your client identify the pros and cons of each. However, it is your client's right and responsibility to make the final choice about what she or he is to do or accept.

It is essential that the worker and client be absolutely clear about the client's needs. Without this clarity, it will be impossible to evaluate the extent to which the resource system has helped. Once clarified, the worker is in a much better position to identify potential resource systems. Chapter 5 addressed the process of as-

sessing client needs in detail. Thus, this chapter will not elaborate further on the process except to note that assessment is essentially the same in most problem-solving situations.

Identifying and Assessing Potential Resource Systems

As the client's needs become clearer, the worker as broker begins to consider which of the available resources will be of most assistance in the particular situation. Perhaps there are informal resources the client has overlooked.

It is important to guide clients who are elderly and demobilized to resource systems that provide for their getting from place to place.

This might include family, friends, coworkers, and others with whom the client has existing relationships. On the other hand, such relationships may be unavailable or inappropriate and then the worker needs to help the client explore other options. This is where a community resource directory can be of inestimable value.

As we've discussed, even if such a document is not available, the worker should have his or her own list of resource systems. You as the worker should know the services provided by various agencies and have a rough knowledge of their eligibility requirements and other pertinent information. For example, you should know whether the agency charges a fee for service and whether financial help is available. You can share this information with the client, along with any other likely problems or obstacles the client may encounter. If the client is likely to be placed on a waiting list for service, you should alert him or her to this. Only when clients are knowledgeable about available options can they make informed choices. You, as the worker, are obliged to help clients make decisions based upon the best information available.

Helping the Client Select the Best Resource System

Many clients know little about existing agencies or services. Other clients will have rudimentary information, but do not understand certain aspects of the service network. Still other clients will be experienced users of available services. By talking to the client, you can figure out the client's understanding of potential resources. If this understanding is inaccurate, you can help the client develop a more factual perspective. It is also your responsibility to help the client make a choice. This can be done by answering client questions. If appropriate, you can recommend a specific service based on your knowledge of its effectiveness.

While a wealth of options may seem positive, it is also possible that the multitude of agencies, organizations, and services will only confuse the client. Also, what is clear to the worker may appear unduly complex to clients not accustomed to formal resource systems. Therefore, you need to make certain the client clearly understands what is involved.

Within the broker role there are essentially four alternatives for connecting clients and resource systems (Connaway & Gentry, 1988). First, a simple approach is to refer the client to an existing service. This option presumes that the client now has sufficient information about different agencies to make an informed decision.

A second option is to provide the resource yourself. This option is appropriate when the expertise needed is within your capacity as a helper and is sanctioned by your agency.

The third choice comes into play when existing services or resources do not meet the client's needs and the worker must be creative in finding or developing a resource. In this situation the worker has a couple of options. One involves tapping the potentially most helpful resource, knowing full well that it will probably not solve the entire problem. This is perhaps the least desirable alternative and should never be chosen without the client understanding that the outcome is likely to be somewhat unsatisfactory.

Another choice is to create a resource. The worker who sought and received assistance from a service club for a client's college tuition pursued this option. No existing service organization provided the kind of financial assistance needed. Nevertheless, the worker targeted an organization whose interests closely matched those of the client. She then convinced the organization's members to stretch their criteria to meet the client's needs. The worker's ingenuity and imaginativeness helped create a resource that had not previously existed.

Frequently, clients have multiple needs requiring the resources of more than one agency or organization. In these situations the responsibility of the worker is coordination of existing resources. The goal is to oversee the timely and efficient distribution of resources to the client. Since this last option relates to the concept of case management, we will discuss it later in this chapter's section on case management.

Making the Referral

Making an appropriate referral requires more than simply giving a client the name and address of an agency. There are several actions you can take which will enhance the success of the referral. Weissman (1976) provides several helpful suggestions. For example, workers can write out the necessary information about the agency and give it to the client. This can include the agency's name and address, telephone number, names of contact persons, and even a brief description of what to expect. For frequently used agencies, you can prepare this information in advance.

Another valuable technique is to send the new agency a written description or referral outlining the client's needs. Sometimes this is helpful because it means clients will not have to repeat all the information they already told you.

You also can set the actual appointment time for the client before he or she leaves your office. For example, you or the client can call the new resource and establish the appointment time right then and there.

A final possibility is to accompany the client to the new agency. This occurs less frequently because it's very time consuming. Still, this option makes sense when clients are hesitant to go and no one else is available to accompany them. This step may be particularly important when the client is under great stress or is undergoing a medical procedure, such as an abortion.

How much you do for the client should depend upon the client's ability. Clients suffering from serious mental impairment, for example, are more likely to rely on the worker. A general rule of thumb is not to do things for clients that they can do for themselves. Creating unnecessary dependency in clients is undesirable.

In addition, you should avoid giving clients a falsely positive impression about what the new resource will or can do. Optimism is appropriate, but painting an unrealistic portrait of the helping agency is not (Hepworth & Larsen, 1990, p. 613). Clients will only become disappointed and disillusioned.

Helping Clients Use Resource Systems

Obviously, part of helping clients use resource systems involves giving them encouragement to do so. For a variety of reasons, clients may be reluctant to approach yet another agency. Many clients find the experience of having to discuss their problems quite traumatic. It may conjure up images of accepting charity or of having failed in a particular role (breadwinner, mother, etc.). It may simply be embarrassing. Other clients will be uncomfortable with anything that suggests accepting "welfare." An example involves an elderly client who feared placement in a nursing home. Her primary worry was that the cost of the nursing home placement would be paid for, in her words, by "the county." For her this meant she would be going "on welfare," which had a distinctly negative connotation for her. The worker reminded the client that she and her husband had spent their entire working lives paying taxes to build roads, maintain schools, provide for needy families, and pay for social service staff. The client had been paying all these years for some services that she was just now getting a chance to use. When put in this context, the client became more comfortable about the impending nursing home placement. She believed she had already paid her fair share.

When clients have to explain their situation to more than one agency you can help them in several ways. First, you can provide a written referral to the new agency. Or you can explain the basic details to a staff person in the new agency. You can also brief clients about the actual procedures used by the new agency and barriers that they might encounter (Anderson, 1981). As mentioned earlier, clients should be given the names of more than one contact person in case the first person is absent when the client contacts the agency. You can also call clients right before their appointments to see if they have any last-minute concerns or problems. Such calls can act as boosters to encourage clients to keep appointments.

Follow-Up and Evaluation of Resource Systems

The most important measure of the success of a referral is whether it met the client's needs. To know this, you must learn the outcome of the referral. This means that either you contact the client or you ask the client to call you back after the referral. You can also schedule an appointment with the client following the referral visit. Such appointments can be set before clients visit the new agencies. In this way you remind clients that you will be following up on the referral, thus providing another form of encouragement. Of course, if you accompany the client to the new agency, follow-up occurs on the spot.

If the client will be having several sessions at the new agency, you could choose to meet the client after each session. This method provides for direct follow-up and may be desirable to reinforce the client's participation. On the other hand, the client whose needs are met by the new agency may not want to continue meeting with you anymore since you're not providing service. Ultimately, it's important to respect the client's rights. Following up on a referral is part of our responsibility as professional social workers to evaluate our practice (Anderson, 1981). We need to know whether the client encountered barriers or whether the referral itself was inappropriate. Perhaps the services were

not available in a timely fashion. Or perhaps the agency did not operate according to your or your client's expectations.

Maybe the agency denied services to which the client was entitled. If so, you may need to assume the role of advocate to help cut through the red tape and bureaucratic subterfuge. Perhaps a higher degree of coordination is necessary if multiple resource systems have been involved. The worker needs this type of information if a realistic evaluation of the referral is to take place.

Workers may discover that a given agency is inadvertently creating problems for clients. Part of the worker's obligation to the client is to provide this knowledge to the agency as a way to help improve the functioning of that resource system.

A referral's success is evaluated according to how the client's identified needs have been fulfilled. If the client was referred for job training, was the training provided? Was the job the client trained for one she or he wanted? Did the client ultimately get a job in that field? Sometimes a client satisfaction questionnaire will provide sufficient information to conclude that the referral was successful (Connaway & Gentry, 1988). Chapter 8 describes several evaluation tools that can be used to assess goal achievement. Many of these can be employed to evaluate the success of the worker acting in the broker role. Choosing the correct one requires experience and good judgment.

Case Management

The concept of case management is not new to the profession of social work. Kaplan (1990) suggests that case management existed since the nineteenth century, but received more attention in the past quarter century. One reason for this attention is that case-management services are now required for specific categories of clients by both federal and state laws and regulations (Greene, 1987). In 1984 the National Association of Social Workers published standards for case-management services to functionally impaired client populations (NASW, 1984).

What Is Case Management?

Moxley (1989, p. 21) defines case management as "a designated person or team who organizes, coordinates, and sustains a network of formal and informal supports and activities designed to optimize the functioning and well-being of people with multiple needs." In practice, this means a practitioner, on the behalf of a specific client, coordinates needed services provided by any number of agencies, organizations, or facilities. Moxley (1989, p. 12) states that "services are said to be coordinated when the principal actors within the helping network are in agreement with one another regarding the client's care, and are moving in the same direction."

For example, take Edward McShane, age thirty-two, who suffers both from a chronic mental illness and from kidney disease. He was institutionalized at a state mental hospital at age nineteen and is now being returned to his home community. Ed has no living family members and no place to live. He needs regular monitoring to ensure that he takes his prescribed medication. Ed needs a variety of services, including housing in the community, medical and mental health services, employment opportunities, and possibly financial aid. All these services must be coordinated so that they are working toward the same goal: keeping Ed out of an institution and functioning as independently as possible in the community.

Case management is the intervention of choice for clients like Ed who have multiple, ongoing needs. The principles of case management have been articulated by Gerhart (1990, p. 216). They include:

Individualization of services: This means developing or designing services specifically to meet the identified needs of the client.

Comprehensiveness of services: Comprehensive services encompass all areas of the client's life including housing, recreation, employment, social, financial, medical care, mental health care, etc. This principle helps ensure that no need will go unfulfilled.

Parsimonious services: The meaning of parsimonious services is that duplication of services will be discouraged and that costs for services will be controlled. Uncoordinated services may result in some needs being met by duplicate agencies while other needs go unmet.

Fostering autonomy: A major focus of case management is on helping clients become as self-sufficient as possible. It also means providing maximum client self-determination so the client makes as many decisions regarding his own care as is possible.

Continuity of care: Continuity of care means that as the client moves through life, requiring in-patient services and help in the community, case management services will ensure continued monitoring of his needs. There is an expectation that most of the clients will require assistance throughout their lives. This is because the conditions from which they suffer are chronic and not subject to quick recovery. This is especially true in the case of chronically mentally ill patients and those with significant developmental disabilities.

Essentially, case management uses the same problem-solving process described throughout this text. The problems are typically multiple ones and need the interventions of many agencies and organizations. Like any worker-client relationship, it is expected that the client will be actively involved in the helping process. Moreover, it is likely that the worker serving as case manager may have to advocate for clients in certain situations. If services or resources to which the client is entitled are not provided, the worker may take necessary steps to correct the problem. Existing resources are used to the maximum extent possible. If services or resources to meet client needs do not exist, the worker has an obligation to work toward development of such resources.

As you can see, the case manager plays several roles. She may be a broker, advocate, counselor, teacher, community organizer, or planner (Intagliata, 1982). Client needs determine the worker's role. Most importantly, however, case managers provide the link between clients and the human services system. Case managers

know the comprehensive needs of clients, connect them to appropriate services, and ensure that those services are provided effectively. This often means that the case manager must encourage clients to use services and give them the emotional support they need to survive day to day. High quality case-management services involve frequent and intense client-case manager contact (Berkeley Planning Associates, 1977).

While case managers play a variety of roles including that of broker, it is important to underscore that the concepts of broker and case manager are not synonymous. The role of case manager goes well beyond that of broker. The broker may refer clients to one or more specific services. The case manager has the broader task of ensuring that a wide spectrum of clients' needs are met in an efficient and effective man-

---

HIGHLIGHT 15.3
An Overview of Case Management

1. *Definition of Case Management*
   A person or team who organizes, coordinates, and sustains a network of formal and informal supports and activities to maximize the functioning of people with multiple needs.

2. *Purpose of Case Management*
   Promoting the skills and capability of the client in using social services and social supports.
   Developing the abilities of social networks and relevant service providers to further the functioning of the client.
   Promoting effective and efficient service delivery.

3. *Focus of Case Management*
   Formulating client support network that integrates client skill development; involvement of social networks, and involvement of multiple providers.

4. *Tasks of Case Managers*
   Assessing of client needs; social network ca-

pacities, and abilities of social service providers.
Developing a comprehensive service plan that includes multi-disciplinary professional involvement and maximum client involvement.
Intervention directly with client to strengthen skills and capacities for self-care and/or indirectly with systems impinging on client.
Monitoring of service plan implementation and tracking of client status, service delivery, and involvement of social network members.
Evaluation of service plan effectiveness and its impact on client functioning, on social network's capacity to support client, and on ability of social service professional to work with client.

Source: Adapted from Moxley (1989), p. 21.

ner. Both brokers and case managers require knowledge of community resources and where such information can be found. Both require good working relationships with service providers and organizations that may be used by clients. Ultimately, it is the case manager who is responsible for coordinating, monitoring, and evaluating the services provided to clients, activities beyond the routine duties of a broker (McMahon, 1990).

Some authors argue that "case management is what most social workers do in most fields of practice most of the time" (Roberts-DeGennaro, 1987, p. 466). This view is understandable because the breadth of the case manager role parallels that of social workers providing services directly to clients. In reality, the case manager typically is directly involved in the care of some clients to an extensive degree. Hepworth and Larsen (1990) point out that the case manager has great responsibility for ensuring that the client receives services to meet a variety of needs.

One other important responsibility of the case manager involves integrating the formal support system (agencies and services) with that of the informal support system (for example, family, friends, and others directly involved with the client). The case manager strives to help the client function independently by facilitating interpersonal relationships (Roberts-DeGennaro, 1987). This may involve negotiations between formal and informal support systems. For example, family members may be reluctant to work with an agency, or they may be unwilling to allow the client the independence needed to function in the community. Perhaps relationships between the client and family members are strained. In either case, the interpersonal problems prevent the client's needs from being met (Lowy, 1985). Describing this dual role, Moore (1990) argues the case manager is both an enabler and a facilitator whose primary responsibility is to help clients function independently. We will discuss Moore's perspectives in more detail in a later section. Finally, Moxley (1989) provides an excellent overview of case management (See Highlight 15.3).

Importance of Case Management for Generalist Practice

Approximately 75 percent of states now require case management for certain categories of clients, such as the chronically mentally ill (Greene, 1987). Of a sample of 350 major companies almost all were using case managers to help employees get appropriate rehabilitative care for job-related injuries and to reduce costs of that care (Institute for Rehabilitation and Disability Management and National Center for Social Policy and Practice, 1988). Interest in case management has spread so rapidly in recent years that private case-management firms are now in existence (Kaplan, 1990). They are helping clients receive homemaker services, alternative housing, day care, transportation services, chore services, and in-home meals. The National Association of Social Workers (1981) identifies case management as one of eleven major functions performed by social workers.

Allen (1990) argues that "more families are likely to be affected by case managers than by treatment providers." Lauffer (1987, p. 320) states "case management has, during the 1980s, emerged as the principle method through which individual case planning is conducted on behalf of clients who are seen by more than a single agency." The Developmental Disabilities Assistance and Bill of Rights Act (Public Law 95-602) specifically lists case management as a priority service. Case management is being used extensively in the developmental disability field, with the chronically mentally impaired, and in the field of child welfare.

Of particular importance for the social work profession is the fact that case management is an approach consistent with social work's emphasis on the rights of the client. Gerhart (1990) notes that the goals of social work and the goals of case management are similar. Both aim to help people increase their problem-solving and coping skills, obtain resources, make organizations responsive to their needs, and facilitate the interaction between clients and their environment. Contrary to the implications of the term, it is not *clients* who are being managed, but the *services* received by the client. Case managers need the skill to intervene with individuals, families, agencies, and the larger community. These are the same skills needed by generalist social workers regardless of their practice settings (Rubin, 1987; Intagliata, 1981). Case managers are currently being used by hospitals and health maintenance organizations with social workers and nurses being the primary professions charged with this responsibility (Greene, 1987).

Several factors are operating to increase the importance of case management for social workers (Stein, 1981). These include:

1. Increased emphasis on maintaining clients in the least restrictive environment;
2. The goal of keeping people out of institutions;
3. The objective of maintaining the elderly in their homes as long as possible;
4. Efforts to reduce or contain costs of providing health and other forms of care to clients;
5. Increased attention to rights of clients who often lack awareness of available resources;
6. Awareness that some clients cannot follow through on the ordinary referral because of their limited capacities (for example, mental retardation);
7. Increased focus on how the environment contributes to client problems;
8. Decreased focus on the medical model of practice (The medical model tends to view clients' problems as "diseases"; hence, the client should be "cured");
9. Expansion of human service programs in

Figure 15.1: A Task Model of Problem Solving

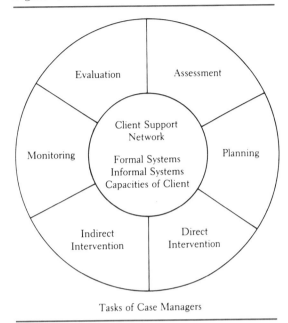

Tasks of Case Managers

Source: Adapted from D. P. Moxley. *The Practice of Case Management* (Newbury Park, CA: Sage. Copyright 1989. Reprinted by permission of Sage Publications, Inc.

the period 1960–1975 and increased complexity and fragmentation of services (that is, greater specialization with no one taking overall responsibility for client service).

Assessment

Assessment is the part of the process where the case manager learns the current and future needs and problems of the client. Because so many clients have long-term needs, future needs have perhaps a higher priority than is true in other areas of social work. The assessment must cover medical, psychological, recreational, social, educational, and vocational areas.

Take, for example, a client who is physically disabled. Here several issues are involved. First, a problem may be *caused directly by the disability* itself. An example would be absence of mobility caused by paralysis of both legs. Second, a need may have *no relationship* at all to the disability. A client who lacks clothing or adequate shelter may have had the same problem even without the disability (for example, if his company laid off many workers who then could not locate other employment).

A third source of problems could be caused by the client's *informal support system*. For example, a parent's attempts to protect a developmentally disabled young adult may prevent that person from learning skills that would help him to become independent.

Fourth, problems may occur in the *formal resource systems* designed to help clients. For instance, an agency may refuse to provide a service to which the client is entitled. The agency's policies may be inappropriately applied. Perhaps the person denying the client service dislikes the client or feels he is taking advantage of the agency. It is also possible that the resource system simply lacks the ability to deliver a specific service. The budget may be inadequate or maybe a specific resource cannot be located. An example of the latter is an agency that has been unable to hire a bilingual social worker to serve as an interpreter for the agency's Hispanic clients.

There are obviously a variety of explanations that can exist for a given need discovered in the assessment process. This means that the assessment must concern itself with at least three areas, each of which is described here:

1. Assessment of the client's ability to meet environmental challenges.

Environmental challenges include a client's self-care ability (for example, to take care of hygiene, dressing, money management, etc.). In this process you need to find out what clients need from their informal and formal resource systems. A need can be anything that you and your client view as necessary for a positive quality of life. The first thing is to determine which needs can be met with little or no outside help.

The focus is on the client's *strengths and capabilities*, not on deficits or shortcomings (Cohen & Johnson, 1987). You also need to determine which available services or resources the client can use. In assessment it is important not to make clients excessively dependent upon others, nor to assume they can do more for themselves than is really the case. A simple example of this is a babysitter who carried a one-year-old baby all around the house because she just assumed that the child could not walk. She was astounded upon her arrival one evening to find the baby toddling after his parents. Thus, you will assess client skills that need to be maintained and those that will need to be enhanced.

It also may be important to find out why the client has sought assistance at this particular time. Does the request for help coincide with important changes in the client's personal resources (for instance, loss of job, eviction), changes in the client's primary support group (for instance, aging parents), or the recent availability of formal resources (for example, a newly created program)? As in any assessment you will want to find out something about the history of the problem as understood by the client or his family. For example, is it a problem for which other interventions have failed, or is it a problem which the client is only now willing to admit? Will the client need on-going service or only that provided in times of stress? Does the client have effective relationships with informal resource systems? What is the client's involvement with formal resource systems?

Finally, as with any assessment, you as the case manager may have a role in determining whether the client is eligible for service. This decision will largely be based on the information gathered above.

2. Assessment of the caretaking ability of the client's informal support group.

How capable are the client's family and friends to meet his needs? These needs may include basic items such as food or shelter, or more abstract things such as social or emotional support. You will want to determine both immediate and extended family members and their relationships with the client. Are there others who serve as informal resources for the client? These might include friends, co-workers, neighbors, storekeepers, members from the same church or club, and schoolmates (Moxley, 1989, p. 44). What kinds of assistance can the primary support group give? How do members of the primary support group interact with the client? How well does this resource system interact with formal resource systems?

3. Assessment of the resources of formal support systems.

The focus here is on the capability of formal resource systems to meet client needs. As we have seen, the formal system may not have the capacity to meet a client's needs (for instance, due to a lack of money). Perhaps it denies the client services for which he is otherwise entitled. This may occur, for instance, because of confusion over eligibility, or because of inappropriately applied policies.

As we assess each of these areas we must focus on the availability, adequacy, appropriateness, acceptability, and accessibility of the resources (Moxley, 1989, pp. 52–53). Sometimes resources are *available* to fill a need, but remain unused because no one knows they exist (Hepworth & Larsen, 1990, p. 450). In other instances a client's needs are not known because the client is isolated or protected by family members or because of the absence of a prior needs assessment.

It's also possible that a client has not shared a need with anyone. It is not unusual for persons with a disability that is not visible to others (for example, a learning disability where they're unable to read) to keep their "secret" from all but a handful of friends. Some may not share the information with

anyone. Often, only an in-depth assessment will disclose the problem.

In other situations the *acceptability* of a resource may be low. Maybe the client refuses to accept help from a specific source. Perhaps the client is too proud to ask for help from a particular agency because of past bad experiences or the negative reputation of the agency. Perhaps the client believes there is a stigma to accepting help from the agency. Any of these factors may reduce the acceptability of the resource, even if it meets all the other criteria.

Accessibility of a resource becomes a problem when the client lacks transportation, mobility, or other means to access the resource. Much of the available housing in this country is not accessible to physically disabled people because of stairs, narrow doorways, or equipment that cannot be reached by clients in wheelchairs.

Assessment also may help us understand the factors that cause or contribute to a particular problem. Allen (1990) points out that knowing a child is physically abused does not provide sufficient information to allow for intervention. Here, we know what the problem is, but not necessarily what's causing it. Intervention needs to target the cause. Child abuse may be "the result of poor parenting skills, a historical pattern of family violence, stresses on the family because of unemployment, or many other potential factors. If the problem is unemployment, parenting classes will not be the most useful intervention" (p. 2).

The process of gathering information needed for assessment for case management is similar to other assessments. For example, the case manager reviews pertinent records (agency, school, etc.), interviews appropriate people (client, family, friends, etc.), and refers the client to specialists who can provide other kinds of data. This may include psychological testing, vocational or educational assessment, medical examinations, and similar evaluations. Moxley (1989, pp. 29–32) summarizes the case management assessment process by noting it is:

1. *Need-based.* This means we focus specifically on client needs.
2. *Holistic/Comprehensive.* This means we attempt to assess clients' needs in all areas, instead of just a few. We will concern ourselves with needs covering income, shelter, work, education, health and mental health, social and other relationships, recreation and leisure time, transportation, legal, etc. (Moxley, 1989, pp. 33–37).
3. *Interdisciplinary.* This suggests the importance of using the expertise of various disciplines to understand clients' needs. Examples include physicians, social workers, psychologists, speech pathologists, occupational therapists, physical therapists, etc.
4. *Participatory.* The client is fully involved in assessing his or her needs and maintains maximum self-determination.
5. *A process.* This concerns a simple recognition that assessment is an ongoing, changing, progressive type of interaction.
6. *Systematic.* This ensures that each area of potential need is explored in sufficient depth and breadth.
7. *A product.* When completed, the assessment should be in written form. It should be a product that guides planning and intervention.

Figure 15.2 provides an overview of case management assessment that emphasizes two perspectives. The first is a focus on identification of client needs. The second involves the assessment of the capacities of the client (self-care), informal support systems (mutual care), and formal support systems (professional care). It also contains a brief description of the assessment process (Moxley, 1989, p. 57).

In summary, the assessment process in case management and that described in chapter 5 are essentially identical. Each must consider the capacities of clients, clients' informal support systems, and formal support systems.

Planning

Coston (1982) describes the planning phase as a "process of locating and procuring services that deliver results the same as, or close to, the client's desired results. These results may be related to diagnosis, evaluation, or service delivery. When received, the results of diagnoses or evaluations are studied by the case manager to determine whether they indicate additional problems or the need for additional service planning" (p. 8).

Service Plans

In planning, the case manager creates a *service plan* that incorporates six dimensions: (1) client needs are prioritized; (2) goals and objectives of service are established; (3) resource systems that will be involved are identified; (4) time frames are identified within which services will be delivered and goals achieved; (5) outcome measures are formulated that will be used to evaluate achievement of case plans; (6) specific tasks are assigned to individuals and groups so that it's clear who is responsible for what.

Impact Goals

Planning in case management often involves setting impact goals. *Impact goals* is a term used in case management to include goals that result in changing some major aspects of the client's life and are the expected results of our intervention. One such goal might involve resolving the transportation needs of a wheelchair-bound young man. Arranging for the acquisition of a vehicle that would accommodate the client's chair would be an impact goal with major consequences for several areas of the client's life. For example, it would provide him transportation to his job, give him increased access to other community resources, and improve his recreational opportunities. Another example would be providing for in-home medical care for a client. This would enable her to remain in her own home rather than being placed in a nursing home.

Service Objectives

Service objectives should be differentiated from impact goals. The term *service objective* is used in case management to describe steps that must be undertaken to achieve an impact goal. For example, let's assume we have a client who lives in a home that is not accessible to someone in a wheelchair. The client is suffering from a condition that restricts her to a wheelchair indefinitely. Service objectives here might in-

clude identifying the physical and structural changes needed in the client's house to make it accessible to her, and locating a carpenter to make the changes (Moxley, 1989, p. 63). Making the home accessible is the impact goal, and service objectives help achieve the impact goal. Figure 15.3 shows one service plan adapted from Coston (1982, p. 9).

The case plan shown in Figure 15.3 describes the impact goal (expected results) and details what the intervention plan will be. It also shows who will do what and sets a date by which the impact goal is to be achieved. The interventions described here are essentially a list of service objectives (e.g., apply for Medicaid, un-

Figure 15.2: The Structure of Case Management Assessment

Characteristic of Assessment	Identification of Client Needs	Assessment of Self-Care	Assessment of Mutual Care	Assessment of Professional Care
Organizing Concepts	Unmet Needs	Client Functioning	Social Network/ Social support	Formal Human Service
Basic Units of Assessment	Income	Physical functioning	Social network structure	Resource inventory
	Housing/shelter	Cognitive functioning	Social network interaction	Availability
	Employment/ vocational training	Emotional functioning	Emotional support	Adequacy
	Health	Behavioral functioning	Instrumental support	Appropriateness
	Mental health		Material Support	Acceptability
	Social/Interpersonal			Accessability
	Recreation/leisure			
	Activities of daily living			
	Transportation			
	Legal			
	Education			
Process of Assessment	Review with client, others, and professionals the needs of client in key areas of daily living	Match needs with client functional areas to assess whether he can fulfill his own needs.	Match needs with mutual care resources to assess whether social network can fulfill client needs.	Match needs with professional care resources to assess whether formal service can fulfill client needs.

Source: Adapted from Moxley (1989), p. 57.

Figure 15.3: A Completed Service Plan

Problem	Expected Results	Intervention/Strategy	Timeline
1	Child has appropriate day care	Client will go to Craven County Child Development Center. Parent will first visit center and make application. Center will provide structured program to enhance developmental skills of client.	9–27–89
2	Family receives food stamps until they are employed and can afford adequate food.	Worker will speak with food stamp worker about emergency stamps. Establish an appointment.	5–20–90
2	The client's parents are employed.	Refer parents to job service. Give job suggestions to parents.	5–20–90
2	Client has medical coverage.	Check eligibility requirements for Medicaid. Refer family to make application with Medicaid. Client will be eligible since spend-down was met in March 1992.	5–30–90
3	Family knows if child has normal vision in both eyes.	Client will visit Dr. Jones for an eye exam.	5–30–90

dergo eye exam). The plan is developed in cooperation with the client or client's family, if the client is a child. As you can see, the case manager must have substantial familiarity with available formal resource systems and a working relationship with many different professionals. Following completion of the service plan, the intervention phase begins.

Intervention

The intervention phase can be regarded as having two parts. One concerns the direct services provided by the case manager. The other involves indirect services provided by other resource systems. Some argue that the case manager should not provide direct services, but simply arrange for others to do so (Stein, 1981). They reason that the time and effort needed to provide direct service may detract from more needed indirect service facilitation. Still, most writers agree that the case manager will provide some direct services to clients.

Direct Services

The case manager may be called upon to provide several direct services to clients. Although these services may not involve counseling or therapy they will still be important to clients. Direct services may include crisis intervention (for example, locating temporary housing for desperate, homeless people), supporting clients making difficult decisions, helping to modify clients' environments (for instance, arranging for transportation within the community), and helping clients overcome emotional reactions to their crisis situations (Moxley, 1989, pp. 83–90).

Other case managers may serve in the role of teacher. For instance, they might instruct clients in money management or personal hygiene. Sometimes, case managers share professional knowledge and judgment with a client or provide important information to clients trying to make decisions. Clients may need to be taught important job-seeking skills before gaining employment. Some teaching techniques available to social workers were described in chapter 3.

Sometimes, case managers will need to motivate clients. This may be required when clients have experienced past failures in attempting to make positive changes in themselves or when they have experienced disappointments in getting the resources they needed. Simple discouragement can make clients doubt that anything could ever possibly be different. Frequently you will need to continue motivating the client throughout the assessment and planning processes (Allen, 1990). Gerhart (1990, p. 213) provides some excellent suggestions for motivating clients that appear in Highlight 15.4.

Workers also will have to support clients through periods of change and help them survive and prosper in their environments. One

Some argue that the case manager should not provide direct services, but simply arrange for others to do so.

way of doing this is to give clients useful information. Another is to praise client changes and growth. As a case manager, you will be working both to help the client change and to assist informal networks in aiding the client. Clients will encounter multiple service and aid programs that are confusing and complex. Eligibility criteria may be unintelligible. Regulations may appear arbitrary. The worker will be providing direct service by helping clients negotiate formal resource systems.

Indirect Services

Indirect services provided by the case manager are largely limited to two roles. The first involves linking clients with needed resource systems. These systems may be formal in that they are existing social agencies. However, they also may include mutual care systems, such as associates from various sectors of the client's life (school, church, work). Self-help groups such as Alcoholics Anonymous, Parents Anonymous, Parents Without Partners, and the National Alliance for the Mentally Ill can also be used to provide mutual care services.

Perhaps it will be necessary for you as case manager to contact other service-providing agencies either in person or in writing. Here the advantage of knowing staff members in other agencies is critical. Johnson (1989, p. 356) emphasizes how important it is for case managers to respect and value the contributions of the other care givers. Whether the needed care is given by you or some other resource system, it is important to remember that the ultimate goal is to help clients help themselves. You should not do things for clients that they can do for themselves.

A second indirect service role involves advocating with various systems on behalf of clients. Much of a case manager's indirect service addresses this latter task. Changing the system to help the client is more difficult than asking the client to change. The case manager may have to develop new resources (often in collaboration with others) or improve access to existing resources. Sometimes this means advocating and intervening with clients' informal resource systems (family and friends). Other times it means coordinating services so that clients get only those they need. It also may require technical assistance and consultation to resource systems as they attempt to deliver needed services to the client (Moxley, 1989, p. 95). As needed, the case manager meets with the client and agency representatives to facilitate referrals and service provision. Meetings also may be held to negotiate problems that exist between the informal system (e.g., family, friends) and formal resource systems.

As in other areas of generalist social work practice, the case manager's responsibilities and activities are determined largely by clients' needs. Those needs change over time, which requires the case manager to provide an ever-changing pattern of direct and indirect service. As the client becomes more involved with existing resource systems (formal or informal) the worker's role shifts to the next phase of the process, monitoring.

Monitoring

Monitoring is one of the primary tasks during the intervention phase. During the monitoring process the case manager continues to communicate with service providers. This involves two tasks. The first concerns determining whether the service plan is being completed. The second focuses on whether or not the original goals are being accomplished.

During the monitoring stage it may be necessary to rewrite the case plan. The case manager maintains necessary records and doc-

---

┌ HIGHLIGHT 15.4
Motivating Techniques

Here are eight techniques that can be used to motivate disgusted, disheartened, or discouraged clients:

1. Begin by asking about the plans a client has for himself. These might include completing school, learning a trade, living independently, getting along better with family members, or establishing an intimate relationship.
2. Contribute realistic suggestions aimed at enhancing the client's life and forestalling relapses. For example, tell the client exactly what to expect when approaching a new agency for help. Suggest ways the client might respond to a negative decision by the agency.
3. Discuss points of disagreement between worker and client and work out realistic compromises. For instance, identify options that satisfy both you and the client.
4. Develop a contract with the client specifying mutual goals.
5. Identify the steps that must be taken and the service providers that can help the client to reach agreed goals.
6. Provide the client with data about service providers. Such information might include eligibility requirements, location, transportation, the nature of services, or the length of service.
7. Discuss any of the obstacles the client can foresee in using the proposed services. For example, suggest the client bring certain forms of identification along when applying for a specific service. This might eliminate typical delays in qualifying for service.
8. Review what the responsibilities of each party will be in completing the linkage with a particular service provider. For instance, ask the client if she understands what you, as the case manager, will do and what the client is responsible for doing herself.

umentation. Managers look for gaps in service and fill them. If clients fail to appear for scheduled appointments, the case manager follows up to see what happened. If the client is receiving medication, the case manager will help assess whether the client is under or over medicated (Cohen & Johnson, 1987, p. 2). If expected outcomes are not being achieved, the case manager will use assessment skills to figure out the cause (Allen, 1990, p. 2). Are new needs emerging? Is the original process being followed, or have changes occurred? What can be done to improve service delivery and effectiveness?

Case managers continue to advocate for the client when the need arises. A case manager also serves as the contact person for the case. Thus, the manager represents the client to resource systems (both formal and informal) and represents those agencies and people in contact with the client (Abrahams & Seidl, 1979). Monitoring also helps ensure that clients do not use the system inappropriately. For instance, a client might receive duplicate services or similar benefits from two or more resource systems. Appropriate coordination of services usually can prevent this from happening. The monitoring function occurs through the use of formal communications, formal and informal meetings, phone contacts, case recording, and formal evaluation devices (e.g., instruments, test results). The primary focus is on how services are provided. Though there is heed paid to the outcomes attained, primary attention to this matter occurs in the evaluation phase.

Additional Roles

The nature of case management is such that the worker provides a vast variety of services or roles. The absence of natural support systems (families, friends) may put the worker in a position of having to help the client develop such a resource. Other clients may infrequently use available services. Thus, the case manager may engage in outreach, namely, reaching out to potential clients who need and qualify for the service. This might include public education about the availability of a service and what the referral process involves. It may involve advocating with an agency to provide services in a different location or during different time frames to fit potential clients not previously served.

Evaluation in Case Management

The importance of evaluating the outcomes of case management services is critical. While some studies show that case management is cost-effective (that is, receiving adequate or better services for the amount they cost), others do not (Kaplan, 1990). There is clearly more research needed to assess the effectiveness of case management.

As we have discussed, some evaluation occurs during the intervention phase. There we were concerned with whether the original case-management plan and goals remained appropriate.

During the evaluation phase we want to determine whether impact goals have been achieved. Perhaps the first task is to decide how data will be collected. Do we use existing case records? Or are external assessments of the client's progress such as your own observations or calls to other agencies necessary?

Another thing we need to do is look carefully at outcomes. Did the client get and keep a job? Has the major health problem that brought the client to our attention been alleviated? Does the client have a reliable form of transportation, thus allowing her to participate in the sheltered workshop program? Is the client taking the medication as prescribed? Has the client quit talking to walls and doors? Is the home now fully accessible to a person in a wheelchair?

Achievement of many of these goals can

be easily assessed because the case manager, significant others, and the client can simply observe results. Other goals are not as observable and require more subjective judgments.

Sometimes we want to know whether the case management services themselves were helpful. If they were helpful, in what ways? What was the impact of service delivery upon the client? Was the client satisfied with the service? Depending upon the ability of the client, client satisfaction questionnaires and surveys might be used. Similar instruments might be created to gather impressions from others involved with the case (for example, family, friends, or formal resources systems).

Other targets of evaluation include the resource systems that served the client. Can these networks provide continued service to the client? Will they need to be augmented (increased or improved) in some way? Were there problems that have been overcome? What barriers remain?

These evaluations require more subjective judgments and are less easily measured. Yet they remain important questions. The answers may determine the continued effectiveness of the helping agencies to many other clients.

Termination in Case Management

It is more difficult to discuss terminating case management services than other short-term interventions. Many clients receiving case management-services have chronic, debilitating conditions. Some case management services continue throughout the client's life. In these situations the only terminations will occur when the worker leaves, or the client dies or moves away. When any of these situations happen, the termination issues described in chapter 9 remain relevant. When case management services end, closure with both the individual or family and with those resource systems that have provided service are involved. As with any termina-

tion, the worker, client, and any others involved will experience a variety of potential feelings that must be dealt with. In addition, the client may need further referral to new and different services. Finally, the case record must be closed. Chapter 16 addresses this issue.

Follow-Up in Case Management

Follow-up of clients receiving case management services is critical. Because of the extreme nature of the problems facing these clients (for example, developmental disabilities, chronic mental illness, or serious physical disabilities), they remain at risk throughout their lives. Gerhart (1990, p. 213) reminds us that follow-up can help prevent reversion to previous problems and other potential catastrophes. The case manager can attempt to contact clients by phone, letter, or home visit as necessary.

Gibelman (1982, p. 16) provides an excellent example of the type of client frequently needing case management services and the ongoing nature of some cases. See Highlight 15.5, which describes how a mentally disabled client's case was managed.

Factors Influencing Case Management Service Delivery

The amount of research on the effectiveness of case management is relatively limited. However, there is some evidence that smaller caseloads influence service delivery. When caseloads become too large the managers only have time to respond to crises. Similarly, there is a corresponding deterioration in the case manager's relationship with clients (Rubin, 1987, p. 218). Caseloads over twenty-five begin to reduce the effectiveness and quality of services provided by case managers (Berkeley Planning Associates, 1977).

Another factor influencing service delivery

HIGHLIGHT 15.5
Case Management for a Mentally Disabled Client

The police brought Oliver to the country crisis unit after he had caused a disturbance in a bank. The Crisis Unit staff had often seen Oliver before. Fifty-six years old, with organic brain syndrome caused by paresis, syphilis, and chronic alcoholism, he had been deteriorating mentally for the last several years. Because he was incoherent and threatening, he was placed in the inpatient unit at Marin General Hospital.

Henja got involved in the case after hospital staff decided that Oliver's crisis had passed. They determined, however, that he needed long-term treatment in a skilled psychiatric nursing facility. But no local facility would accept him for a variety of reasons, including the fact that they had no vacancies, they lacked the proper security, and the patient was dangerous or unmanageable. Henja was asked to find a psychiatric nursing facility in a neighboring county.

She did so, but it wasn't a simple process. The work included:

- Consulting with Marin General Hospital's inpatient staff, the patient's family, and the Transitional Services staff
- Reviewing Oliver's medical, psychiatric, and social history
- Clarifying his legal status
- Interviewing him to assess his current mental status and potential for violence
- Arranging funding through Supplementary Security Income and MediCal, the state's medical benefit plan (similar to other states' Medicaid)
- Presenting the information, including the potential for violence, to the facility's intake worker and convincing the facility to accept Oliver
- Asking MediCal to authorize treatment
- Arranging transportation to the facility

The case wasn't over, though. Oliver got worse. He started assaulting other patients and injured a staff member. Henja got a telephone call: take Oliver away from here. When he returned to the Crisis Unit, a treatment conference determined that he needed to go to Napa State Hospital. But the hospital wouldn't accept him. The director of admissions argued that the hospital was short of beds and that Oliver's prognosis was so poor that he would never be discharged.

Henja got on the phone and at the request of a county mental health supervisor, she spoke to the director at Napa. Since Henja is a state employee who had worked at the hospital and knows the staff, she was in a position to influence the situation. "I worked out an agreement with the director," she recalls. "If he would assure me that the hospital would evaluate Oliver's condition and develop a treatment plan for him, I would promise to place him in a county facility as soon as he was ready."

Henja kept in weekly contact with Oliver and the hospital treatment team. Fortunately, Oliver responded to the lithium and therapy that were prescribed and became generally friendly and cooperative. But he retained symptoms of his organic brain syndrome and refused to acknowledge either his illness or his alcoholism. His plans for the future, he said, were to go back to work, continue drinking, and keep "fooling around with the ladies." Over four months, Henja and the hospital team developed a plan that would allow Oliver to be transferred to a locked skilled nursing facility, where he could continue treatment but also get passes out. With Henja's considerable trepidation, the transfer took place. Because Oliver has continued on lithium and has stopped drinking, the placement has worked well, and Oliver may soon be transferred to a less restrictive facility. In getting Oliver out of the state hospital, Henja kept her promise to the admissions director.

is the extent to which the case manager's responsibilities are clearly delineated. Typically, case managers with vaguely defined responsibilities end up largely providing direct service to the client instead of focusing on the diversity of services needed (Caragonne, 1980; Intagliata, 1982).

The quality of supervision that supervisors provide to case managers has a bearing on the manager's performance. Caragonne (1981) found that supervisors could be an important source of support for case managers; however, many supervisors did not know exactly what the case managers were doing. This lack of knowledge reduces the effectiveness of the supervisor as a source of support.

Stress and burnout of case managers is also a factor influencing service to clients. The relatively high demands on individual case managers has prompted Test (1979) to suggest that the burnout might be prevented by assigning a team of workers to serve as case managers for specific clients. She argued that this also might ensure greater continuity of care. Presumably, the team would share responsibility for the client's well-being, reducing the burden on any single case manager.

Chapter Summary

This chapter began with a discussion of brokering and its importance in generalist social work practice. Effective brokers are those who are experts on the availability of resources, specifics of eligibility criteria, characteristics of resources, and are familiar with contact persons associated with resources. We then reviewed various types of resources and cited where directories of resources might be located. The problem-solving process in brokering was discussed. Its similarities to and differences from the process used in other areas of generalist practice were highlighted.

The last section covered case management, its definition, its importance to generalist social work practice, and the problem-solving process employed by case managers. Finally, factors influencing service delivery of case-management services were discussed briefly.

16 Recording in Generalist Social Work Practice

Setting it in stone

1. The client is a very sick individual.
2. He looked like a disgusting derelict.
3. She was perfectly average.
4. Petey has mongoloid features.
5. The house was disgustingly filthy.
6. We solved all their problems.
7. I'm sure she will have a wonderful life.
8. They should lock him up and throw away the key.

What is wrong or potentially wrong with the above statements? Let's examine them one by one:

1. *The client is a very sick individual.* What does "very sick" mean? Does it refer to physical or mental illness? Does the client have diabetes, brain cancer, or paranoid schizophrenia? Read by itself, the statement is very difficult to understand. It provides great potential for inaccuracy and misinterpretation. It could even resemble a value judgment declared in anger when a person brazenly steps in front of you in a long line at a store.

2. *He looked like a disgusting derelict.* "Disgusting derelict" is not a very flattering term. It labels someone in a derogatory manner. It lacks specificity regarding a person's behavior and appearance. Finally, it's missing any empathy regarding understanding and examining an individual's unfortunate situation.

3. *She was perfectly average.* What does "average" mean? Are you average? Is your best friend average, or your Uncle Donald? Does it mean you're all alike, or just somewhat alike? What does "perfectly average" mean? Is that more average than just plain old "average?" The point is that terms like *average* or *normal* are vague. For each of us, they elicit a different picture. Thus, this statement read alone can conjure up a wide variety of meanings. There is a strong possibility of miscommunication.

4. *Petey has mongoloid features.* Mongolism is defined as "a congenital condition which is characterized by moderate to severe mental deficiency, by slanting eyes, by a broad short skull, by broad hands with short fingers, and by trisomy of the chromosome numbered 21." It is also referred to as Down's Syndrome (*Webster's New Collegiate Dictionary*, 1977, p. 743). The main point about the accuracy of this statement is whether Petey has been formally diagnosed as having mongolism. The statement should only be made if the fact has been medically established.

This particular example is rooted in fact. As a very young, naive, and inexperienced graduate student my field supervisor assigned me the task of writing my first complete assessment of my first client, Petey. I made the mistake of stating in my report that he had "mongoloid features." Unfortunately for me, Petey had not been diagnosed as having mongolism at all. He simply looked "kind of mongoloid" to me. My field supervisor ranted and raved about what horrible repercussions could occur by writing such a thing in a formal record. Petey could be labeled "mongoloid" with all of its ramifications for life. I will never forget that mistake. In actuality, Petey could have been mongoloid, as he had a wide variety of developmental disabilities. However, it was not my place to make up a fact.

5. *The house was disgustingly filthy.* What is "filthy?" How much worse is "disgustingly filthy?" To some people this might mean a week's worth of dust on the bookcase. To others it could mean mounds of dirty dishes in the sink, animal defecation on the floor, and greasy grime on the walls. This kind of statement can have major implications for people if made in a formal record. It might be used against a parent in a custody debate or in an alleged child neglect case. The point is that such a statement needs clarification and more detailed description. It should be clearly stated whether what we're talking about is dust or defecation.

6. *We solved all their problems.* This statement read by itself is simply too general and vague. What were the problems? How did we establish that *all* of them were solved? How were the solutions evaluated? Can anyone ever have *all* of his or her problems solved?

7. *I'm sure she will have a wonderful life.* It is easy for inexperienced students to make this or similar statements when completing their first written assessment or social history. This statement has two primary errors in it. First, how can you ever be absolutely certain about anything in the future? Are you sure that it will rain tomorrow or that you'll get an "A" in this course? There are other ways of stating strong impressions or opinions. For instance, "It is my strong feeling that. . . ." or "It is my impression that. . . ."

The second error in the statement involves the "wonderful life" part. What is a "wonderful life"? Does it mean one completely free of problems? What if this person gets divorced or has

to have a mastectomy? When does a life switch from being "wonderful" to "not wonderful"? Especially when first beginning in social work, it's easy to miss problems. People become adept at concealing and disguising those problems that are most troublesome to them. The real question involves what is hidden behind the "wonderful" part? No one's life is absolutely trouble-free.

8. *They should lock him up and throw away the key.* This sentence makes a strong statement about this person's future. It implies no hope for rehabilitation. Such a statement in a report made to the court could have serious consequences if it influences a judge's decision regarding prescribed punishment. What factors influenced the author to make such a strong statement? By itself the statement gives no clue.

Introduction

The point of the preceding discussion is to emphasize how critically important it is to carefully choose the words you use in social work recording. This chapter will explore social work recording in much greater depth. Most of the principles and issues discussed will apply regardless of micro, mezzo, or macro practice setting. Any setting is unique in terms of the specific types of records it requires you to keep. Specifically, the chapter will:

- Discuss the importance of writing in social work;
- Identify the major types of information included in social work records;
- Describe the most common recording formats, including diagnostic summary recording, the problem-oriented record, standardized forms, process recording, using video and audio tapes, recording for groups, letters, and memos;
- Examine writing skills necessary for good records;

- Investigate the significance of clients' right to privacy, and assess the balance between accountability and confidentiality.

The Importance of Writing in Social Work

Why is what you write so important in social work? The answer is simply that often you *are* what you write. In other words, often you won't be there to testify about a client's problems or accomplishments. Others must rely on what you've written to communicate what both you and your client have done. Additionally, a major national study found that writing was the single most frequently used skill among BSW graduates in the field today (Hull et al., 1992). Kagle (1991) cites ten specific reasons why social work records are important (pp. 2–5).

1. *Identifying the Client and the Need.* Recording information about your clients provides the basis upon which you continue to work. You identify who your clients are and specifically what problems they bring to you. Recording their existence and situations makes them part of your caseload. A caseload includes "all the clients for whom a given social worker is responsible" (Barker, 1987, p. 20). It helps you establish

Writing, according to a major national study, is the single most frequently used skill among Bachelor of Social Work graduates.

that your clients are indeed eligible for services and that your job involves intervention with them.

Recording information helps you explore the nature of your clients' strengths, needs, and problems. It helps you plan and structure how you will proceed with your intervention. It assists you in monitoring your clients' progress. Finally, it allows your agency to oversee how well all of its clients are being served.

2. *Documenting Services*. Recording your work with a client simply provides proof that such work has been done. If a colleague or your supervisor asks what you do, you can refer to your documentation to describe your assessments, plans, interventions, evaluations, terminations, and follow-ups. Documentation proves that you have accomplished what you say you have accomplished. It makes you accountable for what you've done. It can verify the fact that both you and your job are worth having.

Sometimes your client will be involved with the courts. Take, for example, clients on probation or those having child custody disputes. In these cases, your documentation of what occurred in the clients' situations will have significant impact on what will happen in their lives.

3. *Maintaining Case Continuity*. Client problems often change their focus over time. For instance, an unmarried pregnant teen will need different services before and after her baby is born, which often requires the new involvement of other agencies. Recording information about the client, the client's situation, and progress made prevents having to "invent the wheel all over again." In other words, having access to what's been done in the past is much more efficient than "starting from scratch" and doing an assessment from the very beginning.

Workers (including you) come and go as they move on in their careers. Accurate recording allows clients to be transferred with minimal interruption in their continuity of service. Having documented who the client is and what's been done allows for new workers and other professionals working with the client to begin where the last intervention left off rather than starting over from the beginning.

4. *Interprofessional Communication*. We've established that many times clients are involved with numerous agencies and workers. Many clients have multiple problems addressed by multiple agencies. This necessitates accurate communication between social workers and other professionals working with the client, such as psychologists, medical staff, occupational therapists, speech therapists, physical therapists, or psychiatrists, in addition to other social workers functioning in other intervention capacities.

Recording information about the client allows for many professionals to share this information. Some might say that actual meetings of professionals are most effective. Here a group of professionals can dynamically share information, discuss potential alternatives, and develop intervention strategies. Such meetings are often called case conferences. Their dynamic quality encourages the development of creative new ideas that might not occur to individuals working by themselves. Nonetheless, such meetings are time-consuming and expensive due to the involvement of numerous staff. Therefore, recording information and sharing it in writing provides an efficient and effective means of communicating with others involved with the client.

5. *Sharing Information with the Client*. Sometimes it's helpful to share recorded information with the client. For instance, if you're doing a behavioral assessment, showing a client a chart of progress can provide a rich incentive for continuing that progress. Other times, sharing with clients what you've stated about them can clarify for them their strengths, problems, plans, or achievements.

However, you should be aware that laws concerning client confidentiality and agency policies about such sharing with clients and involved others may restrict or prohibit such sharing. You also should be sensitive to how your client might react to the written record. For example, you record on paper that you think your client is a cocaine addict. If the client reads this when you haven't discussed this supposition with her and she is still in a state of denial over the problem, don't expect a pleasant or cooperative reaction on her part. Confidentiality issues will be discussed more thoroughly in a later section of this chapter.

6. *Facilitating Supervision, Consultation, and Peer Review.* Recording your perceptions and your progress will provide a means for you to get direction, feedback, and help from other professionals. Recording your perceptions, for example, can provide a supervisor with a means of evaluating your work. A good supervisor will provide you with constructive criticism, making specific suggestions for how you might be more effective with any particular case. Sometimes you'll be at an impasse with some new problem and simply won't know how to proceed. During times like these, a written record can be very helpful when consulting others for new ideas and suggestions. What you think and what you've done can be clearly presented in writing to them. This provides an opportunity for giving specific feedback.

Peer review involves "a formal evaluation by a relevant peer group of an individual's general competence or specific actions" (Barker, 1987, p. 118). Some agencies provide regular review of practitioners' work. If not done negatively, competitively, and destructively, such review by peers doing similar work to yours can provide a brainstorming think-tank for new, more effective intervention techniques.

7. *Monitoring the Process and Impact of Service.* Throughout this text, we've emphasized the importance of monitoring the effectiveness of your plans and interventions. It helps you to organize your thinking about how to proceed with the client (Austin, Kopp, & Smith, 1986, p. 481). Recording information about clients' progress or lack thereof provides you with clear-cut descriptions of your clients' situations at any

particular point in time. Comparing past records with present ones allows you to measure how much progress has been made.

8. *Educating Students and Other Professionals.* Social work records can provide an excellent means for educating both students and practitioners already in the field about effective interventions. They can help formulate answers to many questions. What are the most important facets of a case to assess? How can clients' strengths best be described? How do other practitioners formulate plans? What types of intervention have worked most effectively in the past with a particular type of problem? What often happens after such cases are terminated? Students and others can scrutinize records and learn much about doing social work.

9. *Providing Data for Administrative Tasks.* Both large and small social service agencies must keep track of the services they provide and how effective these services are. Just like individuals, agencies must be accountable for their work. They need to justify their existence. Additionally, administrative personnel need to attend to issues in service delivery, including "service patterns, workload management, personnel performance, and allocation of resources" (Kagle, 1991, p. 4).

10. *Providing Data for Research.* In order to improve their effectiveness, agencies and organizations need to evaluate the extent to which they are achieving their stated goals. Recording information about large numbers of clients can contribute to a database that is very useful for research. For instance, an agency can develop a typical client profile. Or, an organization can evaluate the effectiveness of a number of models of intervention. What approaches work best with specific types of clients and problems? Research, for instance, can prove that 95 percent of adoptive placements are successful or only 14 percent of clients have to return for services after a one-year period. Recording information then can give an agency and the public it serves significant feedback about how well it's working.

What's in the Record?

Austin et al. (1986) cite seven major types of information that are typically incorporated in agency records. They include:

1. *The date of your interaction with the client.* This can be recorded simply and quickly. For example, you might jot down "6/5/93" in the left-hand margin of a page. You probably should include the year because you don't know who will be picking up the record in the future or when that picking up will be.

2. *Basic information about the client.* This is also referred to as identifying information. Frequently, an agency will consistently use a *face sheet*, which is "a page, usually in the front of a client's case record or in front of a questionnaire, on which specific identifying data about the . . . [client] are recorded, such as age, gender, income, family members, prior contacts with the agency, and so on" (Barker, 1987, p. 53). Specific information requested will vary somewhat according to agency needs. For instance, a Planned Parenthood agency which focuses on helping people with family planning and reproductive health will probably seek information pertaining to the client's health record.

An example of a face sheet is given in Figure 16.1. This sheet provides basic information about a licensed foster home placement. Foster care, of course, involves substitute, full-time care for children who for some reason are unable to live in their own homes. Such placements must conform to specified standards regarding such things as physical conditions and qualifications of the foster parents themselves. They are usually licensed by a public agency in the state in which they live. Licensing means that such placements, after complying with certain standards, are granted "a formal authorization to do something that cannot be done legally without that authorization" (Barker, 1987, p. 90). The face sheet in Figure 16.1 then illustrates the identifying sheet that would be placed at the beginning of a foster family's individual file. The blanks, of course, would be filled in with the information reflecting that particular family's situation.

It should be emphasized that social work records vary drastically in format and content from one agency to another. Examples such as Figure 16.1 are included here only to give you the idea about what to expect in real social work practice. A number of examples will be included in this chapter. Some will be blank forms actually used by individual agencies. Others will be completed examples about what has been recorded about specific clients and cases. The ones you will encounter when you get a job will resemble the examples here in that they will have an established format and will require you to include specific information. However, it is about as unlikely as you winning a state lottery that you will encounter these identical forms in real social work practice.

3. *Reason for client contact.* What is the client's problem and situation? Why is the client coming to you and your agency for help? This can be "a short statement of the major problem as identified by the . . . [client] and clarified by the worker" (Austin et al., 1986, p. 483).

- School referred Arlo to Vocational Enterprises for vocational evaluation services in order to assess vocational strengths and limitations and to assist in vocational planning.
- Mr. C. called Crisis Line and threatened suicide. He said he was depressed and requested counseling.
- Juvenile Court referred Blake and family for counseling following her numerous truancies and recent apprehension for selling illegal drugs.

4. *More detailed information about the client's problem and situation.* Here you must choose which information is more relevant to the client's problem, including his or her strengths, and which is less significant.

Figure 16.1: An Example of a Face Sheet

Foster Home Licensing and Face Sheet

Last Name   Telephone

Address   City   County

HUSBAND or Single Person   WIFE

First Name   Birth Date   First Name   Birth Date

Race   Religion   Race   Religion

Occupation   Occupation

Work Hours and Phone   Work Hours and Phone

Ages of Own Children in Home:_____
                              Boy(s)   Girl(s)

List Name(s) and Age(s) of Foster Children Now in Home:_____

_____

Schools Foster Children Might Attend:_____

Special Child Care Skills:_____

LICENSE INFORMATION

Number of Children:_____   Sex of Children:_____

Age of Children:_____   Other Limitations:_____

DESCRIPTION OF HOME

Total Number of Rooms:_____   Number of Bedrooms:_____

OCCUPANTS IN HOME

Number of Adults:_____   Number of Own Children:_____

Number of Other Persons (excluding foster children):_____

AGENCY RESPONSIBLE FOR LICENSING:_____

AGENCY RESPONSIBLE FOR SUPERVISION:_____

DATE OF LICENSE: From_____To_____

Submitted by:_____   _____
                  Worker   Date

Approved by:_____   _____
                  Supervisor   Date

Source: This form is adapted from one used by the State of Wisconsin Department of Health & Social Services (DHSS). Used with permission of the Wisconsin DHSS, 1 West Wilson, Madison WI.

Figure 16.2: An Example of an Intake Form

CEPHAS HALFWAY HOUSE
Lutheran Social Services

Intake Form

Pre-Intake Date:_____

Intake Date:_____

Name:_____   Birth Date:_____ Place:_____

Address:_____   Ht:_____ Wt:_____ Sex:_____

Telephone:_____   Marital Status: S__ M__ D__ Sep__ W__

Social Security No.:_____   Status: Probation:_____ Parole:_____

Referred by Agency:_____   Person:_____ Phone:_____

On Probation for:_____   Sentence:_____

Present P. O.:_____   Past P. O.:_____
(Probation or Parole Officer)
Court Obligation or Parole Obligation:_____

_____

_____

Is There Any Restriction?:_____   Explain:_____

_____

_____

Reason for Stay at Cephas Halfway House:_____

_____

_____

Notify in Case of Emergency:

Name:_____   Phone: Home_____ Work_____

Relationship:_____   Address:_____

Alternate, if any:_____

Source: This material is reprinted with permission of Luthern Social Services, 3200 W. Highland Blvd., Milwaukee, WI.

Figure 16.2 (*continued*)

CEPHAS HALFWAY HOUSE

Lutheran Social Services

<u>Personal History II</u>

EDUCATIONAL BACKGROUND

Highest Grade Completed: _____ When: _____ GED: _____

Where: _____

College: _____ Other: _____

Vocational Training: _____

Type of Training: _____

_____

When: _____ Where: _____ Skill level: _____

MILITARY

Branch: _____ Dates of Service: _____

Type of Discharge: Honorable: _____ General: _____ Undesirable: _____ Dishonorable: ___

Other: _____

DRIVER'S LICENSE

Yes: _____ No: _____ With/Without Restriction: _____

PAST RECORD

Juvenile

Charges	Disposition	When
1.		
2.		
3.		
4.		
5.		

Adult

Charges	Dispostion	When
1.		
2.		
3.		
4.		
5.		

Figure 16.2 (*continued*)

```
page 3, fc                    CEPHAS HALFWAY HOUSE
                              Lutheran Social Services


                                Intake Form III



How long have you been incarcerated: _____

Where: _____

When: _____


MEDICAL INFORMATION

Cardiac: _____ Epilepsy: _____ Diabetes: _____ Other: _____

Medication, if any: _____ Times/Day: _____

Physical Limitations, if any: _____

_____


INITIAL IMPRESSIONS
```

Agencies vary in the amount and type of information they solicit during the intake process. Intake involves the established procedures for an agency's initial contact with a client. Such procedures might involve telling clients about agency programs, service requirements, and costs. They also include obtaining necessary information about the client, making an initial determination about the client's problem and motivation for service, and designating a specific worker to provide service.

An example of an intake form is presented in Figure 16.2. This form was developed for a halfway house for men on probation or parole who also have alcohol and other drug-related problems. A halfway house provides a "transitional residence for individuals who require some professional supervision, support, or protection but not full-time hospitalization" (Barker, 1987, p. 68).

Depending on why the information is needed and at what point it's gathered in the intervention process, the record can be very detailed or relatively brief and straightforward. The following is an example of a narrative information summary that details the situation where Taylor, a developmentally disabled adult, is referred to an agency for vocational evaluation and placement. All the summary's content related to the vocational planning goal:

Taylor, age fifty-two, lives with his brother and family in Omro. Education consists of a high-school diploma earned through special educational programming in 1956. Taylor reported that he most enjoyed reading classes and least enjoyed arithmetic during his school years. Work history consists of thirty years as a farm laborer. Duties include washing cows, carrying milk, cleaning barns, haying, and driving tractors to haul wagons. Wages were forty dollars per month plus room and board. Taylor also worked at a local theater on weekends as an usher for six years. Disability is listed as Borderline Intellectual Functioning DSMIII V62.89. Full-scale IQ is reported at seventy-three. Academic skills are at the third-grade level. Medical history involves no record of recent hospitalization. Taylor did state that seven years ago he had a farm accident that resulted in a compound fracture of the right arm. Strenuous heavy lifting sometimes bothers him. Leisure activities include fishing and collecting stamps. Taylor stated he would like to work at Vocational Enterprises.

Frequently, more extensive information is gathered. This type of document is often referred to as a *social history*. Specifically, a social history is "an in-depth description and assessment of the current and past client-situation. . . . It is a document that describes the person's family and socioeconomic background and relevant developmental experiences" (Barker, 1987, p. 152). A social history can be organized topic by topic (for example, "employment history" and "extended family"). It can also be written in a chronological, narrative format. Narrative formats refer to those that are written paragraph by paragraph in story-like form. Regardless of format, in addition to information about the client and problem, most social histories include specific recommendations for how to begin the intervention process. Figure 16.3 illustrates an example of a social history format.

5. *Aspects of the intervention process.* This includes your impressions concerning assessment of the client-in-situation, your specific plans for intervention, contacts you've had with clients and others involved in the case over the course of the intervention, progress made, and information about how the case was terminated. Each agency is unique in the specific records it requires workers to keep. As we will discuss in more depth later on, some agencies primarily use reporting forms where you simply fill in the blanks. Other agencies require formatting, which has more of a narrative quality.

Frequently, workers will record a brief entry for each contact with the client and others involved chronologically throughout the intervention process. This includes phone calls

Figure 16.3: An Example of a Social History Format

Name: _____ (d.o.b.): _____

Address: _____

Telephone: _____

School and Grade: _____

Place of Birth: _____

OUTLINE FOR SOCIAL HISTORY

I. FAMILY COMPOSITION
   (Note if any parent or sibling is deceased and date)

   Natural Father: d.o.b.:
   Address:
   Occupation:
   Religion:

   Stepfather: (If appropriate)   d.o.b.:
   Address:
   Occupation:
   Religion:

   Natural Mother: d.o.b.:
   Address:
   Occupation:
   Religion:

   Stepmother: (If appropriate)   d.o.b:
   Address:
   Occupation:
   Religion:

   Siblings:
   Name, date of birth, school and grade. List all siblings including those out of
   home and current situation. If client or siblings are living with others, state
   names, addresses, and relationship.

Figure 16.3 (continued)

Name: _____ (d.o.b.):_____

II. CHILD UNDER CONSIDERATION

Describe personality and physical characteristics.

III. REASON FOR REFERRAL

Short statement about immediate concern, current situation, and by whom referred. Parent and child's attitude about possible placement outside the home.

IV. FAMILY BACKGROUND

A. Mother

1. Relationship to each of mother's parents; relation between mother's parents; evidence of emotional disturbance in family.

2. Mother's educational and vocational history.

3. Medical history if pertinent.

4. Previous marriages, with significant details.

5. History of mother's courting and marriage, including feelings about marriage and children.

B. Father

1. Relationship to each of father's parents, relationship between father's parents; evidence of emotional disturbance in family.

Figure 16.3 (*continued*)

Name: _____ (d.o.b.):_____

 2. Father's educational and vocational history.

 3. Medical history if pertinent.

 4. Previous marriages, with significant details.

 5. History of father's courting and marriage, including feelings about
    marriage and children.

 C. Family Development

   1. Describe parental relationships, who disciplines whom and how, nature
      and reasons for conflicts, family attitude toward current situation,
      family's financial situation and community involvement, family
      involvement with law enforcement and mental health agencies. What do
      you see happening in the family and why? This section should contain a
      historical perspective and comment on the past as well as the present.

   2. Sibling Relationships

      Describe child's relationship with each sibling, to whom is child
      closest and from whom most alienated, reaction to birth of next young-
      est sibling, any specific problems or emotional difficulties siblings
      in family have or have had in the past and how handled by parents.

Figure 16.3 (*continued*)

Name: _____   (d.o.b.):_____

   3. Other Significant Adults

      Grandparents, aunts, uncles, neighbors, and teachers. Indicate who and
      type of relationship and when it began.

   4. Environment

      Significance of neighborhoods family has lived in and their dwellings.

V. PERSONAL HISTORY OF CHILD

  A. Developmental Data

     From pregnancy to current parental realtionship during pregnancy, reaction
     to pregnancy, preferred sex, mother's health (signs of miscarriage,
     emotional state, significant use or abuse of drugs or alcohol)

     Birth

     Delivery, premature or full term, spontaneous, physical condition of mother
     and child, length of hospital stay.

     Early Months

     Note any changes in mother's physical or emotional health. Any difficulties
     in adjusting to the home, was it stable at this time? Did child have colic
     or other problems? Was child breast or bottle fed, any feeding difficulties?
     Note changes in any caretakers and significant losses.

Figure 16.3 (continued)

Name: _____ (d.o.b.):_____

Later Months and Toddler Stage

Note ages at which child walked, talked, and was toilet trained. Note any difficulties with sleeping and eating patterns.

Coordination and Motor Pattern

A general statement as well as noting any hyperactivity, sluggishness, head or body rocking, random or unorganized activity.

Parent's feelings regarding above and how they attempted to handle any difficulties.

B. Personality and Social Growth

Responsiveness

Did child like to be held or did he withdraw from people? Did he play with adults and/or children. Did he play in group or prefer to play alone?

Relationships

Describe relationship with each parent as related by both parents and child --explore any differences. What about relationships with siblings?

Separations from either or both parents

When, why, how long; note also parental and child response toward separating to attend school.

Describe child's outstanding traits and fears if any, e.g., is he happy, sullen, stubborn, dependent, independent, does he have any persistent fears, phobias, or compulsions?

Discipline

How and by whom, how have parents and child reacted to it?

Figure 16.3 *(continued)*

Name: _____   (d.o.b.):_____

Sexual Development

Amount of sex education, provided by whom; unusual behavior or preoccupations; kind of questions or curiosity displayed; masturbation, parental response.

C. <u>Medical History</u>

Any illness or disease suffered; injuries, falls, high fevers, convulsions, fainting or other spells; allergies or other somatic disturbances; child and parent reactions. Also any hospitalization history. Touch on any previous treatment for current problems, previous psychiatric treatment. Type and extent of drug usage, if any.

Birth disfigurements, speech defects, enuresis, handicaps.

Present health.

D. <u>Educational Experiences</u>

Schools and years attended, achievement, testing dates done by schools, M-Team Reports, interpersonal relationships of child; parent's relationship with school systems, extra-curricular activities.

Psychological and Psychiatric Evaluations--previous referrals, contacts, treatment, and progress.

E. <u>Employment Experience</u>

VI. <u>PREVIOUS TREATMENT</u>

Prior placements and services, successful completion of or failure of services and/or placements.

Figure 16.3 (*continued*)

Name: _____ (d.o.b.):_____

Substantiate care and services that would permit the child to remain at home that have been investigated and considered and are not available or likely to become available within a reasonable time to meet the needs of the child.

a. What alternatives to the plan are available?

b. What alternatives have been explored?

c. Why aren't the explored alternatives appropriate?

d. Discuss objectives of rehabilitation, treatment, and care.

VII. REFERENCE SOURCES

Label and date interviews, reports, and letters used to complete the social history.

Date: _____

Prepared by: _____
(Social Worker)

Approved by: _____
(Supervisor)

SS-153 (Rev. '82)

Source: Adapted from form "Outline for Social History." Used with permission of the Community Human Services Department, Waukesha County, 500 Riverview Ave., Waukesha, WI 53188.

made concerning the case. Such notes need not be lengthy or tedious. Frequently, brief phrases will suffice. Dates should always be noted. Even in those rare agencies that don't require this type of recording, it is often wise for you to keep your own notes. An example of one progress note format is presented in Figure 16.4.

A few varied examples of such brief notes follow (the "problem numbers" portion noted in Figure 16.4 will be explained later in the chapter):

3/14/93	Marah's probation officer called. She missed last appointment with him. If that happens once more, he will refer M. back to court. I will call M.'s mother to arrange for a home visit.
5/20/93	Wrote Dr. Morrison that staff noticed Josh's continued odor problems—even the day after Monday's bath.
8/4/93	Held progress review today. Refer to Report for details.
10/8/93	Met with Mr. Petrie. Discussed current job situation. He will follow through on my five referrals and call me back regarding progress by 10/13/93.

6. *Follow-up information.* Is there a plan for follow-up? If so, specifically, who will do what by when?

For instance, a worker might record:

8/5/93	Terminated with Kelly. Summarized progress. I will call within four weeks to determine if alcohol abuse has stopped and if she continues involvement with AA [Alcoholics Anonymous].
9/2/93	Called Kelly. She states she has stopped abuse and continues AA involvement. I will call once more

in mid–November to determine her progress.

7. *Comments and questions to discuss with a supervisor or another worker* (Austin et al., 1986, p. 483). Your own non-validated impressions about a case and questions you'd like to have answered are also appropriate for agency records. Noting these on paper when you think of them can remind you to refer to them during your next meeting with a supervisor.

For example, you might note questions like: "Are resources available in her community for domestic violence?", "Ms. U. seems detached; is schizophrenia resurfacing?", or "What are major symptoms of her disease?"

The Most Common Recording Formats

Three basic types of formats have become the most commonly used in social work agencies today: diagnostic summary recording, problem-oriented recording, and standardized forms that are frequently compatible with computerized record-keeping (Kagle, 1987). In addition to these, we will discuss recording in groups, letter writing, and memos. Finally, we will discuss two common methods of recording that are typically employed to train social work students: process-recording and audio/video recording. Because the last two are the most detailed and basic, we will start with them.

Process-Recording

Wilson (1980) describes process-recording as:

A specialized and highly detailed form of recording. Everything that takes place in an interview is recorded using an "I said then [s]he said"

Figure 16.4: An Example of a Progress Note Format

Client Name: _____		Case ID/MA #: _____
Date Mo/Day/Yr	Problem Number	Progress Note

Source: Adapted from form HSD-004 (3/89) entitled "Waukesha County Community Services Department Progress Notes." Used with permission of the Community Human Services Department, Waukesha County, 500 Riverview Ave., Waukesha, WI 53188.

style. In effect, the social worker writes down everything that would have been heard or observed had a tape recorder and camera been monitoring the interview. Most process-recording uses direct quotes (p. 18).

Additionally, the worker's or student's impressions and comments are noted in a special column right next to what has just been said. Figure 16.5 illustrates an example of a process-recording.

As you can see, Figure 16.5 records word for word what the worker and client say to each other. The worker then comments on her own feelings and impressions about what transpired between herself and her client. Note that you do not have to write a comment concerning each statement. Record one only when you feel it is appropriate and relevant.

Process-recording such as this is very time-consuming. Time is precious, and doing this prevents you from doing other job tasks. Therefore, this type of recording is used primarily for students in their internship. It allows you as a student to analyze in detail your interactions with clients. It also allows your supervisor to give you specific feedback even though he was not present when the interaction occurred.

Using Video- and Audiotapes

Taping your sessions with clients can be tremendously useful. For one thing, taping can sup-

---

Figure 16.5: Portion of a Process-Recording with a Client Who Has Just Entered a Nursing Home

		Comments
Worker:	Good morning, Mrs. Wonderbread. How are you feeling today?	I was worried about her adjustment as this was her third day here.
Client:	Oh, not very well, I'm afraid. My feet hurt and I sure do miss my own home.	It made me nervous when she complained like this. I didn't know what to say.
Worker:	I know you do, Mrs. Wonderbread. It was a very difficult thing for you to do. Leave that house and come here, I mean.	I was trying to show empathy and let her know I really cared.
Client:	Can't I please go home? Please? I promise that I'll eat the way I should.	This made me uncomfortable.
Worker:	You know we worked to keep you at home as long as we could. But you lost forty pounds and fell four times. We were really worried about you.	I tried to review the facts.
Client:	Oh, I know I fell, but I promise I won't anymore. Please let me go home. Please! I hate it here!	
Worker:	You know I wish I could say all right. But you agreed that your health just wouldn't allow you to take care of yourself there anymore.	
Client:	My son, that traitor. He doesn't care about me. Nobody cares about me.	She was expressing her anger.
Worker:	You know I care about you, Mrs. Wonderbread. And I hate hearing you so unhappy. Do you have some time to come out and visit the garden? I'd like to show you the roses. I know how you love flowers.	I think there are things here at the home that she'll learn to enjoy. I'll try to get her more involved.
Client:	Well, I guess so. I do love roses.	

ply you with general feedback about yourself. You may not like to see or hear yourself. Your voice may sound too scratchy to you or you won't like the way you slouch your back. However, viewing or listening to tapes can furnish you with invaluable information about how your clients perceive you. It provides you with a clear picture of your "natural style of interaction" (Ivey, 1983, p. 310). You may decide to try to change some things. For instance, you may determine that you don't speak loudly enough for others to understand you clearly and easily. Or you may notice other habits for the first time such as rolling your eyes and staring deeply into space when concentrating deeply, tapping your feet loudly and rythmically, or tapping the table with your fingers.

Taping your sessions with clients can also be used to gain specific feedback about your interviewing and problem-solving styles. A supervisor viewing or listening to a tape can furnish you with specific suggestions for what you might have said or how you might have proceeded at any particular part of the session. In this way, you can get ideas about alternative and possibly more effective intervention strategies.

It is most likely that video or audiotapes will be used in your student field placement or in your social work practice courses because of their educational value. Although they can be valuable in the real work setting, they, like process-recording, are time-consuming and, thus, expensive.

Kagle (1991) proposes six steps for using audio or videotapes. First, you must get the client's explicit permission to use the tapes. *Never* record an interview without the client's knowledge. It violates their right to confidentiality. Some agencies have established permission forms for such activities.

Although the client (and, perhaps, you) may feel uncomfortable initially during taping, this probably soon will pass. People usually get involved in the ongoing discussion and forget that taping is occurring. This is especially true after the first time.

One creative way of videotaping the session entails having your supervisor observe you during the session from behind a one-way mirror. This, of course, is only possible if the equipment and setting is readily available. As your supervisor observes, she may record comments into an audiotape recorder. Later, you can review both tapes together, getting your supervisor's feedback as you're actually watching yourself proceed with the interview. The supervisor need not be present.

The second step in the taping process is actually doing the taping. The third step involves writing out what transpired during the tape word by word. This resembles a process-recording, although you may or may not include your subjective impressions and concerns. Because this process is so time-consuming, this step is optional.

The fourth step involves writing a summary of the taped session. This may be unstructured in that you summarize what happened during the entire session. You might organize an unstructured summary according to the most important things that happened chronologically. Or you might structure the report by prioritizing what occurred in the interview in order of importance. Either approach involves determining what was most significant in the interview and what amounted to unnecessary detail. Summarizing is one of the most difficult tasks to learn about recording. Accurate discrimination between what is important and what is not generally improves with experience. The more you think about your interviews and make decisions, the easier it is to do the next time.

Your summary report may also follow a more structured format. In other words, it may respond to a series of questions and/or directions. For instance, one format directs you to respond to or answer the following:

1. Briefly summarize chronologically the most significant critical points that oc-

curred during the interview.

2. What specific problems, needs, and strengths surfaced during your meeting?
3. What specific methods did you use during the interview? For each, describe the extent to which you felt they were effective or not effective.
4. Where during the interview do you feel you could have used more effective techniques? Describe your recommended techniques.
5. What are your recommendations for your next meeting with the client?

The fifth step in the taping process involves reviewing your tape, the summary, and, perhaps, the verbatim record with your supervisor. Your supervisor can give you feedback regarding both your intervention approaches and your report writing. The sixth step involves adapting what you've learned during this discussion and writing a report that complies with the conventional format your agency uses.

Diagnostic Summary Recording

Diagnostic summary recordings are among the most commonly used types of agency records. They have several characteristics (Hamilton, 1946; Kagle, 1987). First, they involve ongoing summaries of the progress during intervention. In other words, they are periodic written summaries, not one-time summary reports.

Second, diagnostic summary recordings vary drastically in terms of their actual format. Length, organization or order of topics, and the topics themselves vary widely from agency to agency. Most, however, are structured to include a series of topics. For example, topics might include: "Presenting Problem," "Progress Summary," and "Recommendations." In the actual record or case file the periodic summaries are usually recorded chronologically.

The third characteristic involves a primarily narrative format. In other words, under each topical heading are a number of written narrative paragraphs using, hopefully, correct grammar to describe the case's progress. Highlight 16.1 illustrates an example of a diagnostic summary recording. It was written by a social work "therapist" responsible for providing treatment at a special treatment center that furnished both special education and therapy for behaviorally disordered and delinquent adolescents. Remember that this is only an example and formats vary widely from agency to agency.

Wilson distinguishes five primary differences between process-recording and summary recording (1980). First, content is summarized instead of written verbatim. Second, there is much less, if any, reference to you as the worker and what you do. Rather, the focus is on your impressions and recommendations. Third, only major points are included. Miscellaneous detail is omitted. Fourth, summary recording includes only the intervention's results, not the techniques you used. Fifth, information is usually organized under a variety of topic headings, instead of being recorded in chronological order.

Summaries of Case Conferences

A special type of summary recording involves case conferences. Barker (1987) describes the case conference as follows:

A procedure often used in social agencies and other organizations to bring together members of a professional staff to discuss a client's problem, objectives, intervention plans, and prognoses. The participants in the conference may include the social workers who are providing the direct service to the client or client system and the professional supervisor of these workers. Additional participants might include other agency workers who have special expertise or experience with similar problems or populations, members of other professional groups or disciplines who can provide further information and recommendations, and sometimes personal as-

HIGHLIGHT 16.1

An Example of a Diagnostic Summary Recording

Name of Client: Carol Pulowski
Date of Birth: 11/26/77
Date of Summary: 12/3/93

1. Summary Description

Carol is a heavy, verbal, bright girl who is very sophisticated in social interaction and sensitive to the reaction of others. She has a history of disruptive behavior, including fighting and school problems such as truancy. She has participated in individual therapy and group work with me since September 1992.

2. Presenting Problems

Carol's ability to define alternatives and to examine the results of her behavior realistically is very poor. Her motivation to achieve academically is also very poor. She tends to focus on immediate gratification. When things don't go as she plans, her usual response is to get angry, give up, and go somewhere else, thus shirking any responsibility. Carol has very unrealistic ideas about her future. Her major motivating force at this time is money, but she is unable to utilize available means to improve herself or her status in order to earn that money in the future.

3. Peer Group Relationships

Carol is an accepted and respected member of her peer group. She has much insight into interactions of others but a limited understanding of the effects of her own behavior on herself. For instance, she can easily recognize the expression of painful or angry feelings in her peers. However, she is usually unable to identify similar behavior in herself.

4. Family Situation

Carol is currently living with her guardian, her older sister Royola, her one-year-younger sister Geraldine, and occasionally other aunts. Royola, due to preoccupation with her own problems, is unable to supply Carol with much support or guidance.

5. Treatment Progress

In individual therapy, Carol will sometimes bring up and try to work on her problems. However, she often avoids relevant issues and avoids any negative feedback about the results of her actions.

Individual therapy has focused on the following goals: prevention of Carol's fleeing from responsibility by getting angry or walking out; enhanced confrontation of problems and work toward their solutions; improved self-assessment skills, including focusing on personal strengths, weaknesses, and future job status; and establishment of personal goals and definition of realistic means to attain them. Group therapy has focused on the utilization of positive leadership potential, receiving peer feedback about her behavior, and developing increased understanding of human interaction skills.

6. Recommendations

Continuance in the treatment program is recommended in order to work on the aforementioned goals, with emphasis on taking responsibility for herself and attaining realistic, concrete goals.

Kris Krist, MSW, BSW
Social Work Therapist

sociates or relatives of the client who may be asked to provide information or helping resources (pp. 19–20).

Thus, a case conference may involve a meeting of social workers, professionals in other disciplines, clients, and others involved with clients. As a social worker you are likely to be in the role of leading the conference. You may be the case manager, which involves coordinating virtually all the services provided to one or more clients. This latter role was discussed in greater depth in chapter 15. Sometimes, depending on the agency, case conferences are also referred to as staffings, multidisciplinary team conferences, or interdisciplinary team meetings.

A case conference's purpose is threefold (Austin, Skelding, & Smith, 1977). First, it helps to assess and clearly describe the client's problem. Second, it enhances the involved professionals' grasp of the client's behavior and situation. Third, it provides an arena in which intervention plans may be formulated and ongoing goals reevaluated.

Your own presentation at a case conference should involve the following (Austin et al., 1977):

1. A statement of the . . . [client's] problem;
2. Your observations of the . . . [client];
3. How you have been working with the . . . [client]—the service plan to date;
4. A summary of the results of any . . . [intervention] used or service delivered;
5. The reasons this particular information is being shared with other workers and specific questions highlighting the problem areas that other workers can help you answer (p. 391).

Such a summary may be done either orally or in writing. Frequently, agencies require the written report to be added to the client's ongoing record.

You are also likely to be responsible for summarizing the final findings and conclusions of the entire case conference. Such a summary should follow a similar format in terms of including the preceding information. The specific format of a case conference summary may vary somewhat from agency to agency. One important thing to remember, however, is to clearly specify plans and goals as discussed in chapter 6.

Problem-Oriented Recording

Problem-oriented recording is the second of the three most commonly used methods of recording in social work (Kagle, 1987). Essentially, it involves using a specified format to list problems and another related format to note progress made toward their solutions. Frequently, the problem-oriented record is referred to as *POR*. POR has four primary components; they include a data base, list of problems, intervention plans, and progress in implementing the plans (Kagle, 1991; Sheafor et al., 1988; Weed, 1969). A case example of POR is illustrated in Highlight 16.2.

Database

Sheafor et al. (1988) describe what should be included in the data base:

> The data base consists primarily of the information collected during the intake phase and includes demographic characteristics and a description of the problem that brought the client to the agency. Much of the data base appears on the record facesheet or in the social history. This data should be systematically collected, organized, and recorded, for it provides a foundation for identifying and conceptualizing the client's problems and gives rise to a preliminary problem list (p. 141).

Problem List

Problems can include any that the client is concerned about in addition to those identified

HIGHLIGHT 16.2

An Amended Case Example of Problem-Oriented Recording

The following is an example of problem-oriented recording. The client is a developmentally disabled adult who was referred to an agency offering a variety of services for developmentally disabled people, including evaluation, vocational training, social activities, job placement services, in-home supervision, and group home placement.

This example has been amended somewhat to help overcome the disadvantages mentioned earlier. Specifically, the problem list has been expanded to include both problems and needs. Second, an additional section has been added that lists strengths. Third, a macro orientation has been applied in the last progress note.

Client: Freddie Weaver
Date of Birth: January 13, 1967

1. Database

Freddie was referred by County Social Services on 6/27 for a multiple-level evaluation and subsequent placement in job and living arrangements. He had been living with his elderly mother who died on 6/15. Freddie's brother and his wife have been in regular touch with Social Services and express serious concern over his well-being and future placement. Freddie is residing with them until further plans can be made.

Freddie graduated from high school having taken primarily special education courses. He reports he had difficulty with math and spelling. Achievement grade levels are: reading, 3.4; math, 3.8; and spelling, 3.0. He was employed at a local cheese factory from the time of his high school graduation until two years ago when he was laid off.

His daily activities have included caring for his mother who was bed-bound, shopping for groceries, and watching television. He reports having no friends.

Freddie's sister-in-law (wife of his one sibling) has been regularly involved in Freddie's and his mother's care. Living forty miles away, she has made weekly visits to help with paying bills, cleaning, washing, and other household tasks. She has indicated that he will not be able to continue living with her and her husband because of the brothers' inability to get along.

Freddie appears to be a pleasant individual with a good sense of humor. He speaks slowly and is difficult to understand. He stated that he would like to find both a job and a place to live independently. He indicated that he did not want to continue living with his brother.

2. List of Problems and Needs

Problem	Date	
	Becomes Active:	Inactive/ Resolved:
1. Needs evaluation of intellectual, social, and vocational capacities	7/5/94	
2. Needs permanent place to live	7/5/94	
3. Needs employment	7/5/94	
4. Lack of social support system	7/5/94	
5. Poor relationship with brother	7/5/94	7/10/94

3. Strengths

1. Willingness to cooperate
2. Prior job experience
3. Supportive sister-in-law
4. Pleasant personality
5. Daily living skills developed while caring for his mother

4. Initial Intervention Plans

No. 1: Needs evaluation of intellectual, social, and vocational capacities
- I will refer Freddie to Evaluation Unit by 7/9/94.

No. 2: Needs permanent place to live
- Wait until receive evaluation results and discuss alternatives with family.

No. 5: Poor relationship with brother
- I will meet with Freddie, his brother, and his sister-in-law within two weeks to discuss living alternatives.

5. Progress Notes

7/3/94

No. 1: Needs evaluation

S: Freddie appeared nervous. He states he's anxious to get the testing over with.
O: Accompanied Freddie to evaluation unit. Will receive results by 7/9/94.
P: Will discuss evaluation results with Freddie and family as soon as possible.—B.A.

7/10/94

No. 1: Needs evaluation

S: F.'s very close to his sister-in-law. Relationship with brother not as negative as first appeared.
O: Met with F., brother, and wife to discuss eval. results.

No. 2: Needs permanent place to live

S: F. seems anxious to move out of brother's home.
O: Test results indicate high level of adaptive functioning in all three areas tested.
A: F. capable of living alone in apartment with some staff supervision.
P: Within 2 days I will consult with Living Arrangement supervisor to explore alternative locations.

No. 4: Lack of social support system

S: F. seems personable and lonely.
O: Activities for socialization here appropriate for F. include baseball team, dance group, and bingo.
A: Good potential to fulfill F.'s social needs here.
P: I will discuss available activities with F. during our next meeting on Thurs. and encourage him to attend. If necessary, I'll accompany him the first time.

No. 5: Poor relationship with brother

A: Relationship may improve when F. moves out. They communicate to some extent.
P: Inactive unless further problems—B.A.

7/14/94

No. 2: Needs permanent place to live

S: F. eager to move out.
O: There is no reasonable housing available within close proximity to the agency.

by client and worker during the assessment process. Both client and worker need to agree upon which problems should be the focus of intervention in addition to their priority. In other words, in what order should the problems be worked on? Developing this list can be helpful in that "the process of defining and analyzing a problem critically usually results in an improved understanding of the problem for the . . . [worker]

and the client and a greater ability to set long- and short-term objectives" (Burrill, 1976, p. 67).

It's recommended that the respective problems be numbered (Kane, 1974). Concisely stated problems can provide you with an easily scanned checklist that prevents you from focusing only on one problem. Additionally, when a problem is solved or no longer relevant, it can simply be deleted from the list. An example of

---

HIGHLIGHT 16.2 (continued)

A: Housing needs to be made available. Other clients have similar needs.

P: I will consult supervisor tomorrow to explore ways of locating or developing housing resources.—B.A.

Some Comments about This Particular Record

As we've already noted, a section on client and situation strengths has been added. Strengths provide clues for how to proceed with planning. For example, a willingness to cooperate implies that plans can be made and acted upon relatively quickly with minimal resistance. This willingness to cooperate in addition to Freddie's pleasant personality imply that his social needs have a good chance of being met by the services already provided by the agency. Uncooperative or hostile clients would not readily fit into established social groups.

You might note that the problems are numbered and the strengths alphabetized. This is done arbitrarily to minimize confusion. Additionally, because strengths are difficult to measure and prioritize, they may be listed in any order. For instance, it would be difficult to prioritize whether Freddie's willingness to cooperate or his supportive sister-in-law would ultimately be the most valuable to him. The important thing is that a list of strengths is readily available to you to draw from creatively in your planning.

It should be noted that the exact formats for problem-oriented recording and SOAP vary from agency to agency. For example, the date of the progress note entry may be placed on either the right or the left side of the page. Some agencies have an entirely separate page to list problems. This allows enough room to continue adding and omitting problems in one spot without interfering with the ongoing flow of progress notes. It also allows you to locate and read the problem list quickly.

It's important to include dates both in the active and inactive portions of your problem list and for each of your progress notes. Otherwise, with a busy workload it's very easy to lose your realistic perception of how much time has passed. You might wonder, for instance, whether it's been two weeks or five weeks since you last contacted that particular client.

Additionally, it's suggested that you record the year in addition to the month and day. This is especially important for follow-up and for re-referrals. Years later it's difficult or impossible to figure out when an intervention occurred if the date is not clearly specified.

You might also note that abbreviations are sometimes used in this problem-oriented recording. For example, "F." replaces "Freddie" as the report continues. In real situations, workers will frequently use abbreviations to make their work easier and less time-consuming.

Problem No. 1 is another example of using abbreviation. After being used several times, it is

a format for prioritizing problems is presented in Figure 16.6.

For example, take the problem list noted below of a single mother who has two small children and is living on public assistance:

1. Inadequate food
2. Extremely poor living conditions
3. No job
4. No day care for the children
5. No social support system

If you as the worker help your client find employment, you can simply delete problem number three from the list. Yet, you still maintain a perspective on how problems are prioritized and how much has been accomplished.

---

abbreviated from "Needs evaluation of intellectual, social, and vocational capacities" to "Needs evaluation." This is because the types of evaluation needed were already firmly established within the report. The time it took to write out the additional words was no longer worth it. The important thing is that a person reading the report for the first time can understand clearly what's being said.

This particular record used the word "I" frequently. This is to indicate clearly those tasks the worker had responsibility for. Sometimes, progress notes will omit the "I." For instance, instead of writing, "I will call F.'s sister-in-law tomorrow," the record might state, "Will call F.'s sister-in-law tomorrow." Once again, this is on the behalf of brevity.

In some way you as the worker must make it clear who wrote the note. This may be done using a variety of formats. The one illustrated previously has the worker's initials "B.A." noted after each progress note entry for a specified date. Different agencies require different notations. For example, another one might require the worker to sign her first initial and full last name (for example, B. Aardvark) right after the date at the beginning of the progress note.

Not all of the problems are addressed in the Initial Intervention Plans section because the worker plans to address them later. The worker has determined that Freddie's employment status and social support system can only be addressed after his other evaluations are completed. Then more information will be available with which to develop alternatives and make decisions.

Nor are *all* the problems necessarily addressed under any particular daily entry in the progress notes. Only include the ones upon which some action has been taken. For example, Problems 1, 2, 4, and 5 are recognized on 7/10/94. The worker did not address Problem No. 3, "Needs employment." This is because No. 3 was placed on the back burner to look at sometime in the future. Other aspects of Freddie's situation needed to be settled before he could adjust properly to a job.

Only *portions* of SOAP might be included under any particular problem in the progress notes. For example, no "S" is included in the 7/3/94 progress note entry. This is because the worker decided that an adequate assessment could not be made until tests were completed and results examined.

One of the problems, No. 5, "poor relationship with brother," was noted as going from an active status to inactive on 7/10/94. This was because the worker determined that the brothers' relationship problem would subside when they no longer had to live together on a daily basis.

Finally, you might note that at times progress made involves more than one problem. For example, the worker sat down and talked with Freddie and his family to discuss both his evaluation results and his living situation. Instead of writing a similar SOAP under both progress notes, the worker can decide which problem was more significant and note SOAP only once. Writing essentially the same thing twice is a waste of precious time.

Initial Intervention Plans

Planning in generalist practice was explored extensively in chapter 6. As you recall, plans can involve intervention at the micro, mezzo, or macro levels. Plans should be numbered to correspond to the respective problems they address (Kagle, 1991) and should be updated periodically to respond to changing client problems and needs.

Progress Notes

Progress notes do just that. They reflect any new developments and progress you and your client have made with the case. A frequently used format for progress notes is referred to as SOAP, which is an acronym for the following components (Hepworth & Larsen, 1990; Kane, 1974; Kagle, 1991):

Subjective information: This involves recording the client's perception of the problem and situation. It entails individual perceptions and opinions instead of established fact. For example, you might state, "Ms. G indicated that her apartment is in a shabby rundown condition." Or you might record, "The client perceives the problem as being very severe." Subjective information might also be provided by family members or other people involved in the case.

Objective information: This includes the facts and observations you feel are relevant to record. For instance, have any tests been administered to the client? Are the results of such tests relevant to the client's problem and situation? Additionally, objective information involves your professional observations during a meeting or interview. For example, you might state after an interview with a sixteen-year-old male on probation, "When I asked about his mother, he scowled, opened his jacket, and showed me the hilt of a knife held in an inside pocket." (At some subsequent point, you would probably add that this behav-ior resulted in revocation of his probation and return to incarceration.)

In other words, any objective information involves facts. Perhaps you want to record the fact that your client made a particular statement. In that event, you state verbatim exactly what the client said. Or a fact might be that you called an agency to make a referral for your client. A fact also might be that your client arrived thirty minutes late.

Assessments: Chapter 5 dealt extensively with assessments in generalist practice. In progress notes, assessments involve your impressions about how much progress has been made or not made. What is your client's current condition or state? How has the problem situation changed or not changed?

Sometimes the distinction between subjective impressions and objective information is not perfectly clear. For example, take a client who meets you with a blank look on her face, dilated pupils, and slurred speech. These specific observations are facts. Therefore, they are included in the objective information section. However, your impression that your client has taken an illegal drug is a subjective judgment. In your mind, you are absolutely certain that this is the case but your perception may or may not be fact. Perhaps your client is having a reaction to having taken some prescribed medication for an illness such as diabetes. On the other hand, the fact may be that she did just "shoot up" some heroin.

The important point here is to remain aware of the distinction between subjective and objective information. Sometimes you will make mistakes, as everyone does. You can only try to do your best.

Plans: Chapter 6 addressed planning in generalist practice. In progress notes, a plan needs to be concise and accurate. What is your next step? What have you and your client committed yourself to doing? Recording plans is an ongoing process. As situations change and problems are solved, plans change.

Figure 16.6: An Example of a Format for Prioritizing Problems

<u>PROBLEM AREAS OF MAJOR CONCERN</u>

Please describe below problems or things about you or your situation that you would like to see change as a result of counseling/treatment.

    For each major problem that you list, please describe one or two specific examples of the behavior or feeling about which you are most concerned, telling how often the behavior occurs (e.g., four times per day, three times per week, twice per month, or whatever).

Problem or Concern No. 1:
_____
_____
_____

Problem or Concern No. 2:
_____
_____
_____

Problem or Concern No. 3:
_____
_____
_____

Problem or Concern No. 4:
_____
_____
_____

Problem or Concern No. 5:
_____
_____
_____

                    _____
                    Signature

                    _____
                    Date

Please continue to, "Things I Like Most about Myself and/or Situation".

Figure 16.6 (*continued*)

<u>THINGS I LIKE MOST ABOUT MYSELF AND/OR SITUATION</u>

Positive or Strength No. 1:

_____

_____

_____

Positive or Strength No. 2:

_____

_____

_____

Positive or Strength No. 3:

_____

_____

_____

Positive or Strength No. 4:

_____

_____

_____

Positive or Strength No. 5:

_____

_____

_____

Source: Reprinted with permission of Luthern Social Services, 3200 W. Highland Blvd., Milwaukee, WI 53208.

An example of a format for SOAP progress notes is presented in Figure 16.7.

Advantages of Problem-Oriented Recording

Sheafor et al. (1988) cite a number of advantages of problem-oriented recording. First, it allows others involved with the case to understand how the worker approached the client's problems. Second, although problem-oriented recording depicts how a number of problems are interrelated, it still allows the worker to focus on one problem at a time. Third, it allows for good communication among team members because problems are clearly specified. Fourth, even when one worker leaves the agency, problem-oriented recording allows for continuity of service because of clearly specified plans. Fifth, it provides a useful tool for follow-up. The client's problem status and progress is clearly specified at any point in time, including termination. Sixth, it promotes clear, brief records because of its structured format and brevity.

Disadvantages of Problem-Oriented Recording

A major disadvantage of the traditional problem-oriented record is that there is no specified place to identify and focus upon strengths. As we have discussed in chapters 5 and 6, strengths can provide invaluable keys to solving problems. Plans utilizing strengths already there increase the potential for success.

A second disadvantage to the problem-oriented record involves its focus on problems without explicit identification of needs. Simply expanding the problem portion to include needs will remedy this.

A third disadvantage is the traditional orientation to micro and, to some extent, mezzo practice, thus ignoring macro practice. This disadvantage can be overcome, however, by making certain that macro aspects of the client situation are examined and, where viable, integrated into the intervention plan.

Standardized Forms

The third common type of format used in social work recording involves standardized forms. This means that identical forms are used to gather information from some category of clients. These forms may assume virtually any format and gather virtually any type of information. To some extent all of the recording formats referred to earlier are standardized in that information is recorded in a predictably ordered pattern. However, for our purposes we will consider standardized forms those that minimize the need to do narrative notations. They consist primarily of alternatives that can be checked and brief answers (for example, the date) which can be quickly filled in.

An example of a standardized form is given in Figure 16.8. It's a form workers in a state agency use to summarize information on adoptive families.

Purposes of Standardized Forms

Forms have several purposes. First, they direct the worker to the specific type of information needed and, thus, encourage gathering data quickly.

Second, they provide a means for evaluating data involving a large number of clients. In other words, they assist agencies in quickly inspecting and examining such things as the characteristics of the clientele they are serving. Are they primarily female or equally divided between genders? Are clients mainly young adults or senior citizens? Such characteristics illustrate only some variables in the broad range of information that can be gathered.

A third purpose for standardized forms involves the easy documentation of which services have been provided to which clients. Such

Figure 16.7: An Example of a Format for SOAP Progress Notes

<u>Case Progress Notes</u>

Entry No._____ BGC No._____ Interview Date:_____ Length of Contact:_____
Counselor:_____ People Involved:_____
S:_____
_____
O:_____
_____
A:_____
_____
P:_____
_____

Entry No._____ BGC No._____ Interview Date:_____ Length of Contact:_____
Counselor:_____ People Involved:_____
S:_____
_____
O:_____
_____
A:_____
_____
P:_____
_____

Entry No._____ BGC No._____ Interview Date:_____ Length of Contact:_____
Counselor:_____ People Involved:_____
S:_____
_____
O:_____
_____
A:_____
_____
P:_____
_____
_____

Source: Reprinted with permission of Luthern Social Services, 3200 Highland Blvd., Milwaukee, WI 53208.

Standardized forms assist agencies in quickly inspecting and examining data involving their clients.

documentation employs one avenue where data can be quickly gathered and summarized to reinforce the agency's credibility.

A fourth usefulness for standardized forms concerns their clear compatibility with computerized analyses. Categories of information can be easily quantified, evaluated, and compared with each other. For example, what client characteristics are significantly related to the effectiveness of specific intervention techniques?

Finally, sometimes standardized forms can be given to the clients themselves to complete. Assuming that your clients are literate, this can save a lot of interaction time.

In summary, the advantages of standardized forms involve brevity and easy collection of large amounts of specific information. However, the disadvantages concern making infor-

mation about clients conform to predetermined notions. Narrative recording allows for much greater attentiveness to the client's individuality.

Well-Written Standardized Forms

There are a number of characteristics reflected in a well-written form (Kagle, 1991). It is beyond the scope of this chapter to teach you how to develop your own forms.[1] You will more likely be in the position of using those already

---

1. In the event that you are in the situation of having to develop your own standardized form, we suggest you refer to *Social Work Records*, 2nd ed., by Jill Doner Kagle (Belmont, CA: Wadsworth, 1991). She addresses form development directly and provides numerous examples of forms.

Figure 16.8: An Example of a Standardized Form

DCS ADOPTIVE FAMILY DATA WORKSHEET

	Worker Initials
HEAD OF HOUSEHOLD (Last Name, First Name)	Inquiry Date (mo, day, yr)
Address	Orientation Date (mo, day, y

City State Zip	Telephone	Application Date (mo, day,

Date Assigned to Worker (mo, day, yr)	Date Study Completed (mo, day, yr)	Study Date (mo, day, yr)

STUDY TYPE (check appropriate item)	DECISION (check appropriate item)	MINORITY (check up to 3 choices)
____ SN=Special Needs ____ IN=Independent ____ RE=Relative ____ SP=Stepparent ____ IR=Interstate Request ____ SO=Supervision ____ FC=Foster Home Conversion	____ A=Approved ____ H=Hold ____ T=Transferred to another region/agency ____ W=Withdrew ____ R=Rejected	____ B=Black ____ I=American Indian ____ H=Hispanic ____ O=Oriental ____ M=Black-white ____ Q=American Indian-whit ____ R=Hispanic-white ____ P=Oriental-white ____ X=Other ____ Y=Any Minority Group ____ W=White
Physical Disabilty Level* 0 1 2 3	Emotional Disability Level* 0 1 2 3	
Mental Disability Level* 0 1 2 3	Learning Disability Level* 0 1 2 3	Upper Age Lower Ag
Placement Date (mo, day, yr)	Date Withdrawn (mo, day, yr)	SEX ____ M=Male ____ F=Female ____ E=Either Sex ____ S=Sibling Group

*0 meaning none and 3 meaning severe

Source: This form is adapted from one used by the State of Wisconsin Department of Health & Social Services (DHSS). Use permission of the Wisconsin DHSS, 1 West Wilson, Madison, WI.

established in your agency's practice. However, you will be in the position of evaluating the form's effectiveness and of giving your supervisor and the administration feedback about recommended changes and improvements.

First, the standardized form should have a clearly identified purpose. There should be a need for every piece of information gathered. Neither you nor your client have time to spend on useless information. Additionally, instructions for how to complete the form should be clearly stated.

Second, questions and other calls for information should be clearly articulated. You should immediately be able to understand exactly what type of information the question is designed to solicit. For example, take the query, "Gender ____ male ____ female." The information called for is very clear. You are directed to indicate one of two choices. Unless your client is a transsexual (that is, a person whose mental and psychological identity is in the physiological body of the opposite gender), your choice is easy.

On the other hand, a question asking "What is the client's mental state?" is much more ambiguous. What is the question designed to get at? Depression? Intelligence? Anxiety? The appearance that the client is drugged? In your agency, such a question may be clearly related to the types of information you need. In other words, if you understand the question and know how to answer it, the question is probably appropriate. However, if you find yourself wondering about what the question means and are struggling with how to answer it, you need to consult your supervisor for clarification or to change the question.

A third quality of a good standardized questionnaire involves having appropriate, clearly stated categories of information from which to choose. Take a situation where you're doing juvenile intake at a county social services agency. The standardized form provides the following list of presenting problems: truancy; acting out

in school; running away; fighting with parents; gang involvement; shoplifting, theft, or other delinquent behavior; and depression. Presenting problems are "the perceived symptoms, overt issues, or difficulties the client believes to constitute the problem" that bring the client to you for help (Barker, 1987, p. 124). In the course of your work, you find that in reality a significant number of presenting problems involve drug abuse and incest. Obviously, this presenting problem list is too limited and needs to be expanded.

The fourth quality of a good form concerns its format. Questions should be organized in a logical order. Queries relating to each other should be clustered together. There should be enough space for you to write your answers. In other words, the form should be easy for you to fill out.

Recording Progress in Groups

You might find yourself in the position of running groups and having to record plans and progress. Hepworth and Larsen (1990) make two suggestions for recording in mezzo practice. First, just as records should be kept "for recording functional and dysfunctional responses of individual members," so should a similar type of system be used "for recording the functional and dysfunctional behaviors of the group itself." They state that this can be done by "adding a column to record the growth or changes that you note in the group's behavior" (pp. 312–13). In this column you might focus on such issues as the formation of subgroups and affiliations, who holds power within the group, how the group proceeds to make decisions, what norms develop within the group, and how the group progresses toward achieving group goals.

A second suggestion for recording in groups involves using *sociograms*, which are "representations of alliances in a group at a given point, since alliances do shift and change" (Hepworth

& Larsen, 1990, p. 313). A sociogram illustrates group dynamics by using figures such as circles to represent individuals, and lines between these figures to represent various forms of interaction. Sociograms were explained more thoroughly in the context of families in chapter 5.

Writing Letters

Reasons for writing letters within an agency setting are very diverse. You may need to contact a colleague or another agency for information. You may need to communicate something in writing to a specific client. Or you may need to write a legislator to advocate that an unmet community need be addressed.

Sheafor et al. (1988, pp. 130–31) suggest eight points to remember when writing letters:

1. "Plan carefully before you write even the shortest letter. If it is worth doing, it should be done well because your image as a professional person is shaped by the appearance of your letter."
2. "Revise and polish all drafts of letters and proofread the final version."
3. "Develop several model letters based on situations commonly encountered in your agency. Use these as a starting point when preparing new letters."
4. "Remember that a professional letter will have at least the following parts: letterhead, date, inside address, reference line or subject line, salutation, body, complimentary close, typed signature, and written signature. When appropriate, there should also be an enclosure notation (enc.) and a carbon copy notation (cc) listing names of others receiving the letter."

    You can also send *blind copies* to designated individuals. This refers to sending copies of the letter to people other than the identified recipient without indicating on the letter that you are doing

so. However, you should only send blind copies for some clearly identified reason or purpose.

5. At times you will need to write letters where you're complaining, criticizing, making objections, challenging, or insisting. Be assertive when writing your letter. This means striking an appropriate balance between being overly pushy or aggressive, and ineffectively timid and apologetic. Make your points keeping both your and the other person's rights and feelings in mind. Chapter 13 explores in much greater depth how to become appropriately assertive.
6. Think of the person you're writing to as a real person. Communicate straightforwardly, yet don't appear cold, aloof, and totally unemotional. The person you're contacting is not a machine. Think about how you would speak to the individual if you were interacting face to face. If appropriate, you might thank the individual for already having done something for you. At the very least, you might say something like, "Thank you for your time and consideration." Or you might comment that you look forward to hearing from the person soon. The point is to display a consideration for the other person's feelings.
7. On the other hand, don't be overly friendly, especially when writing formal letters to people in prominent, influential positions. Some degree of politeness and formality conveys to them your respect.
8. Be cautious about using the word "I" too often. It may be appropriate two or three times in one letter. However, be sensitive to how it has the potential to convey the impression that you are an egotistical person.

In addition to these suggestions, Wilson (1980, pp. 129–30) provides seven more:

9. Always type formal letters to agencies or consumers.

10. Avoid sending postcards if they contain confidential information or other information recipients of the cards would not want others to read.

11. Be conscious of who might read the letter after it's sent. For instance, don't include private information about a client that another family member might read.

12. When writing to clients, use words that they can clearly understand. Be sensitive to their level of education and potential comprehension. Don't use long, technical, theoretically impressive words for clients who have little formal education. On the other hand, don't be condescending.

13. Beneath your typed signature, use your appropriate formal title. This conveys to people how to refer to you in their responses.

14. Address people by using appropriate titles. For instance, "Mr.," "Ms.," or "Dr." (if you know the latter is the case) are polite and respectful.

15. *Never* send out a letter without keeping a copy. This provides an ongoing record of communication and progress for a client or an agency. Otherwise, it's too difficult to remember what transpired and when.

Memos

Austin et al. (1986) describe typical memos:

A common type of written report is the memorandum, or memo, which is usually used to announce information or to remind someone about a service that is needed or about an important event. You will probably be using memos to report to administrators in your agency, and you may sometimes use a memo to communicate with other service workers, especially in a large agency. Each agency usually has a set form for memos, and you should be familiar with yours (pp. 495–96).

Although formats vary somewhat, memos are usually entitled "Memorandum" at the top. In an overflowing heap of paper on a desk, this identifies what they are. Additionally, the intended recipient(s) of the memo, the name and position of its sender, the date the memo was written, and a general summary of its content are usually all included right at the beginning. Figure 16.9 is an example of a memo.

When writing a memo, it's useful to keep the following suggestions in mind (Austin et al., 1986). First, make the memo as short and to the point as possible. Second, memos should be *very clear.* You don't want to make readers waste time trying to wade through prolific verbosity to get to the point. Third, memos should be sent out early enough to allow plenty of time for the recipient to respond or comply with your wishes. In other words, don't send a memo requesting a colleague to finish a thirty-page report by tomorrow. Fourth, state the purpose of your memo clearly right at the beginning. Readers need to orient themselves to why they're receiving the memo in the first place. Why do they need to spend valuable time reading it? What might the memo tell them to do? What information does the memo contain that is important for them to know?

There are two other suggestions regarding writing memos. For one thing, address only one topic per memo. If more than one important item is included, it's easy for topics to get lost. For example, where will you file a single copy of a memo that addresses the needs of two different clients? Filing copies of the memo in two different client files violates their respective confidentiality.

One final suggestion for writing memos involves their usefulness in documentation. A memo can clarify and document proposed plans. For example, take the situation where you establish several specific plans over the

Figure 16.9: An Example of a Memo

<u>Memorandum</u>

TO: All Social Work Staff

FROM: Tom Blackwell, Supervisor

DATE: Oct. 19, 1994

RE: Recording

Recently, we received another memo from the state concerning accountability and uniformity relating to record keeping. Through no one's fault, there is little consistency from one worker to another regarding writing regular progress notes for clients.

From now on there will be an individual progress sheet for each of your clients on your individual billing clipboards. Please make a brief entry including date and progress summary each time you see a client. We will discuss format and content further at out next group supervisory meeting.

Please feel free to see me if you have any questions. Thank you for your help and cooperation.

phone with a colleague involved with the same client case. Sending a brief memo to that colleague that clearly summarizes the plans (who will do what by when) documents the fact that the phone conversation took place and who is responsible for which tasks.

A memo can also be used to document for the record your own performance. For instance, you might want to notify your supervisor formally that you had followed through on her specific instructions concerning a case. You might also include the results of your intervention. This provides a clear record of your work for supervisory purposes or for the evaluation of your own on-the-job performance.

Other Types of Recording Formats

There are many other ways of recording information. Chapter 8 addressed some, including single-subject design, goal attainment scaling, and task-achievement scaling. We've established that agencies often vary widely regarding the type of information they need and how they record that information. Recording should always be done for a clearly specified purpose and be as easy to decipher as possible.

Writing Skills and Recording

It is beyond the scope of this text to try to teach basic writing skills. Good grammar and excellent spelling are absolute necessities. Wilson (1980) summarizes the importance of such skills:

> If deficits in writing ability make it impossible for the worker or student to communicate the fact that he is doing effective social work, situations will arise in which it really won't matter whether his skills are any good or not. . . . Thus if a worker's supervisor, professional colleagues, quality control reviewers, and others see only poor, unclear written communication as a reflection of his skills, it will be difficult to convince

them that the individual is actually a highly skilled professional (p. 117).

Writing skills usually improve with practice. In other words, you tend to become more accustomed to writing memos and selecting certain types of words to use.

It's also helpful to use colleagues and supervisors as models. Who in the agency has a reputation for clear communication and exceptional reports? You can identify what formats and phrases these people use and incorporate them into your own writing style. It is especially helpful to target people working with similar client populations and having similar jobs to yours because they will be focusing on the same types of issues and using the same professional jargon that is relevant to you.

Highlight 16.3 summarizes some very basic writing suggestions. Additionally, you are encouraged to have a dictionary and thesaurus on hand. These resources are useful for any type of writing. Finally, a manual of style can be helpful. How often do you forget if a comma should be used or not, or how a reference should be listed? One commonly used manual is the *Publication Manual of the American Psychological Association* (1988). There are a number of others, any of which you can use to make your style consistent.

Privacy Principles

When information is formally recorded about clients, several ethical issues emerge. Although this is discussed more thoroughly in chapter 11, we will briefly approach the subject here.

Kagle (1991) identifies four "privacy principles" that relate to what should be recorded about clients and who should have access to this information. They include "confidentiality, abridgment, access, and anonymity" (pp. 164–65).

Confidentiality refers to "a principle of ethics according to which the social worker or other professional may not disclose information about a client without the client's consent; this information includes the identity of the client, content of overt verbalizations, professional opinions about the client, material from records, and so on" (Barker, 1987, p. 31).

Superficially, the issue may seem simple. What you write about a client should remain confidential, right? But should the client have the right to see what you've written? What if you've recorded some negative things about the client? Should your supervisor be allowed to read what you've written to provide direction and oversee agency operations? What about the information you share at case conferences? How confidential does it remain then? What if a client tells you he's sexually abusing his pre-teen daughter, but specifies that you are not to tell anyone else? What happens in states (for example, Wisconsin) where professionals are legally *required* to report even any *suspected* such abuse?

Here is where the other three privacy principles come into play. *Abridgment* refers to restricting the type of information that is put into the record and the period of time over which the record can be retained. Agency policies and

---

HIGHLIGHT 16.3

Some Basic Good Writing Suggestions

- Choose your words carefully. Specify exactly what you mean. Every word should be there for a good reason.
- Avoid slang. It doesn't sound professional. Use "young men" or "boys," instead of "guys." Use "mother" instead of "mom." Instead of a term like "fizzled out," use "didn't succeed" or something similar.
- Avoid words such as "always," "average," "perfect," or "all." These words can be unclear and misleading.
- Avoid sexist language. Use "Ms." instead of "Mrs." Use "woman" instead of "lady." Use "homemaker" or "woman who does not work outside of the home" instead of "housewife." Don't call adult women "girls."
- Avoid labeling people with terms such as "sleazy," "strange," "punks," "slobs," or "low class."
- Avoid using abbreviations. Some people may not understand them. You can spell the term out the first time used and put the abbreviation in parenthesis right after it. Thereafter, you can just use the abbreviation. For example, "The National Association of Social Workers (NASW) is the major professional organization for social work practitioners.

NASW provides members with a journal and newspaper focusing on current practice issues."
- Be as concise as possible. Determine if a sentence could use fewer words. Consider dividing long sentences into two or more smaller ones.
- Use paragraphs to divide content into different topics, points, or issues. A solid page of text without any paragraph breaks is harder to read. On the other hand, each paragraph should have a unifying theme. Avoid using one sentence paragraphs.
- Distinguish between verified facts and your impression of the facts. Examples of ways to phrase your impressions include "My impression is . . . ," "It appears that . . . ," or "It seems that . . . ."

These suggestions were taken from those presented in the *Student Manual of Classroom Exercises and Study Guide* for *Understanding Human Behavior and the Social Environment*, 2nd ed., by Karen K. Kirst-Ashman and Charles Zastrow (Chicago: Nelson-Hall, 1990), pp. 21–22.

legal restrictions vary drastically from state to state regarding these two issues. Thus, no clear-cut generalization regarding what you should do can be made here. However, you can note that abridgment serves to enhance a client's privacy. For example, only information pertinent to the services the client is receiving may be recorded. Highly personal information not relating to services received may be omitted. Likewise, agencies or laws may specify how long such records may be kept. For instance, an agency might require that the record be disposed of after six months following case termination. This protects clients' privacy to some extent by not allowing access to their records indefinitely.

Access refers to the client's right to see what and how information is being recorded. As with abridgment, client access to records varies widely from state to state and agency to agency. Why might you not feel free to share with your clients everything you write about them? Doesn't such sharing enhance client trust and client-worker communication? Kagle (1991) cites some potential negative consequences:

> Social workers are often wary of the potential for adverse effects if the client or other family members read the record. For example, social workers recognize that clients may not understand or may be upset by what they read. Furthermore, they are concerned about protecting the privacy of others who may have revealed confidential information that is documented in the client's record (p. 167).

Anonymity refers to using recorded information about clients but omitting identifying data. For example, an agency can evaluate its effectiveness of service provision by analyzing information gathered anonymously on all its clientele. No particular case need be identified as a specific individual or family. Or when educating staff or students, specific identifying information such as names and addresses can simply be blocked out in the record. Such cases can still

be used as examples and as training cases. In these instances, names are irrelevant.

Kagle (1991) summarizes the essence of the dilemma by stating that "the goal of social work should be to maximize client privacy while meeting the necessary demands of accountability" (p. 180). Accountability, of course, refers to being answerable to the community and to your clients for the competent, effective provision of the services you as a social worker say you are providing. In order to be accountable, you must record some aspects of the intervention process. As we've discussed, the specific aspects vary widely. Legal and agency policies differ drastically regarding what they require to have recorded and how that information should be shared with others. You need to be well-informed regarding these rules and restrictions. You then need to make professional decisions regarding how to fulfill your responsibilities for being accountable and yet maximize your clients' right to privacy.

Kagle (1991) makes several specific suggestions for achieving this. First, you should seriously consider what information should and should not be kept in the record. What information is necessary to document provision of service and benefit the intervention process? Agency policies that clearly specify what's appropriate and what's not can greatly assist workers in making these sometimes difficult decisions.

A second suggestion for enhancing confidentiality of records involves keeping files and sources of information "physically safe-guarded from unwarranted access" (p. 181). Client records may be kept in locked files or rooms. They may be placed in areas to which only appropriate staff have ready access. Agency staff should be instructed to abide by rules of confidentiality. Case records should not be left haphazardly on desks. Computerized databases need additional safeguards such as passwords for limited access.

A third suggestion for maintaining client con-

Figure 16.10: An Example of a Release of Information Form

```
STATE OF WISCONSIN
DEPARTMENT OF HEALTH & SOCIAL SERVICES        Individual Who Is Subject Of Record
HSS-9 (Rev. 7/84)                          Name:_____
Sections 19.35 & 19.36, Wis. Stats.
                                           Address:_____

                                           City, State, Zip Code:_____

           CONFIDENTIAL INFORMATION        Indentifying Number:_____
           RELEASE AUTHORIZATION
                                           Date of Birth:_____


Name and Address of Agency or Organization
Being Authorized to Release Information          Information May be Released to:

                                           Name:_____

                                           Organization:_____

                                           Address:_____

                                           City, State, Zip Code:_____


Specific Records Authorized for Release (Include dates of records, if applicable)




Purpose or Need for Release of Information (Be specific)




I understand that I may revoke this authorization, in writing, at any time except where
information has already been released as a result of this authorization. Unless
revoked, this authorization will remain in effect until the expiration time I have
indicated and initialed below.

_____ Authorization expires as of _____. (Date)
_____ Authorization expires _____ month(s) from the date I sign this authorization.
_____ Authorization expires after the following action takes place:
```

Source: This form is adapted from one used by the State of Wisconsin Department of Health & Social Services (DHSS). Used with permission of the Wisconsin DHSS, 1 West Wilson, Madison, WI.

Figure 16.10 (*continued*)

As evidenced by my signature below, I hereby authorize disclosure of records to the
person(s) or agency(s) as specified above.

Signature of Individual Who is Subject of Record   Date:

Signature of Other Person Legally   Title or Relationship to   Date:
Authorized to Consent to Disclosure   Individual Who is Subject
(If applicable)   of Record

fidentiality involves having clearly specified release of information forms and procedures. In
general, "information should be released only
with prior, informed, written consent of the client
or the client's guardian. Furthermore, agencies
should seek a separate release of information for
each agency or individual who will receive information" (Kagle, 1991, p. 184). An example of a
release form is provided in Figure 16.10.

A fourth suggestion for enhancing client
confidentiality involves advocating on your clients' behalf. This entails making certain that
established client rights are not violated and reporting them when such breaches occur. It also
concerns becoming very knowledgeable about
legal and agency constraints and evaluating
their effectiveness in maximizing the protection of your clients' privacy.

Chapter Summary

Recording and recording skills are critical aspects of generalist social work practice. There
are many reasons why recording is important,
including enhancing accountability, monitoring interventions' progress, and maintaining
case continuity. Record content typically includes dates, client information, reasons for client contact, detailed information about the client's problems, aspects of the intervention
process, follow-up information, and impressions
and questions about the case.

The most common recording formats used
in agencies today include diagnostic summary
recording, problem-oriented recording, and
standardized forms. Additional methods that
were discussed included process recording,
audio/visual recording, recording for groups,
letters, and memos. The importance of good
grammar, spelling, and conciseness were
stressed. A number of suggestions for good writing were presented.

Four privacy principles for clients, including confidentiality, abridgment, access, and
anonymity, were defined and examined. The
difficult task of finding a balance between accountability and confidentiality was explored,
and some means for attaining such a balance
described.

Bibliography

Abel, G. G. (1988). Behavioral treatment of child molesters. In A. J. Stunkard, & A. Baum (Eds.), *Perspectives on behavioral medicine* (pp. 223–242). New York: Laurence Erlbaum Associates, Inc.

Abrahams, L. & Seidl, H. (1979). *Introduction to effective case management.* Green Bay, WI: Brown County Unified Board.

Abramson, M. (1990). Keeping secrets: Social workers and AIDS. *Social Work, 35*(2), 169–173.

Aguilera, D. C., & Messick, J. M. (1974). *Crisis intervention: Theory and methodology* (2nd ed.) St. Louis, MO: C. V. Mosby.

Alberti, R. E., & Emmons, M. L. (1975). *Stand up, speak out, talk back!* New York: Pocket Books.

Allen, M. (1990). Why are we talking about case management again? *The prevention report.* Oakdale, IA: National Resource Center on Family Based Services.

American Psychiatric Association. (1980). *Diagnostic and statistical manual of mental disorders.* Washington, DC.

American Psychological Association. (1983). *Publication manual of the American Psychological Association* (3rd ed.). Hyattsville, MD: Author.

American Psychiatric Association. (1986). *Diagnostic and statistical manual of mental disorders.* Washington, DC.

Amidei, N. (1982). How to be an advocate in bad times. In F. M. Cox, J. L. Erlich, J. Rothman, & J. E. Tropman (Eds.), *Strategies of community organization* (4th ed., pp. 106–114). Itasca, IL: Peacock.

Amir, M. (1971). *Patterns in forcible rape.* Chicago, IL: University of Chicago Press.

Anderson, J. (1981). *Social work methods and processes.* Belmont, CA: Wadsworth.

Anderson, S. C. (1987). Alcohol use and addiction. In A. Minihan (Editor-in-chief), *Encyclopedia of social work* (18th ed., Vol. 1., pp. 132–192). Silver Spring, MD: National Association of Social Workers.

Apgar, K., & Callahan, B. N. (1980). *Four one-day workshops.* Boston, MA: Family Service Association of Greater Boston.

Arkava, M. L., & Brennen, E. (Eds.) (1976). *Competency-based education for social work: Evaluation and curriculum issues.* New York: Council on Social Work Education.

Austin, M. J., Cox, G., Gottlieb, J., Hawkins, J. S., Kruzich, J. M., & Rauch, R. (1982) *Evaluating your agency's programs.* Newbury Park, CA: Sage.

Austin, M. J., Kopp, J., & Smith, P. L. (1986). *Delivering human services: A self-instructional approach* (2nd ed.). New York: Longman.

Austin, M. J., Skelding, A. H., & Smith, P. L. (1977). *Delivering human services: An introductory programed text.* New York: Harper & Row.

Baer, B. L. (1979). Developing a new curriculum for social work education. In F. Clark and M. Arkava (Eds.), *The pursuit of competence in social work* (pp. 96–109). San Francisco, CA: Jossey-Bass.

Baker, L., & Patterson, J. (1990). The first to know: A systemic analysis of confidentiality and the therapist's family. *American Journal of Family Therapy, 18*(3), 294–299.

Bandler, R., Grinder, J., & Satir, V. (1976). *Changing with families.* Palo Alto, CA: Science and Behavior Books.

Bandura, A. (1977) *Social learning theory.* Englewood Cliffs, NJ: Prentice-Hall.

Bard, M., & Zacker, J. (1971). The prevention of family violence: Dilemmas in community intervention. *Journal of Marriage and the Family, 33,* 677–682.

Barker, R. L. (1987). *The social work dictionary.* Silver Spring, MD: The National Association of Social Workers.

Barker, R. L. (1991). *The social work dictionary* (2nd ed.). Silver Spring, MD: The National Association of Social Workers.

Baruth, L., & Manning, M. (1991). *Multicultural counseling and psychotherapy.* New York: Merrill.

Bauden, D. L. (Ed.) (1984). *The social contract revisited.* Washington, DC: Urban Institute Press.

Beck, A. T. (1967). *Depression.* New York: Harper & Row.

Beck, D. (1973). *Progress on family problems*. New York: Family Service Association of America.

Bellak, A. O. (1984, June 6-7). *Comparable worth: Issue for the 80's, a consultation for U.S. Commission on Civil Rights* (pp. 75-82).

Belle, D. (1991). Gender differences in the social moderators of stress. In A. Monat, & R. S. Lazarus (Eds.), *Stress and coping* (pp. 258-274). New York: Columbia University Press.

Benjamin, A. (1974). *The helping interview*. Boston, MA: Houghton Mifflin.

Benne, K., & Sheats, P. (1948). Functional roles of group members. *Journal of Social Issues, 4*(2).

Berkeley Planning Associates. (1977). The quality of case management process: Final report (Vol. 3). In *The evaluation of child abuse and neglect projects 1974-1977*. Washington, DC: Dept. of Commerce.

Bernal, G., Martinez, A. C., Santisteban, D., Bernal, M. E., & Olmedo, E. E. (1983). Hispanic mental health curriculum for psychology. In J. C. Chunn, P. J. Dunston, & R. Ross-Sheriff (Eds.), *Mental health and people of color* (pp. 65-96). Washington, DC: Howard University Press.

Bertcher, H. J., & Maple, F. (1974). Elements and issues in group composition. In P. Glasser, R. Sarri, & R. Vinter (Eds.), *Individual change through small groups* (pp. 186-208). New York: Free Press.

Berzon, B. (1978). *Sharing your lesbian identity with your children*. In G. Vida (Ed.) *Our right to love: A lesbian resource book*. Englewood Cliffs, NJ: Prentice-Hall.

Bisno, H. (1988). *Managing conflict*. Newbury Park, CA: Sage.

Blau, F. D., & Winkler, A. (1989). Women in the labor force: An overview. In J. Freedman (Ed.), *Women: A feminist perspective* (4th ed., pp. 265-286). Mountain View, CA: Mayfield.

Bloom, M., & Fischer, J. (1982). *Evaluating practice: Guidelines for the accountable professional*. Englewood Cliffs, NJ: Prentice-Hall.

Blythe, B. J., & Briar, S. (1987). Direct practice effectiveness. In A. Minihan (Editor-in-chief), *Encyclopedia of social work* (18th ed., Vol. 1, pp. 399-408). Silver Spring, MD: National Association of Social Workers.

Blythe, B. J., & Tripodi, T. (1989). *Measurement in direct practice*. Newbury Park, CA: Sage.

Bolton, F. G., Morris, L. A., & MacEachron, A. E. (1989). *Males at risk*, Newbury Park, CA: Sage.

Bozett, F. (1980). Gay fathers: How and why they disclose their homosexuality to their children. *Family Relations, 29*, 173-179.

Bozett, F. (1985). Gay men as fathers. In S. Hansen & F. Bozett (Eds.), *Dimensions of fatherhood* (pp. 327-352). Beverly Hills, CA: Sage.

Bozett, F. (1985, April). *Identity management: Social control of identity by children of gay fathers when they know their father is a homosexual*. Paper presented at the 9th Annual Midwest Nursing Research Society Conference, Chicago, IL.

Brandwein, R. A. (1987). Women in macro practice. In A. Minihan (Editor-in-chief), *Encyclopedia of social work* (18th ed., Vol. 2, pp. 881-892). Silver Spring, MD: National Association of Social Workers.

Briar, S. (1967). The current crisis in social casework. *Social work practice* (pp. 19-33). New York: Columbia University Press.

Briar, S. (1987) Direct Practice: Trends and Issues. In A. Minihan (Editor-in-chief), *Encyclopedia of Social Work* (18th ed., Vol. 1, pp. 393-398). Silver Spring, MD: National Association of Social Workers.

Brill, N. I. (1990). *Working with people*. New York: Longman.

Brown, L. N. (1991). *Groups for growth and change*. New York: Longman.

Bryson, R. B., Bryson, J. B., Licht, M. H., & Licht, B. G. (1976). The professional pair: Husband and wife psychologists. *American Psychologist, 31* 10-16.

Burgess, A. W., & Holmstrom, L. L. (1974a). *Rape: Victims of crisis*. Bowie, MD: Robert J. Brady.

Burgess, A. W., & Holmstrom, L. L. (1974b). Rape trauma syndrome. *American Journal of Psychiatry, 131*, 981-986.

Burghardt, S. (1987). Community-based social action. In A. Minihan (Editor-in-chief), *Encyclopedia of social work* (18th ed., Vol. 1, pp. 292-299). Silver Spring, MD: National Association of Social Workers.

Burke, V. (1987). *Welfare and poverty among children*. Washington, DC: Congressional Research Service Review.

Burrill, G. (1976). The problem-oriented log in social casework. *Social Work, 21*, 67.

Caplan, G. (1964). *Principles of preventive psychiatry*. New York: Basic Books.

Caragonne, P. (1980). *An analysis of the function of the case manager in four mental health social services settings*. Report of the Case Management Research Project, Austin, TX.

Caragonne, P. (1981). *A comparative analysis of twenty-two settings using case management components*. Austin, TX: University of Texas School of Social Work.

Card, O., & Wise, O. (1978). Teenage mothers and teenage fathers: The impact of early childbearing on the parents' personal and professional lives. *Family Planning Perspectives, 10*, 199–205.

Carter, E. A., & McGoldrick, M. (1980). *The family life cycle: A framework for family therapy*. New York: Gardner Press.

Carter, E. A., & McGoldrick, M. (1989). *The changing family life cycle: A framework for family therapy* (2nd ed.). Boston: Allyn and Bacon.

Chaplin, J. (1988). *Feminist counseling in action*. Newbury Park, CA: Sage.

Checkoway, B. (1987). Political strategy for social planning. In F. M. Cox, J. L. Erlich, J. Rothman, & J. E. Tropman (Eds.), *Strategies of community organization*. Itasca, IL: Peacock.

Chilman, C. S. (1988). Never married, single, adolescent parents. In C. Chilman, E. Nunnally, F. Cox (Eds.), *Variant family norms* (pp. 17–38). Newbury Park, CA: Sage.

Chilman, C. S., Nunnally, E. W., & Cox, F. M. (1988). *Variant family norms*. Newbury Park, CA: Sage.

Church, D. (1981). *It's time to tell: A media handbook for human services personnel*. Washington, DC: U.S. Department of Health and Human Services.

Clarke, J. (1978). *Self-esteem: A family affair*. Minneapolis, MN: Winston Press.

Cohen, P. B., & Johnson, T. J. (1987). Linking service systems and sharing technologies in behalf of potentially employable long term mentally disabled people. *Arete, 12*(1), 1–10.

Collier, H. V. (1982). *Counseling women: A guide for therapists*. New York: Free Press.

Compton, B. (1983). Traditional fields of practice. In A. Rosenblatt, & D. Waldfogel (Eds.), *Handbook of clinical social work*. San Francisco, CA: Jossey-Bass.

Compton, B., & Galaway, B. (1979). *Social work processes* (2nd ed.). Homewood, IL: Dorsey Press.

Compton, B., & Galway, B. (1984). *Social work processes* (3rd ed.). Homewood, IL: Dorsey.

Conference on Poverty. (1987). *Fact Sheet*. Washington, DC: Author.

Confidentiality in Social Work: Issues and Principles. (1978). New York: The Free Press.

Connaway, R. S., & Gentry, M. E. (1988). *Social work practice*. Englewood Cliffs, NJ: Prentice-Hall.

Corcoran, K., & Fischer, J. (1987). *Measures for clinical practice*. New York: The Free Press.

Coston, N. (1982). System prevents clients from falling through cracks. *Practice Digest, 4*(4), 7–11.

Coughlin, B. (1965). *Church and state in social welfare*. New York: Columbia University Press.

Council on Social Work Education. (1983). *Curriculum policy for the masters degree and baccalaureate degree programs in social work education*. New York: Author.

Cox, F. M. (1987). Alternative Conceptions of Community: Implications for Community Organization Practice. In F. M. Cox, J. L. Erlich, J. Rothman, & J. Tropman, (Eds.). *Strategies of community organization* (4th ed.). Itasca, IL: Peacock.

Cultural Information Service. (1984). *The burning bed: Viewer's guide*. New York: CIStems.

Davis, J. (1982). *Help me, I'm hurt*. Dubuque, IA: Kendall/Hunt.

Day, P. J., Macy, H. J., & Jackson, E. C. (1984). *Social working: Exercises in generalist practice*. Englewood Cliffs, NJ: Prentice-Hall.

Dear, R. B., & Patti, R. J. (1981). Legislative advocacy: Seven effective tactics. *Social Work, 6*(4), 289–296.

Dear, R. B., & Patti, R. J. (1987). Legislative advocacy. In A. Minahan (Editor-in-chief), *Encyclopedia of social work* (18th ed. Vol. 2, pp. 34–42). Silver Spring, MD: National Association of Social Workers.

Dekoven Waxman, L., & Reyes, L. (1987). *The continuing growth of hunger, homelessness, and poverty in America's cities: 1987*. Washington, DC: U.S. Conference of Mayors.

Delbecq, A., Van de Ven, A., & Gustafson, D. (1975). *Group techniques for program planning: A guide to nominal group and delphi processes*. Glenview, IL: Scott, Foresman.

Delgado, M., & Humm-Delgado, D. (1982). Natural support systems: Source of strength in Hispanic communities. *Social Work, 27*(1), 83–89.

Denzin, N. K. (1987). *Treating alcoholism*. Newbury Park, CA: Sage.

DeRisi, W. J., & Butz, G. (1975). Writing behavioral contracts: A case simulation practice manual. Champaign, IL: Research Press.

Devore, W., & Schlesinger, E. G. (1987). *Ethnic-sensitive social work practice.* Columbus, OH: Merrill.

Dewey, J. (1963). *Experience and education.* New York: Collier.

Dieppe, I., & Montiel, M. (1978). Hispanic families: An Exploration. In Montiel, M. (Ed.), *Hispanic families: Critical issues for policy and programs in human services* (pp. 1–8). Washington, DC: Coalition of Spanish-speaking Mental Health Organizations.

Dillard, J. M. (1983). *Multicultural counseling.* Chicago: Nelson-Hall.

Di Nitto, D. M., & Dye, T. R. (1987). *Social welfare: Politics and public policy.* Englewood Cliffs, NJ: Prentice-Hall.

Dixon, S. L. (1987). *Working with people in crisis.* Columbus, OH: Merrill.

Dodson, J. (1983). *An Afrocentric educational manual toward a non-deficit perspective in services to families and children.* Knoxville, TN: University of Tennessee School of Social Work.

Duehn, W. D. (1985). Practice and research. In R. M. Grinnel, Jr. (Ed.), *Social work research and evaluation.* Itasca, IL: Peacock.

Dutton, D. G. (1988). *The domestic assault of women: Psychological and criminal justice perspectives.* Newton, MA: Allyn & Bacon.

Earls, R. & Siegel, B. (1980). Precocious fathers. *American Journal of Orthopsychiatry, 50*(3), 469–480.

Elster, A. B., & Panzarine, S. (1983). Teenage fathers: Stresses during gestation and early parenthood. *Clinical Pediatrics, 22*(10), 700–703.

Englander-Golden, P., & Barton, G. (1983). Sex differences in absence from work: A reinterpretation. *Psychology of Women Quarterly, 8*(2), 185–188.

Epstein, I. (1981). Advocates on advocacy: An exploratory study. *Social Work Research and Abstracts, 17*(2), 5–12.

Epstein, L. (1980). *Helping people: The task-centered approach.* St. Louis, MO: Mosby.

Epstein, L. (1985). *Talking and listening: A guide to the helping interview.* St. Louis, MO: Times Mirror/Mosby.

Erickson, A. G. (1987). Family services. In A. Minahan (Editor-in-chief), *Encyclopedia of social work* (18th ed., Vol. 1, pp. 589–593). Silver Spring, MD: National Association of Social Workers.

Evaluation Research Society. (1982). Evaluation research society standards for program evaluation. In P. H. Rossi (Ed.), *New directions for program evaluation: Standards for evaluation practice.* San Francisco, CA: Jossey-Bass.

Fagan, J., Friedman, E., & Wexler, S. (1984). *National evaluation of the LEAA family violence demonstration program: Summary of major findings.* San Francisco, CA: URSA Institute.

Family Service America. (1984). *Family service profiles: Agency staffing and coverage.* New York: Author.

Farley, L. (1978). *Sexual shakedown: The sexual harassment of women on the job.* New York: Warner Books.

Farmer, R. E., Monahan, L. H., & Hekeler, R. W. (1984). *Stress management for human services.* Beverly Hills, CA: Sage.

Federal Electric Corporation. (1963). *A programmed introduction to PERT.* New York: Wiley.

Filley, A. C. (1978). *The complete manager: What works when.* Champaign, IL: Research Press.

Finckenauer, J. O. (1982). *Scared Straight and the panacea phenomenon.* Englewood Cliffs, NJ: Rutgers University Press.

Fischer, J. (1978). *Effective casework practice: An electric approach.* New York: McGraw-Hill.

Fischer, J., & Gochros, H. L. (1975). *Planned behavior change: Behavior modification in social work.* New York: Free Press.

Fisher, R., & Ury, W. (1981). *Getting to yes: Negotiating agreement without giving in.* Boston, MA: Houghton Mifflin.

Flanagan, J. (1980). *How to sell and how to ask for money.* Chicago, IL: National Committee for the Prevention of Child Abuse.

French, J. R., & Raven, B. (1968). The bases of social power. In D. Cartwright, & A. Zander, *Group dynamics: Research and theory,* (pp. 259–269). New York: Harper & Row.

Friesen, B. (1987). Administration: Interpersonal aspects. In A. Minihan (Editor-in-chief), *Encyclopedia of social work* (18th ed., Vol. 1) Silver Spring, MD: National Association of Social Workers.

Furstenburg, F., & Crawford, A. (1978). Family support: Helping teenage mothers to cope. *Family Planning Perspectives, 10,* 322–333.

Gambrill, E., & Stein, T. J. (1983). *Supervision*. Newbury Park, CA: Sage.

Garvin, C. D., & Cox, F. M. (1987). A history of community organizing since the civil war with special reference to oppressed committees. In F. M. Cox, J. L. Erlich, J. Rothman, J. E. Tropman, *Strategies of community organizing* (4th ed., pp. 26–66). Itasca, IL: Peacock.

Geller, J. (1978). Reaching the battering husband. *Social Work with Groups, 1*(1), 27–38.

Gelles, R. J. (1979). The myth of battered husbands and new facts about family violence. *Ms.*, 65–66.

Gelman, S. (1987). Board of Directors. In A. Minihan (Editor-in-chief), *Encyclopedia of social work* (18th ed., Vol. 1, pp. 206–211). Silver Spring, MD: National Association of Social Workers.

Gerhart, U. C. (1990). *Caring for the chronic mentally ill*. Itasca, IL: Peacock.

Gibbs, L. (1991). *Scientific reasoning for social workers*. New York; Macmillan.

Gibelman, M. (1982). Finding the least restrictive environment. *Practice Digest, 4*(4), 15–17.

Gibson, G. (1980). Chicanos and their support systems in interaction with social institutions. In M. Bloom (Ed.), *Lifespan Development* (pp. 446–459). New York: Macmillan.

Gilbert, L. A. (1985). *Men in dual-career families: Current realities and future prospects*. Hillsdale, NJ: Eilbaum.

Gilligan, C. (1982). *In a Different Voice*. Cambridge, MA: Harvard Univerity Press.

Ginsberg, L. (1990). Selected statistical review. In L. Ginsberg, S. Khinduka, J. A. Hall, F. Ross-Sheriff, A. Hartman (Encylopedia Supplement Committee) *Encyclopedia of social work*, (18th ed., 1990 Supplement, pp. 256–288). Silver Spring, MD: National Association of Social Workers.

Goering, P. N., Wasylenski, D. A., Frakas, M., Lancee, W. J., & Ballantyne, R. (1988). What difference does case management make? *Hospital and Community Psychiatry, 39*(3), 272–276.

Golan, N. (1987). Crisis intervention. In A. Minihan (Editor-in-chief), *Encyclopedia of social work* (18th ed., Vol. 1, pp. 360–372). Silver Spring, MD: National Association of Social Workers.

Good Tracks, J. G. (1973). Native American Noninterference. *Social Work*, 18, 30–35.

Gordon, T. (1970). *Parent effectiveness training*. New York: Peter Weyden.

Gordon, T. (1975). *P.E.T. Parent Effectiveness Training*. New York: New American Library.

Gottlieb, N. (1987). Sex discrimination and inequality. In A. Minihan (Editor-in-chief), *Encyclopedia of social work* (18th ed., Vol. 2, pp. 561–569). Silver Spring, MD: National Association of Social Workers.

Gottman, J., Notarius, C., Gonso, J., & Markman, H. (1976). *A couple's guide to communication*. Champaign, IL: Research Press.

Green, J. W. (1982). *Cultural awareness in the human services*. Englewood Cliffs, NJ: Prentice-Hall.

Green, R. (1978). The burden of proof is on those who say no. In J. P. Brady, H. Keith, & H. Brody (Eds.), *Controversy in Psychiatry* (pp. 813–828). Philadelphia, PA: Saunders.

Greene, R. R. (1987). *Case management. Helping the homeless, mentally ill and persons with AIDS and their families*. Silver Spring, MD: National Association of Social Workers.

Grinnell, R. M., & Williams, M. (1990). *Research in social work: A primer*. Itasca, IL: Peacock.

Haber, D. (1984). Church-based programs for black caregivers of non-institutionalized elders. *Journal of Gerontological Social Work, 7*(4), 43–55.

Hackney, H., & Cormier, L. S. (1979). *Counseling strategies and objectives*. Englewood Cliffs, NJ: Prentice-Hall.

Hagedorn, H., Beck, S., & Werlin, S. (1976). *A working manual of simple program evaluation techniques for community mental health centers*. Washington, DC: Government Printing Office.

Hall, E. (1969). *The Hidden Dimension*. Garden City, New York: Doubleday.

Hamilton, G. (1939). Basic concepts in social case work. In Fern Lowry (Ed.), *Readings in social case work, 1920–1938* (pp. 155–171). New York: Columbia University Press.

Hamilton, G. (1946). *Principles of social case recording*. New York: Columbia University Press.

Hammond, J. L., & Mahoney, C. W. (1983). Reward-cost balancing among coal miners. *Sex Roles*, 9, 17–29.

Harkess, S. (1988). Directions for the future. In A. H. Strombery & S. Harkess (Eds.), *Women working: Theories and facts in perspective* (pp. 358–360). Mountain View, CA: Mayfield.

Harry, J. (1988). Some problems of gay/lesbian families. In C. S. Chilman, E. W. Nunnelly, & F. M.

Cox (Eds.), *Variant family norms* (pp. 96–113). Newbury Park, CA: Sage.

Hartman, A. (1970). To think about the unthinkable. *Social Casework, 51*(8), 467–474.

Hartman, A. (1978). Diagrammatic assessment of family relationships. *Social Casework, 59,* 465–476.

Hartman, A. (1979). *Finding families: An ecological approach to family assessment in adoption.* Beverly Hills, CA: Sage.

Hartman, A., & Laird, J. (1983). *Family-centered social work practice.* New York: Free Press.

Hartman, A., & Laird, J. (1987). Family practice. In A. Minihan (Editor-in-chief), *Encyclopedia of social work* (18th ed., Vol. 1, pp. 575–589). Silver Spring, MD: National Association of Social Workers.

Hasenfeld, Y. (1987). Program development. In F. M. Cox, J. L. Erlich, J. Rothman, J. E. Tropman (Eds), *Strategies of community organization* (4th ed., pp. 450–473). Itasca, IL: F. E. Peacock.

Hawkins, R. P., & Dobes, R. W. (1975). Behavioral definitions in applied behavior analysis: Explicit or implicit. In B. C. Etzel, J. M. LeBlanc, & D. M. Baer (Eds.), *New developments in behavioral research. Theory, methods and applications.* Hillsdale, NJ: Lawrence Erlbaum Associates.

Haynes, K. S. & Mickelson, J. S. (1991). *Affecting change.* New York: Longman.

Helfer, R., et al. (1976). Arresting or freezing the development process. In R. Helfer and C. Kempe (Eds), *Child abuse and neglect: The family and the community* (pp. 55–73). Cambridge, MA: Ballinger.

Hellenbrand, S. C. (1987). Termination in direct practice. In A. Minihan (Editor-in-chief), *Encyclopedia of social work* (18th ed., Vol. 1, pp. 765–770). Silver Spring, MD: National Association of Social Workers.

Hepworth, D. H., & Larsen, J. (1986). *Direct social work practice: Theory and skills.* Chicago, IL: Dorsey.

Hepworth, D. H., & Larsen, J. (1987). Interviewing. In A. Minihan, (Editor-in-chief), *Encyclopedia of social work* (18th ed., Vol. 1, pp. 996–1008). Silver Spring, MD: National Association of Social Workers.

Hepworth, D. H., & Larsen, J. (1990). *Direct social work practice.* Belmont, CA: Wadsworth.

Herman, D. (1984). The rape culture. In J. Freeman (Ed.), *Women: A feminist perspective* (pp. 20–38). Palo Alto, CA: Mayfield.

Hill, R. (1972). *The strengths of black families.* New York: Emerson Hall.

Hitchens, D. (1979/80). Social attitudes, legal standards and personal trauma in child custody cases. *Journal of Homosexuality, 5*(1–2), 89–96.

Ho, M. K. (1983). Social work with Asian Americans. In A. Morales, & B. W. Sheafor (Eds), *Social Work: A Profession of Many Faces* (3rd ed., pp. 274–285). Boston, MA: Allyn & Bacon.

Ho, M. K. (1987). *Family therapy with ethnic minorities.* Newbury Park, CA: Sage.

Holder, W., & Corey, M. K. (1986, revised March 1991). *Child protective services risk management: A decision making handbook.* Charlotte, NC: Action for Child Protection.

Holder, W., & Corey, M. K. (1987, revised August 10, 1990). *The child at risk field system: A family preservation approach to decision making in child protective services forms and instructions.* Charlotte, NC: Action for Child Protection, Inc.

Holman, A. M. (1983). *Family assessment: Tools for understanding and intervention.* Beverly Hills, CA: Sage.

Huber, C. H., & Baruth, L. G. (1987). *Ethical, legal and professional issues in the practice of marriage and family therapy.* Columbus, OH: Merrill Publishing Co.

Hudson, J., & Grinnell, R. M. (1989). *Program evaluation,* in B. R. Compton, & B. Galaway (Eds.), *Social work processes* (pp. 691–711). Belmont, CA: Wadsworth.

Hudson, W. W. (1982). *The clinical assessment package: A field manual.* Homewood, IL: Dorsey.

Hudson, W. W., & Thyer, B. A. (1987). Research measures and indexes in direct practice. In A. Minihan (Editor-in-chief). *Encyclopedia of social work* (18th ed., Vol. 2, pp. 487–498). Silver Spring, MA: National Association of Social Workers.

Hull, G. (1978). *The parents anonymous sponsor: A professional helping role.* Paper presented at the Child Welfare League of America Regional Conference, Omaha, NE.

Hull, G. (1990). *Outcome study of UWEC social work graduates.* Unpublished manuscript.

Hull, G., & Zastrow, C. (1988). *Community services directory for Jefferson, Rock and Walworth counties.* Whitewater, WI: University of

Wisconsin-Whitewater Department of Social Welfare.

Hutchins, T., & Baxter, V. (1980). Battered women. In *Alternative social services for women* (pp. 179–234). New York: Columbia University Press.

Hutchison, N. (1989). Application of process in a community change endeavor. In B. R. Compton, & B. Galaway (Eds.), *Social work processes* (pp. 407–410).

Hyde, J. S. (1984). How large are gender differences in aggression: a developmental meta-analysis. *Developmental Psychology, 20,* 722–736.

Hyde, J. S. (1990). *Understanding human sexuality.* New York: McGraw-Hill.

Institute for Rehabilitation and Disability Management and National Center for Social Policy and Practice (1988). *Case management: The present and future tool for improving employment opportunities for people with disabilities.* Unpublished proposal.

Intagliata, J. (1981). Operationalizing a case management system: A multi-level approach. *Case management: State of the art.* Washington, DC: National Conference on Social Welfare.

Intagliata, J. (1982). Improving the quality of community care for the chronically mentally disabled: The role of case management. *Schizophrenia Bulletin, 8*(4), 655–674.

Ivey, A. E. (1983). *Intentional interviewing and counseling.* Belmont, CA: Brooks/Cole.

Ivey, A. E. (1988). *Intentional interviewing and counseling: Facilitating client development* (2nd ed.) Monterey, CA: Brooks/Cole.

Jacobs, M. R. (1981). *Problems presented by alcoholic clients.* Toronto: Addiction Research Foundation.

Janosik, E. G. (1984). *Crisis counseling: A contemporary approach.* Belmont, CA: Wadsworth.

Janzen, C., & Harris, O. (1986). *Family treatment in social work practice.* Itasca, IL: F. E. Peacock.

Johnson, D. W. (1973). *Educational psychology.* Englewood Cliffs, NJ: Prentice-Hall.

Johnson, D. W. (1986). *Reaching out.* Englewood Cliffs, NJ: Prentice-Hall.

Johnson, D. W., & Johnson, F. P. (1975). *Joining together: Group theory and group skills.* Englewood Cliffs, NJ: Prentice-Hall.

Johnson, L. C. (1989). *Social work practice: A generalist approach.* Needham Heights, MA: Allyn and Bacon.

Jones, L. (1987). Women. In A. Minihan (Editor-in-chief), *Encyclopedia of social work* (18th ed., Vol. 2, pp. 872–881). Silver Spring, MD: National Association of Social Workers.

Jones, M., & Biesecker, J. (1977). *Goal planning in children and youth services.* Millersville, PA: Training Resources in Permanent Planning Project.

Jung, M. (1976). Characteristics of contrasting Chinatowns: Philadelphia, Pennsylvania. *Social Casework, 57*(3), 149–154.

Kadushin, A. (1972). *The social work interview.* New York: Columbia University Press.

Kadushin, A. (1990). *The social work interview* (2nd ed.). New York: Columbia University Press.

Kadushin, A., & Martin, J. A. (1988). *Child welfare services* (4th ed.). New York: Macmillan.

Kagle, J. (1987). Recording in direct practice. In A. Minihan (Editor-in-chief), *Encyclopedia of social work* (18th ed., Vol. 2, pp. 463–467). Silver Spring, MD: National Association of Social Workers.

Kagle, J. (1991). *Social work records.* Belmont, CA: Wadsworth.

Kahn, A. J. (1987). Social problems and issues: Theories and definitions. In A. Minihan (Editor-in-chief), *Encyclopedia of social work* (18th ed., Vol. 2, pp. 632–644). Silver Spring, MD: National Association of Social Workers.

Kaimowitz, 42 USLA 2063, (1973).

Kamerman, S. B. (1984). Women, children and poverty in industrialized countries. *Signs, 10*(2), 249–271.

Kamerman, S. B., & Kahn, A. J. (1981). *Child care, family benefits, and working parents.* New York: Columbia University Press.

Kane, R. (1974). Look to the record. *Social Work, 19*(4), 412–419.

Kaplan, K. O. (1990) Recent trends in case management. In A. Minihan (Editor-in-chief), *Encyclopedia of social work* (18th ed., 1990 Supplement, pp. 60–77). Silver Spring, MD: National Association of Social Workers.

Kazdin, A. E. (1989). *Behavior modification in applied settings* (4th ed.). Pacific Grove, CA: Brooks/Cole.

Keefe, T., & Maypole, D. E. (1983). *Relationships in social service practice: Context and skills.* Monterey, CA: Brooks/Cole.

Keniston, K., & Carnegie Council on Children. (1977). *All our children: The American family under pressure.* New York: Harcourt Brace Jovanovich.

Kennedy, E. (1980). *On becoming a counselor.* New York: Continuum.

Kettner, P., Daley, J., & Nichols, A. (1985) *Initiating change in organizations and communities*. Monterey, CA: Brooks/Cole.

Kingery-McCabe, L. G., & Frances, A. C. (1991). Effects of addiction on the addict. In D. C. Daley, & M. S. Raskin (Eds.), *Treating the chemically dependent and their families* (pp. 57–78). Newbury Park, CA: Sage.

Kirst-Ashman, K. (1989, March). *Enhancing the relevance of human behavior and the social environment content*. Paper presented at the Council on Social Work Education Annual Program Meeting, Chicago, IL.

Kirst-Ashman, K. (1991). *Feminist values and social work: A model for educating non-feminists*. Paper presented at the Council on Social Work Annual Program Meeting, New Orleans, LA.

Kitano, H. H. (1991). *Race relations*. Englewood Cliffs, NJ: Prentice-Hall.

Kohlberg, L. (1968). The child as a moral philosopher. *Psychology Today, 2*(4), 25–30.

Kohlberg, L. (1969). Stage and sequence: The cognitive developmental approach to socialization. In A. A. Goslin (Ed.), *The handbook of socialization* (pp. 347–480). Chicago, IL: Rand McNally.

Kohlberg, L. (1981). *The philosophy of moral development*. New York: Harper & Row.

Kohlberg, L., & Gilligan, C. (1971). The adolescent as a philosopher: The discovery of the self in a postconventional world. *Daedelus, 100*(4), 1051–1086.

Kolodny, R. C., Masters, W. H., & Johnson, V. E. (1979). *Textbook of sexual medicine*. Boston: Little, Brown.

Konle, C. (1982). *Social work day-to-day*. New York: Longman.

Koss, M. P., Dinero, T. E., Siebel, C. A., & Cox, S. L. (1988). Stranger and acquaintance rape: Are there differences in the victim's experience? *Psychology of Women Quarterly, 12*(1), 1–24.

Kravetz, D. F., & Rose, S. D. (1973). *Contracts in groups: A workbook*. Dubuque, IA: Kendall/Hunt.

Kuramoto, F. H., Munoz, F. U., Morales, R. F., & Murase, K. (1983). Education for social work practice in Asian and Pacific American Communities. In J. C. Chunn, P. J. Dunston, and F. Ross-Sheriff (Eds.), *Mental health and people of color* (pp. 127–156). Washington, DC: Howard University Press.

L'Abate, L., Ganahl, G., & Hansen, J. C. (1986). *Methods of family therapy*. Englewood Cliffs, NJ: Prentice-Hall.

Larson, C. E., & LaFasto, F. M. (1989). *Teamwork*. Newbury Park, CA: Sage.

Lasater, M. (1980). Sexual assault: The legal framework. In C. G. Warner (Ed.), *Rape and sexual assault* (pp. 231–264). Germantown, MD: Aspen Systems Corp.

Lauffer, A. (1987). Social planners and social planning in the United States. In F. M. Cox, J. L. Erlich, J. Rothman, & J. E. Tropman (Eds.), *Strategies of community organization* (pp. 311–325). Itasca, IL: Peacock.

Lauffer, A., Nybell, L., Overberger, C., Reed, B., & Zeff, L. (1977). *Understanding your social agency*. Beverly Hills, CA: Sage.

League of Women Voters of the United States. (1976). *Making an issue of it: The campaign handbook*. Author.

Lebbers, R. (1978). *Getting a grant*. Englewood Cliffs, NJ: Spectrum.

Levant, R. F. (1984). *Family therapy: A comprehensive overview*. Englewood Cliffs, NJ: Prentice-Hall.

Levine, B., & Gallogly, V. (1985). *Group therapy with alcoholics: Outpatient and inpatient approaches*. Newbury Park, CA: Sage.

Lewis, K. G. (1980). Children of lesbians: Their point of view. *Social Work, 25*(3), 203.

Lewis, R., & Ho, M. (1975). Social work with Native Americans. *Social Work, 20*(5), 378–382.

Lippitt, R., Watson, J., & Westely, B. (1958). *The dynamics of planned change*. New York: Harcourt.

Lloyd, J. C., & Bryce, M. E. (1984). *Placement prevention and family reunification: A handbook for the family-centered service practitioner*. Iowa City, IA: University of Iowa.

Locke, P. (1973, August). Indian gifts of culture and diversity. In *Cultural diverse exceptional children conference presentations* (Cassette tape). Reston, VA: The Council for Exceptional Children.

Loevinger, J. (1976). *Ego development*. San Francisco: Bass.

Loewenberg, F. M. (1977). *Fundamentals of social intervention*. New York: Columbia University Press.

Loewenberg, F., & Dolgoff, R. (1985). *Ethical decisions for social work practice* (2nd ed.). Itasca, IL: Peacock.

Loewenberg, F., & Dolgoff, R. (1988). *Ethical deci-*

sions for social work practice (3rd ed.). Itasca, IL: Peacock.

Logan, S., Freesman, E. M., & McRoy, R. G. (1990). Social work with black families: A culturally specific perspective. New York: Longman.

Lott, B. (1987). Women's lives: Themes and variations in gender learning. Monterey, CA: Wadsworth.

Lovece, F., & Edelstein, A. J. (1990). The old Brady's versus the new. TV Guide, 38, 12–15.

Lowy, L. (1985). Social work with the aging: The challenge and promise of the later years. New York: Longman.

Lum, D. (1986). Social work practice and people of color: A process-stage approach. Monterey, CA: Brooks/Cole.

Lum, D. (1992). Social work practice and people of color. Pacific Grove, CA: Brooks/Cole.

Magura, S., & Moses, B. S. (1986). Outcome measures for child welfare services: Theory and applications. Washington, DC: Child Welfare League of America.

Mailick, M. D., & Ashley, A. A. (1989). Politics of interprofessional collaboration: Challenge to advocacy. In B. R. Compton & B. Galaway (Eds.), Social work processes (pp. 622–628). Belmont, CA: Wadsworth.

Maluccio, A. N. (1990). Family preservation: An overview. In Family preservation: Papers from the Institute for Social Work Educators 1990, 17–28. Riverdale, IL: National Association for Family-Based Services.

Maple, F. F. (1985). Dynamic interviewing: An introduction to counseling. Newbury Park, CA: Sage.

Marion, T. D., & Coleman, K. (1991). Recovery issues and treatment resources. In D. C. Daley and M. S. Raskin (Eds.), Treating the chemically dependent and their families, (pp. 100–127). Newbury Park, CA: Sage.

Marsden, D., & Owens, D. (1975). The Jekyll and Hyde marriage. New Society, 32, 334.

Martin, D. (1976). Battered wives. San Francisco, CA: Glide Publications.

Martin, H.P.I., & Beezley, P. (1976). Personality of abused children. In H. P. Martin (Ed.), The abused child (pp. 105–111). Cambridge, MA: Ballinger.

Martin, S. E. (1984). Sexual harassment: The link between gender stratification, sexuality and women's economic status. In J. Freeman (Ed.), Women:

A Feminist Perspective (pp. 54–69). Palo Alto, CA: Mayfield.

Massella, J. D. (1991). Intervention: Breaking the addiction cycle. In D. C. Daley and M. S. Raskin (Eds.), Treating the chemically dependent and their families (pp. 79–99). Newbury Park, CA: Sage.

Masson, H. C., & O'Byrne, P. (1984). Applying family therapy: A practical guide for social workers. New York: Pergamon Press.

Masters, W. H., Johnson, V. E., & Kolodny, R. C., (1985). Human sexuality (2nd ed.). Boston, MA: Little, Brown.

Masters, W. H., Johnson, V. E. & Kolodny, R. C. (1988). Human sexuality. Glenview, IL: Scott, Foresman.

Mayer, A. (1983). Incest: A treatment manual for therapy with victims, spouses, and offenders. Holmes Beach, FL: Learning Publications, Inc.

Maypole, D. E., & Skaine, R. (1983). Sexual harassment in the workplace. Social Work, 28(5), 385–390.

McAdoo, H. (1977). Family therapy in the black community. Journal of the American Orthopsychiatric Association, 47(1), 75–79.

McAdoo, H. (1987). Blacks. In A. Minihan (Editor-in-chief), Encyclopedia of social work (18th ed., Vol. 1, pp. 194–206). Silver Spring, MD: National Association of Social Workers.

McCormick, I. A. (1984). A simple version of the Rathus assertiveness schedule. Behavior Assessment, 7(1), 95–99.

McGee, E. (1982). Too little, too late: Services for teenage parents. New York: Ford Foundation.

McGowan, B. G. (1974). Case advocacy: A study of the interventive process in child advocacy. Doctoral dissertation, New York: Columbia University.

McGowan, B. G. (1987). Advocacy. In A. Minihan (Editor-in-chief), Encyclopedia of social work, (18th ed., Vol. 1, pp. 89–95). Silver Spring, MD: National Association of Social Workers.

McGrath, C. (1980). The crisis of domestic order. Socialist Review, 11–30.

McMahon, M. (1990). The general method of social work practice. Englewood Cliffs, NJ: Prentice-Hall.

Meenaghan, T. M. (1987). Macro practice: Current trends and issues. In A. Minihan (Editor-in-chief), Encyclopedia of social work (18th ed., Vol. 2, pp. 82–89). Silver Spring, MD: National Association of Social Workers.

Meyer, C. H. (1987). Direct practice in social work: An overview. In A. Minihan, (Editor-in-chief), *Encyclopedia of social work* (18th ed., Vol. 1, pp. 409–422). Silver Spring, MD: National Association of Social Workers.

Middleman, R. R., & Goldberg, G. (1987). Social work practice with groups. In A. Minihan (Editor-in-chief), *Encyclopedia of social work* (18th ed., Vol. 2, pp. 714–728). Silver Spring, MD: National Association of Social Workers.

Miller, N. B. (1982). Social work services to urban Indians. In J. W. Green, *Cultural awareness in the human services*. Englewood Cliffs, NJ: Prentice-Hall.

Minihan, A. (Editor-in-chief). (1987). *Encyclopedia of social work*, (18th ed., Vol. 1–2). Silver Spring, MD: National Association of Social Workers.

Minuchin, S. (1974). *Families and family therapy*. Cambridge, MA: Harvard University Press.

Minuchin, S., & Fishman, C. H. (1981). *Family therapy techniques*. Cambridge, MA: Harvard University Press.

Mish, F. (Editor-in-chief). (1991). *Webster's Ninth New Collegiate Dictionary*. Springfield, MA: Merriam-Webster, Inc.

Monat, A., & Lazarus, R. S. (1991). *Stress and coping*. New York: Columbia University Press.

Moody, J. D., & Hayes, V. (1980). Responsible reporting: The initial step. In C. G. Warner (Ed.), *Rape and sexual assault* (pp. 27–45). Germantown, MD: Aspen Systems Corp.

Moore, S. T. (1990). A social work practice model of case management: The case management grid. *Social Work, 35*(5), 444–448.

Morris, R. (1986). *Rethinking social welfare: Why care for the stranger?* New York: Longman.

Morris, R. (1987). Social welfare policy: Trends and issues. In A. Minihan (Editor-in-chief), *Encyclopedia of social work* (18th ed., Vol. 2, pp. 664–681). Silver Spring, MD: National Association of Social Workers.

Moses, A. E., & Hawkins, R. O. (1982). *Counseling lesbian women and gay men: A life-issues approach*. St. Louis, MO: Mosby-Year Book.

Moxley, D. P. (1989). *The practice of case management*. Newbury Park, CA: Sage.

Murray, C. (1984). *Losing ground: American social welfare policy 1950–1980*. New York: Basic Books.

Mutschler, E. (1987). Computer utilization. In A. Minihan, (Editor-in-chief), *Encyclopedia of social work* (18th ed., Vol. 1, pp. 316–326). Silver Spring, MD: National Association of Social Workers.

Nadelson, C. C. (1982). A follow-up study of rape victims. *American Journal of Psychiatry, 139*(10), 1266–1270.

National Association of Social Workers. (1979). *Code of Ethics*. Silver Spring, MD: Author.

National Association of Social Workers. (1980). *Code of ethics*. Silver Spring, MD: Author.

National Association of Social Workers. (1981). *Guidelines for the selection and use of social workers*. Silver Spring, MD: Author.

National Association of Social Workers. (1983). *Program advancement fund: A step-by-step guide to the job search process*. Silver Spring, MD: Author.

National Association of Social Workers. (1984). *Standards and guidelines for social work case management for the functionally impaired: Professional standards*. Silver Spring, MD: Author.

National Association of Social Workers. (1987). *Salaries in social work: A summary report on the salaries of NASW members*. Silver Spring, MD: Author.

National Association of Social Workers, Inc. (1990). *Code of Ethics of National Association of Social Workers*. Silver Spring, MD: Author.

Neiding, P. H., & Friedman, D. H. (1984). *Spouse abuse: A treatment program for couples*. Champaign, IL: Research Press.

Nelson, J. (1983). *Family treatment: An integrative approach*. Englewood Cliffs, NJ: Prentice-Hall.

Netting, F., Thibault, J., & Eller, J. (1990). Integrating content on organized religion into macropractice courses. *Journal of Social Work Education, 26*(1), 15–24.

Nichols. (1984). *Family therapy: Concepts and methods*. New York: Gardner Press.

Norman, E., & Mancuso, A. (1980). *Women's issues and social work practice*. Itasca, IL: F. E. Peacock.

Northen, H. (1982). *Clinical social work*. New York: Columbia University Press.

Northen, H. (1987). Assessment in direct practice. In A. Minihan (Editor-in-chief), *Encyclopedia of social work* (18th ed., Vol. 1, pp. 171–183). Silver Spring, MD: National Association of Social Workers.

Northwood, L. K. (1964). Deterioration of the inner city. In N. E. Cohen, (Ed.), *Social work and social problems* (pp. 201–269). New York: National Association of Social Workers.

Nunnally, E., & Moy, C. (1989). *Communication basics for human service professionals*. Newbury Park, CA: Sage.

Okun, B. F. (1976). *Effective helping: Interviewing and counseling techniques*. Belmont, CA: Duxbury.

Okun, B. F., & Rappaport, L. J. (1980). *Working with families: An introduction to family therapy*. North Scituate, MA: Duxbury.

Olmstead, M. (1959). *The small group*. New York: Random House.

Osborne, O., Pinkleton, N., Carter, C., & Richards, H. (1983). Development of African American curriculum content in psychiatric and mental health nursing. In J. C. Chunn, P. J. Dunston, & F. Ross-Sheriff, *Mental health and people of color* (pp. 335–376). Washington, DC: Howard University Press.

Papalia, D., & Olds, S. W. (1989). *Human development*. New York: McGraw-Hill.

Patterson, G. R. (1975). *Families: Applications of social learning to family life*. Champaign, IL: Research Press.

Patti, R. J., & Dear, R. B. Legislative advocacy: One path to social change. *Social Work* 20(3): 108–114.

Patti, R. J., & Resnick, H. (1972). Changing the Agency from Within. *Social Work, 17*(4), 48–57.

Pearson, J., & Varderkooi, L. (1983). Mediating divorce disputes, mediator behavior, styles, roles. *Family Relations, 32*(4), 557–566.

Perez, J. E. (1979). *Family counseling theory and practice*. New York: Van Nostrand Reinhold.

Peters. (1982). The legal rights of gays. In A. I. Moses, & R. O. Hawkins (Eds.), *Counseling lesbian women and gay men: A life issues approach* (pp. 21–26). St. Louis, MO: Mosby-Year Book.

Piaget, J. (1970). *Science of education and the psychology of the child*. New York: Viking Press.

Pierce, D. M. (1989). Farewell to alms: Women's fare under welfare. In J. Freeman (Ed.), *Women: A feminist perspective* (pp. 493–506). Palo Alto, CA: Mayfield.

Pietrzak, J., Ramler, M., Renner, T., Ford, L., & Gilbert, N. (1990). *Practical program evaluation*. Newbury Park, CA: Sage.

Pincus, A., & Minahan, A. (1973). *Social work practice: Model and method*. Itasca, IL: F. E. Peacock.

Pippin, J. A. (1980). *Developing casework skills*. Beverly Hills, CA: Sage.

Poll: Women belong in the workplace. (1986, June 17). *Providence Evening Bulletin*, A1–A2.

Presidential Commission on the Human Immunodeficiency Virus Epidemic. (1988). *Report of the presidential commission on the human immunodeficiency virus epidemic*. Washington, DC: U.S. Government Printing Office.

Presley, J. H. (1987). The clinical dropout: A view from the client's perspective. *Social Casework, 68*(10), 603–608.

Pyke, S. W., & Kahill, S. P. (1983). Sex differences in characteristics presumed relevant to professional productivity. *Psychology of Women Quarterly, 8*(2), 189–192.

Radloff, L. (1975). Sex differences in depression: The effects of occupation and marital status. *Sex Roles, 1*(3), 249–265.

Rapoport, L. (1977). Consultation in social work. In J. Turner (Editor-in-chief), *Encyclopedia of social work* (17th ed., Vol. 1, pp. 193–196). Washington, DC: National Association of Social Workers.

Raskin, M. S., & Daley, D. C. (1991). Assessment of addiction problems. In M. S. Rasking, & D. C. Daley (Eds.), *Treating the chemically dependent and their families* (pp. 22–56). Newbury Park, CA: Sage.

Rauch, J. B., & Tivoli, L. (1989). Social workers' knowledge and utilization of genetic services. *Social Work* 34(1) 55–56.

Rawlings, E. I., & Carter, D. K. (Eds.). (1977). *Psychotherapy for women: Treatment toward equality*. Springfield, IL: Charles C. Thomas.

Reamer, F. G. (1987). Values and ethics. In A. Minihan (Editor-in-chief), *Encyclopedia of social work* (18th ed., Vol. 2, pp. 801–809). Silver Spring, MD: National Association of Social Workers.

Reid, W. J. (1978). *The task-centered system*. New York: Columbia University Press.

Reid, W. J. (1985). *Family problem solving*. New York: Columbia University Press.

Reid, W. J. (1987a). Research in social work. In A. Minihan, (Editor-in-chief), *Encyclopedia of social work* (18th ed., Vol. 2, pp. 474–487). Silver Spring, MD: National Association of Social Workers.

Reid, W. J. (1987b). Task-centered approach. In A. Minihan (Editor-in-chief) *Encyclopedia of social work* (18th ed., Vol. 2, pp. 757–765). Silver Spring, MD: National Association of Social Workers.

Reid, W. J., & Epstein, L. (1972). *Task-centered casework*. New York: Columbia University Press.

Resnick, M. (1976). *Wife beating counselor training*

manual no. 1. Ann Arbor, MI: AA NOW/WIFE Assault.

Rice, S., & Kelly, J. (1988). Choosing a gay/lesbian lifestyle: Related issues of treatment services. In C. Chilman, E. Nunnally, & F. Cox (Eds.), *Variant Family Norms* (pp. 114–132). Newbury Park, CA: Sage.

Richardson, E. (1981). Cultural and historical perspectives in counseling American Indians. In D. W. Sue, (Ed.), *Counseling the culturally different* (pp. 216–255). New York: John Wiley.

Richmond, M. (1917). *Social diagnosis.* New York: Free Press.

Riddle, D. (1977). *Gay parents and child custody issues.* Unpublished manuscript, University of Arizona-Tuscon, Department of Psychology.

Robert, H. M. (1971). *Robert's rules of order revised.* New York: William Morrow.

Roberts-DeGennaro, M. (1987). Developing case management as a practice model. *Social Casework, 68*(8), 466–470.

Robinson, D. (1969). Our surprising moral unwed fathers. *Ladies Home Journal, 86*(8), 48–50.

Roffman, R. A. (1987). Drug use and abuse. In A. Minihan (Editor-in-chief), *Encyclopedia of social work* (18th ed., Vol. 1, pp. 477–487). Silver Spring, MD: National Association of Social Workers.

Romero, J., & Williams, L. (1985). Recidivism among convicted sex offenders: A 10 year followup study. *Federal Probation, 49*(1), 58–64.

Rose, S. D. (1981). Assessment in groups. *Social Work Research & Abstracts, 17*(1), 29–37.

Roskies, E. (1991). *Stress management: A new approach to treatment.* New York: Columbia University Press.

Rothman, J. (1987). Community theory and research. In A. Minihan (Editor-in-chief), *Encylopedia of social work* (18th ed., Vol. 1, pp. 308–316). Silver Spring, MD: National Association of Social Workers.

Rothman, J., & Tropman, J. (1987). Models of community organization and macro practice perspectives: their mixing and phasing. In F. M. Cox, J. L. Erlich, J. Rothman, & J. Tropman (Eds.), *Strategies of community organization* (pp. 3–26). Itasca, IL: Peacock.

Rubin, A. (1987). Case management. In A. Minihan (Editor-in-chief), *Encyclopedia of social work* (18th ed., Vol. 1, pp. 212–222). Silver Spring, MD: National Association of Social Workers.

Rubin, H., & Rubin, I. (1986). *Community organizing and development.* Columbus, OH: Merrill.

Russell, A. B., & Trainor, C. M. (1984). *Trends in child abuse and neglect: A national perspective.* Denver, CO: American Humane Association, Children's Division.

Russell, D. E., & Howell, N. (1983). The prevalence of rape in the United States revisited. *Signs, 8*(4), 688–695.

Russo, J. R. (1985). *Serving and surviving as a human-service worker.* Prospect Heights, IL: Waveland.

Rutman, L., & Mowbray, G. (1983). *Understanding program evaluation.* Newbury Park, CA: Sage.

Safran, C. (1976, November). What men do to women on the job: A shocking look at sexual harassment. *Redbook, 148*(1), 149.

Sager, C. J., Brown, H. S., Crohn, H., Engel, T., Rodstein, E., & Walker, L. (1983). *Treating the remarried family.* New York: Brunner/Mazel.

Salter, A. (1988). *Treating child sex offenders and their victims: A practical guide.* Newbury Park, CA: Sage Publications.

Sapiro, V. (1990). *Women in American society.* Mountain View, CA: Mayfield.

Scheidel, T., & Crowell, L. (1979). *Discussing and deciding: A deskbook for group leaders and members.* New York: Macmillan.

Schmitt, B. (1980). The child with non-accidental trauma. In C. H. Kempe (Ed.), *The battered child* (pp. 129–146). Chicago, IL: University of Chicago Press.

Schoech, D. (1987). Information systems: Agency. In A. Minihan (Editor-in-chief), *Encyclopedia of social work* (18th ed., Vol. 1, pp. 920–931). Silver Spring, MD: National Association of Social Workers.

Schreiner, T. (1984, May 29). A revolution that has just begun. *USA Today,* p. 40.

Schwab, D. P. (1984). Using job evaluation to obtain pay equity. In *Comparable worth: Issue for the 80's: A consultation for the U.S. Commission on Civil Rights, 1*(June 6–7), 83–92. U.S. Government Printing Office, 1984–524 722/30008.

Schwaber, F. H. (1985). Some legal issues related to outside institutions. In H. Hidalgo et al. (Eds.), *Lesbian and gay issues: A resource manual for social workers* (pp. 92–99). Silver Spring, MD: National Association of Social Workers.

Schwartz, W. (1976). Between client and system: The mediating function. In R. W. Roberts, &

H. Northen (Eds.), *Theories of social work with groups* (171–197). New York: Columbia University Press.

Seabury, B. A. (1987). Contracting and engaging in direct practice. In A. Minihan, (Editor-in-chief), *Encyclopedia of social work* (18th ed., Vol. 1, pp. 339–345). Silver Spring, MD: National Association of Social Workers.

Selman, R. (1976). A developmental approach to interpersonal and moral awareness in young children: Some educational implications of levels of social perspective-taking. In T. Hennessey (Ed.), *Values and moral development* (pp. 142–146). New York: Paulist Press.

Selye, H. (1956). *The stress of life*. New York: McGraw-Hill.

Sharwell, G. R. (1982). How to testify before a legislative committee. In M. Mahaffey and J. Hanks (Eds.), *Practical politics: Social workers and political responsibility* (pp. 85–98). Silver Spring, MD: National Association of Social Workers.

Sheafor, B. W., Horejsi, C. R., & Horejsi, G. A. (1988). *Techniques and guidelines for social work practice*. Boston, MA: Allyn & Bacon.

Sheafor, B. W., Horejsi, C. R. & Horejsi, G. A. (1991). *Techniques and guidelines for social work practice* (2nd ed.). Boston: Allyn & Bacon.

Sheafor, B. W., & Landon, P. S. (1987). Generalist perspective. In A. Minihan (Editor-in-chief), *Encyclopedia of social work* (18th ed., Vol. 1, pp. 660–669). Silver Spring, MD: National Association of Social Workers.

Shelton, J., & Ackerman, J. M. (1974). *Homework in counseling and psychotherapy*. Springfield, IL: Charles C. Thomas.

Sherman, S. N. (1977). Family services: Family treatment. In A. Minihan (Editor-in-chief), *Encyclopedia of social work* (18th ed., Vol. 1, pp. 435–440). Silver Spring, MD: National Association of Social Workers.

Shortridge, K. (1989). Poverty is a woman's problem. In J. Freeman (Ed.), *Women: A feminist perspective* (pp. 485–492). Palo Alto, CA: Mayfield.

Shulman, L. (1979). *The skills of helping individuals and groups*. Itasca, IL: Peacock.

Shulman, L. (1981). *Identifying, measuring, and teaching helping skills*. New York: Council on Social Work Education.

Shulman, L. (1982). *Skills of supervision and staff management*. Itasca, IL: Peacock.

Shulman, L. (1984). *The skills of helping individuals and groups*. Itasca, IL: Peacock.

Shulman, L. (1987). Consultation. In A. Minihan (Editor-in-chief), *Encyclopedia of social work*, (18th ed., Vol. 1, pp. 326–331). Silver Spring, MD: National Association of Social Workers.

Shulman, L. (1991). *Interactional social work practice*. Itasca, IL: Peacock.

Shulman, M. (1979). *A survey of spousal violence against women in Kentucky*. Washington, DC: U.S. Department of Justice, Law Enforcement Assistance Administration.

Sieber, S. (1981). *Fatal remedies*. New York: Plenum.

Siegel, L. M., Attkisson, C. C., & Carson, L. G. (1987). Need identification and program planning in the community context. In F. M. Cox, J. L. Erlich, J. Rothman, & J. Tropman (Eds.), *Strategies of community organization* (pp. 71–97). Itasca, IL: Peacock.

Siporin, M. (1975). *Introduction to social work practice*. New York: Macmillan.

Slater, P. E. (1958). Contrasting correlates of group size. *Sociometry, 21*(2), 129–139.

Smith, S. A., & Tienda, M. (1988). The doubly disadvantaged: Women of color in the U.S. labor force. In A. H. Stromberg & S. Harkness (Eds.), *Women working* (pp. 61–80). Mountain View, CA: Mayfield.

Solomon, B. B. (1989). Social work with Afro-Americans. In A. Morales, & B. W. Sheafor (Eds.), *Social work: A profession of many faces* (3rd ed., pp. 567–588). Boston, MA: Allyn & Bacon.

Sosin, M., & Caulum, S. (1989). Advocacy: A conceptualization for social work practice. In B. R. Compton, & B. Galaway (Eds.), *Social work processes* (pp. 533–540). Belmont, CA: Wadsworth.

Spanier, G. B. (1976). Formal and informal sex education as determinants of premarital sexual behavior. *Archives of Sexual Behavior, 5*(1), 39–67.

Spaulding, E. (1991). *Statistics on social work education*. Alexandria, VA: Council on Social Work Education.

Spergel, I. A. (1987). Community development. In A. Minihan (Editor-in-chief), *Encyclopedia of social work* (18th ed., Vol. 1, pp. 299–308). Silver Spring, MD: National Association of Social Workers.

Star, B. (1987). Domestic violence. In Minahan, A. (Editor-in-chief), *Encyclopedia of social work* (18th ed., Vol. 1, pp. 463–476). Silver Spring, MD: National Association of Social Workers.

Stark, R., & McEvoy J. (1970). Middle class violence. *Psychology Today, 4*(6), 52, 53, 54, 110–112.

Stein, T. J. (1981). Macro and micro level issues in case management. In *Case management: State of the art.* Proceedings of the national case management conference, National Conference on Social Welfare, Indianapolis, IN. Washington, DC: Administration on Developmental Disabilities.

Straus, M. A. (1974). Leveling, civility and violence in the family. *Journal of Marriage and the Family, 36*(1), 13–29.

Straus, M. A. (1978). Wife-beating: How common and why? *Victimology: An International Journal, 2*(3–4), 443–458.

Straus, M. A., Gelles, R. J., & Steinmetz, S. (1980). *Behind closed doors: Violence in the American family.* Doubleday, NY: Anchor Press.

Stromberg, A. H., & Harkess, S. (1988). *Women Working.* Mountain View, CA: Mayfield.

Strong, B. (1983). *The marriage and family experience.* New York: West.

Stuart, R. B. (1983). *Couple's therapy workbook.* Champaign, IL: Research Press.

Tarasoff v. Regents of the University of California. 13 Cal. 3d 177 (1974).

Tayler, R., & Chatters, L. (1986). Patterns of informal support to elderly black adults: Family, friends and church members. *Social Work, 31*(6), 132–438.

Termination of parental rights: The legal aspects. (pp. 85–116). Urbana, IL: Center for Legal Studies.

Test, M. (1979). Continuity of care in community treatment. In L. Stein (Ed.), *Community support systems for the long-term patient* (pp. 15–23). San Francisco, CA: Jossey-Bass.

Thompson, D. G. (1977). *Writing long-term and short-term objectives.* Champaign, IL: Research Press.

Thompson, J. W., Smith, C. R., Blueye, H. B., & Walker, R. D. (1983). Cross-cultural curriculum content in psychiatric residency training. In J. C. Chunn, P. J. Dunston, and F. Ross-Sheriff. *Mental health and people of color* (pp. 269–288). Washington, DC: Howard University Press.

Thorman, G. (1982). *Helping troubled families: A social work perspective.* New York: Aldine.

Toomey, B. G. (1987). Sexual assault services. In A. Minihan (Editor-in-chief), *Encyclopedia of social work*, (18th ed., Vol. 2, pp. 569–575). Silver Spring, MD: National Association of Social Workers.

Toseland, R. W. (1987). Treatment discontinuance: Grounds for optimism. *Social Casework, 68*(4), 195–204.

Toseland, R. W., & Rivas, R. F. (1984). *An introduction to group work practice.* New York: Macmillan.

Tower, C. (1989). *Understanding child abuse and neglect.* Needham Heights, MA: Allyn & Bacon.

Trattner, W. I. (1979). *From poor law to welfare state: A history of social welfare in America.* New York: Free Press.

U.S. Bureau of the Census. (1985a). *Estimates of poverty including the value on noncash benefits: 1984.* Washington, DC: U.S. Government Printing Office.

U.S. Bureau of the Census. (1985b). Money, income and poverty status of families and persons in the United States: 1984. *Current Population Reports.* Washington, DC: U.S. Government Printing Office.

U.S. Bureau of the Census. (1987a). A *statistical abstract of the United States.* Washington, DC: U.S. Government Printing Office.

U.S. Bureau of the Census. (1987b). *Male-female differences in work experience, occupation, and earnings, 1984.* Washington, DC: U.S. Government Printing Office.

U.S. Bureau of the Census. (1988a). *Household and family characteristics: March, 1987.* No. 424. Washington, DC: U.S. Government Printing Office.

U.S. Bureau of the Census. (1988b). *Statistical abstract of the United States.* Washington, DC: U.S. Government Printing Office.

U.S. Department of Commerce. (1990). *Statistical abstract of the United States,* 110th ed. Washington, DC: Author.

U.S. Department of Health Education and Welfare. (1979). Resource materials: A curriculum on CAN DHEW. (DHEW Publication No. 79-30221). Washington, DC: Author.

U.S. Department of Health and Social Services. (1989). *Social security programs throughout the world.* Washington, DC: U.S. Government Printing Office.

U.S. Merit Systems Protection Board (MSPB). (1981). *Sexual harassment in the federal workplace: Is it a problem?* Washington, DC: U.S. Government Printing Office.

Van Den Bergh, N., & Cooper, L. B. (Eds.). (1986). *Feminist visions for social work.* Washington, DC: National Association of Social Workers.

Van Den Bergh, N., & Cooper, L. B. (1987). Feminist social work. In A. Minihan (Editor-in-chief), *Encyclopedia of social work*, (18th ed., Vol. 1, pp. 610–618). Silver Spring, MD: National Association of Social Workers.

Visher, E. B., & Visher, J. S. (1988). Treating families with problems associated with remarriage and step relationships. In C. S. Chilman, E. W. Nunnally, & F. M. Cox (Eds.), *Variant family norms* (pp. 222–244). Newbury Park, CA: Sage.

Vosler, N. K. (1990). Assessing family access to basic resources: An essential component of social work practice. *Social Work*, 37(5), 434–441.

Walker, L. E. (1979). *The battered woman*. New York: Harper & Row.

Warheit, G. J., Bell, R. A., & Schwab, J. J. (1977). *Planning for change: Needs assessment approaches*. Washington, DC: National Institute of Mental Health.

Warren, R. B. (1978). *The community in America* (3rd ed.). Chicago, IL: Rand McNally.

Warren, R. B., & Warren, D. I. (1984). How to diagnose a neighborhood. In F. Cox, J. L. Erlich, J. Rothman, & J. E. Tropman (Eds.), *Tactics and techniques of community practice* (2nd ed., pp. 27–40). Itasca, IL: Peacock.

Warren, R. L. (1972). *The community in America*. Chicago, IL: Rand McNally.

Wattenberg, E. (1987). Family: One parent. In A. Minihan (Editor-in-chief), *Encyclopedia of social work* (18th ed., Vol. 1, pp. 548–555). Silver Spring, MD: National Association of Social Workers.

Weatherley, R. A., & Cartoof, V. G. (1988). Helping single adolescent parents. In C. Chilman, E. Nunnally, & F. Cox (Eds.), *Variant family norms* (pp. 39–55). Newbury Park, CA: Sage.

Webster's New Collegiate Dictionary. (1977). Springfield, MA: Merriam Co.

Webster's Ninth New Collegiate Dictionary. (1991). Springfield, MA: Merriam-Webster.

Weed, L. L. (1969). *Medical records, medical education and patient care*. New York: Garland STPM Press.

Wegscheider, S. (1981). *Another chance: Hope and health for the alcoholic family*. Palo Alto, CA: Science Behavior Books.

Weissman, A. (1976). Industrial social services: Linkage technology. *Social Casework*, 57(1) 50–54.

Weitzman, L. J. (1985). *The divorce revolution*. New York: Free Press.

Wells, E. (1987). Food stamp program. In A. Minihan (Editor-in-chief), *Encyclopedia of social work* (18th ed., Vol. 1, pp. 628–634). Silver Spring, MD: National Association of Social Workers.

Wells, R. A. (1981). *Planned short-term treatment*. New York: Free Press.

White, G. D., Nielsen, G., & Johnson, S. M. (1972). Timeout duration and the suppression of deviant behavior in children. *Journal of Applied Behavior Analysis*, 5(2), 111–120.

White, V. P. (1975). *Grants*. New York: Plenum.

Whitham, F. L., & Mathy, R. M. *Male homosexuality in four societies*. New York: Praeger.

Whittacker, J. K., & Tracy, E. M. (1989). *Social treatment: An introduction to social work practice*. New York: Aldine de Gruyter.

Wicks, R. J., & Parsons, R. D. (1984). *Counseling strategies and intervention techniques for the human services*. New York: Longman.

Wilensky, H., & LeBeaury, C. (1965). *Industrial society and social welfare*. New York: Free Press.

Williams, J. B. (1981). DSM-III: A comprehensive approach to diagnosis. *Social Work*, 26(2), 99–111.

Williams, J. B. (1987). Diagnostic and statistical manual (DSM). In A. Minihan (Editor-in-chief), *Encyclopedia of social work* (18th ed., Vol. 1, pp. 389–393). Silver Spring, MD: National Association of Social Workers.

Williams, L. F., & Hobbs, J. G. (1990). The social work labor force: Current perspectives and future trends. In A. Minihan (Editor-in-chief), *Encyclopedia of social work*, (18th ed., Vol. 2, pp. 289–306). Silver Spring, MD: National Association of Social Workers.

Wilson, S. J. *Recording guidelines for social workers*. New York: The Free Press.

Wolf, D. (1979). *The lesbian community*. Berkeley, CA: University of California.

Wolman, B. B. (1973). *Dictionary of behavioral science*. New York: Van Nostrand Reinhold.

Wolock, I., & Horowitz, B. (1984). Child maltreatment as a social problem: The neglect of neglect. *American Journal of Orthopsychiatry*, 54(4), 530–543.

Wong, H. Z., Kim, Li I. C., Lim, D. T., & Morishima, J. K. (1983). The training of psychologists for Asian and Pacific American communities. In J. C. Chunn, P. J. Dunston, and F. Ross-Sheriff (Eds.), *Mental Health and People of Color* (pp. 23–41). Washington, DC: Howard University Press.

Yalom, I. D. (1975). *The theory and practice of group psychotherapy*. New York: Basic Books.

Yalom, I. D. (1985). *The theory and practice of group psychotherapy*. New York: Basic Books.

Zabin, L. S. (1986). Evaluation of a pregnancy prevention program for urban teenagers. *Family Planning Perspectives, 18*(3), 119–126.

Zabin, L. S., Hirsch, M. B., Smith, E. A., & Hardy, J. B. (1984). Adolescent sexual attitudes and behaviors: Are they consistent? *Family Planning Perspectives, 4*, 181–185.

Zander, A. (1983). *Making groups effective*. San Francisco, CA: Jossey-Bass.

Zastrow, C., & Kirst-Ashman, K. (1987). *Understanding human behavior and the social environment*. Chicago, IL: Nelson-Hall.

Zelnick, M., & Kim, Y. J. (1982). Sex education and its association with teenage sexual activity, pregnancy, and contraceptive use. *Family Planning Perspectives, 14*(3), 117–125.

Name Index

Subject Index

Photo Credits